Asian Christian Theologies
A Research Guide to Authors, Movements, Sources

Edited by
John C. England, Jose Kuttianimattathil sdb,
John Mansford Prior svd, Lily A. Quintos rc,
David Suh Kwang-sun, Janice Wickeri

VOLUME 3
Northeast Asia

ISPCK/Claretian Publishers/Orbis Books
2004

Asian Christian Theologies–Vol. 3—Published by the Rev. Ashish Amos of the Indian Society for Promoting Christian Knowledge (ISPCK), Post Box 1585, Kashmere Gate, Delhi-110006 in association with Claretian Publishers, Quezon City; Orbis Books, Maryknoll, NY.

First Published 2004

© The Editors 2004

Library of Congress Control Number: 2003040526

ISBN: 1-57075-483-7

Cover design: TONY SMITH

Laser typeset and cover design by **ISPCK,** Post Box 1585, 1654 Madarsa Road, Kashmere Gate, Delhi-110006, Tel: 23866323, Fax: 91-11-23865490.
E-Mail–ispck@nde.vsnl.net.in, Publishing@ispck.org.in
Internet-www.ispck.org.in
Printed at Cambridge Press, Kashmere Gate, Delhi–110006

*Dedicated by the editors to
their forebears throughout the region
who have handed on the
rich heritage of Asian theologies,
and to colleagues in all Asian countries who,
despite few resources and every obstacle,
persevere in writing, teaching and living
Asian theology with people in context.*

Contents

The Genesis of this Work	ix
Acknowledgements	xi
Foreword 1: Dr Theresa Chu Mei-fen	xv
Foreword 2: Dr Kim Yong-Bock	xxi
A Note on Languages, Terms, Style	xxiii
Abbreviations	xxvii
Table of Contents Vols. 1 & 2	xxxv
Note on Illustrations & Artists	xxxvi
Illustrations	xxxvi-a
Introduction	xxxix
1. Contextual Christian Theology in Asia	1
2. Groundwork for Asian Christian Theologies: Northeast Asia	9
3. Contextual Theology in China	34
4. Contextual Theology in Hong Kong	216
5. A Note on Inner Asia	293
6. Contextual Theology in Japan	302
7. Contextual Theology in Korea	475
8. A Note on Contextual Theology in North Korea	645
9. A Note on Contextual Theology in Macau	652
10. Contextual Theology in Taiwan	663
Key Bibliographical Sources	730
Contributors to Volume 3	732
Editors	734
Index of Persons	737
Index of Subjects	757

The Genesis of this Work

In this third volume the first publication of a Research Guide to *Asian Christian Theologies* is completed, following preparations over some decades. During the last twenty years in particular, the extent of our knowledge of Asian Christian theologies and of their extensive written sources, has greatly increased, as has the number of those studying these and of the courses offered for them in seminary or university. There has been, however, no attempt as yet to provide an Asia-wide and comprehensive guide to study or research in these theologies, despite a growing tide of deep interest, study and teaching. Some of this concern has been fostered through the work of the Commission for Theological Concerns (CCA-CTC), the publications of the Federation of Asian Bishops' Conferences (FABC), the Theological Seminar-Workshops held regularly over the past 20 years by the Programme for Theology and Cultures in Asia (PTCA), and activities of regional bodies such as the Asia-Pacific Association for Missiological Research (ASPAMIR).

Impetus came from all these, along with the more recent Congress of Asian Theologians (CATS), for the undertaking at last of a more comprehensive and fully ecumenical guide to study and research, despite the scale and the complexity of work necessary for such a project. A small group shared by mail their enthusiasm and commitment for this in mid 1997, and in early 1998, a team of co-editors was forming in order to initiate the writing. A fully ecumenical team of contributors was sought with participation from each country in the region and the co-editors first met for planning and co-ordination in December, 1998.

Approaches were made to CCA, ASPAMIR and PTCA for their approval, and to MWI Missio (Aachen) and the Council for World Mission (CWM, London) for seed funds to assist in co-ordination and publication. There has also been a generous anonymous donation.

Principal concerns have throughout been to make available as wide a range as possible of Asian Christian theologies in all their varied forms, and to provide adequate guidance for their discovery, study and research.

The demanding work of obtaining adequate contributions from across the region, and of themselves preparing major sections of the text, demanded considerable dedication of the editors and co-ordinator over the next three years along with the work of many other colleagues across the region who have assisted with information, bibliographies, translations and advice. It is hoped that many more colleagues will now continue and expand the research and interpretation which is here begun.

Acknowledgements

The following chapters of volume 3 represent the work not only of those whose writing is included here but of an almost countless number of colleagues throughout the region, and also in other countries, who have in their writings, teaching and co-operative study made possible the compilation of this volume of *Asian Christian Theologies*. Along with the Contributors (listed elsewhere), some have provided personal knowledge and counsel, while others have given indispensable assistance in the research, drafting and compilation of particular sections. Many eminent theologians, writers and activists throughout the Asian region and beyond have given valued encouragement and advice, and librarians both of theological colleges and of universities in many countries have also provided wide-ranging support. It is of course impossible to acknowledge by name here all who have assisted with their expertise and sustaining help.

Amongst the many colleagues who have given particular assistance, the following at least, must be mentioned for this volume:

Mrs Margaret Allen of the China Desk, Churches Together in Britain and Ireland, London; Ms Aiko Carter, formerly of the Woman's Desk, National Christian Council of Japan, Tokyo; Dr Cho Kwong, Department of History, Korea University, Seoul, Korea; Dr Hyondok Choe of the Asia Desk, Institute of Missiology, Missio, Aachen, Germany; Dr Peter Choi Wai Man, Rector of Holy Spirit Seminary, Hong Kong; Dr Choi Ki Young, Head of Research at the Research Foundation of Korean Church History, Seoul; Dr Theresa Chu Mei-fen of the National Seminary in Beijing, China; Dr Luis Gutheinz sj, Graduate School of Theology, Fujen University Theological Faculty, Taipei, Taiwan; Dr. Huang Po Ho, President of Tainan Theological College and Seminary, Tainan, Taiwan; Dr Im Tae-soo, Director of the Research Institute of Minjung Theology,

Seoul; Sr Leo Kim Jeong-ja of the Little Servants of the Holy Family of Seoul; Kim Sung-hee, PhD candidate, Drew University, NJ, USA; Sr Theresa Shun Sil Kim of the Korean Catholic Women's Community for a New World, Seoul; the Rev'd Kwok Nai Wong, former Director of the Hong Kong Christian Institute, Hong Kong; Dr Archie Lee Chi Chung, Dept of Religious Studies, Chinese University of Hong Kong; the Rev'd Lee Jae-chun, PhD candidate, Drew University, NJ; Lee Sook-jin, PhD candidate, Ewha Womans University, Seoul; Dr Loh I-to, formerly president of Tainan Theological College and Seminary, Tainan, Taiwan; Sr Betty Ann Maheu of Holy Spirit Study Centre, Hong Kong; Dr Noh Yong Pil, Researcher of the Institute of Anthropology, Catholic University of Korea, Seoul; Dr Oda Takehiko, Bishop and associate professor of Theology, Sapientia University, Osaka, Japan; Dr Martin Repp of the NCC Center for the Study of Japanese Religions, Kyoto, Japan; the Rev'd Carl Smith, historian and archivist, Hong Kong; Prof. John Jyigiokk Tin, formerly of the Tainan Theological College and Seminary, Tainan, Taiwan; Dr John Tong, formerly director of Holy Spirit Study Centre and now Assistant Bishop of Hong Kong; Dr Philip Wickeri, formerly of Amity Foundation, Nanjing, China, now professor of mission and evangelism, San Francisco Theological Seminary; the Rev'd Yamano Shigeko, of the Central Theological College, Tokyo; Ms Yoshida Megumi, consultant, Tomisaka Christian Centre, Tokyo; Zhou Tailiang of the Bishops' Conference Office of the Catholic Church in China, Beijing, China; and Dr Rachel Zhu Xiaohong of Fudan University, Shanghai, China.

Thanks must go especially to those colleagues who have greatly assisted in the final editing of country chapters: Dr Theresa Chu Mei-fen, Dr Oda Takehiko, Dr Huang Po Ho, Sr Betty Ann Maheu, Dr Kwan Sui-man, Dr Philip Wickeri and Dr Hwang Jong Ryul; to Dr Chu Mei-fen and to Dr Kim Yong Bock who have generously contributed Forewords; and to Dr Judo Poerwowidagdo and the staff of the Asian Christian Art Association who have again assited with the illustrations here included. Special mention must also be made of the additional editorial work done by Dr David Suh Kwan-sun and Dr John M. Prior svd, of the professional services as copy and detail editor in addition to her other editorial responsibilities

Acknowledgements

given by Janice Wickeri and to Rita M. England who has undertaken supplementary research, editorial and proof-reading responsibilities at every stage. Co-ordination of writing and editing has been done by John C. England. The Editors wish to also acknowledge the careful work of the Rev'd Ashish Amos, Rachna Singh and their staff at the ISPCK throughout the production of these volumes.

Foreword 1

All Asian Christian theologies live and grow in the context of world religions and ancient cultures and East/Northeast Asia is a multi-racial and multi-religious region where different Asian nationalities have also their own native religions. Encounter with world organized religions such as Islam, Buddhism, or Christianity only came later, so much so that a layer of Shamanism lies buried underneath Korean Christianity, for example, and the same can be said of ancestor-worship in China and Shintoism in Japan. Once world religions entered this part of Asia, however, they circulated from one nationality to another, touching and transforming mores and thought in diverse ways. Confucianism and Buddhism, Christianity and (to a lesser extent in this region) Islam, encountered and sometimes blended with Taoism, Shintoism, Shamanism and other primal religious traditions, in periods when major socio-political changes erupted and extensive encounters between eastern and western cultures also occurred. This is the setting for the reflection and writings presented below.

Consideration of this history clearly calls for the reviewing of Christian theology in order to find a deeper connection between theology and one's specific culture, especially during times of large-scale changes. Culture here is understood not only to include philosophical systems, artefacts and styles of life in general, but also the unspoken-of value system underlying a people's way of thinking, their religion and politics. Of course the way people understand God, the meaning of life, human beings and their relationship to God and to one another is also an integral part of culture as are political systems. So much so that a systemic change in politics or in religion is not likely to last unless it is deeply rooted in culture. For all Asians, encounter with the West represented a challenge, and Christianity was perceived, in this period at least, as a thing of the West. Yet it will be seen that discernment and articulation of the roots of theology in culture and in the specific experiences of a given people, has a long and rich tradition in the East and Northeast Asia region. Complex and sometimes catastrophic historical changes have also stimulated creative developments in theological reflection. The chapters which follow present many of the writings and authors responsible for these.

As an example, the Chinese experience of the modern missionary movement, of westernization and of revolution illustrates processes common to much of the region as well as the relationship between socio-political change and contextual theological reflection. Throughout the 19th and early 20th centuries, much of Catholic theology for example, put its strongest emphasis on the after-life and on the salvation of individual souls. In this, missionaries found a great incentive for their heroic approach to China. To baptize dying babies found in streets became most rewarding although few seemed to ask why the babies were there to be found. That question would have to wait until after the Vatican II Council in order to be clearly heard in the Catholic Church. Till then (and perhaps even up to the present moment for some in our countries), the emphasis on after-life made the clergy, and especially western missionaries, benefactors bringing eternal life to the Chinese believer, who assumes a humble position as receivers. Chinese Catholics were rightly grateful to the missionaries, but their uncritical and unthinking stance often prevented them from growing into mature Christians. They were content to be good Catholics, since that was sufficient for them to attain the aim of life. Given the prevalent theology at the time, it is perhaps understandable that, as a rule, missionaries did not raise the social or nationalistic consciousness of their Chinese believers.

At the time of the Vatican II ecumenical council (1962-65), the Roman Catholic Church outside China experienced a major paradigm shift in all branches of theology. Had this change come earlier, Chinese Catholics might have been better equipped to face the challenge of the revolution, simply because the new theology is more universal, less western culture -bound. Ironically, China - that most needed such a change - was excluded from the experience. Earlier in the century Protestant theologians further developed more

Foreword 1

open and localised theologies and more recently under Bishop K. H. Ting and colleagues have launched a major effort towards constructive theological thought. Chinese Catholics have worked towards the same goals, recently under the leadership of Bishop Tu Shihua. The task is of course immense and long-term. For, while the present generation has the advantage of closeness to contemporary history, future generations will have that of distance and objectivity. For these tasks this Research Guide is so valuable, providing as it does theological resources that are both contemporary and drawn from long centuries of history.

The success of the Chinese revolution leading to the proclamation of the People's Republic on October 1st, 1949 took Chinese Catholics by surprise. They were accustomed to obeying authority. Their Confucian past as well as their Catholic upbringing had led to this. But now that there were two mutually competing authorities, which one were they to obey and why? The new situation invited grassroots laity as well as clergy to think for themselves and to make personal decisions. At the same time, the concrete reality after 1949 - political movements as well as individual contacts - showed them the darker side of the Church whereas they were used to think of her as a spotless Mother! As well, they were shown the positive side of the revolution whereas they were told that the government ushered in by the revolution was the enemy of the Church. They truly needed a new paradigm, but it could not be obtained overnight. So these good-willed individuals, full of faith in God, struggled, suffered, and became divided. Theology would now have to articulate these ongoing experiences.

Of course very similar conditions and responses occurred in the other countries of Northeast Asia. For Korea and Japan, Formosa/Taiwan and Hong Kong also until the early 20th century, it was only exceptional expatriates or nationals who showed in life and thought a theology that was socially and nationally aware. As in China, revolutionary changes occurred in these territories; massive social needs shaped Christian response; and nationalistic consciousness grew amongst many who recognised the ambiguities of modernisation or the evils of imperialism. In society at large many agreed that western science and technology could be utilised, but it was widely emphasised that China, Korea, Japan and (later) Hong Kong and Taiwan must keep their own, local, non-negotiable identity. One can see in following chapters some of the many theological questions raised by experience in China and other Northeast Asian countries from the mid-18th century up to now, among these being: What does salvation in fact mean in local context? What is the relationship between religion and culture? Between religion and politics? What resources does the Christian faith offer for social and political reconstruction? And what are the forms of Christian community which are both rooted in, and nourish, the human community in which they are set?

If major historical events and life situations in China demand that Chinese Christians reflect theologically within their own culture, it would be possible to similarly trace the impact of social and political changes upon the self-understanding and theology of Christian Commuities in Japan and Korea, Taiwan and Hong Kong. In Japan, Christian identity would be shaped by centuries of persecution and the seemingly miraculous re-emergence of Catholic believers in the mid-19th century; by the turmoils of the Meiji restoration and the emergence of Protestant scholars and universities; by the tides of western thought and technology and the conflicts and injustices arising from military and economic imperialism; and by the pervasive traditions of Shintoism and Buddhism. In Korea, long persecution also ended in the last quarter of the 19th century, and western influence early supported nationalist movements. Here the social and political consciousness of Christians was long sharpened by the suffering in successive periods of oppressive domination, by China, Japan and a series of military dictatorships until the late 20th century. The painful division of Korea into North and South, the social consequences of unbridled industrialisation, and the resurgence of *minjung* identity have also brought major issues for Christian understanding. Taiwanese Christian consciousness has also been permanently shaped by the hegemony of neighbouring powers: by imperial China, by Japan, and by the Kuo Min Tang, until recent decades. Rapid industrialisation, ethnic diversity and Taiwanese identity have

Foreword 1

been no less important as challenges to Christian reflection. For Hong Kong, theological issues have also been sharply raised by long comprador experience under British rule, by economic inequalities, and by questions of 'hybrid' identity, of democratic process and of Chinese tradition.

Creative Christian leaders and theologians in each country of East/Northeast Asia, as will be clearly seen in following pages, have therefore reflected upon the path of God's Spirit in their histories, have often participated in forward-looking social or political movements, and have allowed their theology to be shaped by their people's suffering and aspiration. The Research Guide seeks to place the rich story of Christian theologies firmly within these diverse social and political contexts and thus provide historically-rooted introductions to centuries of theological thought and life. Each historical situation has its uniqueness and the invitation to read one's own situation or that of others in the light of faith is addressed to all. The Chinese Catholic situation but gives us an example. Would a post-Vatican II position based on liberal humanism be enough for an Asian country? How do Asian cultural roots provide resources for our theological reflection? What do our reflections say to our culture? How does a living theology inspire and sustain our Christian communities to discern and join the work of God throughout the whole of our people's life? These and many related questions are fully considered throughout *Asian Christian Theologies*. I deeply hope therefore that future generations will take these and other questions most seriously in their study, teaching and writing. Then, editors of the Research Guide would be doing Christian Churches in Asia a tremendous service, they would have provided a stepping stone towards a bright future for Christian theology and Christian presence in Asia.

Theresa Chu Mei-fen
National Seminary, Beijing, China.

Foreword 2

It is indeed wonderful for the Asian theological community to celebrate the publication of this very important third volume in the series on resources for Asian theology. It is the first time in Asian history that such works have been made available. There are several important points to be made concerning this event. First of all it is now possible to "construct" a comprehensive history of Asian theology based upon this publication. Up to the present time scholars could only find and use partial and fragmentary materials on the history and materialsof Asian theology: now it is possible to build a historiography of Asian theology. Secondly, this publication will make possible a specifically Asian history of theology for the three volumes contain not only English and Western language materials, but also materials in the original languages. This then makes the Asian construction of historical theology fully credible and I believe that this is a truly major step in the construction of Asian theology with Asian resources. Thirdly, these three volumes allow Asian theological scholars to share in an unprecedented way their theological insights among themselves as well as with theologians outside the continent.

I am very happy to note that all three volumes are truly ecumenical in editorial policy. In the first place they contain materials from all Asian Christian churches and traditions. Previously we could not find such ecumenical scope in works on Asian theology. The publication will therefore facilitate ecumenical dialogue in theology in Asia. But it is ecumenical not only in scope, but also in content, so that all volumes clearly include ecumenical issues such as interfaith, societal and ecological questions along with other issues. Also it is a very gender-conscious publication with strong emphasis placed upon enlisting theological works of and by women theologians in a distinct way.

The publication of these volumes lays many foundations for further work. The basis for much further research and intrepretation in each country is here provided. There is much now to do in studying and assimilating the range of resources here assembled, but much yet also to uncover and assemble from our autonomous Christian theologies. In addition, for future compilations, the theological work of Asian Christian diaspora communities in Asia, as well as outside of Asia, should be gathered and included. The publications and source materials produced by missionaries and other theologians, which are held in Western mission archives and Western theological libraries and institutions must also be eventually included. Of course, these additional materials must be collected and selected, as in these volumes, from an Asian theological perspective both regarding their historical context and their content.

I want to express my personal thanks to the editors and supporters of these three grand volumes of Asian Christian Theology. It is indeed an important historical event to cause congratulation and celebration among the Asian theological community. Now we can confidently talk of Asian Christianity in historical and theological terms. I hope that the various levels of subsequent work will now be widely taken up and pursued in conscientious, liberated and autonomous ways..

Kim Yong-Bock
Chancellor, Advanced Institute for the Study of Life,
Seoul, Korea

A Note on Languages, Terms, Style

Much of the theological writing and scholarship done today in Asia is written or published in English. As Michael Amaladoss points out in his Foreword to volume I, English is the link language of Asia, "less an embodiment of culture than a medium of communication." But the grounding of this Research Guide in what has become the default language of international communication will, we hope, make these resources more broadly available within the region itself.

The English language, however, and by extension the varieties in use in Asia, is far from uniform. Its varieties give only a hint of the greater linguistic and cultural diversity in which they exist. The history of a community, often its experience of colonisation, and the unique character of its encounter with Christianity all bear on the choice of 'Englishes'. We have avoided standardization beyond the chapter level, for the multiplicity of usage, punctuation and spelling that a work of this scope embraces reflects, in its sometimes jarring, hybrid nature, the realities and diversities of the Asia region.

Extensive research has been undertaken to ensure that a wide range of vernacular materials are included and outlined. Care has also been taken to provide translation where necessary, along with correct forms for romanization. In very many cases, alternative forms are widely used in the region, both for key terms in discourse and for personal names, and these proliferate further in secondary language sources

Any work in English which refers to Chinese, Japanese and Korean sources for non-readers of these languages, must contend with a variety of romanization systems, a dilemma only made worse for heavily historical works by the sometimes substantive changes in such systems over time.

The Chinese case is the most complicated. Jesuit missionaries formed the first romanization systems in the 17th century; however, since the 1970s, the contemporary mainland Chinese system of *pinyin* has come into widespread use. Tone markings are frequently omitted however, since the general reader would have little understanding of or use for them. Nineteenth century (and earlier) materials in English, and scholarship based on them, generally use the Wade-Giles system. Examples of the difference would be Tao (Wade-Giles) vs. Dao (*pinyin*) or Mao Tse-tung (Wade-Giles) vs. Mao Zedong (*pinyin*). For historical materials, the waters can be further muddied by retention of forms used in the Postal System, such as Foochow (Fuzhou in *pinyin*) or Szechuan (Sichuan). Wade-Giles and *pinyin* are Mandarin-based. There are systems based on other dialects: Sun Yat-sen for example (Cantonese) or the theologian N.Z. Zia (Shanghai). In the U.S., there is also the Yale system, though this is little used now.

For ease of use and understanding, Chinese titles are given in *pinyin* where possible, while many individual terms are given in both forms. Personal names are given in the form most preferred by the person, if that is known (K.H. Ting); in the most widely used form, if well-known; or in *pinyin*. For individual entries, all commonly used forms are given. For example: T.C. Chao/ Chao Tse-ch'en/ Zhao Zichen. For those who use an English name as well, this is given first to preserve the form of the name in the original language; for example, Angela Wong Wai-ching. Hong Kong names are most commonly romanized in Cantonese, and for these, the Mandarin is given in parentheses: Angela Wong Wai-ching (Huang Huizhen).

A number of different systems are used in Taiwan for both Han characters (as in Mandarin Chinese), and for Taiwanese. For the former there are also a number of special characters sometimes used which are unique to Taiwan. Taiwanese (Tâi-oân-oe or Ho-ló-oe) is the variant of Hokkien spoken widely in Taiwan. The romanized form most often used follows the system originally developed by Christian missionaries (Peh-oe-ji, "vernacular writing"), and many writers included here employ this.

Several systems exist for Japanese ideographs (*kanzi*) and syllabary (*kana*) - for example Hepburn, National *roomazi* and *monbusho;* and for Korean *hangul* as well - McCune-Reischauer, Yale, and revised romanization. These are not however as entrenched either historically or in common usage, so it is unnecessary to give more than one form. Representation of personal names in Japanese is generally given in these pages surname first as is the traditional and widespread practice in Japan. Korean names are also given surname first, usually in three discrete syllables: Ryu Dong Shik; though some, following personal preference or published materials, may make use of a hyphen, as Lee Chang-Sik. For all three languages, whether in the text or in bibliographical listings, surname is given first, followed by the "given" name, with no comma between. A Christian name will usually come first.

English spelling and punctuation follow that which is customary within the country under consideration. Apart from some minor variations made necessary by particular cultural traditions, the style followed is that of *The Chicago Manual of Style*. Particular terms and usages - and in some cases formats - native to the area concerned have been retained where possible, both to remain true to the wide diversity of texts and authors, and also to signify important aspects of localised context and reflection. A glossary, which can be only partial for such vast geographical areas and such immense bodies of writing, is provided for abbreviations, special terms and acronyms, along with full indexes to subjects and to personal names.

Abbreviations

ABCFM	-	American Board of Commissioners for Foreign Mission
ABS	-	The American Bible Society
ACISCA	-	Association of Christian Institutes for Social Concern in Asia
ACPO	-	Asian Committee for people's Organization
ACPP/CCP	-	The Asian Centre for the Progress of Peoples, Hong Kong
AILM	-	Asian Institute for Liturgy and Music, Quezon City, Philippines
ARENA	-	Asia Regional Exchange for New Alternatives, Hong Kong
ARMS	-	*The Annual Report of the Missionary Society of the Methodist Episcopal Church*
ARPC	-	*Annual Reports of the Board of Foreign Mission of the Presbyterian Church in the USA*
ATESEA	-	Association for Theological Education in Southeast Asia
ATLA	-	American Theological Libraries Association
AWRCCT	-	Asian Women's Resource Centre for Culture and Theology, Kuala Lumpur, Malaysia
BCCCC	-	Bishops' Conference of the Catholic Church in China
BFBS	-	British and Foreign Bible Society

CAN	-	*China News Analysis*
CASS	-	publisher in Shanghai, China
CBCK	-	Catholic Bishops' Conference of Korea
CCA	-	Christian Conference of Asia
CCA URM	-	Christian Conference of Asia - Urban Rural Mission
CCPA	-	Chinese Catholic Patriotic Association
CCRAI	-	Centre for Christian Response to Asian Issues, Japan
CGST	-	China Graduate School of Theology, Hong Kong
CIC	-	Christian Industrial Committee, Hong Kong
CIIR	-	Catholic Institute for International Relations, London
CIM	-	China Inland Mission (now OMF)
CIS	-	publisher in Beijing, China
CISJD	-	Christian Institute for the Study of Justice and Development, Korea
CLS	-	Christian Literature Society - (in Japan, Kyo Bun Kwan)
CLSK	-	Christian Literature Society Korea
CMYB	-	*The China Mission Year Book*
CNWS	-	Centre of Non-Western Studies, Leiden University
CPC	-	China Patriotic Committee
CPH	-	Catholic Publishing House, Korea
CPPCC	-	Chinese People's Political Consultative Conference
CR	-	*Chinese Recorder*
CR*	-	*Chinese Repository*

Abbreviations

CSCCRC	-	Christian Study Centre on Chinese Religion and Culture, Hong Kong
CTC	-	Commission for Theological Concerns (CCA)
CTR	-	*Chinese Theological Review*
CUHK	-	Chinese University of Hong Kong
CWC	-	Currents of World Christianity, Cambridge, England
CWM	-	Council for World Mission
DPP	-	Democratic Progressive Party, Korea
EACC	-	East Asia Christian Conference (now Christian conference of Asia)
EAPR	-	*East Asia Pastoral Review*
EATWOT	-	Ecumenical Association of Third World Theologians
EMI	-	publisher in Bologna, Italy
EWS	-	Economic Welfare Society
EYCK	-	Ecumenical Youth Council of Korea
FABC	-	Federation of Asian Bishops' Conferences
FKC	-	Federation of Korean Christians
FM	-	*Foreign Missionary*
HKCC	-	Hong Kong Christian Council
IBMR	-	*International Bulletin of Missionary Research*
ICMICA	-	International Catholic Movement for Intellectual and Cultural Affairs
ICU	-	International Christian University, Tokyo, Japan
IDOC FME	-	(*IDOC Future of the Missionary Enterprise*)
IISR	-	International Institute for the Study of Religious Responsibility

IKCH	- Institute of Korean Church History, Seoul
ISCS	- Institute of Sino-Christian Studies, Hong Kong
JOC	- Young Catholic Workers
KACWWM	- Korea Association of Christian Women for Women Minjung
KAFT	- Korean Association of Feminist Theology
KAWT	- Korean Association of Women Theologians
KCA	- Korea Christian Academy
KCCJ	- Korean Christian Church in Japan
KCFM	- Korea Catholic Farmers' Movement
KCWC	- Korean Catholic Women's Community for a New World
KCWU	- Korean Church Women United
KMF	- *The Korean Mission Field*
KMT	- Kuomintang, China and Taiwan
KRP	- *The Korean Repository*
KSCF	- Korean Student Christian Federation
KTSI	- Korean Theological Study Institute
KWC	- Korea Women Church
LMS	- London Missionary Society (now CWM)
LWF	- Lutheran World Federation
MHCC	- Mission to the Higher Classes in China
MRW	- *The Missionary Review of the World*
NAC	- National Administrative Commission of the Catholic Church, China
NAE	- National Assembly of Evangelicals
NBSS	- *Quarterly Record of the National Bible Society of Scotland*

Abbreviations

NCCCUSA	-	National Council of Churches of Christ in the USA
NCCJ	-	National Christian Council of Japan
NCCK	-	National Council of Churches in Korea
NCCT	-	National Council of Churches of Taiwan
NCPCRJ	-	National Catholic Priests' Corps for the Realization of Justice, Korea
NDB	-	*Nuduobao* journal, China
NEAJOT	-	*Northeast Asia Journal of Theology*
NPC	-	National People's Congress, China
NPCCRJ	-	National Protestant Clergy's Corps for the Realization of Justice, Korea
NUTS	-	Nanjing Union Theological Seminary
OMF	-	Overseas Missionary Fellowship
PCK	-	Presbyterian Church of Korea
PCROK	-	Presbyterian Church in the Republic of Korea
PCT	-	Presbyterian Church of Taiwan
PCUSA	-	Presbyterian Church in the USA
PLA	-	Peoples' Liberation Army, China
PRC	-	People's Republic of China
PROK	-	Presbyterian Church in the Republic of Korea
PTCA	-	Programme for Theology and Cultures in Asia
RAWA	-	Revolutionary Association of the Women of Afghanistan
ROC	-	Republic of China (Taiwan)
SATHRI	-	South Asia Theological Research Institute
SCM	-	Student Christian Movement
SDSC	-	Student Development Service Corps of the YMCA and the Korean Student Christian Federation

SEAGST	- Southeast Asia Graduate School of Theology
SEAJOT	- *Southeast Asia Journal of Theology* (now *Asia Journal of Theology*)
SEMINEX	- Seminary in Exile, Tokyo, Japan
SM	- *Sheng Ming* (Life Quarterly), China.
SMC	- publisher in Taipei, Taiwan
SMCO	- Seoul Metropolitan Community Organization, Korea
SoCo	- Society for Community Organization, Hong Kong
SPG	- Society for the Propagation of the Gospel
TDWX	- *Tianzhujiao dongchuan wenxian xubian* (A collection of writings of Catholicism's Orient mission)
TEF	- Theological Education Fund (now WCC ETE)
TFS/TFSEC	- Tao Fong Shan Ecumenical Centre
TSPM	- Three-Self Patriotic Movement, China
TTCS	- Tainan Theological College and Seminary, Taiwan
UBF	- publisher in Tokyo, Japan
UCAN	- *Union of Catholic Asia News*
UCCJ	- Kyodan / United Church of Christ in Japan
UIM	- Urban Industrial Mission
UPMR	- Missionary Journal, Korea, 1870s/1880s
URM	- Urban Rural Mission
UV	- *Union Version* (of the Bible), China
WARC	- World Association of Reformed Churches
WCC	- World Council of Churches
WCTU	- Women's Christian Temperance Union

Abbreviations

WS	-	*Wenshe yuekan* (Literature Monthly), China.
WSCF	-	World Student Christian Federation
WWFE	-	*Women's Work in the Far East.*
YMCA	-	Young Men's Christian Association
YWCA	-	Young Women's Christian Association

Table of Contents: Volumes 1 & 2

Volume 1 - Regional, South and Austral Asia.

Forewords
Introduction

I Asia as Region.
   1   Groundwork for Asian Theology 1 (7-15th Cents)
   2   Groundwork for Asian Theology 2 (16-18th Cents)
   3   Asia-wide and Ecumenical Theologies .

II South Asia
   4   Contextual Theology in Bangladesh
   5   Contextual Theology in India
   6   A Note on Nepal
   7   Contextual Theology in Pakistan
   8   Contextual Theology in Sri Lanka

III Austral Asia
   9   Contextual Theology in Aotearoa New Zealand
   10 Contextual Theology in Australia

Key Bibliographic Sources
Indexes; Contributors

Vol. 2 Southeast Asia

Forewords

Introduction

1   Asia Regional Survey (Summary)
2   Southeast Asia 16-18 Cents.
3   Contextual Theology in Burma (Myanmar)
4   A Note on Contextual Theology in Cambodia and Laos
5   Contextual Theology in Indonesia
6   Contextual Theology in Malaysia and Singapore
7   Contextual Theology in the Philippines
8   Contextual Theology in Thailand
9   Contextual Theology in Vietnam

Key Bibliographic Sources
Indexes, Contributors

ILLUSTRATIONS
Volume Three: Northeast Asia

1.a. & 1.b. He Qi - China
Print: NATIVITY
(Source: *Image* 81, p.4.)
Print: CRUCIFIXION 83
(Source: *Image* 83, p.10.)

Dr He Qi is a professor at the Nanjing Union Theological Seminary and a tutor for master candidate students in the Philosophy Department of Nanjing University. He is also a member of the China Art Association and a council member of the Asian Christian Art Association. He has been committed to the artistic creation of modern Chinese Christian art for over a dozen years. He hopes to help change the "foreign image" of Christianity in China by using artistic language, and at the same time, use Christian art to supplement Chinese art the way Buddhist art did in ancient times. In his works, He Qi has blended Chinese folk customs and traditional Chinese painting techniques with the western painting art of the Middle and Modern Ages, and has created an artistic style of colour-on-paper painting.

In his "old paintings" He Qi painted in a kind of Chinese traditional style—brush and ink with water, which is called 'scholarly painting', emphasising only water and ink without colour (also called Zen Art).

Here are his comments: "As a Christian artist, I start from the story of Creation (Genesis) - when God said 'Let there be light', he made a colourful world. In my travels, I have seen so many original works of impressionism, post-impressionism, expressionism, cubism, even American abstract-expressionism....., I am interested in doing a kind of art style which is a mixture of Chinese traditional style and western modern style. In my point of view, our Chinese traditional art not only includes the 'Zen painting' but should also include

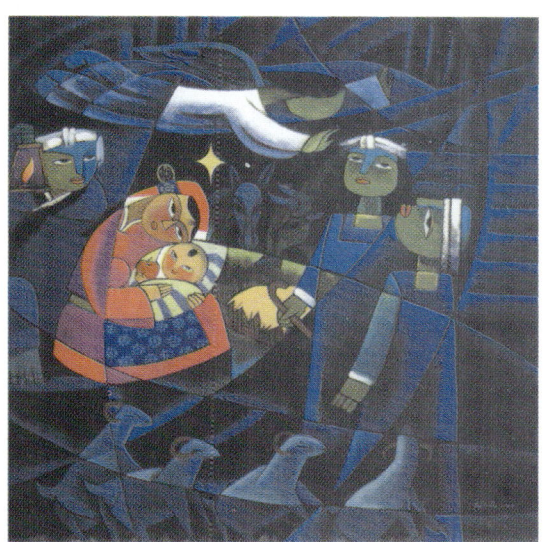

He Qi – Nativity

He Qi – Crucifixion

Wang Honyi – Safe in His Mother's Arms

Ding Fang – Go into Belief - (Detail)

An Dong-Sook – Temptation of Christ

Kim Hak Soo – The Sermon on the Mount

Sadao Watanabe – The Angel Ascends from the Rising of the Sun

Chinese folk art and minority national art—which are very colourful!"

2 Wang Honyi - China
Print: SAFE IN HIS MOTHER'S ARMS
Source: *The Bible through Asian Eyes*, p.81.

Wang Hon-yi was born in China in 1942. He is a professional artist painting in the *nanga* (Chinese brush-painting) style. His Christmas painting was used by the Chinese church in its annual calendar in 1984. He works for the Jiangsu Provincial Art Museum.

3 Ding Fang - China
Print: GO INTO BELIEF (detail)
Source: *The Bible through Asian Eyes*, p.95.

Ding Fang was born in Nanjing, China, in 1956. Graduating from the Nanjing Art College with a degree in oil painting, he became a teacher of art at the Nanjing Art College. Since 1988 he has been a member of the Chinese Art Academy.

4 An Dong-Sook - Korea
Print: TEMPTATION OF CHRIST
Source: *The Bible through Asian Eyes*, p.91.

An Dong-Sook was born in Korea in 1922. Through the influence of another artist, he was converted to Christianity and baptised in 1950. He has been chairperson of Oriental Art at Ewha Women's University in Seoul. His abstract art works are often based on biblical texts. He experiments with different styles: the "Temptation" was painted in watercolours in 1990 and exhibited at the annual exhibition of Korean Christian art.

5 Kim Hak Soo - Korea
Print: THE SERMON ON THE MOUNT
Source: *The Bible through Asian Eyes*, p.101.

Kim Hak Soo was born in Pyongyang in 1919 and studied with Kim Un Ho in Seoul in the 1940s. While recovering from a serious illness at the age of 40, he felt "a calling" to begin his life anew, returning more closely to his Christian faith. He was encouraged by the Rev'd Kim Yang Son to begin religious painting and he did so using the traditional methods of old Chosun. Events are drawn in careful, correct detail using traditional Korean brush and ink with additional colour. To mark the centennial of the Protestant church in Korea, Kim Hak Soo completed two large projects: 66 historical paintings of the early history of the church in Korea and an additional series on the life of Christ. There are 36 paintings in the portrayal of the life of Christ and each shows Jesus' ministry in a Korean context. "The Sermon on the Mount' is part of this series.

6 Sadao Watanabe

Print: THE ANGEL ASCENDS FROM THE RISING OF THE SUN
Source: *The Bible through Asian Eyes*, p.191.

Sadao Watanabe of Japan is one of Asia's best-known Christian artists. His works are found in collections from the Vatican museum to the White House in Washington. His distinctive graphic style makes the prints particularly useful for illustration and a Watanabe art work will often be seen on the cover of a book or as a poster.

Introduction

The central aim in preparing this volume of the Research Guide - as with the previous two volumes - has been to introduce and chart the range and significance of Asian Christian theologies in historical context, and to provide the resources and tools for *their* study. The focus of this volume is East and Northeast Asia. Responses thus far to volumes 1 and 2 have been very gratifying and helpful comments have been recorded for possible revised editions. It must also again be recognised that however much research and collaboration has been undertaken in preparing this volume, there may still be omissions of significant items or inaccuracies in some entries. For these we ask your pardon and also your fuller cooperation in order to correct and complete this guide to contextual Christian thelogies throughout the region. The general introduction to the series here follows.

It is of course impossible within even three volumes to provide an exhaustive coverage of Christian reflection and writing from half the Christian world over more than fifteen centuries. Within scores of diverse cultures and religious traditions - Shinto or Taoist, Primal Hindu, Confucian, Buddhist or Islamic - Christian faith has lived and interacted since the earliest centuries. From this presence has come

- bodies of Christian writing from at least the 4th century with particular creativity in the periods of the 4th-5th centuries (west Asia in particular), 7th-8th centuries (west and central Asia), 16th-17th centuries (east and south Asia), late 19th century and second half of the 20th century (throughout the region).

- writings in a wide variety of literary and oral-record forms - frequently shaped by local tradition - along with richly diverse expressions in art, architecture and community life.

- reflection, scholarship, and devotion amidst the widest range of movements and endeavours for not only spiritual nurture and 'church-planting', 'leadership training', and many-sided educational and medical programmes, but also in community and inter-religious movements for social reform or political reconstruction, for rural development and environmental protection, for women's concerns and human rights, for peace, social justice, community reconciliation, and the empowering of the destitute and powerless.

A Different Focus

A large part of this theological work and writing can indeed be studied with the help of resources here provided, but the primary focus in the following sections is more limited. It is rather to outline the key sources for a study of 'Asian theologies' which have arisen from, and fed, Christian life in a particular country and region; 'reflective' responses to God's historic and present work in Tamilnadu or Tomohon, Guangdung or Luzon, Cholla, or Kyushu. The focus is therefore upon contextualizing, incarnational or 'local' theologies which discover within a people's present struggle and aspiration, and in their creative cultural and religious traditions, the presence of the same liberating and transforming Spirit known in Jesus the Christ.

From early centuries on, and now in the midst of sharp socio-economic and cultural discord, we can recognise theological reflection and construction which is both critical and doxological, non-dualistic and communitarian, dialogical and confessional, dissident and devotional, historical, incarnational, pilgriming, heuristic and pragmatic. Beyond the motives of communicating the faith or nurturing believers, creative theological reflection is here often a wrestling with such issues as:

- "what understanding of Christian faith in our culture will make possible social reconstruction and spiritual reform for our nation and people?" (in the 17th or 18th centuries: such authors as Yang Tingyun, Fucan Fabian, and Chong Yak-jong; in the 19th and early 20th centuries: such authors as Krishna Mohan Banerjea, Jose Burgos, Nguyen Truong To and Kozaki Hiromichi, amongst many others);

- "what faith and spirituality will nourish our people in prophetic and holistic mission?" (in the 20th century: such theologians - out of very many - as C.L. Wickremasinghe, Khin Maung Din,

Park Sun-ai, T.B. Simutupang, Shoki Coe, Horatio de la Costa).

Such bodies of reflection and insight are not easily classified according to non-Asian theological movements or western theological disciplines. The long and autonomous traditions of Asian theologies have not only other sources and intentions, but frequently question, even reject, the elements or frameworks of western or westernising theologies. In this, many Asian theologies are "post- (or pre-) colonial", and reject either explicitly or implicitly the categories of imperial or neo--imperial theories and theologies, especially where these would claim an "objective" or normative role in assessing or interpreting theological reflection.

Whatever similarities can be found to the theologies of other regions, those of Asia have long held quite distinct qualities. There is in Asia a special seriousness of concern for indigenous culture and religion, and a particular apprehension of life in community as it is shaped by these. The vast scale of human suffering in Asian countries and the sharpness of the struggle for human survival has yielded also a vitality of prophetic insight and an immediacy in gospel interpretation, while the unrivalled diversity of peoples, of Christian traditions and of historical experience in the region give a unique character to each of Asia's theologies.

In this sense, these theologies, like all others, are local theologies. They arise at a particular point of history, in the dynamic interaction of gospel, church, and culture. They grow out of and serve national or regional Christian traditions and retain the marks of a unique cultural experience. This can be thought to undermine the universality of the Christian gospel only by ignoring the particularity and historicity of God's dealings with Israel and of the life of Jesus himself. Those who would reject the localised character of theological construction are often in fact imposing their own formulations as in some sense normative for all others. And this often veils only thinly a westernising or ethnocentric oppression brought about by cultural (and economic) domination.

Theological reflection is Asian therefore, not because of the characteristics shared with other parts of the region: far less because of the nationality or geographical location of the theologian. Rather it will be Asian, and a witness to the one living God, in so far as it discerns and responds to the unique incarnation of the Gospel in a local Asian context.

'The Lord has a personal and particular controversy' with the people of Thailand or Sri Lanka, the Philippines or Korea as much as with Israel; with the people of Indonesia or Vietnam, India or Japan as with Judah. And in each of Asia's peoples, this presence and 'controversy' comes as a different summons.

In their vast extent, their wisdom and witness, such writings and reflections are also a continuing challenge to any assumptions that Asian theologies are of secondary importance or that western theologies are somehow normative for all others. Extensive libraries of Christian writing, from many countries over many centuries, and the vitality of reflection and insight they contain, demonstrate that Asian theology is a major study in its own right, with independent sources and experience and with its own autonomy of intention and interpretation.

It must be recognised, however, that the thought patterns, the terminology, and the interpretive principles used in incarnational Asian theologies are frequently markedly different from those which are often assumed to be normative in some other regions. The systematic metaphysical construction that emerged in the post-medieval West for example, has seldom been an indispensable - or even recognised - element in incarnatonal Asian theologies. And it will be clear throughout this Guide that Asian Christians have long possessed different models - of insight and wisdom, discernment and truth-seeing, of heart-knowledge and life-shaping - by which they "do theology", reflecting upon and living the faith.

The forms of thought and writing included for study here, include therefore not only treatises and volumes, articles and theses, but also many other forms, including letters and poetry, liturgies, homilies and confessions, declarations, meditations, and life-stories. And because 'spirituality' and devotion has from the earliest centuries been integral to the doing of theology in Asian cultures, the 'theology' presented often demonstrates a unity of life-

Introduction xliii

experience and mysticism, of cultural identity and critical reflection, which goes beyond particular 'disciplines' while also drawing on a wide range of Christian resources. The reflection and writing may in fact be incidental to ministry, to vocation or to activism, arising from present needs to "take the next step in pilgrimage", rather than from any desire to contribute to systematic thought, although this too will appear in many entries. Certainly it will be seen that Christian theology in Asian countries includes all deeply human issues and concerns within its content, and that it arises as much in a dynamic unity of words and life - an alternative hermeneutic of prophetic witness - as in the formulation of creative expositions.

Charting Resources

Scores of national bibliographies, surveys, histories, and anthologies have attempted to introduce sections of these large bodies of material, and many regional studies, collections, and surveys have been published in recent decades. In addition there are now over two hundred theological journals published regularly in the region along with publications by networks of Christian publishers, Study and Social Concern Centres, People's Movements, Pastoral Institutes, and Theological Schools. A guide-to-study which attempts to be more comprehensive, and practical, in aim has become increasingly necessary in order to introduce and chart a fuller range of the resources available. And such a charting must be based on careful work, to assemble as well as reclaim a wide spectrum of theological sources which are genuinely contextualizing or incarnational. These include both unique national and local bodies of thought and witness, and also the writings which have arisen from regional movements and complex theological interactions. We recognise the significance not only of creative individuals, and scholarly teachers, but also of groups and collectives, of 'non-professional'/lay women and men, and of thinkers, witnesses or activists, some having only tenuous relationship to an institutional church. The attempt has also here been made to include such thought and writings from those of 'Orthodox', 'Catholic' or 'Protestant' communions, in all parts of

Asia/Austral-Asia, from all cultural traditions and from the period of the 7th to 20th centuries.

In order to do this, the approach chosen for this 'guide-to-study' presents study-outlines by country and region. These may include brief historical introductions, mini-studies of selected texts and writers, and bibliographies for these as well as for additional sources. Although most sections appear in the form of individual, group or theme entries, followed by selected references, some are largely annotated and categorised bibliographies. In view of the wide diversity of theological context and tradition being included, such minimum diversity in format is appropriate. Supplementary bibliographies are also provided where necessary; further works by authors cited can be found in such serials as *Theology in Context* (Bi-annual, Aachen); *International Review of Mission* (Quarterly, Geneva); *Bibliographia Missionaria* (Annual, Rome); and *PTCA Bulletin* (Bi-annual, Kyoto and Chiangmai). Special attention has been given to, but is not limited to, the work and writings of nationals, both 'lay' and professional, with particular recognition of women's thought and work. But the primary reason for inclusion in all cases has been the intention by the author(s) to 'incarnate' the gospel in a particular Asian context in response to the realities of a people's life and God's presence within them.

It is hoped that the combination of historical contexts, textual and biographical notes, bibliographies and other tools will form a practical guide to the people, movements, and literatures which offer, for the life of our people now, the wealth of Asian theological reflection and insight.

Use of the Guide

A chapter for each country of Northeast Asia is here provided, comprising entries for individuals, groups and movements, as well as for historical contexts and diverse categories of writing. These all include selected bibliographies which are enlarged in extensive supplementary bibliographies for each country. Quick reference to particular authors, movements, sources or contexts can be found by use of the listing that commences each chapter and/or by use of the indexes

Introduction

In using this guide for individual or group study, the following approaches are suggested:

i) Country studies - centred in theological movements and leaders within a particular period.

ii) Thematic studies - selecting writings on Christian ethics; theologies of struggle, spirituality or mission; cross-cultural or inter-faith interpretation ... within a group of countries.

iii) Study of regional movements in, for example, women's theology, story theology, contextualising/incarnational theologies, ecumenical action and reflection, biblical hermeneutics.

iv) Study of selected texts, by country, period or movement - or surveys of theological literature within a particular historical context.

v) Research that uses this Guide as basis for the investigation of further primary sources from a country, movement or period.

A note must be added concerning the accessibility of many materials here referred to. Few theological libraries in Asia have as yet any comprehensive collection of the sources, and although some libraries in other regions have selected items, these collections also are individually fragmentary. For most countries there are extensive sources held outside the region which should be copied and returned. It has been thought best, however, to include reference to any source up to the year 2000 which is important for the further study of Asian 'theologies', regardless of its location, so that at least the necessary signposts for subsequent research are given.

The Tasks Ahead

The editors have no illusions that these volumes offer an exhaustive guide to Asian theologies but believe them to be thoroughly representative of their range and content. No similar guide has yet been attempted, and it has become increasingly clear during preparation of this study-guide that large tasks remain if the full extent and significance of the region's reflection and writing is to be recognised (and included in such a Research Guide). This work is therefore also a signpost, and hopefully a stimulus, to some of the major investigation which still needs to be undertaken.

For some countries, peoples and historical periods, we are still in the 'excavatory' stage of discovering and identifying texts and authors: much research and reclaiming is still needed, not least because the writings of nationals, of lay people, clergy, or of women have often been disguised, or even suppressed. Many studies of writings, as yet unrecognised or interpreted in their context, wait to be done. We warmly invite you to collaborate in this venture to unearth, collect, and share theological sources in our region, assuring you that the Editors will gratefully acknowledge all contributions sent to:

Research Guide to Asian Theologies,

[Either at] Puslit Candraditya, Jalan Lero Wulan No. 1,
Wairklau - Maumere 86112, Flores NTT, Indonesia;

[Or at] 13 Hilldale Place, Christchurch 8002, New Zealand.

It is now the time to give priority to the study of Asia's many living theologies, within the life of our societies - through carefully planned courses both in 'academic' and non-formal settings, in local or national seminars and workshops, and in programmes of study by individuals or groups. Increasing numbers of our colleagues beckon us to do this, and partners beyond the region ask us to share our resources with them.

The related tasks of collection, translation, publication or reprinting call for much fuller commitment and active promotion if our libraries are to possess any significant body of even fundamental texts. And for this we must seek active co-operation with the librarians of our seminaries, institutes, study and social concern centres, and with translators, publishers and distributors. For despite the collaboration of scores of scholars from the region and the very extensive research which has made this Guide possible, it remains only the first wide-ranging attempt to chart the vast materials of Asian theologies.

There then remains for us the enriching exchanges across cultures, the reinterpretation shaped by our people's struggles, and the collaboration in putting-theology-to-work, by which we together seek the transformation of society, culture, and faith which God's coming Commonwealth brings.

The Editors

1 Contextual Christian Theology in Asia
Historical Regional Survey (Summary)

1 Theological Heritage

As in other sub-regions of Asia, in order to understand contextualising theologies as these have developed in the countries of Northeast Asia in the past two centuries, it is necessary to recognise their beginnings and their diverse contributions in previous centuries also. The theological heritage of Christians throughout Asia is in fact much vaster than is usually recognised and brief surveys for this are provided below for the periods 7th-15th centuries, 16th-18th centuries, and the 19th century. For fuller outlines see: *Groundwork for Asian Theologies* I and II (chapters 1 and 2 of volume 1), and country chapters throughout.

In each country of Northeast Asia also, pioneering work prior to the 19th century has provided groundwork for contextual theological reflection, in linguistic, historical and anthropological studies, as well as in theological and inter-faith studies. As the basis for understanding later theological developments, selected examples of this groundwork are outlined in chapter 2 of this volume below. For the period since 1800, country chapters given in this volume give the fuller treatment for authors, movements and sources.

The outline below provides an overall summary for the region as a whole, as context for the resources of Northeast Asia.

1.1 Theological Heritage Before 1500
(See *Groundwork for Asian Theologies I*, volume I, chapter 1.)

In the manuscripts from writers of Turkestan and west China, from the 7th to 11th centuries, Christian scriptures and teaching are found not only in the Syriac of the parent 'Oriental Orthodox' tradition, but also in the Sogdian, Uighur and Chinese vernaculars. They utilize imagery, terminology and literary forms then current in Central Asian communities, especially those of Buddhist tradition.

Along with many translations of liturgical and ecclesiastical texts, the sutras and fragments thus far translated present a Christian faith which preserves orthodox doctrine - as in the Nestorian Motwa Hymn: *Honouring the Majestic Three, and the Credo of Rabban bar Sauma,* and also interprets the Gospels contextually - as in *The Lord of the Universe's Discourse on Almsgiving.* Some stress simplicity of life-style and compassionate service - as in the *Sianfu* (Xi'anfu) *Stele* inscription (sometimes called the Nestorian Monument) and many reflect a sympathetic dialogue with those of other living faiths - as in the sutras of Alopen such as *The Discourse on the Oneness of the Universe, Parable Part II* and the *Jesus Messiah Sutra.*

These and other writings are outlined in the books below, and additional texts are still being discovered and translated. Together these offer a growing body of Christian literature that has been significantly shaped by its context, and which has abiding significance for Christian life and mission in the region.

Selected References:
    See Supplementary Bibliography, vol. 1: Moffatt 1992; England 1998; Philip 1998.
    Gillman, Ian and Hans-Joachim Klimkeit. *Christians in Asia before 1500.* Richmond: Curzon, 1999.
    Kitagawa, Joseph Mitsuo. *The Christian Tradition: Beyond its European Captivity.* Philadelphia: Trinity Press International, 1992.
    Palmer, Martin. *The Jesus Sutras. Rediscovering the Lost Scrolls of Taoist Christianity.* New York: Ballantyne, Forthcoming.
    Saeki, Paul Yoshiro. *The Nestorian Documents and Relics in China.* Tokyo: Maruzen, 1951.
    Standaert, Nicholas. *Handbook of Christianity in China.* Vol.1: 635-1800. Leiden: Brill, forthcoming.
    van der Ploeg, J.P.M. *Syriac Manuscripts of St. Thomas Christians.* Bangalore: Dharmaram, 1983.

See also the journals *Harp* (Kottayam); *Numen* (Leiden); *SOAS Bulletin* (London); and those listed in Gillman and Klimkeit (1999).

1.2 Theological Heritage 1500-1800

(See also *Groundwork for Theologies II*, volume I, chapter 2; and *Southeast Asia 16th-18th Centuries*, chapter 2 below.)

Christian writings of the 16th to 18th centuries - most of which have yet to receive serious study - include many confessional, historical and apologetic documents, many of which translate or imitate European models. Although these often reveal the imagery and thought of indigenous translators, there are also, however, extensive writings which openly draw on indigenous tradition and display contextualising insight. And these come both from the hands of 'local' clergy, lay women, and men, and from 'foreign' lay men, and women, and clergy.

Treatises and narratives modify or reject western teaching (see for example Chong Yak Jong in Korea, Lu Y Doan in Vietnam and Fukansai Fabian in Japan); indigenous poetry and drama reshapes Christian thought (see for example Paulo Yoho-ken in Japan and Aquino de Belen in the Philippines); dialogues and treatises restore local religious tradition (see for example Yang Ting-yun, China, and the Christ Veda writers in India). There is also sometimes a complete integration of vocation, life-style, and writing in the lives of some authors, notably women (see for example, Candida Hsu (Xu) in China and Gracia Hosokawa in Japan).

Fully traditional literary or art forms are also often employed: those such as encyclopaedia (Korea and India), *babad* (East Indies), *pasyon* (Philippines), and *Maria-Kannon* (Japan).

Selected References:

Ba, Vivian. *The Early Catholic Missionaries in Burma.* A collected series of articles from Guardian Monthly, Rangoon, c. 1957-1964. Rangoon Reprint 1997.

Baago, K. *A Bibliography. Library of Indian Christian Theology.* Madras: Christian Literature Society, 1969.

Cho Kwong. *A Historical Study of Catholicism in the Late Chosun Dynasty* (in Korean). Seoul: 1988.

England, John C. "Bamboo Groves in Winds from the West: Indigenous Faith and Westernization in Asian Christian Writings of 16th-18th Centuries." In *Christen und Gewürze*, edited by Klaus Koschorke. Göttingen: Vandenhoeck & Ruprecht, 1998.

Laures, Johannes. *Kirishitan Bunko: A Manual of Books and Documents on the Early Christian Mission in Japan.* Tokyo: Sophia University, 1957.

Lumbera, Bienvenido L. *Tagalog Poetry 1570-1898: Tradition and Influences in its Development.* Quezon City: Ateneo de Manila University Press, 1986.

Nguyen Van Truong et al. *Ve Sach Bao cua Tac Gia Cong Ciao: The Ky XVII-XIX* (Books and Newspapers by Catholic Authors - Vietnam 17th-19th Centuries). Ho Chi Minh City: University of Ho Chi Minh, Literature Department, 1993.

Pieris, Edmund. *Studies Historical and Cultural.* Colombo, 1978.

Standaert, Nicholas. *Handbook of Christianity in China. Vol.1: 635-1800.* Leiden: Brill, forthcoming.

Streit, R. and J.Dindinger, eds. *Bibliotheca Missionum.* Rome: Herder, 1963: Vols. 4-8.

1.3 Theological Heritage 1800-1900

(See also Country chapters, volumes I, II, III.)

Despite continuing proscription of Christianity in many countries of the region in this period, the number of theological writings which recognise the historical and indigenous, inter-church and inter-faith dimensions of Christian faith and practice, steadily increase in this century. This is largely because of the growth of the 'modern missionary movement' throughout the region, but it also drew on continuing and renewed sources of reflection and writing within the Christian traditions of particular peoples.

In India, for example, theological and contextual writing was greatly stimulated by a cultural and religious renaissance from the 1820s on, by nationalist movements, and by inter-faith encounter. (See Volume I). In the Philippines, the traditions of the *pasyon,* folk-poetry, and narrative, often as vehicles for subversive Christian insight, continued to develop, along with strongly nationalist theology and advocacy. (See Volume II).

Contextual Christian Theology in Asia

In China, study of the Chinese culture and classics remained central for many, often placed in the context of social and educational reform, or of ecumenical co-operation. In Japan, many Kakure Kirishitan communities continued their traditions of accommodation even after the return of Catholic missionaries, while by the late 19th century, Japanese theology and identity-within-culture are being clearly expressed. (See Volume III)

In Korea and Vietnam, confessional literature arose from continuing persecution which, however, eases by mid century, to be later followed by a growing body of nationalist and reformist writing. (See Volumes II and III). In Sri Lanka, Malaya, Burma, and the East Indies, the circumstances of colonial domination largely restricted the growth of indigenous writing. Nevertheless there are many examples in each place of sustained contextual study and reflection which are now being recovered. (See Volumes I and II).

Selected References:

Bays, Daniel H., ed. *Christianity in China: From the Eighteenth Century to the Present.* Stanford: Stanford University Press, 1996.

Boyd, Robin H.S. *An Introduction to Indian Christian Theology.* Madras: Christian Literature Society, 1969, 1975.

Deats, Richard L. *Nationalism and Christianity in the Philippines.* Dallas: Southern Methodist University Press, 1967.

Furuya, Yasuo, ed. *A History of Japanese Theology.* Grand Rapids: Eerdmans, 1997.

Germany, Charles H. *Protestant Theologies in Modern Japan: A History of Dominant Theological Currents from 1920-1960.* Tokyo: IISR Press, 1965.

Handbook of Christianity in China. Vol.2: 1800-2000. Leiden: Brill, forthcoming.

Hoekema, Alle Gabe. *Deken in dynamisch evenwicht: de wordingsgeschiedenis van de nationale protestantse theologie in Indonesie (ca. 1860-1960).* Goudstratt: Uitgeverij Boekencentrum, B.V., 1984.

Lam, Wing-hung. *Chinese Theology in Construction.* Pasadena: William Carey Library, 1983.

Nguyen Van Truong et al. *Ve Sach Bao cua Tac Gia Cong Ciao: The Ky XVII-XIX.* (Books and Newspapers by Catholic

Authors, 17th-19th Centuries.) Ho Chi Minh Ville: University of Ho Chi Minh Ville, 1993.

Ryu Dong Shik. *A History of Korean Theological Thought* (in Korean). Seoul: Jun Mang Sa, 1982.

Scheiner, Irwin. *Christian Converts and Social Protest in Meiji Japan.* Berkeley & Los Angeles: University of California Press, 1970.

Schumacher, John N. *Revolutionary Clergy: The Filipino Clergy and the Nationalist Movement, 1850-1903.* Quezon City: Ateneo de Manila University Press, 1981.

Thomas, George. *Christian Indians and Indian Nationalism 1885-1950: An Interpretation in Historical and Theological Perspectives.* Frankfurt a.M: Lang, 1979.

Thomas, M.M. *The Acknowledged Christ of the Indian Renaissance.* Confessing the Faith in India 5. Madras: C.L.S. 1970.

1.4 Asian Regional and Ecumenical Theologies (19th-20th Centuries).

For a full treatment see *Asian Regional and Ecumenical Theologies* (volume I, chapter 3).

In the last two centuries theology in the Asian region has been greatly stimulated and nourished by regional and ecumenical movements in mission, study and reflection. These have emerged in rich interaction between Christian faith and the shared realities of history and culture, and have often exercised strong influence upon the development of both national and Christian identity in witness, action and theology. Churches and communities across the region have "found each other in mission", developed a wide range of networks and associations which further their common mission and produced many volumes of contextual theology.

Key movements here have been the Asia-wide council of churches - the Christian Conference of Asia (formerly the East Asia Christian Conference, 1957-) and its forerunners since the mid-19th century, and the Federation of Asian Bishops' Conferences (1970-). Both organizations operate a range of commissions and study programmes, and provide focus for many tributary institutions, centres and scholars. Both publish regular bulletins and journals addressing the theologies and practice of mission, church and society concerns, international affairs, theological formation and inter-religious life and dialogue.

From these and similar movements - Roman Catholic, Protestant and Orthodox - has come a stream of creative theological reflection, writing and collaboration. (See especially the *FABC Papers,* and *CTC Bulletin,* along with *In God's Image, East Asia Pastoral Review* and *Asia Journal of Theology).* Notable here is the role of multiplying movements and associations of women in ministry and theology, as well as of lay centres and movements and of those active in a wide variety of frontier and social ministries.

The largest proportion of the country chapters following are devoted also to this period.

Selected References

Alangaram, A. *Christ of the Asian Peoples: Towards an Asian Contextual Christology Based on the Documents of the FABC.* Bangalore: Asian Trading Corporation, 1999.

Christian Conference of Asia and Federation of Asian Bishops' Conferences. *Living and Working Together With Sisters and Brothers of Other Faiths in Asia. An Ecumenical Consultation, Singapore, 1987.* Hong Kong: CCA & FABC, 1987. Also published as *FABC Paper 49.*

Christian Conference of Asia. *Colombo to Tomohon: Christian Conference of Asia 1995 - 2000.* Hong Kong: CCA, forthcoming.

Chung Hyun-kyung. *Struggle to be the Sun Again: Introducing Asian Women's Theology.* Maryknoll, NY: Orbis Books, 1991.

England, John C. and Archie C.C. Lee, eds. *Doing Theology with Asian Resources: Ten Years in the Formation of Living Theology in Asia.* Auckland: Pace Publishing (for the Programme for Theology & Cultures in Asia), 1993.

Fabella, Virginia and Sun Ai Lee Park. *We Dare to Dream. Doing Theology as Asian Women.* Hong Kong: Asian Women's Resource Centre for Culture and Theology, 1989.

Kwok Pui-lan. *Introducing Asian Feminist Theology.* Sheffield: Sheffield Academic Press, 2000.

Philip, T.V. *Ecumenism in Asia.* Delhi: ISPCK & CSS, 1994.

Rosales, Gaudencio, C.G. Arevalo and Eilers, F.J. eds. *For All the Peoples of Asia.* 2 vols. Federation of Asian Bishops'

Conferences Document from 1970-1997. Manila: Claretian, 1992; Maryknoll, NY: Orbis Books, 1995 and 1997

Sugirtharajah, R.S., ed. *Frontiers in Asian Christian Theology: Emerging Trends.* Maryknoll, NY: Orbis Books, 1994.

Weber, Hans-Ruedi. *Asia and the Ecumenical Movement 1895-1961.* London: SCM Press, 1966: Chap. 3.

Yap Kim Hao. *From Prapat to Colombo. History of the Christian Conference of Asia 1957-1995.* Hong Kong: CCA, 1995.

2 Groundwork for Asian Christian Theologies : Northeast Asia
A Selection from Christian Writings of the 16th to 18th Centuries - an Annotated Bibliography
[See also "Asia-wide and Ecumenical Theology" volume 1, 1.1 and 1.2.]

1 Introduction

This second period in the history of Asian theologies is marked by strong influences from European thought and doctrine and yet also includes many examples of independent theological reflection by Christian Asian writers. We are, however, in the 'excavatory phase' for a study of these materials, in order to unearth, recognise and name both the writings and traditions themselves, and the characteristics of Asian thought and literature which largely shape them.

The sheer diversity of contexts, agents and partners in the encounters between 'natives' and 'foreigners' in the period requires extensive study and explication. Theologies which are either transplanted/colonising or 'incarnational'/ 'liberating' are found in the work of both local Christians and missionary teachers. Cultural-political assumptions regarding the host culture, rather than nationality or ethnicity, are primary here, and we will see that either "nationals" or "expatriates" may perform either contextualising or colonising functions.

The determining role of indigenous socio-cultural concerns (rather than purely religious responses) is a specially important feature of major Asian writings which is yet to receive recognition. In country after country, careful study of major writings reveals that urgent issues of national reform and social reconstruction, rather than questions of doctrine or religious allegiance, primarily shape the indigenous response in clearly contextualised writings The larger setting for Asian Christian writings in the 'post-classical' period (14th to 19th centuries) is that of abundant and creative interpretations within Buddhism, Confucianism, Islam and Christianity alike, which reshaped and indigenised the 'classical' traditions, at the very time when missionary agents absolutised their own (and other) thought-forms and practice. There was also a rich diversity which we must note, of other sources of thought and creativity available, in native humanist traditions, indigenous art and literary forms, and in contemporary socio-political movements and structures.

An overview of the 'types of discourse' found in 'contextual' Northeast Asian theologies in these centuries - other than a simple acceptance or imitation of introduced forms - and represented in literary or art forms from the hands of 'local' clergy, lay women and men, and from expatriate laymen and clergy, could be outlined as follows:

Local Christians encounter, but also modify, or even reject, western teachings or doctrinal formulations in commentaries, treatises, narratives;

– Indigenous verse, drama and art forms express and reshape Christian thought as brought by western missionaries;

– Indigenous religious tradition is restored and reconciled with Christian teaching in dialogues, verse-forms and treatises;

– A complete integration of vocation, lifestyle, and writing can be observed in the works of some authors/artists, and is especially notable in the lives of a number of women.

– The following selection of texts, which contain contextualising elements, is made from much larger bodies of writing which are emerging across the region.

2 China

2.1 Amongst writings by Christians in China in the 16th to 17th centuries are found letters, essays and treatises, dialogues, poetry, prefaces and memoirs. These include humanist and philosophical writings, as well as catechetical, devotional, biographical, theological, and apologetic writings. Major theological themes dealt with in the context of Chinese culture include monotheism, the Incarnation, the passion and redemption, creation, and the Trinity. Amongst the writers and extant writings should be noted:

2.1.1. Li Zhizao (Li Chih Tsao) (c.1540-1630) completed the *Tianxue zhuan*, a collection of writings - some of them contextualising - by the Jesuits and their Chinese colleagues concerning Christianity and science. Li also wrote many prefaces for the Jesuit writings which he edited. Others who also contributed to these include Xu Xuchen, Zhang Wendao and Yang Tingyun (2.1.3 below).

> Li Zhizao. *Tianxue zhuan* (First anthology of Christian learnings). 6 volumes. Taipei: Hsueh-sheng, 1966.

2.1.2. The principal writings of Li Madou (Li Ma Tou) (Matteo Ricci) (1552-1610) in collaboration with Feng Yingqing, Li Qizhao and others, include:

> *Tianzhu shiyi* (T'ien-chu shih-i) (The true meaning of the Lord of Heaven), first printed in 1603 at Beijing, largely written (as The True Record of the Lord of Heaven) between 1579-1584. First complete English translation published in bilingual edition by the Ricci Institute (Taipei-Paris-Hong Kong, 1985) as *Variétés Sinologiques* - Nouvelle Series 27. This dialogue on Christian faith in the context of Chinese culture had wide influence throughout East Asia in succeeding centuries.
> *Bianxue yidu* (Letters on Buddhism and Christianity) in *Tianxue zhuan 2* (1966): 637-687.
> Ricci's memoirs were issued by Nicholas Trigault (1576-1628) in *De Christiana expeditione apud sinas* (Augustae Vindekorum 1615), French edition in 1618 (Paris: P. le-Mur). English version in Luis J. Gallagher, 1953.

2.1.3. Yang Tingyun (1557-1627) was both a Neo-Confucian scholar and an orthodox Christian and his works are central to the dialogue between Neo-Confucianism and Christianity. For him God is both Father and Mother. Writings, from the years 1617-1627, include:

> *Tianshi Mingbian* (Clear discussion on [the teaching of] Heaven and Buddhism), n.d., last printed in Tianzhujiao dongchuan wenxian xubian (TDWX): I.229-417, 1996.

Xiaoluan bu bingming shuo (The owl and the phoenix do not sing together), n.d., TDWX: I.37-47.

Daiyi pian (Treatise to supplant doubts). First edition 1621. TDWX 1965.

Daiyi xupian (Sequel to "Treatise to Supplant Doubts"). First printed 1635. (Courant 1912: 7111-7112.)

Shengshui jiyan (Recorded words [of the Society] of the Holy Water) compiled by Sun Xueshi. Courant 1912: 6845.

A full study of Yang Tingyun's life and thought is provided by Standaert (1988) - References following 2.2.3.

2.1.4. Li Jiubiao and Li Jiugong (fl. 1630) compiled:

Koude Richao (Diary of oral exhortations) 1630-1640, recording the teachings of the Jesuits Rudomina and Aleni. Bibliothèque Nationale de France, Chinois 7114.

Lixiu Yijian (A mirror to encourage self-improvement) c.1644, Fujian, a compilation of stories, teachings and events chosen to show the divine power at work. See Michele Boin's "When the Twain met ..." (*Itinerario* VIII.I 1984: 58-76).

2.1.5. Xu Guangqi (Hsu Kuang-ch'i) (d. 1633) was one of the most prolific of 17th century Christian writers, not only expounding aspects of Christianity and Confucianism but also the responsibilities of government for peasant welfare and reform, agricultural methods and scientific processes. The main sources for his religious and political thought are found in:

Xu Guangqi ji (The collected writings of Xu Guangqi) edited by Wang Zhongmin. Peking: 1963; Shanghai: Guji chubanshe, 1984.

Xu wending jiashu moji (Facsimile reproductions of Xu Guangqi's family letters). Taipei, 1962.

Bianxue zhangshu (Memorial written to defend the teachings [1616] of t'ien) translated in *The Chinese Repository* [Canton] 19.3 (1850).

Xushi baoyan (Kitchen talks of Mr Hsu) [1617]. Shanghai: Zikawei Cathedral Collections, 1933, 5 juan.

Pi wang (Refuting heterodoxy) in *Tianzhujiao dong chuan wenxian xubian.* Vol. 2, 1625-1628.

2.1.6. Wang Zheng (d.1644) was the Assistant Surveillance Commissioner, baptised in 1616. He collaborated with the Jesuits in extending their work in Shaanxi, and in publications. He was active in charitable work and had a strong ethical concern, establishing the "Humanitarian Society" in Jinyang, ca. 1634. Collections of his writings have been published in:

> *Wang Zheng yi zhu*, edited by Li Zhiqin. Xi'an: Shaanxi Renmin chubanshe, 1987.
> *Ming Jingyang Wang Zheng Xiansheng Nianpu*, edited by Song Boyin. Xi'an: Shaanxi Shifan Daxue chubanshe, 1990.

2.1.7. Xu Candida (1607-1680) (Granddaughter of Xu Guangqi.) Her life, including extracts from her letters and conversation, is given fully by Philippus Couplet in his *Histoire d'une dame Chretienne de la Chine* (Paris, 1688). This narrates her founding of 30 churches, two congregations of women catechists, and also of orphanages, along with her extensive work for the poor and in support of missionaries. Her son Basil composed a work of several volumes which has apparently not survived. Xu Candida is only one of many women who were thus active. (See Standaert forthcoming, Selected References following 2.2.3.).

2.1.8. Chinese Christians in this period who were widely known as poets include:

> Wei I-chieh (Wei Yijie) (1616-1686). His poems appear in a number of anthologies, most recently in the 1960 edition of *Jingshi duo*, edited by Zhang Yingchang (1790-1874) reprinted in Beijing (Zhonghua shuju, 1983).
> Wu Li, alias Wu Yu-shan (1632-1718). An acknowledged master of early Qing dynasty painting who also pioneered a Chinese Christian poetry which used traditional forms to express orthodox Christian theology. This is found in:
> *Wu Yushan yanjiu lunji* (Collection of Wu Yu-shan's admonitions), edited by Chou Kang-hsieh. Hong Kong: Chung-wen Bookstore, 1971. Includes the "Compendium of Orthodox Sounds of Heavenly Music", probably Wu's greatest work, first printed in 1950.
> *Mojing ji* (Inkwell anthology), edited by Li Ti. Shanghai: Xujiahui (Zikawei) Press, 1909.
> *Mojing shichao* (Inkwell Poetry) in *Xiaoshi shanfang congshu* (Pebble Cottage Series) edited by Ku Hsiang, 1874.

A recent study of Wu Li including his collected poetry is that of Chaves 1993, Selected References following 2.2.3.

2.1.9. Zhang Xingyao (1633-c.1725). A senior licentiate of the literati, whose writing shows the compatibility of Neo-Confucianism with the "Lord of Heaven's Teaching from the Far West". His principal writings are:

Tongjian jishi benmo buhoubian (Supplement to the history of the comprehensive mirror) 50 juan, 1690.

Shengjiao zanming (Inscriptions in praise of the sage teaching Christianity) 38 poems, c.1680. MS (Bibliotèque National de Paris).

Tianjiao Rujiao tongyi kao (Examination of the similarities and differences between the Heavenly Teaching and the Literati Teaching). 3 juan, 1672-1715. MS (Zikawei Library, Shanghai).

Sidian shuo (Discussion of sacrificial rites). c.1685. MS (Jesuit Archive, Rome).

—, with Ding Yuntai. *Tianjiao mingbian* (Clearly distinguishing the Heavenly Teaching [from heterodoxy]), 1711.

—, with Hong Ji. *Pi Lueshuo tiaobo* (abridged Refutation of disputable points [with Buddhists]). Hangzhou, 1689.

A full study of Zhang's life and work is given in Mungello 1994, Selected References following 2.2.3.

2.1.10. Among other writings by literati contemporaries of Zhang, are:

Shengjiao xinzheng (Evidence of Christian Faith) by Han Lin and Zhang Geng, 1647, and the *Tianxue chuan 'gai* (Summary of the Spread of the Heavenly Teaching) edited by Li Zubo et al., in 1664. (Reprinted in TDWX II, 1966, Selected References following 2.2.3.)

Duo Shu (Book of the Bell), written by Han Lin, expounds the Chinese Catholic principle of "revering Heaven and loving human beings", along with traditional Confucian ethical teachings of China prevalent in his time.

The Tian Ru yin (Comparison of the Heavenly and literati teachings) was written in 1664 by Shang Weitang (Huquuig) in collaboration with Li Andang (Caballero a Santa Maria) who also wrote *Zhengxue Liushi* (Touchstone of true learning)

1698. (TDWX II, 1966 and TDWX I, 1972, Selected References following 2.2.3.)

2.1.11. Yan Mo (d. c.1720) has left extensive writings which include:

> *Ditiankao* (Investigation into the concepts of Lord and Heaven) c.1685. Argues from Chinese classical sources, that *t'ien* (*tian*) and *shang-ti* (*shangdi*) are sacred names of the Christian God.
>
> *Bianji* (Discerning sacrifices) c.1693 (and its sequel *Bianji houzhi*, 1695) which counter the arguments against the practice of revering ancestors.
>
> Five detailed studies of the basis, history, and validity of rites honouring ancestors: *Jizuokao* (Investigation into ancestral ancestral worship), *Kaoyi* (Investigation into doubts), *Lishi tiaowen* (Successive questions of Fr. Li), *Miaocikao* (Ancestral temple and shrine), and *Muzhukao* (Investigation into the ancestral tablet).

2.1.12. Liu Ning (ca.1625-ca.1715) wrote many works on Chinese antiquities, language, and religion, also making Christian interpretations of ancient Chinese characters and texts. His works include: *Juesi lu*, a collection of five apologetic essays; and *Tianxue jijie*, a collection of 284 texts dealing with Christianity and western science.

2.1.13. Other writings by Chinese authors of the period are collected in *Tianzhujiao dongchuan wenxian xubian* [TDWX] (A collection of writings of Catholicism's Orient mission), 3 volumes., compiled by Wu Hsiang-hsiang. Taipei: Hsueh-sheng, 1964, 1966-7, 1972; also in Li zhizao's *Zhizao's First Anthology of Christian Learnings*. See Courant 1912 and Standaert forthcoming, Selected References following 2.2.3.

2.1.14. Writings of Ricci's more eminent Jesuit colleagues or successors in the 16th and 17th centuries include:

> The letters and instructions of Alessandro Valignano (1539-1606), written in Macao 1578-79, listed in Schutte 1985, Selected References following 2.2.3.
>
> Michele Ruggieri (1543-1607) Letters, and poems in Chinese (*Monumenta Serica* v.41, 1993), as well as the early Chinese

Catechism in dialogue form which he composed with assistants, printed in Macau in 1584.

Alfonso Vagnone (d. 1640) *Tianzhu jiaoyao jielue* (Explanation of the essentials of the teaching of the Master of Heaven), 1615; *Tianzhu shijie jielue* (Explanation of the ten commandments of the Master of Heaven), n.d.; *Simo Lun* (On the four utmosts), 1624.

Adam Schall (1591-1666) *Historica Relatio de ortu et progressu fidei orthodoxae in regno Chinensi* (Ratisbon: August Hanckwitz, 1672), and *Lettres et memoires d'Adam Schall* edited by Henri B. Maitre (Tientsin: Hautes Etudes, 1942).

Giulio Aleni (d. 1649) *Dizui zhenggui* (Correct rules of confession), n.d.; *Xixue fan* (Account of western studies), 1623; *Zhifang waiji* (Record of areas beyond the tribute states), 1623; *Sanshan lunxue ji* (Record of the discussions about the teaching in Sanshan), 1627; *The Dialogues with Buddhists at Hangzhou*, TDWX II, 1966; (with Ding Zhilin) *Yang Xiansheng chaoxing shiji* (Achievements of the surpassing nature of Yang Xiansheng), n.d.

Ferd. Verbiest (1623-88)*Bu deyi bian* (Pu-Te-i-Pien) (A rebuttal of the 'I could not do otherwise'). A debate in two parts, co-authored by Luis Buglio, establishing the Jesuit understanding of the Master of T'ien (Peking, 1665-70).

2.2 Eighteenth century

Apart from the later writings of Zhang Xingyao, Yan Mo and Wu Li (above), few other Chinese Christian writings appear to have survived from the 18th century, when there were severe persecutions. Those extant include:

2.2.1. Andrew Ly (Li) (1692-1774). *Journal d'Andre Ly, Pretre Chinois, Missionaire et Notaire Apostolique 1746-1763*. Introduction by A. Launay. Paris: Picard, 1906; Hong Kong: Imprimerie de Nazareth, 1924. In manuscript the journal fills 831 pages of fluent Latin. In a time of persecution, Ly laments the dearth of indigenous clergy, and records the racist attitudes of expatriates.

Between the years 1746-1762 Ly also wrote (in Chinese) a treatise on the Seven Deadly Sins, Catechisms on the Eucharist and Extreme Unction, a critical study of Chinese 'superstitions', a *Mirror of the Virtues of Good Servants* (1762), and revised a three-volume book of *Meditations on the Gospel* composed by a Jesuit in 1620 (1747).

Groundwork for Asian Christian Theologies : Northeast Asia

2.2.2. Pierre-Martial Cibot (1727- 1780), a Chinese Jesuit and Figurist (finding the seeds of Christian belief in traditional Chinese culture), countered Voltaire's elevation of Chinese virtues over against Judaism or Christianity, by presenting biblical roots for Chinese civilisation in his *Essai sur l'antiquité des chinois*, (Paris, c.1777). He also wrote in *Memoires concernant les Chinois* (Paris, 1782) on this and related subjects, and elsewhere on Taoism and Chinese botany.

2.2.3. The work of Ricci was continued into this century, notably by

>Kilian Stumpf (d. 1720) *Acta Pekinensia* and other writings.
>Jean Francis Foucquet, (1665-1741), in *Zhongguo Jingben yu tian* (Chinese classics come from heaven) (BAV, Rome. Borg.cin 380 (5), c.1712); *Yijing Zongshuo* (Commentary on the I-Ching) (BAV, Rome. Borg.cin 317 (3), c.1714); *New Chronological Table of Chinese History* (in Latin). Rome, 1729 and Augsberg, 1746. Foucquet's letters appear in *Lettres edifiantes* (below), and other essays upon *tai ji* (*T'ai chi*), the *Yi jing*, and Yin and Yang are extant.
>Note: For further writings for these periods see Bernard (1945 and 1960) and Standaert's collection of texts (1996 and forthcoming), both in Selected References below.

Selected References

>Bays, Daniel H., ed. *Christianity in China: From the Eighteenth Century to the Present*. Stanford: Stanford University Press, 1996.
>Bernard, Henri. "Les Adaptations Chinoises d'Ouvrages Européens: Bibliographie Chronologique ...." *Monumenta Serica* 10 (1945), and 19 (1960).
>Chaves, Jonathan. *Singing the Source - Nature and God in the Poetry of the Chinese Painter Wu Li*. Honolulu: University of Hawaii Press, 1993.
>Cordier, Henri. *L'imprimerie sino-europeenne en Chine: bibliographie des ouvrages publies en Chine par les europeens au XVIIe et au XVIIIe siecle*. Paris E. Leroux,1901.
>Courant, M. *Catalogue des Livres Chinois* etc. Paris: 1912.
>Criveller, Gianni. *Preaching Christ in Late Ming China*. Taipei: Ricci Institute; Brescia: Fondazione Civilta, 1997.

Dehergre, Joseph. *Les lettres annuelles des missions jesuits de Chine au temps des Ming 1581-1644*. Roma: Institute Historique de la Compagnie de Jesus, 1980.

Dudink, Adrianus. "The Rediscovery of a Seventeenth Century Collection of Chinese Christian Texts: the Manuscript Tianxue jijie." *Sino-Western Cultural Relations Journal* 15 (1993).

Entenmann, Robert E. "Chinese Catholic Clergy and Catechists in Eighteenth-Century Szechwan." In *Actes du VIe Colloque International de Sinologie de Chantilly. Variétés Sinologiques*, nouvelle série 78, 389-410. Paris: Institut Ricci, Centre d'Etudes Chinoises (1995).

Gallagher, Luis J., trans. *China in the Sixteenth Century: the Journals of Matthew Ricci, 1583-1610*. New York: Random House, 1953.

Harris, George L. "The Mission of Matteo Ricci S.J.: A Case Study of Guided Cultural Change in the 16th Century." *Monumenta Serica* 25 (1966).

Jacques, Ch. *Choix de lettres edifiantes*. Volume. II. Brussels: 1838.

King, Gail. "Candida Xu and the Growth of Christianity in China in the Seventeenth Century." *Monumenta Serica* 46.1, 1998.

Lin Jinshui. "Chinese Literati and the Rites Controversy." *Rites Controversy* (1994).

Maitre, Henri Bernard. *Sagesse chinoise et philosophie chrétienne, Les Humanités d'Extrême-Orient*. Paris: Cathasia, 1950.

Moule, A.C. "Gregory Lopez, Bishop." *New China Review 1* (Shanghai) (1919): 480-487; *New China Review* 3 (1921): 138-9. (Reprinted Taipei: 1964).

Mungello, D.E. *The Forgotten Christians of Hangzhou*. Honolulu: University of Hawaii, 1994.

Olichon, A. *Aux Origines du Clergé Chinois: Le Prêtre Andre Ly*. Paris: Bloud et Gai, 1933.

Schurhammer, George, ed. *Epistolae S. Francisci Xavierii aliaque euis scripta*. Roma: Historical Institute of the Society of Jesus, 1944-45.: Vol. 2.

Schutte, Joseph F. *Valignano's Mission Principles for Japan*. Anand: Gujurat Sahitya Prakash, 1985: vol. I, 401-428.

Standaert, Nicolas. *The Fascinating God: A Challenge to Modern Chinese Theology Presented by a Text on the Name of God Written by a 17th Century Chinese Student of Theology*. Inculturation: Working Papers on Living Faith and Cultures XVII. Rome: Editrice Pontificia Universita Gregoriana, 1995.

—. *Yang Ting Yun - Confucian and Christian in Late Ming China: His Life and Thought*. Leiden: Brill, 1988.

—. et al. *Chinese Christian Texts from the Zikawei Library*. 5 volumes. Taipei: Fujen Catholic University, 1996.

—., ed. *Handbook of Christianity in China*. Volume One: 635-1800. Leiden: Brill. Forthcoming.

TDW - Documents on the Spread of Catholicism to the East. Taipei: 1965: 471-631.

TDWX - Second Collection of Documents on the Spread of Catholicism to the East. 3 vols. Taipei: 1966.

Wang, Xiaochao. *Christianity and Imperial Culture: Chinese Christian Apologetics in the 17th Century and their Latin Patristic Equivalent*. Boston: Brill, 1998.

Young, John D. *Confucianism and Christianity - The First Encounter*. Hong Kong: Hong Kong University Press, 1983.

Zurcher, Erik. "Christian Social Action in Late Ming Times: Wang Zheng and his Humanitarian Society." In *Linked Faiths: Essays on Chinese Religious and Traditional Culture* ..., edited by J.A.M. de Meyer and P.M. Engelfreit. Leiden: Brill, 1999.

—, Nicolas Standaert and Adrianus Dudink. *Bibliography of the Jesuit Mission in China (ca.1580-ca.1680)*. CNWS publications 5. Leiden: Leiden University Centre of Non-Western Studies, 1991.

(Xavier) *The Letters and Instructions of Francis Xavier*, translated and introduced by Joseph M. Costelloe. Anand Gujurat: Gujarat Sahitya Prakash, 1993.

3 Formosa (Taiwan)

The Dutch were present in Formosa from 1624 to 1661, with the pioneer Reformed missionary George Candidus arriving in 1627. By 1647, over 50 Formosan catechists are recorded as working for Reformed churches and the Consistory of Formosa grew to include 29 clergy at the height of its activity. Letters, narratives, sermons, catechisms, journals and vocabularies are extant in Formosan dialects, and in Dutch from Dutch ministers for the period 1624-1661, along with an extensive series of Day Journals, Council and Consistory letters and reports. Writings by Formosan catechists have yet to be discovered.

A station of the Spanish Dominicans was established from the Philippines in 1625 of which the pioneer leader was Fr Bartholomew Martinez (d.1642), followed later as leader by Fr Jacintho Esquivel del Rosario. Spanish and French Jesuits were in Formosa for varying periods between 1582 and 1715. Writings from Dominicans in particular, include letters, narratives, catechisms and grammars.

Administration of the mission work of both Reformed and Roman Catholic missioners was closely identified with Dutch and Spanish colonial policies. Few writings have yet been discovered from the remainder of the 18th century, during Chinese colonial rule.

(See Taiwan, volume 3 of this work.)

Amongst those whose work and writings provide part of the groundwork for contextual theology in Formosa/Taiwan are:

3.1 George Candidus (Reformed, in Formosa from 1627). Memos, letters, and bilingual prayers are given in Campbell 1903, Part II, and outlines of his work there and in Campbell 1915, chapter 48, in Selected References following 3.6. See his "A Short Account of the Island of Formosa in the Indies", in A. and J. Churchill, *Collection of Voyages and Travels*. 3rd ed. London: 1732, 1744.

3.2 Jacintho Esquivel del Rosario (Dominican, in Taiwan from 1627), who left a Grammar and a Dictionary, founded a school for "latin, liberal arts and theology", and worked to establish peace between warring villages. (Blair and Robertson 1906: chaps. 32 and 35; Rowald 1974, Selected References following 3.6.)

3.3 Daniel Gravius (Reformed, in Formosa from 1647) translated sections of the Bible with local assistance, and compiled *Patar ki Tna'msing an ki Christang. T'formulier des Christendoms met de verklaringen van dien inde Sideo-formosa-ansche taal.* (Outline of the Christian faith in Formosan). Amsterdam: 1662.

3.4 Gilbert Happert (Reformed, in Formosa from 1649) has left sermons, tracts, a catechism and prayers in Formosan, along with a manual on *The Practice of the Christian Life*, listed in Campbell 1903.

3.5 Robertus Junius (Reformed, d.1656). Extensive letters and reports, and collections of bilingual prayers and sermons are given in Campbell 1903 (Selected References following 3.6.). Amongst these are accounts of indigenous concepts - regarding marriage for example. Outlines of his often controversial work are given in Campbell 1903, and 1915 (Selected References following 3.6.). See also his controversial *Formulary of Christianity.* (bilingual), printed Camp-Vere: 1662.

3.6 Joseph-Anna-Marie de Moyria de Mailla sj. "Notes on Formosa". In *Lettres Ediifiente et Curieuse*, vols xiv, xviii. (Shanghai: 1715). Reprinted as *The Early History of Formosa* (Shanghai: Souriero, 1874). He later completed the *Histoire générale de la Chine, ou Annales de cet Empire; traduit du Tong-kiere-kang-mou par de Mailla.* (13 volumes, Paris: 1777-1785).

Selected References

Alvarez, Jose Maria. *Formosa geografica e historicamente considerada.* Barcelona: L. Gili, 1930. Vol. 2, *Dominicans in Formosa,* includes "Bibliografia de Formosa".

Blair, E.H. and J.A.R. Robertson, eds. *The Philippines Islands 1493-1898.* Cleveland: Arthur H. Clark, 1906: chapters. 24, 26, 32, 35.

Blusse, Leonard, Natalie Everts and Evelien Frech, eds. *The Formosan Encounter: Notes on Formosa's Aboriginal Society. A Selection of Documents from Dutch Archival Sources* (in Dutch and English). Taipei: Shung Ye Museum of Formosan Aborigines, 1999.

Campbell, W. *Formosa Under the Dutch Described from Contemporary Records.* London: Trubner, 1903; Taipei: Cheng-wen, 1967; Taipei: SMC Publishing, 1992. Extensive Bibliography.

—. *Sketches from Formosa.* London: Marshall Brothers, 1915: chapter xlviii.

—, ed. *An Account of the Missionary Success in Formosa (1650).* London: Trubner, 1889.

Cordier, Henri. *Bibliographie des ouvrages relatifs a l'isle Formose.* Extracted from *Bibliotheca Sinica.* Chartres: Imprimerie Durand, 1893.

Ferrando, Juan. *Historia de los P.P. Dominicos en las islas Filipinas y en susmisiones del Japon, Tung-kin y Formosa*. Madrid: M. Rivadeneyra, 1870-72.

Ginsel, Willy Abraham. *De Gereformeerde Kerk op Formosa: of de lotgevallen eener handelskerk onder de Oost-Indische-Compagnie, 1627-1662*. Leiden: Mulder, 1931.

Kuepers, Jacobus Joannes Antonius Mathias. *The Dutch Reformed Church in Formosa 1627-1662: Mission in a Colonial Context*. Schriftenreihe der Neuen Zeitschrift fur Missionswissenschaft. Immensee: Neue Zeitschrift fur Missionswissenschaft, 1978.

Mendiburu, Francisco. *Un Navarro en China: memorias de un hermano jesuita Bilbao*. (Includes Jesuits in Formosa.) *Biblioteca Testimonios* 14. Ediciones Mensajero, c1996.

Rowald, H. "Seventeenth Century Roman Catholic Missions in Taiwan." *Southeast Asia Journal of Theology* 15.2 (1974).

Rubinstein, Murray A., ed. *Taiwan; A New History*. Armonk: M.E. Sharpe, 1999.

Compare: the constructions of George Psalmanazar (pseudonym) in *An Historical and Geographical Description of Formosa* (2nd ed. London, 1705; Explorer's Club in 1926), and *A Dialogue between a Japanese and a Formosan about Some Points of the Religion of the Time* (London, 1707 and 1896).

4 Japan

4.1 The "Christian century" following Xavier's arrival in 1549 saw the emergence of Christian writings in a wide variety of forms, both by Japanese converts, and through their collaboration, by Jesuit scholars. By the mid-17th century, no further Christian writings were published, being replaced by the underground literature and artefacts of the Kakure Kirishitan.

Amongst the earliest Christian writers for whom some localised writings are extant are the following:

4.1.1. Paulo Yoho-ken (1510-1596) has been termed the "father of Japanese Christian literature". Physician, catechist and later member of the Society of Jesus, his writings include plays on Christ's Passion, and on Christmas, and the stories *Kurofune Monogatari* (Tale of the black ship) and *Bungo Monogatari* (Tale of Bungo) of which only extracts are extant. He was also a prolific co-author, and translator, of many other works.

4.1.2. Vincente Hoin (b. 1538, son of Yoho-ken) was said in the *Catalogue* of 1593 to have "written and translated the greater part of the spiritual and learned books which have thus far been written in Japanese" (Laures, 1957: 40, Selected References following 4.6.3.). See volumes listed below for the years 1586-1600 (See 4.3).

4.1.3. Hosokawa, Tama Gracia (1563-1600), wife of Hosokawa Tadaoki, wrote a series of letters to Gregorio de Cespedes sj (Laures, 1959: 98ff., Selected References following 4.6.3.) and also a number of poems (Heuvers 1938: 277; Laures 1956: 113f., Selected References following 4.6.3.) in the years 1587-1600. (Her life is given in Boxer 1934-5, Laures 1956, and Laures 1959, Selected References following 4.6.3.), and exhibits a unity of Christian devotion, insight and action in the context of 16th century Japan.

4.1.4. Fucan Fabian (b. 1565) is noted for both the first Japanese work of apologetic, and (later) for the first anti-Christian book in Japan:

Myotai Mondo (Dialogue between Myoshu and Yutei) contains an outline of Christian doctrine and a refutation of Confucianism, Shinto, and Buddhism. (1605, trans. Pierre Humbertclaude, 1939; published in Ebisawa, 1960, Selected References following 4.6.3.)

Ha-Deus (Deus refuted), a 'pamphlet' printed in 1620, refutes the Christian doctrines of Myotai Mondo systematically. Fucan rejects in particular the doctrines of original sin and eternal damnation, and bases his criticisms on Christianity's failure to recognise Japanese spirituality, or to bring peace and national salvation. (Published in Hibberd 1962, Ebisawa 1960, Selected References following 4.6.3.)

Fucan also compiled *Heike Monogatori* (1592), a colloquial and condensed version of the classical original in the form of a dialogue. (Laures 1957: 106f., 46f., Selected References following 4.6.3.; Reprinted in Tokyo, 1927.)

4.2 Amongst the many letters extant from the 16th and 17th centuries, those of Francis Xavier (in Japan 1549-1551: see Schurhammer 1973-1982, Selected References following 4.6.3.) and Alessandro Valignano (in Japan for periods between 1579 and 1602) are of particular importance. Valignano's writings and instructions shaped far-reaching policies throughout the region, adapting Christian mission to local cultures and contexts. (Valignano's extensive writings in catechetics, 'missiology', and history are fully listed in Schutte 1980: 401-428, Selected References following 4.6.3.)

4.3 For approximately 40 years, books were composed and translated into Japanese by the Jesuits and their colleagues in Japan, and circulated in printed or manuscript form. These included translations of the New Testament and of the lectionary Gospels, devotional works and sermons. (Jennes 1973: 78f., Selected References following 4.6.3.)

Early printed Japanese Christian literature of this period having theological significance, and published 'In Collegio Iaponico Societatis Iesu' between 1586 and 1600 include:

> *Catechismus Christianae Fidei*, written in Japan by Valignano and Japanese scholars and published in Lisbon in 1586.
> *Sanctos no Go-sagyo no uchi Nugigaki* (Extracts from the Acts of the Saints). Compiled from various sources and translated into *romaji* by Yoho-ken and Hoin. (Kazusa: 1591.)
> *Orashio no Honyaku* (a prayer book and catechism) published by Goto Thome Soin, "on all that a Christian should know". (Nagasaki: 1600.)
> *Roei Zafitsu* (Poems for recital) a collection of Japanese and Chinese poems on life and death, and heroes. (Nagasaki: 1600.)

4.4 Important writings from the first decades of the 17th century include:

> *Konchirisan no ryaku* (Guide to contrition), and abridgement of the contrition in manuscript (1603) including rules, 'considerations', and act of contrition. Found at Urakami and printed by Petitjean (1869).
> *Maruchirio no Susume* (Exhortations to martyrdom) and *Maruchirio no Kokoroe* (Instructions for martyrdom) circulated in manuscript (c.1615 and 1620 respectively). See Laures 1957: 73ff. and Anesaki 1931: 35-65, Selected References following 4.6.3.

4.5 Biographical materials and lives are extant for many Japanese Christians of the 16th and 17th centuries, including those of Gamo

Ujitsato-ki (fl. 1595), Hosokawa Tama Gracia (1563-1600), Itasaka Bokusai (1578-1655), Matsudaira Nobutsuna (1596-1662), Kumkuzawa Banzan (1619-1691), who also left a number of essays on economics, Bai Buntei (1633-1721), and Arai Hakuseki (1652-1725), who completed three volumes in 1716, along with a multi-volume diary, essays and letters. (All annotated in Ebisawa 1960: 9-67, Selected References following 4.6.3.)

4.6 Following intensified persecution, the eviction of all missionary priests, and the suppression of Christian faith (from 1614 on), writings and manuals of the Kakure-Kirishitan (crypto-Christians) survived largely through oral transmission and in manuscript, to be collected and printed only in succeeding centuries.

4.6.1. Amongst many collections of documents from 16th and 17th centuries, the more significant include:

Kirishitan shomono (Christian notebook, 1) on the Mass, the litany, daily meditations, mental prayer. (MS discovered 1920, provenance 16th century.)

Kirishitan sho (Christian notebook, 2) on the rosary, capital sins, the Ten Commandments. (MS discovered 1922, dated to c. 1610 or c. 1630 and printed Tokyo, 1952.)

The Takasuki Documents. Including a letter of allegiance to the Companha (Society of Jesus), a Christian calendar and name list (c.1596), printed by Ganshodo Shoten, Tokyo, 1933.

The Mito Documents. Eleven handwritten documents including a Book of Directions, sections of liturgy, the calendar, lives of the saints, and a Christian Doctrine. (All dated to c.1615-1630, published in *Kirishitan Sosho,* by Mainichi Shinbun, Osaka, 1928-1929.) (Refer Laures 1957: 112ff., Selected References following 4.6.3.)

4.6.2. Collections of often anonymous documents dated to the 18th century include the following:

Tenchi Hajimari no Koto (Origin of the universe). Compiled and circulated throughout the 18th century - brought to Fr. Petitjean at Nagasaki, 1865; reprinted by Tagita 1954. Differing manuscripts are extant from Urakami, Sotome and Ikitsuki. (See also Harrington 1993: chap 4. and Whelan 1996, Selected References following 4.6.3.)

Nagasaki Kirishitan Monjo (Christian documents of Nagasaki) c.1750.

Kirishitan Shiryo (Christian documents) 1781-1800; all listed in Ebisawa 1960, Selected References following 4.6.3.

Orasa no Mitsuji (Mysterious prayers) a manuscript (c.1794) printed and annotated by Ebisawa, Tokyo, 1953.

4.6.3. Kirishitan art forms. These are particularly valuable as sources of Christian history and theology in the period. Apart from the many relics brought into Japan by missionaries and converts (e.g. from China or Europe), the Japanese-made artefacts are of two kinds. Those from the period 1574-1615, when the Kirishitan faith was approved, openly depict Christian figures and symbols on, for example, sword hilts, candle stands, hand mirrors or tea utensils. (Suzuki, 1961: plates 1-12, in Selected References below.)

Following the proscription of Christianity (nationally enforced from 1638) the Kakure-Kirishitan concealed or disguised the Christian features of their artefacts. (Suzuki 1961: plates 13-32, Selected References following.) This led to the creation of an indigenous Christian folk art in which Buddhist or Shinto images were adapted to represent Christian figures or symbols. The most widespread examples depict the Madonna and Child in the form of Maria Kannon (Kuan Yin, goddess of mercy) or of Kishiboshin (Hariti) both of whom could be represented holding a child. One class of Maria-Kannon has both a distinct cross upon her breast, but also holds a budding lotus flower instead of a child. Ten-jin (the Shinto deity of learning) also came to symbolize God, for the name translates as "God-in Heaven".

Selected References

Anesaki Masaharu. *Proceedings of the Imperial Academy. Kirishitan Literature.* Tokyo: 1924-1933.

Boxer, C.R. "Hosokawa Tadaoki and the Jesuits, 1587-1645." *Japan Society Transactions and Proceedings* 32 (1934-35).

de Charlevoix, Pierre-Francois-Xavier. *Histoire de l'etablissement, des progres et de la decadence du christianisme dans l'empire du Japon, ou l'on voit les differentes revolutions qui ont agite cette monarchie pendant plus d'un siecle.* Rouen: J.J. le Boullenger, 1715.

Ebisawa Arimichi. *Christianity in Japan: A Bibliography of Japanese and Chinese Sources.* Tokyo: International Christian University, 1960.

England, John C. and Martin Repp, eds. *Kirishitan - Early Christianity in Japan.* Special issue of *Japanese Religions*, 19.1 & 2 (1994).

Furuno Kiyoto. *Kakure Kirishitan.* Tokyo: Shibundo, 1959.

Harrington, Ann M. *Japan's Hidden Christians.* Chicago: Loyola University Press, 1993.

Heuvers, von Hermann. "Gratia Hosokawa in Mintono." *Monumenta Nipponica* I.1 (1938).

Hibberd, E.L. *Refutation of Deus by Fabian.* English version, Tokyo: 1962.

Humbertclaude, P. "La litterature chrétienne au Japon il y a trois cents ans." *Bulletin de la Maison Franco-Japonaise* 8.2-4. (1937).

—. "Myotei Mondo: Une apologétique chrétienne japonaise de 1605." *Monumenta Nipponica* 1.2 (1938); and 2.1 (1939).

Jarrett-Kerr, Martin. *Patterns of Christian Acceptance: Individual Response to the Missionary Impact 1550-1950.* London: OUP, 1972.

Jennes, Joseph. *A History of the Catholic Church in Japan.* Tokyo: Oriens Institute, 1973.

Laures, Johannes. *Gracia Hosokawa.* Kalden Kirchen: Steyler, 1956.

—. *Kirishitan Bunko: A Manual of Books and Documents on the Early Christian Mission in Japan.* Tokyo: Sophia University, 1957.

—. *Two Japanese Christian Heroes.* Rutland, VT: Bridgeway Press, 1959.

Mayer, Oskar. *Zur Genesis neuzeitlicher Religionskritik in Japan: Fukansai Fabian, Japanismus und japanisches Christentum.* Frankfurt am Main: Herchen, c1985.

Moran, J.F. *The Japanese and the Jesuits: Alessandro Valignano in Sixteenth-century Japan.* London: Routledge, 1992; New York: Routledge, 1993.

Nagayama Tokihide. *Collection of Historical Materials Connected with the Roman Catholic Religion in Japan* (In Japanese). Nagasaki and Tokyo: Maruzen, 1927.

Schurhammer, Georg. *Francis Xavier: His Life, His Times.* 4 vols., translated by M. Joseph Costelloe. Rome: Jesuit Historical Institute, 1973-1982.

Schutte, Joseph Franz. *Valignano's Mission Principles for Japan.* Volume. I. Anand: Gujurat Sahitya Prakash, 1980.

Suzuki Hidesaburo. *Crypto-Kirishitan Relics in Japan.* Kyoto: Hidesaburo Suzuki, 1961.

Tagita Koyo Paul-M. *Study of Acculturation among the Secret Christians of Japan.* Tokyo: Privately Printed, 1954.

Turnbull, Stephen. "Acculturation Among the Kakure Kirishitan: Some Conclusions from the 'Tenchi Hajimari no Koto'." In Breen, J.L. and Mary Williams, eds. *Japan and Christianity: Impact and Responses.* London: MacMillan, 1996.

—. *The Kakure Kirishitan of Japan.* Richmond: Curzon, 1998. (See especially Bibliography).

—, ed. *Japan's Hidden Christians 1549-1999.* Richmond: Curzon, 2000.

Whelan, Christal. *The Beginning of Heaven and Earth: The Sacred Book of Japan's Hidden Christians.* Honolulu: University of Hawaii Press, 1996.

5 Korea

5.1 Sixteenth to seventeenth centuries:

5.1.1. Extant writings by Korean Christians in this period are almost all in the form of letters from Japan where they were either prisoners or refugees. Of the many Korean martyrs, six have left such writings containing Christian reflections:

Pedro and Miguel - 'proto-martyrs' (d. 1614), Catalina Kuzaemon (d. 1623), Francisco - 'aged 12 years' (d. 1623), Vincent Kaun - member of Society of Jesus (d. 1626), Gayo Iemon - novice in Society of Jesus (d. 1627) (de Medina, 1986/1991).

Other letters by Korean writers in Japan include those of:

Maxima - 'Dama Coreana' (imprisoned 1613);

Pak Marina (1572-1636) member of Julia's company (see below) - to, for example, Francisco Colin;

Naizen Joao (d. 1626) companion of Kaun - to, for example, his sister;

Ota Julia (forms sisterhood, imprisoned, dies c.1652) - to, for example, Pedro Morijon and Francisco Pasio.

(See de Medina, 1986/1991, Selected References following 5.5.)

5.1.2. Amongst early Sirhak ('western learning') scholars who quote or summarize the *T'ien-chu Shih-I* (Tianzhu shiyi, The true meaning of the Lord of Heaven) of Matteo Ricci, are:

> Yu Mong-in (1559-1623), I Su-kwang (1563-1628) - see e.g. *I Sukwang Chibong yusol* (Collected essays of Chibong); and the encyclopaedist Yi Ik (1681-1763), who wrote a commentary (Ch'onju sirui bal) on Ricci's *The True Meaning of the Lord of Heaven* and edited a version of his *Of Friendship*. Yi Ik also wrote a critique of the *Qike* (Seven victories), and through his disciples An Tjong-pok (An Chong-bok 1712-1791) and Hong Iou-han (b. 1736) later influenced I Py-ok and Chong Yak-jong. His collected works appear in *Songho Saesol* where he recognises continuity between Confucian and Catholic teachings. (Yu 1996: 49ff., Selected References following 5.5.)

Of those who wrote comparative/critical studies of Ricci's teaching, Lou Mong-in (1569-1623) and An Chong-bok (1712-1791) are notable.

5.2 By the end of the 18th century, a library of Christian writings had developed in Korea, numbering almost 150 items in both original works and translations from the Chinese: the vast majority dated from the last two decades of the century. All were written by Korean lay Christians and included writings on such subjects as:

> Biblical teachings, Christian feasts, commemorations, and sacraments;
> the Nativity and Passion of Jesus Christ;
> the Ten Commandments, the Life of Apostolic Faith, the Rule and Ministry of the Mass, the Rosary of St Mary;
> the Feasts of All Saints, of the Nativity of Jesus Christ, and Easter;
> the Rule and Practice of Confession;
> Stigmata of Jesus Christ;
> Introductions to Christianity and to Catholicism;
> Rules for Mission Work;
> Guides to Prayer, Meditation, or particular Christian doctrines;
> and on the lives of apostles and saints (including Korean martyrs), along with calendars, litanies, guides to devotional practices, and catechisms.

A detailed listing is given in Cho Kwang 1988, Selected References following 5.5.

5.3 Major Christian writings from the period were shaped both by extensive knowledge of western and Chinese philosophy, religion, and science and by Korean theological insights and social concerns which were formed independently of missionary teaching. Christianity is most frequently presented as their own religion for Koreans, and as a faith which would solve this world's suffering and bring national reconstruction.

The writings also include hymn sequences and extensive catechisms or outlines of the faith, and include those of:

5.3.1. I Py-ok (1753-1786) - pioneer Christian teacher of the Sirhak movement.

Song Gyo Yo Ji (Essentials of the holy teaching). Seoul, c. 1784. Outline of Christian faith by a leading 'Sirhak' scholar. I Py-ok also wrote letters and a Catechism, along with hymns, notably *Ch'ou Ju Gong Ga* (Hymn of the Lord's adoration) c.1786. In his writings, I harmonized the ethical ideas of traditional Confucianism with the moral theology of Roman Catholicism.

5.3.2. Chong, Yak-jong Augustine (1760-1801) - scholar in theology and oriental culture.

Chu-Gyo Yo-Ji (Essence of the Lord's Teaching), 2 vols., c.1795. Systematic presentation of Christian doctrine in Confucian and Korean context and the most significant Christian writing of the period. (Reprinted in *Martyrs And Witnesses* (1982) and in Diaz 1986, Selected References following 5.5.)

Song-Gyo Jon-So (The complete book of the holy teaching) - an anthology of Christian doctrine not now extant, in which Chong was assisted by Kim Kon-sun Josaphat (c.1801).

5.3.3. Yi Sung-hun (1756-1801), wrote a defence of his reasons for accepting Christianity. His poetry was collected posthumously in *Manch'on yugo*, which pictures the quest for true friendship and includes songs of praise to *Tianzhu*, some also by Chong Yak-jong, I Py-ok and Yi Ka-hwan; these being entitled *Ch'onju kasa* (Songs to Tianzhu).

5.3.4. Chong, Yak-yong ("Tasan", 1762-1836) - expert on Confucianism, encyclopaedist and advocate of systematic reform in all areas of government, economy and law. He regarded I Pyok as his mentor.

Sip Kye Myong Ga (Hymn of the Ten Commandments). Seoul, c.1787.

Mongmin Simso (A book for the mind of the shepherds of people). 4 vols. (Originally 48 vols., completed in 1818). Reprinted Seoul: Hwangsong, 1902.

Kyonse, Yap'yo, also known as *Pongnye Ch'obon* (Proposals for government reform). Originally 40 volumes, but unfinished in 1817.

5.3.5. Pak Che-ga (1750-1815) - advocate of *Pakhakpa* (Northern Learning of socio-economic reform).

Pakhagui (Discourse on northern studies) 1779. (Reprinted by South Korean Education Ministry, 1962.) Proposals for industry, international trade and the improvement of rural and urban life, which included advocacy for the legalisation and use of Christianity and its teachers.

5.3.6. Chong Ha-sang (fl.1820, son of Chong Yak-jong) is known for his *Sang chaesang so* (To the heavenly Lord, a letter to the prime minister) which he wrote when in prison. In this he draws similarities between Confucian and Catholic teachings, but also affirms the universal characteristics of truth, and the universal appeal of Christianity.

5.4 Statements are extant from those martyred between 1798 and 1830, including those of Yi To-gi (d.1798), Kang Wan-suk (d.1801) and Sin Tae-bo (d.1827). Yi To-gi is notable for his statement regarding the human conscience being God's law, and his belief in the universal nature of truth to which all cultures are open. Sin Tae-bo was eloquent in affirming the social equality which true faith brings. (Dallet 1874, Selected References following 5.5.)

5.5 Catholic hymns in Hangul (Korean characters) date from the time of persecution in early decades of the 19th century, with a large number appearing in the mid-century. These were written both to confess Christian faith and also to defend its place within Korean society. In this they show different emphases from the earlier songs to *Tianzhu*.

Selected References

Cho Kwang. *A Historical Study of Catholicism in the Late Chosun Dynasty.* (In Korean) Seoul: Korea University, 1988.

Courant, Maurice. *Bibliographie Coréene.* 3 vols. Paris: Libraire de la Société Asiatique de l'Ecole des Langues Orientales Vivantes, 1894-96.

Dallet, Charles. *Histoire de L'Eglise de Corée.* Paris: Victor Palme, 1874.

de Medina, Juan G. Ruiz. *Origenes de la Iglesia Catolica Coreana desde 1566 hasta 1784.* Rome: Institute of History, Society of Jesus, 1986. English translation, Seoul: Royal Asiatic Society, 1991.

Diaz, Hector M.G. *A Korean Theology. Chu-Gyo Yo-Ji: Essentials of the Lord's Teaching by Chong Yak-jong Augustine (1760-1801).* Immensee: Neue Zeitschrift fur Missionswissenschaft, 1986.

Grayson, James Huntly. *Early Buddhism and Christianity in Korea: A Study of the Implantation of Religion.* Leiden: Brill, 1985.

Hahn Moo-sook. *Encounter: A Novel of Nineteenth-Century Korea.* Berkeley: University of California Press, 1992. (Closely based on historical sources.)

Han Woo-keun. *The History of Korea.* Honolulu: University Press of Hawaii, 1971.

Institute of Korean Church History, ed. *Martyrs and Witnesses.* Seoul: IKCH, 1982.

Joe, Wanne J. *Traditional Korea: A Cultural History.* Seoul: Chung'ang University Press, 1972.

Kang W.J. (Wi-jo). "Early Korean Contact with Christianity and Korean Response: an Historical Introduction." In *Korea's Response to the West,* edited by Jo, Yung-hwan. Kalamazoo, Mich.: Korea Research and Publications, 1971.

Kim, Andreas Jeong-soo. *Katechese und Inkulturation: Dargestellt am Beispiel der Geschichte der Katholischen Kirche im Korea 1603-1983.* Frankfurt: Peter Lang, 1987.

Kim Kyu. "The Encounter between Neo-Confucian Literati and Roman Catholicism in the Yi Dynasty: A Case Study in

Eighteenth and Early Nineteenth Century." Thesis, Seoul, 1982.

Korean National Commission for UNESCO, ed. *Main Currents of Korean Thought*. Seoul: Si-sa-yong-o-sa Publishers; Arch Cape: Oregon, 1983.

Ri, Jean Sangbae. *Confucious et Jesus Christ. La Première théologie chrétienne en Corée d'apres l'oevre de Yi Piok, Lettre Confucien 1745-1786*. Paris: Beauchesne, 1979.

Setton, Mark. *Chong Yagyong: Korea's Challenge to Orthodox Neo-Confucianism*. Albany NY: State University of New York, 1997.

Takashi Konoi. "The History of the Relationship between Japanese and Korean Christianity in the 16th/17th Centuries." *Samok* 252, 1999.

Yi Won-sun. "The Consciousness of Western Learning Among Scholars of the Practical Learning in the Latter part of the Chosun Period." *Yoksa kyoyuk* (Historical education) 17 and 18 (1973).

Yu Chai-shin, ed. *The Founding of the Catholic Tradition in Korea*. Mississauga, Ont.: Korean and Related Studies Press, 1996.

3 Contextual Theology in China

1 **Resources for Research**
   1.1 Bibliographies and Guides
   1.2 Other Key Texts, most including Bibliographies
2 **Contextual Catholic Theology in China**
   2.1 Catholic Communities 1800-1950
      2.1.1. Introduction; **2.1.2.** Jesuits at Zikawei
   2.2 Catholic Scholars - late 19th / early 20th centuries
      2.2.1. Li Wenyu, Laurent (1840-1911); **2.2.2.** Ma Xiangbo (c.1840 -1939); **2.2.3.** Pierre Teilhard de Chardin sj (1881-1955); **2.2.4.** Vincent Lebbe (1877-1940), and colleagues; **2.2.5.** Lou Tseng-tsiang, Pierre Celestine (1871-1949)
   2.3 Response to Civil Conflict and War
   2.4 Journals and the Debate on "Atheism"
   2.5 Supplementary Bibliography I
3 **Contextual Catholic Theology Since 1949**
   3.1 Revolution, Response, Division: 1949-1975
   3.2 Theological and Contextual Writings
      3.2.1. The 1950s-1960s
         3.2.1.1. The Patriotic Association of Chinese Catholics - Documents; **3.2.1.2.** Maurus Fang Hao (1910-); and Wei Tsing-sing (fl.1960); **3.2.1.3.** John C.H. Wu (Wu Ching-hsiung 1899-1986)
      3.2.2. Reconstruction, Convergence and the Doing of Theology: 1980-2000;
         3.2.2.1. Theological Writings: Post-Cultural Revolution; **3.2.2.2.** Bishops' Conference of the Catholic Church in China; **3.2.2.3.** Tu Shihua (1919-); **3.2.2.4.** Laszlo Ladanyi sj (1914-1990); **3.2.2.5.** Zong Huaide (1917- 1997); **3.2.2.6.** Chu Mei-fen, Theresa (1924-); **3.2.2.7.** Liu Yuanren, Joseph (1925-); **3.2.2.8.** John B. Zhang Shijiang (b. 1964); **3.2.2.9.** Major Journals

3.3 Supplementary Bibliography II

4 **Contextual Protestant Theology in China, 1800-1920**
4.1 Theology and Mission
4.2 Protestant Interpreters (to mid-19th Century)
    4.2.1. Liang Fa (Leung Faat/Leong Kung-fa, 1795-1855);
    4.2.2. Other Protestant Interpreters
4.3 Theology and Society
    4.3.1 The Taiping Movement (1850-1864)
4.4 Women's Writing 1 (late 19th Century)
4.5 Expatriate Scholars, Educators and Journalists: 1. 19th Century
4.6 Biographies of Chinese Christians (19th century)
4.7 Expatriate Scholars, Educators and Theologians: 2. Late 19th Century/early 20th Century
    4.7.1. Timothy Richard (1845-1919); **4.7.2.** Gilbert Reid (b. 1857); **4.7.3.**; Other Expatriate Scholars and Interpreters
4.8 Chinese Protestant Interpreters / Writers 2. (late 19th / early 20th centuries)
4.9 Women's Writing 2 (early 20th Century.)
    4.9.1. Other Women Theologians and Writers
4.10 Periodicals and Booklets
4.11 Supplementary Bibliography III

5 **Contextualization in the Chinese Protestant Church: Fully Chinese and Fully Christian: 1915-**
5.1 May Fourth: First Generation
    5.1.1. Contextual writings; **5.1.2.** The Anti-Christian Movement and the Christian Apologetic; **5.1.3.** T.C. Chao (Zhao Zichen; Chao Tze-ch'en, 1898-1979); **5.1.4.** L. C. Wu (Wu Leichuan, 1870-1944); **5.1.5.** P.C. Hsu (Hsu Pao-ch'ien; Xu Baoqian) (1892-1944); **5.1.6.** Jia Yuming (1879-1964); **5.1.7.** N.Z. Zia (Xie Fuya, 1892-1991); **5.1.8.** Y.T. Wu (Wu Yaozong, 1893-1979); **5.1.9.** Cheng Jingyi (Andrew C.Y. Ch'eng, 1881-1939); **5.1.10.** Liu Tingfang, Timothy (T.T. Lew, 1891-1947)
5.2 The Indigenous Church Movement
    5.2.1. In Pursuit of Autonomy; **5.2.2** Indigenization; **5.2.3.** National Christian Conference 1922; **5.2.4.** Church of

Christ in China: 1927; **5.2.5.** Indigenous churches and sects; **5.2.6.** Wang Ming-tao (Wang Mingdao, 1900-1991); **5.2.7.** Watchman Nee (Ni Tuosheng, 1903-1972)

5.3 1930s and 1940s: Decades of Social Program and Political Upheaval

5.3.1. The Modernist Debate and Theological Conservatism in China; **5.3.2.** Women in the Life and Work of the Church; **5.3.3.** Expatriate Activists, Educators and Theologians 3 (1900-1950)

5.4 1950s: Christianity and New China

5.4.1. The Christian Manifesto 1950; **5.4.2.** The Denunciation (or Accusation) Movement; **5.4.3.** Three-Self Patriotic Movement of Protestant Churches in China (TSPM); **5.4.4.** Theological Reorientation at the Grassroots; **5.4.5.** K.H. Ting (Ding Guangxun, 1915-); **5.4.6.** Chen Zemin (1917-); **5.4.7.** Zhao Fusan (1926? -); **5.4.8.** Journals and writings

5.5 Cultural Revolution Era 1966-1976

5.6 The Resurgence of Church Life and Theology: 1980s

5.6.1. Wang Weifan (1928-); **5.6.2.** Shen Yifan (1929?-1995); **5.6.3.** Publications; **5.6.4.** Lay Leadership and the Church at the Grassroots; **5.6.5.** The Younger Generation; **5.6.6.** Women and Theology; **5.6.7.** Minority Christians

5.6.7.1. Wang Zhiming (1907-1973)

5.7 The Academic Study of Religion and the Dialogue with Intellectuals

5.7.1. Research Institutes and Study Centers

5.8 Theological Reconstruction

5.9 Supplementary Bibliography IV

1 Resources for Research

See Northeast Asia: 16th - 18th centuries - China, see chap. 2 above.

There are very extensive resources for research in Chinese Christian history since 1800, including not only bibliographies and guides along with many diverse studies and collections, but also the archives of many church and mission organizations. A selection from the more important resources follows.

1.1 Bibliographies and Guides

Chinese Christian Monograph Collection. (Microform.) American Theological Library Association. Princeton: ATLA Board of Microtext, ?1981.

Chinese Periodicals. (Microform.) American Theological Library Association. Princeton: ATLA Board of Microtext, ?1981.

Chung-hua fu yin shen hsüeh yüan. *Chung-kuo chi tu chiao shih yen chiushum : Chung, Jih wen chuan chu yü lun wen mu lu* (A bibliography of the history of Christianity in China). Taipei : Chung-hua fu yin shen hsüeh yüan, 1981.

Crouch, Archie R., et al., eds. *Christianity in China: a Scholar's Guide to Resources in the Libraries and Archives of the United States.* Armonk, NY: M.E. Sharpe, 1989.

Zhonghua fuyin shenxue yuan. *Zhongguo jidujiao shi yanjiu shumu: Cong riwen juanzhu yu lunwen mu lu* (A bibliography of the history of Christianity in China). Taipei: Zhonghua fuyin shenxue yuan. 1981.

Heyndrickx, J. *Historiography of the Chinese Church: 19th and 20th Centuries.* Leuven: Ferdinand Verbiest Foundation, 1994.

Hunter, Alan, and Don Rimmington. *Methodological Questions in the Study of Christianity in China.* Leeds East Asia papers 9. Leeds: University of Leeds, Department of East Asian Studies, 1992.

Lai Yung-hsiang. *Catalog of Protestant Missionary Works in Chinese.* Harvard-Yenching Library. Boston, MA: G.K. Hall, 1980.

Marchant, Leslie R. *A Guide to the Archives and Records of Protestant Christian Missions from the British Isles to China, 1796-1914.* Nedlands, W. Aust.: University of Western Australia Press, 1966.

Tiedeman, G.R., ed. *Handbook of Christianity in China. Vol. II, 1800-2000.* Leiden: Brill, Forthcoming.

Wang, Peter Chen-main. "Jidu jiao caihuashi zhongwen shumu xuanyao" (Selected Chinese bibliography on Christianity in China). In *Christian Missions in China - Evangelists of What?,* edited by Jessie G. Lutz. Boston: Heath, 1965 (Chinese trans. Taipei: Academia Historica, 2000).

Xu Zongze. *Ming Qing jian Yesuhui shi yizhu tiyao* (Bibliography of Chinese Catholic authors). Taibei: Taiwan zhonghua shuju, 1958.

Zhongguo tianzhujiao zhinan (Guide to the Catholic Church in China). (In Chinese and English.) Singapore: *China Catholic Communication*, 1986, 1989, 1997, 2000.

See also :

<http://ricci.rt.usfca.edu/> Ricci 21st Century Roundtable Database on the History of Christianity in China. Ricci Institute, University of San Francisco. <http://www.iscs.org.hk/eng/main.shtml> website of institute of Sino-Christian Studies, Tao Fong Shan.

1.2 Other Key Texts, most including Bibliographies, include:

Bays, Daniel H. *Christianity in China: From the Eighteenth Century to the Present.* Stanford CA: Stanford University Press, 1996.

Cary-Elwes, Columba. *China and the Cross: Studies in Missionary History.* New York: Longmans, Green, 1957.

Charbonnier, Jean. *Histoire des Chrétiens de Chine.* Paris: Joint edition Desclée and Bégédie, 1992.

Cohen, Paul A. *China and Christianity: The Missionary Movement and the Growth of Chinese Antiforeignism, 1860-1870.* Cambridge, Mass.: Harvard University Press, 1963.

d'Elia, Paschale M. *Catholic Missions in China.* Shanghai: Commercial Press, 1934.

Hiyane Antei. *Shina kirisutokyo shi* (A history of Christianity in China). Tokyo: Seikatsusha,1940.

Gu Changsheng. *Chuanjiao shi yu jindai Zhongguo.* (History of missions in China). Shanghai: Shanghai renmin chubanshe: Xinhua shudian, 1981.

Ku Wei-ying and Koen De Ridderl. *Authentic Chinese Christianity. Preludes to its Development (Nineteenth and Twentieth Centuries).* Leuven Chinese Studies volume 9. Leuven: Leuven University Press, 2000.

Lam Wing-hung. *Chinese Theology in Construction.* Pasadena: William Carey, 1983.

Latourette, Kenneth S. *A History of Christian Missions in China.* New York: Macmillan, 1929.

Li Zhigang. *Zaoqi Jidujiao zaihua chuanjiao shi* (History of early Protestant missions in China.) Taibei: Commercial Press, 1985.

MacGillivray, Donald. *A Century of Protestant Missions in China* (1807-1907). Shanghai: American Presbyterian Mission Press, 1907.

Tang, Edmond and Jean-Paul Wiest. *The Catholic Church in Modern China*. Maryknoll, NY: Orbis Books, 1993.
Soetens, Claude. *L'Eglise catholique en Chine au XXe siècle*. L'histoire dans l'actualité 6. Paris: Beauchesne, c1997.
Whyte, Bob. *Unfinished Encounter: China and Christianity*. London: Collins, 1988.
Wickeri, Philip L. *Seeking the Common Ground: Protestant Christianity, the Three-Self Movement, and China's United Front*. Maryknoll, NY: Orbis Books, 1988.
Wolferstam, Bertram. *The Catholic Church in China 1860-1907*. London: Sands, 1909.
Yamamoto Sumiko. *History of Protestantism in China: The Indigenization of Christianity*. Tokyo: Toho Gakai (Institute of Eastern Culture), 2000.
Zha Shijie. "Minguo Jidujiaohui shi (1), 1911-1917" (History of Christianity in the republican period, part I: 1911-17). *Guoli Taiwan daxue lishi xuexi xuebao* (Journal of Historical Studies of National Taiwan University) 8 (1981).

2 Contextual Catholic Theology in China
2.1 Catholic Communities 1800-1950
2.1.1. Introduction

By the death of Louis de Poirot sj at Peking in 1814, there had been, over the previous two centuries, 69 Jesuit authors who published over 200 books. The large majority of these books were either presentations of classical Catholic authors such as Aquinas, or volumes of selected readings from sacred Scripture, catechisms, collections of maxims, prayers, and devotions, along with liturgies and hagiographies. It was, however in a small number of writings such as the journal of André Ly (1692-1774), that beginnings of localized reflection upon contemporary experience can be discerned. A century or more would pass before any similar attempts were made.

Despite persecution continuing until 1842, the often compact nature of Catholic communities, along with indigenous leadership, had enabled them to survive political and social changes, as it would in succeeding periods. But this would still be in the main a church on the margins of society, usually both suspect and suspicious. There had been, however, a slow increase in membership, and in Chinese clergy, in some major provinces, before the return to former districts of missionaries and religious orders. Many of these latter were influenced by post-Jansenist and post-revolution movements in French theology which were highly conservative and anti-humanist. They therefore imposed the inflexibility and dogmatism of European Catholic theology upon Catholic communities which, although deeply faithful and devout, had been more influenced by indigenous conditions in the previous century.

Such inflexibility would only be reinforced by the establishment of the French Protectorate - by the treaties of 1844, 1858 and 1860 - which further alienated Catholic missions from Chinese society, and also by the ultra-montane and centralizing positions taken by the Vatican Council of 1869-70. Despite the appearance of periodicals like *The Chinese Church News* (1868) edited by Li Lezhi, scope for Chinese Catholics to exercise leadership, or to articulate experience and thought, was very limited. Although there would be some Chinese priests ordained by 1885, orders such as the Jesuits and the Lazarists, along with many missioners arriving later from America, would actively restrict the access to leadership for Chinese throughout the century and beyond. And although by the 1890s there were in some provinces attempts to recognize differences in Chinese custom and tradition, leading to adaptations in liturgy and festivals, this accommodation was almost always made without any contextual theological reflection.

Nor was there much contribution to the thought of the wider community or to the intellectual ferment of Chinese social and cultural movements, until late in the century when Catholic educational, publishing and "localizing" movements began to take shape. These slowly came to recognize the place of China's historical and cultural context and included the development of collections and publications by the Xujiahui (Zikawei) Library of Shanghai (established by the Jesuits originally in 1850), with its publication of journals like *Les variétés sinologiques* (1892), and writings on religious and cultural issues from the presses at Peking, Hsien Hsien and Hong Kong. Also significant was the work of Ma Xiangbo and colleagues in education and publishing and the establishment of Catholic universities (1903 and 1912); the later Hautes Etudes industrielles et commerciales (1923); and the "nationalist" campaigns associated with Vincent Lebbe and later, Cardinal Constantini. These led to a marked increase in the number of Chinese priests and bishops, to movements for inculturation of the faith, and to the end of the French Protectorate. In 1912, also, Chang Yutang and colleagues founded the *Union de l'Action Catholique Chinoise* with chiefly evangelistic aims which by the 1930s had broadened to include education, publication and social issues.

By the middle of the 20th century, the number of Catholic periodicals, of which the first was founded by Lebbe in 1912, burgeoned, there being 15 in print by 1926. The most considerable journal was *Monumenta Serica*, issued in Peking in 1935. Catholic lay associations had begun, following the foundation of the Union for Catholic Action (1912), including those established by Vincent Lebbe (1923), and by the Jesuits in the early 1930s. Following seven regional synods the Catholic Council of the Church in China held its first Plenary meeting in May 1924, and six Chinese bishops were consecrated soon after (1926). There would be 27 by 1949 (out of 139). By 1948 fourteen major seminaries were functioning with scores of minor seminaries active.

From the late19th century we therefore have contextual writings from a number of exceptional scholars in historical, cultural and religious studies. In early decades of the 20th century we also have publications of the College of Bishops and pastoral letters from individual bishops which applied Christian teaching to contemporary issues, supported the causes of nationalism and peace, and opposed atheistic Communism. By 1948, some individual scholars were able to continue studies and writing amid the turmoils and transitions of civil and international warfare, but much of their work is still to be collected and interpreted. In these, and in selected publications from the Catholic publishing houses, are found significant writings which provide the resources of context and Catholic thought from which further contextualizing theology would grow.

Selected References

Brou, A., sj. "Notes pour servir a l'histoire des origines du clergé indigéne en Chine." *Revue d'historie des missions* (1926 and 1927).

Cary-Elwes, Columba. *China and the Cross: studies in missionary history*. New York: Longmans, Green, 1957.

Charbonnier, Jean. *L'interprétation de l'histoire en Chine contemporaine*. 2 vols. Lille: Université de Lille, 1980.

—. *Histoire des Chrêtiens de Chine*. Paris: Joint edition Declée and Bégédie, 1992.

Constantini, C. *Le Missioni Cattoliche e la Cultura dell' Otiente*. Rome: Instituto Italiano per Medio ed Edtremo Oriente, 1943.

d'Elia, Paschale M. *Catholic Missions in China*. Shanghai: Commercial Press, 1934.

—. *Catholic Native Episcopacy in China, being an Outline of the Formation and Growth of the Chinese Catholic Clergy (1800-1926)*. Shanghai: T'ousewei Print Press, 1927.

Heyndrickx, J. *Historiography of the Chinese Church: 19th and 20th Centuries*. Leuven: Ferdinand Verbiest Foundation, 1994.

Huppertz, Josefine. *Ein Beispiel katholischer Verlagsarbeit in China: eine zeitgeschichtliche Studie*. Studia Instituti Missiologici Societatis Verbi Divini 54. Nettetal: Steyler Verlag, 1992.

Jennes, Jos, Albert van Lierde and Tien Paul Yung Cheng. *Four Centuries of Catechetics in China: Historical Evolution of Apologetics and Catechetics in the Catholic Mission of China from the 16th century until 1940*: Taipei, Huaming Press, 1976.

Ku Wei-ying and Koen De Ridderl. *Authentic Chinese Christianity. Preludes to its Development (Nineteenth and Twentieth Centuries)*. Leuven Chinese Studies volume 9. Leuven: Leuven University Press, 2000.

Latourette, Kenneth Scott. *A History of Christian Missions in China*. London: SPCK, 1929.

Masson, Joseph. *Vers l'Église indigène: catholicisme ou nationalisme?* Bruxelles: Éditions universitaires, 1944.

Piolet, J.B. *Les Missions Catholiques Francais au XIXe siècle*. 5 vols. Paris, n.d.

Soetens, Claude. *L'Eglise catholique en Chine au XXe siècle*. L'histoire dans l'actualité 6. Paris: Beauchesne, c1997.

Streit, P. Robert. *Bibliotheca Missionum. Vol. 12, Chinesische missionsliteratur; 1800- 1884*. Freiburg: Verlag Herder, 1958.

Tiedeman, G.R. ed. *Handbook of Christianity in China. Vol. II, 1800-2000.* Leiden: Brill, Forthcoming.
Triviere, Leon. *The Catholic Church in Mainland China* (L'église catholique en Chine continentale). Hong Kong: 1959.
Wolferstam, Bertram. *The Catholic Church in China 1860-1907.* London: Sands, 1909.

2.1.2. Jesuits at Zikawei

The Jesuit foundation at Xujiahui (Zikawei), originally established in1847, was by 1872 a center for Chinese scholarship and scientific research, with both an extensive library based on collections begun two centuries earlier, and a printing press which became notable particularly for learned sinological studies. From 1892 on, these were issued as the series *Variétés Sinologique*, which included 66 volumes by 1938. Here were published the writings of such Chinese scholars as Huang Po-lu (1830-1909) - in many volumes on Chinese history, geography, law and government; Simon Kiong sj - on Chinese culture; Wang Tch'ang-tche sj - on the philosopher Wang Yangming; and Mathias Tchang (1852-1929), from whom there are historical and biographical writings in Chinese studies, including Catholic writers. Other writers included Henri Havret sj - on the Nestorian Monument; Joseph Tardif de Moidrey sj, Louis Gaillard sj and Louis Pfister sj - on Chinese church history; H. Dugout sj and Albert Tscepe sj - on Chinese history and geography; Henri Dore sj and Jerome Le Tobar - in a series on religion and superstition. These and other volumes include contextual studies, which provide significant sources for a contextualizing theology, although in some cases later superceded. Many have since been reprinted by other publishers including Brill, Johnson Reprint, Kraus Reprint, Ch'eng Wen and Kuangchi presses. They would be followed by the new series of *Variétés Sinologiques*, commencing in 1982.

Selected References

Dore, Henri, sj. *Recherches sur les superstitions en Chine.* 18 vols. *Variétés sinologiques.* Shanghai: T'ou-sè-wè Press, 1911-1938.
Dudink, A., N. Standaert, et al. *Xujiahui zangshulou Ming Qing tianzhujiao wenxian* (Chinese Christian texts from the Zikawei

Library). 5 vols. Taibei: Fu Jen Catholic University Press, 1996.

Gaillard, Louis, sj. *Crois et Swastika en Chine. Variétés sinologiques* 3. 2nd ed. Shanghai: T'ou-sè-wè Press, 1904.

Huang Po-lu. *Mélanges sur l'administration. Variétés sinologiques* 21 (1902).

Huang Zhiwei. "The Xujiahui (Zikawei) Library." *Tripod* (July-August 1992).

King, Gail. "The Xujiahui (Zikawei) Library of Shanghai." *Libraries and Culture* 32.4 (1997).

Pfister, Louis, sj. *Notices biographiques et bibliographiques sur les Jésuites de l'ancienne missionde Chine 1552-1773.* 2 vols. *Variétés sinologiques* 59-60. Shanghai: T'ou-sè-wè Press1932, 1934.

Tardif deMoidrey, Joseph. *La hiérarchie catholique en Chine, en Corée et au Japon (1307-1914). Variétés sinologiques* 38. Zi-ka-wei, Chang-Hai: Imprimerie de l'Orphelinat de T'ou-sé-wé, 1914.

Tchang, Mathias and Pierre de Prunelle sj. *Le Pere Simon A. Cunha S. J. (Ou Li Yu-Chan 1632-1718). L'homme et l'œuvre artistique. Variétés sinologiques* 37. Shanghai: T'ou-sè-wè Press, 1914.

2.2 Catholic Scholars - late 19th/ early 20th centuries

Many Catholic scholars in this period have left writings in history or philosophy, in literature, theology or scientific studies which include contextual elements and reflections. Among Chinese writers are those already mentioned (above): Huang Po-lu (fl.1900); Simon Kiong sj; Wang Tch'ang-tche sj; and Mathias Tchang (fl. 1912); along with Li Kang-chi (1872-1915) who made careful studies of church history and of "foreign" religions in China; and Li Wenyu (1840-1912) who wrote many works on religion and philosophy (see 2.2.1.). The layman Vincent Ying Lianzhi, in his *Exhortation to Study* (1917), addressed to the clergy of his time, and later to the Pope, an appeal for much greater seriousness in education and for the foundation of a Catholic university. (See Ma Xiangbo 2.2.2.). This eventuated in 1925, with its initial department being a school of Chinese Studies. Thaddeus Yang (1905-1982) also later wrote and campaigned for the establishment of an Intellectual Apostolate in the following period.

Among expatriate scholars and writers, apart from those mentioned above in connection with the *Variétés Sinologiques*, and others leaving many historical and apologetic writings, a number stand out for their contributions to church history, and to cultural and religious studies. Seraphin Couvreur wrote and translated widely in Chinese religion, language and literature, and Emille Butruille studied and wrote on Buddhism. Henri Bernard has left works on the history of Christianity in China in the 13th and 17th centuries, and upon the relation between Chinese wisdom and Christian philosophy. L. Wieger wrote historical, linguistic and philosphical texts, including studies of Chinese religion. Evariste Régis Huc has left a series of important church histories, Jean de la Servière produced standard histories of the Jesuit presence in China, and Pasquale M. d'Elia wrote extensively on Matteo Ricci and on the formation of the Chinese Catholic clergy. Edward Licent and Antoine Mostaert reported their extensive researches in Mongolia (see Teilhard de Chardin, 2.2.3.). Among the many biographers of both national and expatriate Catholics are F.M.J. Gourdon, Gu Luodong, A.G. Foucauld, Jean Guennou and Antoon Hullen.

Selected References

Adams, Archibald G. et al. *T'an Tau lu* (Dialogue on Christianity for my Chinese friends). Shanghai: YMCA Press, 1922; Bologna: EMI, 1976.

Bernard, Henri. *Sagesse Chinois et Philosophie Chrétienne, essai sur leurs relations historiques.* Tientsin: En vente à la procure de la Mission de Sienshien, 1935.

Charbonnier, Jean. *Histoire des Chrétiens de Chine.* Paris: Joint edition Desclée and Bégédie, 1992.

Couvreur, Seraphin S.J. *Li ki; ou, Mémoires sur les bienséances et les cérémonies.* Texte chinois avec une double traduction en français et en latin. 2 vols. 2nd. ed. Ho Kien Fou: Imprimerie de la Mission catholique, 1913.

d'Elia, Pasquale sj., ed. *Fonti Ricciane. Original Documents concerning Matteo Ricci ...* 3 volumes. Rome: Libreria dello Strato, 1942-1949.

Huc, Evariste. *Christianity in China, Tartary and Thibet.* New York: Sadlier, 1857.

—. *Empire Chinois, faisant suite a l'ouvrage intituli Souvenirs d'un voyage dam la Tartarie et le Thibet.* 2 vols. Paris: A l'Imprimerie Imperiale, 1854.

Li Kang-chi. *La Chine & les religions étrangères: Kiao-ou ki-lio ... "Resume des affaires religeuses."* Shanghai: Imprimerie de la Mission Catholique, 1917.

—, and Chou Fu. *Chiao wu ji lue.* Taibei: Wen hai chu ban she, 1986. Reprint. Originally published: *Nan-yang kuan pao chü,* 1905.

Liang Tingnan. *Hai guo sishuo.* Beijing: Zhonghua shuju (distr. by Xinhua shudian), 1993.

Wieger, L. *A History of the Religious Beliefs and Philosophical Opinions in China.* Reprint. New York: Dover, 1969.

Wang Zhaoxian. "Tianzhujiao de chuban shiye" (On Catholic publishing). *Wenshe Monthly* 2.5 (1927).

Zu Zongze. *Zhongguo Tianzhujiao gailun* (An introduction to Chinese Catholicism). Shanghai: Shanghai shengjiao zazhishe, 1938.

2.2.1. Li Wenyu, Laurent (1840-1911)

Li Wenyu was a disciple of Angelo Zottoli of Zikawei, assisted in the formation of the library there, and was rector of a minor seminary and later rector of *Zhendan daxue* (Aurora University), succeeding Ma Xiangbo (see 2.2.2. below) in 1906. He had earlier commenced pioneer work in both journalism and religious studies, in 1879. In 1898 he founded and edited the weekly *Yiwen Lu* (Useful News), which combined with *Ge Zhi Hui Magazine* to become the *Yi Wen Ge Zhi Hui Magazine* (from 1907 entitled the *Recueil de nouvelles et de sciences*). He had also founded (1887) the *Shengxin bao* (Le Bulletin du Sacré-Coeur). Apart from almost 60 translations and four collections of biographies he also wrote 17 works on religion and philosophy, with special attention to the history of Catholicism in China, "Translation of the New Scripture" and "Annals of the Believers." He made particular studies of the writings of Paul Xu and the poems of the early priest Wu Yushan. Through these and other writings Li has been acknowledged as assisting the Church in China to better understand its roots and to become more aware of its identity. He recognized the demands for modernization in Chinese society, but was even more passionately concerned to recover Chinese Christian tradition. Many colleagues believed he was able to present a faith which was both fully Christian and fully Chinese in his studies of this.

Selected References

"Li Wen Yu (1840-1912)." *Tripod* 12 (1970).

Fang Hao. *Zhongguo Tianzhujiao shi renwu zhuan* (Biographies of Catholic historical figures in China). 3 vols. Hong Kong: Gongjiao zhenli xuexi, 1970. Reprint, Beijing: Zhonghua shuju, 1988.

Charbonnier, Jean. *Histoire des Chrétiens de Chine*. Paris: Joint edition Declée and Bégédie, 1992.

2.2.2. Ma Xiangbo (c.1840 -1939)

Scholar and priest, educator and ardent nationalist, human rights advocate and theologian, Ma Xiangbo is chiefly remembered as the founder of *Zhendan daxue* (Aurora University) and later the *Fudan daxue*, for his contribution to the establishment of *Furen daxue* (a catholic university in Beijing), and as "the most influential Chinese Catholic thinker of the modern period." Although he became a Jesuit (1862), he later left the order (1874), not being able to accept a wholly European framework for the life of a religious, as he was later unable to accept the overly French shaping of *Zhendan daxue*. Later he married and undertook public service, donating much of his family property to establish *Fudan gongxue* (Fudan Public School). With his close colleague Ying Lianzhi, Ma had worked for the establishment of *Furen daxue* and other schools, and the university expanded to include all faculties and to publish three sinological journals. In 1935, at the invitation of the Communist Party, Ma wrote the *Declaration of the Shanghai Culture Rescue Movement* with Sheng Junyu and Zuo Taobei. Although he was at times placed under surveillance by warlord regimes for his political activities, he nonetheless made significant contributions to religious, educational and political movements in China, exploring in his extensive writings the issues of Chinese modernization, the role of political parties and of the Church within the state, the relationship of religion to society and the indigenization of Christianity.

Many of Ma's writings were published as *Collected Works* in 1947, but many more have since come to light. These include articles written before the 1911 Revolution, on constitutional and political responsibility, and on educational and professional innovation. They appeared in such newspapers and journals as the *Shi bao* (The Times), *Guangyi congbao* (The Serial of Broad Benefit), *Minguo bao* (The Republican), and *Huanqiu Zhongguo xuesheng bao* (The Global Newspaper of Chinese Students). He was also a skilful linguist, translating the Four Gospels and a number of Christian classics. Letters, lectures and other documents of his have also only recently been rediscovered, and these, along with a collection of Ma's speeches during the Sino-Japanese War, are absent from the *Collected Works*. The full measure of his thought and writing is yet to be gauged, but a four-volume collection of his works - general, religious, political and educational - is now being prepared. In particular, the contribution of Ma Xiangbo to the development of Chinese Catholic theology by his application of classical Confucian and also Christian insights to the major social and political questions of a Chinese society in transition is yet to be adequately studied and received.

Selected References

> Fang Hao, ed. *Ma Xiangbo wenji* (Ma Xiangbo's collected writings). Beijing: Shangzhi Publishing, 1947.
> Hayhoe, Ruth. "A Chinese Catholic Philosophy of Higher Education in Republican China." *Tripod* 48 (1988).
> —, and Lu Yongling, eds. *Ma Xiang Bo and the Mind of Modern China 1840-1939*. Armonk, NY: M.E.Sharpe, 1996.
> Lu Yongling, et al., eds. *Ma Xiangbo ji* (A compilation of Ma Xiang Bo's writings). Shanghai: Fudan University Press, 1996.
> Malatesta, Edward J. "Two Catholic Universities and a Major Chinese Catholic Thinker: Zhendan daxue, Furen daxue and Ma Xiang Bo." In *Historiography of the Chinese Catholic Church,* edited by J. Heyndrickx. Leuven: Ferdinand Verbiest Foundation, 1994.

2.2.3. Pierre Teilhard de Chardin sj (1881-1955)

It is not widely acknowledged that Teilhard de Chardin's major thought and many of his writings matured in China, where he lived and worked, apart from brief intervals, from 1923 until 1946. It was during these years, and from his extensive travels and studies as a paleontologist and geologist there - often with Edward Licent, W.C. Pei or Pierre Leroy as colleagues- that his intensive study and reflection bore fruit in a stream of writings, most of which were also first published in China. In all these, de Chardin's central concern is to understand the role of the "the human phenomenon" in its total breadth, and to uncover the "thinking and knowing level of the universe" which is, he affirms, evolving through increased socialization of the human condition to an infinite future (the "noosphere"). A comprehensive theology of humanity within the universe had thus been formed amid the ancient and turbulent expanses of China, but de Chardin's mystical dialogue with place, people and history in China still awaits full assimilation.

The development of his thought, within the experiences in China which clearly shaped it, is most clearly traced in the modest volume containing his letters from the year 1923 until that of his death: *Letters from a Traveller* (1956), the vast majority of which were written in China. Here can be seen the growth of his mystical theology, sometimes termed "neo-humanism," which effected a synthesis of the material and physical world with the world of the mind and spirit, personalizing "the world in God" through Jesus Christ, in the universal community of a fulfilled humanity. The fuller articulation of Teilhard de Chardin's theology is found in many writings written during the China years and is found to be closely linked to particular experiences there. *The Mass on the World* (originally shaped in Ordos as *The Mass on Things*), appeared in Tientsin in 1924, and *My Universe*, there a year later. He then writes his treatise on spirituality, *The Divine Milieu* (Tientsin 1930), and his second study for *The Human Phenomenon* (Tientsin 1931). Following work in Liangzhou (Gansu) comes *The Spirit of the Earth* (1931) and in 1933, *The Meaning of Suffering* (Peking). After travels to Henan, and the Yangtze, *How I Believe* was written (Peking). In quick succession come a series of other writings, most of them also written in Peking in between various travels, including *Design of a Personal Universe*, and *We Can Save Mankind* (both in 1936); *The Human Energy* (1937); *The Human Phenomenon*, (completed in 1939); *The Granitization of China* and *The Expected Word* (1940); *Primitive Man in China* (1941); *The Evolving Christ* (1942); and *Super-Humankind, Super-Christ, Super-Charity* (1943). The works of his last years, included: *Reflections on the Spiritual Resonance of the Atomic Bomb* and *Design for a Dialetics of the Spirit* (1946), *Spiritual Market of the Extreme Orient* (1947), *The Modern Neo-Humanism* (1948), and *The Place of Humanity in Nature* (1949).

Selected References
Works by Pierre Teilhard de Chardin
> *Les oeuvres complètes*. Paris: Editions du Seuil, 1955-1976.
> *Letters from a Traveller*. Paris: Bernard Grasset ,1956; London: Collins, 1962.
> *Le Milieu Divin*. Paris: Editions du Seuil, 1957; London: Collins, 1960.
> *The Phenomenon of Man*. London: Collins; New York: Harper, 1959.
> *L'Energie Humaine*. Paris: Editions du Seuil, 1962.
> *Man's Place in Nature*. London: Collins; New York: Harper, 1966.
> Faricy, Robert L. *Teilhard de Chardin's Theology of the Christian in the World*. New York: Sheed and Ward, 1967.
> King, Ursula. *Spirit of Fire: The Life & Vision of Teilhard de Chardin*. Maryknoll, NY: Orbis Books, 1996.
> La Héronnière, Edith de. *Teilhard de Chardin: une mystique de la traversée*. Paris: Pygmalion/G. Watelet, 1999.
> Lubac, Henri. *The Religion of Teilhard de Chardin*. Paris: Aubier, 1962; London: Collins, 1967.

2.2.4. Vincent Lebbe (1877-1940) and colleagues
Frédéric Vincent Lebbe (Lei Mingyuan) was priest, activator and advocate for the autonomy of the Catholic Church in China and for the development of its native clergy. He was a strong critic of the liaison between colonial power and missions in China, of the arrogance and eurocentric mindset of most missionaries there, and worked to end the French protectorate. Almost from his arrival in China (1901), and working first among intellectuals in Tientsin, he began to identify himself closely with Chinese colleagues and with their lifestyle, took Chinese nationality and devoted himself to study of the Chinese language and writing, culture and history. On this

basis he was to become a unique leader in missiological reform, in the recognition and formation of Chinese leadership, and in the articulation of Chinese Christian selfhood. "I believe," wrote Lebbe, "that we owe it to the Christians here, and even to the non-Christians, to be to them what the Church is wherever it exists - the last refuge of what is right and proper, where justice need never fear to make its voice heard."

Lebbe quickly developed his own catechism, the so-called "method of Tientsin," in order to "inculturate the Christian message in the Chinese context," and then undertook an intensive program of lecturing on these issues and upon Christian social doctrine. With Chinese colleagues and his confrère Anthony Cotta he formed Catholic lay associations and founded the first Catholic weekly newspaper in China (1912), the Catholic daily paper *Yi shi bao* - "the public well-being" (1915) for north China, as well as a *Mission Magazine* and one for children and women. In these and other periodicals he wrote regular "religious" columns. Transferred to Ningpo for his outspoken criticism (1917), he nonetheless prepared the *Memoir on the Catholic Mission in China* which led directly to the promulgation of Pope Benedict XV's encyclical *Maximum Illud*. This and the later *Rerum ecclesiae* of Pius XI (1926) marked a radical change in mission practice, but it was through the association of Lebbe with Celso Constantini, who was appointed Apostolic Legate in 1922, that effective moves to form an indigenous Catholic Church were made. The French Protectorate was ended, six Chinese bishops were consecrated (1926) and increasing numbers of Chinese were ordained priests. Lebbe continued to write, to organize lay movements and to mobilize auxiliary associations for the Chinese Church and later for patriotic causes during the Sino-Japanese War. His theological contributions are recognized by "Vincent Lebbe Centres" established in both China and Belgium.

Selected References
Works by Vincent Lebbe
> "Mouvement des Idées et des Choses en Chine au cours de ces quinze dernières années." *Bulletin Société Géographique* 60 (1913).

"Le Clergé National. Lettre à Mgr Reynaud." (Ning-po, 18 septembre 1917). *Cahiers des Auxiliaires Laïques des Missions* 10.4 (1951).
"*Memoir on the Catholic Mission in China and Formation of an Indigenous Clergy.*" In *Sagra Congregazione De Propaganda Fide, Ponente.* Roma: 1922.
Pour l'Église chinoise. Introduction et notes par Cl. Soetens. Recueil des Archives Vincent Lebbe. Louvain: Faculté de Théologie, 1982-83.
Lettres du Père Lebbe, Choisies et présentées par P. Goffart. Tournai-Paris: A. Sohier, 1960.
Goffart, Paul. "La Genèse des Idées des missionnaires du Père Lebbe." *Église Vivante* 1 (1949).
Leclercq, Jacques. *Thunder in the Distance: Life of Père Lebbe.* New York: Sheed and Ward, 1958 (Paris, 1954).
Rivinius, Karl Josef. "Lebbe, Frédéric Vincent." In *Biographisch Bibliographisches Kirchenlexicon.* Herzberg: Verlag Bautz, 1992.
Soetens, Claude. *Inventaire des Archives Vincent Lebbe.* Louvain: la-Neuve, 1982.
Thoreau, Vincent. *Le tonnerre qui chante au loin. Vie et mort du Père Lebbe, âpotre des chinois (1877-1940).* Bruxelles, 1990.

2.2.5. Lou Tseng-tsiang, Pierre Celestine (1871-1949)

Lou Tseng -tsieng, already imbued with both Confucian and Christian traditions, studied foreign languages in Peking and entered China's diplomatic service, first in St Petersburg (1893-1896). His mentor Shu King-shen urged him to study Christian history and particularly the history of Catholicism at Zikawei where, he writes, he encountered many problems in the relationship between China and Christianity. These he continued to study and reflect on, in Europe and China, while being instrumental in reforming China's Department of Foreign Affairs, and taking significant roles in meetings of the League of Nations. Following the death of his wife (1926), Lou moved towards a fuller religious vocation as Catholic priest, later entering the Benedictine Order in Belgium (1928). In doing this he believed he was not only fulfilling his vocation, but that he was also continuing that of his beloved wife, as well as uniting the callings of diplomat, peace-maker and monk.

In his book *Ways of Confucius and of Christ,* Lou outlines these experiences with reflections upon Christianity as the completion

Contextual Theology in China

of the Confucian tradition. He came to affirm that the Greek "Logos" corresponded directly to the Chinese "Tao" and this was revealed in Jesus Christ who rendered supreme familial piety to God. Through long meditation he had also found the rejuvenation and deepening of the ancient national culture of China to lie in a renewed understanding of the Christian Gospel, and called upon his people to see the harmony of this with the purpose of Confucius "to bring peace to the universe." Here, and in other writings, Lou draws on the earlier history of Catholicism in China, and on recent policies of the Propaganda Fide, to portray a fully Chinese church, able to contribute both its culture and its witness to the Graeco-Latin church. He also pleads for genuine inter-cultural learning, and for both ecumenical and international reconciliation and joint action. To this end, he finds in a broadened concept of filial piety, in the universal principle of human relationships and, in the creative tradition of Ricci and Lebbe, sources for the renewal of the Catholic apostolate and for the reconstruction of China.

Selected References
Works by Lou Tseng-tsiang
"La vie et les oeuvres du grand chrétien Paul Siu Kouang-k'i."
Bulletin des missions 13 (1934).
"Preface" to *The Voice of the Church in China 1931-1932, 1937-1938*. London: Longmans Green, 1938.
Souvenirs et Pensées. Paris: Desclée & De Brouwer. 1945.
Ways of Confucius and of Christ. London, Burns and Oates, 1948.
La Rencontre des humanités et la découverte de l'Evangile. Paris; Desclée de Brouwer, 1949.
Garnier, H. "Etude sur M. Lou Tseng-Tsiang." In *Introduction à la vie réelle du père Lebbe*, Duxième partie. Dijon: Bernigaud et Privat, 1951.
Wu Ching-Hioung, Jean. *Dom Lou: sa vie spirituelle*. Préface du R.P. Garrigou-Lagrange. Bruges: Desclee de Brouwer, 1949.

2.3 Response to Civil Conflict and War

Conditions of civil and later international war from 1925 on brought strongly localized theological response from leading Catholic bishops during the 1930s. Although strongly opposed to Communism, and in some cases later implicated in the repressive policies of the Kuomintang (KMT), some of their writings yet contain genuine insights for a contextual theology. Archbishop Mario Zanin, in Pastoral Letters, and the Circular Letter "Inter Arma Caritas" (Oct. 1937), moved from biblical examples to an advocacy for peace and justice in China, as well as for prayer and works of service. This was to include charity for the relief of the wounded and homeless in co-operation with secular and national organizations. Bishop Auguste Haouissé (Shanghai), echoed Zannin's appeal for solidarity with secular societies in relief work, and in his Pastoral Letter "Devotion to the Country" (July 1937) outlined the "Kingdom of Christ" as the spiritual principle not only of personal devotion, but of public, social and national devotion. Archbishop Chou Chi-shih Joseph, issued similar Pastorals, and the College of Bishops published joint letters on the same subjects, especially after the outbreak of the Sino-Japanese War. Selected Pastoral letters and articles also appeared in such journals as the weekly *Kung-i-lou*, the *Nouvelle Revue Théologique* and *L'osservatoro Romano*. In these, bishops and others applied the social demands of Christian teaching and a larger theology of the "kingdom of God" to contemporary turbulent conditions, by advocating the peace and welfare of Chinese society as a whole.

Bishop Paul Yu Bin (1901-1978, Nanjing), has left in his writings some of the fullest theological reflections of the time, and despite his strong anti-Marxist position and controversial political role (also later in Taiwan), he takes significant theological 'leaps' in particular documents. In Pastorals and in treatises on "War in the Far East" (Dec. 1937), "Christian Patriotism" (Dec. 1937), and "The Communist Question in China" (March 1938), he opposes atheistic materialism, presents the current war as an international psychological problem for both China and other nations caused by Japanese aggression, and outlines the basis for non-revengeful defence of one's own people found in Catholic teachings on the justice of God. His most creative theological insights arise as he presents the role of China's suffering as being on behalf of others, and bringing renewal and human dignity for all. The latter theme is further elaborated in an "Address to the International Eucharistic Congress, May, 1938." Here he declares that because the Chinese

Contextual Theology in China

people have offered to God so much suffering "for the salvation of their brothers," they resemble Jesus Christ, can receive his charity and are embraced by his salvation. This is a clear affirmation, provoked by the tragic events of war, that universal salvation is available to *all* who sacrifice themselves for others in the Sino-Japanese War. In the following year he also welcomed the return to Ricci's method of approach to the literati which was signalled by the Vatican's revised instructions on the acceptability of Confucian rites (1939), later also writing on China's reconstruction 1939-1951.

A note should be added concerning the literature of biography, autobiography and martyrology which arose from the imprisonment and death of many Christians at the hands of revolutionary forces. Examples of these writings and reflections can be studied in such periodicals as *China Missionary Bulletin* (CMBA), *Religion in Communist Lands*, *Bulletin de la Société des Mission Etrangères* (BSMEP), *China Bulletin* and *Fides*; and in such volumes as that by Monsterleet (1955).

Selected References

Catholic Association for International Peace (US). Asia Committee. *Manchuria: the Problem in the Far East. Study Presented to the Catholic Association for International Peace by the Asia Committee.* New York: Paulist Press, 1934.

Collectanea Commissionis Synodalis. *Digests of the Synodal Commission of Catholic Church in China, 1928-1947: Guide to the Microfiche Collection.* Bethesda, MD: CIS Academic Editions, c1988.

d'Elia, Pascal, ed. *Le triple Démisme du Sun Wen.* Shanghai: Zikawei Institute, 1929.

Hanson, Eric O. *Catholic Politics in China and Korea.* Maryknoll, NY: Orbis Books, 1980.

Haouissé, Auguste. Foreword to *Fifty-six years a Missionary in China: the Life of Mother Dominic, Helper of the Holy Souls.* London: Burns, Oates & Washbourne, 1935.

Kearney, James F. *Four Horsemen Ride Again.* Portraits of China Series 2. Shanghai: Imprimerie de T'ou-se-we, 1940.

Maryknoll Mission Letters, China: Extracts from the Letters and Diaries of the Pioneer Missioners of the Catholic Foreign

Mission Society of America 1923-1942. New York: Macmillan, ?1943.

Masson, Joseph. *Vers l'Église Indigène: Catholicisme ou Nationalisme?* Collection "chrétienté nouvelle" 1. sér., 2. Bruxelles: Éditions universitaires, 1944.

Monsterleet, J. *Martyrs in China.* London: Longmans, Green, 1955.

The Chinese Bishops Archbishop Mario Zanin, Bishop Haouissé sj, and Bishop Yu Bin, with a Preface by Dom Pierre-Celestin Lou Tseng-tsiang. *The Voice of the Church in China, 1931-1932, 1937-1938.* London, New York, Longmans, Green, 1938.

Yü Pin, Bp. *Eyes East.* Paterson, N.J.: St. Anthony Guild Press, 1945.

Whyte, Bob. *Unfinished Encounter. China and Christianity.* London: Collins, 1988.

2.4 Journals and the Debate on "Atheism" (see also 3.2.1. et seq.)

The history of Chinese Catholic churches in part predisposed them to reject the claims of revolutionary movements and to ignore or opposing Communist policies. Assumptions on the part of missionary priests were most often that the central issue was that of "belief" in God, equated with faithful performance of Catholic liturgical and devotional practices, opposed to "disbelief," which was equated with all social, moral and religious evils. Few, even of the above bishops, wrestled with the demands of faith for a religious life in which the urgent demands for social justice and reconstruction in Republican China were central to the Gospel and to Christian discipleship. Lebbe (2.2.4.) and some of his co-workers made some beginnings in this, but there was no comparable group to those among Protestants, of thinkers and theologians who were studying to clarify the extent to which Christians could, to be faithful to the Gospel, collaborate in programs obviously directed towards the correction of gross injustices and to the genuine relief of poor peasants and oppressed workers. The vast majority of writings upon the political and military turmoils of the 1930s and 1940s are therefore strongly anti-Marxist.

Articles supporting the incompatibility between theism and atheism can be found particularly in Catholic journals among which are:

Xin Bei Chen (New Northern Stars), began publication in 1936. Number 3 is a special issue advocating anti-communism; it might help to remember that civil war was still going on as well as the war of resistance against Japan.

Yi Shi Bao (For the Good of the World - Social welfare) (Tientsin), began with the Oct. 10, 1915 issue and ceased in 1949 (see Lebbe 2.2.4.). There was a daily and a weekly under the same name, which later presented writings opposing atheism. Some issues were accompanied by supplements. This was also published in various regional editions after 1945, in Peking, Chongqing and Xian.

Other Catholic periodicals which were significant in this period include: *Fu jen ta hsüeh (Furen daxue)* - Bulletin of the Catholic University of Peking (1926-1934); *China Missionary: Review of the Catholic Missions in China* - Missionnaires de Chine, Shanghai (continued in Hong Kong after 1949); *Monumenta Serica - Universitatis Catholicae Peking* (1936?); *Journal of Oriental Studies* (later published in Tokyo, 1949-1963, Los Angeles, 1964-1971 and St. Augustin, Germany, 1972-); *Bulletin de la Société des Mission Etrangères*; *China Missionary Bulletin* (Shanghai and Hong Kong).

Selected References

Bays, Daniel H. "Chinese Popular Religion and Christianity Before and After the 1949 Revolution: A Retrospective View." *Fides et Historia* 23.1 (1991).

Cary-Elwes, Columba. *China and the Cross: Studies in Missionary History.* New York: Longmans, Green, 1957.

Catholic Missions and Annals of the Propagation of the Faith. New York: 1924-

Maryknoll Mission Letters, China: Extracts from the Letters and Diaries of the Pioneer Missioners of the Catholic Foreign Mission Society of America 1923-1942. New York: Macmillan, ?1943.

Eber, Irene, Sze-kar Wan and Knut Walf, in collaboration with Roman Malek, eds. *Bible in Modern China: The Literary and Intellectual Impact.* Sankt Agustin: Institut Monumenta Serica; Nettetal: Steyler, 1999.

Latourette, Kenneth Scott. *A History of Christian Missions in China*. London: SPCK, 1929.

Löwenthal, Rudolf. *The Catholic Press in China*. Peiping: s.n., 1936.

Wang Zhaoxian. "Tianzhujiao de chuban shiye" (On Catholic publishing). *Wenshe Yuekan* 2.5 (1927).

Yi Shi Bao (Microfilm.) Washington, DC: Center for Chinese Research Materials, Association of Research Libraries, 1973.

2.5 Supplementary Bibliography I

Annales de la Congrégation de la Mission. Paris: Congregation de la Mission, 1835-1963.

Annales de la propagation de la foi, receuil periodique, Collection faisant suite aux lettres édifiantes. Lyon: 1842 et seq. English translation, Dublin and New York: 1838-1923. Vols. 22, 23, 26, 27, 28.

Archives des Missions Etrangères. Societe des Missions Etrangères. Paris.

Beckman, Johannes. *Die katholische Missionsmethode in China in neuester Zeit (1842-1912): geschichtliche Untersuchung über Arbeitsweisen, ihre Hindernisse und Erfolge*. Immensee, Missionshaus Bethlehem, 1931.

Bibollet, A. *Le clergé indigène dans les misions de Chine confiées aux congrégations francaises*. Paris: Oeuvre de Saint-Pierre-Apotrre, 1945.

Collectanea S. Gongregationis de Propaganda Fide, seu Decreta, Instructiones, Rescripta pro Apostolicis Missionibus. 2 vols. Rome: Ex Typographia Polyglotta S.C. de Propaganda Fide, 1907.

Catalogus librorum, mapparum et imaginum religiosarum quae prostant in orphanotrophio. Shanghai: Typographia Missionis Catholicae, 1896.

Chicoine, F. (Fidèle). *Petit catechisme des missions*. Tientsin: Chihli Press, 1938.

Constantini, Celso. *Con i missionari in Cina*. 2 vols. Rome: Unione missionaria del clero in Italia, 1946.

Couvreur, S. with Li Chi. *Memoires sur les Bienseances et les Ceremonies*. Paris: Cathasia, c.1950.

Duperray, E. "La Littérature Chrétienne Chinoise." *Eglise Vivante*. 1954.

Kervyn, Louis M. *Méthode de L'apostolat Moderne en Chine*. Hongkong: Société des Missions-Étrangères, 1911.

Launay, Adrien. *Histoire de la Mission de Chine: Mission du Se-Tchouan.* 2 vols. Paris: Tequi, 1920.

Li Shiqiang. *Zhongguo guanshen fanjiao de yuanyin, 1860-1874* (The causes of anti-Christian movement by Chinese officials and gentry, 1860-74). Institute of Modern History, Academia Sinica, 1966.

Little Brothers of St. John. *La règle des Petits Frères de Saint-Jean-Baptiste.* (In French & Chinese.) Louvain-la-Neuve: Faculté de théologie, 1986.

Hauth, Thomas. *Russian Literary and Ecclesiastical Life in Manchuria and China from 1920 to 1952: Unpublished Memoirs of Valerij Perelesin.* Russian emigre literature in the 20th century, Studies and texts 6. The Hague: Leuxenhoff, 1996.

Saint Martin, Jean-Didier de. *Doctrine de la Sainte Religion a l'usage des missionnaires en Chine et leurs neophytes.* Paris: Typ. Henri Pion, 1859.

Shengjiao yaoli (Essential doctrines of the holy religion). Chongqing: Zeng-jiayan shengjiao shuju, 1926.

The New Glories of the Catholic Church, translated by the Fathers of the London Oratory. London: Richardson & Son, 1859.

Wang, R. *A Witness behind the Curtain. Biography of Fr. Francis Xavier Chu.* Taipei: Kuang-chi, 1987.

Wiest, Jean-Paul. *Maryknoll in China: a History, 1918-1955.* Armonk, NY: M.E. Sharpe, c1988.

Wolf, Ann Colette. *Against all Odds: Sisters of Providence Mission to the Chinese, 1920-1990.* Saint Mary-of-the-Woods, IN: Sisters of Providence, 1990.

Xiao, Joseph. *Shengjiaoshilue* (History of Chinese Catholic Church). 2 vols. Xianxian, Hebei: 1905.

Zu Zongze. *Zhongguo Tianzhujiao gailun* (An introduction to Chinese Catholicism). Shanghai: Shanghai shengjiao zazhishe, 1938.

3 Contextual Catholic Theology Since 1949

3.1 Revolution, Response, Division: 1949-1975

Following the establishment of the People's Republic of China in 1949, Roman Catholics entered into a period of intense ambiguity. A situation of religious and political confrontation in both urban and rural districts demanded of them individual choices, and personal decisions and difficulties were all the greater because the political situation changed completely almost without warning. There were less than 30 Chinese bishops remaining in China, for over 100 expatriate bishops had left along with (eventually) all other expatriate personnel. There were also no precedents to follow in reconstructing ecclesial leadership or theological training in the wake of major conflict and continuing social division. No matter which side was chosen - in church allegiance or in ideological and theological interpretation - great risks were involved. Sudden and strong political positions were therefore taken, not as the result of deliberate and mature thought, but rather of discernment done in the depths of people's consciences.

Although the legacy of recent decades in debate, writings and in statements from the hierarchy, was such that many Catholics strongly opposed Communist rule in the first few years, overt resistance largely ended after 1955, although divisions within the church were to harden and go underground from then on. By 1960, the patriotic movement among Chinese Catholics had grown in influence and the Catholic Patriotic Association was formed under the leadership of Bishop Li Boyu and Archbishop Pi Shushih. (It would be re-organized in 1980, when the College of Bishops was also formed (see 3.2.1.1.). Theologically the past 50 years have therefore been a period for many of either inactivity or frantic action. Some theologians also have chosen to go underground from whence they might write their reflections, although these are seldom published within China. Others who have chosen to continue the visible life of the Church and to minister to the millions of Catholics who openly profess their faith, have not been able, either because of their age or their lack of resources, to greatly assist in theological reflection. They have been busy repairing churches and opening Catholic educational institutions to raise new generations of priests and religious women. By and large it has been a period for action rather than prolonged reflection. People did reflect, naturally, but not in a way as to produce what one might call 'systematic' theology. Their actions might well be found inspiring, but their writings have often not yet caught up with their life and action.

Looking particularly at theological writings, this half century can be divided into the three periods of before, during, and after the Cultural Revolution. Before, that is from 1949 to 1966, the Catholics' struggle was at an initial period. Emotions caused by the sudden changes tended to take precedence over cool debate. Under the guidance of Pope Pius XII, a majority of the Chinese bishops coined and adopted the phrase "Theism and atheism are incompatible" as an overall guiding principle for all Catholics. Gradually this became the watershed dividing believers into two groups: one strongly supporting this principle and the other questioning it. There were articles written by proponents for either side, but most resemble political statements rather than theological treatises. There were manifestos calling for a "three-self" Catholic Church and also personal narratives and memoirs written by those such as Michael Yeung and Bishop Tang, in which theological and political reflection were blended. The issues for the indigenization of theology in China at that time clearly included those of church authority and ecclesial structure, of the role and expression of indigenous leadership, and of interpreting the localized responses to revolutionary change by clergy and laity.

During the Cultural Revolution era (1966-1976), religious activities came to a virtual standstill. Nothing was then published by Catholics in the way of position statements or theological reflection and unpublished writings are yet to be assembled and their implicit theology interpreted (for following years see 3.2.2. below).

Selected References

Periodicals which provide diverse selections of source materials include:
> *Bulletin de la Société des Mission Etrangères*; *China Missionary Bulletin*; *China News Analysis* (CNA, Hong Kong, 1953-); *China Notes*; *Xin Ge* (Catholic newspaper, Shanghai).

Bush, Richard. *Religion in Communist China*. Nashville: Abingdon, 1970.
Ch'en Ch'i-pin. "Report to the Catholic Congress in Harbin ... (July 1959)." In *Religious Policy and Practice in Communist China. A Documentary History*, edited by Donald E. McInnis. New York: Macmillan, 1972.

Dufay, F. *En Chine l'étoile contre la Croix*. Tournai: Casterman, 1955.

Liu, J. (Michael Yeung). *Inside China, Experience of a Chinese Catholic: 1948-1980*. Hong Kong: Privately published, 1981.

Lo Kuang. *Jiaoting yu Zhongguo shijie shi* (A history of Vatican relations with China). Taichung: Kuangqi, 1961.

Pi Shushih. "Life of Catholics in China." In *Religious Policy and Practice in Communist China, A Documentary History*, edited by Donald E. McInnis. New York: Macmillan, 1972.

Trivière, L. *Catholic Church in Mainland China*. Mimeo'd. Hong Kong: 1959.

Wei, Louis Tsing-sing. "The Vatican and China: 1949-1974." In *Christian Faith and the Chinese Experience*. Geneva: Lutheran World Federation and Pro Munid Vita, 1974.

3.2 Theological and Contextual Writings
3.2.1. The 1950s-1960s

The Nanjing Synod (1953) saw the first attempt by Chinese clergy to seek a modus vivendi for the Church in the long-venerated, largely Confucian, "Ten Articles." Journals that stated a patriotic position and that were often critical of foreign missionaries' involvement in, and imperialistic behavior towards, China also began in the early 1950s in Tianjin, Shanghai, Nanchang, Guiyang, Wuhan, Changsha and other cities. These included the journals: *Guang Yang*, *Xin Ge*, *Ai Guo*, *Hui Kang*, *Xiao Ming*, *Xin Sheng* and others. *Guang Yang*, the first to appear, was published in Tianjin. In 1952 and the first half of 1953, Catholics wrote articles in these journals to show their patriotic position, accusing the imperialists of unjust actions criticizing the position of their opponents, and telling stories of their own experiences to affirm the achievements of new China.

A representative example can be found in an article entitled "How My View of the Communist Party Changed" written by Father Lee De Pei (*Guang Yang*, July 1st, 1952). In this article, Father Lee wrote of earlier reactionary associates, and his ignorance of the Communist Party, except for rumours of immorality and mass killings that made him very fearful. After Liberation, he wrote: "I saw that Communist cadres lived simple lives, they are practical people, so the country has moved forward rapidly. I have understood then that the government under the leadership of the Communist Party is one that seeks to benefit the people. When the 'Policy Guidelines of the Communist Party' published the principle of religious freedom, I realized that the People's Government is concerned about all aspects of people's lives; not only does it seek happiness for the people in the material sense, but it also gives people freedom in religion." This partly exemplifies the patriotic position of many Catholics at that time.

Church leaders such as Bishop Li Poyu would later affirm (1957) that the church was then in good heart, despite the growing persecution, and Archbishop Pi Shushih reported on Catholics being credited as model workers. On the other hand Sister Suen Tsong-yi wrote in the Tianjin (T'ientsin) Catholic paper (1959) on the oppressive labor conditions for clergy and sisters, and Li Han recounted her survival under intense harassment for being Catholic (from 1958-1963). Theology here provided the assurances of traditional Catholic piety and of eternal succour for faithfulness in persecution. There were also writings that voiced the beliefs of those who could not accept the atheistic principles believed to be behind all government-approved policies, seeing the issue to be primarily one of belief or unbelief, but these appeared only outside China.

However, biblical studies were also undertaken by such scholars as Ludovicus Liu Xutang, Antonius Li Shiyu, Marc Chen Weitong and others, of the biblical grounds for a patriotic church and, by some, for support of the Chinese government. Only a few other theological writings are seemingly extant from before the Cultural Revolution, again mostly written by Chinese who were by now outside China, such as T. Hang's work on the Catholic Church in China. Others are found in such periodicals as *China Missionary Bulletin, Religion in Communist Lands* (from 1962), *Bulletin de la Société des Mission Etrangères,* and occasionally in European theological journals. Apart from the *Collection of Reports Given at the Assembly of Chinese Catholic Delegates* (1957, see below), most of these documents are yet to be collected.

An article by a Mr. Zhang (1951), recently cited in *Zhongguo Tianzhujiao,* is representative of many written by believers at that time. This dealt fully with questions of patriotism and faith, of church authority, and of the line of Christian obedience. Zhang affirmed that "to have the Catholic faith and to oppose imperialism are not mutually contradictory. Love of country and love of religion can be united in one." As to whether or not ecclesiastical authorities (including the Pope), should be obeyed implicitly, the author draws on much Christian history to show that authorities on various levels have committed errors historically and that there are always limits to spiritual authority, which should not be abused.

Selected References
> The periodicals *Guang Yang, Xin Ge, Ai Guo, Hui Kang, Xiao Ming, Xin Sheng,* and *Zhongguo Tianzhujiao,* along with *China Missionary Bulletin, Religion in Communist Lands, Bulletin de la Société des Mission Etrangères, China Bulletin* and *Fides.*
> Bush, Richard. *Religion in Communist China.* Nashville: Abingdon, 1970.
> Lam, Anthony S.K. *The Catholic Church in Present-Day China. Through Darkness and Light.* Leuven: Ferd Verbiest Foundation; Hong Kong: Holy Spirit Study Centre, 1994.
> MacInnis, Donald E., ed. *Religious Policy and Practice in Communist China. A Documentary History.* New York: Macmillan, 1972.
> Monsterleet, J. *Martyrs in China.* London: Longmans, Green, 1955.
> Tang, Edmond and Jean-Paul Wiest. *The Catholic Church in Modern China.* Maryknoll, NY: Orbis Books, 1993.
> Whyte, Bob. *Unfinished Encounter. China and Christianity.* London: Collins, 1988.

3.2.1.1. The Patriotic Association of Chinese Catholics - Documents

The fullest collection from the 1950s of writings from leaders and members of the Association is found in the volume *Collection of Reports Given at the Assembly of Chinese Catholic Delegates*, edited by the Patriotic Association of Chinese Catholics, September 1957. The setting for the first ever assembly of Catholic representatives from all over the country, from which the papers

Contextual Theology in China 65

came, was the gathering for 40 days of 241 delegates from over 100 dioceses in 26 provinces and autonomous regions. The occasion was shaped by revolutionary events in the previous few years which included: explicit orders from bishops forbidding Catholics to take part in patriotic movements (the volume gives details); the arrest of Bishop Gong Pingmei of Shanghai on September 8, 1955; and the request of the Shanghai diocese addressed to Pope Pius XII, asking for authorization of Bishop Elect Zhang Shilang to replace Bishop Gong. There was a similar request in favor of the Bishop Elect Dong Guangqing of Wuhan. The Vatican refused authorization and condemned the two candidates as well as all those who might be involved in the autonomous consecrations; while giving "extraordinary rights" to only those priests who were in "peaceful communion" with Rome.

The theme of the assembly was: "Is it a sin to be patriotic?" This was no mere theoretical debate; it involved, on the contrary, intellect, emotions, knowledge and experience. There were small group discussions and general assemblies: there was careful listening as well as open criticism. Several people confessed to have changed their point of view through listening and debate. Content of the discussions showed two clearly different positions, one insisting on the correctness of following orders from church authorities, from the Pope downwards, and the other distinguishing:

i) between religion and politics, stating acceptance of the authority of the Holy See in all matters concerning religion, morality and in spiritual matters, but claiming independence when it comes to political decisions regarding social systems and political parties;

ii) between natural law and man-made laws including canon law. "No penance without sin" and three other principles were cited by Bishop Pi Shushih as justifying patriotic attitudes and actions. Careful mention was made re religious practice, meaning no one was subscribing to any atheistic position on this.

Those participating included church leaders such as Bishop Pi Shushih, who laid down clear principles on the basis of which he took the patriotic stance, and bishops (some of whom were consecrated later) Zhang Shilang, Duan Yinming, Zhang Jiashu, Li Side, and Li Boyu. Among others were Sister Wang Boren; Sister Shi Junpu, who quoted many passages of the New Testament to justify patriotism; Mr. Jin Yican, a layman, of Korean nationality; and Fathers Yang Lingde, Xu Zonghai (11th - generation descendent of Xu Guangqi, the colleague of Matteo Ricci), and Wu Muyi. Over 200 people spoke; even the *Collection* did not include all the speeches. The people who spoke were often simple people; many lay men and women began their speech with the remark: "I don't understand law, but ...". Apart from these individuals, 123 small groups made collective reports.

The discussions also included strong objection to the special rights granted to those in "peaceful communion" with Rome, stating that such communion is rooted in one's relationship with Christ and that was not to be hindered by one's political stance in supporting a new government, no sin being involved in that supportive stance. There were statements also on the new socialist system citing many of its advantages and indicating their conformity to Gospel values. Several reports showed it was a time of conscientization on the part of Chinese Catholics, especially of religious women and priests. Experiences of discrimination were mentioned, although some of the discriminatory practices were recognized as being built-in to church institutions. But Chinese Catholics were then doing contextual theology, in recognizing that God is living and cannot be confined within the framework of law, no matter how holy.

The discussions were also in reaction to events, both in China and in international politics. Without tools and without adequate preparation, Catholics simply responded with their hearts, but they firmly believed that God was there in their new situation. It would be doing them a disservice to discard the value of these discussions under the rubric of "political education." The reports show that for the Catholics, it was a question of their relationship with God, therefore a question of life or death of the total person. There may have been external pressure, but such as it was, it came from both the government and from Rome. One might even say that, precisely because of pressure from both sides, these Catholics were forced to do theology and interpret their faith. They may not have written theological treatises, neither have they produced volumes, but the reality as seen and interpreted by them can be judged valid and authentic.

Selected References

Periodicals to be consulted for this period include:
> *Ching Feng* (Christian Study Centre, Hong Kong since 1957), *China and Ourselves* (Canadian Council of Churches, Toronto), *China Talk* (China Liaison Office, Hong Kong), *China Notes* (NCC/USA, New York) and *China News* and *Church Report* (Chinese Church Research Centre).
> Bush, Richard. *Religion in Communist China.* Nashville: Abingdon, 1970.
> Hang Tuijie, Thaddeus. *Die Katholische Kirche im chinesischen Raum: Geschichte und Gegenwart.* Munich: Pustet, 1963.
> MacInnis, Donald E., ed. *Religious Policy and Practice in Communist China. A Documentary History.* New York: Macmillan, 1972.
> Patriotic Association of Chinese Catholics, ed. *Collection of Reports Given at the Assembly of Chinese Catholic Delegates.* (In Chinese). Beijing: The Patriotic Association of Chinese Catholics, 1957.
> Tang, Bishop. *How Inscrutable His Ways! Memoir 1951-1981.* Hong Kong: Aidan Publicities and Printing, 1987.
> Zhang Yushi. "Imperialism: Pharisees, and Enemy of Catholics." *Renmin Ribao* (People's Daily) (Sept. 20 1959).

3.2.1.2. Maurus Fang Hao (1910-); and Wei Tsing-sing (fl.1960)
Maurus Fang Hao, formerly of the University of Taiwan, was a Christian essayist, historian and biographer who wrote extensively on the history of Catholicism in China and on its leading figures. These included Matteo Ricci and the "Three Pillars of the Catholic Church in China" - Paul Hsu, Michael Yang, and Leo Lee, writer of the 20 books in the *First Collection of the Celestial Science.* Fang Hao also carried out research on the earliest Catholic writings published in Asia and discovered another Chinese *Doctrina* in the Bibliotica Nacional in Madrid. This was printed xylographically in the Philippines in 1593. His other writings include studies of

particular Catholic texts from the 17th and 18th centuries in China and especially of the use made by them of Confucian sources.

Although also living for many years outside China, Louis Wei Tsing-sing made regular visits to China, and wrote studies of Catholicism in relation to the movements within Chinese culture, and for nationalism and reform. He studied in particular the relations of the Chinese Church to the Vatican as this was evolving in the years after 1949 and participated in ecumenical study programs on this and other aspects of theology in the new China. He provided a middle path of critical appreciation for the development of the post-revolutionary Catholic Church, and when travelling in China in the mid-1960s judged the newly appointed bishops to be "acting in good faith and with a sincere pastoral intention." His writings also include historical studies of Catholicism in China and in particular of the work of Vincent Lebbe (2.2.4.).

Selected References

Works by Maurus Fang Hao

Zhongguo Tianzhujiao shi luncong. jiaji (Essays on the history of Catholicism in China). Chungking: Shangwu yinshuguan, 1944.

Essays of Fang Hao. Shanghai: n.p., 1948.

Collected Works of Maurus Fang Hao. 2 vols. Rev. and ed. by the author. Taipei: Student Book Co., 1969.

Zhongguo Tianzhujiao shi renwu zhuan (Biographies of Catholic historical figures in China). 3 vols. Hong Kong: Gongjiao zhenli xuexi, 1970. Reprinted Taipei: Guoli Zhengzhi daxue, 1981, and Beijing: Zhonghua shuju, 1988.

"Notes on Matteo Ricci's De Amicitia." *Monumenta Serica* 14 (1949-1955).

"Adaptation by Catholics of Confucian Tenets during the late Ming and Early Ch'ing Dynasties." *Bulletin of the College of Arts* 11, National Taiwan University (1962).

Works by Wei Tsing-sing, Louis

La Politique Missionaire de la France en Chine 1842-1856. Paris: Nouvelles Editions Latines, 1960.

Le Saint Siège et la Chine de Pie IX à nos jours. Sotteville les Rouens: Editions Allais, 1971.

"Le Père Lebbe et l'Abbaye de Saint-André lez-Bruges (1877-1940)." *Rythmes du Monde* 34 (1960).
"Open Letter to the West." *Information Catholiques Internationales* (Sept. 15, 1966).
"Le confucianisme chinois et l'enterrement." *Concilium Revue Internationale de Théologie* 32 (1968).
"The Vatican and China 1949-1974." In *Christian Faith and Chinese Experience.* Geneva: Lutheran World Federation and Pro Mundi Vita, 1974.

3.2.1.3. John C.H. Wu (Wu Ching-hsiung 1899-1986)
Wu Ching-hsiung was a research scholar at the Harvard Law School (1929-30), a judge and lawyer in Shanghai (1930-1941), and a prisoner of the Japanese. Appointed the Republic of China's Minister to the Vatican in 1946, he was later professor of Chinese Philosophy at the University of Hawaii (1949). Among prime influences upon his thought, he found in Saint Therese of Lisieux "the heart of the Buddha, the virtues of Confucius, and the philosophic detachment of Lao Tsu." He writes in particular of his debt to Taoism and Mahayana Buddhism.

In May 1935, the *T'ien Hsia* (Everything under heaven) *Monthly*, was founded by John Wu to be a cultural and literary journal in English, interpreting Chinese culture to the West. He translated many Chinese poems into English, and then began in many writings to present a "living synthesis between all pairs of opposites, such as humility and audacity, freedom and discipline, joys and sorrows, duty and love, strength and tenderness, grace and nature, folly and wisdom, wealth and poverty, corporateness and individuality." Here love is the "highest principle of the cosmos; standing above Yin and Yang, for it brings them together in a holy commerce; [where] the 'feminine' qualities of the East are to be married with the 'masculine' qualities of the West." Christianity weaves together the two inherited strains of Taoism and Confucianism "into a perfect harmony," he writes, and for him Confucius and Mencius, Buddha and Lao Tsu (Laozi), are the "Pedagogues to lead men (sic) to Christ."

Christianity is not to be termed 'western,' Wu declared, for it is universal, and the East has major contributions to make. "The

East has gone farther in its *natural* contemplation than the West has in its *supernatural* contemplation," he wrote, and compared the wide knowledge amongst Buddhists in China of the three stages in spiritual life of Abstention, Concentration and Wisdom, with the widespread ignorance among Christians of the three purgative, illuminative, and unitive paths. Yet while Christianity is for him the only possible synthesis between East and West, he is careful to stress that it has no exclusive hold upon truth for there are "fellow-seekers" in all living faiths. In major studies he also made "oriental" evaluations of the role of science, technology and law. Central to his theology was the role of grace in the Gospels, which nonetheless, for "anyone who has tasted the infinite goodness and wisdom of God," are yet understatements of the truth. Many of Wu's concerns would be continued by his godson Sih Paul Kwang Tsien.

Selected References
Works by John C.H. Wu
> "The Science of Love." *T'ien Hsia Monthly* 10.4 (1940).
> *Beyond East & West*. London: Sheed and Ward, 1951.
> *The Interior Carmel: the Threefold Way of Love*. New York: Sheed & Ward, 1953.
> *Fountain of Justice: a Study in the Natural law*. London, Sheed and Ward, 1959 (c1955).
> *Chinese Humanism and Christian Spirituality,* edited by Paul K.Y. Sih. New York: St John's University Press, 1965.
> —, tr., *Tao Teh Ching* - by Lao Tzu, translated into English by John C. H. Wu. Boston: Shambhala; New York: Distributed in the United States by Random House, 1989 (c1961).
> Sih, Paul K. T. (Kwang Tsien). *Chinese Culture and Christianity; Selected Works of Paul K. T. Sih* (Chung-kuo wen hua yü chi tu chiao i.). Taipei: China Culture Publishing Foundation, 1957.
> —. *From Confucius to Christ*. New York: Sheed and Ward, 1952.

3.2.2. Reconstruction, Convergence and the Doing of Theology: 1980-2000

After Deng Xiaoping's open policy was introduced (1978), religious movements were able to return to public life and activity. By the end of 1980, mass was being publicly celebrated in over 15 cities and many rural areas, and the Chinese Conference of Bishops had been established. A new sense of identity and self-reliance had developed which independently also reflected insights affirmed by the Vatican II Council. In early 1982 the first seminary in this period opened (20 years later there would be 36) and by 1983, 120 churches were open (as of this writing in 2000, there are over 4,500). Since 1980, publications also began to appear. In some dioceses like Beijing, Shanghai, and Shijiazhuang, diocesan weekly papers and/ or monthly journals were commenced that contained articles by clergy and laity alike. By and large, the purpose of these publications was to re-educate the people of God in matters of faith and to help them in their spiritual life after a ten-year hiatus. Some publications have for their aim the sharing of information regarding activities and events in churches outside China, but most have been mainly concerned with the rebuilding of churches, the re-commencement of seminaries and religious congregations for women, and - for some - with assimilating the new teachings of the Vatican II Council.

But there are other reasons for divided energies which inhibit theological reflection. Village-centered Catholics have been observed to "focus more on vertical relationships of authority and dependence rather than on horizontal relations of reciprocity and cooperation," which would lead them to participate more fully in and to reflect upon, the life and issues of their people. This along with the norms of an agrarian society, the authoritarian culture, and the history of harsh political repression, combine to produce a self-containment in many Catholic communities, and a preoccupation with maintaining traditional beliefs and practices. This continues to prevent full Catholic unity and sometimes provokes government repression. The State Council's *Document 3* (1989), although permitting "purely religious relationships with the Holy See," granting authority over the Catholic Patriotic Association to the Bishop's Conference, and implementing the return of church property, nevertheless outlined a severe policy regarding the "underground" church. Yet despite increased government restrictions, and continuing arrests in some provinces, numerous Catholic communities have been expanding, and many bishops are "taking new initiatives in pastoral work, training of clergy, and in the social apostolate."

Historically, Catholicism has often been regarded as a "foreign religion" with little understanding of China's Christian history. Today, many Chinese Catholics are beginning to recognize the resources of their own history and culture, including their long Christian history (since at least the 7th century) which has in recent decades been highlighted by further remarkable discoveries. Many, too, recognize the role which they can play in the larger community, both critically but also in solidarity with their people's aspirations. On the one hand, the role of many Catholics of the underground church has become recognized as being prophetic in their struggle for religious freedom, while on the other, that of many in the open churches is described as more priestly: working within the social system to minister to the spiritual needs of all.

Tensions remain between movements for ecclesial independence and a localized theology, and those who give priority to the church's place within international Roman Catholicism and the universal Church. There is also need for the Church to meet present demands for the nurture of church and ministry and for taking its place within a rapidly changing Chinese nation; and yet at the same time to come to terms with its own long Christian history, and that of sister Christian communities in the Asian region. These issues are sometimes highlighted by the important moves towards Vatican II renewal. Even though tensions still exist, however, many scholars in China and overseas conclude that the Catholic Church in China remains one church, albeit giving two testimonies, but both retaining the essentials of Catholic faith. A new image of the Chinese Church is also taking shape in the spirit of the 2nd Vatican Council and theologians, liturgists and other religious experts from oversees have been invited to teach in six seminaries to support this renewal. Similarly, as reported by *Zhongguo tianzhujiao zhinan* (1997), by then more than 100 priests, seminarians and sisters had been sent overseas for further theological studies in the last few years. Friendly relations of exchange with Catholics outside China are also now approved by the government.

Selected References

Periodicals which provide diverse selections of source materials include:

China Bulletin (Louvain, since 1979); *Ching Feng* (Hong Kong, since 1957); *China Study Journal* (London, formerly *Religion in the PRC: Documentation* 1979-1985; and *China Study Project Journal* 1983-1985); *China Update* (Louvain, since 1981); *Tripod* (Hong Kong, since 1981); *Union of Catholic Asian News* (UCAN, Hong Kong since 1979); *Zhongguo Tianzhujiao* (Catholic Church in China, Beijing, since 1980); *Zhonglian* (China Catholic Communication, Singapore, since 1981). cf. *Cardinal Kung Foundation Newsletter* (from ?1994).

Chu Li-teh, Michael. "China and the Christian Church Tomorrow." *Studies in the International Apostolate of Jesuits* 4 (1975).

Jin Luxian. "The Church in China Past and Present." *Tripod* 36 (1986).

—. "Pastoral Letter: 'Embracing the Third Millennium'." *China Study Journal* 11.1 (1996).

Lam, Anthony S.K. *The Catholic Church in Present-Day China. Through Darkness and Light.* Leuven: Ferd Verbiest Foundation: Hong Kong: Holy Spirit Study Centre, 1994.

Leung, Beatrice. "The Impact of Modernisation on the Catholic Church in China." *Missiology* 13 (1985).

Madsen, Richard. *China's Catholics. Tragedy and Hope in an Emerging Civil Society.* Berkeley: University of California, 1998.

Maheu, Betty Ann. "China's Religious Policy 1881-1999." *Tripod* 113 (1999).

Malek, Roman, ed. *"Fallbeispiel" China: Okumenische Beitrage zu Religion, Theologie, Kirche im Chinesischen Kontext.* Sankt Augustin: China-Zentrum; Netteral: Steyler Verlag, 1996.

Pro Mundi Vita. *The Catholic Church in the People's Republic of China.* PMV *Studies* 15 (1990).

Tang, Edmond and Jean-Paul Wiest, eds. *The Catholic Church in Modern China.* Maryknoll, NY: Orbis Books, 1993.

Zhongguo tianzhujiao zhinan (Guide to the Catholic Church in China). (In Chinese & English.) Singapore: *China Catholic Communication*, 1986, 1989, 1997, 2000.

3.2.2.1. Theological Writings: Post-Cultural Revolution

All these elements (3.2.2.) are discernible in recent narratives and theological writing. Catholic theology in China therefore, although largely still accepting the neo-Scholastic forms of Tridentine thought, is being enriched by many streams of experience and reflection, both from study of Chinese culture and Christian history, and from ecumenical exchanges. Declarations, articles and statements for the open Churches appear regularly in *Zhongguo Tianzhujiao* while other publications, not always approved by the CPCA and the National Administrative Commission of the Catholic Church (NAC), include catechetical and liturgical materials privately printed or imported. At the same time, however, in the realm of thought, many Catholics have been studying and following the teachings of the Vatican II Council in areas that concern the practical life of Catholic communities, such as liturgical reform. Much theological reflection in these areas is yet to be collected and interpreted, and even more is yet to be recorded adequately.

Theologically, following the Cultural Revolution, the question was "how to formulate a contextual theology in the framework of post-Mao society?"; with "patriotism as the framework for the theology of an independent, self-ruled Catholic Church in a reborn sovereign nation." Many accepted to greater or lesser degree that the government would exact guidance in the social and political spheres, and sought to work through an understanding of the faith and its expression which could co-exist with this. This was done not by systematic analysis but through a pragmatic wrestling with pastoral and ecclesial issues, which was in fact exploring the contextual basis for integrating church and society. This reflected a change in methodology from that of the 1950s - which moved through a response to experience - to a more inductive theology, using also pragmatic terminology and vernacular values. In this, elements of a unity of action and knowledge like that of Wang Yangming, of the Taoist dialectic of *yin-yang*, and of a "Maoist" theory of practice have also been discerned, along with traditional attitudes to autocracy and a philosophy of survival.

A series of articles in *Zhongguo Tianzhujiao* (1980-1984) shows the growth of a contextualizing theology. Bishop Zong Huaide of

Contextual Theology in China

Shandong outlined in 1980 a full theological rationale for patriotism which was to be echoed by other bishops and vicars capitular. This included the christological basis for patriotic acts, the divine ordinance for national authority, its basis in the traditional teaching of the church, and in God's commandment of love. Others presented the need to love both church and country, in a more dualistic interpretation of service to both soul and body, or viewed patriotism as the clear obligation of all citizens. A new theology of patriotism emerged in the wake of the conference in 1983 which developed a new methodology for theological construction. Tenets of faith found their proof not from proof-texts or authoritative statements but by "the lived-out experience of a certain community in an actual living environment ...." While this must be grounded in Scripture it must also "reflect the social and political context of Chinese society." Patriotism then places a moral obligation upon Catholics to be in solidarity with the Chinese people and to share their aspirations, becoming thereby a community which is integral to Chinese society. Obviously there had been a significant move in theological interpretation from a largely dogmatic methodology to one which is more 'biblical' and contextualizing.

Anonymous writings questioning the primacy of Rome (1980) were later used by Bishop Tu Shihua and Fr. Zhang Zhilai to show how early traditions and church history supported the authority of local bishops, rather than the Bishop of Rome, Bishop Tu affirming that all bishops receive apostolic power from God and not from the Pope, and that both history and Chinese experience are the basis for the independence and selfhood of the Chinese church (1981). Bishops such as Huang Ziyu (Xiamen), Aloysius Jin Luxian (Shanghai) and Joseph Lin Quan (Fuzhou) affirmed in interviews (1985 and 1988), the autonomy of the Chinese Church, also stressing that the Church must serve the people, and in the case of Bishop Lin Quan, that while retaining relations with Rome and the world Church, the authoritative head of the Church in China was Jesus Christ. Bishops like Fu Tieshan (Beijing) and Zong Huaide (Shandong) have also stressed (1984 and 1987) the equality of national and international ecclesial bodies, being critical of Rome in this regard.

On the other hand Bishop Fan Xueyan circulated "13 Points" (1988) which condemned the practices of the open church on principles of Papal superiority. Other bishops such as Ma Ji issued statements which argued for the end of the Catholic Patriotic Association and the restoration of Papal primacy, on the basis of such doctrines as that of Papal infallibility and the traditional disciplines of the Church.

A new initiative in 1986 was the formation of the Association of Catholic Intellectuals in Shanghai. Links were established in Hong Kong the following year and the Association is now related to the international programs of Pax Romana, directed to provide relevant perspectives and alternative policies in the fields of the social pastoral and international affairs of the Church, in inter/intra-religious dialogue and cooperation and concerning the global economic crisis. Women however are yet to be accorded full place in such associations, as in the church itself, but highly educated women such as Theresa Chu Mei-fen (see 3.2.2.6 below) and Elizabeth Hui Zhou of People's University (Renmin Daxue), Beijing, are contributing to national and international colloquia. Elizabeth Hui Zhou has also given a critique of the re-patriarchalized discourses in the *Chinese Union Version with New Punctuation* of the Bible.

In theological education, some seminaries are also using volumes from the series issued for various branches of theological study, by the publishing house of the *Guangqi she* in Shanghai. These are collections of transcripts for lectures by various authors which have been formerly broadcast by radio, but no individual authors are given. They concentrate on presenting core Catholic teaching, including material from the documents of Vatican II, but with little explicit reference to Chinese cultural, religious or political contexts.

Some of the fullest of contextual theological studies for church life and thought in China since 1980 have come from Chinese theologians working in Hong Kong or Taiwan. Among these, Maria Goretti Lau has proposed a "praxical ecclesiology" which would be more compatible with Maoist ideology; Chan Kim-kwong has assessed and developed this approach, and outlined Chinese ecclesiology as being pragmatic, contextual and localized; and Aloysius Chang Ch'un-shen has written many articles on the theology and life of the Church in China (See in particular *Tripod* and *Collectanea Theologica*, in chaps. below).

Selected References

Castro, Loreta N. and Arij A. Roest Crollius, eds. *Poverty and Development: the Call of the Catholic Church in Asia.* Rome: International Jacques Maritain Institute, 1995.

Chan Kim Kwong. *Struggling for Survival: The Catholic Church in China from 1949 to 1970.* Hong Kong: Christian Study Center on Chinese Religion and Culture, 1992.

—. *Towards a Contextual Ecclesiology. The Catholic Church in the People's Republic of China (1979-1983): Its life and Theological Implications.* Hong Kong: Phototech System, 1987.

Chang Ch'un-shen, Aloysius. *The Catholic Church in Mainland China: Pastoral and Theological Reflections.* Taipei: Wisdom Press, 1998.

Chu, Michael, ed. *The New China: a Catholic Response.* New York: Paulist Press, c1977.

Fan Xueyan. "The 13 Points of Bishop Fan Xueyan." In *The Catholic Church in Present-Day China. Through Darkness and Light*, by Anthony S.K. Lam. Leuven: Ferd Verbiest Foundation; Hong Kong: Holy Spirit Study Centre, 1994.

Fu Tieshan. "Witnessing to Christ by Chinese Catholic Clergy and Laity." In *A New Beginning. An International Dialogue with the Chinese Church*, edited by Theresa Chu and Christopher Lind. Toronto: Canadian Council of Churches, 1983.

Jin Luxian. "Christian Faith in the Far East - A Chinese Perspective." *Verbum SVD* 27.4 (1986).

Kwok, M.T. "To Know the Past and to Look at the Future: the Task is Heavy." *Zhongguo Tianzhujiao* (The Catholic Church in China) 8 (Dec. 1983).

Lau, Maria Goretti. "The Possibility of a Praxical Eccesiology." *Tripod* 5 (1981).

—. *Towards a Theology of the Local Church.* Leuven: Catholic University, 1989.

—. *Chinese Catholic Church: Contemporary Perspectives; the Formation of New Church Leaders in China*. South Orange, NJ: Catholic China Bureau, 1990.

Lazarotto, Angelo. "The Church in China: A Fifteen Year Review." *Tripod* 90 (1995).

Madsen, Richard. *China's Catholics. Tragedy and Hope in an Emerging Civil Society*. Berkeley: University of California, 1998.

Ma Ji. "Bishop Ma Ji and his 'My Statement'." In *The Catholic Church in Present-Day China. Through Darkness and Light*, by Anthony S.K. Lam. Leuven: Ferd Verbiest Foundation; Hong Kong: Holy Spirit Study Centre, 1994.

Zhang Suyuan. "The Chineseness of the Church under Socialism: Independence Paramount." *China Study Journal* 4.1 (1989).

Zhongguo Tianzhujiao (ZT) 1980-1984, passim.

Zhong Huaide. "Theology of Patriotism." *Zhongguo Tianzhujiao* 1 (1980).

3.2.2.2. Bishops' Conference of the Catholic Church in China

There are significant differences between the purpose and functions of the Chinese Conference of Bishops and the Chinese Catholic Patriotic Association. The latter is a "mass organization" with the aim of "uniting the clergy and Catholics of the whole country to manifest a patriotic spirit, to support the Socialist system, ... assist the government in implementing its policy of freedom of religious belief; ... [and] assist the church in implementing the principles of independence, self government and self management ..." The Conference of Bishops however is "the leading national structure for church affairs of the Chinese Catholic Church," with purposes of studying and explaining doctrine and church rules, examining and approving the election and ordination of diocesan bishops, establishing pastoral guidelines [and] developing pastoral ministries. It is also to unite clergy and laity in observance of the laws and policies of the country, and to "implement the principles of independence, self government and administration which is in accordance with the situation in China." All this is to be done "in accordance with the Bible and based on the traditional spirit of the one, holy, catholic and apostolic church."

The bishops, both corporately and individually, along with their consultants, have remained a key - sometimes the only - source for theological reflection and writing in this period, although no collection of their materials has yet been made. Official Church statements are contained in the journals *Zhongguo Tianzhujiao* (Catholic Church in China), and in *Shenxue yanjiu* (Theological Study). Individual bishops have written articles or given interviews, and some have been translated (see 3.2.2.8.). Bishop Aloysius Jin Luxian, has written and also given frequent interviews concerning the policies of the Bishops' Conference and of the Catholic Patriotic Association. The Bishops' Conference has issued Pastoral Letters on such matters as "The Dignity and Responsibility of Women" (1995), and "The Meaning of the Millennium" (2000), and held special meetings for the 40th and 50th anniversaries of the Chinese hierarchy, and for discussion on such issues as "the church and socialist spiritual civilization in theory and practice." Besides these, articles are issued by the Catholic Delegates Conference and official government statements are published in a government journal on religion in general, called *Zhongguo Zongjiao* (Religions in China), published by the Religious Affairs Bureau of the State Council of China and available to the general public. *Zhongguo Tianzhujiao* is the journal of the Catholic Patriotic Association (since 1980).

Selected References

"Constitutions of the Chinese Bishop's Conference." Translated by Peter Barry, mm. *Tripod* 13.75 (1993).

Jin Luxian, Aloysius. "Opening Speech at the Study Meeting of the Catholic Patriotic Association in the City of Shanghai." *Tianzhujiao yanjiu ziliao* Huibian 19 (1990/91); *China Study Journal* 6.1 (1991).

—. "Role of the Patriotic Association." In *The Catholic Church in Modern China,* edited by Edmond Tang and Jean-Paul Wiest. Maryknoll, NY: Orbis Books, 1993.

—. "La Formation des Futurs Pretres dans les Seminaires de Chine." *Missions Etrangère de Paris* (1996).

Lam, Anthony S.K. *The Catholic Church in Present-Day China. Through Darkness and Light.* Leuven: Ferd Verbiest Foundation; Hong Kong: Holy Spirit Study Centre, 1994.

Unofficial Bishops' Conference. "The Chinese Bishops' Conference: A Proposal." *Tripod* 14.79 (1994).

Catholic Bishops' Conference. "Pastoral Letter: The Dignity and Responsibility of Women." *China Study Journal* 10.3 (1995).

Unofficial Bishops' Conference. "Pastoral Letter Commemorating the 700th Anniversary of Blessed John of Montecorvino, First Archbishop of Peking (Beijing)." *Tripod* 86 (1995).

"Pastoral Letter of the China Mainland Catholic Bishops' Conference." *Tripod* 96 (1996).

"Open Church Bishops' Conference Pastoral letter on Jubilee 2000." *China Study Journal* 15.1 (2000).

3.2.2.3. Tu Shihua (1919-)

Tu Shihua entered the Franciscan Order in 1944 and was ordained the following year. Following studies at Furen University, Beijing, he taught philosophy in Lianghu Seminary from 1953, becoming rector there in 1959. Consecrated bishop in the Diocese of Hanyang in 1962, he also became responsible for the diocese of Hankou in 1980, and the year after became vice-president of the Conference of Catholic Bishops. Until 1990 he was also rector of the National Catholic Seminary in Beijing. Currently he continues as vice-president of the Chinese Catholic Patriotic Association and is also director of the Commission on Theological Research for the Catholic Bishops Conference of China.

Tu Shihua has had a leading role in the articulation of theology for both the self-understanding and the ministry of the Chinese Catholic church. (See also 3.2.1.) He has written extensively upon the independent nature and policies of the Catholic Church in China, and on its relationship to the Vatican, grounding this in the practice and theology of the early church. His writings also include studies of the early history of Christianity in China, of particular pastoral and social issues being faced by the Chinese church, and of the Second Vatican Council. There are also collections of his devotional writings which have been published. The Bishops' Conference and the Patriotic Association offices are preparing the publication of a collection of articles written by Bishop Tu which will be published under the title of *Tu Shihua Zhujiao wenji* (Collected works of Bishop Tu Shihua).

Selected References
Works by Tu Shihua

"Exalt the Traditional Spirit of the Apostles, Autonomously and Independently Run the Chinese Church Well." *Zhongguo Tianzhujiao* 1 (1980).

"To Have an Independent, Self-ruled and Self-managed Church is our Sacred Right." In *A New Beginning. An International Dialogue with the Chinese Church*, edited by Theresa Chu and Christopher Lind. Toronto: Canadian Council of Churches, 1983.

"Autonomy and Independence of Local Churches." Article Series. *Zhongguo Tianzhujiao* 3 (1990), 4 (1990), 5 (1991), 2 (1992), 3 (1992), 1 (1993). First article also in *China Study Project Journal* 5.3 (1990).

"Family Planning and Pastoral Care." *Shenxue yanjiu* (Theological Study) 1 (1996).

"The Vatican II Council." *Guoji Tianzhujiao cankao ziliao* (Reference materials on the international Catholic Church) 1 (1999).

"New Life in Christ, Retreat Meditations." *Zhongguo Tianzhujiao* 2 (1999), 3 (1999).

"The Position of *Jing jiao* (Nestorianism) in the Mission History of Chinese Catholicism, Its Rise and Fall." *Jidujiao wenhua pinglun* (Critique of Christian culture). (Sept. 1999).

"Discussing the Autonomous and Independent Running of the Church in Our Country." *Zhongguo Tianzhujiao* 4 (2000).

3.2.2.4. Laszlo Ladanyi sj (1914-1990) and Colleagues.

After study and work in Hungary, Laszlo Ladanyi studied theology at Zikawei in Shanghai. His first ministry was among university students there (1946) and later at the University of Hong Kong (1949). During the following years, he was also active in helping refugees and contributing reports on China to the *China Missionary* under the pen name of A. Road. On 25 August 1953 the first issue of *China News Analysis* appeared, at the request of his superior, in order to inform the Catholic Church abroad of developments in China. For the following 30 years, Ladanyi produced 1,250 issues of CAN, some 8,750 pages in all (a weekly at first, it became a fortnightly in January 1979).

Along with careful analysis of a wide range of publications, followed by synthesis and interpretation, Ladanyi was concerned to critique the policies and actions of the Chinese government and of any who collaborated with them. Ladanyi also wrote studies of *The Catholic Church in China* and *The Chinese Communist Policy Towards Christianity,* and reported writings and interviews of Chinese Catholics during three decades. P.J. Honey (University of London) was a regular contributor for 21 years, and other Jesuit collaborators included Mark Hardy, Frank Doyle, Fernando Mateos, Joseph Sebes (Georgetown University), Frs. Alan Birmingham and Jerry McCarthy, with long-term assistance from Ms Helen Lee. In 1969 he started a monthly bulletin in Chinese, *Hai Nei Hai Wai*, focussing on Chinese culture in today's world and *Letters from Asia* appeared in 1973, aiming to provide an Asian commentary on current affairs in the region.

Selected References
Works by Laszlo Ladanyi
> *The Church in China: Yesterday, Today and Tomorrow.* Hong Kong: China News Analysis, 1975.
> *Behold, The Catholic Church in China.* Hong Kong: n.p., 1983.
> *The Catholic Church in China.* Perspectives on freedom 7. New York: Freedom House, 1987.
> *The Communist Party of China and Marxism, 1921-1985*: *A Self-Portrait.* Stanford, CA: Hoover Institute Press, Stanford University, c1988.
> *Law and Legality in China: the Testament of a China-watcher*, edited by Marie-Luise Nath. Honolulu: University of Hawaii Press, c1992.
> "The Church in China at the end of 1980." *The Month* 242 (1980).
> —, with Vincent Lo and Jurgen Domes, John Dolfin and Frank Ching. *The China Watch;* also *China News Analysis* 1953-1983.

3.2.2.5. Zong Huaide (1917-1997)

Zong Huaide was ordained a priest in 1943, entered Furen University in 1948, became vicar general of Zhoucun diocese, Shandong province, in 1949, and in 1958 became bishop of the same diocese. He was among the first group of bishops

Contextual Theology in China 83

autonomously consecrated. In 1980, he was elected president of the CCPA, along with other posts of deputy director of the Church Affairs Commission, and vice- president of the CCBC. In 1992, he became the president of the CCPA, president of the CCBC, and rector of the National Seminary. Zong was widely known as a man of faith and dedication, who while living in the seminary personally cared for individual students, was unstinting in help to others and extremely simple in lifestyle.

Zong's writings have now been collected and include his sermons and speeches given on various occasions. In these he stresses both authentic witness to the Gospel, and the autonomous life of the Church in China. Included are the papers: On Loving Our Neighbor, Glorifying the Cross, Let Our Light Shine in the Midst of People, Safeguarding Our God-given Right to Run Our Church, Let's Go Forward Courageously on the Road of Autonomy and Selfhood, In Praise of St.Joseph, Patron of China.

Selected References
The Collected Writings of Bishop Zong Huaide. (In Chinese.) Beijing: CCPA (Chinese Catholic Patriotic Association) and the CCBC (Chinese Catholic Bishops' Conference). Forthcoming.

3.2.2.6. Theresa Chu Mei-fen (1924-)
Chu Mei-fen entered the Society of the Sacred Heart in Shanghai (1947), was principal of a women's college in Korea (1956-1971) and completed her doctoral study at University of Chicago (1977). Following two years with the China Liaison Office in Hong Kong she was director of the Canada China Programme of the Canadian Council of Churches (1981-1991), and a key person in the international networks which were in solidarity with - and responding to - the emerging Catholic Church in China. After six years teaching spirituality and the Old Testament in Shanghai (1991-1996) at the Noviciate of the Sisters of the Presentation, along with two years at the Seminary in Sheshan, she has been teaching spirituality and Christology at the National Seminary in Beijing.

Along with thorough research into the thought of Mao Tsetung (Mao Zedong), Chu Mei-fen has striven to understand the dilemmas and stresses facing Catholics in China, and the responses and sacrifices made by those striving to be fully Christian and fully Chinese. She has therefore undertaken careful study of China's recent social and religious history, both through extensive travel and through her residence in China again since 1991. She has been particularly concerned to learn from Catholics in particular provinces of China of their contemporary experience and has written many reports and articles on the issues facing the Catholic Church there. The process of inter-action between Roman Catholics and Chinese government officials. Since 1950, she believes, has been laden with prejudices, faux-pas, and over-reaction on both sides. The ensuing result has been suffering on the part of all Catholics in China. Reconciliation between divided groups is not only a matter of principle, but a question of justice as well, Chu writes. For her there is much in post-Vatican II theology that could ease the tension that divides Catholics in China and this animates her work in Beijing. Her intention remains that of sharing more fully with seminarians and religious women their life and ministries, and of also sharing in the endeavors for balanced views, justice, and above all, hope for reconciliation. In a real way, the tension which arose in the 1950s continues and the patriotic stance as rooted in faith demands recognition, she believes. "Justice on the international level remains to be done to those Chinese Catholics who chose to be both good Catholics and good Chinese under a new socialist government."

Selected References
Works by Theresa Chu Mei-fen
"The Religious Dimension in Mao Tsetung Thought." Dissertation, Microfilm. University of Chicago, the Divinity School, 1977.
"L'église catholique dans la République populaire de Chine." *Univers* 57 (1981).
"Canada China Programme: An Introduction." *Tripod* 11 (1982).
"The Chinese Catholic Patriotic Association." *Ecumenist* 22 (1984).
"Catholicism, Chinese Traditional Values and Marxist Thought." *Missiology* 13 (1985).
"Learning from Catholics in Wuxi." *China Study Project Journal* 2.3 (1987).

"Post-Vatican II Spirituality and the Church in China Today." *China Study Project Journal* 5.3 (1990).
"Dear Friends in Canada ... My First Year in China." *China and Ourselves* 17.3 (1992).
—, and Christopher Lind, eds. *A New Beginning. An International Dialogue with the Chinese Church.* Toronto: Canadian Council of Churches, 1983.

3.2.2.7. Joseph Liu Yuanren (1925-)

Liu Yuanren studied at Shanghai major seminary and was ordained priest in 1953. He was consecrated by a bishop approved by the Vatican and is currently bishop of Nanjing. Although he has spent years in prison because of his loyalty to Rome, he has been since January 1998 president of the Bishops' Conference of the Catholic Church in China (BCCCC). Over some decades he has provided strong theological leadership, both in his diocese and as lecturer at the national seminary in Beijing. He has often travelled overseas and is now head of the BCCCC committee for seminary education, with responsibility for a theological research center and five special committees covering teaching, theological seminaries, rituals, liaison with foreign religious organizations, economic development and social services.

His theological concerns include the development of a genuinely Chinese Church which knows its history and "spiritual roots," the spiritual formation and continuing education of priests and religious, and the development of ecumenical cooperation with Protestants, based on mutual respect, with the aim of "real unity" between Catholics and Protestants being eventually established. In his writings he has also focused upon the methods to be used in indigenizing the Chinese Church and in particular its theology.

Selected References
Works by Liu Yuanren
"On the Question of Theological Construction in the Chinese Catholic Church." *Shenxue yanjiu* (1999).
"On the Indigenization of the Chinese Church." *Shenxue yanjiu* 1 (2000).

Jin Luxian. "Christian Faith in the Far East - A Chinese Perspective." *Verbum SVD* 27.4 (1986).

Tang Boduo. "Wodui 'Dulizizhu Zibanjiaohui' de Sikao" (My reflection on the independent and self-governing church). *Catholic Church in China* 30 (1990).

Tu Shihua. "Being Relevant to Society and Serving the Cause of the Gospel." *Zhongguo Tianzhujiao*. Forthcoming.

3.2.2.8. John B. Zhang Shijiang (b. 1964)

John B. Zhang Shijiang is the director of the Hebei Catholic Faith Service Center in Shijiazhuang, Hebei. He studied at the Shenyang Catholic Seminary and Shanghai Sheshan Seminary, and later at the East Asian Pastoral Institute, Manila. He was ordained a priest in 1989, at Xianxian, Hebei, and after working at the Guangqi Press, in Shanghai, founded the Service Center there in 1991.

In his recent volume *Toward a Wider Reconciliation* (1997), Zhang reflects on the divisions, and possible reconciliation, within the church in China. Beginning with a review of the literature on these divisions, he here seeks to contribute to the search for an inculturated Christology for Catholics in China through a Jesus-centered theology of reconciliation. For this he studies the political and canonical aspects of the divisions and then the relevant resources of Chinese culture in contrast to western concepts. He then outlines the bases in both biblical and Chinese tradition for reconciliation within the Chinese church, as well as reconciliation between church and state, and between Chinese culture and Judaeo-Christian tradition.

Selected References

Zhang, Shijiang, John B. "Toward a Wider Reconciliation: A Cultural-Theological Reflection on the Division within the Church in China." *East Asia Pastoral Review* 34.1&2 (1997).

—. "Consensus on 'Reconciliation and Unity' in the CCC Gradually Gaining Acceptance." *Tripod* 61 (1981).

Leung, Beatrice. *Sino-Vatican Relations: Problems in Conflicting Authority 1976-1986*. London School of Economics and Political Science Monographs in International Studies. New York: Cambridge University Press, 1992.

Lin Ruiqi. *Shui Zhu Chen Fu* (Historical reflections on the CCC at the present time). Hong Kong: Holy Spirit Study Centre, 1995.

Liu Bainian. "The Last Fifty Years of the CCC." *China Catholic News* 2.6 (1996).

Tang, Edmond and Jean-Paul Wiest. *The Catholic Church in Modern China*. Maryknoll, NY: Orbis Books, 1993.

3.2.2.9. Major Journals

At present, two Catholic journals on the national level encourage publication of theological reflection:

1) *Zhongguo Tianzhujiao* (Catholic Church in China). Begun in 1980, this journal is a bi-monthly published by the Chinese Catholic Patriotic Association and Catholic Bishops' Conference of China. It states the official position of the Catholic Church on important events, publishes government rules and regulations concerning religion, pastoral letters of the bishops, and articles on theological reflection, spiritual life, biblical knowledge and interpretation, poems and essays on current liturgical feasts, news of various dioceses, exchanges with foreign countries.

2) *Shenxue yanjiu* (Theological Study). Begun in 1996, it is published by the 'theological study center' of the Chinese Catholic Patriotic Association and the Catholic Bishops' Conference of China. This journal is irregular and contains translated articles as well as original writings.

These two journals contain a number of articles contributed by bishops, priests, religious women and believers in general. Notable names include the following: Bishops Liu Yuanren, Tu Shihua, Jin Luxian, Fu Tieshan. Others include Ma Yinglin, Liu Yuanlong, Li Guoliang, Wang Wei, Liu Minglian, Lu Yunpeng, Ren Bing and Xie Meng. Father Ma Yutian writes a series on introduction to the Old Testament, and Lue Yuting comments on the Psalms. Father Wang Zizheng has also contributed.

The *China Study Journal* (U.K.) has regularly carried (since 1979) articles and reports from the Catholic Church in China, including translations from *Zhongguo Tianzhujiao* and *Shenxue yanjiu* and items from *Tianzhujiao ziliao weibian* and the *Union of Catholic Asian News* (UCAN*)*. Included also have been articles on the Chinese church by such scholars as Anthony Lam, Theresa Chu (3.2.2.6.), John May and Peter Barry. A series of papers by Liu Xiaofeng, and by of the group of intellectuals sympathetic to Christianity, has also been published in the *China Study Journal* 7.3 (1992).

Tripod (See Hong Kong - vol 3, chap. 4.) has, for more than 20 years, carried a watching brief on developments in the Church in China, sometimes publishing theological or historical articles from mainland writers. Among these has been an unusual series of articles by Yang Ni (1993-94), which present aspects of a new spirituality for Chinese Catholics. This semi-autobiographical account of a faith-journey from house-church family, to study in Beijing and overseas, and returning to China to become a priest, reflects on a faith and ministry which meets people's aspirations and thinks critically in a changing society. It finds a fulfilment of filial piety in the life of prayer and priesthood in a church both fully Chinese, fully participatory and universal.

A number of articles written anonymously in various provinces have also appeared in journals such as *Tripod, China Study Journal, Zhonglian* and *Union of Catholic Asian News* during this period, on such topics as "challenges facing the Chinese church," "China Modernisation, the Church and the Spirit," and "the Prophetic Role of the Church in China," along with a series of "appeals from the Underground Church." *Catholic Documentation* has been issued by the Guangqi Research Center, Shanghai, since 1985; *Faith,* the monthly Catholic periodical from Hebei Province since 1991, now also has a national circulation; and *Yi-China Message* has been published from Hong Kong throughout this period.

In a different field, the new series of *Variétés Sinologique* was commenced in 1982, by the Ricci Institutes of Paris and Taipei, in association with such publishers as Desclée de Brouwer and volumes continue to appear. The associated institutes specialize in the study and the teaching of Chinese philosophy, medicine and spirituality, particularly of Taoism, and of the relationship between this and Christian theology and spirituality. Since 1982 more than 20 volumes have appeared, including those listed below.

Theological reflection may only now (2000) be receiving a firmer priority - among intellectuals and church leaders, but the past 50 years have been, for Catholics in China, an intense period of 'doing theology' at many different levels. There has been enormously rich content, but it may take another generation to draw from these lived experiences their fullest theological import.

Selected References

Criveller, Gianni. *Preaching Christ in Late Ming China: the Jesuits' presentation of Christ from Matteo Ricci to Giulio Aleni. Variétés Sinologique* 86 (1997).

Jin Luxian. "Embracing the Third Millennium in Hope and Expectation - Pastoral Letter of Bishop Jin Luxian, Shanghai." *Tianzhujiao ziliao weibian* 40 (1995); *China Study Journal* 11.1 (1996).

Ko Ha Fong, Maria. "Reading the Bible in an Asian Context." *Bulletin Dei Verbum* 3-4, 1996.

—. "The Church in China facing the Challenge of Formation. The Formation of Seminarians and Sisters in China Today." *Sedos Bulletin* 28 (1996).

Larre, Claude and Elizabeth Rochat de la Vallée. *Zhuangzi - La conduite de la vie: De vide en vide* 84 (1995).

Lin Ke. "A Preliminary Proposal on Seminary Training." *Zhongguo Tianzhujiao* 4 (1991); *China Study Journal* 7.1 (1992).

Liu Yuanren. "On the Question of Theological Construction in the Chinese Catholic Church." *Shenxue yanjiu* (1999).

Masson, Michel. *Philosophy and Tradition. The Interpretation of China's Philosophic Past: Fung Yu-lan 1939-1949. Variétés Sinologique* 71 (1984).

O'Brien, Roderick. "Catholic Publishing in the People's Republic of China." *East Asia Pastoral Review 30* (1993).

—. "Catholic Publishing in the People's Republic of China at the Turn of the Century." *East Asia Pastoral Review.* Forthcoming.

"Resolutely Develop Bible Study and Sanctify Spiritual Growth." *Zhongguo Tianzhujiao* 3 (1999); *China Study Journal* 14.2 (1999).

Ricci, Matteo. *The True Meaning of the Lord of Heaven*, translated and edited by D. Lancashire and Peter Hu Kuo-chen. *Variétés Sinologique* 72 (1985).

"The Prophetic Role of the Church in China Today." No author given, translated by Michael Sloboda. *Tripod* 87 (1995).
Yang Ni. "Longqui: Dragon Prays." *Zhu Ai Zhonghua. Tripod* (May-Sept issues, 1993; July-August 1994).

3.3 Supplementary Bibliography II

Bao Sidong. "Today's Church in Mainland China." *Tripod* 103 (1998).
Bresciani, Umberto. "Towards a Chinese Theology of the Incarnation." *Tripod* 118 (2000).
Chang, A.C.S. "Critical Review of Chinese Catholic Thinking." *Ching Feng* 22.3 (1979).
Chang Sang-loi, Anthony. "The Chinese Catholic Church In Search of its Future." *Yi* (China Message) 8.5 (1989).
"First Conference with Regard to Teaching Material on Chinese Catholic Theology and Philosophy: Held in March at Beijing." *Yi* (June 1984).
Dunch, Ryan. *Fuzhou Protestants and the Making of Modern China 1857-1927*. London: Yale University Press, 2000.
Fleming, John R. "Religion and the Churches in China Today." *China Notes* 11.1 (1972).
Forristal, Desmond. *The Bridge at Lo Wu: a Life of Sister Eamonn O'Sullivan*. Imprint Veritas, 1987.
Fu Lean, Ren Yanli, Shi Liubin and Feng Jiafang. *Dangdai Tianzhujiao (The Contemporary Catholic Church)*. Beijing: Dong fang chu ban she, 1996.
Hsiang T'ui-chieh *Liming qian de Zhongguo Tianzhujiao*. Taichung: Chengxiang, Guangqi, 1963.
Laurentin, Rene. *Chine et Christianisme: aprés les occasions manqués*. Paris: Desclée de Brouwer, 1977.
Lazarotto, Angelo. *The Catholic Church in Post-Mao China*. Hong Kong: Holy Spirit Study Centre, 1982.
Lefeuvre, Léon. *Shanghai: Les Enfants dans la Ville*. Paris: Casterman, 1962.
Leung, Beatrice and John D. Young, eds. *Christianity in China: Foundations for Dialogue*. Centre of Asian Studies occasional papers and monographs. Hong Kong: Centre of Asian Studies, University of Hong Kong, 1993.
Liu Xiaofeng. "A Theological and Socio-Cultural Commentary on 'The Way'and 'The Word'." *China Study Journal* 7.3 (1992).

Lozada, Eriberto. *God Aboveground: Catholic Church, Postsocialist State and Transnational Processes in a Chinese Village.* Stanford: Stanford University Press, Forthcoming.

Madsen, Richard. "The Catholic Church in China: Cultural Contradictions, Institutional Survival, and Religious Renewal." In *Unofficial China: Popular Culture and Thought in the People's Republic,* edited by Perry Link, Richard Madsen, and Paul G. Pickowicz, 103-20. Boulder, CO: Westview Press, 1989.

Malek, Roman, ed. "Fallbeispiel" China : ökumenische Beiträge zu Religion, Theologie, und Kirche im chinesischen Kontext. Sankt Augustin : China-Zentrum, 1996.

— and Werner Prawdzik, eds. *Zwischen Autonomie und Anlehnung. Die Problematik der katholischen Kirche theologisch und geschichtlich gesehen.* Nettetal: Steyler Verlag, 1989.

— and Manfred Plate, eds. *Chinas Katholiken suchen neue Wege.* Freiburg im Breisgau: Herder, 1987.

McInnis, Donald. *Religion in China Today. Policy and Practice.* Maryknoll, NY: Orbis Books, 1989.

Ng, Esther. "Christianity and Its Indigenization in China: An International Symposium." *CGST Journal* 7 (1989).

Ng Tse Ming, Peter. "On Dialogue Between Christianity and Chinese Culture." *Chinese Theological Journal* 1.2 (1986).

O'Reilly, Luke. *Passing the Torch.* Blackrock, Dublin: Columba Press, 1995.

Orr, Robert G. *Religion in China.* New York: Friendship Press, 1980.

Roberts, Leo. *Mary in their Midst: The Legion of Mary in Action in China.* Dublin: Clonmore and Reynolds, 1960.

Shih, Joseph. "The Problem of an Indigenous Chinese Theology." *Omnis Terra* 11 (1976/77).

Tan Xing. "'Culture Christianity' in Mainland China." *Tripod* 60 (1990).

Tang Chun-i. *Chung-kuo jen-wen ching-shen chih fa-chan* (The development of the Chinese humanist spirit). Hong Kong: 1958.

Vermander, Benoit, ed. *Le Christ chinois* (homage to Fr. Yves Raguin). Paris: Desclée de Brouwer, 1998.

Von Collani, Claudia. "Recent European Research regarding the Catholic Mission and Catholic Church History in China." *China Study Journal* 5.3 (1990).

Welte, Paul. "Basic Problems of a Chinese Contextual Theology." *Tripod* 17 (1983).

Yang Kao-chien and Li Chen-lin. "On the Four Problems of the Catholic Church." *Hsin Hunan Pao* (Changsha) (June 3, 1957).

Tang Yi-Jie. *Confucianism, Buddhism, Daoism, Christianity and Chinese Culture.* Washington DC: University of Peking and Council for Research in Values and Philosophy, 1991.

Yamamori, Tetsunao and Kim-Kwong Chan. *Witnesses to Power: Stories of God's Quiet Work in a Changing China.* Waynesboro, GA: Paternoster Press, 2000.

Wurth, Elmer, ed. *Papal Documents Related to the New China.* Maryknoll: Orbis Books, 1985.

Zhongguo tianzhujiao zhinan (Guide to the Catholic Church in China). (In Chinese & English.) Singapore: China Catholic Communication, 1986, 1989, 1997.

4 Contextual Protestant Theology in China, 1800-1920
4.1 Theology and Mission

Protestant presence in China is usually dated from Robert Morrison's arrival in Canton (Guangzhou) in 1807. The numbers of expatriate missionaries would escalate in following decades in the wake of the treaties enforced by foreign powers (1840, 1860); the establishment of more stations in the interior (by the 1890s); and the socio-political changes which followed revolutions in 1901 and 1911. Among the major church and mission societies involved were the LMS (from 1807), the ABCFM (1823), the Protestant Episcopal Church (1835), the Church Missionary Society (1848), and by this time also the mission boards of the American Presbyterian, Baptist and Methodist churches and of the English Wesleyen and Presbyterian churches. In the second half of the century these were followed by the Rhenish, Basel and Berlin societies from Germany, the British Baptists, the SPG, the China Inland Mission and the Christian and Missionary Alliance, along with missionaries from many other countries including Finland, Sweden, Scotland, Canada and Norway. By 1864, 24 missionary societies were active, by 1889, there were 41 societies, and by 1919 the number had reached 130.

For the vast majority of missionaries the primary aim of all activity was the discipling of people and the planting of churches. Direct proclamation of the Gospel, and whatever made this possible therefore had supreme importance. This was most often accompanied by the dismissal of all Chinese religion and culture as superstition and heathenism and the equation of western culture with Christian culture. With some, like Hudson Taylor and leaders of the CIM, there was nevertheless a deep identification with the concerns, situation and life-style of Chinese people. From the beginning, also, attention was given by main-line missions to establishing schools, medical clinics and literature services, and later, relief agencies, lay movements and universities. These agencies inevitably came to include larger purposes of education, community welfare and cultural enrichment, especially in the hands of exceptional missionaries such as Morrison, Legge, Martin, Allen, Soothill, Richard or Reid (see 4.7). Despite imperialist implications which missionary activity frequently carried because of the "unequal treaties," and continuing hostility to such provisions as extra-territorial legal rights for Christians, such scholars and writers were also often able to demonstrate that Christian presence could foster Chinese culture and contribute to nationalist and indigenous concerns. (See 5 below). They also frequently showed deep respect for the best of Chinese tradition and belief and opened new paths for their appreciation. Some missionaries also contributed directly to such movements as the Self-strengthening Movement (1860s), the Reform movements of the 1890s and the New Culture Movement (1920s), and through literature and education societies they published widely in Chinese language journals and books on Chinese religion and culture, western learning and Christian teaching (see 4.5 below).

Leading Chinese Christians such as Liang Fa, Wang Tao and Yen Yung-kiung (Yan Yongjing) and later, those such as Wang Chih-hsin (Wang Zhixin), Wang Cheng-tin, Yen Yang-ch'u, (Ms)Cheng Wanzhen, (Ms) Zeng Baosun and (Ms) Hu Binxia, would hold similar roles at many levels of China's national life (see 4.2.1.; 4.2.2.; 4.7.3.). Writings by these and others would produce, by the end of this period, a substantial body of indigenous theology, albeit mostly in article or booklet form. By the 1890s a series of ecumenical mission conferences had been held, although Chinese participation was still minimal. However, organizations such as the YWCA, the YMCA, the WCTU and the WSCF were developing under largely Chinese leadership and had as their central aims not only personal but also social transformation. Spiritual strengthening from the life of Jesus Christ was linked directly to the work for effective social and political reconstruction. From such localized ecumenical movements came a flow of contextual theological reflection in many diverse and often unexpected forms. Women leaders in movements and colleges in particular provided ecumenical and theological leadership in these developments (see 4.4., 4.9., 4.9.1.), along with male colleagues in colleges, lay movements and independent associations. By the end of the century it was clear that although many nationals and expatriates responded to China's faiths and social realities by reaffirming western, and even millenarian, patterns of belief, others had responded with open and contextualized theologies and ecumenical collaboration. The division between these groupings would harden in the Republican period.

Selected References

Barnett, Suzanne Wilson, and John King Fairbank, eds. *Christianity in China: Early Protestant Missionary Writings*. Cambridge, MA: Harvard University Press, 1985.

Bays, Daniel H. *Christianity in China: from the Eighteenth Century to the Present*. Stanford, CA: Stanford University Press, 1996.

Cohen, Paul. "Missionary Approaches: Hudson Taylor and Timothy Richard." *Papers on China* (Harvard University) 11 (1957).

Fan Tzu-mei. "Chi-tu-hua yü Chung-kuo Chiao-hui" (Christianization and the Chinese church). *CNCP* 52 (1922).

Kwok Pui-lan. *Chinese Women and Christianity 1860-1927*. Atlanta: Scholars Press, 1992.

Latourette, Kenneth S. *A History of Christian Missions in China*. New York: Macmillan, 1929.

Lutz, Jessie G. *China and the Christian Colleges 1850-1950*. Ithaca, NY: Cornell University Press, 1971.

Soothill, William. *A Typical Mission in China*. New York: Young People's Missionary Movement, 1907.

Vermander, Benoit, ed. *Le Christ Chinois.* Paris: Desclée de Brouwer, 1998.
Wang, Zhixin. "Jidujiao yu Zhongguo wenhua" (Christianity and Chinese culture). *Zhenguang zazhi* 26.6 (1927).
Whyte, Bob. *Unfinished Encounter: China and Christianity.* London: Collins, 1988.
Yamamoto Sumiko. *History of Protestantism in China: The Indigenization of Christianity.* Tokyo: Toho Gakai (Institute of Eastern Culture), 2000.

4.2 Protestant Interpreters (to mid-19th Century)
4.2.1 Liang Fa (Liang Ah-Fa, 1795-1855)

Along with Roman Catholic and other assistants, Liang Fa was an associate of Robert Morrison and William Milne, and "the first major Chinese Protestant apologist." He learned wood-block printing in Canton, became printer for the LMS in Malacca and assistant to Morrison in Canton. He found in Christianity a monotheism which could be the focus for filial and moral piety, a source for personal transformation in the Holy Spirit along with the ideas and motive for cultural critique. Having found in Christianity a transformed and morally serious personal life himself, he devoted his writings and teaching to sharing this with those who otherwise, he believed, would lose eternal life.

Liang's writings include a commentary on *Hebrews* (ca. 1824), a paraphrase of *Romans* (1827), tracts on "holy doctrine," along with collections of prayers and (as co-author) a tract against the opium trade. Among the more than twenty 'tracts' which he wrote, the most important is the *Ch'üan Shih Liang Yen(Quanshi liangyan)* (Good words to admonish the age - 1832). This work of over 500 pages outlines biblical teaching from Genesis to Revelation, with a final chapter on eternal life. In part a summary of the teaching of Protestant missionaries, *Ch'üan Shih Liang Yen* rejects much of Chinese religious and cultural life, drawing on both biblical prophetic sources and Chinese texts on morality. He recognizes however, parallels to Christian teaching in Confucianism regarding the "five constant virtues" of benevolence (*ren*), sense of rightness (*yi*), propriety (*li*), rationality (*zhi*) and good faith (*xin*). "For Liang, Christianity not only magnified but in fact perfected Confucian morality" (Bohr: 46). He also found links with the insistence on individual accountability seen in Taoism and Buddhism, but along with Buddhists and Taoists, Confucianists would be judged for their failings in social justice and in universal love and morality. Nevertheless he affirmed that Confucian virtues, which rightly underlie the political order also, could be extended through devotion to God, to include "filiality on a cosmic scale."

Selected References
Works by Liang Fa
> *Zhendao Wenda Qianje* (A Catechism on the True Way). Canton: 1829.
>
> *Quanshi Liangyan[Ch'üan Shih Liang Yen]* (Good words to admonish the age). Canton: London Missionary Society Religious Tract Society, 1832; Taipei: Chungkuo shih hsueh tsung shu, 1965. Also printed in *North China Herald* 161 (1853).
>
> Bohr, P. Richard. "Liang Fa's Quest for Moral Power." In *Christianity in China: Early Protestant Missionary Writings*, edited by Suzanne Wilson Barnett and John King Fairbank. Cambridge, MA: Harvard University, 1985.
>
> Harrison, Brian. *Waiting for China*. Hong Kong: Hong Kong University Press, 1979.
>
> Lovett, Richard. *The History of the London Missionary Society 1795-1895*. 2 vols. London, H. Frowde, 1899.
>
> McNeur, George H. (Mai Zhan'en). *Liang Fa zhuan* (Life of Liang Fa). Hong Kong; Council on Christian Literature, 1959.

4.2.2. Other Protestant Interpreters

Among these scholars and writers, some were colleagues of early Protestant missionaries like Robert Morrison or James Legge, some were affiliated to missionary societies such as the LMS or the Rhenish mission, and some were independent evangelists or lay people. Examples would include those below.

Ho Tsun Sheen (Ho Fuk Tong - 1818-1871), was a pastor from Guangdong who worked also under the LMS in Hong Kong as a close associate of James Legge and as co-pastor of Union Church. His writings include pastoral letters, commentaries in Chinese on the gospels of Mathew and Mark, and booklets expounding the Ten Commandments and also the significance of the Bible for Chinese. In a pastoral letter of October 1848 he writes in apostolic form to present "the Chinese Christian world as he knew it, to others from 'outside'"(Pfister: 237). He preferred the use of *Shangdi* (as opposed to *Shen*) to designate God, and in tracts and commentaries he has been judged to integrate, in a dynamic way, Christian faith and understanding with the fundamental teachings of Confucian texts.

Wang Tao (1828-1897), was a Confucian scholar who worked closely with James Legge during his stay in Hong Kong, in the translation of Chinese classics into English. Beginning in 1849, Wang worked for the LMS Press (the Mohai shuguan) in Shanghai for a period of 13 years, where he assisted W.H. Medhurst with his translation of the Bible into Chinese. Wanted by the Qing government because of his early contacts with the Taipings, he later fled to Hong Kong. He was a social reformist, if not a revolutionist, who called for the adoption of western economics, industrial institutions and armaments to regenerate the nation (see also vol. 3, chap. 4 - Hong Kong). In spite of his close association with missionaries and long working relationship with Legge, it is not certain that Wang himself was a confessing Christian. (See also chap. chap. 4, Hong Kong, 3.1.2).

Yen Yung-kiung (Y.K. Yen, 1838-1898) labored as Anglican parish priest at Wuchang, Hankow and Shanghai, and also served on the faculty of St John's University, Shanghai. He and his wife were the only Chinese participants in the General Missionary Conference, Shanghai 1890. Yen was not only pastor, scholar, teacher and writer, but also an active advocate in causes of justice for poor workers. In addition to the translation of prayer books and philosophical works, he wrote (in Chinese) *Outline of Christian Doctrine*, a *History of China* and the *Ladder of Learning*, and translated many Christian works in Chinese. (See also Hong Kong, chap. 4.)

Wang Yuk-ch'o (b. 1843) studied in Canton and Hong Kong, becoming a teacher and preacher with the Rhenish Mission at the Berlin Foundling House, Hong Kong, and later at the London

Missionary Society's Independent Church in Hong Kong. Apart from an autobiography, Wang wrote three books: a tractate on the reasons why the church is hated by the rulers; an appeal to the rulers to help their unhappy people to True Reformation (through a better understanding of Christianity); and a treatise on the reform necessary within the church to cause the Gospel to spread far and wide through the country. (See also Hong Kong, chap. 4.)

Cao Jingrong (Cao Ziyu - fl. 1870) was an evangelist from Beijing who in presenting religious reasons for the elimination of foot-binding, outlines a theology of female-male equality. He argues (1875) "that God created both men and women perfect and complete and that it was therefore unnatural to alter the shape of a girl's feet to make them more beautiful" (Kwok: 112). He also declares that, in the light of Paul's teaching on parenthood, inflicting such pain and suffering contradicted the benevolence which the Gospel requires from parents.

Another who early advocated indigenous Christian responses was **Chen Mengnan** (1840-1882), founder of Chinese Alliance Churches. There are biographies, autobiographies, prayers and hymns for some other Confucian (or Buddhist) scholars who became Christian, such as Pastor Hsi of Shanxi (Hsi Shengmo - d. 1896), pastors Chang and Ch'u, or pastor Ren Ch'eng-yuan of Hankow (Hangzhou) (1852-1929). Such scholars do not however seem to have articulated in writing any inter-relationship between Confucian or Buddhist teaching and their Christian faith, although their ministries were partly shaped by such relationships.

Selected References

Barnett, Suzanne Wilson and John King Fairbank, eds. *Christianity in China: Early Protestant Missionary Writings.* Cambridge, MA: Harvard UniversityPress, 1985.

Bentley, W.P. *Illustrious Chinese Christians.* Cincinatti: Standard Publishing, 1906.

Eber, Irene. "A Transmitter but not a Creator: Ho Tsun-Sheen (1817-1871), the First Modern Chinese Protestant Theologian." In *Bible in Modern China: the Literary and Intellectual Impact,* edited by Irene Eber et al. Monumenta serica Monograph 43. Nettetal: Steyler, 1999.

Ho Tsun-sheen. *Shengjing zhengju* (Evidences for the Holy Scriptures). Hong Kong: 1855.
Kwok Pui-lan. *Chinese Women and Christianity 1860-1927*. Atlanta: Scholars Press, 1992.
Latourette, Kenneth S. *A History of Christian Missions in China*. New York: Macmillan, 1929.
Pfister, Lauren. "Reconfirming the Way: Perspectives from the Writings of Ho Tsun-sheen." *Ching Feng* 36.4 (1993).
Soothill, W.E. "Native Sermons." In *A Typical Mission in China*, by W.E. Soothill. New York: Young People's Missionary Movement, 1907.
Taylor, Mrs Howard. *Pastor Hsi: Confucian Scholar and Christian*. London: Hodder & Stoughton, 1902.
Tsa Shih-chieh. *Zongguo Jidijiao renwu xiaozhuan* (Biographies of famous Christians in China). Taipei: Zhonghua fuyin Seminary, 1983.
Wang Tao. *Taoyuan we lu wa bian: 12 juan* (Wang Tao's anthologies). Hong Kong: Tao yuan lao min, 1883.
Wang Zhixin. "Bense jiaohui yu bense zhuzuo" (Indigenous churches and indigenous writings). *Wenshi Monthly* 1.6 (1926).

4.3 Theology and Society

The many levels of publication, education, medical and relief work, along with socio-political advocacy, were sources of much theological reflection and publication. Translation and literary production commenced with the issue of Robert Morrison's Bible in 1819 and the tracts of colleagues such as Liang Fa and William Milne. (See 4.2.1., and vol.2, chap. 6 - Malaysia). Christian literature would later be a central concern for missionaries such as Alexander Williamson, Young J. Allen, Timothy Richard and their Chinese colleagues (see section 4.7). Numerous journals were established for both Christian and general education, beginning with Elijah Bridgman's *Chinese Repository* (later the *Chinese Recorder*) in 1832 and many literary endeavors would by the 1880s be developed through the Society for the Diffusion of Christian and General Knowledge among the Chinese (later the Christian Literature Society - see 4.7.1. and 4.10 below).

Since the formation of the Morrison Education Society in 1839, educational mission would include not only catechetics, and training for evangelists, ministers and Bible women (see 4.4.), but also participation in a full range of "secular" education in schools, colleges and universities, including government institutions. W.A.P. Martin for example (see 4.7.3.) was president of the Beijing Tongwenguan, 1869-1895. A central issue would remain the provision and nature of women's education, especially in relation to their role in the church and the recognition of their social status, symbolized by the campaign against foot-binding (see 4.2.2., 4.3., 4.4., 4.9., 5.3.2.). These issues led to wide-ranging theological teaching and writing, by Chinese such as Cao Jingrong (see 4.2.2.) and Bao Guanxi.

Medical and relief work was early a major concern for both expatriates and nationals, along with the alleviation of destitution and succor during the famines which had assumed massive proportions by the 1870s. By 1890 there were 61 mission hospitals in China and 44 dispensaries. Missionaries like Timothy Richard (4.7.1.) and Gilbert Reid (4.7.2.) along with their Chinese colleagues, not only publicized such disasters but mobilized major campaigns of relief and modernization, which were both theologically and scientifically informed.

In the areas of social, educational and political reform the work of leaders such as Allen, Reid, Richard, Martin and Soothill contributed to nationalist and "self-strengthening" movements, and to the Reform Movement of K'ang Yu-wei (Kang Youwei), Chang Chih-tung (Zhang Zhidong) and Liang Ch'i -ch'ao (Liang Qichao) in the late 1890s. The apparent failure of this led many Chinese to recognize that only a more radical revolution would achieve reform, and for this the influence of Protestant educators and reformers would prove to be most significant. Their writings for this bring together the insights of Christian theology, principles from western learning and proposals for political action. (See 4.5 below).

A number of theological reflections by women in this period focused upon many of these major social issues, including war, nationalism, labor and industry, foot-binding, education and the condition of women (see 4.3., 4.4. below).

Selected References

Bohr, Paul R. *Famine in China and the Missionary: Timothy Richard as Relief Administrator and Advocate of National Reform, 1876-1884*. Cambridge, MAss.: Harvard University Press, 1972.

Cao Jingrong, "Chanzu lun" and "Le Chengrenmei lun." (The Pleasure of Helping Others Attack Foot-binding). *Wanguo Gongbao* (Globe Magazine) 7 (1875).

Garrett, Shirley S. *Social Reformers in Urban China: The Chinese YMCA, 1895-1926*. Cambridge, MA: Harvard University Press, 1970.

Reid, Gilbert (Li Jiabai). "Chuangshe xuexiao yi" (Educational reform is urgent). *Wanguo gongbao* (Globe magazine) 7.84 (1896).

Kwok Pui-lan. *Chinese Women and Christianity 1860-1927*. Atlanta: Scholars Press, 1992.

Lian Xi. *The Conversion of Missionaries: Liberalism in American Protestant Missions in China, 1907-1932*. University Park, PA: Pennsylvania State University Press, 1997.

Marchant, Leslie R. *British Protestant Christian Evangelists and the 1898 Reform Movement in China*. Nedlands WA: University of Western Australia, 1975.

Martin, W.A.P. *The Awakening of China*. New York: Doubleday, Page, 1907.

Richard, Timothy. *Forty-five Years in China*. New York: Frederick A. Stokes, 1916.

Smith, Carl T. "The Protestant Church and the Improvement of Women's Status in the 19th Century China." In *A Sense of History*, by Carl T. Smith. Hong Kong: Hong Kong Educational Publishing, 1995.

4.3.1 The Taiping Movement (1850-64)

The Taiping Movement, or Taiping Rebellion, is remembered as the most important political and religious upheaval in China in the 19th century. It irreversibly altered the fate of the Qing dynasty (1644-1911/12). Though the religious nature of the movement is still largely debatable, it did take the form of a syncretised Protestantism. The movement was initiated by Hong Xiuquan (1814-64), a man who believed he had been transported to Heaven during his mental breakdown. Later he claimed to be the brother of Jesus, the second Son of God, sent by God to save China. In 1847 Hong went to Canton to study Christianity with an American missionary, Rev. I.J. Roberts.

Hung's ideology was reformist, syncretic and initially Christian-influenced. The purpose of this 'kingdom of God' was to bring political reforms, economic development through the use of western science, and the public ownership of all property. In its later years the movement garnered increasing popular support, but also led to spreading conflict, extensive corruption and finally to its suppression. However the genesis, theology and diverse elements within the movement have been, and continue to be, a subject for extensive studies.

Selected References

Boardman, Eugene Powers. *Christian Influence upon the Ideology of the Taiping Revolution, 1851-1864*. Madison: University of Wisconsin Press, 1952.

Jen Yu-wen. *The Taiping Revolutionary Movement*. (With the editorial assistance of Adrienne Suddard). New Haven, Yale University Press, 1973.

Michael, Franz and Chang Chung-li. *The Taiping Rebellion: History and Documents*. Vol. 1: *History*. Seattle & London: University of Washington Press, 1966. Vol. 2: *Documents and Comments*. Seattle: University of Washington Press, 1971.

Shih Vincent Yu-chung. *The Taiping Ideology : its Sources, Interpretations, and Influences*. Publications on Asia / Far Eastern and Russian Institute, University of Washington 15. Seattle : University of Washington Press, 1967.

Spence, Jonathan D. *God's Chinese Son: the Taiping Heavenly Kingdom of Hong Xiuquan*. London: Flamingo, 1997.

—. *The Taiping Vision of a Christian China 1836-1864*. Waco, Tex.: Markham Press Fund, Baylor University Press, 1998.

Wang Qincheng. *Taiping Tianguo de wenxian he lishi: haiwai xinwen xiankanbu he wen xian shishi yan jiu* (The sources and history of the Taiping). Beijing: Shehui kexue wenxian chubanshe: Xinhua shudian jing xiao, 1993.

4.4 Women's Writing 1 (late 19th Century)

Chinese women had, of course, been significant for the life of Protestant communities since their inception and expatriate women had also played important roles since the 1830s. But from the 1860s on, issues regarding the role and responsibility of women in the church emerged more and more in women's writings, and these writings would eventually address a full range of social and theological concerns. Church practices which discriminated against women or which restricted their roles, were criticized first by missionaries such as William Soothill, J.V.N. Talmage, Elizabeth M. Fisher, Emma D. Smith and Mary H. Porter. Services and activities specially shaped for women's participation multiplied in the 1880s, along with the training and employment of women as evangelists, Bible women, deacons and volunteers in many capacities. Despite continuing debates regarding their role and also continuing marked discrepancy in income, many came to hold important teaching, preaching and pastoral positions, along with the leadership of house-churches or congregations.

By 1885 there were annual women's conferences in some districts, along with a proliferation of women's mission societies, auxiliaries and reform associations. In these decades also Chinese women first gained access to advanced education in, for example, medical training, and also became increasingly active in such organizations as the WCTU which commenced in China in 1886 and in the YWCA which was founded in 1890. From such associations would come periodicals and other publications which included contextual elements. Journals such as *The Chinese Recorder*, *Jiaohui xinbao* (The Church News), *Nuduobao* (The Woman's Messenger), *Wanguo Gongbao* (The Globe Magazine), *Shengming* (Life) and *Woman's Work in the Far East* (see also 4.9, 4.10 below) carried articles by such women authors as Cheng Guanyi (Ruth Cheng), Ding Shujing (Ting Shu-ching) and Xie Wanying (Bing Xin). These, along with Shi Meiyu, Cheng Wanzhen, Wang Liming and Zeng Baosun (see 4.9.) continued to contribute articles in the following decades.

Particular issues for society and mission became the focus for some writers and activists and among those women in the second half of the 19th century whose teaching and writing focused on social concerns were Zhang Zhujun of Guangzhou and (Mrs) Ding Si-ngok of Fuzhou Girls Boarding School. Zhang Zhujun, a medical doctor, was reported to be the first Chinese woman to preach from the pulpit. In her preaching she clearly denounced Paul's prohibition of women preaching as wrong and illogical: "Women and men have equal rights," she argued, "there is no reason why women should not preach in church" (*WWFE* 9.2 :,1886, cited Kwok 112f.). Ding Si-ngok wrote movingly of her suffering from foot-binding when "a step an inch long was attended with pain, so no matter how many doors there might be open for the Gospel, I could not enter them. Now I can go wherever I want to go. I can now present my "body a living sacrifice, holy and acceptable ..." (*WWFE* 1896).

Expatriate colleagues in awareness-building and writing included Mary Porter, Emma D. Smith, Mary Elizabeth Andrews, Mary Martin Richard, Maria Brown, Helen Newell and Alice Little. In this period also, as in earlier years, a number of male colleagues such as Cao Jingrong, Bao Guanxi, Charles Hartwell, Arthur H. Smith, Chester Holcomb, John Macgowan, Young J. Allen and Timothy Richard advocated changes for Chinese women and popularized more liberal images for them, including that of "educated motherhood." During the 19th century, too, missionaries, especially women, were active in the development and use of romanized dialect vernaculars to ease the path to literacy for the less educated, many of whom were, of course, women. This was an ideal also supported by the prominent Chinese reformers Kang Youwei and Liang Qichao.

Selected References

Andrews, Mary Elizabeth. *Shengjing yaoyan*. (Important words of Scripture). Beijing: Huabei Shuhui, 1890.

Burton, Margaret. *Notable Women of China*. New York: Fleming H. Revell, 1912.

——. *The Education of Women in China*. New York: Fleming H. Revell, 1911.

Ding Si-ngok. "Results of Unbinding my Feet." *WWFE* 17.2 (1896).

Kwok Pui-lan. *Chinese Women and Christianity 1860-1927*. Atlanta: Scholars Press, 1992.

Li Yuning, and Zhang Yufa, eds. *Jindai Zhongguo nuquan yundong shiliao 1842-1911* (Documents on the Feminist Movement in China 1842-1911). Taipei: Chuanji 4.2.1Wenshu, 1975.
Miner, Luella. "The Place of Women in the Protestant Missionary Movement in China." *China Year Book* 9 (1918).
Nevius, Helen. *Yesujiao wenda* (Catechism of sacred doctrine). Fuzhou: ABCFM Collection, 1880.
Shaw, Ella C. "The Work of Bible Women in China." *CMYB* 6 (1915).
Smith, Carl T. "The Protestant Church and the Improvement of Women's Status in the 19th Century China." In *A Sense of History*, by Carl T. Smith. Hong Kong: Hong Kong Educational Publishing, 1995.
Yuan Yuying. "Funü yu zhanshi zhi guanxi" (The relationship between women and war). *NDB* 2.3 (1913).
"Zhang Zhujun nushi lishi"(History of Miss Zhang Zhujun). In *Jindai Zhongguo nuquan yundong shiliao 1842-1911* (Documents on the Feminist Movement in China 1842-1911), edited by Li Yuning and Zhang Yufa. Taipei: Chuanji Wenshu, 1975: vol. 2.

4.5 Expatriate Scholars, Educators and Journalists: 1 (19th Century)

Many early Protestant - and some Orthodox - missionaries are remembered for their educational, translation and theological work. Much of this provided groundwork for later scholarly and theological writing. Protestant scholars include Robert Morrison (1782-1934), William Milne (1785-1822), W.H. Medhurst (1796-1857), Elijah C. Bridgman (b.1801), Karl F.A. Gutzlaff (1803-1851) and James Legge (1815-1897) along with Nikita Yakovlevich Bichurin (1777-1853) and the Archimandrite Palladius (1817-1878).

Nikita (Iakinf) Bichurin graduated from Khazan Seminary and headed the 9th Orthodox mission to Beijing from 1808 to 1821. He translated many Chinese classics and historical records into Russian and the Orthodox liturgy into Chinese. He became recognized as a scholar of Chinese and East Asian history and culture. Among his writings are *The Record of Tibet*, and *Reading Notes on Mongolia*.

Morrison's principal work was the translation of the Bible into Chinese (1807-1832) along with compilation of Christian tracts and dictionaries (see also vol. 3, chap. 9 - Macau). His close associates in this work were Liang Fa (see 4.2.1.above), two Chinese Roman Catholic colleagues, and for varying periods, William Milne. Milne served chiefly in Malacca, as printer, educator and writer of tracts. Notably among these, was the apologetic dialogue *Two Friends*, which shows a sensitivity to other faiths (see vol. 2, chap. 6 - Malaysia).

Following periods in Malacca and Batavia, Medhurst worked in Shanghai as printer, translator and writer on Chinese dialects and philological matters, especially on the rendering of the divine names in Chinese. He also wrote with Milne a Christian version of the *San-tzu ching* (*Sanzi jing*) (Trimetrical Classic), and also utilized the *Lun-yü* (Analects) of Confucius in preparing Christian materials.

There was strong emphasis in these writings, as in those of Bridgman also, upon the communication of 'secular learning.' Bridgman also worked at translation and the production of tracts and articles on western culture, in which he combined Christian and Confucian concepts in works on world geography. He is chiefly remembered for his founding of the *Chinese Repository* (later the *Chinese Recorder*). This was to become a journal of major importance for historical, cultural and theological scholarship in China.

Karl F.A. Gutzlaff worked in Malacca and along the China coast, before periods spent in Guangzhou, Ningbo and Hong Kong. Much of his work was in translation, the training of evangelists and in voluminous writings. Apart from evangelization, Gutzlaff's main aim was the "sinification" of Christianity by presenting it through Chinese colleagues using local dialects and tracts, Chinese in tone and idiomatic style. He valued much of Confucius' teaching and employed Confucian categories in some of his writings.

James Legge is chiefly known for his translation of the central corpus of the Confucian classics and his wideranging Chinese scholarship (see also chap. 4 - Hong Kong). He advocated the use of *Shangdi* for God, and also pictured God as having both male and female characteristics - both parental authority and maternal care - as earlier neo-Confucian literati had done.

Archimandrite Palladius (Benedict Petr Ivanovich) was a Russian sinologist, attached to the 12th, 13th and 15th Orthodox mission groups to China. Along with a direct involvement in policies of Russian expansion, he was a gifted linguist, and undertook historical, religious, archaeological and ethnological studies, especially in the Ussuri area, Heilongjiang. His works include *The Historical Essentials of the Ussuri Area; The History of Early Buddhism; The Documents of Early Islam in China;* and *Travel Notes from Beijing to Manchuria.*

Selected References

Barnett, Suzanne Wilson and John King Fairbank, eds. *Christianity in China: Early Protestant Missionary Writings.* Cambridge, Mass.: Harvard University, Department of History, 1985.

Drake, Fred W. "Protestant Geography in China: E.C. Bridgmen's Portrayal of the West." In *Christianity in China: Early Protestant Missionary Writings,* edited by Suzanne Wilson Barnett and John King Fairbank, 89-106. Cambridge, Mass.: Harvard University, Department of History, 1985.

Girardot, Norman J. *The Victorian Translation of China: James Legge's Oriental Pilgrimage.* Berkeley: University of California Press. Forthcoming.

Gutzlaff, Karl. *A Journal of Three Voyages Along the Coast of China in 1831, 1832 and 1833 ...* London: n.p. 1834.

—. *Gaihans Chinesische Berichte von der Mitte des Jahres 1841 his zum Schluss des Jahres 1846.* London: Cassel, 1850.

Lai Yung-hsiang. *Catalog of Protestant Missionary Works in Chinese.* Harvard-Yenching Library. Boston, MA: G.K. Hall, 1980.

Legge, James. *The Notions of the Chinese Concerning God and Spirit ...* Hong Kong: Hong Kong Register Office, 1852.

—. *The Religions of China. Confucianism and T'aoism Described and Compared with Christianity.* London: Hodder & Stoughton, 1880.

Leonard, Jane Kate. "W.H. Medhurst: Rewriting the Missionary Message." In *Christianity in China: Early Protestant Missionary Writings,* edited by Suzanne Wilson Barnett and

John King Fairbank, 47-59. Cambridge, MA: Harvard University Press, 1985: 47-59.

Lutz, Jesse. "The Missionary-Diplomat Karl Gutzlaff and the Opium War." In *Proceedings of the First International Symposium on Church and State in China*, edited by Li Chi- fang, 215-38. Taibei: Danjiang (Tamkang) University, 1987.

Medhurst, Walter Henry. *An Inquiry into the Proper Mode of Translating ruach & pneuma, in the Chinese Version of the Scriptures.* Shanghai: Printed at the Mission Press, 1850.

Schlyter, Herman. *Der China-Missionar Karl Gutzlaff und seine Heimatbasis.* Lund: C. W K. Gleerup, 1976.

Skachkov, P. Yeo. *Iakinf Bichurin: Materialy K Biographi.*(Materials for biography). n.l., n.p.,1933.

4.6 Biographies of Chinese Christians (19th century)

Numerous biographies and some autobiographies are extant for Chinese Christians in this period. Christian living at that time in China was necessarily contextualized in many respects, not least because of the scale of social and political disturbance as well as of natural or military disasters. Full study of these, therefore, will reveal many elements of contextual biblical reflection or teaching. References for a small selection of these, other than those mentioned in 4.2, 4.4, 4.8, and 4.9, are given in this section. Many more are recorded in mission histories, missionary biographies and histories such as Latourette (1929, and 1945- vol. 6), Jen Yu-wen (1957) or Garrett (1970).

Some, such as those for Agnes Tsao Kuei (d. 1856) or Laurence Pe Mu (d. 1856), are brief accounts and testimonies of those martyred. Others like Yen Yung-kiung (Y.K. Yen) (1838-1898), Wang Yuk-ch'o (b. 1843) or Soong Chiao-shun (fl. 1880-1900) are given full accounts in volumes such as those by Bentley (1906), MacGillivray (1912), Margaret Burton (1912), Arthur W. Hummel (1943) or Bays (1996). Some, like Hou Sheng-ch'ing (fl. 1870), Ho Tsun-sheen or Ding Limei, appear in individual articles in journals such as the *Chinese Recorder*, *Nüqingnian bao* or *Shengming,* while others such as Cheng Mao (1851-1898) of Fukien, Zeng Baosun (4.7.5.), Pastor Hsi Sheng-mo (Xi Shengmo) (d.1896) of Shansi, Pastors Chang and Ch'u, or Wang Ying-ming of Manchuria have full volumes devoted to them. A smaller number such as Mi Hu Yong (1837-1893), Ren Ch'eng-yuan (1852 -1929) and (Ms) Cai Sujuan (Christiana Tsai) have left full autobiographies.

Selected References

> Bays, Daniel H., ed. *Christianity in China from the Eighteenth Century to the Present.* Stanford, CA: Stanford University Press, 1996.
> Bentley, W.P. *Illustrious Chinese Christians.* Cincinatti: Standard Publishing, 1906.
> Broomhall, Marshall. *In Quest of God. The Life Story of Pastors Chang and Ch'u, Buddhist Priest and Chinese Scholar.* London: China Inland Mission, 1921.
> Brown, C.C. *A Chinese St Francis or the Life of Brother Mao.* London: Hodder & Stoughton, 1911.
> Burton, Margaret. *Notable Women of China.* New York: Fleming H. Revell, 1912.
> Cai Sujuan. *Anshi zhi hou* (Queen of the dark chamber). Hong Kong: Bellman House, 1982.
> Garrett, Shirley S. *Social Reformers in Urban China: The Chinese YMCA, 1895-1926.* Cambridge, MA: Harvard University Press, 1970.
> Jen Yu-wen. *Pioneers of the Protestant Church in China.* Hong Kong: Chinese Christian Literature Council, ?1957.
> Latourette, Kenneth S. *A History of Christian Missions in China.* New York: Macmillan, 1929.
> —. *A History of the Expansion of Christianity, Vol. 6. The Great Century in Northern Africa and Asia A.D. 1800-A.D. 1914.* London: Eyre and Spottiswoode, 1945- .
> MacGillivray, Donald. *A Century of Protestant Missions in China.* Chicago: Fleming H. Revell, 1912.
> Mi Hu-yong. *The Way of Faith Illustrated: Autobiography of Hu-yong Mi of the China Mission Conference.* Cincinnati: Curts & Jennings, 1896.
> Ren Ch'eng-Yuan. *A Tamarisk Garden Blessed with Rain.* London: China Inland Mission, 1930.
> Wei Waiyang. "Ding Limei Lijie xiongdi hezhuan" (A combined biography of the brothers Ding Limei and Ding Lijie). *Xiaoyuan* (Campus) 22.2 (1980).
> *Zha Shijie Zhongguo Jidujiao renwu xiaozhuan* (Concise biographies of Chinese Christians). Taibei: China Evangelical Seminary Press, 1983.

4.7 Expatriate Scholars, Educators and Theologians: 2 (Late 19th /early 20th Century)

Among the very large number of expatriate Protestants who worked for lengthy periods in the later 19th century with the Chinese churches and communities, were a number of exceptional scholars, writers and theologians. Although only a small minority of the missionary community, these writers contributed on many levels to both the growth of scholarly disciplines regarding Chinese religion and culture and also to the development of deeper and broader Christian understanding of church and mission in China. The lives and work of some in particular have continuing theological significance for Chinese contextual theology. Prominent among these are Timothy Richard and Gilbert Reid.

4.7.1. Timothy Richard (1845-1919)

Timothy Richard began his work with the Baptist Missionary Society in Shandong (Shantung) (1870), and with John Nevius undertook extensive famine relief (1876-) for which he became widely known. He fostered relationships with Roman Catholics and those of other religious faiths whose genuine work for China he recognized. The suspicion which this aroused in some fellow missionaries would later increase when he wrote and lectured on the truths to be found in other faiths. He consistently advocated that Christianity be adapted to its Chinese setting and that more comprehensive systems for higher education and for Christian publication were the key areas of mission. He became secretary of what was later the Christian Literature Society (1906), and commenced the publication of series of periodicals, books and pamphlets along with initiating lecture programs and reading-rooms. With Gilbert Reid, Young J. Allen and W.A.P. Martin he also exerted considerable influence upon leaders of the Reform Movement of Liang Qichao and Kang Youwei. He later became Chancellor of Shansi (Shanxi) University of which he was a co-founder.

Through such life experience, Richard's theology came to stress the place of bodily, and not only "spiritual," welfare; of national, and not only personal, salvation; and the Gospel within Buddhism as well as the Gospel of Christianity. Like many other missionaries he had undergone "multiple conversions": from conventional evangelism to study of the Chinese people and context; to famine relief and to being a prophet of structural reform; to a theologian of religions and inter-faith pioneer: to worker for peace and champion of the submerged. His recognition of affinity between the Christian faith and two Mahayana texts in particular, occasioned most theological reflection and writing. He found the "Gospel in Chinese" in the *Lotus Scripture* of the Tien Tai school and, in the *Awakening of Faith* of the Pure Land School, salvation by faith, a God both immanent and transcendent, deep compassion for people, and a Messiah (*Zhenru*) for all humankind. He later believed that such affinities could be traced to Nestorian Christian influence in China. His highly suggestive writings and translations here are found in *New Testament to Higher Buddhism* (1910), and *Guide to Buddahood* (sic) (1907). Other important works include *Conversion by the Million in China* (1907), and *Forty-Five Years in China: Reminiscences* (1915).

Selected References
Works by Timothy Richard
   Guide to Buddahood (sic) : being a Standard Manual of Chinese Buddhism. [Trans.] Shanghai : Christian Literature Society, 1907.
   A Dictionary of Philosophical Terms: chiefly from the Japanese. Shanghai: Christian Literature Society for China, 1913.
   Forty-Five Years in China: Reminiscences. New York: Frederick A. Stokes, 1916.
   Epistle to all Buddhists throughout the World. S.l.: s.n., 1916.
   A Mission to Heaven, A Great Chinese Epic and Allegory by Ch'iu Ch'ang Ch'un, A Taoist Gamaliel who became a Nestorian Prophet and Advisor to the Chinese Court. Shanghai: The Author, 1940.
   "Christian Persecutions in China - Their Nature, Causes, Remedies." CR 15 (July-Aug. 1884).
   —. trans. and ed. A'svaghosa. Mahayana'sraddhotpada'sastra (The New Testament of Higher Buddhism). Edinburgh: T. & T. Clark, 1910.
   Bohr, Paul R. *Famine in China and the Missionary: Timothy Richard as Relief Administrator and Advocate of National Reform,*

1876-1884. Cambridge, MA: Harvard University, Council on East Asian Studies, 1972.

Evans, Edward Willliam Price. *Timothy Richard: A Narrative of Christian Enterprise and Statesmanship in China.* London: Carey Press, 1945.

Johnson, Rita T. *Timothy Richard's Theory of Christian Missions to the Non-Christian World.* Microform. Ph.D. diss., St. John's University, New York, 1966. Published: c1968.

Soothill, W.E. *Timothy Richard of China.* London: Seeley Service, 1924.

4.7.2. Gilbert Reid (b. 1857)

Gilbert Reid first worked in Shandong (Shantung) (1882), studied Confucianism and formed (1892) the Mission to the Higher Classes in China (MHCC - from 1897, the *Shang Xian Tang*: International Institute). He also wrote for the London *Times* on educational and political reform in China and published, in Chinese writings, his advocacy of "Confucius plus Jesus." Regarding famine relief, Reid advocated more scientific methods of prevention and was closely associated with Timothy Richard and others in petitioning the Chinese government on wide-ranging reforms. He also wrote many articles on reform to the Zongli Yamen (Office of foreign Affairs) - also published in the *Wanguo Gongbao* - and was later director of the *Peking Post* (1917-1921).

Deeply concerned for China's future, Reid first believed that in the Chinese context Christianity would have to blend its teachings with the creative elements of Confucianism, and that this along with the spread of western knowledge would lead to acceptance by local elites. He presented in his writings many similarities between Confucianism and Christianity and in his reports for the MHCC wrote that he worked "with the Bible in one hand and the Four Books in the other", not in order to proselytise but to "bring about harmony and union between the votaries of various faiths." His full study of Confucian texts is revealed in many of his writings and for this his work was honored by Chinese leaders. His understanding of national reform also reflected Confucian doctrine in stressing the livelihood of people and the fostering of security and morality, before any rapid establishment of representative forms

Contextual Theology in China 113

of government. And only through a society where "natives and foreigners, Christians and non-Christians" lived and worked together, he believed, could China become independent, peacefull and prosperous.

Selected References
Works by (John) Gilbert Reid (Li Jiabai)
"Chuangshe xuexiao yi" (Educational reform is urgent). *Wanguo gongbao* (Globe magazine) 7.84 (1896).
"The Duty of Christian Missions." *CR* 19.8-10 (Aug.-Oct. 1888).
"Guang xinxue yifu jiuxue shuo" (Supplementing old learning with new learning). In *Chouhua chuyan* (The question of the time for the good of China), by Gilbert Reid, 43a-46a. Shanghai: Commercial Press, 1904.
"The Importance of Christian Evangelization." *CR* 22.2 (Feb. 1891).
"Mengzi zhushi" (Explanation of Mencius with notes). *Guoji gongbao* (International journal) 5.39-40 (Aug. 1927); 5.41-42 (Sept. 1927).
"Minjiao xiang'an yi" (On harmony between non-Christians and Christians). In *Chouhua chuyan* (The question of the time for the good of China), by Gilbert Reid, 32a-37a. Shanghai: Commercial Press, 1904.
Renxu yanjianglu (The lectures of 1923). Shanghai: American Presbyterian Press, 1923.
"Gilbert Reid's Biographical Record." Manuscript, Presbyterian Historical Society, Philadelphia.
Sunderland, J.T. "Dr. Gilbert Reid and His Unique Mission to China." *Unity* (24 Oct. 1924).
Tsou Mingteh. "Christian Missionary as Confucian Intellectual: Gilbert Reid (1857-1927) and the Reform Movement in the Late Qing." In *Christianity in China from the Eighteenth Century to the Present*, edited by Daniel H. Bays. Stanford, CA: Stanford University Press, 1996.

4.7.3. Other Expatriate Scholars and Interpreters

A number of other expatriates developed theologies in this period which were shaped by full study of Chinese culture, by deep and practical concern for Chinese people and their nation, and by their experience in education, relief, scholarship and cultural exchange. The following provide just a few examples.

W.A.P. Martin (1827-1916) was author and educator, president of the University of Wuchang and an authority on international law. He also advocated baptism for families and communities following their basic acceptance of Christianity, with fuller understanding to follow later. Although his paper on Chinese Ancestral Rites, which he declared was a cultural form and therefore not idolatrous, was rejected by the General Missionary Conference, Shanghai 1890, he continued in extensive educational and literary work until his death.

Young J. Allen (1859-1907) was a prolific journalist, founder of magazines and disseminator of knowledge concerning Christianity along with scientific, economic, educational and moral development, for Chinese Christians and the wider community. He was an outstanding pioneer in cross-cultural communication and exchange.

William Soothill (1861-1935) was also a prolific writer, linguist, educator and founder of colleges. He was principal of Shansi Imperial University and later, professor of Chinese at Oxford. His principal scholarly work was as an interpreter of Chinese religions, especially Confucianism; Confucius being for him the "chief classical master and moral philosopher" - although not the "saviour" - of China. He also valued the work of Richard in presenting a new mode of responding to Mahayana Buddhism.

Herbert A. Giles (1845-1935) devoted most of his work in China to the study of Chinese language, literature and religion, and was later professor of Chinese at Cambridge. His purpose was to spread knowledge of China's "immense bulk of authorship" along with deeper understanding of Chinese culture and its faiths. He also wrote on China's contemporary problems.

Others to be studied in this period include Charles Hartwell, Ernst Faber, Arthur Evans Moule, Alexander Williamson, Henry McKee Woods, Alexander Wylie, Hudson Taylor, George Hunter McNeur and Karl Ludwig Reichelt (See chap. 4 - Hong Kong).

Selected References

Allen, Young J. "Our China Mission." *Methodist Review* 4 (1882).
—. (Lin Lezhi). *Zhongdong zhanji benmo* (A history of the Sino-Japanese War). 13 vols. Shanghai: Christian Literature Society, 1896.
Bennett, Adrian A. *Missionary Journalist in China, Young J. Allen and his Magazines 1860-1883.* Athens, GA: Georgia University Press, 1883.
Cook, Edmund F. *Young J. Allen, D.D., LL.D., 1859-1907: Statesman, Author, Missionary.* Nashville: MECS Women's Board of Foreign Missions, 1910.
Cohen, Paul. "Missionary Approaches: Hudson Taylor and Timothy Richard." *Papers on China* (Harvard University) 11 (1957).
Duus, Peter. "Science and Salvation in China: The Life and Work of W.A.P. Martin." *Papers on China* (Harvard University) 10 (1956).
Giles, H.A. *A History of Chinese Literature.* London: Heineman, 1901.
—. *Chaos in China.* Cambridge: Heffer & Sons, 1924.
—. *Confucianism and its Rivals.* New York: AMS Press, 1979.
Hartwell, Charles *Zhengdao qimeng* (Enlightenment on truth). Fuzhou: Taiping jie fuyin tang, 1871.
—. *Shangdi zonglun* (On the doctrine of God). Fuzhou; n.p., 1878.
Marchant, Leslie R. *Ernst Faber's Scholarly Mission to Convert the Confucian Literati in the Late Ch'ing Period.* Nedlands: University of Western Australia, Centre for East Asian Studies, 1984.
Martin, W.A.P. *Hanlin Papers. Essays on the History, Philosophy, and Religion of the Chinese.* Shanghai, etc.: Kelly and Walsh, 1894.
—. *A Cycle of Cathay; or, China, South and North. With Personal Reminiscences.* New York, Chicago, etc.: Revell, 1896.
Moule, Arthur Evans. *Half a Century in China. Recollections and Observations.* London: SPCK, 1911.
Soothill, William. *A Typical Mission in China.* New York: Young People's Missionary Movement, 1907.
—. *The Three Religions of China.* 3rd ed. London: Oxford University Press, 1929.

4.8 Chinese Protestant Interpreters / Writers 2 (late 19th / early 20th centuries)

The final decades of the 19th century and the first decades of the 20th were a period of increasing social and political turbulence, along with new intellectual and revolutionary movements. It was, not surprisingly, also a time when growing numbers of Chinese Christians articulated both their faith and their political commitment. (See also 4.9 and 5.1). We therefore have numerous articles, books and statements on such subjects as Jesus Christ in the new China; Jesus and revolution; indigenization of the church; the future of an independent China; nationalism, socialism and reconstruction; Confucian and Christian ethics; Christianity and Chinese culture; the anti-Christian movements; and Christian education, service and citizenship. A small selection of those who were writing before 1920 follows, and others whose main writings are in the subsequent period appear below (5.1).

Xu Qian (Hsü Ch'ien, 1871-1940) was a scholar, a judge, a founder of the Kuomintang (KMT) (1912), president of the General Association for Religious Freedom, Minister of Justice for Sun Yat-sen (1918) and leader of the National Salvation Movement formed by Protestants (1918). He was appointed Chancellor of the Sino-Russian University (1925) and member of the KMT Central Executive, but was deemed a dissident nationalist and socialist by Chiang Kai-shek. Though an Anglican, he edited the Catholic *Yishibao* (See Lebbe 2.2.4.) and later also founded the newspaper *Ping Jih Bao*. His writings include volumes on law, religion, calligraphy and economics, along with a body of poetry.

Wang Zhixin (Wang Chih-hsin, b. 1881) of Chekiang, taught Chinese before becoming professor of Chinese studies at Nanjing Theological Seminary (1921). He had edited the *Christian Advocate* (1913-1918) and would later be chief editor for the Christian Literature Society, Dean of the Arts College of Fukien (Fujian) Christian University and professor of Chinese at the University of Shanghai. He was a Confucian scholar and prolific author of books and articles on Chinese culture, education and philosophy, on Sun

Yat-sen's thought, the indigenization of Christianity and on people's livelihood, as well as upon the life of Jesus, on socialism and contemporary movements. For Wang, Christianity was a universal culture into which both eastern and western cultures could be synthesized, yet both the Chinese church and its literature must be indigenous by assimilating Chinese thought and ethics. Drawing parallels between progressive elements in Confucianism and the teaching of Jesus he proposed a "middle way" which was deeply ethical, and harmonized in piety and service, love-for-others and love-for-self.

Wang Zhengting (C.T. Wang, 1882-1961) was born in Ningpo, joined the YMCA at Tientsin (Tianjin), and served as a national secretary of the YMCA until 1911 when he became successively a Red Cross worker, provisional minister of Foreign Affairs and vice-president of the Senate. He spoke at the Edinburgh 1910 Conference, was from 1915 the first Chinese General Secretary of the YMCA along with government appointments, and later became vice-chairperson of both the WSCF and the World's YMCA. His writings, chiefly in articles, reflect a wide ecumenical understanding of China's political problems, of the ways by which Christianity may be indigenized in China and of the roles of lay and student movements in this.

Fan Zimei (Fan Tzu-mei; T.M. Van, fl. 1920) received full Confucian education, and became prominent in the sphere of Christian literature by 1920. He was editor of the *Wanguo gongbao*, the *Chih-pu Tsa-chih* (*Zhibu zazhi*) and later of the *Ch'ing-nien Chin-pu* (*Qingnian jinbu*). In many articles and books he wrote on issues of Christianization; on Confucian views of the family (of which he was critical), of personality, politics and of revolution; of the search for truth; and of cultural diversity and exchange. Fan recognized the naturalistic and humanistic aspects of Chinese tradition yet believed that harmony was possible between pristine forms of Christianity and undistorted Confucian doctrine. After all, both are eastern teachings, he declared, and both exalt virtues above power, peace above violence, ethical service above status or possessions.

Others who wrote on Jesus Christ in China and related topics, included Hu Yiku (Y.K. Woo), Hsieh Hung-lai (Xie Honglai), Lo Lun-yen (Luo Lunyan), Lin Han-ta (Lin Handa) and Pao Kuang-lin (Bao Guanglin); on national salvation and reconstruction, Hsu Ch'ien, Ying Yuan-tao (Ying Yuandao) and Chao Kuan-hai (Zhao Guanhai); and on an indigenous church and its theology, Chien Yu-wen (Jian Youwen), Zhu Baoyuan, Ying Yuan-tao and Hsieh Hung-lai. To these must be added the number of theologians dealt with more fully in section 5 below: Wu Leichuan (1870-1944), Jia Yuming (1879-1964), Cheng Jingyi (Andrew C.Y. Ch'eng, 1881-1939), T.C. Chao (Zhao Zichen, 1888-1979), Liu Tingfang, Timothy (T.T. Lew, 1890-1947), P.C. Hsu (Hsu Pao-ch'ien; Xu Baoqian, 1892-1944), N.Z. Zia (Xie Fuya, 1892-1991. See also vol 3, chap 4 - Hong Kong), Y.T. Wu (Wu Yaozong, 1893-1979), Wang Mingtao (Wang Mingdao, 1900-1991) and Watchman Nee (Ni Tuosheng, 1903-1972).

Others for whom we have contextual writings include Hu Shih, Y.Y. Tsu, M. Thomas Tchou, Wei Francis Cho-min (See Taiwan, chap. 10, 2.1), T.Z. Koo, L.T. Chen, David Z.T. Yui, (Yu Rizhang), Sanford C.C. Chen, Chester S. Miao, Yen Yang-ch'u (James Y.C. Yen (1893-1990), Chang Fu-liang / Huang Siu-chi (Miao), Marcus Cheng, Xu Dishan (1893-1941), Shen Szu-chuang, H.L.Zia, Ting Limei and Yu Bin. In these years their expatriate partners in such writing included such people as John S. Barr, C. Stanley Smith, Henry T.Hodgkin, John Leighton Stuart, Frank Rawlinson, Paul Hutchinson, Lucius Porter, Frank Price and Paul Monroe. (For women colleagues see 4.9).

By the 1920s, Protestant theological writing was developing rapidly. This was to further develop in the wake of the May Fourth Movement (ca. 1915-1919), especially as this was a time of political, intellectual and social ferment (see 5.1).

Selected References
> Barnett, Suzanne Wilson and John King Fairbank, eds. *Christianity in China: Early Protestant Missionary Writings.* Cambridge, MA: Harvard University Press, 1985.

Bays, Daniel. "Foreign Missions and Indigenous Protestant Leaders in 20th-century China: Chen Chonggui (Marcus Cheng) and the Issues of Identity and Loyalty in an Age of Nationalism." *CWC Position Paper*. Cambridge: Currents of World Christianity, Sept. 2000.

Ch'eng, Marcus. *Echoes from China: The Story of My Life and Lectures*. Chicago: Covenant Book Concern, 1921.

Chien Yu-wen (Timothy Jen; Jian Youwen). "Minzu jiaohui" (The people's church). *CNCP* 52 (1922).

Fan Tzu-mei. "Wozhi guocui baocun guan" (My view on preserving the national essence). *CNCP* 26 (1919).

—. "Jiduhua yu Zhongguo jiaohui" (Christianization and the Chinese church). *CNCP* 52 (1922).

—. "Dongfang de Jidujiao." (Christianity of the East). *CNCP* 79 (1925).

Hsieh Hung-lai. *Shengdao yu Guankui* (The character of Jesus). Shanghai: Association Press, 1920.

—, ed. *Zheng Dao ji* (Reasons for Christian faith). Shanghai: Association Press, 1919.

Hsü Ch'ien. "Gongde zhenli" (Christianity the basis for a republic). *SM* 1.1 (1919).

Hu I-ku. "Shijie gaizao yu Yesu Jidu de yansheng" (World reconstruction and the birth of Jesus Christ). *CNCP* 58 (1922).

Lam Wing-hung. *Chinese Theology in Construction*. Pasadena: William Carey, 1983.

Rawlinson, Frank Joseph. *Naturalization of Christianity in China: (A Study of the Relation of Christian and Chinese Idealism and Life)*. Shanghai: Presbyterian Mission Press, 1927.

Stauffer, Milton, ed. *China Her Own Interpreter. Chapters by a Group of Nationals Interpreting the Christian Movement*. London: SCM Press, 1928.

Wang, Zhengting. *The Youth Movement in China*. New York: New Republic, 1928.

—. "On Christ as an Oriental." Papers of the WSCF Conference in Tokyo, 1907.

—. "Some Effects of the Christian Student Movement on Chinese Public Life." *Student World* 1915.

—. "Making Christianity Indigenous in China." *Chinese Recorder* 52 (1921).

Wang Zhixin. "Bense jiaohui yu bense zhuzuo." (Indigenous churches and indigenous writings). *Wenshe Monthly* 1.6 (1926).

—. "Ruhe shi Jidujiao wenzi dadao shehui zhongxin" (How to make Christian literature gain the center of society). *WS* 1.2 (Nov. 1925).

—. "Jidujiao yu Zhongguo wenhua" (Christianity and Chinese culture). *Zhenguang zazhi* 26.6 (1927).

Xu Run. *Xuyuzhai zixu nianpu fu Shanghai zaji* (Xu Run's autobiography and Shanghai miscellanies). Xiangshan: Xushi yin, 1927.

4.9 Women's Writing 2 (early 20th Century)

The first decades of the 20th century saw rapid growth in the education, ministries and writing of women, especially in the years following the Revolution of 1911. By 1920 there were over 50 Bible Schools for women, and a quarter of the women teaching in Christian schools and one-fifth of church evangelists were Chinese women. But along with these developments and the licensing and appointment of women preachers a few years later, large disparities in status and income continued. Many outstanding women, however, came to hold prominent roles in ecumenical, provincial and national associations. The actions of women in revolutionary activities and the dissemination of feminist concerns through periodicals also influenced the aspirations of large numbers of Christian women

Following the establishment of the China (Edinburgh) Continuation Committee in 1913 which included women for the first time, women were soon also to speak and write in national Christian forums. Among these leaders were the medical doctor Shi Meiyu (Mary Stone), Cao Fangyun of the Shanghai YWCA, Yu Cidu (Dora Yu) of the Methodist Episcopal Mission, Mei Yunying of the WCTU, Ding Shujing and Cheng Wanzhen of the YWCA, and Chen Yuling of the Chinese Missionary Society. Cheng Guanyi, Fan Yurong, Kang Chen (Ida Kahn) and Zeng Baosun (Tseng Pao-suen) also became members of the National Christian Council. Four of the seven founders of the Chinese Missionary Society (1918) also, were women: Shi Meiyu, Cai Sujian (Christiana Tsai), Kate Woo and (Mrs.) F.H. Sung.

Writings are extant for most of the above in such journals as *The Chinese Recorder, Jiaohui xinbao* (The Church News), *Nüduobao* (The Woman's Messenger), *Wanguo Gongbao* (The

Globe Magazine), *Shengming* (Life) and *Woman's Work in the Far East*. Examples of significant theological reflection are found in the writings of Yuan Yuying, Zhang Zimou, Cheng Wanzhen, Hu Binxia, Laura White and Zeng Baosun (for these see below).

Cheng Wanzhen was a staff-member of the YWCA's industrial department and a pioneer advocate for the justice implied in a theology of the Kingdom of God. She urged the Chinese church to take a stand in applying the standards of the International Labor Conference for all labor and she opposed the industrial system which treated human lives as "of less value than soulless machinery." Writing of the Kingdom of God, in contrast to the church's readiness for charitable work, she used the repeated " cry of the exploited poor ... 'We want no charity - we want justice'" and she challenged the church to "again lay the foundation stone of standing for social justice and humanity ..."

Hu Binxia (Mrs. T.C. Chu), first Chinese chairperson of the national YWCA, and a member of the revolutionary *Gongaihui* (Common Love Society) which worked for the overthrow of the Manchu regime. She was outspoken in her criticism of the "three-fold subordination" Chinese women were subjected to, and linked the emancipation of women to the future destiny of China. Strongly patriotic, she urged women on biblical grounds to join the struggle for a new China.

Laura White presents in two articles the goddess symbolism of purity, compassion, patience and gentleness, and compares Mary, the mother of Jesus, and Guanyin, Chinese deity and bodhisattva. She concludes that both Mary and Guanyin serve to symbolize incarnation, prayer and salvation, self-cultivation and the union between the human and the divine" (Kwok: 55). Christian women can value, therefore, the contribution of creative elements within their own culture along with the gospels and biblical teaching.

Yuan Yuying, secretary of the WCTU, writing of foot-binding and related issues, declared that women were equally created by God and went on to relate the cause of nationalism to the liberation of women's bodies. This was both for women themselves and for the Chinese nation as a whole. For women were to be strong and whole for the Chinese people and also 'living sacrifices' to the Lord.

In writing on church reform, **Zhang Zimou** refers to Jesus' care for and relationships with women in preaching, healing and respect, as recorded in the gospels. In these she finds, as does Peng Jinzhang, that "Jesus treated women as equals with men," and outlined the grounds for declaring that he would reject "customs that regard women as inferior to men" (Kwok: 50).

Zeng Baosun (P. S. Tseng) was headmistress of a girls' school in Hunan who in her writings presents the long quest of women for a recognized identity, and their struggle for liberation from social and cultural suppression. She draws on China's history to show that women had not always been subordinate, and were often more compassionate and religious in community life. The perfect humanity and self-sacrifice of Jesus shows us "how to attain God's favor" and how women are to become "free in mind and behaviour, eager to learn and serve ... and striving to set right the social and economic wrongs of her nation." In a creed-like statement Zeng affirms that "Chinese women can only find full life in the message of Christ, who was born of a woman, revealed his messiahship to a woman, and showed His glorified body after His resurrection to a woman" (Kwok: 172f.)

Selected References

Beahan, Charlotte L. "Feminism and Nationalism in the Chinese Women's Press, 1902-1922). *Modern China* 1 (1975).

Cheng Wanzhen. "The Chinese Church and the New Industrial System." *CR* 53 (1922).

—. "Nüzi zhiye wenti" (Women's employment issues). *Nüqingnian Bao* (The YWCA magazine) 5.1 (1921).

—. "The Women's Movement in China." *The YWCA magazine* (June 1923).

Hu Binxia. "The Emancipation of Chinese Women." *CR* 50 (1919).

—. "Nüzi yu guoyun." (Women and the destiny of the nation). *NDB* 11.2 (1922).

Kwok Pui-lan. *Chinese Women and Christianity 1860-1927*. Atlanta: Scholars Press, 1992.

Li Yuning, and Zhang Yufa, eds. *Jindai Zhongguo nüquan yundong shiliao 1842-1911.* (Documents on the Feminist Movement in China 1842-1911). Taipei: Chuanji Wenshu, 1975.

Wang Huiwu. "Nüquan yundong yu nü Jidutu." (The Feminist Movement and female Christians). *Nüqingnian Bao* 2 (1922).

White, Laura. "Maliya tu shuo" (A portrait of Mary). *NDB* 1.1 (1912).

—. "Maliya de Muyi" (The motherhood of Mary). *NDB* 11.7 (1922).

—. "Xiawa beiyu tu" (A portrait of the temptation of Eve). *NDB* 1.3 (1912).

Yuan Yuying. "Funü yu zhanshi zhi guanxi" (The relationship between women and war). *NDB* 2.3 (1913).

—. "Chanzu lun" (On foot-binding). *NDB* 8.11 (1920).

Zhang Zimou. "Jiaohui Gaizao de Wojian" (My opinion on church reform). *Shengming* (Life). 2.9-10 (1922).

Zeng Baosun. "China's Women and their Position in the Church." *Church Missionary Review* 68 (1917).

—. "Wo de Jidujiao xinyang" (My Christian faith). In *Jidujiao yu xin Zhongguo* (Christianity and a new China), edited by Wu Yaozong. Shanghai: Qingnian Xiehui Shuju (Association Press), 1940.

—. *Zeng Baosun huiyilu* (Memoir of Zeng Baosen). Hong Kong: Chinese Christian Literature Council, 1970.

4.9.1. Other Women Theologians and Writers 3

Many of the women for whom we have contextual theological writing in this period were, as can be already seen in 4.9. above, members of, or affiliated to either the WCTU (formed in 1886) or the YWCA (from 1890). Although these movements were introduced by women from western countries, they quickly came to emphasize leadership by Chinese women. In the face of confining traditions in both society and church and of major social problems, and amid revolutionary changes and sporadic conflict, these and related associations developed networks, institutions and programs which were able to respond quickly to the needs of Chinese people. Their aims included the education and betterment of women in all their home, work and social settings; national aspirations for self-determination; the dissemination of Christian teaching and ideals for these; along with the abolition of social evils such as destitution, illiteracy, economic injustice and discrimination.

At the same time, many members and leaders articulated in articles and books their theological understanding of personal and social change, of transformed communities and of women's role in these. The model for this role was found again and again in the perfectly human life of Jesus who so closely identified himself with women. In addition to those mentioned in 4.4 and 4.9 above, such as Shi Meiyu (Mary Stone), Cheng Guanyi and Ida Kahn (Kang Cheng), others for whom we have theological reflection include Xie Wanying (the poet Bing Xin), Guo Fangyun, Fan Yurong, Huang Ying, Wang Liming, Li Guanfeng, Jiang Hezhen (Anna Kong Mei), Xu Baoqian, Deng Yuzhi (Cora Deng), Cai Kuei, and (Mrs.) Cheng Cheng-yi. Expatriate colleagues in writing during these years included Luella Miner, Sarah Goodrich, Ella C Shaw, Kate L. Ogborn, Ella J. Newton, Mildred Cable, Francesca French, Jane Shaw Ward and Irma Highbaugh.

Amongst those who were widely recognized for their leadership and writing in these and subsequent decades the following must be mentioned:

Cheng Guanyi (Ruth Cheng), sister of Cheng Jingyi (see 5.1.9), was a graduate of North China Union College and active in the *Shengming she* (Life Fellowship). She wrote especially on women's education as the means to both reform in the church (including women ministers), and to develop a free society. Using many incidents in the gospels, she particularly stressed Jesus' revolutionary attitude to women in all situations.

Deng Yuzhi (Cora Deng) was student secretary, industrial secretary and then general secretary of the YWCA with particular concerns for industrial and mass education. In these she collaborated with communist cadres and later became an important national leader for women following the revolution.

Ding Shujing, General Secretary of the Beijing YWCA was also a member of *Shengming she* (Life Fellowship) and wrote on both personal development and national reconstruction. She held particular concern for the masses of rural women, declared that the (human) life of Jesus is "unique in both the past and in the present, and presents a full ecclesiology when writing of women in the church.

Ida Kahn, colleague of Shi Meiyu, criticized aspects of women's revolutionary involvement and drew on the gospels in contrasting in her writing women who were more flamboyant in political activity to those who served with more subtle and womanly self-abnegation.

Shi Meiyu (Mary Stone) was a leader in the WCTU and also active in the NCC. She wrote of the means to a new self-consciousness amongst women. From her theological understanding of church and mission she also worked to integrate the participation of women in all aspects of ecumenical activity.

Wang Liming (Mrs. Herman C.E. Liu) was national president of the WCTU, and chairperson of the Shanghai Woman's Suffrage Association, advocating both political equality and marriage based on love. She also, with Ding Shujing, worked to make YWCA programs more accessible to rural women.

Selected References

Bagwell, May. "An Account of the Industrial Work of the Shanghai YWCA, 1904-29." In *A Study of the YWCA of China, 1891-1930*, 221-26. World YWCA Archives, Geneva.

Cheng Guanyi. "Funü duiyu ziyou de gongxian" (Women's contribution to freedom). *NDB* 10/11 (1922).

—. "Women and the Church." *Chinese Recorder* 53 (1922).

Deng Yuzhi (Cora Deng). "The Industrial Work of the YWCA in China." 29 Nov. 1934. *World YWCA Archives*, Geneva.

—. "The Ping Erh Yuen (A Report on the Children's Home Visited by Sociology 41, October, 1925)." *Ginling College Magazine* 12.1 (Dec. 1925).

Ding Shujing. "Fengmen de shengming" (Fullness of life). *Nüqingnian bao* (The YWCA magazine) 7-4 (May 1928).

—. "Funü zai jiaohui zhong de diwei" (The position of women in the church). *Nüqingnian bao* (The YWCA magazine) 7.2 (1928).

Drucker, Alice. "The Role of the YWCA in the Development of the Chinese Women's Movement, 1890-1927." *Social Service Review* 53.3 (1979).

Goodrich, Sara. "Woman's Christian Temperance Union." *CMYB* 7 (1916).
Haass, Lily K. "The Social and Industrial Programme of the YWCA in China." 9 May 1939. *World YWCA Archives*, Geneva.
Herman C. E. (Mrs.) (Wang Liming). "The Woman's Christian Temperance Union." *CMYB* 11 (1923).
Kahn, Ida. *An Amazon in Cathay*. Boston: Women's Foreign Missionary Society, 1912.
—. "The Place of Chinese Christian Women in the Development of China." *CR* (1919).
Ogborn, Kate L. "A Self-Propagating Church, the Goal of all Mission Work." *CR* 45 (1914).
Shi Meiyu. "What Chinese Women have Done and are Doing." *Chinese Yearbook* 5 (1914).
—. "Zhongguo xianjin funü jiaoyu shiye zhi jinbu" (Progress in progressive education for Chinese women). *Nianjin* 1 (1914).
Wang Liming. *Zhongguo funü yundong* (Chinese Women's Movement). Shanghai: Commercial Press, 1934.
—. "Funü wenti" (Women's issues). *Jiezhi yuekan* 5.10 (1926).
Xie Wanying. (Christian poetry). *Shengming* 1.8, 2.1, 2.2 (1921).

4.10 Periodicals and Booklets

Christian presses had been established early in the century, following Morrison's work in Guangzhou: Roman Catholic presses at Beijing and Hong Kong (see 2.1); Presbyterian presses at Macao (1844) and Shanghai (1860); the American Board at Guangzhou (1856) and Beijing (1868); as well as those of Methodists, Episcopalians and others later. Already by 1877, 43 books or booklets of biblical commentary, 521 books of theology, 82 catechisms and 117 books of prayer or liturgies had been published. The Christian Literature Society was formed in 1887 (formerly Society for Diffusion of Christian and General Knowledge) and in 1915 the Christian Publishers' Association followed. The YMCA (from 1885), the WCTU (from 1886), the YWCA (from 1890) and the Student Volunteer Movement (from 1910), were all active in publication, as was the National Christian Council and its forerunners (from 1877). Many articles and statements are only accessible in the archives of ecumenical and mission associations (see 1.1 above). But by the 1920s, books and booklets of all kinds were being published and of these the more contextual writings have been outlined above. Others such as the *New Collection of Tracts for the Times* (CLS, 1890s) are yet to be fully studied.

Often more valuable as vehicles of contextual reflection were the many periodicals published regularly from the 1830s until the 1920s. The more important of these periodicals for research, include:

The Chinese Recorder (1867-1941. Formerly *The Chinese Repository* 1831. Index 1986); *Wanguo Gongbao* (Globe Magazine, A Review of the Times - from 1874. Formerly *Chiao-hui Shinpao*); *Christian Literature Society for China Annual Report*, (1887-1947); *T'ung Wen Pao (Christian Intelligencer* - from 1902); *Ta T'ung Pao* (Chinese Weekly - from 1904); *China Christian Year Book* (CCYB - 1925. Formerly *The China Mission Year Book, CMYB,* 1910-1925); *Wenshe yuekan* (Literature Monthly - 1924-1928); *The Bulletin of the National Christian Council* (1922-1937); along with *Women's Work in the Far East; Ginling College Magazine; Nüduobao* (The Woman's Messenger); *Nüqingnian bao* (The YWCA magazine); and *Shengming* (Life Magazine). (See also *Missionary Periodicals from the China Mainland*, University Publications of America, 35 microfilm reels, Greenwood Press. - mainly Protestant periodicals 1900-1949)

The concerns most often reflected upon in this period included movements towards an indigenous Church, Jesus Christ in Chinese context, wholistic evangelism, Chinese culture and tradition, excessive control by missionaries, the training of ministers and lay people, the contribution of women, social, political and labor reform, the development of Christian literature, family life, general education and temperance.

Selected References

Chen Xun. "Shengjing wenxue yu Jidujiao wenzijie de zeren" (Biblical literature and the responsibility of Christian literary circles). *Wenshe Monthly* 1.3 (1925).

Cheng Xiangfan. "Wo duiyu Jidujiao wenzi shiye zhi yijian" (My opinion of Christian literature). *Wenshe Monthly* 1.2 (1925).

Ho, Herbert Hoi-Lap (He Kaili). "Zhonghua Jidujiao wenshe yu bense shenxue zhuzuo" (The National Christian Literature

Association and the indigenous Chinese literature movement). *Journal of China Graduate School of Theology* 5 (July 1988).

Jian Zhe. "Zhongguo Jidujiao wenzi shiye fanlun" (A general discourse on Christian literature). *Wenshe Monthly* 1.4 (1926).

Lodwick, Kathleen, ed. *Chinese Recorder Index: A Guide to Missions in Asia, 1867-1941*. Wilmington, DE: Scholarly Resources, 1986.

Rawski, Evelyn. *Education and Popular Literacy in Ch'ing China*. Ann Arbor: University of Michigan Press, 1978.

Shen Sizhuang (J. Wesley Shen). "National Christian Literature Association." *China Christian Year Book* 15 (1928).

Wang, Peter Chen-main (Wang Chengmian). *Wenshe de shengshuai - er ling niandai Jidujiao bensehua zhi ge'an yanjiu* (The rise and fall of the Wenshe - a case study of indigenization of Christianity in China in the 1920s). Taibei: Yuzhouguang, 1993.

Whitefield, Brent. "Reforming China: the Christian Literature Society for China, 1887-1911." *CWC Position Paper 120*. Cambridge: Currents of World Christianity, 2000.

Zhao Zichen (T.C. Chao). "Wo duiyu Zhonghua Jidujiao wenzi wenti de ganxiang" (My impression of Chinese Christian literature). *WS* 1.1 (Oct 1925).

Wang Zhixin. "Zhongguo Jidujiao wenzi shiye zhi guoqu xianzai yu weilai" (Past, present and future of Chinese Christian publications). *WS* 1.8 (1926).

4.11 Supplementary Bibliography III

Arkhangelov, S.A. *Nashi Zagranichnye Missii* (Nashi Zagranichnye Missions). St Peterburg: P.P. Soikina, 1899.

Band, Edward *Working His Purpose Out: The History of the English Presbyterian Mission, 1847-1947*. London: Presbyterian Church of England, 1948.

Boorman, Howard L., ed. *Biographical Dictionary of Republican China*. Vol. 2. New York: Columbia University Press, 1967-79.

Brown, Margaret H. *MacGillivray of Shanghai: The Life of Donald MacGillivray*. Toronto: Ryerson Press, 1968.

Cai Sujuan. *Anshi zhi hou* (Queen of the dark chamber). Hong Kong: Bellman House, 1982.

Chappell, E. B., ed. *Heroes of Faith in China*. Nashville: Publishing House of the MECS, 1915.

Chu, Mrs. T.C. (Hu Binxia). *Zhongguo nüqingnianhui xiaoshi* (A short history of the Chinese YWCA). n.p., 1923.

Cohen, Paul A. "Christian Missions and Their Impact to 1900?" In John K. Fairbank, ed., *The Cambridge History of China. Vol. 10, Late Ch'ing 1800-1911.* Cambridge, Eng.: Cambridge University Press, 1978, 543-590.

Ding Shujing. "Beijing Jidujiao nüqingnianhui" (The Beijing YWCA). *Nianjin* 5 (1918).

Endicott, Stephen *James G, Endicott: Rebel Out of China.* Toronto: University of Toronto Press, 1980.

Freytag, Mirjam. *Frauenmission in China: die interkulturelle undpedagogische Bedeutung der Missionarinnen untersucht anhand ihrer Berichte von 1900 bis 1930.* Ann Hasseltine Judson Collection of Mission Studies. Munster; New York: Waxmann, c1994

Foster, John. *The Chinese Church in Action.* London: Cargate Press, 1933.

Garrett, Shirley S. *Social Reformers in Urban China: The Chinese YMCA, 1895-1926.* Cambridge, MA: Harvard University Press, 1970.

Hummel, Arthur, ed. *Eminent Chinese of the Ch'ing Period, 1644-1912.* 2 vols. Washington, DC: Government Printing Office, 1943.

Kesson, John *The Cross and the Dragon, or the Fortunes of Christianity in China.* London, Smith, Elder, 1854.

Li Zhigang. *Zhongguo funu yundong* (The Chinese women's movement). Shanghai: Commercial Press, 1934.

John, Griffith. *The Christian Three Character Classic.* n.p.: Korean religious Tract Society, 1908.

Lin Chih-p'ing. *Jidujiao yu Zhongguo jindahua lunji.* Taipei: Taiwan shangwu yinshuguan, 1970. (about Robert Morrison, W.A.P. Martin).

Littell-Lamb, Elizabeth. "To Seek a Place in the Social Revolution: Christian Women's Institutions; the Chinese Women's Movement, and Feminist Objectives in Republican China 1911-1949." Ph.D. diss., Carnegie Mellon University, 2000.

Lu Shiqiang *Zhongguo guanshen fanjiao de yuanyin, 1860-1874* (The causes of the anti-Christian movement by Chinese officials and gentry, 1860-74). Taibei: Institute of Modern History, Academia Sinica, 1966.

Martin, W.A.P. *The Awakening of China.* New York: Doubleday, 1907.

Miner, Louella. "Jidujiao nüzi jiaoyu" (Christian women's education). *Nianjian* 1 (1914).

Oi Ki Ling *The Changing Role of the British Protestant Missionaries in China, 1945-1952.* Fairleigh Dickinson University Press, 1999.

Records of the General Conference of the Protestant Missionaries of China, Held at Shanghai, May 10-24, 1877. Shanghai: American Presbyterian Mission Press, 1878.

Records of the General Conference of the Protestant Missionaries of China, Held at Shanghai, `May 7-20, 1890. Shanghai: American Presbyterian Mission Press, 1890.

Soothill, William. *The Analects of Confucius.* New York: Dover Publications, 1995 (Yokohama, 1910).

—. *The Lotus of the Wonderful Law; or, The Lotus Gospel, Saddharma pundarika sutra, Miao-fa lien hua ching.* Oxford: Clarendon press, 1930.

Wang Liming. "The Woman's Christian Temperance Union." *CMYB* II (1923).

Wang, Zhengting. *Some questions answered on the Chinese-Japanese situation.* N.p.: n.p., 1937.

Ward, Jane Shaw. *Shanghai Sketches.* New York: Woman's Press, 1917.

Ying Yuandao. "Baiyu nianlai zai Hua Xi jiaoshi duiyu Jidujiao wenzi shiye zhi gongxian" (Western missionary contributions to Christian literature in China in the last hundred some years). *Wenshe Monthly* 1.4 (1926).

Yung Wing. *My Life in China and America.* New York: Arno Press, 1978.

Zeng Baosun. "The Chinese Woman Past and Present." In *Symposium on Chinese Culture,* edited by Sophia H. Chen. Shanghai: China Institute of Pacific Relations, 1931.

5 Contextualization in the Chinese Protestant Church: Fully Christian and Fully Chinese (1915-)

5.1 May Fourth: First Generation

A quite new development of Chinese Protestant theology by Chinese theologians began in the May Fourth era, or New Culture Movement (ca. 1915-1920), a time of political, intellectual, and social ferment, as China struggled to define its modern political and cultural identity amid the ruins of the old order. Wu Leichuan (5.1.4.) ascribed this relatively late flowering to the failure of the missionaries to take Chinese culture seriously. T.C. Chao (5.1.3.) blamed it on an over-emphasis in the church on education, medical work, publishing, and relief activities, as a result of which, "the weakest aspect of Christianity became the church itself, and the weakest aspect of the church was its doctrinal theology" (1950).

This generation was nurtured in traditional Chinese culture: many had classical educations, were proficient in the literary language, and were molded by traditional thinking and character. At the same time, many were profoundly influenced by the awakening of democratic consciousness and the spirit of inquiry that were hallmarks of the New Culture Movement. This new mindset led Christian intellectuals to question the western expression of their faith and the western domination of their churches. The rising tide of nationalism and the desire for self-determination that grew through the 1920s and 30s led to a new political consciousness among Christians that deplored the identification of western mission efforts with imperialism and colonialism. The spiritual and ethical dilemma they faced, the choice between loyalty to Christ and filiality to culture (and later loyalty to the new nation), has in a real sense shaped the Chinese pilgrimage of Christian theology throughout the 20th century.

Broadly, there were two kinds of issues for the contextualization of theology: 1) the relationship with traditional culture: Was Christianity against Chinese culture? Could it complement and strengthen traditional culture? Could it be a means to modernizing culture? and 2) the Christian response to China's political, social and economic crises: Did Christianity have a contribution to make to social reformation and national salvation, as the survival of China as a nation in the face of Japanese aggression was termed at the time?

Among intellectuals generally, involved in the intellectual ferment of imported Japanese and western thinking and its implications for China that was the New Culture Movement in the early to mid-1920s, the idea of reforming the society through reform of the individual appealed as a path to China's "national salvation." Writers such as Lu Xun, the great luminary of modern Chinese letters, and political theorists like Chen Duxiu, one of the founders of the Chinese Communist Party, both espoused the idea. Chen wrote a famous essay praising the noble and lofty personality of Christ - while discounting the need for the religion that bore his name - and other prominent writers and thinkers were attracted by the figure of Christ and the ethical model of self-sacrificing service Christ represented.

Many Christian thinkers, too, identified with the ideals of the New Culture Movement. The person of Jesus Christ and his saving grace became an important focus for theological reflection, one which, in conjunction with Chinese humanism, had the potential to break through the confines of western theology, as well as to transcend the borders between Christian and non-Christian in the quest for personal regeneration and social construction. Christian faith and theology, as developed in the Chinese context, were marked by a unity of faith, knowledge, and action, as opposed to the Western path of faith proved by knowledge, and by a concern for "external expression" of one's "inner formation" - the ethical foundation of service.

Selected References

Chen Duxiu. *Jidijiao yu Zhongguo ren* (Christianity and the Chinese people). *New Youth* (Xin qingnian), 7:3 (1920).

Duan Qi. *A Draft History of the Indigenization of Christianity in China* (in Chinese). Unpub. Ms.

Fan Bihui. "Zhongguo lunli de wenhua yu Jidujiao" (Chinese ethical culture and Christianity). *Youth Advance* 84 (1925).

Lam Wing-hung. *Zhonghua shenxue wushi nian: 1900-1949* (Fifty years of Chinese theology: 1900-1949). Hong Kong: China Alliance Press, 1998. Extensive bibliography of works in Chinese and English.

Wang Weifan. "The Pattern and Pilgrimage of Chinese Theology." *CTR*:1 990.

—, and Ji Fengwen. "Forty Years of Chinese Christianity." *CTR*: 8 (1993).

Wang Zhixin. "Zhongguo bense jiaohui de taolun" (Discussion on an indigenous Chinese Church). *Youth Advance* 79 (1925).

Whyte, Bob. *Unfinished Encounter: China and Christianity*. London: Collins/Fount Paperbacks, 1988.

Ying Fuk-tsang. *Chinese Christians and Cultural Accommodation (1860-1911)*(in Chinese). Hong Kong: Alliance Bible Seminary, 1995.

—. *Christian Faith and National Salvation: Case Studies from the early 20th century* (in Chinese). Hong Kong: Alliance Bible Seminary, 1997.

Yui, David Z.T. "The Present Situation in China and its Significance to the Christian forces in China and throughout the World." In *Report of the Jerusalem meeting of the International Missionary Council, March 24th-April 8th, 1928*. VIII. London: Oxford University Press, 1928. 75 ff.

5.1.1. Contextual writings

The publication of the long-awaited (Mandarin) Union Version (UV) of the Bible in the vernacular in 1919 was a groundbreaking event in Christian circles. The translation, representing years of labor by Chinese and western missionary translators, had considerable impact in intellectual circles outside the church as well. Part of the May Fourth heritage was a bold step in the creation of a modern vernacular literary language that would reflect people's everyday speech. The UV was hailed as a model for written vernacular by some of the best secular writers of the day, including Zhou Zuoren, the brother of Lu Xun (see above) and Guo Moro, poet and essayist. The role of the Chinese translators, referred to as "assistants" and seldom mentioned by name, deserves to be better known and studied for the entire history of Chinese Bible translation (see Zetsche below).

The secular *New Youth* magazine, begun in 1915 by Chen Duxiu, was published in the vernacular. Several Christian publications followed suit, most notably *Shengming* (Life), launched in 1919, which was published in various permutations until 1937. *Shengming* emerged from a forum of western missionaries and Chinese faculty at Yenching (Yanjing) University, known initially as the Peking Apologetic Group (see 5.1.2 below). Its board was interdenominational and international, and included men and women: Ruth Cheng Guanyi for example, the sister of Cheng Jingyi (5.1.9.), was a member. Other Chinese members of the editorial staff included T.C. Chao, Cheng Jingyi, T.T. Lew, P.C. Hsu, Y.T. Wu, L.C. Wu and Z.T. Yui. Among others contributing contextual writings were Andrew Tsu Yuyue of St John's University; Marcus Cheng Chonggui of Chungking (Chongqing)

Theological seminary; Koo Tsezung (see also p.237 below); (Ms) Wu Yifang of Ginling (Jinling) College, Nanjing; and Li Chuwen of the YMCA.

Shengming provided a link between intellectuals inside and outside the church, carrying articles from both, as well as articles by concerned western missionaries, and included translations, fiction, poetry, and prayers. T.C. Chao (5.1.3.) was a frequent contributor. The early Christian poetry, heavily based on biblical models, of famed woman poet Xie Wanying (Bing Xin), then a student at Yenching Women's College, was published in its pages. Other publications of the time include:

Zhenli (Truth), founded in 1923 by L.C. Wu (Wu Leichuan), with Y.T. Wu, Bao Guanglin, Hu Xuecheng, Chen Guoliang and others in reaction to the foreign involvement in *Life*, was similar in content. But it included only Chinese among its editors and contributors. In 1926, the two merged, becoming *Truth and Life*.

Publications of the *Zhonghua Jidijiao wenshe* (National Christian Literature Association of China). The Wenshe was formed in 1924 jointly by missionaries and some Chinese Christian leaders for the express purpose of fostering indigenous literary talent to produce a Chinese Christian literature rooted in and responsive to China's needs. Lack of such a literature in Chinese hindered effective evangelization. The Wenshe published a monthly (*Wenshe*), pamphlets, and books, and planned a new translation of the Bible with modern punctuation by a well-known secular scholar. *Wenshe* became an influential Christian journal, outspoken on issues of indigenization. This offended some western missionaries and led to the mainly overseas-financed publication being forced to shut down in 1928. The organization disbanded in 1930. (See also 4.10 above).

Selected References

    Chen Xun. "Shengjing wenxue yu jidujiao wenzijie de zeren" (Biblical literature and the responsibility of Christian literary circles). *Wenshe Monthly* 1.3 (1925).

    Duan Qi. *A Draft History of the Indigenization of Christianity in China* (in Chinese). Unpub. Ms.

Ho, Herbert Hoi-Lap. "Zhonghua jidujiao wenshe yu bense shenxue zhuzuo" (The National Christian Literature Association and the indigenous Chinese literature movement). *CGST Journal*, 5 (1988).

Ling, Samuel D. "The Other May Fourth Movement: The 'Chinese Christian Renaissance', 1919-1937." unpub. Ph.D. diss., Temple University, 1980.

Wang, Peter Chien-Main. "Contextualizing Protestant Publishing in China: The Wenshe, 1924-1928." In *Christianity in China from the Eighteenth Century to the Present*, edited by Daniel H. Bays, 292-306. Stanford, CA: Stanford University Press, 1996.

Wickeri, Janice. "The Union Version of the Bible & the New Literature in China." *The Translator, Studies in Intercultural Communication*, vol. 1, no. 2 (1995).

Yamamoto, Sumiko. *History of Protestantism in China: The Indigenization of Christianity*. Tokyo: Toho Gakkai, 2000.

Zetzsche, Jost Oliver. *The Bible in China: The History of the Union Version or The Culmination of Protestant Missionary Bible Translation in China*. Monumenta Serica Monograph Series XLV. Nettetal: Steyler Verlag, 1999.

5.1.2. The Anti-Christian Movement and the Christian Apologetic

The critique of Christianity gained momentum in the early 1920s. Christian thinkers faced challenges from traditional culture as well as from non-Christian Chinese intellectuals armed with imported western critiques of Christianity as anachronistic and unscientific. Imported western ideas, characterized in the press as Mr. Science and Mr. Democracy, were seen as evidence that Christianity had been superseded on its own cultural ground. With increased organization of students and workers by the nationalist Kuomintang (KMT) and the newly formed (1921) Chinese Communist Party, the most serious challenges were directed at the use of Christianity as a western imperialist tool and a cultural aggressor. The anti-Christian movement was sparked by the April 1922 meeting at Qinghua (Tsinghua) University in Beijing of the WSCF, its first meeting in Asia. This particular anti-Christian activity was part of a broader 'anti-religion' climate of opinion and activity. The movement peaked and ebbed in several stages during the years

1922-1927, focusing especially on Christian-run schools and on the unequal treaties, and resulted in curtailed missionary influence, particularly in the area of primary and secondary school education.

The Peking Apologetic Group was formed to present and defend the faith to the broader non-Christian public, and to intellectual circles in particular (See also 5.1.5). The pages of its journal, *Life* (5.1.1.) addressed a Christian response to the anti-Christian forces, as well as involvement in social causes, and student work and educational issues. Particular emphasis was given to promoting study and discussion of Christianity, demonstrating the relevance of the Christian message for China, reinterpreting Christianity in the Chinese context and applying the latest scientific knowledge to this reinterpretation. Christian thinkers further sought a melding of Christianity and Confucian ideals, as a way of approaching a fully Chinese Christianity. Yet this could not in itself be the basis of a Chinese theology, since Confucianism and traditional culture were also under attack by progressive secular thinkers.

The anti-Christian movement may be said to have brought home to some Christian thinkers the need to critique the links between their Christian faith and western imperialism, and the necessity for an intentional Chinese Christian patriotic stance as a bridge to identification with their own people. It crystallized for Christian leaders and thinkers the weaknesses and inequalities that had come to plague the church, raised their consciousness regarding the political and social role of the church and Christianity and set them to ponder how the Christian essence might be expressed in Chinese terms. (See also 5.2.2.) The second wave of the anti-Christian movement ended in 1927, the same year as the Nationalist-Communist split and the Northern Expedition. This was a time of suffering and setbacks for missions and Chinese Christians, which functioned to push forward reforms in church organization and church-related education. Christian publications carried articles on a Christian assessment of the current situation in China, centering around the May 30th incident, the Northern Expedition and patriotism.

Selected References
See also references following 5.2.2. below.

The Anti-Christian Movement. Papers translated for the Student YM & YWCA of China. 2nd. ed. Shanghai, 1925.

Chao, T.C., trans. "Christian Renaissance in China: Statement of the Aims of the Peking Apologetic Group." *CR* (1920).

Chao, Jonathan T'ien-en. "The Chinese Indigenous Church Movement, 1919-1927: A Protestant Response to the Anti-Christian Movement in Modern China." Ph.D. diss., University of Pennsylvania, 1986.

Cohen, Paul A. *China and Christianity: The Missionary Movement and the Growth of Chinese Antiforeignism 1860-1870*, Harvard East Asian Series, 11 Cambridge, Massachusetts: Cambridge University Press, 1967.

Dan Cui. *The Cultural Contribution of British Protestant Missionaries and British-American Co-operation to China's National Development During the 1920s.* University Press of America, 1998.

Duan Guanglu. "Jidujiao yu Zhongguo wenhua" Christianity and Chinese Culture). *Youth Advance* 82 (1925.

Duan Qi. *A Draft History of the Indigenization of Christianity in China* (in Chinese). Unpub. Ms.

Fenn, William A. *Christian Higher Education in Changing China, 1880-1950.* Grand Rapids, MI: Eerdmans, 1976.

Hsu, P.C. "The Anti-Christian Movement and What I Should Do Now" (in Chinese). *Life* vol. 6, no. 5 (1926).

Jian Youwen. "Jiuguo yu Jidujiao" (National salvation and Christianity). *True Light* 24 (1925).

Lew, T.T. "How Christianity in China Can Respond to Criticisms" (in Chinese). *Life* (vol. 6, no. 2 (1925).

Lutz, Jessie G. *Chinese Politics and Christian Missions: The Anti-Christian Movements of 1920-28.* Cross Cultural Publications Crossroads Books, 1988.

Lutz, Jessie G. *China and the Christian Colleges, 1850-1950.* Ithaca: Cornell University Press, 1971.

Stauffer, Milton T. *The Christian Occupation of China.* Shanghai: China Continuation Committee, 1922.

Yamamoto, Sumiko. *History of Protestantism in China: The Indigenization of Christianity.* Tokyo: Toho Gakkai, 2000.

Yip Ka-che. *Religion, Nationalism and Chinese Students: The Anti-Christian Movement of 1922-1927.* Bellingham, WA, 1980.

Zhang Shizhang. "Zhongguo Jidujiao yu shehui zhuyi" (Chinese Christianity and socialism). *Youth Advance* 56 (1922).

5.1.3. T.C. Chao (Zhao Zichen; Chao Tze-ch'en, 1898-1979)

Chao received a classical education and graduated from Soochow (Dongwu) University in 1910. He received his B.D. and M.A. degrees from Vanderbilt University in the US, where he was influenced by western liberal theology and the ideals of the social gospel. Returning to China, he taught at Soochow University briefly and then served as professor of theology and dean of the School of Religion at Yenching (Yanjing) University for over 20 years. He was ordained an Anglican deacon and priest in Hong Kong in 1941. A man of letters and an accomplished poet in the classical style, he wrote prolifically in both Chinese and English, producing books, articles, poems, hymns and translations. He was active nationally in the National Christian Council and the national committee of the YMCA. A leading educator, he was also a church leader of international standing, widely respected in the West, and a delegate to Jerusalem in 1928; Tambaram, 1938; and Whitby, 1947. He was elected as one of the first presidents of the World Council of Churches at the Amsterdam Assembly in 1948, but resigned his presidency in 1951 in protest at the WCC statement attributing the Korean War to the North's invasion of the South, which he saw as bowing to western imperialism.

In the 1920s he emphasized the humanity of Christ and his moral excellence. Salvation depended upon moral striving, not only for the sake of the individual, but for society. Christianity would be the basis for social reconstruction in China. He wrote in *Jesus' Philosophy of Life* (1926) that "China's weakness... lies in the dejection of the Chinese personality." Christianity could aid in the reformation of individuals who would then reform society (see above). People needed to change from the inside out. Yet the church must also proclaim Christ and work for a spiritual goal beyond social service.

As a Chinese intellectual of his times and a Christian, Chao sought a synthesis of the personal gospel with the social gospel. He was early concerned with indigenization, seeking to synthesize traditional culture and the essence of western theology while creating a theology of relevance that would relate faith to China's social needs. His essay "Christianity and Chinese Culture," set out his plan for indigenization, which involved getting to the essence of Christianity by purifying it of its western accretions; "cutting away" both practices which were culturally unsuitable to China, and doctrines which Chao felt could not be squared with reason, such as the virgin birth and the resurrection of the body. Doctrines must be adjusted to the times and their context. His *Life of Jesus*, too, aimed at a re-telling for Chinese, removing what was purely "Western veneer," interpreting Jesus' death on the cross, for example in eastern terms: "to preserve virtue complete" (Yamamoto 2000).

Denominationalism, too, was an "unintelligible confusion" for Chinese. His aesthetic temperament and grounding in Confucian, Buddhist and Taoist sensibilities were expressed in a range of theological language that transcended Christianity's western roots.

Chao linked his efforts at indigenization with a concern for China's social and political ills - Christianity as a basis for national salvation and regeneration. Yet this was eventually a dead-end for Chao and others: Christianity proved unable to solve China's urgent social problems. In the 1930s he began to move away from social relevancy, inward to a more spiritual understanding of Christian fellowship. This break between his faith and social action led him back into a type of spiritual self-cultivation that has been called more Confucian than Christian.

With the end of the Sino-Japanese War and the founding of the People's Republic, Chao was a Christian delegate to the Chinese People's Political Consultative Conference (CPPCC) and a leader of the Three-Self Movement (5.4.3.). In the mid-1950s, he came under attack during the three-anti's campaign. and had to resign his positions at Yenching. In his later years, Chao suffered from a sense that his theology was a failure, and came to distance himself from the beliefs he once held. Yet he remains a pioneer in the search for an indigenous Christian theology for China, always seeking to push the church forward in this endeavor.

A critical edition of his Collected Work is in preparation in Beijing.

Selected References
Works by T.C. Chao

Jidujiao zhexue (Christian philosophy). Shanghai: CLS, 1925.

Yesu zhuan (Life of Jesus). Shanghai: Association Press, 1935; Hong Kong: CCLC, 1965, 1986.

Jidujiao jinjie (Interpretation of Christianity). Shanghai: Association Press, 1947.

Sheng Baolo zhuan (Life of St. Paul). Shanghai: Association Press, 1947.

Xiyu ji (My prison experience). Shanghai: Association Press, 1948. Chao was imprisoned by the Japanese in 1942.

Shenxue sijiang (Four talks on theology). Shanghai: Association Press, 1948.

Jidujiao jinjie (A progressive interpretation of Christianity). Shanghai, 1948.

"The Appeal of Christianity to the Chinese Mind." *CR* 49 (1918.

"Christian Renaissance in China." *CR* 51 (1920).

"Can Christianity be the Basis of Social Reconstruction in China?" *CR* 53 (1922).

"Zhongguo jiaohui de qiangdian yu ruodian" (Strengths and weaknesses of China's churches). *Life*, 3:5 (1923).

"Jidujiao yu Zhongguo wenhua" (Christianity and Chinese culture). *Truth and Life* 2 (1927).

"Fengchao zhong fenqi de zhongguo jiaohui" (The Chinese church that rises out of the storm). *Truth and Life* 2:2 (1927).

"Jidujiao yu zhengzhi" (Christianity and politics). *Truth and Life*, 2:11 (1927).

"Xin shidai xuanjiao fa de shangque" (The Debate over evangelistic methods for the new age). *Truth and Life*, 5:3 (1931).

"Christian Unity." *CR* Apr (1935.

"Christian Faith and China's Crisis." *CR* Mar (1936).

"The Message of the Cross for China." *CR* 67 (1936).

"Christianity and the National Crisis." *CR* 68 (1937).

—, R.O. Hall, and Roderick Scott. "The Christian Movement in China in a Period of National Transition: three papers prepared at the request of the Department of Social and Industrial Research for the Tambaram meeting of the International Missionary Council, 1938.

Chao, Samuel H. "The Chinese Church and Theology: A Discussion." *The East Asia Journal of Theology* 2:1 (1984). On Chao's essay "The Possibility of Development of Christian Theology in China for the Next Forty Years."

Duan Qi. *A Draft History of the Indigenization of Christianity in China* (in Chinese). Unpub. Ms.

Gluer, Winfried. *Christliche Theologie in China: T.C. Chao 1918-1956*. Missionswissenschaftliche Forschungen, V 13, Gutersloher Verlagshaus Gerd Mohn, Gutersloh, 1979. Chinese translation by Deng Zhaoming (Joe Dunn). Hong Kong: CCLC, 1998.

Lam Wing-hung. *The Life and Thought of Chao Tze-ch'en*. Hong Kong: China Graduate School of Theology, 1994.

Ng Lee-ming. "An Evaluation of T.C. Chao's Thought." *Ching Feng*, vol. 14, nos. 1&2 (1971).

—. "A Bibliography of T.C. Chao and Y.T. Wu." *Ching Feng*, vol. 16, nos. 3&4 (1973).

Whyte, Bob. *Unfinished Encounter: China and Christianity*. London: Collins/Fount Paperbacks, 1988.

Wickeri, Philip L. *Seeking the Common Ground: Protestant Christianity, the Three-Self Movement, and China's United Front*. Maryknoll, NY: Orbis Books, 1988.

Wan Sze-Kar. "The Emerging Hermeneutics of the Chinese Church: Debate between Wu, Leichuan and T.C. Chao and the Chinese Christian *Problematik*." In *The Bible in China: The Literary and Intellectual Impact,* edited by Irene Eber, Sze-Kar Wan, and Knut Wolf, 351-382. Monumenta Serica Monograph Series XLIII. Nettetal: Steyler Verlag, 1999.

Yamamoto, Sumiko. "T.C. Chao's Life of Jesus." In *History of Protestantism in China: The Indigenization of Christianity* by Yamamoto Sumiko, 237-262. Tokyo: Toho Gakkai, 2000.

Zi Zhu. "The Transformation of a Chinese Theologian: T.C. Chao's Journey from Humanism to Theocentrism." *CTR: 1991*.

5.1.4. L.C. Wu (Wu Leichuan, 1870-1944)

In 1898 Wu gained his *juren* and *jinshi* degrees under the imperial examination system and became a member of the Hanlin Academy of scholars. Following the 1911 revolution, he became chief secretary of education in Beijing, a post he held from 1912-1925. He began teaching at Yenching University in 1924, becoming a full-time professor there in 1926, and later vice-chancellor. Wu was a leading proponent of indigenization in the 1920s, and is representative of those who saw Christianity as a complement to Confucianism, making up for its weaknesses. In this period he believed Christianity would bring new strength to traditional culture and help preserve its value.

In his "Character - Jesus and Confucius" (Life Quarterly 5.2, 1924), he compared the two religious leaders, concluding that Christianity and Confucianism would meld into a harmonious whole in future: their common points - harmony and reconciliation. From Confucianism, he appropriated the concept of *ren* or humanheartedness, identifying it with the character of the Holy Spirit. *Ren* must be allowed to permeate the world. His aim was not so much to preserve the tradition as to seek a path for China's future. One searches for personal salvation and truth for the sake of society, he affirmed. In the mid-1930s, he felt it was no longer necessary for Christianity to identify itself with traditional culture, because Chinese culture itself was searching for a new direction. He eventually saw Jesus as a political leader whose aim was the reform of society; who when unsuccessful in this, decided to begin with the reformation of human hearts.

Selected References
Works by Wu Leichuan

> *Jidujiao yu Zhongguo wenhua* (Christianity and Chinese culture). Shanghai: Association Press, 1936.
> "The Chinese Renaissance." *CR* 51 (July 1920).
> "Jidujiao yu rujiao" (Christianity and Confucianism). *Truth Weekly* 1: 43 (1923).
> "Jidujiao zhi shengling yu rujiao zhi ren" (The Holy Spirit in Christianity and the Confucian concept of *ren*). *Life Quarterly* 6: 5 (1926).
> "Jidujiao yu geming" (Christianity and revolution). *Truth and Life Journal* 5: 4 (1931).
> "Jidutu ruhe shixing jiuguo de gongzuo" (What Christians can do in the work of national salvation). *Truth and Life Journal* 6: 5 (1932).
> "Jidujiao duiyu Zhonghua minzu fuxing neng you shenma gongxian?" (What contribution can Christianity make to the

regeneration of the Chinese people?). *Truth and Life Journal* 9: 2 (1935).

"Jidujiao yu shehui gaizao" (Christian faith and social reform). In *Jidujiao yu xin Zhongguo* (Christianity and new China), edited by Y.T. Wu, vol 2: 151-160. 2 vols. Shanghai: Association Press, 1940.

Chan Sin-Jan. *Wu Lei-chuan: A Confucian-Christian in Republican China*. New York: Peter Lang, 1995.

Duan Qi. *A Draft History of the Indigenization of Christianity in China* (in Chinese). Unpub. Ms.

Ng Lee-ming. "Christianity and Social Change in China." 1981.

West, Philip. "Christianity and Nationalism: the Career of Wu Leich'uan at Yenching University." In *The Missionary Enterprise in China and America*, edited by John K. Fairbank, 226-246. Cambridge, MA: Harvard University Press, 1974.

Wan Sze-Kar. "The Emerging Hermeneutics of the Chinese Church."

Yamamoto, Sumiko. "L.C. Wu's *Christianity and Chinese Culture*." In *History of Protestantism in China: The Indigenization of Christianity* by Yamamoto Sumiko, 263-300. Tokyo: Toho Gakkai, 2000.

5.1.5. P.C. Hsu (Hsu Pao-ch'ien; Xu Baoqian) (1892-1944)

Hsu became a Christian in 1913 while studying at the Beijing Customs College and in 1915 he became a student secretary with the YMCA. In 1921 he went to Union Theological Seminary in New York to study theology and later studied philosophy at Columbia University. Returning to China in 1924, he served as executive secretary of the Christian School Association and taught philosophy at Yenching University. In 1919, Hsu thought of publishing a quarterly as a Christian response and counterbalance to the New Culture Movement. The group that formed, consisting of missionary educators and Chinese Christians at Yenching University, was originally known as the Peking Apologetic Group (see 5.1.2.), which met informally each month to discuss issues of common interest. Hsu became co-editor of the *Shengming* (Life), and the name of the group was later changed to the Life Fellowship.

Hsu, who became secretary of the Fellowship of Reconciliation in China, felt that the Christian way to achieve change must be founded on love and reconciliation. In the 1930s, he resigned from teaching to accept the position of general secretary of the Lichwan (Lichuan) Project, a rural reconstruction project in Jiangxi province that was one of the most significant church-related projects of the time. Though the project ultimately failed, Hsu saw in rural reconstruction the type of service he espoused as a means to national salvation.

Like many theologians and church leaders of his generation, Hsu believed that China needed a regeneration of the Chinese people themselves. In Christianity he found a more profound doctrine than Confucianism, but felt it was unnecessary to abandon Confucianism altogether. One could be true to the spirit of both. The essence of Christianity for Hsu was Christ's life and service, which was an approach to solving China's ills.

Selected References
Works by P.C. Hsu
> *Ethical Realism in Neo-Confucian Thought.* Beiping: Yenching University Press, 1933.
> "Xin sichao yu Jidujiao" (The New Thought Movement and Christianity). *Life* 1: 2 (1920).
> "Jinggao jinzhi tichang guojia zhuyi zhe" (A caution to those promoting nationalism today)." *Truth and Life* 5: 4 (1925): 1-3.
> —, ed. "The Future of Christianity in China." *Truth and Life* 2.3, Special English Number (February 1927).
> "Christianity and Politics." *Wenshe Monthly* 3: 2 (1927).
> "Christian Rural Reconstruction in China." *China Christian Yearbook* 20 (1936-1937).
> Duan Qi. *A Draft History of the Indigenization of Christianity in China* (in Chinese). Unpub. Ms.
> Ling, Samuel D. "The Other May Fourth Movement: The Chinese Christian Renaissance, 1919-1937." Unpub. Ph.D. diss., Temple University, 1980.
> Ng Lee-ming. "Hsu Po Ch'ien-A Christian Model of Unification of Knowledge and Practice." *Ching Feng* XXI: 1 (1978).

5.1.6. Jia Yuming (1879-1964)

As a young man in Shandong, Jia joined the Presbyterian Church. Ordained in 1904, he served local churches for 12 years. He then worked in seminaries and theological schools, including Jinling Women's Seminary in Nanjing, where he was principal for seven years. He later established the Lingxue Yuan, or Spiritual Study Academy. In 1936 he moved to the newly-established China Theological Seminary, also in Nanjing, following it to western China during the war years, and back again to Shanghai after 1945. As an educator, his goal was to lay down a firm theological foundation for the Chinese Church and to address the 'anti-religion' movement.

His *Shendao xue* (The Study of Theology), the first volume of systematic theology to be published in China, appeared in 1921. It was a major work of conservative theology, modeled on that of American theologian Augustus H. Strong. The book proved popular and went through six editions prior to the Sino-Japanese War. Jia, however, took a narrower view of inerrancy than Strong and found his view of culture too optimistic. In Jia's understanding, redemption was of paramount importance, culture and social reform a far second: Jia stated that the liberals were preaching another gospel.

As an evangelical hermeneutical scholar, Jia maintained that the whole Bible was a revealed text, inerrant, a standard for believers' faith and action. The Bible was the complete way of salvation, the treasury of truth, a portrait of life and the path to God's presence. Yet his hermeneutics was eclectic, making use of a variety of approaches to biblical interpretation. He emphasized prayer, a life of commitment and faith, and witnessing to the Lord as true and living God. For him, knowledge and action were integrated:

"What I believe is what I know; what I know is what I believe and also what I do. With actual experience I will know what I believe and do what I know....But the good works or actions advocated by Christian faith are not merely ethical virtues. They are the very sacred fruits of a life saturated by the truth, filled with the Holy Spirit and radiating the fragrance of Jesus Christ." His was a pre-critical approach which continues to be influential among a large section of Chinese Christians in China and overseas.

In 1948, Jia was a delegate to the World Evangelical Conference held in the Netherlands, and was elected one of its vice-presidents. At first wary of the Three-Self Movement, he later supported it and was elected a vice-chair in 1954. Jia was much loved as a pastor and exerted a wide and lasting influence in the Chinese Church through his pastoral work. His work includes over 20 volumes of biblical exegesis and theology. He was also a prolific hymn writer and edited four hymnals. Jia lived all his life in a church and seminary environment, training a great number of evangelists. He also wrote prolifically in the field of theology and hermeneutics, especially commentaries.

Selected References
Works by Jia Yuming
> *52 lingchen jiangti* (52 topics in spirituality). Nanjing: Lingguang baoshe, 1930; Hong Kong: Chenxing press, 1986.
> *Wanquan jiufa* (Total salvation). 3rd edition. Hong Kong, 1987.
> *Loma xin jiangyi* (A new discourse on Romans). 4th ed. Hong Kong: Chenxing Press, 1986.
> *Yuehan fuyin jiangyi* (A discourse on John). New ed. Hong Kong: Xuandao Press, 1967.
> *Shengjing yaoyi* (The essential meaning of the Bible).
> *Shengjing yanjiu rumen* (Primer of biblical research).
> Kwok Wai-luen. "Spiritualization and Interpretation. A Study on Jia Yuming's Hermeneutics." *Jian Dao* 7 (1997).
> Zhao Qiusheng. "The Old Testament Commentaries of Rev. Jia Yuming." *CTR* 9 (1994).

5.1.7. N.Z. Zia (Xie Fuya, 1892-1991) (see Hong Kong 3.2.2.)

5.1.8. Y.T. Wu (Wu Yaozong, 1893-1979)
Y.T. Wu studied at the Customs College in Beijing and worked seven years in various customs offices including that in his native Guangzhou. He became a Christian in 1918, as a result of personal encounter with the personality of Jesus while reading the Sermon on the Mount and participation in a Sherwood Eddy rally. He was baptized in Beijing in 1920. Wu was early on concerned with the concrete problems of Chinese society and the fate of the nation. In the personality of Jesus and the ethical teachings of the Sermon on the Mount, he found a way to understand the meaning of life and action.

In 1920, Wu joined the YMCA and became involved in student work. He was attracted to the ideas of the New Culture Movement, and like other Christian intellectuals of his generation, saw the role of Christianity in terms of a spiritual basis for the regeneration of China. This also made him an indigenizer, seeking to bring Christianity more in line with Chinese culture. In 1923, he went to study in the US at Union Theological Seminary and Columbia University, receiving an M.A. in 1927. He was very much influenced during this period by the work of Harry Ward, Reinhold Niebuhr, John Dewey and William James.

Returning to Shanghai he became editor-in-chief of the YMCA's Association Press and remained involved in publication work for most of his career. He later became editor of the church monthly *Tian Feng*, though he had to resign following the uproar over his article, "The Present Day Tragedy of Christianity in China" (1947), in which he included a strong attack on foreign missions as part of his social and political critique of Christianity and its relationship to imperialism and capitalism.

Wu's theology was oriented toward humanism and this-worldliness. His was a kind of "political theology," the core of which was Christian materialism. In the early 1930s, he was an advocate of the social gospel, reconciliation and pacifism, at one time a member of the Fellowship of Reconciliation. But the Sino-Japanese War changed his thinking on the necessity for violence under certain circumstances. He moved from western approaches of reconciliation and the social gospel to become a socialist Christian.

Wu believed that God is "truth," and that salvation is a matter for society, and not solely an individual matter. Heaven is an ideal society and can be realized on earth. Like similar thinkers of the early 20th century in China, both in and outside the church, he focused on Christ's personality in the conviction that a new humanity could be created on this model. While emphasizing the role of harmonious human relationships, he also stressed the importance of a close human relationship to God. In this regard, prayer is important in Christian life: "Prayer is harmony, light, and strength." In the 1940s, he grew increasingly outspoken on the political corruption and moral decadence of the Chinese society of his day and looked for Christianity to play an active part in its reform.

Perhaps his best-known work is *No One Has Seen God,* a popular book that went through five printings from 1943 to 1948. In articles he affirmed that God, as the "objective truth of the universe" finds "first and only complete expression" in Christ; as truth, love, justice, freedom, which are historical realities to be realised in concrete situations. Salvation, by definition, cannot be limited to personal salvation, for it is salvation from selfishness.

A founder of the Three-Self Reform Movement, he was active in it from 1949-1966, serving two terms as its first chair and contributing immeasurably to the reform and building up of the Chinese Church. He published many articles in *Tian Feng* during this period and was very active politically, as a delegate to the National People's Congress and a member of its Standing Committee.

In September 1950, Wu drafted the text of the "Christian Manifesto", calling upon Christian groups and believers to rid themselves and the church of imperialist influences and to foster patriotism, moving toward the three-self goal of self-government, self-propagation, and self-support. Wu's pioneering thinking on the accommodation between Christianity and socialism in China helped to ensure the continued existence of the church and provided it with a social and political frame of reference as it found its way in post-1949 China.

"Christianity must learn that the present period is one of liberation for the people, the collapse of the old system, a time when the old dead Christianity must doff its shroud and come forth arrayed in new garments. It must learn that it is no longer the sole distributor of the panacea for the pains of the world. On the contrary, God has taken the key to the salvation of mankind from its hand and given it to another. In a word, Christianity must come to a new thorough understanding of itself, discarding the dead body and entering into new life... ("The Reformation of Christianity," 1950).

Wu became for many a symbol of Christian accommodation with the new government after 1949, in both the positive and negative senses.

Selected References

Works by Y.T. Wu

—, ed. *Wo suo renshi de Yesu* (The Jesus I know). Shanghai: Association Press, 1929.
Shehui Fuyin (The social gospel). Shanghai: Association Press, 1934.
Meiyou ren kanjianguo shangdi (No one has seen God). Shanghai: Association Press, 1943.
Heian yu Guangming (Darkness and light). Shanghai: Association Press, 1949.
Talks on Christianity. Shanghai: Association Press, 1950.
Jidujiao gexin yundong xuexi shouce (A study manual of the Christian Reform Movement). Shanghai: Association Press, 1952.
"Zongjiao jingyan tan" (My Personal Religious Experience). *Life Quarterly* (1923).
"Confucius and Christ: A Personal Experience." *Student World* 18 (1925).
"The Task of the Chinese Student Christian Movement." *Truth and Life* (1929).
"Can Modern Man be Real Christians." *CR* 60 (1929).
"Christianity and China's Reconstruction." *CR* (1936).
"Whither the Chinese Church." *CR* 67 (1936).
"The Present Day Tragedy of Christianity in China," *Tian Feng* 116 (1948). Translated in *Documents of the Three-Self Movement*, edited by Wallace C. Merwin and Francis P. Jones. New York: NCCCUSA, 1963.
"The Reformation of Christianity." *Ta Kung Pao*, July 15, 1950.
"How to Carry Out the Christian Reform Movement." *Tian Feng* 237 (1950).
"Results of the Three-Self Reform Movement in Eight Months." *Tian Feng* 262 (1951).
"The Communist Party Has Educated Me." *Tian Feng* 271 (1951).
Chen Chi-rong. *Wu Yao-Tsung:ein Theologie im sozialistischen China 1920-1960.* Munster: Lit Verlag, 1992.
Chen, Zemin. "Y.T. Wu: A Prophetic Theologian." *CTR* 10 (1995).

Leung Ka-lun. *Y.T. Wu's Understanding of Christianity and its Relation to Chinese Communism*. Hong Kong: Alliance Bible Seminary, 1996.

Ng Lee-ming. "A Study of Y.T. Wu." *Ching Feng* XV: 1 (1972).

Ting, K.H. "What Can We Learn From Y.T. Wu Today?" *CTR* 1989.

——. "Forerunner Y.T. Wu." In *Love Never Ends*. Nanjing: Yilin Press, 2000.

Studies of Y.T. Wu's Life and Thought: Remembering Y.T. Wu on the 100th Anniversary of his Birth (in Chinese). Shanghai: TSPM, 1995.

Whyte, Bob. *Unfinished Encounter: China and Christianity*. London: Collins/Fount Paperbacks, 1988.

Wickeri, Philip L. *Seeking the Common Ground: Protestant Christianity, the Three-Self Movement, and China's United Front*. Maryknoll, NY: Orbis Books, 1988.

Yamamoto, Sumiko. "Y.T. Wu's *No Man Hath Seen God*." In *History of Protestantism in China: The Indigenization of Christianity* by Yamamoto Sumiko, 301-322. Tokyo: Toho Gakkai, 2000.

Xu Rulei. "A 'True Israelite'." *CTR* 1990.

5.1.9. Cheng Jingyi (Andrew C.Y. Ch'eng, 1881-1939)

Better known as a churchman than a theologian, Cheng Jingyi was very active in encouraging the development of an independent and unified Protestant Church in China. He initiated the China for Christ Movement and helped found the Chinese Home Mission Society. At the age of 22, Cheng went to England with George Owen of the LMS to work with him on a revised translation of the New Testament. The translation being finished in 1906, Cheng studied theology at Glasgow Bible Training Institute, graduating in 1908. He put off ordination until his return to China where at age 27 he was ordained pastor of Rice Market Church in Beijing, an independent church.

Cheng was active in the ecumenical movement throughout his career. As one of three Chinese delegates to the World Missionary Conference in Edinburgh, 1910 when he was in his early 20s, he stunned the gathering with a tightly-constructed 7-minute speech in which he pressed for indigenization and an end to denominationalism: "If the missionaries cannot supply this demand for leadership in the practical development of Christian unity, ... that leadership will undoubtedly arise outside the ranks of the missionaries, and perhaps even outside the ranks of the duly authorized ministers of the Christian Church in China" (Gairdner 1910). He was subsequently elected to the continuation committee of the International Missionary Council. In 1922, he chaired the National Christian Conference in Shanghai, an important gathering for the indigenization endeavour, and became head of the National Christian Council that was formed as a result.

His concern for the realization of a genuine Chinese church is reflected in his article "Discussing an Indigenous Church." He speaks of the need to adapt the church to the needs of eastern peoples and for Chinese Christians to assume responsibility for all affairs of their church. "...Like *bonsai* (dwarf potted trees) we have been carefully nurtured and kept safe from rain, frost and damage to our limbs; but we have been but objects for hobby and show. The question is how we can grow and develop like wild flowers resistant to blizzards and living off the rain and dew provided by nature."

Selected References
Works by Cheng Jingyi
>*China Today Through Chinese Eyes*. Second series. London: SCM Press, 1927.
>"The Chinese Church in Relation to Its Immediate Task." *International Review of Missions* 8 (July 1919).
>"Zhongguo de jiaohui" (The Chinese Church). *Youth Advance* 52 (1922).
>"The Development of an Indigenous Church in China." *International Review of Missions* 12 (1923).
>"Discussing an Indigenous Church" (in Chinese). *Wenshe Monthly* (1925).
>"The Road Not Yet Travelled." In *China Her Own Interpreter*, edited by M.T. Stauffer, 96-105. New York: Mission Education Movement of the US and Canada, 1927.
>"Problems of the Chinese Church." In *China Her Own Interpreter*, edited by M.T. Stauffer. New York: Mission Education Movement of the US and Canada, 1927.
>"An Interpretation of the Five-Year Movement in China." *International Review of Missions* 20 (April 1931).

Gairdner, W.H. T. *Echoes of Edinburgh 1910: an Account and Interpretation of the World Missionary Conference*, with an Introduction by John R. Mott, 183-186. London: Fleming H. Revell, 1910.

5.1.10. Liu Tingfang, Timothy (T.T. Lew, 1891-1947)

Born in Wenzhou, Zhejiang, Liu studied at St. John's University in Shanghai, but finished his education in the U.S.A. with a B.D. from Yale in 1918 and a Ph.D. from Columbia Teachers' College in 1920. In 1918, he taught religious education at Union Theological Seminary, the first Chinese to teach a non-Chinese subject in an American seminary. He returned to China in 1920 to become concurrently dean of the graduate school of education at Peking University and professor of theology in the Yenching School of Religion (becoming dean in 1921).

A multi-talented, cosmopolitan figure, he also served as editor of *Life, Truth,* and the merged *Truth and Life*. He was a close associate of John Leighton Stuart at Yenching, where he served as chancellor (*xiaozhang*) when Stuart headed the school.

Liu was more an educator than a theologian, one who moved widely in non-Christian circles as an eloquent spokesman for Christianity. An ecumenist, he was well-known abroad as a delegate to important international church gatherings, including Edinburgh, 1937. He was chief editor of the Protestant hymnal, *Hymns of Universal Praise*, published in 1936, which contained 171 hymns that Liu had written or translated. This hymnal was used until a major revision incorporating new Chinese hymns was published in 1986.

Liu was a founding member and cooperating secretary of the National Christian Council of China and gave one of the three major addresses at the first annual meeting of the NCC in May 1923, where 38 of 64 delegates were Chinese. He became a member of the Legislative Yuan of the nationalist government in 1936. He was living in the U.S. at the time of his death.

Selected References
Works by Liu Tingfang
"China's Renaissance-The Christian Opportunity." *CR* 52 (May 1921).
"Xin wenhua yundong zhong Jidujiao xuanjiaoshi de zeren" (Missionary responsibility in the New Culture Movement). Speech during a meeting of the China Continuation Committee, May 5, 1921.
"Zhongguo de Jidu jiaohui" (The Chinese Christian Church). *Life* 2 (1922).
"Jidutu de jingji guan he Jidujiao hui de zeren" (Christians' view of economics and the churches' responsibility). *Life* 3:1 (1922).
"Jidujiao quanguo dahui" (The National Christian Conference). *Life* 2:3 (1922).
"Zhonghua jidutu aiguo wenti de pingyi" (An assessment of the patriotism issue for Chinese Christians). *Life* 4:8 (1924:4); continued 4:9 & 10 (1924:6).
"Zhongguo jiaohui lijie yishi de wenti" (Liturgy in the Chinese Church). *Life* 5:3 (1924).
"Wei bense jiaohui yanjiu zhonghua minzu zongjiao jingyan de yige caoan" (A draft study of the Chinese folk-religious experience done for the indigenous church). *Truth and Life*: 1: 7 (1926:8).
"Guonan zhong jiaohui de shiming" (The church's mission in the national crisis). *Truth and Life*: 6:3 (1931).

5.2 The Indigenous Church Movement
5.2.1. In Pursuit of Autonomy

Scattered instances of Chinese Christians running their own churches in the latter half of the 19th century, notably Chen Mengnan who established an independent church in Guangzhou in 1872, grew in number with the advent of the 20th. An early example was the Christian Union (Jidutu hui) formed by Yu Guozhen, Xie Honglai, and Song Yuru among others. In 1906 Zhu Baoyuan of the Church of the Savior in Shanghai announced that his church would no longer accept foreign funds, constructing a new church in traditional Chinese architectural style, and proclaiming "self-administration, self-support and self-propagation." They also called for the repeal of the unequal treaties that protected the church.

Others who wrote and reflected on independence and indigenization in this period include Wang Zhixin, Shen Sizhuang, Yong Yuandao, K.T. Chung and T.Z. Koo. Post May Fourth, the trend continued, bolstered by the rising spirit of nationalism and ethnic self-determination. Shi Meiyu (see 5.3.2.) was among those who left the Jiangxi Presbyterian Mission to set up the Bethel Church. Jia Yuming (5.1.6.) began the Chinese Presbyterian Church in Jiangsu and Shangdong. Yu Guozhen, an early independence activist, pastor of the Zhabei Church in Shanghai, also founded the Chinese Christian Independent Church in 1920 and branches of this sprang up in 16 provinces. Magazines published by these churches include *Sheng bao* and *Zhongguo xintu*. Cheng Jingyi (5.1.9.) was a promoter of independence in his Beijing congregation and stood for its goals in his subsequent career in the mainstream church. Other independent churches appeared in over 600 cities and provinces across the nation. Yamamoto (2000) also notes independent missionary work by groups such as the Chinese Home Mission Society founded in 1918.

5.2.2 Indigenization

The Anti-Christian Movement and the New Life Movement made thoughtful Christians ask questions that led them toward issues of patriotism and indigenization. The growing thrust toward indigenization was linked to the patriotic awakening of Christians as citizens of China who must act to save their country. Many authors sought evidence for such a patriotic stance in the Bible and a Christian Committee for National Salvation was founded. The warmth of feeling and discussion on such issues was generated by the increased contact such Christians had with the New Culture Movement, and their response to their country's plight improved public opinion of Christians (Duan, see below) and led to a lessening of the gap between Christians and those who had been accustomed to thinking that "one more Christian means one less Chinese." The spirit of inquiry that marked the movement helped Chinese Christians to be more critical of the West, and increased contacts also gave added impetus to calls for indigenization and all that meant. Christians became more aware of the links between imperialism and the missionary movement and of the need to recover church sovereignty and independence from the mission boards (Chen and Cao 1982). In a sense, the anti-Christian movement benefited the movement for a more fully Chinese Church in that it raised the consciousness of Chinese Christians with regard to the role of women, the need for unity, independence and selfhood, and to patriotism and indigenization.

Along with discussions that took place in the China Continuation Committee (see 5.2.3. below), numerous articles considering its significance and the meaning and challenges of indigenization of Christianity in China appeared in such publications as *Life* (under the editorship of T.T. Lew); *Truth, True Light* (Zhang Yijing, editor), *Youth Advance* (YMCA organ, Fan Tzu-mei [Fan Zimei] editor) etc. in the lead up to the 1922 National Christian Conference. The dominance of western missionaries and the need for unity were also addressed. These writings greatly enriched the discussions at the Conference.

Selected References

Bays, Daniel H. "Indigenous Protestant Churches in China, 1900-1937: A Pentecostal Case Study." In *Indigenous Responses to Western Christianity*, edited by Steven Kaplan, 124-143. New York: New York University Press, 1995.

—. "The Growth of Independent Christianity." In *Christianity in China from the Eighteenth Century to the Present*, edited by Daniel H. Bays, 307-316. Stanford, CA: Stanford University Press, 1996.

—. "Christian Revival in China, 1900-1937." In *Modern Christian Revivals*, edited by Edith Blumhofer and Randall Balmer. Urbana: University of Illinois Press, 1993.

Chao, T.C. "Bense jiaohui de shangque" (A consideration of the indigenous church). *Youth Advance* 76 (1924).

—. "Xuanjiaoshi yu zhenli" (Missionaries and truth). *Life,* vol.3, no. 3 (1922).

Chen Zemin and Cao Shengjie. "The Patriotic Tradition within Chinese Christianity in Light of the Independence Movement in the Chinese Church." Unpub. Paper, 1982.

Cheng Jingyi. "Zhongguo de jiaohui" (The Chinese Church). *Youth Advance* 52 (1922).

Duan Qi. *Brief History of the Indigenization of Christianity in China* (in Chinese). Unpub. Ms.

Grubb, Violet M. *The Chinese Indigenous Church Movement*. London and New York: World Dominion Press, n.d.

Jian Youwen. "Minzu de zongjiao" (Religion of the people-1). *Youth Advance* (1922).

—. "Sanyi hui yu Jidujiao" (The Sanyi Church and Christianity). *Life* 4:6 (1924).

Lam Wing-hung. *The Emergence of a Protestant Christian Apologetics in the Chinese Church During the Anti-Christian Movement in the 1920s*. Ph.D. diss., Princeton Theological Seminary, 1978.

Li Daohui. "Shandong Zhonghua Jidujiao hui" (The Shandong Church of Christ in China). *Shenxue zhi* 10:3 (1924).

Lew, T.T. "Xuanjiaoshi de wenti" (On the missionary issue). *Life*, vol. 3, no. 3 (1922).

Shen Sizhuang. "Xuanyan sanzhong" (Three kinds of manifesto). *Shenxue zhi* vol. 8, no. 1 (1922).

Ling, Samuel D. "The Other May Fourth Movement: The Chinese Christian Renaissance, 1919-1937." Unpub. Ph.D. diss., Temple University, 1980.

Whyte, Bob. *Unfinished Encounter: China and Christianity*. London: Collins/Fount Paperbacks, 1988.

Yamamoto, Sumiko. *History of Protestantism in China: The Indigenization of Christianity*. Tokyo: Toho Gakkai, 2000.

Yao Minquan. "Indigenization in China in the First Half of the Twentieth Century." *CTR:*11:1(1996).

Xie Fuya (N.Z. Zia). "Jidujiao xin siqiao yu Zhongguo minzu genben sixiang" (The Chinese Christian renaissance and the basic mindset of the Chinese). *Youth Advance* 82 (1925)

—. "Bense jiaohui wenti yu Jidujiao zai Zhongguo de qiantu" (The question of indigenization in the church and the future of Christianity in China). *Wenshe Monthly* 1:4 (1926).

Xing Wu (Jia Yuming). "Jinri zhi Zhonghua Jidujiao hui" (The Chinese Church today). *Shenxue zhi* vol. 8, no. 1 (1922).

5.2.3. National Christian Conference 1922

In 1877, a group of Protestant missionaries met in Shanghai for the first General Conference of Protestant Missionaries of China. Further meetings were held in 1890, 1907 (the centenary of Protestant missions in China), and 1913. Movement toward more cooperation among missionaries and denominations and increased Chinese participation was given added impetus by the formation of the China Continuation Committee as a result of the World Missionary Conference held in Edinburgh 1910. The membership of the committee was one-quarter Chinese, in a venue in which, for the first time, Chinese Christians and western missionaries discussed Chinese Christianity on an equal footing (Yamamoto 2000); a focus of their discussions was the relationship of the New Culture Movement to Christianity with an emphasis on the patriotic movement within the church and the call for indigenization (Duan, see below). Extensive preparation for the next missionary conference to be held in 1922 included publication (in both English and Chinese editions) of a detailed survey of the current state of Protestantism in China, *The Christian Occupation of China*. The 1922 meeting was a watershed for the formation of a Chinese Protestant Church.

1922 was the first such meeting which was truly national in terms of representation and the first at which Chinese delegates accounted for over half of those attending, 568 out of 1025. The theme of the conference was The Chinese Church, rather than mission work in China, aiming to foster a church independent of missionary administration and finance, and the development of a theology relevant to China's needs, and topics discussed reflected the changing concerns of that church. In addition to evangelism, medical work, education and other traditional concerns, the meeting was concerned with rural and urban problems and economic and industrial conditions. Important addresses were given in both English and Chinese. In Chinese articles, it was frequently referred to as the May 2nd meeting to illustrate that its national importance was equivalent to that of the May 4th Movement (Duan, see below). Cheng Jingyi (5.1.9.) chaired the meeting, with K.T. Chung as one of three vice-chairs.

A more open attitude was evident, especially among more liberal missionaries, toward cooperation with Chinese colleagues on an equal footing and a greater sympathy for traditional Chinese culture and religion. Another hallmark of the meeting was the active role played by Chinese women. The Conference culminated in the constitution of the National Christian Council (NCC), formed as a permanent body to supplant the China Continuation Committee, to play an advisory role in matters excepting church doctrine and administration. The first Council chair was Z.T. Yui, with Cheng Jingyi as chief secretary. Women played a role in this new body as well.

Increasing social and political pressures however, eventually took their toll on the NCC during the turmoils of following years, not least the events of 1925-27. As concerned Christian leaders and intellectuals grappled with the Chinese Christian response to the May 30th incident (1925), in which British police in the Shanghai International Concession fired on Chinese protesters, killing 13 and wounding a dozen others, some western mission organizations drew back when the NCC made statements deploring the incident. The CIM withdrew in October 1926 and the Lutherans later followed.

Selected References

> Callahan, Paul E. "Christianity and Revolution as Seen in the National Christian Council of China." *Papers on China*. East Asian Research Center, Harvard University 5 (1951).
> Duan Qi. *Brief History of the Indigenization of Christianity in China* (in Chinese). Unpub. Ms.
> Fan Yurong. "Zhonghua quanguo Jidujiao hui xiejin hui" (The National Christian Council). *YWCA* 12 (1922).
> National Christian Council of China. *The Chinese Church as Revealed in the National Christian Conference Held in Shanghai, Tuesday, May 2, to Thursday, May 11, 1922*, edited by Frank J. Rawlinson, Helen Thoburn, and Donald MacGillivray. Shanghai: Oriental Press, 1927.
> Stauffer, Milton T., ed. *The Christian Occupation of China*. Shanghai: China Continuation Committee, 1922.
> Yamamoto, Sumiko. *History of Protestantism in China: The Indigenization of Christianity*. Tokyo: Toho Gakkai, 2000.

5.2.4. Church of Christ in China: 1927

The animus toward denominationalism as a western imposition dividing Christians in China was a moving force in the movement for indigenization and independence. The National Christian

Conference of 1922 had hailed the birth of an indigenous Chinese Church; the formation of the Church of Christ in China (C.C.C.) was aimed at making it a reality. Presbyterian and Congregationalist groups had joined with the LMS in 1922. Formally established in 1927, one article of incorporation for the Church of Christ in China read in part: "The Church shall have as its object to unite Christian believers in China, to plan and promote with united strength the spirit of self-support, self-governance and self-propagation, in order to extend Christ's Gospel, practice His Way of Life and His Kingdom throughout the world" (in Yamamoto 2000). The church was to be autonomous, independent and non-aligned with any church overseas. The church's scope was gradually broadened to include all other denominational bodies that held a modicum of beliefs in common and desired an end to denominational divisions.

Its first general assembly in October 1927 gathered 16 denominational groups with 87 commissioners from 17 provinces representing 120,000 Protestant Christians, making it the most powerful member of the new NCC. Cheng Jingyi became the first moderator.

A number of important writings on ecumenical mission have arisen from the circles of the C.C.C. since its foundation, and the Hong Kong Council of the Church of Christ in China is still active.

Selected References

Duan Qi. *Brief History of the Indigenization of Christianity in China* (in Chinese). Unpub. Ms.

Fisher, A.J. *The History of the Church of Christ in China*. MSS. General Assembly of the CCC, 1943.

Merwin, Wallace. *Adventure in Unity: The Church of Christ in China*. Grand Rapids: Eerdmans, 1974.

Morton, T. Ralph. *Life in the Chinese Church*. London: SCM Press, 1931.

Kepler, A.R. "What is the Church of Christ in China?" *CR* 58 (1927): 27-32.

Whyte, Bob. *Unfinished Encounter: China and Christianity*. London: Collins/Fount Paperbacks, 1988.

Yamamoto, Sumiko. *History of Protestantism in China: The Indigenization of Christianity*. Tokyo: Toho Gakkai, 2000.

Zhonghua Jidujiaohui. *Papers of the Border Service Department of the Church of Christ in China, 1939-1949* (inclusive). Yale University Library (3 boxes).

Zhonghua Jidujiaohui. *Records and minutes of the second annual meeting of the General Council of the Church of Christ in China. Shanghai, October 9-18, 1929 and ad-interim actions to date.* April 1, 1930. Shanghai: CCC, 1930.

—. *Important actions of the fourth meeting of the General Assembly, Church of Christ in China.* Shanghai: CCC, 1948.

—. *Digest of the minutes and reports of the General Council of the Church of Christ in China.* Amoy: [s.n.], 1933.

—. *Important actions of the fifth meeting of the General Assembly, Church of Christ in China.* Shanghai: CCC, 1948.

—. *An Adventure in Church Union in China. Origin, nature and task of the Church of Christ in China.* New York, 1944.

5.2.5. Indigenous churches and sects

Wang Mingdao's Christian Tabernacle and Watchman Nee's "Christian Assembly" or Local Church Movement, are the best known of these (see below for both). Paul Wei, one of the founders, with Barnabas Tung, of the True Jesus Church in 1917, was originally a follower of the London Missionary Society, who drifted from that to the Mormons and then to Pentecostalism. He made the revelation of the Holy Spirit to the leader of the church the sole basis of the gospel and the foundation of his church. The church had no systematized doctrine, no links with other Christian groups, and tapped into traditional Chinese beliefs of fortune-telling using dreams and signs. Churches sprang up rapidly in the countryside, where it taught faith healing and glossalalia. The True Jesus Church may have been the largest of the independent churches but it was disbanded in the 1950s as counter-revolutionary, while continuing today in overseas Chinese communities.

The Jesus Family was founded in Shandong in 1921 by Jing Dianying. The church practiced a primitive communism of equality in poverty, stressing the spirit over material goods and spiritual bonds over blood ties. The church was strongly Pentecostal, and stressed orderly production based on a communal life of spiritual discipline. It grew rapidly in rural Shandong, the scene of frequent military skirmishes, natural disasters, and great poverty from the 1920s to the 1940s. It, too, was disbanded in the early 1950s.

The Little Flock, or Local Church Movement, tradition remains strong in many rural areas, including the northeast, east and southeast (Zhejiang and Fujian) Its pietistic practices and cohesive organization gave many the strength to persevere as Christians through the trials of the Cultural Revolution period. Like the True Jesus Church and the Jesus Family, its theology is exclusivist and premillennarian, heir to the conservative side of the fundamentalist/ modernist split that began among western missionaries in China. Organizationally diffuse, it has no ordained clergy. Their traditions of complete independence in church government and organization, church support and evangelization gave the group an adaptability which served to sustain it through the departure of western missionaries and the Cultural Revolution.

Many regard the Little Flock as it exists today within mainland China as a completely indigenous church; yet its conservative traditions and theological viewpoint make it difficult for these churches to reach beyond themselves to become active segments of a broader Chinese society. Their beliefs would preclude efforts to bring Christianity closer to culture; for the strong emphasis is rather on a separation from culture as at best secular and at worst under the domination of Satan.

In 1958, these more sectarian and fundamentalist traditions became, at least organizationally, part of the unified Protestant church (see 5.4). This was however an uneasy alliance and other churches (even then) remained independent : some are still not related to the TSPM/CCC today.

Selected References
> Bays, Daniel H. "The Growth of Independent Christianity." In *Christianity in China from the Eighteenth Century to the Present*, edited by Daniel H. Bays, 307-316. Stanford, CA: Stanford University Press, 1996.
> Rees, D. Vaughn. *The Jesus Family in Communist China: A Modern Miracle of New Testament Christianity*. London: Paternoster Press, 1959.

Wang Xipeng. *Ji Yesu jiating* (Remembering the Jesus Family). Shanghai: National Christian Council, 1950.

—. "Yesu jiating de gongchan zhidu" (The Jesus Family's communist system). 1950.

Wang Zhixin. "Bense jiaohui yu bense zhuzuo" (Indigenous churches and indigenous writings). *Wenshe Monthly* 1.2 (1925).

Zhen Yesu hui sanshi zhou nian jinian zhuankan (Thirtieth Anniversary Special of the True Jesus Church). 1951.

5.2.6. Wang Ming-tao (Wang Mingdao, 1900-1991)

Wang Ming-tao was educated in schools run by the London Missionary Society and baptized at the age of 14. He wanted to be a politician, but turned to ministry through an experience of healing from a serious illness. He taught for a time at a Presbyterian school, with plans for further education and theological studies, possibly overseas. But he was dismissed over his desire to be rebaptized by immersion. After a time of soul-searching and Bible reading, he turned from "worldly" pursuits to the pursuit of eternal life. He decided he did not need seminary training to do God's work and began his independent ministry in 1924. His Christian Tabernacle, established in 1937, grew out of a Bible study group in his home. It was a three-self church, for few from outside were invited to preach, most of the preaching being done by Wang himself. He made frequent preaching trips and became one of the most popular Christian preachers in China.

Wang did not set down a theology, his writings mainly consisting of articles in his *Spiritual Food Quarterly*, begun in 1927 to combat modernist influence. Through this magazine he was one of the most prolific Christian writers. Certain concepts defined his message: salvation from death; justification by faith; the assertion that the Bible was "dictated" by God; and a highly moralistic approach to Christian conduct. The new person in Christ must be not only internal but external: a sign of faith and a means of evangelism. Social action or charity was an entirely secondary consideration, necessary only as a form of witness. It was futile to try to save the world and believers must guard their purity from corruption by the evils of society.

Wang's message was not that Christianity was a corrective to the problems of China; faith should be separate from political and social action. Rather, Wang's message was that Christianity represented another way of living in a world under the dominion of Satan. And though indigenous in origin and order, the Christian Tabernacle made no attempt to bring Christianity closer to Chinese culture.

He rebuffed both political and theological "outsiders" and had minor problems with the Japanese authorities during the occupation. After the war, he continued to work until the TSPM was established in 1954. Wang refused to join this and was strongly criticized as part of the denunciation movement (5.4.2.). He went to prison for a year, made a confession, was released, retracted his confession and was again detained, spending some time under house arrest and becoming well known in the West through reports of his persecution. His "We Because of Faith" (1955) is an explanation of his reasons for refusing to join the TSPM: "We will not unite in any way with these unbelievers, nor will we join any of their organizations. And even with true believers and faithful servants of God we can enjoy only a spiritual union. There should not be any kind of formal, organizational union, because we cannot find any teaching in the Bible to support it."

After the Cultural Revolution, the TSPM made several attempts to win Wang Mingdao over, but were rebuffed each time.

Selected Resources
Works by Wang Mingdao
> *Shouku youyi* (The Blessing of Suffering) (1934). *Wang Mingdao wenku* (The Wang Mingdao Library) vol. 6: 385-402. Taiwan: Douliu zhen Taiwan Baptist Press, 1976-1978. Hong Kong: Alliance Press, 1962.
> *Horn Blast* (1930) (in Chinese). Hong Kong: Grace Press, 1967.
> *Sermons of Mr. Wang Ming-tao* (1932) (in Chinese). Hong Kong: Hong Dao Press, 1967.
> *Wushi nian lai* (These Fifty Years) (autobiography; 1950). Hong Kong: The Bellman House, 1957, 1982. Arthur Reynolds, partial trans. *A Stone Made Smooth*. Sholing, U.K.: Mayflower, 1981.
> "We Because of Faith."
> Lyall, Leslie. *Three of China's Mighty Men*. London: OMF Books, 1973.

Ng Lee-ming. "Wang Ming-tao: An Evaluation of His Thought and Action." *Ching Feng* XVI: 2 (1973).

Wang Mingdao Library (Wang Mingdao wenku). Wang Zhongzheng, ed. Douliu zhen Taiwan Baptist Press. 1976-1978.

5.2.7. Watchman Nee (Ni Tuosheng, 1903-1972)

Watchman Nee is the founder of the indigenous Chinese sect known variously as the Little Flock, the Christian Assemblies, or the Local Church Movement. Nee was classically educated and attended Anglican schools, but in 1920 he attended a gospel meeting with a Chinese Methodist evangelist and, and, attracted to that message, spent a year at a Bible school in Shanghai. Nee's influences were the Keswick Movement and the Brethren Movement, though he had his differences with both, and was often hostile to missionaries and foreign Christians.

It has been said that Nee's movement was a model for the development of an independent, non-denominational church for China. The Little Flock began with a small house gathering in Shanghai, with many local churches springing up in the area on this model. Nee's approach was three-self with the addition of clear locality. It was an exclusivist approach: there could be only one true church in each place.

During WWII, Nee took a job with his brother to help the church financially, but was criticized by the elders in the Shanghai church for taking a secular job, and was forbidden to preach as a result. In 1947 he gave his financial assets over to the church and was reinstated. He responded with a new structure, the Jerusalem Principle, which limited the power of the elders and asserted a centralized control. Nee was arrested in 1952 on charges of corrupt business practices and sentenced to fifteen years after a public trial in 1956. He died in prison in 1972. His associate Li Changshou transferred the church to Taiwan and it is today based there and in the U.S.A.

Selected References

Works by Watchman Nee

His many works include: *A Balanced Christian Life; The Basic Lesson Series.* 6 vols.;

The Communion of the Holy Spirit; Church and the Work. 3 vols.; *Grace for Grace; Authority and Obedience* (in Chinese); *On Church Affairs* (in Chinese); *What Shall This Man Do?* In adition to :
The Release of the Spirit. Indianapolis: Premium Literature Co., 1965.
The Normal Christian Life. Angus I. Kinnear, ed. Fort Washington, Penn.: Christian Literature Crusade, 1968.
The Spiritual Man. Stephen Kaung, trans. 3 vols. New York: Christian Fellowship Publishers, 1968.
Kinear, Angus. *Against the Tide: The Story of Watchman Nee.* Wheaton: Tyndale House, 1973.
Cliff, Norman Howard. *The Life and Theology of Watchman Nee, Including a Study of the Little Flock Movement Which He Founded.* Ann Arbor, Mich.: University Microfilms International Dissertations Services, 1987.

5.3 1930s and 1940s: Decades of Social Program and Political Upheaval

Since 1927, when the Nationalist-Communist alliance broke apart and the anti-Christian movement was at its peak, many Christians had been seriously concerned with their role as Christians in social change and modernization. It was a time for action and the social gospel, but one that produced little in the way of genuine theological reflection. The churches sponsored many social and relief programs. The YMCA and YWCA continued to train many future Christian leaders in student and social work. Christian social organizations were involved in mass literacy projects, such as that spearheaded in Ding County, Hebei, by James Yen (Yen Yangchu) and development programs like the Lichwan Project. Involvement in such rural development and education programs was a new departure for church groups. In 1931, a department of rural churches was set up at Nanking Theological Seminary, with Frank W. Price as its chair. The department had a field station in rural Jiangxi for research and training rural missionary specialists. Other Christian intellectuals such as Xu Shikang and Tao Xingzhi were also active promoters of churches' involvement in rural development.

Worsening economic and social conditions, flood and famine in the countryside, and the subsequent eradication of law and order there, banditry and the growing political struggle between the KMT and the CPC, the war with Japan and its occupation of parts of China, all contributed to the eventual decline of the liberal program espoused by many Christian thinkers. Then as the 1930s became the 1940s, the hope of reform gave way to the inevitability of revolution. Though individual Christians became involved in progressive causes, the church lost incisive attention to more radical approaches. Movements such as the "Five-Year Movement" were seen as more ethical than political and the discussion of indigenization issues received less active attention. Because of the exigencies of national crisis, most Christians found themselves unable to develop a well-defined theological alternative. A small number of contextual reflections however did appear, often in the setting of sharp disturbances or conflicts.

Selected References

Bi Fanyu. "Xiangcun chuandaozhe de xunlian" (Training for rural evangelists). *Nanjing Theological Review* 14, no. 7-8 (1932).

Chen, W.Y. "The State of the Church in China." *International Review of Missions* 36 (1947): 141-152.

Duan Qi. *Draft History of the Indigenization of Christianity in China* (in Chinese). Unpub. Ms.

Garrett, Shirley S. *Social Reformers in Urban China: The Chinese YMCA, 1895-1926*. Cambridge, Mass.: Harvard University Press, 1970.

Hayford, Charles W. *To the People: James Yen and Village China*. New York: Columbia University Press, 1990.

Hsu, P.C. "Christian Rural Reconstruction in China." *China Christian Yearbook* 20 (1936-1937): 319-329.

—. "Theory and Practice of the Leichwan Project" (in Chinese). *China Christian Yearbook*, vol. 13 (1934-1936).

National Christian Council of China. *Report on Rural and Literacy Work Submitted to the Biennial Meeting of the NCCC, May 3-11, 1933*. Shanghai: NCCC, 1933.

—. *Christian Cooperation in China*. Biennial meeting. Shanghai, May 5-11, 1937. Shanghai: NCCC, 1937.

Tian Ligong. "Theory and Practice of New Village Churches" (in Chinese). *Nanjing Theological Review* 19, no. 5 (1938).

Wu Leichuan. *Christianity and Chinese Culture* (in Chinese). Shanghai: YMCA Press, 1937.

Wu, Y.T. "China's Challenge to Christianity-Make Christianity Socially Dynamic." *CR* 65 (1934): 7-11.

Yamamoto, Sumiko. *History of Protestantism in China: The Indigenization of Christianity.* Tokyo: Toho Gakkai, 2000.

Yen, James Y.C. *The Mass Education Movement in China.* Shanghai: Commercial Press, 1925.

5.3.1. The Modernist Debate and Theological Conservatism in China

The modernist/ fundamentalist division formed with a report on China missions and a dispute among missionaries there that the social gospel emphasis on education and social activism came at the expense of Bible-believing Christianity (Hutchison 1987). Latourette notes that those groups in which the conflict was greatest were strongly represented in China, so that conservatives were especially numerous. The powerful CIM and many smaller missions saw 'modernism' as inimical to the very life of the church in China. The Bible Union (1920) was founded to reaffirm a strongly literal faith in which the Bible was the inerrant word of God and the ultimate authority for Christian faith and practice.

It is tempting but too simplistic to set the split entirely along urban-rural lines. Yet liberalism may be mainly identified with the urban setting, where there were more well - often western - educated church leaders and progressive Christian thinkers. The conservative, more fundamentalist missionaries were more numerous in rural areas, and the indigenous sects and churches influenced by their theology grew rapidly and well in the socially and economically beleaguered countryside.

The revivalist movement of the 1920s and the popularity of conservative itinerant and revivalist preaching by renowned conservative evangelical preachers such as Wang Mingdao, John Sung (Song Shangjie), and Andrew Gih (Ji Zhiwen), were not limited to rural congregations: they found a ready audience in urban churches as well. But there is a blurring of the differences between fundamentalism and evangelicalism in the history and the present of the Chinese church which needs to be addressed. For the strength and endurance of a conservative faith perspective, especially in the countryside, cannot simply be ascribed to a 19th century legacy of hidebound missionary theologies.

Selected References

Bays, Daniel H. "Christianity and the Chinese Sectarian Tradition." *Ch'ing-shih wen-t'i* 4:7 (June 1982).

—. "The Growth of Independent Christianity." In *Christianity in China from the Eighteenth Century to the Present*, edited by Daniel H. Bays, 307-316. Stanford, CA: Stanford University Press, 1996.

Hutchison, William R. *Errand to the World: American Protestant Thought and Foreign Missions.* Chicago & London: University of Chicago Press, 1987.

Latourette, Kenneth S. *A History of Christian Missions in China.* London: SPCK, 1929. Reprint. New York: Paragon Book Gallery, Ltd., n.d.

Lyall, Leslie T. *John Sung.* London: Overseas missionary Fellowship, 1956.

5.3.2. Women in the Life and Work of the Church (See also 4.9, 4.9.1).

Women were a special focus of missionary work on the basis that through women, whole families could be reached and converted. Women's roles in society began to undergo a fundamental change with the advent of the May Fourth movement, as women students in particular became involved in political and social protests, the new literary movements, higher education, medicine, and an independent approach to love and marriage. Educated in mission schools and Christian colleges such as Hwa Nan Women's College in Fujian and Jinling Women's College in Nanjing, Christian women were active in the social reform movements spanning the turn of the century: against foot-binding, concubinage, and opium and in the temperance crusade. They became doctors (cf. Mary Stone (Shi Meiyu), 4.9.1.), nurses and health care workers, greatly extending health care available to women and children. The YWCA provided leadership training for many.

Contextual Theology in China

In rural areas, women had long served as Bible women; as the century progressed they began to take a more active role in church leadership. Many whose careers continued in these years are mentioned above in 4.9.1, including Ding Limei, Shi Meiyu (Mary Stone), Phoebe Shi, Cheng Guanyi (Ruth), Deng Yuzhi (Cora), and Ding Meiyu (Mary Ting), among others. Following the 3 women who were memebrs of the China Continuation Committee (1913), at the formation of the National Chinese Christian Conference in 1922, 19 women were elected as denominational representatives and at-large members, including Cheng Guanyi and Fan Yurong. It should also be noted that Christian educational institutions and wider work with women had an impact beyond the Christian community; many women activists who would not identify themselves as Christian received some or all of their education in such institutions.

Women's writings can be found in a number of journals and newspapers including *The Chinese Recorder*, *Jiaohui xinbao* (Church News), *Woman's Work in the Far East*, *Shengming* (Life) and its successor *Life and Truth* (see also 4.4 above). Among others, Shi Meiyu, Cheng Wanzhen, Ding Shujing, Wang Liming and Zeng Baosun (4.9.) wrote on Christian mission, women's role in the Church, women's concerns and social issues. The *Shengming she* (Life Fellowship) included women among its members and as writers for its journal, *Life*. Those whose work appeared in its pages include Cheng Guanyi (Ruth Cheng), Ding Shujing (Ting Shu-ching), among others. The early poetry of the well-known poet Xie Wanying (Bing Xin/ Ping Hsin) also appeared there.

Kwok Pui-lan has done foundational work on women and Christianity in China, including women's writings and publications. Much has also been done on American and British women missionaries (see Supplementary Bibliography below). Though their numbers were small, well-educated Christian women played important roles in both Church and society, especially in education, social service and reform movements. Their contributions deserve further study. (See also 4.4 and 4.9 above.) Others like P.S.Tseng (Zeng Baosun) participated in the ecumenical conferences at Jerusalem (1928) and Tambaram (1938).

Selected References

Cai Shujuan. *Anshi zhi hou* (Queen of the dark chamber). Hong Kong: Bellman House, 1982.

Cheng, Ruth Guanyi. "Women and the Church." *CR* 53 (1922).

Chu, Mrs. T.C. (Hu Binxia). "Magazines for Chinese Women." *CMYB* 8 (1917).

Deng, Cora Yuzhi. "The Industrial Work of the YWCA in China." 29 Nov. 1934. World YWCA Archives, Geneva.

Ding Shujing. "Funu zai jiaohui zhong de diwei" (The position of women in the church). *Nuqingnian* (The YWCA Magazine) 7.2 (1928).

Drucker, Alice. "The Role of the YWCA in the Development of the Chinese Women's Movement, 1890-1927." *Social Service Review* 53.3 (1979).

Kwok, Pui-lan. *Chinese Women and Christianity, 1860-1927.* Atlanta: Scholar's Press, 1992.

Kahn, Ida (Kang Cheng). "The Place of Chinese Christian Women in the Development of China." *CR* (1919).

Shaw, Ella C. "The Work of Bible Women in China." *China Mission Yearbook* 6 (1915).

Wang Liming (Mrs. Herman C.E. Liu). *Zhongguo funu yundong* (The Chinese Women's Movement). Shanghai: Commercial Press, 1934.

5.3.3. Expatriate Scholars, Educators and Theologians 3 (1900-1950)

The turbulent times, vast social problems and increasing pressure for a self-governed church and a fully Chinese expression of Christian faith brought forth a variety of responses from expatriates working with and in the churches of China who were themselves supporters, to a greater or lesser extent, of contextualizing forces. Toward the end of the period, some among them became supporters of the growing Communist movement. Of those who returned after Liberation, many became interpreters of China to their own countries. A partial list would include:

Roland Allen (1868-1947), served in China as a missionary attached to the Anglican Society for the Propagation of the Gospel from 1895-1900. He experienced the Boxer Rebellion and siege of the Peking Legation firsthand. His critique of Christian mission as an instrument of colonization was shaped by his experiences there and continues to be important for the study of mission, along with his proposals for the formation of indigenous ministries.

R.O. (Ronald Owen) Hall (1895-1975) (see chap. 4, Hong Kong), was a delegate to the WSCF Conference in Peking in 1922, where he formed close relationships with young Christian leaders like T.Z. Koo and Y.T. Wu. These led him always to seek to understand the Chinese situation from the Chinese standpoint. As Bishop of Hong Kong, 1932-1966, he played an important role both in advocating for the poor and in showing support for the Chinese revolution. In 1944, he ordained the first Anglican woman priest, Li Tim-oi, to serve Christians in an isolated area of China during wartime.

Frank W. Price (1895-1974), born in China to Southern Presbyterian missionaries, he served as a missionary-professor at Nanking Theological Seminary where he became involved in educational reform, as well as ecumenical efforts resulting in the establishment of the Church of Christ in China. He helped to establish the Rural Training Center at Nanking Seminary. He was a personal friend of Chiang Kai-shek and because of his connections with the KMT, spent some months under virtual house arrest before leaving the country in 1952. He became director of the Missionary Research Library in 1956 and remained an influential voice on China in North America.

Francis Price Jones (1890-1975), was a missionary of the Methodist Episcopal Church in Fujian, 1915. In 1930 he went to teach at Nanking University where he also served on the hymnal committee with Bliss Wiant for *Hymns of Universal Praise*. In 1937 he went to teach New Testament at Nanking Theological Seminary where he founded a school of church music. He was a prodigious translator, spearheading during the war a planned 54-volume series of translated and edited Chinese classics.

David M. Paton (1913-1992), went to China in the 1940s as an Anglican missionary, serving first as a YMCA secretary and then with the CMS, until 1945. His critique of the arrogance of western churches and missions toward Chinese culture shaped his

Christian Missions and the Judgment of God (1953) which has had wide recognition.

Frank Joseph Rawlinson (1871-1937), came to China in 1902 as a Southern Baptist missionary but left and joined the ABCFM because of his liberal views. He served as editor of the *Chinese Recorder* until his death in 1941, was long active in the National Christian Council and was a supporter of Chinese nationalism and indigenization.

Randolph C. Sailer (1898-1981), a Presbyterian missionary, taught psychology at Yenching (Yanjing) University for over 20 years and knew or taught many who became leaders in later years. Recognized as a great friend of China, he was one of the first invited to visit, in 1973, following the Cultural Revolution, when he met personally with Zhou Enlai.

Maud Muriel Russell (1893-1989), went to China in 1917 with the YWCA and after language study, worked in Changsha, Hunan. In late 1927, because of anti-foreign sentiment and the split between the KMT and CCP, she was moved from Wuhan to Shanghai. The experience radicalized her and she began to study Marxism in a study group made up of foreigners and Chinese, including Rewi Alley, Talitha Gerlach and Cora Deng. She remained in China until 1943, then returned to the US where she eventually founded the *Far East Reporter*, in spite of having been under scrutiny by the House Un-American Activities Committee.

Talitha Gerlach (1896-198?), worked with the YWCA in the US, and in China along with Cora Deng. She lived in China for most of her life, was associated with Maud Russell and headed the China Welfare Institute in Shanghai.

James G. Endicott (1898-198?) was a United Church of Canada missionary to China, from 1925-1944. He was a champion of Chinese causes in the West, crusading against American involvement in the Korean War. He was awarded the Stalin Peace Prize in 1952 and was active for many years in the Canada-China Friendship Association and published *The Canadian Far Eastern Reporter*.

Selected References

Allen, Roland. *Missionary Methods: St. Paul's or Ours?* London: Robert Scott, 1912.

—. *The Spontaneous Expansion of the Church and the Causes which Hinder It.* London: World Dominion Press, 1927. Reissued 1949, 1956, 1960. First American edition, Eerdmans, 1962.

Chiow, Samuel. "Religious Education and Reform in Chinese Missions: The Life and Work of Frank Wilson Price (1895-1974). Ph.D. diss., St. Louis University, 1988.

Endicott, Stephen. *James G. Endicott: Rebel out of China.* Toronto: University of Toronto Press, 1980.

Hall, R.O. *A Missionary Artist Looks at His Job.* New York: International Missionary Council, 1942.

—.*T.Z. Koo.* London: SCM Press, 1950.

Jones, Francis P. *The Church in Communist China: A Protestant Appraisal.* New York: Friendship Press, 1962.

— .*Theological Thinking in the Chinese Protestant Church under Communism.* Reprinted from Religion in Life, Nashville, Autumn, 1963.

Lian Xi. *The Conversion of Missionaries: Liberalism in American Protestant Missions in China, 1907-1932.* University Park, Pa.: Pennsylvania State University Press, 1997.

Paton, David M. *Christian Missions and the Judgment of God.* London: SCM Press, 1953. 2nd. ed. with biographical essay by his son. Grand Rapids and Cambridge: William B. Eerdmans, 1996.

—. *"R.O."The Life and Times of Bishop Ronald Hall of Hong Kong.* 1985.

—, with Charles Long. *The Collected Writings of Roland Allen.* 1983.

—. *Christian Missions and the Judgment of God.* London: SCM Press, 1953.

Price, Frank W. "Christian Presuppositions for the Encounter with Communism." In

Rawlinson, Frank. *Progressive Ideals of Christian Work in China, by Resident Workers.* Shanghai: E. Evans & Sons, Ltd., (192?).

—. *Naturalization of Christianity in China (a study of the relation of Christian and Chinese idealism and life).* Shanghai: Presbyterian Mission Press, 1927).

—. *Revolution and Religion in Modern China, a brief study of the effects of modern revolutionary movements in China on its religious life*. Shanghai: Presbyterian Mission Press, 1929.
—. *The Rural Church in China*, 2nd. ed. 1948.
—. *Marx Meets Christ*. Philadelphia: Westminster Press, 1957.
Sailer, Randolph C. "Cooperative Thinking between Americans and Chinese." *China Notes*, vol. XVII, no. 2 (Spring 1979).
Wickeri, Philip L. "Roland Allen and the Decolonization of Christianity." Unpub. Paper.

5.4 1950s: Christianity and New China

The church found itself in an ambiguous and difficult situation following Liberation and the establishment of the PRC. Though progressive church people, especially in Shanghai and other urban areas, had a history of knowing counterparts among radical political activists and the communist underground, others in the church had prayed for the Yangtze to swallow up the approaching PLA ! In conservative rural areas where land reform was underway, there was of course resistance to the new order. To define and consolidate a positive role for the Church within the new order was therefore a twofold task: to unite Christians to participate in the new society; and identify Christians as part of the Chinese people, with a contribution to make to modernization. Progressive Christians embraced the new situation, others were opposed because they felt the church should remain aloof from politics, and still others felt the church should be Chinese, but were uncertain about the CPC. This became less a theological process than a political and social one: love country, love church (*aiguo aijiao*). In the exigencies of the Chinese revolution, the first step was to break with the past. Before theological reflection could take place, the very existence of Christianity in the new society had to be addressed.

5.4.1. The Christian Manifesto 1950

The Manifesto came out of a meeting between 19 protestant leaders and Zhou Enlai, first premier of the new PRC. It was a document to address the political situation of the church in the new order, a statement of support for the new government and the Chinese Communist Party, inaugurating the movement to identify politically with the new order, as well as a controversial document whose designers' attitudes ranged from a need to placate the communist government to outright agreement with the new regime. It called upon churches to acknowledge the problem of imperialism and work for the selfhood of the churches. Many felt reluctance over any political statement coming from the churches. Numerous drafts and revisions were necessary, with discussions taking place among Christian leaders in Shanghai, north and east China. The final document was issued with a covering letter signed by 40 prominent Christians and published and endorsed on the front page of the national newspaper, *People's Daily*. The final tally of signatures to the Manifesto was 417,389, of a total Protestant Christian population of approximately 700,000.

Selected References

Bush, Richard. *Religion in Communist China*. Nashville and New York: Abingdon, 1970.

Chao, Jonathan, and Rosanna Chong. *Dangdai Zhongguo Jidujiao fazhan shi, 1949-1997* (A History of Christianity in Socialist China, 1949-1997). Taipei: CMI Publishing Co., Ltd., 1997.

Duan Qi. *Draft History of the Indigenization of Christianity in China* (in Chinese). Unpub. Ms.

Ferris, Helen. *The Christian Church in Communist China*. Montgomery, AL: The Human Research Institute, Air University, 1952.

Hockin, Katherine. *Servants of God in People's China*. New York: Friendship Press, 1962.

Hood, George A. *Neither Bang Nor Whimper: The End of a Missionary Era in China*. Singapore: Presbyterian Church in Singapore, 1991.

Jones, Francis Price. *The Church in Communist China: A Protestant Appraisal*. New York: Friendship Press, 1962.

—. "Theological Thinking in the Chinese Protestant Church Under Communism." *Religion in Life* 32:4 (Autumn 1963).

—, ed. *Documents of the Three-Self Movement: Source Materials for the Study of the Protestant Church in Communist China*. New York: National Council of Churches of Christ in the USA, 1963.

Lee, Renesalaer. "Chinese Communist Religious Policy." *China Quarterly* 19 (1964): 161-173.

Miao, Chester. *Christian Voices in China*. New York: Friendship Press, 1948.
Sih, Paul K.T. *Decision for China: Communism or Christianity*. Chicago: Regnum, 1959.
Whyte, Bob. *Unfinished Encounter: China and Christianity*. London: Collins/Fount Paperbacks, 1988.
Wickeri, Philip L. *Seeking the Common Ground: Protestant Christianity, the Three-Self Movement, and China's United Front*. Maryknoll, NY: Orbis Books, 1988.
Yamamoto, Sumiko. *History of Protestantism in China: The Indigenization of Christianity*. Tokyo: Toho Gakkai, 2000.

5.4.2. The Denunciation (or Accusation) Movement

In the political movements of the early years of the PRC, the critique of the past and those seen as complicit with it became a prelude to reform and change. The Denunciation Movement, begun in April, 1951, was the Christian counterpart to the political study and ideological remolding movements of the early 1950s, whose goals were the denunciation of foreign influence and Chinese complicity with that. It was a movement within the broader TSPM to deepen criticism of American imperialism in particular. Meetings were held in the NCC, the YM and YWCAs, the Christian Literature Society and other organizations with strong overseas connections. Certain individual missionaries and Chinese church leaders were singled out for attack by former colleagues and associates. It was a divisive and agonizing chapter in the church's life, and one which engendered considerable resistance in many forms.

Selected References

Chedi geduan jidujiao yu meiguo diguozhuyi de lianxi (Sever the links between Christianity and American Imperialism). Beijing: Renmin wenxue xhubanshe, 1951.
Jiang Wenhan. "Guangxuehui shi zeyang yige jigou?" (What Kind of Organization was the Christian Literature Society?) *Wenshi ziliao xuanji*, ed. National Committee for Research on Literary and Historical Sources of the CPPCC. Beijing: Zhongguo shuju 43 (1981).
Ying Yuandao. *Jidujiao de kongsu yundong* (The Christian Denunciation Movement). Shanghai: YMCA Press, 1953.

Jones, Francis Price, ed. *Documents of the Three-Self Movement: Source Materials for the Study of the Protestant Church in Communist China*. New York: National Council of Churches of Christ in the USA, 1963.

Yamamoto, Sumiko. *History of Protestantism in China: The Indigenization of Christianity*. Tokyo: Toho Gakkai, 2000.

5.4.3. Three-Self Patriotic Movement of Protestant Churches in China (TSPM)

Three-Self - self-government, self-support- and self-propagation - was a concept adopted from abroad, first formulated by Henry Venn, Rufus Anderson and John Nevius in the 19th century. Missionaries first applied it to the situation of the church in China but although the three-self ideal was taken up by the independence movement churches in early 20th century, it was not really adopted until the late 1940s.

The Three-Self Patriotic Movement Committee was formally established in 1954 at the first NCC meeting held after Liberation, to serve as "the patriotic and church-loving organization of Chinese Christians (and) undertake patriotic education and relationships with the government." It was shaped by the forces of the times: including the Christian Manifesto; support for China's entry into the Korean War; and the denunciation movement. In the 1950s it was given some theological content, for example, by Zhao Fusan who saw it as calling Chinese churches to repentance and renewal, expressing both judgement and the grace of God. Disbanded in 1966 during the Cultural Revolution, it was reorganized in 1980.

Y.T. Wu was the first Chairperson of the TSPM at its inception. Among others associated with the formation of the TSPM in various capacities were Shen Derong, Luo Guanzong, Shen Zigao, Jiang Wenhan (Kiang Wenhan), Li Chuwen, Deng Yuzhi (Cora Deng) and Liu Liangmo.

In 1980, the China Christian Council was founded as the organization to oversee church affairs. During the late 1980s, there were rumors that the TSPM, having fulfilled its task, would be abolished. Instead, its achievements were affirmed and the two national organizations, commonly referred to as the *lianghui* (two bodies or associations) were said to work as two hands of the same body.

Selected References

    Deng Zhaoming. *The Vicissitudes of the Three-Self Patriotic Movement in the 1950's and its Predicament Today*. Ching Feng Series No. 8. Hong Kong: Christian Study Centre on Chinese Religion & Culture, 1997.

    Duan Qi. *Draft History of the Indigenization of Christianity in China* (in Chinese). Unpub. Ms.

    Jones, Francis Price, ed. *Documents of the Three-Self Movement: Source Materials for the Study of the Protestant Church in Communist China*. New York: National Council of Churches of Christ in the USA, 1963.

    Luo Guanzong, ed. *Zhongguo jidujiao sanzi aiguo yundong wenxuan: 1950-1992* (Selected Documents and Writings from the Chinese Christian Three-Self Patriotic Movement: 1950-1992). Shanghai: TSPM and CCC, 1993.

    Shen Derong. *My Fifty Years with the TSPM* (in Chinese). Shanghai: CCC/TSPM, 2000.

    Ting. K.H. "Three-Self and the Church: Re-ordering the Relationship." In *Love Never Ends*. Nanjing: Yilin Press, 2000.

    Whyte, Bob. *Unfinished Encounter: China and Christianity*. London: Collins/Fount Paperbacks, 1988.

    Wickeri, Philip L. *Seeking the Common Ground: Protestant Christianity, the Three-Self Movement, and China's United Front*. Maryknoll, NY: Orbis Books, 1988.

    Yamamoto, Sumiko. *History of Protestantism in China: The Indigenization of Christianity*. Tokyo: Toho Gakkai, 2000.

    Ying Fuk-tsang and Leung Ka-lun. *Wushi niandai sanzi yundong de yanjiu* (The Three-Self Patriotic Movement in the 1950s). Hong Kong: Alliance Bible Seminary, 1996.

5.4.4. Theological Reorientation at the Grassroots

The necessity for Chinese Christians to reflect theologically in a new context - how to reconcile Christian faith with the new reality - produced heated debate. Between 1953 and 1955, articles appeared in the church magazine, *Tian Feng,* that criticized extreme theological views. In 1956 *Tian Feng* spearheaded a mass discussion, with emphasis on the exchange of theological views among lay people and pastors, with church leaders and intellectuals consciously trying to relate themselves to the concerns of Christians at the grassroots. The focus of debate was on those theological issues that most concerned Christians: namely attitudes toward the world and toward non-Christians.

It was a theological attempt to resolve the contradictions of being "yoked together with unbelievers" and to emphasize the continuity between prevailing conservative views on the necessity of redemption and a more creation-centered theological approach. This new approach was characterized as "new light": the leading of the Holy Spirit toward a new framework of understanding the biblical message. Emphasis was on seeking the common ground (while reserving differences) in faith matters as well as identifying with the Chinese people, which theologically meant affirming the goodness revealed in nature and history. All good works come from God, thus Christians could learn from and work with non-believers. They could play an active and positive role in new China.

It was a diffuse rather than systematic theological approach that made it possible for conservatives to affirm the new reality. Human nature was not totally depraved; the world was not completely fallen.

In 1958, the contradictions of denominationalism were resolved by the adoption of unified worship and organization. Though the trend toward unity was of long-standing, its realization was an administrative move, undertaken under pressure from the government. The new situation would require "mutual respect," that is, "seeking the common ground in matters of faith and worship, and reserving differences." Thus Protestant Christians from a wide and disparate variety of faith backgrounds were drawn together into a single entity, though individual churches retained their inherited patterns of Baptism and Communion. Some were more willing and others less, but the political vicissitudes of the coming years made of the "post-denominational church" one body, and in practice brought many who might be labeled "conservative" or "liberal" into a closer and more fluid relationship than such loaded terms as "open" and "underground" do not do full justice to. In many ways this constitutes a unique heritage of Chinese Protestantism.

Selected References

Chen, Zemin. "The Task of Theological Construction in the Chinese Church (II)" (in Chinese). *Nanjing Theological Review* 7 (1957).

Duan Qi. *Brief History of the Indigenization of Christianity in China* (in Chinese). Unpub. Ms.

Wickeri, Philip L. *Seeking the Common Ground: Protestant Christianity, the Three-Self Movement, and China's United Front.* Maryknoll, NY: Orbis Books, 1988, 243-280.

Ting, K.H. "Theological Mass Movements in China." In *Love Never Ends.* Nanjing: Yilin Press, 2000, 137-150.

—. "Another Look at Three-Self." In *Love Never Ends.* Nanjing: Yilin Press, 2000, 90-106.

Yamamoto, Sumiko. *History of Protestantism in China: The Indigenization of Christianity.* Tokyo: Toho Gakkai, 2000.

5.4.5. K.H. Ting (Ding Guangxun, 1915-)

K. H. Ting has been a key figure in the Chinese churches for over half a century. He received his B.A. and B.D. from St. John's University in Shanghai and his M.A. in religious education in 1948 from Union Theological Seminary in New York. He was ordained in 1942 and consecrated Bishop of Chekiang (Zhejiang) Province in 1955. After student work with the YMCA, Ting served in the SCM of Canada and with the WSCF in Geneva. He returned to China in 1951, against the advice of his overseas friends, and became Principal of Nanjing Union Theological Seminary when it was formed in 1953, a post he still holds. Prior to the Cultural Revolution, he was a delegate to both the Chinese People's Political Consultative Conference (CPPCC) and the National People's Congress (NPC). In 1978, he was made a member of the Standing Committee of the CPPCC and the following year became a delegate to the NPC. In the 1980s, he was chair of the Chinese Christian Three-Self Patriotic Association and president of the China Christian Council, and also President of the Amity Foundation. He retired from his posts in the CCC and TSPM in 1997. Ting is a solidly ecumenical church leader of international standing.

In the 1950s, K.H. Ting published a series of theological essays addressing concrete problems which the church faced. In "Evangelism and Church Building (1953), he criticized the tendency to overemphasize the doctrine of justification by faith, enumerating its negative consequences. In 1957, he gave a powerful address to graduating students at Nanjing Seminary, later published as "On Christian Theism." Coming at the end of the anti-rightist movement, the address is a forthright defense of Christian belief in God, rejecting the simplistic division between Christianity as "idealism" and Marxist materialism. Disputing the idea that Christianity is in essence the "opiate of the people," he speaks of the relationship between nature and revelation: grace in no way denies nature, but fulfills it.

In this early period, he focused on building up the Chinese Church in the new situation and on finding a theological foundation for cooperation among people of various denominational backgrounds, one that would help those who formerly wanted to escape the world to engage with it. He was removed from all his church and political posts at the start of the Cultural Revolution in 1966, but began to appear in public and meet with overseas visitors again in the early 1970s. In the early 1980s, as President of the China Christian Council and Chair of the TSPM, Ting worked to unite as many believers as possible within the purview of the two organizations, emphasizing seeking the common ground while reserving differences. He also played an active role throughout the 1980s and 90s in interpreting religion in general and Christianity in particular to government officials, working to increase the space for religious activities in Chinese society. He did much to discredit the simplistic idea of religion as opium, and his writings aimed at secular and political audiences set out a Christian apologetic for the 1980s, a defense of Christianity using Marxist language.

He has published numerous theological essays on a variety of theological themes, including Incarnation, Christology, ecclesiology, the nature of God, the nature of humanity, nature and revelation, etc. He begins theologically from the Chinese social and political context and creatively merges western theology and Chinese culture. So that while it is clear that his theological thinking has been influenced by many western scholars, at the same time his is a completely Chinese theology, creative and grounded in the contemporary Chinese social situation. He is perhaps best known for his theology of love: both love for God, love for each other in the church, and love for people who are not Christians. And he sets these familiar terms within both the Chinese and a cosmic context. We are all, both Christian and non-Christian, God's children; God is love, and love is the uniquely essential attribute of God, therefore, we should love one another. Love is our best witness for God to our fellow people. These ideas are perhaps best set out in relation to the "cosmic lover", in his 1991 address, "The Cosmic Christ."

"That Christ is cosmic gives us assurance that God is the cosmic lover, not any cosmic tyrant or punisher. He works by education and persuasion rather than coercion and forced obedience. He lures and invites and waits for free response and does not resort to scolding and reprimanding. That is why many of us in China find the Gospels' analogy of the transformation of seeds and the growth of plants in air, rain and sun more appealing than that of beating and controlling the sheep with rod and staff. God's is the will-to-fellowship, not the will-to-power. For Chinese Christians, to discard the image of a vengeful, frightening God, God the omnipotent in dealing with humans, and to come to adore God the Lover, the Sympathizer, the fellow-sufferer who comes to us, is a shift that is truly liberating. . . . . This emphasis on God as the great Lover working out his purpose for the world brings in its train an understanding of reality as becoming. It gives us hope for and beyond history. We cannot fathom the actual time and manner the end of history as we know it will come about, but are sure it will be the triumph of love and grace. The way from alpha to omega is never a straight line, but love accompanies the pilgrims."

His thinking on Christology, ecclesiology, and elsewhere has thus been very helpful in directing the reconstruction of the Chinese church, and in helping the church to become reconciled with the Chinese people. In some sense, his theology is a theology of reconciliation, both reconciliation with God, reconciliation with church members, and reconciliation with non-Christians. And this approach is of course most important for Chinese society, both within and beyond the church.

Selected References
Works by K.H. Ting
> *How to Study the Bible*. English trans. Hong Kong: Tao Fong Shan Ecumenical Centre, 1981; excerpts in *CTR 1985*.
> —, ed. *Liangguang de guang* (Seeing Light in the Light). Shanghai: CCC, 1988.
> "Fourteen Points." In *A New Beginning: An International Dialogue with the Chinese Church*, edited by Theresa Chu and Christopher Lind, 104-108. Toronto: Canada China Programme, 1986.
> *Christianity with a Chinese Face*. Cincinnati: Forward Movement Publications, 1989.
> *Ding Guangxun wenji* (Writings of K.H. Ting). Nanjing: Yilin Press, 1999.
> *Love Never Ends* (English edition of *Ding Guangxun wenji*). Nanjing: Yilin Press, 2000.
> Translations of other writings and sermons appear in the pages of the *Chinese Theological Review:* 1985 -. No. 10 (1995) is a festschrift with appreciations by colleagues and friends.
> Duan Qi. *Draft History of the Indigenization of Christianity in China* (in Chinese). Unpub. Ms.
> Whitehead, Raymond L., ed. *No Longer Strangers*. Maryknoll, N.Y.: Orbis, 1989.
> Whyte, Bob. *Unfinished Encounter: China and Christianity*. London: Collins/Fount Paperbacks, 1988.
> Wickeri, Philip L. *Seeking the Common Ground: Protestant Christianity, the Three-Self Movement, and China's United Front*. Maryknoll, NY: Orbis Books, 1988.
> —, and Janice K. Wickeri, eds. *A Chinese Contribution to Ecumenical Theology: Selected Writings of K.H. Ting*. Geneva: World Council of Churches. Forthcoming.
> Yamamoto, Sumiko. *History of Protestantism in China: The Indigenization of Christianity*. Tokyo: Toho Gakkai, 2000.

5.4.6. Chen Zemin (1917-)
With a background in social service and hospital chaplaincy, Chen has been Associate Dean and Dean of Nanjing Theological

Seminary, becoming Vice-Principal in 1981. He is also a professor of systematic theology and senior pastor of St. Paul's Church in Nanjing, as well as a Vice-President of the China Christian Council.

Chen wrote an important essay during the theological reorientation movement titled "Theological Construction in the Chinese Church" (written in 1956, and originally appearing in the *Nanjing Theological Review*, 1957), in which he wrote that theology could not be separate from the social context of the church. To continue to exist in the midst of the new socialist society, the Chinese church must recognize its duty and complete its mission. It already has sufficient experience and material upon which to reflect, and must use the language of theology to review the road along which it has come, through faith and in the context of the history of Christianity. The church should also make use of this same mode of thinking to determine and indicate its future direction. In this essay, he saw both the theological poverty of the pre-1949 Chinese church and the awakening of theology in a new era, both the problem which the church was facing and the path by which the church could reach its future. He also attempted to reflect theologically from the perspective of the Chinese social and cultural context.

"In our understanding of redemption, we oppose making sin the foundation of the gospel or basing the future of the church on human despair…Rather, we find the source in the just and loving nature of God. The necessity of the gospel and the future of the church are not based on the hopelessness of this world or of humanity, but on the fact that God, in His plan of creation, chose redemption as His method. It was not humanity's utter depravity that caused God to seek us, but that humanity is the crown of creation, created in the image of God to help God oversee this world. It is only because of all this that we are worthy of God's redemption." ("The Task of Theological Construction in the Chinese Church (II)" *Nanjing Theological Review* (August 1957).

With the reopening of the Chinese Church in the early 1980s, Chen Zemin has been active in teaching and writing and in introducing contemporary western theologies to China, as well as reflecting on Christian theology and issues of Christ and culture in China. He is well known as a Christian scholar in religious studies circles and considers it crucial to train Chinese Christian scholars to engage in dialogue with non-Christian scholars of religion.

A theological liberal, Chen Zemin advocates a broadly creation-based theology which allows the church to be in dialogue with all sectors of society and with its culture. He summarizes aspects of contemporary Chinese theological reflection on this basis: 1) God is love and God's love is universal; 2) the Cosmic Christ: Christ is God become flesh, in whom humans can see salvation and renewal. Christ is the cosmic Christ, thus his salvation is beyond the church; 3) the Holy Spirit moves in the whole universe, not just in the church. All truth, goodness and beauty are from the Spirit of God; 4) Humans are not totally depraved; they have fallen, but have not totally lost the image of God within themselves; 5) Christian life should emphasize justification by faith, but there should be a balance between faith and works; 6) The Chinese Church has an urgent need for ecclesiology, in which it is very weak; and 7) In terms of eschatology, many people still hold pre-millenarian views, but most Chinese theologians have turned to post-millenarianism, allowing some room for social development and progress.

Selected References
Works by Chen Zemin
> *Pillar of Cloud; Pillar of Fire.* 1950. reprint, Nanjing, 1991.
> Senior ed. of Christianity portion of the Religion Section of the *Chinese Encyclopedia.*
> "Evangelical Movements in History," *Nanjing Theological Review* 2 (1954).
> "Living as Christians Today: Biblical Insights," *China Study Project Journal*, vol. 3, no. 2 (1988).
> "Protestant Christianity Facing Challenges of Modernization." In *Christianity and Modernization: A Chinese Debate*, edited by Philip Wickeri and Lois Cole. Hong Kong: DAGA Press, 1995.
> "Self-Propagation in the Light of the History of Christian Thought." *CTR* 1986.

"Theological Construction in the Chinese Church". *Nanjing Theological Review* 6 and 7 (1957); reprinted with new preface, *Nanjing Theological Review* 14/15 (1991); *CTR* 1991.

—,ed. *Selected Theological Writings from Nanjing Theological Seminary (1952-1992)*. Nanjing Theological Seminary Publications, 1992.

"Inculturation of the Gospel and Hymn Singing in China." *CTR* 11:2 (1998).

"On Nanjing Theological Seminary," *CTR* 1987.

"The Church's Approach to Intellectuals." *CTR* 13 (1999).

"Theological Construction of the Chinese Church," *Nanjing Theological Review* 18(1993).

"Y.T. Wu: A Prophetic Theologian." *CTR* 10.

5.4.7. Zhao Fusan (1926? -)

Zhao was a vice-chair of the TSPM and became a deputy director of the Chinese Academy of Social Sciences in 1985. Ordained an Anglican priest, Zhao did not study overseas, but traveled widely outside China: he was present at the 1956 WSCF assembly in Tutsing, and accompanied K.H. Ting to the First All-Christian Peace Assembly in 1961. Like K.H. Ting, Zhao wrote many essays in the mid-1980s, refuting the claims of scholars in the so-called "third opium war" that religion was no more than the opiate of the people. Zhao demonstrated the cultural contribution of Christianity in the West, to show that religion could play a positive role in society, just as Christianity was part of the West's heritage, its spiritual culture, to be passed on when any great change takes place. It was not the class nature of religion that was important, but its essence. Zhao was one of those who argued for the complex nature of religion, and the need for a new departure in religious studies at a meeting of the CPPCC in 1985.

Zhao did not return to China after June 4, 1989. He now resides in the U.S.

Selected References
Works by Zhao Fusan

"The Penitence and Renewal of the Church in China." In David M. Paton, ed. *Essays in Anglican Self-Criticism*, 86-98. London: SCM Press, 1958.

"Church Autonomy from a Theological Perspective." In *A New Beginning: An International Dialogue with the Chinese Church*, edited by Theresa Chu and Christopher Lind, 95-97. Toronto: Canada China Programme, 1986.

"Colonialism and Missionary Movement." In *A New Beginning: An International Dialogue with the Chinese Church*, edited by Theresa Chu and Christopher Lind, 94-95. Toronto: Canada China Programme, 1986.

"Religion, Spiritual Culture and Unity." *CTR* 1985.

Christianity in China. Theresa Carino, ed. Manila: De La Salle University Press, 1986.

Whyte, Bob. *Unfinished Encounter: China and Christianity*. London: Collins/Fount Paperbacks, 1988.

Wickeri, Philip L. *Seeking the Common Ground: Protestant Christianity, the Three-Self Movement, and China's United Front*. Maryknoll, NY: Orbis Books, 1988.

In addition to the individuals mentioned here, others less known for their writings who nonetheless worked for the contextual formation of the Protestant church in China in this and subsequent periods include, Jiang Wenhan, Zheng Jianye, Bishop of Zhejiang and Peter Tsai (Cai Wenhao), among others

5.4.8. Journals and writings

The weekly church magazine, *Tian Feng*, began publication in 1945 in Chongqing (Chungking) with Y.T. Wu as editor. In 1951, it was designated the official organ of the TSPM by the Three-Self Preparatory Committee. It became a monthly in 1961 and was closed in 1964.

Other journals continued in the early 1950s: *Xie jin*, the official publication of the NCC, was reorganized in 1951 and closed in 1954; the *Nanjing Theological Review* published seven issues between 1953 and 1957, carrying important theological and interpretive essays.

Specialized publications, such as *Tian jia* (Christian Farmer) and *Enyou* (for youth) ceased by the mid-1950s. The publication of pamphlets, study manuals, devotional literature, and reference materials by the TSPM, undertaken in the 1950s, had all ceased publication by the early to mid-1960s. (See further below 5.6.3, 5.9).

5.5 Cultural Revolution Era 1966-1976

From the late 1950s through the early 1960s, the increasing leftist political line in national life grew in its impact on the life of the church and in most areas little theological reflection was possible. Nanjing Union Theological Seminary, closed six years earlier in 1955, reopened in 1961. Other seminaries closed in 1963. Although the church was able to maintain itself until the mid-1960s, a slight political relaxing in 1961 ended in 1966 with the Cultural Revolution. Churches and church organizations were closed, their properties being taken over by other units. The practice of meeting together in homes for prayer, Bible study and worship grew in the late 1950s and some house gatherings continued throughout the Cultural Revolution, especially in the countryside. This tradition of house gatherings sustained a church that had been deprived of all institutional expression. From memoirs and anecdotes, we know that some groups tithed, and that hand-copied, mimeographed bible portions and Bibles were cherished. For the most part, clergy and seminary professors were reassigned to factory jobs or manual labor in the countryside. In 1972, it began to be possible for more groups to meet across the country. Though secular studies and memoirs of the movements of the 1950s and 1960s, and of the Cultural Revolution, have appeared in China, the experience of Christians and the survival of church life is little discussed or studied. Detailed analysis of the impact of the Cultural Revolution on Christianity in China has yet to be done.

Selected References

Adeney, David H. *China: Christian Students Face the Revolution.* Downer's Grove: Intervarsity, 1975.

—. *China: The Church's Long March.* Robesonia, PA: OMF Books, 1985.

Bush, Richard. *Religion in Communist China.* Nashville and New York: Abingdon, 1970.

Chao, Jonathan. *Wise as Serpents, Innocent as Doves: Christians in China Tell Their Story.* Pasadena: William Carey Library, 1988.

Clark, William H. *The Church in China: Its Vitality, Its Future.* New York: Council Press, 1970.

Digan, Parig. *The Christian China Watchers: A Post-Mao Perspective*. Brussels: Pro Mundi Vita, 1978.
Green, H. Gordon. "A Canadian Look at the Church in China." *Christian Century* (24 August 1966).
Hockin, Katherine. *Servants of God in People's China*. New York: Friendship Press, 1962.
Jones, Francis Price. *The Church in Communist China: A Protestant Appraisal*. New York: Friendship Press, 1962.
—, ed. *Documents of the Three-Self Movement: Source Materials for the Study of the Protestant Church in Communist China*. New York: National Council of Churches of Christ in the USA, 1963.
Lacy, Creighton B. "Protestant Missions in Communist China." Ph.D. diss., Yale University, 1953.
Lutheran World Federation and Pro Mundi Vita. *Christianity and the New China*. vol. I. *Christianity and the New China* (Papers presented at the Ecumenical Seminar held in Båstad, Sweden, Janaury 29 - February 2, 1974). vol II. *Christian Faith and the Chinese Experience*(Papers and Reports from an Ecumenical Colloquium held in Louvain, Belgium, September 9 - 16, 1974). South Pasadena: Ecclesia Publications (William Carey Library), 1976.
Mac Innis, Donald. *Religious Practice and Policy in Communist China*. New York: MacMillan, 1972.
Patterson, George. *Christianity in Communist China*. Waco: Word Books, 1969.
Whitehead, Raymond. *Love and Struggle in Mao's Thought*. Maryknoll, NY: Orbis, 1977.

5.6 The Resurgence of Church Life and Theology: 1980s

The first service of public worship in a reopened church took place at Christmas, 1978. Reinstatement of publications, the reopening of Nanjing Seminary and other seminaries, the reorganization of the TSPM and formation of the CCC all took place in 1980.

A resurgence in Christianity began to be felt, developing into a "Christianity fever," especially in rural areas, as both Christian faith and Christian ethics spoke to people out of the void left by the Cultural Revolution. It was a time of broadening unity, with an emphasis on bringing as many believers as possible into the TSPM/CCC fold, and renewed calls for seeking the common ground.

Writings in the *Nanjing Theological Review* explored the biblical grounds for Three-Self, and the contribution of religion to "socialist spiritual civilization." The government promulgation of Document 19 was seen as increasing space for religion in society. There was a sense that Christians had changed the foreign image of their religion by suffering with all Chinese people in the Cultural Revolution. Reports of the good image of Christians in villages and factories through donated labor and harmonious personal relationships abounded; individual Christians were recognized as advanced workers. This may be seen as Christians living out their own sense of the Christian life through an ethical witness of good deeds.

The survival of the church through the Cultural Revolution was a powerful experience of resurrection from suffering and death that led to new insights on the theological issues that shaped Chinese Christianity. The Incarnation, that God became incarnate in the flesh, meant an affirmation of the flesh (society) as well as of the spirit: both are of God. This opened the way to acceptance of truth, goodness, and beauty outside the church and an affirmation of human nature. Theologically, it opened the way for some conservative Christian leaders, like the woman evangelist Sister Jiang Peifen (see 5.6.6.), to unite with Three-Self.

A deeper understanding of the meaning of the Cross was explored: that of God with us in suffering and suffering as God's pedagogy. This was seen as potentially a way of transcending the conflict between a personal and social gospel. Ultimately humankind can be reconciled to God only through redemption, yet the paradoxical truth of the Cross is verified through the sacrificial and noble deeds of people, whatever their beliefs. Reconciliation, both within the church and with society was important, healing enduring theological conflicts, as well as the wounds of the Cultural Revolution. Many Chinese become Christians through an experience of healing - physical, in some cases, but more importantly emotional and personal. Christ as healer and the healing love of God are themes that can be explored more fully in studies of Chinese theology.

Contextual Theology in China 191

In the mid-1980s, need for an ecclesiological grounding was increasingly felt. Three-self became "three wells," with an emphasis on Christian stewardship and transparency in financial affairs, democratic decision-making in the church, and a strengthening of the institution through regularized management structures. Lay-training courses were instituted to deal with the shortage of ordained ministers and to channel orthodox theological training to the many lay leaders who had come forward during the Cultural Revolution and the rapid growth that followed. Growth outstripped the church's institutional capacity to deal with it, further underscoring the need for ecclesiology both structurally and theologically. A draft church order was adopted at the Sixth National Christian Conference in early 1997, but has no binding power.

The 1980s saw an increasing openness in theological writings, with discussion of a wide variety of viewpoints, the call to liberate theological thinking, and to learn from international theological developments. In the aftermath of June 4, 1989, there was a drawing in, but continuing emphasis on theological education and lay training, harmonization with socialism, and upon running the church well. There was greater recognition of the theological gap with conservative viewpoints, as well as of the need to reach out to intellectuals and open dialogue with the growing study of religion and Christianity outside the church.

Overseas visits and exchanges were revitalized, notably "A New Beginning: An International Dialogue with the Chinese Church," held in Montreal in 1981 and attended by Catholic and Protestant leaders from China, including Fu Tieshan, Tu Shihua, K.H. Ting, Han Wenzao, Jiang Peifen, Chen Zemin, Shen Yifan, Jiang Wehan, Zhao Fusan and others, along with 150 Christians from around the world (see refs. above).

This period also witnesses a resurgence and growth in the social witness of the church. The Amity Foundation was begun in 1985 with the purpose of "making Christian presence better known in society." For this funding was received from overseas partners as well as Chinese sources to carry out a variety of projects in rural development, education, community health, etc. Many individual churches also began locally-based social service projects: orphanages, kindergartens, homes for senior citizens, clinics, etc.

Selected Resources

Bao Zhimin. "Facing Reality and Responding to Challenges: On Ten Years of Chinese Church Reconstruction." *CTR:* 1989.

Brown, G. Thompson, ed. *Christianity in the People's Republic of China.* Atlanta: John Knox Press, 1986.

CCA Consultation with Church Leaders from China. Singapore: CCA, 1981.

Chen Fu Tien. *The Current Religious Policy of the People's Republic of China (January 1, 1976 - March 15, 1979): Part I: An Inquiry.* Norwalk, CT, 1983.

Chinese Theological Review: 1985 contains church statements and documents from the Third NCCC held in 1980; 1987 from the Fourth; 1991 from the Fifth; and vol. 12 (1998) from the Sixth.

Chu, Theresa and Christopher Lind. *A New Beginning: An International Dialogue with the Chinese Church.* Toronto: Canada China Programme, 1986.

Covell, Ralph. *Confucius, the Buddha and Christ: A History of the Gospel in Chinese.* Maryknoll, NY: Orbis Books, 1986.

Duan Qi. *Draft History of the Indigenization of Christianity in China* (in Chinese). Unpub. Ms.

Dunch, Ryan. "Protestant Christianity in China Today: Fragile, Fragmented, Flourishing." In *China and Christianity: Burdened Past, Hopeful Future,* edited by Stephen Uhalley, Jr., and Wu Xiaoxin, 195-216. Armonk, NY. and London: M.E. Sharpe, 2001.

"EATWOT Visits China, May 2-13, 1986." Ecumenical Association of Third World Theologians, 1986.

Fung, Raymond. *Households of God on China's Soil.* Geneva: World Council of Churches, 1982.

Glasser, Arthur. "China Today-An Evangelical Perspective." *Missiology* 9:3 (July, 1981).

Hood, George A. *Neither Bang Nor Whimper: The End of a Missionary Era in China.* Singapore: Presbyterian Church in Singapore, 1991.

Hunter, Alan and Kim-Kwong Chan. *Protestantism in Contemporary China.* Cambridge: Cambridge University Press, 1993.

Lambert, Tony. *The Resurrection of the Chinese Church*. London: Hodder and Stoughton, 1991. Rev. ed. Wheaton, Ill.: Harold Shaw, 1994.

Luo Zhufeng, ed. *Zhongguo shehui zhuyi shiqi de zongjiao wenti* (The Religious Question during China's Socialist Period). Shanghai: CASS, 1987. Translated by Donald E. MacInnis and Zheng Xi'an as *Religion Under Socialism in China*. Armonk: M. E. Sharpe, 1991.

MacInnis, Don. *Religion in China Today: Policy and Practice*. Maryknoll, NY: Orbis, 1989.

Oblau, Gotthard. "Protestant Sermons in China-Harbingers of an Evolving Contextual Theology." *China Study Journal* 11: 1 (April 1996).

Pas, Julian F., ed. *The Turning of the Tide: Religion in China Today*. Hong Kong: Oxford University Press with the Hong Kong branch, Royal Asiatic Society, 1989.

Towery, Britt. *Churches of China: Taking Root Downward, Bearing Fruit Upward*. 3rd edition. Waco: Baylor University Press, 1990. The Tao Foundation Missionary Heritage Edition, *Christianity in Today's China: Taking Root Downward, Bearing Fruit Upward*. 1st Books Library, 2000.

Whitehead, James, Yuming Shaw and N. J. Giradot, eds. *China and Christianity: Historical and Future Encounters*. South Bend: Center for Pastoral and Social Ministries, University of Notre Dame, 1979. A collection of articles on American perceptions and interpretations of China in the early Deng Xiaoping era.

Xiao Yue. "Chinese Theology in the Early 1980s." *CTR* 14 (2000).

Yamamoto, Sumiko. *History of Protestantism in China: The Indigenization of Christianity*. Tokyo: Toho Gakkai, 2000.

Yip, Francis Ching-wah. *Chinese Theology in State-Church Context: A Preliminary Study*. Hong Kong: Christian Study Center on Chinese Religion and Culture, 1997.

Zhao Fusan. *Christianity in China*. Edited by Theresa Carino. Manila: de La Salle University, 1986.

5.6.1. Wang Weifan (1928-)

Prolific and popular devotional writer, preacher, theologian, Wang was a 1955 graduate of Nanjing Union Theological Seminary. Following the Cultural Revolution he became Associate Professor of New Testament at Nanjing Theological Seminary and head of its Publications Department. As a theological educator, Wang instilled his own love for Chinese literary tradition in his students and encouraged them to find roots of Christian faith in traditional Chinese culture and its classic writings, thus nurturing a new generation of Chinese Christian writers. For Wang, the mystical and the socio-political interact and complement each other as modes of discourse. He is generally a more evangelical thinker, but not a conservative one. He sees change as providing new opportunities for witness bearing, while as a socially committed intellectual he is not afraid to say that he is sustained by the gracious love of God in Jesus Christ. Christocentric mysticism threads through his life and thought and he draws deeply on western mystical sources, as well as on Chinese sources. His view of the encounter of Christian faith with traditional Chinese values allows him to adapt in the twists and turns experienced by the Chinese people over the last 45 years.

His theological thinking is informed by a broad and deep grasp of traditional Chinese culture (encompassing its Confucian, Buddhist and Taoist expressions) and western theology. Like K.H. Ting, he focuses on the Incarnation, but for him the emphasis is somewhat different. In merging western theology and Chinese culture to create an indigenous Chinese theology, he sees the possibility for the "Word becoming flesh," in cultures beyond Bethlehem and Judah - in every culture, including Chinese culture. Just as God did not abandon Jewish culture, but rather fulfilled it, so God will fulfill Chinese culture. In comparison to K.H. Ting, who is more concerned with the church's social and political context, Wang's concern with Chinese culture makes an indigenous theology in some ways more complete. In his *Chinese Theology and Its Cultural Sources*, he writes:

> "To be Christians, we should 'according to the principle of *ren* (human-heartedness; benevolence), help others.' But this *ren* differs from the *ren* of Confucianism, which means human relationships through human kindness and love. Instead, it is the *ren* of the *Yi jing*, which is the seed of grasses, trees and fruits. This seed is the very source of life. The theological assumption of Nestorian Christians is that all good works and virtues are meant to help people live and to live a better life.

"Therefore, God is an ever-generating God who creates and sustains life and Christ is an invitation to life through the destruction of death, making life more complete and full. Christians are dependent upon the power of heaven for self-transformation and also to protect life. This is the theological reflection of Christians living in the Tang and Yuan dynasties, arrived at with the influence of Chinese traditional culture: an ever-generating God, firmly rooted in the Chinese notion of 'unceasing generation'." (Foreword)

Through an examination of classic works such as the *Yi jing* (Book of Change), Wang identifies points at which traditional Chinese culture influences Chinese theological reflection and explores them theologically, seeking the spiritual sources of Chinese civilization and how these may inform Christian faith.

Selected References
Works by Wang Weifan
> *Lilies of the Field.* Shanghai: China Christian Council, 1985; English edition, Philip and Janice Wickeri, trans. and eds. Hong Kong: Foundation for Theological Education in South East Asia, 1988; U.S. edition, Nashville: Upper Room Books, 1993, 1996.
> "Changes in Theological Thinking in the Church in China." *CTR* (1986).
> *Commentary on 1 and 2 Corinthians.* Chinese Theological Education Series. Shanghai: Theological Education Commission of CCC, 1989.
> "The Pattern and Pilgrimage of Chinese Theology." *CTR* (1990).
> *Xunzhao nide puren* (Seek Out Your Servant). Shanghai: CCC/TSPM, 1994.
> *The Way Home.* Shanghai: CCC/TSPM, 1996.
> *Chinese Theology and Its Cultural Sources.* Foreword in *CTR* 13 (1999). Forthcoming.

5.6.2. Shen Yifan (1929?-1995)

Son of the former Bishop of Shanxi, T.K. Shen, Shen Yifan was general secretary of the China Christian Council and director of the Theological Education Commission. He was consecrated Bishop in 1988.

He has published less than other theologians mentioned here, but wrote of his concerns for the construction of Chinese theology in the new context following 1949. His essays such as "Chinese Christianity in Theological Reflection," and "Theological Reflection in the Chinese Church," outline Chinese theological reflection since 1949. He was widely appreciated as a pastor and preacher. Generally speaking, his theological thinking followed that of K. H. Ting and focused on the concrete Chinese social situation in which the church exists. Like most contemporary Chinese theologians, he gave a central emphasis to the doctrine of the Incarnation. This he found to be clearly helpful in eliminating the tension between such areas as the sacred and the profane, God and the world, Christian and non-Christian, and similar dualisms.

Selected References
Works by Shen Yifan
> *Jiangtai shifeng; Luntan xinsheng-Shen Yifan zhujiao wenji* (Collected Sermons of Bishop Shen Yifan). vols.1 & 2. Shanghai: CCC publication, 1996.
> "Chinese Christianity in Theological Reflections." *CTR* (1985).
> "How New China Helps Christians Think Anew Theologically," and "Freedom as Viewed by a Chinese Christian." In *A New Beginning: An International Dialogue with the Chinese Church*, edited by Theresa Chu and Christopher Lind, 52-57; 29-32. Toronto: Canada China Programme, 1986.
> "Theological Reflection in the Chinese Church." *CTR* (1988).
> "Tasks of the Church in the Process of Modernisation." *China Study Journal*, vol. 7, no. 1 (April 1992).
> "Religious Liberty: A Chinese Perspective." *CTR* 8 (1993).
> "Your Young Men Shall See Visions." *CTR* 11:1 (1996).
> Li Yading. "In Memoriam: Bishop Shen Yifan." *CTR* 11:1 (1996).

5.6.3. Publications (See also 5.4.8 and 5.9).

Tian Feng returned as the church monthly in 1980 in a new series. *Nanjing Theological Review* (Jinling Shenxue zhi) also returned in a new series. *Jiao cai* (Study Materials) is a theological correspondence course sent out from Nanjing Seminary to over 50,000 subscribers. *Jiangdao ji* (Collected Sermons) is published by the Hangzhou Christian Council in Zhejiang. *Yanjing*

Theological Journal is published by the Beijing Seminary; other seminary magazines have been published by East China Theological Seminary in Shanghai and Zhejiang Seminary in Hangzhou. Bible publication under the joint auspices of the CCC and the United Bible Societies reached 26 million in 1999. Other publications of the CCC and other Christian Councils include devotional works, simple readers on Christian topics for new readers, calendars, collections of sermons, a revision of Fenn's Chinese-English concordance, hymnals, commentaries, textbooks, and many more.

Local and provincial governments have published a series of historical materials on religions that often include recollections or contributions from or about Christian figures.

Selected References
> Gong Liang. "Twenty Years of Studies of Biblical Literature in the People's Republic of China (1976-1996)." In *The Bible in China: The Literary and Intellectual Impact,* edited by Irene Eber, Sze-Kar Wan and Knut Wolf, 383-408. Monumenta Serica Monograph Series XLIII. Nettetal: Steyler Verlag, 1999.
> *Jindai Jiangsu zongjiao* (Religion in modern Jiangsu). Jiangsu Literary and Historical Materials, no. 38. Nanjing, 1991.
> Peng Shengyong. *Jiaomu yu jiaomu gongzuo* (Pastoral Care: Concept and Practice). Chinese Christian Theological Education Series, no. 2. Nanjing: CCC Commission on Theological Education, 1989.
> Xu Sixue. *Jiuye gailun* (Overview of the Old Testament). Nanjing: CCC Commission on Theological Education, 1995.
> —. *Xinyue gailun* (Overview of the New Testament). Hangzhou: Zhejiang Christian Council, 1996.

5.6.4. Lay Leadership and the Church at the Grassroots (See also 5.4.4).
House gatherings and house churches have long been an important feature of the development of Christianity in China, in both urban and rural areas, but particularly in the latter. It is estimated that 80% of Chinese Christians live in the countryside. Many groups are led by lay people, though where possible, there has been a

generally welcome program of visits, however irregularly at times, from pastors from churches in cities.

The church at the grassroots has grown rapidly, at times chaotically. Rapid growth has also given rise to sects and unorthodox beliefs and practices. Experiences of healing play an important role in bringing people to Christian faith. Efforts at channeling the energy of the grassroots church have resulted in a proliferation of lay training courses of various lengths and to the founding of at least one school bringing candidates together for further, more intense and structured training, at the Jiangsu Bible School outside Nanjing. Both Chinese and overseas scholars have begun to pay attention to the study of popular Christianity in China, speaking of the "folk-religionization" of Christianity.

Selected References

Gao Shining. "Twenty-first Century Chinese Christianity and the Chinese Social Process." *China Study Journal* 15: 2/3 (August-December 2000).

Ji Zhongwen. "How to Deal with the 'Local Church'-A Survey of Northern Zhejiang." *China Study Journal* 11: 1 (April 1996).

Jiang Peifen. "Church Life at the Grassroots." In *A New Beginning: An International Dialogue with the Chinese Church*, edited by Theresa Chu and Christopher Lind, 43-47. Toronto: Canada China Programme, 1986.

Leung Ka-lun. *Gaige kaifang yilai de Zhongguo nongmin jiaohui* (The Rural Churches of Mainland China Since 1978). Chinese Study Series 4. Hong Kong: Alliance Bible Seminary, 1999.

—. "Rural Christianity and Chinese Folk Religion." *China Study Journal* 14: 2 (August 1999).

Ma Jianhua. "Development of Rural Christianity in China and its Challenges." *CTR* 13 (1999).

"Self-Support Difficulties in Mountain Churches." *CTR* 12 (1998).

Währisch-Oblau, Claudia. "Healing Prayers and Healing Testimonies in Mainland Chinese Churches." *China Study Journal* 14: 2 (August 1999).

"Working Well at the Grassroots." *CTR* 12 (1998).

Ying Jie. "The Formation of Christian Home Meeting-points and Our Approach to Them." *China Study Journal* 11: 1 (April 1996).

5.6.5. The Younger Generation

Those who received their theological education in the 1980s and 1990s have begun to engage in theological reflection, among them some who have studied theology overseas after their first theological study in China. In general their interests are in indigenization and contextualization, the encounter of Christianity with both traditional Chinese culture and modern social issues, and for some, doing theology *in* Chinese. Women have begun to reflect theologically on their own situation and to investigate the encounter between Chinese women and Christianity.

Writings here include a wide range of biblical, contextual, historical and cultural, doctrinal, missiological and pastoral concerns, along with the concerns of spiritual life, homiletics, social issues, Christian art, education, ecumenical relations, biography and church order. These writings can be found in *Nanjing Theological Review, Tian Feng, Chinese Theological Review, China Study Journal.*

5.6.6. Women and Theology

Women have taken leadership roles in the work of the church both before and after the Cultural Revolution. In rural areas, their steadfast toil has been responsible for the growth of the church and often, for the physical construction of church buildings as well as their upkeep. Their role in the history of the Chinese church is being studied both in China and overseas. Among the older generation of church women, Rev. Cao Shengjie (1931-) has served many years as a vice-president of the China Christian Council and of the Shanghai Christian Council; Sister Jiang Peifen (d. 1996) taught at Nanjing Theological Seminary and was a popular devotional writer of a more evangelical bent (*Faith and Service*, (Nanjing: Nanjing Theological Seminary Publications, 1988). One of the best-known Christian women leaders of the last 50 years, Dr. Wu Yifang, president of Jinling Women's University, and Head of the Jiangsu Provincial Education Department, as well as Deputy-Governor of Jiangsu Province, continued to be an important force in education until her death in 1986. She also held national-level positions as a delegate to the NPC and to the CPPCC.

In addition to those of the younger generation mentioned above, women serve as pastors, theological educators, in the programs of the Amity Foundation, in the ongoing programs of the YWCA, and in many other capacities.

Their writings can be found in the *Nanjing Theological Review* and *Tian Feng*, and the latter frequently includes, as well, profiles of and interviews with women, lay and ordained, at all levels of the church. Protestant women also produced and presented a video on women in the church for the NGO Forum at the UN Women's Meeting in Beijing, 1996.

No in-depth study of women in the church since liberation has yet been done.

Selected References

    Lutheran World Federation. *The Situations of Women in the Church in China*. LWF Studies. China Study Series, vol. 2. Hong Kong: LWF, 1997.

    Peng Yaqian. "The Feminist Awakening Among Chinese Christian Women." *CTR* 11:1 (1996).

    Ting, K.H. "Speech at the Memorial Service for Ms. Wu Yifang." In *Love Never Ends*, 271-275. Nanjing: Yilin Press, 2000.

    Wu Mingfeng. "Ministry to Women, Children and Minorities in China." *CTR* 14 (2000).

    Wu Ying. "Humanity, Women, and God's Work." *CTR* 1991.

    Zhang Yan. "Christianity and the Modern Chinese Women's Movement." *CTR* 11:1 (1996).

    Zhu Xuebo. *Wu Yifang*. Nanjing: Jiangsu PPCC Committee and Nanjing Normal University, 1993.

    Cao Shengjie. "Feminist Theology and the Chinese Church." (In Chinese.) *NTR* 2 (2000).

    —. "Learning from the Grass-roots Churches." *CSP Bulletin* 2 (988).

    Meng Yanlin. "The Biblical View of the Position of Women as seen in the Context of Traditional Chinese Culture." *NTR* 2 (2000).

    Gao Ying. "On Women's Work in the Church in China." *NTR* 3 (2000).

    Sun Meici. "The Role of Women in Church and Society as seen in the Bible." *NTR* 3 (2000).

    Chen Zhaohe. "Ideal Womanhood in Ancient Chinese Culture and in the Book of Proverbs: A Comparison." *NTR* 3 (2000).

5.6.7. Minority Christians

Through the efforts of mainly British missionaries in the 19th century, Christianity became a major religious force among a number of non-Han minority peoples in southwest China, including especially the Miao, Lisu, Yi, Gobu and Nosu.

Protestant missions among the Miao began in Guizhou in the late 1890s with the arrival of J.R. Adams of the CIM. The first Miao Christian is recorded as Pan Sheoshan. The English Methodist Samuel Pollard, known as the "apostle to the Miao," is to this day highly regarded in local government circles for having introduced the potato to the region (Guizhou and Yunnan), thus saving many from starvation. Centers of the work were in Zhaotong, Kunming, Wuding County (Yunnan), and Shimenkan (Guizhou). Christian primary schools were built and a writing system for the Miao language created, which is still in use. By 1949, Christianity was well established among the Miao.

In 1951, Miao Christians were among 30,000 to sign a statement promoting the TSPM and endorsed government policies and programs. Because of their history, the Miao Christians felt a close bond with the Christian missionaries who had worked among them, and a significant number refused to denounce missionaries as imperialists in the 1950s. According to Prof. Tien Ju-Kang, Christianity helped to reinforce Miao identity and provided a basis to resist assimilation or sinification into the broader society (Tien 1993).

5.6.7.1. Wang Zhiming (1907-1973)

Wang Zhiming was a highly respected Miao pastor in Wuding County, Yunnan. He showed his loyalty to new China, but refused to take part in denunciation meetings held to humiliate landlords or foment hatred against foreign powers. When the Cultural Revolution came to Wuding, he was known to be a critic of the atheistic campaigns of local Red Guards. In May 1969 he and other members of his family were arrested. Four years later he was condemned to death and executed in December 1973 at the age of 66. At the mass rally where he was executed chaos broke out among the crowd and the prosecuting official was assaulted by furious

Christians. In October 1980 Wang was "rehabilitated," his family was offered an official apology, and his death at government hands termed unlawful. A stone tablet inscribed with his story and the facts of his martyrdom stands at his tomb in the family graveyard. A statue of Wang is one of ten depicting 20th century martyrs that stand on the west front of Westminster Abbey, London, dedicated in 1998.

Selected References
> Covell, Ralph. *The Liberating Gospel in China: The Christian Faith among China's Minority Peoples*. Grand Rapids, MI: Baker, 1995.
> Han Junxue. *Jidujiao yu Yunnan shaoshu minzu* (Christianity and Minority Peoples in Yunnan). Kunming: People's Publishing House, 2000.
> Mackerras, Colin. *China's Minorities:Integration and Modernization in the Twentieth Century*. Hong Kong: Oxford University Press.
> Tien Ju-Kang. *Peaks of Faith: Protestant Mission in Revolutionary China*. Leiden, New York & Cologne: E.J. Brill, 1993.
> Wickeri, Philip L. "The Abolition of Religion in Yunnan: Wang Zhiming." In *The Terrible Alternative. Christian Martyrdom in the Twentieth Century*, edited by Andrew Chandler, 128-143. London: Cassell, 1998.

5.7 The Academic Study of Religion and the Dialogue with Intellectuals

Since the organization of the Institute of World Religions under the Chinese Academy of Social Sciences in Beijing and the Institute of Religious Studies at Nanjing University in the early 1980s, the study of religion and of Christianity in particular has become extremely popular among secular scholars. Some have developed a deep and abiding sympathy for Christian faith that has prompted the use of the term "culture Christians" to refer to the phenomenon. The term "culture Christians" was first used by Bishop K.H. Ting as a means of expressing appreciation and welcome. The limitations of "culture Christians" as a category have become evident as the diverse nature of the scholarly interest in Christianity grows more apparent, as Christian scholars in and outside China respond to it, and as some (though few in number) "culture Christians" are baptized and become Christian in fact. The meaning of the term is so vague that it gave rise to a heated debate among Chinese Christian and non-Christian scholars, not only on the mainland, but in Hong Kong and overseas.

Academic studies of Christianity have made a great contribution, not only to the study of religion, but through ambitious programs of translation and research. Through their translations the works of many more western theologians are now available in Chinese. Their research has illuminated the social background and context of Christian believers in China and explored reasons for the growth of Christianity. Through their writings, which include popular introductions to the various religions as well as schoalrly treatises, they have helped to make Christianity known to a much broader segment of the Chinese population.

In the 1990s, centers for the study of religion and/or Christianity have increasingly appeared at major universities. New journals and book series have joined the long standing *Religion*, published by the Institute of Religious Studies at Nanjing University. Leading figures in the academic study of religion are the staff members of the Christian Study Center on Chinese Religion and Culture in Hong Kong, Liu Xiaofeng editor of the journal *Logos and Pneuma*, He Guanghu, deputy director of the Center for Christianity at the Chinese Academy of Social Sciences, and Zhuo Xinping, director of the Institute of World Religions in Beijing, among many others.

For various reasons, there is no genuine and promising cooperation between "culture Christians" and the Chinese church. This is unfortunate for the Chinese church and perhaps for the "culture Christians" as well. True dialogue awaits the maturing of a generation of Chinese Christian intellectuals who can participate on equal footing, neither despising their scholarly counterparts as unbelievers, nor feeling inadequate to the conversation. For their part, scholars must further develop a knowledge of the Bible as a spiritual book informing a living faith, and an appreciation for the institutional church.

5.7.1. Research Institutes and Study Centers

Over the past 20 years, the secular study of religion, and especially of Christianity, has developed rapidly in China. Specialized research institutes now exist in government departments. There are also religious studies institutes and centers for the study of Christianity in tertiary educational institutions. Government bodies include, most importantly, the Institute of World Religions of the Chinese Academy of Sciences, founded in 1964; research in Christianity is led by its Office of Research in Christianity and the Center for Research in Christianity. The Shanghai Academy of Social Sciences set up its Religious Studies Institute in 1980, the Religious Studies Institute of the Yunnan Provincial Academy of Social Sciences was established in 1984, and the Institute for the Study of Historical Religion of the Shaanxi Provincial Academy of Social Sciences in 1995. All carry on research in Christianity. Government departments rely mainly on the religious studies center of the Religious Affairs Bureau of the State Council, whose emphasis is on the current state and development of Christianity. It publishes the monthly *Religion and World*, providing a great deal of news and information for the study of contemporary Christianity.

Related departments in tertiary educational institutions and their religious research institutes whose research involves Christianity include the religious studies departments of Beijing University and Wuhan University, the Religious Studies Institute of Nanjing University, the Religious Studies Institute of Fujian Normal University, the Christian Culture Research Institute of People's University (Beijing), the Center for the Study of Christianity at Fudan University (Shanghai), the Center for the Study of Christianity at Zhejiang University, the Central China Normal University's Research Center on the History of Church-Run Universities in China, Zhengzhou University's Institute of Religious Studies, the Beijing Foreign Languages University's Center for the Study of Foreign Sinology, Shandong University's Institute for the Study of Modern Chinese Christianity (which became the Shandong University Institute of Religious Studies in 1998), Zhongshan University's Institute for the Study of Religious Culture, the Institute for the Study of Christian Culture at Shaanxi Normal

University, and related research bodies at other institutions, such as the Yanjing Research Institute, the Matteo Ricci group of the Chinese Ming History Association, etc.

Selected References

The following represent only a sampling of what is available. Not mentioned here are the many publications that have resulted from an ambitious program of translation of classic and modern western theological works.

*Among important **journals and series** are*:

Jidu zongjiao yanjiu (Study of Christianity), 1999- . Zhuo Xinping and Xu Zhiwei (Edwin Hui), eds. Published by Beijing CASS.

Jidujiao wenhua pinglun (Christian Culture Review), 1990- . Liu Xiaofeng and He Guanghu, eds. Contents of previous issues in each volume.

Logos and Pneuma. Liu Xiaofeng, ed. Hong Kong: Tao Fong Shan.

Jidujiao wenhua yuekan (Christian Culture Journal), 1999- . Yang Huilin, ed. Published at People's University, Beijing.

Zongjiao yu sixiang (Religion and thought series). Includes some translations.

Dialogue & Comparison of Religions. Zhuo Xinping, general ed. 3 vols. published in 2000.

Zongjiao zhishi congshu (Religious knowledge series). Short histories of Catholicism and Protestantism in China by Yao Mingquan and Luo Weihong. Also separate volumes on the major religions in China published in 1999, including Catholicism, Protestantism, Buddhism, Taoism and Islam.

Other series include: A Library of Academic Studies on Christianity through the Ages (Liu Xiaofeng, editor-in-chief); Library of Academic Studies on Christianity; Religion and World Series; Chinese Academic Library of Christian Thought in History; Studies in Modern Christianity Series; Christian Culture Series; and others.

Books (in Chinese, unless otherwise noted):

A Dictionary of Christianity. Beijing: Beijing Languages Institute Press, 1994.

A Study on Church Cases in Modern China. Edited by the Sichuan Social Sciences Association. Sichuan: Provincial Social Science Academy Press, 1987.

Bai Yunxiao. *A Dictionary of New Testament Names.* Tianjin: Tianjin People's Publishing House, 1989.

China Encyclopedia Press, Shanghai Branch. *A Concise Encyclopedia on Christianity.* Shanghai: China Encyclopedia Press, 1992, 1993.

Christianity Studies Section, ed. *A Panorama of Christian Culture.* Institute of World Religions, Chinese Academy of Social Sciences, Qilu Press, 1991, 1992.

Dai Kangsheng, Zhang Xinying and Michael Pye (eds.): *Religion and Modernization in China.* Proceedings of the International Association for the History of Religions held in Beijing, China, April 1992. Cambridge: Roots and Branches, 1995. Collection of reports from the first IAHR conference held in Beijing, China, in April 1992. 34 articles, arranged into four sections: *Religion in China, Religion and modernization, Foreign religions and Chinese culture,* and *Theoretical reflections on religion.* (English)

Duan Qi. *Draft History of the Indigenization of Christianity in China* (in Chinese). Unpub. Ms.

Gao Shiliang, ed. *History of Missionary Schools in China.* Hunan Education Press, 1994, 1995.

Gu Weimin. *Jidujiao yu jindai Zhongguo shehui* (Christianity and modern Chinese society). Chinese Society Series. Shanghai: Renmin chubanshe, 1996.

Han Junxue. *Christianity and Ethnic Minorities in Yunnan.* Study of Religious Culture in Yunnan series. Yunnan People's Publishing House, 2000.

He Guanghu. *The Pluralist Outlook on God - A General Survey of Western Religious Philosophy in the 20th Century.* Guizhou People's Publishing House, 1991.

—, and Gao Shining, eds. *Christian Culture and Modernization.* China Social Science Press, 1996.

—. "Religion and Hope: A Perspective from Today's China." *China Study Journal* 13: 2 (August 1998).

—. *Zixuan ji* (Selections from my writings). Guilin: Guangxi Normal University Press, 1999.

—. "Religious Studies in China 1978-1999 and their Connection with Political and Social Circumstances." *China Study Journal* 15: 1 (April 2000).

Hui, Edwin C. and He Guanghu, co-ed. *Dialogue: Confucianism, Buddhism, Daoism and Christianity.* Vols. 1&2. Beijing: Chinese Social Science Documentation Press, 1999.

—."Christian Doctrine of Trinity and Confucian Concept of Immanence and Transcendence." In *Christian Philosophy in the Chinese Intellectual Context*, co-edited with Zhao Dunhua. Beijing: Chinese Academy of Social Science Press, 2000.

Institute of Sino-Christian Studies. *Wenhua Jidutu: xianxiang yu zhenglun* (Cultural Christians: phenomenon and argument). Hong Kong: Institute of Sino-Christian Studies, 1997.

Institute of Sino-Christian Studies, ed. *Cultural Christian: Phenomenon and Argument*. Hong Kong: Institute of Sino-Christian Studies, 1997.

Jiang Wenhan. *Christianity in Ancient China*. Shanghai: Zhishi (Knowledge) Publishing House, 1982.

Li Pingye. *Religious Reformation and Ideological Trends in Contemporary Western Society*. China Today Press, 1992.

—, and Chen Hongxing, eds. *Taking History as a Mirror*. Religious Culture Press, 2000.

Liang Gong, ed.-in-chief. *An Encyclopedic Dictionary of the Bible*. Liaoning People's Publishing House, 1990.

Ling, Samuel and Stacy Bieler, eds. *Chinese Intellectuals and the Gospel*. Phillipsburg, NJ: P & R Publishing, 1999.

Liu Xiaofeng. *Zou xiang shizijiashang de zhenli* (Moving toward the truth on the cross). Hong Kong: Joint Publishing (H.K.) Co., Ltd., 1990.

—, ed. *Deeds and Words*. Sanlian Bookstore, 1995.

—. *Yuanjiu yu xiaoyao* (Salvation and freedom). Humanist Studies Series. Shanghai: Renmin chubanshe, 1988.

Luo Fangguang. *Matteo Ricci in Zhaoqing*. Literature and History of Zhaoqing, vol. 2. Zhaoqing: Literary and Historical Data Committee under CPPCC, 1985.

Sprenger, Arnold, svd. "Liu Xiaofengs neue Vision fur China." In Malek, 299-324.

Sun Jiang. *The Cross and the Dragon*. Zhejiang People's Publishing House, 1990.

Sun Shangyang. *Christianity and Confucianism at the End of the Ming*. Shanghai: Shanghai People's Publishing House, 1994.

Tang Yi, ed. *A History of Christianity*. China Social Science Academy Press, 1993, 1994.

Tian Jiayou. "Christianity and Modern Chinese Intellectuals." M. A. Thesis. Pacific School of Religion. March 12, 1994.

Wang Lixin. *American Missionaries and China's Modernization in the Late Qing: A Study of Social, Cultural and Educational*

Activities by Protestant Missionaries in Contemporary Times. Tianjin: Tianjin People's Publishing House, 1997.

Wang Weifan and K.H. Ting. "Recent Developments in the Study of Religion." *CTR* (1988).

Wickeri, Philip and Lois Cole, eds. *Christianity and Modernization: A Chinese Debate.* Hong Kong: DAGA Press, 1995. (English)

Xiong Yuezhi. *The Spread of Western Culture to the East and the Society in the Late Qing.* Shanghai: Shanghai People's Publishing House, 1994.

Yang Huilin. *Sin and Redemption - On the Spirit of Christian Culture.* Xi Jiang Yue series. Dongfang Press, 1995.

Yang Tianhong. *Christianity and Modern China.* Sichuan People's Publishing House, 1994.

Zhang Jiuxuan. *Stories from the Bible.* China Social Science Press, 1982.

Zhang Li and Liu Jiantang. *A History of Church Cases in China.* Sichuan Provincial Social Science Academy Press, 1987.

Zhao Dunhua. *1500 Years of Christian Philosophy.* A Library of Philosophers series. Beijing: People's Publishing House, 1994.

—, and Edwin C. Hui, eds. *Christian Philosophy in the Chinese Intellectual Context.* Beijing: Chinese Academy of Social Science Press, 2000.

Zheng Tianxing. *Marx and Engels on Atheism, Religion and Church.* Huawen Publishing House, 1991.

Zhu Weizheng, ed. *Jidujiao yu jindai wenhua* (Christianity and Modern Culture). Shanghai: Renmin chubanshe, 1994.

Zhuo Xinping. *Dangdai Xifang Tianzhujiao shenxue* (Contemporary Theology of the Western Catholicism). Shanghai: Shanghai Joint Publishing Co., 1998.

—. *Dangdai Xifang Xinjiao shenxue* (Contemporary Theology of the Western Protestantism). Shanghai: Shanghai Joint Publishing Co., 1998.

—. "Dangdai Zhongguo Jidu zongjiao yanjiu"(Contemporary Chinese Research in Christianity). *Jidu zongjiao yanjiu* 2 (1999).

Zhuo Xinping. *A Discourse on the Origin of Religion.* Hunan People's Publishing House, 1988.

—. "Chinese Intellectuals and Christianity." *Jian Dao* 7 (1997).

—. *Appreciating the Bible.* China Social Science Press, 1992.

—. *Historical Christianity and Judaism in China.* Shanghai People's Publishing House, 1998, 1999.

—. *Essential Knowledge of Christianity in China*. Knowledge of Religion series. Religious Culture Press, 1999.

—, and Zhang Xiping, eds. *Exploring Indigenization: A Collection of Academic Papers on China's Christian Culture in the 20th Century*. China Radio and Television Press, 1999.

—. *A Reader of Christian Knowledge*. Religious Culture Press, 2000.

—. *A Reader on Christianity. A Handbook for Cadres*. Religious Culture Press, 2000.

—. *About Christianity*. Social Science Document Press, 2000.

5.8 Theological Reconstruction

The call for theological reconstruction was raised at the second meeting of the 6th National Christian Conference held in Jinan, Shandong, November 1998, was given impetus by the publication of K.H. Ting's book of a selection of his writings, personally-chosen and, in a breakthrough for China, commercially published. The book became part of the discussion at meetings and at special forums on its contents. It has become part of the standard curriculum for theological education.

Apart from eliciting papers and responses that have appeared in the pages of the *Nanjing Theological Review* and other church publications, the discussion has again raised issues, old and new, crucial to the future of the church. At this point, two stand out. One is an effort to rid Chinese theology of what are characterized as received fundamentalist viewpoints held over from the missionary legacy of the 19th century. This appears in an ongoing exploration of a creation-centered vis-à-vis salvation or redemption-centered theology. There is a concern for the hard-won fruits of the struggle to be accepted as fully Chinese and fully Christian in the socialist context, which has eroded to some extent the desire for the broadest possible unity among Christians. Many feel that genuine identification and dialogue with "unbelievers"- the church's ability to open itself to its largely secular and socialist social context - is key to its future and will be a positive witness in Chinese society. These are crucial issues for theological education, where the call is for a greater diversity in theological viewpoints in the context of a modernizing society.

The second is a call for new overtures to intellectuals and an openness to insights from the academic study of Christianity, another issue which is related to theological education. In addition to ongoing exploration through articles in seminary journals, especially the *Nanjing Theological Review*, familiarization and training sessions have been organized in several cities, notably Shanghai and Nanjing, and this effort will no doubt be broadened to other areas.

The diversity and pluralism often spoken of in the context of theological reconstruction does not point to the task of relating in a multi-religious society, but rather relating to and accepting in a broad sense, non-Christians, and the possibility of participating in secular society. From the Chinese government's view, this means adapting religions to socialist society. From the Church's perspective, it is an issue of how the church can be accepted by society with recognition of its rightful role; and just as crucially, how it can meet the challenges of modern society in a globalized world and find a language that speaks to Chinese people today, inside and outside the church.

Selected References:

CTR 14 (2000) contains essays on the need for theological reconstruction by several church leaders, including Chen Zemin.

Wang Aiming. "Self-Government in the Light of Church Dogmatics." *CTR* 14 (2000).

Kan Baoping. "Further Thoughts on Creation and Redemption." *CTR* 14 (2000).

Xu Rulei. "The Three Rises and Three Falls" in the History of Christianity in China, and the Three-Self Movement and Theological Reconstruction." *NTR* 2 (2000).

Fu Xianji. "Redaction of the Gospels and Theological Reconstruction." *NTR* 2 (2000).

Ting, K.H. "Readjustments in Theological Thinking: Necessary and Unavoidable." *NTR* 2 (2000).

Cao Shengjie. "The Three-Self Patriotic Movement and Theological Renewal." *NTR* 4 (2000).

—. "Theological Up-building and Self-Propagation." *NTR* 3 (2000).

Wang Aiming. "The Nature and Purpose of Theological Construction in the Chinese Church." *NTR* 1 (2000).

5.9 Supplementary Bibliography IV

Any comprehensive listing for additional materials relevant to the contextual theologies of China would require much more space. The following are offered as a selection of those resources likely to be of more immediate use.

Journals

Chinese Theological Review: 1985-. Published annually by the Foundation for Theological Education in Southeast Asia. English translations of theological essays and sermons from *Nanjing Theological Review* and other seminary journals; church statements and documents from the National Chinese Christian Conferences.

ANS (*Amity News Service*): 1992-. Published by the Amity Foundation, Hong Kong. Carries summaries and/or translations of important theological statements; some translation of articles.

Jian Dao. A Journal of Bible & Theology: 1994-. Published by the Alliance Bible Seminary, Hong Kong.

China Study Journal. From the China Desk of Churches Together in Britain and Ireland (CTBI). Begun in 1979 as *Documentation*; then appeared in booklet form as *Religion in the People's Republic of China*; in 1986 became the *China Study Project Journal*; and then in 1991, the *China Study Journal*.

Tripod. Published by the Holy Spirit Study Center, Hong Kong. Some archived issues online:
<http://www.hsstudyc.org.hk/>

Ching Feng. Formerly published by Tao Fong Shan Center for the Study of Christianity and Chinese Culture.

Books

Anderson, Gerald, ed. *The Theology of the Christian Mission*. New York: McGraw-Hill, 1961, 158-167.

Bagwell, May "An Account of the Industrial Work of the Shanghai YWCA, 1904-29." In *A Study of the YWCA of China, 1891-1930*. n.p., n.d. 221-226. YWCA Archives, Geneva.

Baoping, Kan "Theology in the Contemporary Chinese Setting." *Chinese Theological Review* 11:2, 1995, 112-124.

Bates, M. Searle "Christianity in the People's Republic." *China Notes* 6.2 (1968).

Bays, Daniel H. "Chinese Popular Religion and Christianity Before and After the 1949 Revolution: A Retrospective View." *Fides et Historia* 23.1 (1991).

Brown, G. Thompson. *Christianity in the People's Republic of China.* Revised Edition. Atlanta: John Knox Press, 1986.

Camps, Arnulf and Vriend, John "The People's Republic of China: From Foreignness to Contextualization." In *Missiology: An Ecumenical Introduction: Texts and Contexts of Global Christianity*, ed. A. Camps, L. A. Hoedemaker, M. R. Spindler and F.J. Verstraelen, 49-64. Grand Rapids: Eerdmans, 1995.

Chan, Kim-Kwong and Alan Hunter. *Prayers and Thoughts of Chinese Christians.* London: Mowbray, 1991. (Also Boston: Cowley, 1991.)

Chao, Jonathan T'ien-en [Zhao Tianen]. *A Bibliography of the History of Christianity in China.* Waltham, MA: CGST, 1970.

— "The Chinese Indigenous Church Movement, 1919-1927: A Protestant Response to the Anti-Christian Movement in Modem China?" Ph.D. Thesis. University of Pennsylvania, 1986.

— *A History of the Church in China since 1949: a Reader, and Expanded Study Guide.* Grand Rapids, Mich, Institute of Theological Studies, c1995.

Chao, T.C. and T.T.Lew. *The Church in China and the Church Universal.* Shanghai: 1923.

Danyun. *Lilies Amongst Thorns: Chinese Christians Tell Their Story Through Blood and Tears.* Tonbridge, UK: Sovereign World, 1991.

Deng Yuzhi [Cora Deng] "The Industrial Work of the YWCA in China." 29 Nov. 1934. *World YWCA Archives*, Geneva.

Gu Changsheng. *Chuanjiaoshi yu xiandai zhongguo* (Missionaries and Modern China). Shanghai: Renmin chubanshe, 1981.

Feng Shangli. "The Contours of Chinese Theology." *Ching Feng* 13.1 (1970).

Gray, G. F. and Smalley, Martha Lund. *Anglicans in China: a history of the Zhonghua Shenggong Hui (Chung Hua Sheng Kung Huei)*. Episcopal China Mission History Project, 1996.

Hass, Ilse. *Die Portestantische Christenheit in der Volksrepublik China und die Chinaberichterstattung in der Deutchen Evangelischen Missionliteratur*. Hamburg, 1974.

He Guichun. "A Summary of Research in the Last Ten Years into the History of Christianity in China". *China Study Journal* 8 (1993).

Hsü Sung-shih. *Chao-liu-chü-shih chu Chung-hua min tsu yen li ti Yeh-su* (Jesus Through the Eyes of the Chinese People). Oakton, Va.: Center for Chinese Research Materials, 1992.

Huang Pi-yun. *Kuo nan, min yun, hsin yang fan ssu* (Some christian reflections on the June 4 massacre and the democratic movement). Chiu-lung, Hsiang-kang Chi-tu tu hsueh hui, 1990.

Hunter, Alan "Continuities in Chinese Protestantism, 1920-1990". *China Study Journal* 6.3 (1991).

Hunter Alan and Rimmington Don. *Methodological questions in the study of Christianity in China*. Leeds East Asia papers ; no.9. University of Leeds Department of East Asian Studies, 1992

— eds. *All under heaven : Chinese tradition and Christian life in the People's Republic of China*. Kampen: J.H. Kok, 1992.

Jinling shenxueyuan (Nanking Theological Seminary) *Jinling shenxueyuan sishi zhounian jiniantekan* (Special issue commemorating the 40th anniversary of the Nanking Theological Seminary.) Nanjing: Jinling shenxueyuan, 1950.

Kiang, Wen-han [Jiang Wenhan] *The Ideological Background of the Chinese Student Movement*. New York: King's Crown Press, Columbia University, 1948.

Laaman, Lars. *Christian heretics in Late Imperial China: the Inculturation of Christianity in 18th and 19th Century China*. Guildford: Curzon, Forthcoming.

Lee-ming, Ng "The Promise and Limitations of Chinese Protestant Theologians, 1920-50." *Ching Feng* 21:4 (1978).

Lyall, Leslie T. *Come Wind Come Weather*. Chicago: Moody Press, 1960.

Lyon, D. Willard "Dr. C. Y. Cheng's Thoughts on the Indigenization of the Chinese Church." *Chinese Recorder* 6.12 (1925).

Maclnnis, Donald E. *Religious Policy and Practice in Communist China.* New York: Macmillan, 1971.

Rawlinson, Frank. *Evolution of "Christian" Treaty "Rights" in China.* [s.l.: s.n.], 1925.

—. *Western Money and the Chinese Church, an Attempt to find a Modern Approach to an Old Practice.* Shanghai: Presbyterian Mission Press, 1929.

Rawlinson, John Lang. *Rawlinson, the Recorder, and China's Revolution: A Topical Biography of Frank Joseph Rawlinson (1871-1937).* Notre Dame: Cross Cultural, 1990.

Robinson, L.S. *Double Edged Sword.* Hong Kong: Tao Fong Shan Ecumenical Centre, 1986.

Shih, Vincent Y.C. "The Ideology of the Taiping T'ien Guo." *Sinologica* III (1951).

Ting, K.H. et al. *Chinese Christians Speak Out - Addresses and Sermons.* Beijing: New World Press, 1984.

Tsu, Y. Y. *The Chinese Church: Partner in a World Mission.* New York: Friendship Press,1944.

Veith, Gene Edward. "Christianity and culture: the China challenge" in *Christ and Culture in Dialogue: Constructive Themes and Practical Applications*, ed. by Angus J.L. Menuge, St. Louis: Concordia Pub. House, 1999.

Wu Liming [Ng, Lee-ming] *Jidujiao yu Zhongguo shehui bianqian* (Christianity and social change in China). Hong Kong: Chinese Christian Literature Council, 1981.

Währisch-Oblau, Claudia and Gotthard Oblau. *Kein Geheimnis Christ zu sein: Lebens-Bilder aus Chinas Gemeinden heute.* Neukirchen-Vluyn Aussaat, c1992.

Wang Xiaochao. *Christianity and Imperial Culture.* Leiden, Brill; 1997.

Yeo, Khiok-khng *What has Jerusalem to do with Beijing?: Biblical Interpretation from a Chinese Perspective.* Harrisburg, Penn., Trinity Press International, 1998.

YWCA of China. *Introduction to the Young Women's Christian Association of China, 1933-1947*. Shanghai National Committee of the YWCA of China, n.d.

Zha Shijie. *Zhongguo Jidujiao renwu xiaozhuan* (Concise biographies of Chinese Christians). Taibei: China Evangelical Seminary Presss, 1983.

Zhang Zhidong. *Zhang Wenxiang-gong quanji* (Complete work of Zhang Zhidong.) Edited by Wang Shutong. 6 vols. Taibei: Wenhai chubanshe, 1963 .

- JCE and JW, with CMF, CYT

4 Contextual Theology in Hong Kong

1 **Introduction**
   1.1 Place and People
   1.2 Criteria of Inclusion
2 **On Early Hong Kong History**
   2.1 Eitel, Ernest John (1838-1908) and Tsai Jung-fang (1936-);
   2.2 Smith, Carl T. (1918-)
3 **Protestant Contextual Theology - the Period 1840-1930**
   3.1 The Context and Response
      3.1.1. Legge, James (1815-1897); **3.1.2.** Wang Tao (1828-1897); **3.1.3.** Sun Yat-sen (1866-1925); **3.1.4.** Chang Wen-k'ai (Zhang Wenkai, 1871-1931); **3.1.5.** The Taiping Movement (1850-64); **3.1.6.** The Anti-Mui Tsai Campaign (1920s); **3.1.7.** *Da-guang Bao* (1913-1949)
   3.2 The Period 1930-1960
      3.2.1. Karl Ludwig Reichelt (1877-1952); **3.2.2.** Xie Fuya (N.Z. Zia, 1892-1991); **3.2.3.** Xu Dishan (1893-1941), and Inter-religious Encounter; **3.2.4.** Ronald O. Hall (1895-1975)
   3.3 The Period 1960-1980
      3.3.1. People and Centres; **3.3.2.** Ho Sai-ming (He Shiming, 1911-1996); **3.3.3.** Wu Mingjie (1916-1990); **3.3.4.** Peter Lee King-hung (Li Jingxiong, 1930-); **3.3.5.** Hong Kong Christian Industrial Committee (HKCIC) (1967-); **3.3.6.** The Society for Community Organization (SoCo) (1972-);
   3.4 The Period 1980-2000
      3.4.1. Changed Identities; Developing Theologies; **3.4.2.** Declarations or Statements; **3.4.3.** The Historic Event of "1997"; **3.4.4.** Alan Chan Chor-choi (Chen, Alan Zuocai,

1935-); **3.4.5.** Kwok Nai-wang (Guo Naihong, 1940-); **3.4.6.** Raymond Fung (ca 1940-); **3.4.7.** Kaung Tai-wai (Jiang Dahui, 1949-); **3.4.8.** Archie Lee Chi-chung (Li, Archie Zhiqiang, 1950-); **3.4.9.** Lo Lung-kwong (Lu Longguang, 1951-); **3.4.10.** Liu Xiaofeng (1956-); **3.4.11.** Kwok Pui-lan (Guo Pei Lan); **3.4.12.** Angela Wong Wai-ching (Huang Huizhen (); **3.4.13.** Other Writers/Animateurs of Contextual Theology

4 Catholic Contextual Theology
 4.1 Introduction
 4.2 Contextual Theological Concerns
  4.2.1. *Tripod* (since 1981); **4.2.2.** *Theology Annual* (since 1986); **4.2.3.** *Spirit* (since 1989); **4.2.4.** Women Doing Theology; **4.2.5.** Centres and Movements;
    4.2.5.1. Holy Spirit Study Centre (1981); **4.2.5.2.** The Asian Centre for the Progress of Peoples (ACPP);
  4.2.6. A Selection of Theologians
    4.2.6.1. Edward Chau; **4.2.6.2.** Maria Goretti Lau (Lau Choi-mei) spb; **4.2.6.3.** Kwong Lay-kuen, Madeleine (Magdalena) spb; **4.2.6.4.** Robert Ng Chi-fun sj; **4.2.6.5.** John Tong; **4.2.6.6.** Other Catholic Writers of Contextual theology

5 Supplementary Bibliography
 5.1 Book Titles
 5.2 Periodicals

1 Introduction
1.1 Place and People

As a geo-political entity, "Hong Kong" refers to "Hong Kong Island", the "Kowloon Peninsula" and the "New Territories", plus 235 adjacent islands. It covers a total of 386 square miles of land which houses a population approaching seven million, 98% of whom are ethnic Chinese. Chinese religious traditions are therefore widely preserved, especially those of Buddhism, Taoism and folk religious variations of these, along with the pervasive morality and pieties of Confucianism. Christians number approximately 8% of the total population.

Before it was officially given the name "Hong Kong" in 1840, as a part of China it was named variously as "Red Incense Burner", "Girdle Road", or "Naked Pillar". The 1840s were very decisive years for the development of Hong Kong, for not only was it given its official name then but also its history of colonisation began: Hong Kong Island was ceded to Britain in perpetuity in 1842, Kowloon in 1860, and the New Territories were granted to Britain under a 99-year lease in 1898.

Missionary Christianity first arrived in 1841, that is, one year before Hong Kong's cession to Britain. The first Catholic missionary to set foot in Hong Kong was a Swiss called Theodore Joset. The first Protestant missionary, Jehu Lewis Shuck from the American Baptist Missionary Union, came in 1842. Increasing numbers of missions would be established over the next century - Catholic, Protestant and most recently Orthodox - often closely related to mission initiatives in China. During this period Hong Kong developed rapidly to become a significant international city for trade, transport, education and cultural exchange.

1.2 Criteria of Inclusion

The entries included below are of those writings and authors that show aspects of a locally rooted and contextual theology. However, the meaning of "locally rooted and contextual theology" can be ambiguous. In this regard, Hong Kong is beyond doubt a case in point. It is culturally and politically a part of China, but it has been cut off from the contemporary China mainland both culturally and politically due to its history of colonisation. It has now returned to its mother country, but under the policy of "one country, two systems". To best serve the purpose, we will thus try to adopt the widest possible meaning of "locally rooted and contextual theology" with reference to the phrase "movements in context". This will be theology that reflects on and responds to God's presence and activity; which manifests itself through the "movements" it creates in the cultural, social, economic and political realms, within local histories. However, as was mentioned above, Christianity in Hong Kong has only a very brief history and thus it can be expected that the Christian voice, not to mention the theological voice, during the early period of colonial history is not clearly audible. This theological silence, of course, does not imply God's inactivity during the period, but indicates that the voice has yet to be uncovered. For this reason, we also include those archival materials in which the voice may be embedded. Most of these archival materials contain materials concerning the socio-political or cultural movements that were initiated or participated in by various Christian groups.

Also included are those Christian authors who were diasporic mainlanders but who for one reason or another (mostly political) migrated to or sojourned in Hong Kong during the 1930s and 1940s. Though they were not local authors in the strictest sense of the word, nor were their theological concerns, strictly speaking, locally rooted (most of them being interested in the dialogue between Christianity and Chinese culture), their writings did have some impact on the local culture and society, particularly through their work in reforming local education.

The 1997 handover of Hong Kong to China, which was an event of world note, was surely one of the most decisive moments in the history of Hong Kong. Many different kinds of locally rooted theology were nurtured in response to this event. We will also adopt the widest possible meaning of the word "theologian", so that besides academic theologians, Christian writers, Christian cultural workers and Christian social activists will also be included. It must be stressed lastly, that research into theological movements of a particular place requires an understanding of its history which will be introduced here through a number of scholarly works on the early history of Hong Kong, both from within and outside Christian circles.

2 On Early Hong Kong History
2.1 Eitel, Ernest John (1838-1908) and Tsai Jung-fang (1936-)

Eitel was a historian, a long-time resident, an official and a scholar who had very rich first-hand experience of what went on in the early colonial history of Hong Kong. His works were regarded as an indispensable reference, though elements of racism, colonialism and imperialism could be found embedded in these.

Tsai Jung-fang is professor of history at the College of Charleston, South Carolina. He is an expert in Hong Kong history, and in contrast to the colonial approach and European elitist perspective, he has attempted to write the social history of Hong Kong from the perspectives of Chinese people.

Selected References

Eitel, Ernest John. *Europe in China: the History of Hongkong from the Beginning to the Year 1882.* London: Luzac; Hong Kong: Kelly & Walsh, 1895.

—. *Hand-book of Chinese Buddhism: being a Sanskrit-Chinese Dictionary with Vocabularies of Buddhist Terms in Pali, Singhalese, Siamese, Burmese, Tibetan, Mongolian and Japanese.* 2nd ed., rev. and enl. Tokyo: Sanshusha, 1904.

—. "Ethnographical Sketches of the Hakka Chinese." *Notes and Queries on China and Japan* 1.5-11 (1867).

Tsai Jung-fang. *Hong Kong in Chinese History: Community and Social Unrest in the British Colony, 1842-1913.* New York: Columbia University Press, 1993.

2.2 Smith, Carl T. (1918-)

Carl Smith is a Protestant missionary, an ordained minister, a historian, an archivist and one of the leading scholars in the field of Hong Kong studies. His works have advanced the understanding of how Chinese Christian communities and Chinese social organisations came to their important social status in the early colonial history of Hong Kong. His importance as an archivist and a historian is indicated by the fact that the Public Records Office has collected and compiled two volumes of his essays entitled *The Rev. Carl T. Smith Collection.*

Smith has been living in Hong Kong since 1961 when he was sent here as a missionary of the United Board for World Ministries to teach theological students at the Theological Institute of the Church of Christ in China, Ho Fuk-Tong Centre, Hong Kong. Since then, he has been meticulously studying the colonial history of Hong Kong, and in particular the role of Chinese Christians within this. He was research associate at the Tao Fong Shan Ecumenical Centre for many years and has been an active member of the Hong Kong Branch of the Royal Asiatic Society for decades, since 1985 serving as vice-president of the Society.

Selected References

Works by Carl T. Smith

> *The Rev. Carl T. Smith Collection.* Hong Kong: Public Records Office, 1985.
> *Chinese Christians: Elites, Middlemen, and the Church in Hong Kong.* Hong Kong: Oxford University Press, 1985.
> *A Sense of History: Studies in the Social and Urban History of Hong Kong.* Hong Kong: Hong Kong Educational Pub., 1995.
> "The Early Hong Kong Church and Traditional Chinese Family Patterns." *Ching Feng* 20.1 (1977).
> "The Adaptation of the Protestant Church to a Chinese and Colonial Situation." *Ching Feng* 26.2&3 (1983).
> "Protected Women in 19th Century Hong Kong." In *Chinese Patriarchy: Submission, Collusion and Escape among Chinese Women*, edited by Suzanne Meyers and Maria Jaschok. London: ZED Books, 1993.

See also:

> Ash, Robert F. *Hong Kong in Transition : the Handover Years.* New York: St. Martin's Press, in association with Centre for the Study of Globalisation and Regionalisation, University of Warwick, 2000.
> Brown, Judith M. and Rosemary Foot. *Hong Kong's Transitions, 1842-1997.* Basingstoke: Macmillan, in association with St Antony's College, Oxford, 1997.
> Endacott, George B. *A History of Hong Kong.* London: Oxford University Press, 1958.
> Fok, K.C. *Lectures on Hong Kong History: Hong Kong's Role in Modern Chinese History.* Hong Kong: Commercial Press, 1990.
> Lethbridge, H.J. *Hong Kong, Stability and Change.* Hong Kong: Oxford University Press, 1978.
> Miners, Norman. *Hong Kong under Imperial Rule, 1912-1941.* East Asian historical monographs. Hong Kong and Oxford: Oxford University Press, 1987.

Ng Lee-ming. *Christianity and social change: the case in China, 1920-1950*. Microform, Princeton and Yale University Libraries, 1970. Also serially in *Ching Feng* 1971-1972.

Ngo Tak-wing, ed. *Hong Kong's History: State and Society under Colonial Rule*. London and New York: Routledge, 1999.

Roberts, Elfed Vaughan, Ling Sum Ngai and Peter Bradshaw. *Historical Dictionary of Hong Kong & Macau*. Asian historical dictionaries 10. Metuchen, NJ; London: Scarecrow Press, 1992.

Tang Kwong-Leung. *Colonial State and Social Policy: Social Welfare Development in Hong Kong 1842-1997*. Lanham, MD.: University Press of America, c1998.

Tsai Jung-fang. *Hong Kong in Chinese History: Com*munity and Social Unrest in the British Colony, 1812-1913. New York: Columbia University Press, c1993.

3 Protestant Contextual Theology - the Period 1840-1930
3.1 The Context and the Response

In the decades following 1840 Hong Kong developed rapidly as an entrepot port, as a regional centre for cultural and religious exchange, and as a base for Christian study of, and presence in, China. Development of the Christian community in Hong Kong itself was also greatly assisted by the work of theological scholars and educators. Following early work by James Legge, Wang Tao and their colleagues, there were by the 1860s Chinese Christians prominent in social, political and church movements. Amongst these were Wong Shing, Wung Wing, Ho Kai, Tong King-shing, and Wu Ting-fang. Some were also active in the HK Christian Churches Union (from 1915). Widely known Christians such as Wang Tao (3.1.2.) and Sun Yat-sen (3.1.3.) were amongst those politically active before and after the turn of the century, and others also participated in the work of the *Da-guang bao* (see 3.1.4.; 3.1.7.), which was founded in 1913. The 1920s were a period of widespread civil disturbance and conflict in China which disrupted the work of seminaries and other Christian centres and increased demands on the Christian communities of Hong Kong. Partly because of such disturbances, Karl Reichelt, along with Chinese colleagues such as Pan Lok-sam and Kuantu, with Axel Hamre and Bishop

Contextual Theology in Hong Kong

Ronald Hall, brought his "mission to Buddhists" to Tao Fong Shan (1930). (See 3.2.1.).

Locally rooted Christian concerns during this period can, however, be characterised by two types of processes: dialogue between the Chinese cultures and the teachings of missionary Christianity, and endeavours, participated in or initiated by Christians, in transforming the society through socio-political movements. As in China itself there were both scholarly nationals and exceptional missionaries who collaborated in pioneering the translation and study of Chinese cultural resources. A selection of these is given below. Many Christians both local and expatriate were also concerned for the issues of social and cultural reform; therefore included below are not only authors, but also a number of the relevant socio-political movements. Furthermore, the Christian voice which is embedded in these movements still remains largely in the form of archives. Therefore some important local newspapers from the period are also included below.

Selected References

    Bays, Daniel H., ed. *Christianity in China: From the 18th Century to the Present*. Stanford: Stanford University Press, 1996.

    Catholic Hong Kong: a Hundred Years of Missionary Activity: On the Occasion of the Centenary Year of the Arrival in Hong Kong of the Pontifical Foreign Missions Institute. Hong Kong: Catholic Press Bureau, 1958.

    Coulson, Gail et al. *The Enduring Church: Christians in China and Hong Kong*. New York, Friendship Press, 1996.

    Endacott, George B. and Dorothy E. She. *The Diocese of Victoria, Hong Kong. A Hundred Years of Church History, 1849-1949*. Hongkong: Kelly & Walsh, 1949.

    Kwok Nai Wang. "Christian Churches in Hong Kong under Colonial Rule." *Tripod* 98 (1997).

    Kwong Ha Seong, Louis. "The Foundation of the Catholic Mission in Hong Kong 1841-1894." PhD dissertation. Hong Kong: University of Hong Kong, 1998.

    Niemeijer, Hendrik E. "The Beliefs, Aspirations and Methods of the First Missionaries in British Hong Kong, 1841-5." In *Missions and Missionaries. Studies in Church History*. Subsidia 13, edited by Pieter N. Holtrop and Hugh McLeod.

Woodbridge, Suffolk, UK; Rochester, NY: Published for the Ecclesiastical History Society by the Boydell Press, 2000.

Smith, Carl T. *Chinese Christians: Elites, Middlemen, and the Church in Hong Kong.* Hong Kong: Oxford University Press, 1985.

—. "The adaptation of the Protestant Church to a Chinese and colonial situation." *Ching Feng* 26.2&3 (1983).

Woodman, Sophia. *Hong Kong's Social Movements: Voices from the Margins.* Hong Kong: July 1 Link and Hong Kong Women Christian Council, 1997.

3.1.1. Legge, James (1815-1897)

Legge was a world-renowned sinologist and foremost scholar of Chinese philosophy and religion. Following work in Malacca (1839-1843), he came to Hong Kong as a missionary sent by the London Missionary Society, to be the principal of the Anglo-Chinese Theological Seminary. To introduce Chinese culture to the West, he completed, with the help of scholars such as Wang Tao (3.1.2.), the first complete translation of the central corpus of the Confucian classics into a European language. He also wrote tracts and articles on Christian history and thought. In the long-running debate upon the proper term for God in Chinese he supported the use of Shang Di (*Shangdi*). He appreciated Confucian thought and was willing to utilise natural theology to expound truths in the Chinese classics, writings which sometimes resulted in conflict with other Christians in China. He was later professor of Chinese studies at Oxford.

Selected References

Works by James Legge

An Argument for Shang-te as the Proper Rendering of the Words Elohim and Theos in the Chinese Language. Hong Kong: Hong Kong Register Office, 1850.

The Notions of the Chinese Concerning God and Spirit ... Hong Kong: Hong Kong Register Office, 1852.

Confucianism in Relation to Christianity: a Paper read before the Missionary Conference in Shanghai, on May 11th, 1877. Shanghai: Kelly & Walsh, 1877.

The Religions of China: Confucianism and Taoism described and compared with Christianity. London: Hodder, 1880.

The Chinese Classics. Original Text with a Translation, Critical and Exegetical Notes, Prolegomena, and Copious Indexes. 7 vols. Oxford: Clarendon Press, 1893.

The Nestorian Monument of Hsi-an Fu in Shen-hsi, China, Relating to the Diffusion of Christianity in China in the Seventh and Eighth Centuries with the Chinese Text of the Inscription, a Translation, and Notes, and a Lecture on the Monument. London: Trubner, 1888.

Girardot, Norman J. *The Victorian Translation of China: James Legge's Oriental Pilgrimage.* Berkeley: University of California Press. Forthcoming.

3.1.2. Wang Tao (1828-1897)

It is not certain that Wang was a converted Christian although some scholars have argued so quite convincingly. Wang is remembered as one who worked closely with James Legge in the translation of Chinese classics into European languages during his stay in Hong Kong. Since 1849, Wang had been working for the London Missionary Society Press in Shanghai and was famous for refining the language in the Delegate's version of the Bible while he was working for the press there. In 1862, hunted by the Manchu government on suspicion of association with the Taiping Movement, he fled to Hong Kong.

Wang was a social reformist, if not a revolutionist, who called for the adoption of Western economics, industrial institutions and armaments to regenerate the nation. Some scholars even argue that he served as a source of inspiration to the leaders of the Reform Movement of 1898 which was led by K'ang Yu-wei (Kang Youwei) and Liang Ch'i-ch'ao (Liang Qichao). In 1874, he founded the *Xunhuan ribao*, which is remembered as the first local daily newspaper solely owned by Chinese; he himself serving as the chief editor. Here he wrote almost daily to urge the Manchu government to take remedial steps to save the country. Paul Cohen (1974) gives a very good introduction to Wang in relation to his contributions as a social reformist.

Selected References
Works by Wang Tao
    Xunhuan ribao (Circular Daily News). Microform. Hong Kong: Xunhuan Ribao Press.
    Taoyuan wenlu waibian: 12 juan. (Wang Tao's anthologies.) Hong Kong: Taoyuan lao min, 1883.
    My Life in China and America. New York: 1980.
    McLeavy, H. *Wang T'ao ... (1828-?1890), the Life and Writings of a Displaced Person; with a Translation of Mei-li hsiao chuan, a Short Story by Wang Tao.* [Based on a lecture delivered before the China Society, on the 22nd May, 1952, at the China Institute, London]. London: The China Society, 1953.
    Cohen, Paul A. *Between Tradition and Modernity: Wang Tao and Reforms in Late Ching China.* Cambridge, Mass: Harvard University Press, 1974.

3.1.3. Sun Yat-sen (1866-1925)

Sun is known as the father of modern China. Influential in overthrowing the Qing dynasty (1911), he served as the first provisional president of the Republic of China (1911-12) and later as de facto ruler (1923-25). Sun received his education mainly in Hong Kong, coming there as a secondary school student in 1882. In either 1884 or 1885 he was baptised by an American missionary. In 1892, he graduated as a medical doctor from the College of Medicine for Chinese in Hong Kong. However, he soon forsook his medical practice because of his love for the country and travelled to Hawaii in 1894 where he founded the Revive China Society; in effect a secret revolutionary group. He came back to Hong Kong in 1895 and plotted with colleagues for an uprising in Canton.

    His political thought is summarised in his *Three Principles of the People* (nationalism, democracy, and people's livelihood). To what extent his political thought has been influenced by his Christian faith has yet to be fully articulated. His ties with Christianity have been studied by a number of scholars including Zheng Yongfu, Carl T. Smith and many others.

Selected References
Works by Sun Yat-sen

Fundamentals of National Reconstruction. Chungking: Chinese Ministry of Information, 1945.

San min chu i (The three principles of the people), edited by L.T. Chen. New York: Da Capo Press, 1975.

Prescriptions for Saving China: Selected Writings of Sun Yat-sen, edited by Julie Lee Wei, Ramon H. Myers and Donald G. Gillin. Stanford CA.: Hoover Institution Press, c1994.

Hensman, C.R. *Sun Yat-sen.* London: SCM Press, 1971.

Liu Yaozhong, ed. *Guofu, zongtong jiang gongji furen zongjiao yanlun jiyao* (Selected works of the father of the nation). Taipei: zhong yan wen wu, 1979.

Smith, Carl T. "Sun Yat-sen's Baptism and some Christian Connections." *Ching Feng* 22.4 (1979).

Zheng Yongfu. *Sun Zhong-shan yu ji du jiao guan xi de li shi kao cha* (A Historical investigation into the relation between Sun Zhongshan and Christianity). Wuchang, 1991.

3.1.4. Chang Wen-kai (Zhang Wenkai, 1871-1931)

Chang was a Christian writer, who before his stay in Hong Kong, worked in Guangzhou as the editor of a Christian magazine called *Zhenguang* (True Light). In 1917, he came to Hong Kong and was employed as the chief commentator of a local Christian-owned newspaper, *Da-guang bao*, established in 1913. Chang is remembered as an apologetic writer and polemicist who defended the Christian faith against Confucian attacks during the second decade of the 20th century. His arguments were later collected and published in the form of a book titled *Da-guang po-an ji*.

Selected Reference
Works by Chang Wen-kai (Zhang Wenkai)

Da-guang po-an ji (Relative value of Christianity and Confucianism). Hong Kong: Da-guang bao, 1917.

Da-guang bao (The Great Light News, 1913-1949). Hong Kong: Da-guang bao.

Qu jing chu: you ming Du Chen Huanzhang boshi Kong jiao jiang yi bian miu (Destroying the thistle). S.l.: s.n., ?1984.

3.1.5. The Taiping Movement (1850-64) and Hong Kong
(See chap. 3, China, 4.3.1)

The Taiping Movement, or Taiping Rebellion, is remembered as the most important political and religious upheaval in China in the 19th century.Though the religious nature of the movement is still largely debatable, it did take the form of a syncretised Protestantism. Founder of the movement was Hong Xiuquan (1814-64), who studied Christianity in Canton.

Though the movement was largely confined to China, there was another connection with Hong Kong. The Gan Wang, that is, the prime minister of the Taiping Kingdom, was a man from Hong Kong called Hong Rengan. When the rebellion broke out, he fled to Hong Kong, where he was baptised and educated by a Protestant missionary, and later studied with James Legge. In 1859, under the auspices of missionaries in Hong Kong, he finally made his way to the Taiping camp with the intention of "rectifying" the syncretistic teachings of the Taipings. However, he finally had to relinquish that purpose.

Selected References

> Boardman, Eugene Powers. *Christian Influence upon the Ideology of the Taiping Revolution, 1851-1864*. Madison: University of Wisconsin Press, 1952.
> Hong, Rengan. *Ying Jie Gui Zhen* (The Missionaries). Taipei: Dahua yinshu guan, 1968.
> *Yangzhou shifan xueyuan zhongwen xi. Hong RenGan xuan ji* (Selections from the writings of Hong Rengan). Beijing: Zhonghua shuju, 1978.
> Wang Qincheng. *Taiping Tianguo de wenxian he lishi: haiwai xinwen xiankanbu he wen xian shishi yan jiu* (The sources and history of the Taiping). Beijing: Shehui kexue wenxian chubanshe: Xinhua shudian jing xiao, 1993.

3.1.6. The Anti-Mui Tsai Campaign (1920s)

The purchase of girls (i.e. mui tsai) for domestic service was a long-standing Chinese custom. The Anti-Mui Tsai campaign is remembered as the first major effort of various Chinese Christian bodies and individuals to campaign for social change. This campaign had its origin in 1919, when a colonial official, H.L. Haslewood, came to Hong Kong and discovered the Mui Tsai system, finding it ethically and socially abhorrent in every way. Because of his advocacy against the system, tension intensified with the colonial office, which at that time depended upon the support of wealthy locals to enforce colonial rule effectively. Haslewood was recalled to Britain over the issue; however, he continued his efforts, seeking the support of his compatriots. Supported by some British personnel, some groups of Christians in Hong Kong began to join in advocating for reforms, and their actions very soon turned into a campaign. An Anti-Mui Tsai Association was formed in 1921 following the publication of an article by Rev'd Wang Ai-tang in the Christian-owned newspaper *Da-guang Bao* (3.1.7.). The dynamics of the whole campaign were in fact highly intricate, involving a struggle between the colonial office - the colonial master - and the colonial people, both the wealthy of Hong Kong and members of the Christian communities. The story of this campaign, and any reflection arising from it, remains at present only in documents and archives. More work must be done if we are to understand how Christians organised their efforts to respond to the issue and the particular roles they played both in advocacy and action.

Selected References

    Haslewood, Hugh Lyttleton. *Child Savery in Hong Kong, the Mui Tsai System*. London: The Sheldon Press, 1930.

    Mui tsai Commission. *Mui tsai in Hong Kong and Malaya*. London: H.M. Stationery office, 1937.

    Smith, Carl T. *A Sense of History: Studies in the Social and Urban History of Hong Kong*. Hong Kong: Hong Kong Educational Pub., 1995.

    Xianggang Fandui Xubi Kuai. *Fandui Xubi Shilue* (A brief history of the Anti-Mui Tsai Movement). Hong Kong: Xianggang Fandui Xubi Kuai, 1933.

3.1.7. *Da-guang bao* (1913-1949)

The newspaper *Da-guang bao* (Great Light News) was established shortly after the founding of the Republic of China (1911). Once the Qing had been overthrown, Sun Yat-sen realized that the revolution could not achieve its end without reforming the society as well as the minds of the people. With this goal in mind, Sun called for the establishment of the *Da-guang bao*. Several Christians, including Ou Feng-chi and Yin Wen-ka, who finally took the leadership in establishing the newspaper, aspired to reform China in accordance with biblical teachings, and enthusiastically responded to Sun's invitation. On 8 February 1913, the first issue of *Da-guang bao* appeared. According to Chang Wen-kai, chief editor from 1917, the newspaper was named on the basis of texts such as Luke 2:32 and Matthew 4:16 concerning the coming of the "great light". (See also 3.1.4.)

Selected References

>   *Da-guang bao* (The Great Light News, 1913-1949). Hong Kong: *Da-guang bao*.
>   Liu Yaozhong, ed. *Guofu, zongtong jiang gongji furen zongjiao yanlun jiyao*. (Selected Works of the father of the nation). Taipei: Zhongyan wenwu, 1979.
>   Sun Yat-sen. *Prescriptions for Saving China: Selected Writings of Sun Yat-sen,* edited by Julie Lee Wei, Ramon H. Myers and Donald G. Gillin. Stanford CA.: Hoover Institution Press, c1994.

3.2 The Period 1930-1960

These years were traumatic decades for Catholics as for Protestants, not least because of: Sino-Japanese and world wars; violent occupation by Japanese forces; imprisonment and malnutrition; post-war turmoil and repercussions of civil conflict; the 1949 Revolution; and China's "great leap forward". Throughout this period, continuing flood-tides of migrants, military, displaced missionaries and refugees of all categories brought exhaustive demands upon all resources of medical care, housing and accommodation, relief and welfare services, and also on pastoral ministries. Many critical events in the turbulent growth of Hong Kong over the next two decades ensured that Christian energies were largely absorbed in such events and the people's response to them.

Contextual Theology in Hong Kong 231

There were, however, particular lay men and women who led in these endeavours, and among them Leung Sui-choh, Karl Reichelt (3.2.1.) and Teng Chih-hui stand out. Teng was active in the Christian Alliance Church and a number of Chinese Christian communities. Leung was formerly a leader in the YMCA in Canton and Shanghai, and became chairperson of the HK Council of the Church of Christ in China. He was also active in regional and world ecumenical bodies, and a number of his writings are extant. N.Z. Zia and S.K. Lee were also active in the study of religion and church history in China and Hong Kong. In the 1950s, the ecumenical Chung Chi College - part of the nucleus for the later Chinese University of Hong Kong - was founded (1951), the HK Christian Council was reconstituted (1954), and the Christian Study Centre (see 3.3.1.; 3.4.1.) was established at Tao Fong Shan.

These twenty years witnessed, however, two important events with reference to the development of contextually sensitive theologies in Hong Kong. First, there were some mainland Christian scholars who came to Hong Kong, in the main because of the unstable socio-political conditions on the mainland, and these loosely formed a diasporic scholarly community in Hong Kong. Although of diverse theological and social backgrounds, these Christian scholars had at least two things in common: their existential as well as academic concerns for the possibility of a confluence between Chinese culture and the Christian faith; and their common concerns for and involvement in educational work at various levels. Their influence upon Hong Kong naturally fell mostly in the areas of fostering the development of a more genuinely Chinese Christianity, and in advocacy for educational reforms. For some, a key concern was also the recognition of truth and wisdom in China's major religious traditions. Expatriates also played important roles in these three concerns.

During these decades as well, the neo-Confucian manifesto titled *Wei zhongguo wenhua jinggao shijie renshi xuanyan* (Manifesto on the crisis in Chinese culture) appeared, drawing forth lively Christian response. The manifesto was jointly signed by four world-renowned neo-Confucianists: Mou Zongsan, Xu Fuguan, Zhang Junmai and Tang Junyi. Six months after its publication, about 30 local Christian scholars and church leaders called for a conference to discuss the ways Christians should respond to Chinese cultures. The participants included figures such as Li Zhaojiang, Gu Baoluo, Zhou Yuxi, Wu Xianli, Zheng Xinrong, Rui Tao'an, and others. From this conference, one can sense that the indigenisation of Christian faith found in Hong Kong was quite different from that which was proceeding in the China mainland. The latter placed considerable stress on the socio-political implications (such as national salvation) of the dialogue. The emphasis seen in Hong Kong concerns for indigenisation of the faith was, however, relatively more cultural and existential.

Selected References

> *Catholic Hong Kong: a Hundred Years of Missionary Activity: On the Occasion of the Centenary Year of the Arrival in Hong Kong of the Pontifical Foreign Missions Institute.* Hong Kong: Catholic Press Bureau, 1958.
> Leung Sui-choh. "On Selfhood of the Chinese Church." In *Report of the Jerusalem Meeting of the International Missionary Council, March 24-April 8, 1928.* London and Melbourne: Oxford University Press, 1928: vol. III.
> —*Evaluation of the Christian universities in China.* Hong Kong : Chung Chi College, 1958.
> Paton, David M. *'R.O.' The Life and Times of Bishop Hall of Hong Kong.* Hong Kong: Diocese of Hong Kong and Macao, 1985.
> Ryan, Thomas F. *China through Catholic Eyes.* Hong Kong: Catholic Truth Society of Hong Kong, 1942.
> Sharpe, Eric J. *Karl Ludvig Reichelt. Missionary, Scholar, Pilgrim.* Edited by Mary Kay Hobbs. Hong Kong: Tao Fong Shan Ecumenical Centre, 1984.
> Smith, Carl T. *Chinese Christians: Elites, Middlemen, and the Church in Hong Kong.* Hong Kong: Oxford University Press, 1985.
> Xie Fuya (N.Z. Zia). *Jidujiao yu zhongguo sixiang* (Christianity and Chinese thought). Hong Kong: Chinese Christian Literature Council, 1971.

3.2.1. Karl Ludwig Reichelt (1877-1952)

Karl Ludwig Reichelt is remembered as a pioneer in the study and experience of Mahayana Buddhism and in Buddhist-Christian encounter. Arriving in China in 1903 he was soon immersed in studies of Buddhism and became internationally known as both Buddhist scholar and creative teacher. In 1920 he founded in Shekow, the "Christian Brotherhood among China's Buddhists" on the basis, shared by Buddhist friends, that "our Mahayana scriptures point forward to Christianity as their true fulfilment". Reichelt developed there what became a fully inculturated *Wan Seui Tong* (Hall for Pilgrims) where enquirers and pilgrims could stay in friendship and mutual learning. Reichelt's dream was of "an independent church among Buddhists" - a Retreat and Study Centre - where all followers of the Tao would share "an inward spiritual power". The dream would be partly fulfilled in Nanking and Shanghai, and most fully at *Tao Fong Shan* (Hill of the Wind of the Way) in Hong Kong from 1930-1952. Here, where the architecture, symbolism and chapel art fully reflected Buddhist forms, a large library was collected, many writings were published, and a college was added for pilgrims who sought fuller Christian training. From here Reichelt and colleagues travelled extensively throughout China, and later throughout Asia, meeting, studying and teaching, as well as frequently lecturing in Europe.

Reichelt's own writings received increasing recognition as authoritative studies of both Buddhism and of Christian response to its faith and quest. He had discerned the Spirit of God at work in the faith of Buddhist monks and believed he had found in Mahayana Buddhism the Cosmic Christ of John's Gospel. He would frequently stress that this could be grounded in the reality of God's creative activity everywhere, eternally, so that the Tao and the Logos could be seen as identical. And this he found demonstrated in the close parallels between Buddhism and Christianity regarding faith, new birth, the "paradise in the west", and in Trinitarian forms. He remained critical of other features of Buddhism, however, still holding central the goal of God's Reign, a faith that comes through reconciliation to God, and which is revealed by individual and social fruits.

Selected References
Works by Karl Ludvig Reichelt
> Truth and Tradition in Chinese Buddhism. Shanghai: Commercial Press, 1927.

Religion in Chinese Garment. Translated by Joseph Tetlie. London: Lutterworth Press, 1951.

Meditation and Piety in the Far East: A Religious-Psychological Study. Translated by Sverre Holth. London: Lutterworth Press, 1953.

The Transformed Abbot. Translated by G.M. Reichelt and A.P. Rose. London: Lutterworth Press, 1954.

"The Johannine Approach." In *The Authority of the Faith. International Missionary Council, Tambaram, December 1938.* Tambaram Series vol. 1. London: Oxford University Press, 1939.

Noren, Loren E. "The Life and Work of Karl Ludvig Reichelt." *Ching Feng* 10.3, 1967.

Eilert, Hakon. *Boundlessness: Studies in Karl Ludvig Reichelt's Missionary thinking with Special Regard to the Buddhist Christian Encounter.* Studia Missionalia Upsaliensia 24. Aarhus: Forlaget Aros, 1974.

Sharpe, Eric J. *Karl Ludvig Reichelt. Missionary, Scholar, Pilgrim.* Hong Kong: Tao Fong Shan Ecumenical Centre, 1984.

3.2.2. Xie Fuya (N.Z. Zia, 1892-1991)

Xie is remembered as a prominent Christian philosopher who was an expert in the dialogue between Chinese culture and the Christian faith. His endeavour in arguing that the two were mutually critical and at the same time enriching, was highly influential. He was an educator and professor of philosophy at various famous Chinese universities, such as Lingnan University, Zhongshan University (both in Guangdong) and Jinling University (in Nanjing). Xie was also a prolific writer not only of philosophical and theological articles and books but also of poetry. He came to Hong Kong in the 1940s and in 1952 was appointed by Chung Chi College (which later became a constituting college of the Chinese University of Hong Kong) as professor of the history of Chinese philosophy.

Amongst his chief writings are studies of the convergences between Confucianism, Taoism and Chinese Buddhism, and the relationship of Chinese culture to Christianity and to western thought. One of the unforgettable contributions Xie made to the Chinese Christian community was his work as chief editor, starting from 1958, for the translation project entitled the Christian Classics

Library. The purpose of this series of books was to make available to the Chinese community the great wealth of Christian thought enshrined in the Christian literature of the past 19 centuries. This translation project contributes resources for the indigenisation of the Christian faith in Chinese soil.

Selected References
Works by Xie Fuya (N.Z. Zia)
> *Zhongguo sanjiao de gongtong benzhi* (Common ground of Confucianism, Taoism, and Chinese Buddhism). Hong Kong: Christian Study Centre on Chinese Religion and Culture, 1966.
> *Jidujiao yu zhongguo sixiang* (Christianity and Chinese thought). Hong Kong: Chinese Christian Literature Council, 1971.
> *Nanhua xiaozhu shan fang wenji* (Works written during a brief stay in the mountains of southern China). Hong Kong: Nantian shuye, 1974.
> *Xie Fuya wannian wenlu* (The later writings of Xie Fuya). Taibei: Chuanji wenxue, 1977.
> *Zhongyong yu daoli: Zhong xi lidai zhexiao bilun* (Chinese thought and Western counterparts). Hong Kong: Hong Kong Baptist College, 1986.
> *Xie Fuya wannian jidujiao sixiang lunji* (N.Z. Zia's thoughts on Christianity in his old age). Hong Kong: Chinese Christian Literature Council, 1986.
> *Zi bianzi zhi dianzi: Xie Fuya bainian shengping jilue* (From pigtail to electron). Hong Kong: Chinese Christian Literature Council, 1992.

3.2.3. Xu Dishan (1893-1941) and Inter-religious Encounter

Xu was a native of Fukien (Fujian) Province. After obtaining a BA degree from the Yenching (Yanjing) University, he continued his studies at Columbia University (MA) and at Oxford University. He is remembered as an educationalist and professor at Yenching University, Peking University and Tsinghua (Qinghua) University. His association with Hong Kong began in 1936 when he was appointed by Hong Kong University (founded by the colonial government) to be dean of the department of Chinese literature. Soon after the appointment, he applied himself to reformation of the educational system. Faced with entrenched colonialism in the university, one of his most important contributions was the effort to introduce Chinese culture, language and traditions as a necessary dimension of the curriculum. Predictably, he encountered great difficulties which prevented the full implementation of his reforms.

Xu was also a writer of some note, regarding not only literature but also on Christianity and other faiths, as well as in fictional works. The influence of China's encounter with Christianity has been noted in a variety of ways in the works of writers of the 20s, 30s and 40s. As a professed Christian, Xu is distinctive for the Christian themes and symbolism of his work, as well as broader religious elements from his encounter with other Chinese faiths. Xu converted to Christianity in 1916, although his religious faith was characterised by an extensive syncretism that also included elements of Chinese Buddhism, Taoism, and Confucianism. He embraced his syncretistic religious identity without difficulty. Inter-religious encounter and debate were central concerns for scholars like Xu.

Selected References
Works by Xu Dishan

> *Dao-jiao shi* (History of Taoism). Shanghai: Shang-wu, 1934.
> *Fu-ji mi-xin di yan-jiu* (A Study on the superstition of Planchette). Zhang sha: Shang wu yin shu guan, 1941.
> *Wei-chiao Chui-chien* (Letters from an endangered home). Shanghai: Commercial Press, 1947.
> *Hsü Ti-shan Hsüan-chi (Selected Works of Hsü Ti-shan)*. Peking: Jenmin Wen-hsüeh, 1958.
> *Kong-shan ling-yu* (Raining in the mountain). Taipei: Tai-wan shang-wu, 1966.
> *Fo-jiao yi-shu lun-ji* (On Buddhist art). Taipei: Mi-lei, 1984.
> *Xu Di Shan Ji* (Xu Di Shan collections). Chen Yang: Chen Yang Chu Ban She, 1998.
> Robinson, Lewis S. "Christianity through the Eyes of Chinese Writers." In *Double-Edged Sword. Christianity and 20th Century Chinese Fiction,* by Lewis S. Robinson. Hong Kong: Tao Fong Shan Ecumenical Centre, 1986: part II.

See also Issue of *Ching Feng* 2 (Dec. 1958).

3.2.4. Ronald O. Hall (1895-1975)

Ronald Hall was Anglican bishop in Hong Kong for 34 years, and exercised a deep influence there and in China, upon student and worker leaders, upon generations of leaders in frontier ministries and local churches, and upon key leaders of the churches in mainland China. He was strongly shaped by the Student Christian and ecumenical movements, by such thinkers as Teilhard de Chardin, and by Chinese leaders such as Timothy T. Lew, Y.T. Wu, T.C. Chao, and Cheng Cheng-yi. Hall was committed not only to the educational, welfare and spiritual needs of peoples in Hong Kong and south China, but also to ecumenical, inter-faith and social ministries; a mentor to pioneers in industrial mission and workers' organisations, to theological teachers and Chinese leaders such as T.Z. Koo and K.H. Ting. He was deeply concerned for social issues, the relationship between liturgy and society, and befriended communists. He also ordained the first Anglican woman priest, Florence Li Tim-oi (1944).

Hall's expressed goal was the "demonstration of Christian love in action in the modern world". This meant for him following an "incarnational principle in social action", as well as in church administration and pastoral ministry, where steps were to be tried, outcomes relearnt, and further steps taken to meet the most urgent human needs. He formed a deep appreciation for living aspects of Chinese religious tradition, and directly supported the work of Karl Ludvig Reichelt (3.2.1.) at Tao Fong Shan. His vision for Hong Kong churches was that of a truly Chinese Christianity, and his contribution to the formation of the Three Self Patriotic Movement in China was acknowledged (by K.H. Ting) as being indispensable. His writings were very much 'tracts for the times', and dealt with Christian responses to contemporary needs in church, in mission and in society, where God's love was to be acted out.

Selected References
Works by Ronald O. Hall
>   *New Church Order, the Future of the World-wide Episcopal Church; the Twenty-seventh Annual Hale Memorial Sermon, delivered*

November 14, 1941, by the Rt. Rev. Ronald Owen Hall. Evanston: Seabury-Western theological seminary, 1941.

The Art of the Missionary: Fellow-workers with the Church in China. London: Student Christian Movement Press, 1942.

China's Fight for Freedom. London: Odham Press, 1943?

The Missionary-artist Looks at his Job. New York: International Missionary Council, 1942.

—, with T.C. Chao and Roderick Scott. *The Christian Movement in China in a Period of National Transition.* Mysore City: Wesley Press and Publishing House, 1938.

Paton, David M. *'R.O.' The Life and Times of Bishop Hall of Hong Kong.* Hong Kong: Diocese of Hong Kong and Macao, 1985.

Li Tim-oi, Florence. *Raindrops of My Like: Memoirs of the Reverend Florence Li Tim-oi.* Toronto: Anglican Book Centre, 1996.

3.3 The Period 1960-1980
3.3.1. People and Centres

These decades witnessed the continuing effort to elaborate the ways in which Chinese culture (especially that in the name of Confucianism) and Christianity could be mutually enriched. Studies of re-emerging Christianity in China also multiplied in Hong Kong along with further attempts to develop more contextual theological reflection. Scholars and writers who contributed to the growth of a more localised theology at this time included faculty members of Chung Chi College, the Chinese University of Hong Kong, such as Andrew Roy, Philip Shen, Ng Lee-ming, Paul Newman, Chiu Teng-kiat, Richard Deutsch and James Pan; and staff of the two Lutheran theological seminaries such as Manfred Berndt, Andrew Chiu and Tim Hoffman. Other contributors, who were active in the Hong Kong Christian Council, included Paul Webb, Ralph Lee, William Tung, Ng Sui-lai, Kwok Nai-wang (3.4.5.), Alan Chan Chor-choi (3.4.4.), and Raymond Fung (3.4.6.). Those in related groups included Victor Liu Bo-chin and (Ms) Chung Yuk-sum (SCM), (Ms) Ko Siu-wah (YWCA), Denis Rogers (Hong Kong Union Church), (Ms) Lee Ching-chee (Church of Christ in China), Milton Wan Wai-yiu (China Church Research Centre) and Francis Yip (Holy Carpenter Church).

Contextual Theology in Hong Kong

It is generally agreed that many social movements active in conscientisation, advocacy and reflection in Hong Kong emerged more fully from the late 1960s. Amongst the movements there were many led by, shared in, or funded by Christian bodies. Prominent here were student and worker groups, the Holy Carpenter Church, Hong Kong Observers, the Christian Industrial Committee, and the Society for Community Organization (for the CIC and SOCO see 3.3.5 and 3.3.6.). In China study and reflection, Protestant centres which were active along with the CSCCRC / TFSEC (see below), were the China Liaison Office led by Ewing Carroll, and the China Church Research Centre led by Jonathan Chao and Christopher Morris, both centres being active in publication. (See under Contextual Theology in China vol. 3, chap. 3.)

The Christian Study Centre on Chinese Religion and Culture (CSRCRC), and the Tao Fong Shan Christian Institute were active in research, theological reflection and publication. Earlier staff included Chiu Teng-kiat, Feng Shang-li, Sverre Holth, Frederick Brandauer, Eric Kvan, Gilbert Baker and Winfried Gluer. The two centres merged to become the Tao Fong Shan Ecumenical Centre (TFSEC) in 1979 (until 1986, when they separated again). The then Director was Peter Li Jing xiong (3.3.4.) and full-time staff included Deng Zhao-ming, Paula Chui, Grace Lam, Rita M. England and John C. England. The Study Centre and later Ecumenical Centre conducted a range of seminars, and by the end of this period, the TFSEC was also responsible both for local workshops and international study courses on the church in China and on Asian theology. The CSCCRC and TFSEC have published the academic journal *Ching Feng* (formerly *Quarterly Notes*) since 1957, *Bridge Magazine* and a series of publications on Chinese Christian writings and the church in China.

Selected References

    Baker, Gilbert. *Bishop Speaking*. Hong Kong: Hong Kong Diocesan Office. 1981.

    Berndt, Manfred H. *The Diakonia Function of the Church in Hong Kong.* Hong Kong: s.l., 1970.

    Deutsch, Richard. "Cultural Heritage Versus the Old Testament?" *Ching Feng* 29.1 (1971).

England, John C., ed. *Living Theology in Asia*. London: SCM Press, 1981; New York: Orbis , 1982.

Hong Kong Christian Council. *The Mission of the Church in Hong Kong in the 70s.* (Papers from the Conference). Hong Kong: HKCC, ca.1971.

Lee Ching-chee. *Half the Sky* and *Frankly Speaking* (both in Chinese). Hong Kong: Choi Tao Christian Publishers, 1993.

Lee, Shiu Keung. *The Cross and the Lotus*. Hong Kong: Christian Study Center on Chinese Religion and Culture, 1971.

Ng Lee-ming. *Christianity and Social Change in China*. Chinese Theological Education Series. Hong Kong: Chinese Christian Literature Council, 1981. (Reprinted from *Ching Feng,* vols 14, 15, 16, 20 and 21 (1971-1978).

Shen, Philip. "Our Theological Tasks in Relation to our Theological and Cultural Heritages." *Ching Feng* 21.4 (1978).

Smith, Carl T. "A Look at Ching Feng over the Past Twenty-Five Years." *Ching Feng* 25.4 (1982).

Wan, Milton Wai-yiu. *A Christian Introduction to Communism*. Hong Kong: Tien Dao Publishing House, 1979.

See also *Change* and *Monthly Memo* (CIC), *Chung Chi Journal, Theology and Life* (LTS), *News and Views* (HKCC).

3.3.2. Ho Sai-ming (He Shiming, 1911-1996)

Ho Sai-ming obtained his BA degree from the National Sun Yat-sen University, and his PhD in Humanities in the United States. A canon of the Hong Kong Anglican Church, his chief work for many years was with the Hong Kong Chinese Christian Literature Council. He is remembered as a prolific writer whose main writings have been collected under the series entitled "Collected Writings of Rev. Canon Simon Ho Sai Ming", 28 volumes in all. His life-long endeavour was to firmly root the Christian faith in Chinese soil, and for this purpose he wrote many books and articles. These considered in particular the relationship between Confucianism and Christianity, Christianity in Chinese piety, indigenous Christian theology and Christianity, and Christian faith in daily life. His writings on works of the Confucian canon have recently been reprinted. He also fostered the publishing of a wide range of writings by Hong Kong Christians.

Selected References
Works by Ho Sai-ming (He Shiming)

Twelve Talks on Christianity. Hong Kong: Chinese Christian Literature Council, ?1956.

Ts'ung Chi-tu chiao k'an Chung-kuo hsiao tao (Christianity and filial piety). Oakton, VA: Center for Chinese Research Materials, 1991? (1963).

Jidu jiao ru xiao si jiang (Christian viewpoint on Confucianism). Hong Kong: Chinese Christian Literature Council, 1982.

Jidu jiao yu ru xiao duitan (Dialogue between Christianity and Confucianism). Hong Kong: Chinese Christian Literature Council, 1986.

Jidu jiao bense shenxue congtan (On Indigenous Christian theology). Hong Kong: Chinese Christian Literature Council, 1987.

Zhonghua Jidu jiao rongguan shenxue chu yi (A tentative proposal on Chinese Christianity). Hong Kong: Chinese Christian Literature Council, 1987.

Da xue xuan shi (Explanations of selected passages from "The Great Learning"). Hong Kong: Christian Cultural Society, 1998.

Lunyu xuan shi (Explanations of selected passages from the *Analects*). Hong Kong: Christian Cultural Society, 1998.

Mengzi xuan shi (Explanations of selected passages from Mencius). Hong Kong: Christian Cultural Society, 1998.

Zhongyong xuan shi (Explanations of selected passages from the "Doctrine of the Mean"). Hong Kong: Christian Cultural Society, 1998.

3.3.3. Wu Mingjie (1916-1990)

Wu completed his doctoral degree in the United States and came to Hong Kong after the Communist Party came to power in mainland China. He was a pastor of the Evangelical Lutheran Church of Hong Kong and was appointed president of the Lutheran Church in 1960. He was also appointed vice-president of the Lutheran Theological Seminary. Wu is remembered as a local church leader of more evangelical tendencies who also made efforts to indigenise the Christian faith in Hong Kong by relating it to both the living elements of Chinese culture and also to the lives of lay Christians in Hong Kong. He wrote two books on this theme.

Selected References
Works by Wu Mingjie
> *Xintu yu shenxue* (Christian theology for layman). Hong Kong: Tian dao, 1981.
> *Jidu jiao yu zhongguo wenhua de jiechu dian* (Points of contact between Christianity and Chinese culture). Hong Kong: Dao sheng, 1990.

3.3.4. Peter Lee King-hung (Li Jingxiong, 1930-)

Lee was ordained in the United Methodist Church in 1959, and obtained his PhD from Boston University School of Theology in 1973. Though he is a pastor of the Hong Kong Methodist Church, most of his time has been spent in ecumenical ministries, as chaplain to Chung Chi College and as director of the Christian Study Centre on Chinese Religion and Culture (and TFSEC) from 1974 to1994. During the same period he served as editor of the internationally known theological journal *Ching Feng,* for which he wrote many locally-rooted theological articles. With his colleagues (see 3.3.1.) he fostered seminars, conferences and workshops on many aspects of Chinese spirituality, theology and church life, both for local movements and for international networks committed to ecumenical study and reflection. He has been especially active in facilitating the dialogue between Christianity and Confucian thought in association with theological schools and ecumenical associations of theologians. He has also been active in teaching theology in the Lutheran Theological Seminary from 1978 to the present.

During these last two decades, Lee has studied sources in Chinese religion and culture and worked at contextualising the Christian faith, especially in relation to the developing history of China and Hong Kong and to the Confucian tradition. In line with the Asian theological movement of the 1970s, he sharply criticised older understandings of indigenisation, advocating that dialogue between the Christian faith and Chinese culture be done critically and in the contemporary context. It was therefore his contention that a Chinese Christian must be critical both of Christianity and of his/her own cultural traditions. He also contributed to ecumenical symposia on Chinese religion, Asian Christian spirituality and use of Asian resources in doing theology.

Selected References
Works by Peter Lee King-hung (Li Jingxiong)

Romance and Theology. Hong Kong: Taosheng Publishing, 1997.

"Indigenous Theology - Overcropped Land or Under- developed Field?" *Ching Feng* 17.1 (1974). In *Ching Feng*, Chinese edition, "Bense shenxue - Jiu geng yi xin ken." Vol. 40.1 (1974).

"From Mission to Buddhists to Possibilities of Multifacet Religious Dialogue." *Ching Feng* 21.3 (1978).

"1997 and the Church of Hong Kong: An Exercise in Contextualization." *Ching Feng* 25.4 (1982).

"Some Critical Issues in Asian Christian Thinking." *Ching Feng* 31.2-3 (1988).

"Hong Kong: From the Shadow of the Third World to a People's Theology of Liberation." *Ching Feng* 32.3 (1989).

"The Search for Spirituality in the Modern Word: The Hong Kong-Taiwan-China Orbit." *Ching Feng* 36.4 (1993).

"Naming the Divine: The Christian-Chinese Cross-cultural Experience." *Ching Feng* 39.2 (1996).

—, with Virginia Fabella and David Kwang-sun Suh, eds. *Asian Christian Spirituality: Reclaiming Traditions*. Maryknoll, NY: Orbis Books, 1992.

3.3.5. Hong Kong Christian Industrial Committee (HKCIC) (1967-)

In the face of exploitative labour conditions and often severe suffering by Hong Kong workers and poor families leading to large discontent in 1960s, the Hong Kong Christian Council established its industrial mission work. With early leadership by Margaret Kane, the Hong Kong Christian Industrial Committee was born in 1967. As a part of the Hong Kong Christian Council, HKCIC identified itself as a mission work of the Hong Kong Protestant Church to workers. Since its birth, HKCIC has committed itself to stand alongside workers in their attempts to rectify abuses and injustices, by providing education, negotiation and advocacy. The Committee does not attempt to become a leader of workers, but rather wishes to struggle alongside workers, assisting them to organise in order to fight for their own rights. It has also been active in a range of campaigns for people's human rights and democratic freedoms in

Hong Kong. Long-time leaders in the Committee's work have been Raymond Fung and Lau Chin-shek as secretary-organisers, Hans Lutz as close associate, and Ding Lik-kiu as chairman.

All these activities have been done on the basis of both social analysis and a theology of human dignity and equity, and out of a belief that only through such struggle will workers and citizens be able to change their poor situation and a fuller community be achieved. The movement is notable for its combination of forthright protest and advocacy with Bible study, theological reflection and 'church-planting'. From it has come a flow of writing on all these parts of its work, in Newsletters, Memos, and collections of articles, along with the creation of Christian Worker Fellowships, which have all the necessary features of a local church. Raymond Fung, in particular (see 3.4.6.), has written extensively on both the practice and theology of urban and industrial mission.

Selected References

>Fong, Bernard. *Out of the Shadow. Life and Times of Ding Lik-kiu.* Hong Kong: Haven of Hope and Yang Memorial Methodist Social Centre, 1994.
>Fung, Raymond. "Industrial Mission and Evangelism." *International Review of Mission* (July 1975).
>—. "Ten Theses on Labour Evangelism." *Change* (Newsletter of Hong Kong CIC) 36 (May 1976).
>—. "A Spirituality and Strategy for Industrial Mission." *Change* 43 (Sept. 1978).
>Ding Lik-kiu. "Annual Reports" of the HKCIC, Mimeo'd (1969-).
>Recent reports and statements are downloadable from webpage: http://www.cic.org.hk/

3.3.6. The Society for Community Organization (SoCo) (1972-)

SoCo was formed in 1972 by church members to assist people to solve their community problems through solidarity and organisation, and therefore to build up the power of citizens through community work. Its establishment was largely under the auspices, and with the support of the East Asia Christian Conference who, at their meeting in 1970, confirmed the emphasis on urban industrial

Contextual Theology in Hong Kong

mission and strengthened URM networks for this. Concretely its objectives are: 1) to organise and provide social welfare services for the people of Hong Kong; 2) to promote development and a sense of community among the people of Hong Kong; 3) to guide and help citizens to take responsibility on their own through participation in efforts to solve community problems; and 4) to promote a caring and equal society. Leaders in SoCo's programmes have included Ho Hei-wah, Calina Tsang Ka-wai and Sze Lai-shan.

The Society has declared its belief that "all human beings are born equal; everyone has equal political rights and equal opportunity of participation in the community; and fair distribution of social resources is the foundation of human rights. Only when the social system and policies are based on this foundation, can the paradigm of 'all members of the human family are equal' be recognized", and a society that respects humanity and the dignity of all persons be built. Some of SoCo's projects include: i) a Civic Rights Education Centre; ii) helping to found the Hong Kong Human Rights Commission; iii) action on Cage Homes and Old Private Housing Development Projects; iv) the Nam Cheong Neighbourhood Level Community Project; v) the Elderly Rights Project; and vi) Kwun Tong and Wong Tai Sin Community Development Projects. A number of publications present the motivations, planning and reflection on which such projects are based and carried out.

Selected References
Works produced by SoCo
  Annual Report. Hong Kong: SoCo, 1973-92.
  Da- keng- dong zhi sheng. (Voices From Da-keng-dong). Hong Kong: SoCo, 1973-87.
  Project Report. Hong Kong: SoCo, December 1979, 1980.
  People's Power in this Decade. Hong Kong: SoCo, 1982.
  Society for Community Organization. Tenth Anniversary Special. Hong Kong: SoCo, 1982.
  Gongmin quanyi zhi duo shao zhi tousu quan. Ziliao ce. (Handbook of Civic Rights-Right to Complain). Hong Kong: SoCo, 1984.
  Hong Kong Human Rights Reports. Hong Kong: SoCo, 1991-1992, 1993.

Violations and the Poverty Problem in Hong Kong. Hong Kong: SoCo and Hong Kong Human Rights Commission, 1994.

Ji gang quan huodong ziliao ce: Tongshi xianggang ren. (Activity Handbook of Right to Abode). Hong Kong: SoCo, 1999.

3.4 The Period 1980-2000
3.4.1. Changed Identities; Developing Theologies

Hong Kong entered into its process of decolonisation starting from 1984 after the signing of the *Joint Declaration of the Government of the United Kingdom of Great Britain and Northern Ireland and the Government of the People's Republic of China on the question of Hong Kong*. This affirmed that Hong Kong was an inseparable part of mainland China and that the latter had decided to resume the exercise of sovereignty over Hong Kong with effect from 1 July 1997. Suddenly, Hong Kong people were thrown into an identity crisis, for the inhabitants were faced with questions as to who they were and where they belonged. Younger generations brought up in Hong Kong's apolitical and utilitarian culture were forced to ask in what sense they were Chinese, and to what extent Hong Kong was rather a cosmopolitan society. Some felt that Hong Kong should be returned to the People's Republic of China (PRC), while others asked why not the Republic of China (Taiwan)? Still others wished that Hong Kong could continue its colonial status. Culturally, the majority of people in Hong Kong are Chinese; politically, however, it has been sheltered by its colonial status which kept it apart from mainland China and direct involvement in the political turmoil experienced by mainland Chinese during the past several decades. Hong Kong people, including of course local theologians - whether women or men, lay or clergy - were thus ambivalent towards the restoration of Chinese identity.

Many theological discourses that arose during this period were inevitably conditioned by this ambivalence. Besides, these two decades also witnessed the growth of different types of locally or culturally rooted theologies. The work and publications of centres and movements mentioned above - the Hong Kong Christian Council and associated units; the Tao Fong Shan Ecumenical Centre (from 1987 known as the Christian Study Centre); student, worker,

Contextual Theology in Hong Kong

pastoral and China Study centres; groups within some of the theological seminaries; and related Catholic movements - continued and expanded. At Chung Chi College, the Chinese University of Hong Kong, there were now also a number of other staff who wrote extensively, including: Joseph Kaung Tai-wai (see 3.4.7.), Eric Chong, Archie Lee Chi-chung (3.4.8.) and Kwok Pui-lan (3.4.11.), Philip Shen, Ng Lee-ming, Alan Chan Chor-choi (3.4.4) and others. Many of their writings appeared in the *Tolo Theological Series* of volumes and other theological monographs dealing with the theology of Hong Kong, citizenship and education, pastoral theology, and biblical studies in Hong Kong.

The Evangelical Lutheran Seminary continued publishing *Theology and Life*, and along with the Lutheran World Federation, a series of volumes in the *China Studies Series*, surveying life of the churches in China, the role of women in them, and the role of biblical interpretation and liturgical renewal. At the TFSEC/CSC, new staff included Chung Yuk-sum, Mary Kay Hobbs, and Philip L. and Janice K. Wickeri, and the centre produced significant contextual writings (in *Ching Feng* and elsewhere). Other institutes and associations which now produced volumes of Christian analysis and reflection upon the life and situation of Hong Kong's people included the Hong Kong Women Christian Council, the Hong Kong Christian Institute, the China Graduate School of Theology, ARENA, and the Asian Human Rights Association. Other individual authors of volumes included (Ms) Lee Ching-chee, Winnie Ho Hsiao-hsin, Carver Yu, Deng Zhao-ming, Leung Ka-lun, Ying Fuk-tsang, Lam Wing-hung, Chan Shun-hing, and Yeo Khiok-khng.

Selected References

Chan Shun-hing. "Secularization and Social Change in Hong Kong: A Sociological Interpretation." *Ching Feng* 38.4 (1995).
—. "Conceptual Differences Between Hong Kong and Chinese Theologians. A Study of the 'Cultural Christians' Controversy." *Asia Journal of Theology* 12 (1998).
China Graduate School Journal Special Issues: *National Identity and Commitment*. Vol. 23 (1997); *The Church in Hong Kong: the Past 50 Years*. Vol. 25 (July 1998) (Note Siu-lun Lau

The Indigenization of the Church in Hong Kong after 1949: Two Case Studies; and Carver Yu. *Theological Development of the Hong Kong Christian Community in the Last Forty Years*); *Theological Trends in the 21st Century I & 2*. Vols. 28 & 29 (2000).

Chong, Eric. "Fellow Pilgrims on the Road to Truth." In *Turn Around: Called to Witness Together Amidst Asia Plurality*, edited by Henriette Hutabarat and Dhyanchand Carr. Hong Kong: CCA, 1995.

Hong Kong Christian Council. *The Mission of the Church in Hong Kong in the 80s. Official Report of the Consultation November, 1980*. HKCC, 1981.

Ho Hsiao-hsin, Winnie. *Hua jen fu nu shen hsueh ch'u t'an* (Towards a Chinese feminist theology). Hong Kong: Hsiang-kang hsin i tsung shen hsueh yuan: Fa hsing che Tao sheng, 1988.

Kaung, Joseph, ed. *Hong Kong Christians' Political Theology*. Tolo Theological Series 3. Hong Kong: Chung Chi Theology Division, 1985.

Kwok Pui-lan, ed. *1997 and the Theology of Hong Kong*. Tolo Theological Series 1. Hong Kong: Chung Chi Theology Division, 1983.

Lee, Archie Chi-chung. *The Old Testament in Context*. Tolo Theological Series 6. Hong Kong: Chung Chi Theology Division, 1988.

Lee Ching-chee. *Half the Sky*. Hong Kong: Choi Tao Christian publishers, 1993.

Romaniuk, Susan and Denise Tong, eds. *Uncertain Times: Hong Kong Women Facing 1997*. Hong Kong: Hong Kong Women Christian Council, 1995.

Woodman, Sophia. *Hong Kong's Social Movements: Voices from the Margins*. Hong Kong: July 1 Link and Hong Kong Women Christian Council, 1997.

Yeo Khiok-khng. *What Has Jerusalem to do with Beijing. Biblical Interpretation from a Chinese Perspective*. Harrisburg: Trinity Press International, 1998.

Yu, Carver. *Being and Relation: A Theological Critique of Western Dualism and Individualism*. Edinburgh, Scottish Academic Press, 1988.

3.4.2. Declarations or Statements

In this period many declarations or statements were formulated and published by a wide range of Christian churches and groups,

Contextual Theology in Hong Kong 249

concerning such matters as religious freedom, the mission and role of the church in Hong Kong, and the future of Christian communities there. Below is a selected list of documents in off-print or mimeo'd form, since 1984.

"Statement on the Catholic Church and the Future of Hong Kong." Signed by Cardinal John Baptist, Wu Cheng-Chung. Diocese of Hong Kong, 1984.

"A Manifesto Of The Protestant Church In Hong Kong On Religious Freedom." Hong Kong Christian Council, 1984.

"The Convictions Held By Christians in Hong Kong in The Midst of Contemporary Social and Political Change." Evangelical Christian Leaders in Hong Kong, 1984.

"A Position Paper on the Future of Hong Kong." The Delegation of Hong Kong Protestant Church Leaders, 1984.

"March into the Bright Decade." A Pastoral Exhortation issued by Cardinal John Baptist Wu Cheng-Chung, 1989.

"Mission 2000." Hong Kong Church Renewal Movement Limited, 1989.

"A Manifesto of the Mission of Church in Hong Kong for the 90s." By the *Consultation on the Mission of the Churches in Hong Kong in the 1990s* organised by the Hong Kong Christian Council, 1990.

"A Reaffirmation of the Role of the Hong Kong Church - A Position Paper of the 1991 Hong Kong Church Delegation to China." The 1991 Hong Kong Church Delegation to China, 1991.

"Towards 2000 - Hong Kong Church Mission Declaration." Hong Kong Church Renewal Movement, Limited, 1993.

"Hong Kong Mid-decade Church Consultation Pastoral Letter to All Christians in Hong Kong." *Hong Kong Mid-Decade Church Mission Consultation* organised by the Hong Kong Christian Council, 1994.

"Towards the Special Administrative Region: A Declaration of the Mission of the Hong Kong Churches." *The Second Consultation on Evangelism* organised by the Hong Kong Church Renewal Movement Limited, 1995.

"The Vision of Hong Kong." *Conference on the Vision of Hong Kong* jointly organized by the Theology Division Chung Chi College the Chinese University of Hong Kong, the Hong Kong Christian Institute, the Christian Times and Christian Study Centre on Chinese Religion and Culture, 1996.

3.4.3. The Historic Event of "1997"

The prospect, and completion, of Hong Kong's retrocession to China generated theological reflection in Christian writings of many different kinds. Here is a selected and chronological book list - see also Kwok Nai-wang (Guo Naihong, 3.4.5.):

> Hong Kong Christian Council, ed. *Xianggang jiaohui yu Xianggang qiantu* (Hong Kong Church and Hong Kong Future). Hong Kong Christian Council, 1982.
> Kwok Pui-lan, ed. *1997 yu Xianggang shenxue* (1997 and Hong Kong Theology). Hong Kong: Chung Chi College Theology Division, 1983.
> Chin Pak Tau et al, eds. *1997: Zhuanbian yu gengxin* (Articles on 1997). Rev. ed. Hong Kong: Fellowship of Evangelical Students, 1984.
> Kaung, Joseph Tai-wai and Kwok Pui-lan, eds. *Fengcheng de fuyin: Cong "jiu-qi" suo yinfa de fanxing* (The Fullness of the Gospel: Reflections on 1997). Hong Kong: Chung Chi College Theology Division, 1984.
> Christian Witness Press, ed. *1997 yu jiaohui shiming* (1997 and the Church's Mission). Hong Kong: Christian Witness, 1984.
> Kaung, Joseph Tai-wai, ed. *Jidutu yu zhengzhi* (Christians and Politics-in the Hong Kong Context). Hong Kong: Chung Chi College Theology Division, 1985.
> Lawrence, Thomas, ed. *Facing 1997-What Hong Kong Pastors are Saying-A Survey Report,* translated by Richard van Houten. Hong Kong: China Church Research Centre, 1987.
> Chan Hak-ping. *Xianggang de zhuanbian yu jiaohui jiaodao celu.* (A strategy for the teaching ministry of the Hong Kong Churches as they face transition). Hong Kong: Christian Witness, 1987.
> Hong Kong Christian Council, ed. *Heyi chengdan mu wanmin: 90 niandai Xianggang jiaohui shiming zixun huiyi.* Hong Kong: Hong Kong Christian Council, 1990.
> Kwok Nai-wang. *Hong Kong 1997 - A Christian Perspective.* Hong Kong: CCA-URM, 1991.
> Chui, Jane C.L. *Huiying jiuqi: Jidutu qunti de jianzheng* (Some Christian responses on 1997 issues). Hong Kong: Hong Kong Christian Institute, 1992.
> Chan, Sequire S.H., ed. *Xianggang de yuanxiang* (The vision of Hong Kong). Hong Kong: Chinese Christian Literature Council, 1998.

3.4.4. Alan Chan Chor-choi (Chen Alan Zuocai, 1935-)

Chan was born in mainland China and educated in Hong Kong and the United States. He was ordained in 1962 and has long been a canon of the Anglican Cathedral in Hong Kong. He has contributed to many ecumenical councils and symposia and has also been a member of the Presidium of the Christian Conference of Asia (1981-85). While serving as head of the Theology Division at the Chinese University of Hong Kong, he also taught practical theology and made many contributions to the development of a contextualising theology.

Chan sees the particular history of the Christian Church in Hong Kong as being that of a comprador institution, benefiting from government policies and subsidies, while providing services to the government in return. This has effectively prevented the churches in the past from taking any prophetic role in the community, except for one or two charismatic figures. Drawing on the experience of urban mission in Hong Kong and Asia, as well as on the history of Christianity in China, he affirms that Christian mission must take the world seriously and recognise the total need and potential of the people, respond both to sinners and to the sinned against, and seek a Christian identity which can be expressed through diverse racial, national, cultural or professional identities. Chan has also written pastoral manuals, as well as utilising reflection on contemporary Chinese novels, and on stories of martial arts, in the doing of Christian theology.

Selected References
Works by Alan Chan Chor-choi (Chen Alan Zuocai)
    Wuxia yu rensheng (Martial arts stories and life*)*. Hong Kong: Breakthrough Publishing, 1990.
    Kaishi weiyi de lu: Xianggang xuanjiao shenxue keti de tantao (Is this the only path? Issues on mission theology in Hong Kong). Hong Kong: Theology Division, CUHK, 1995.
    Wuxia rensheng: Jinyong bi xia de xinling yu qinghuai (The mind of martial arts). Shanghai: Shanghai renmin chubanshe, 1999.

"Mission in the 80s. Three Lectures to the HKCC Consultation" *HKCC Message,* (Jan., Feb., April, 1980).

"Theological Issues Involved in the Characters of Wei Sui-bo and Shui Fung - Two distinctive personalities in Ching Yung's 'Wuu Shiar' Novels." Theological Seminar-Workshop, July 1984. Hong Kong; mimeo'd.

"Mission Theology: A Hong Kong Chinese Understanding." In *Crossroads are for Meeting,* edited by P. Turner and F. Sugeno. Sewanee: SPCK, 1986.

3.4.5. Kwok Nai-wang (Guo Naihong, 1940-)

Kwok is an outspoken local theologian who has written more than 20 books and edited five others. For many years as an ordained minister of the Hong Kong Council of the Church of Christ in China, he was pastor of Sam Oi Church, located in a densely populated slum area. He has also been general secretary of the Hong Kong Christian Council (1978-1988) and was founding director of the Hong Kong Christian Institute (1988-2000). In all these roles Kwok has been mentor to many ministers, lay people and theological teachers. All aspects of ecumenical mission have received his active support; whether emergency relief for victims of flood and fire, vocational training for Vietnamese refugees, or the development of study centres and of courses in contextual theology which he currently teaches at the Chinese University.

In his writings, he ranges from issues of political identity and democratic or religious rights, to the nurture of Christian spirituality in Hong Kong, to immediate questions of legal procedure or social inequities, to theological issues for contemporary Christian mission. He sees the social fabric of Hong Kong disintegrating as China's control strengthens and he expresses his concern for the building of full human community, where social justice and human rights are fully respected. Much of his writing is therefore highly critical of the government of Hong Kong, of local churches and of the PRC government. His vision of the Church within such a human community is one that exists for others through the gospel of self-emptying, thus being able to rebuild a people's 'humanness' in a humane society.

Contextual Theology in Hong Kong 253

Selected References
Works by Kwok Nai-wang (Guo Naihong)

Some Christian Reflections of the June 4 Massacre and the Democratic Movement. Church and Society Series 1. Hong Kong: Hong Kong Christian Institute, 1989.

In Search of a Future: 1997 and the Mission of the Church in Hong Kong (in Chinese). Church and Society Series 2. Hong Kong: Hong Kong Christian Institute, 1990.

Hong Kong 1997. A Christian Perspective. Hong Kong: CCA Urban Rural Mission, 1991.

Weizhe chengqiu shengming (Seeking spirituality in a precarious city: a collection of sermons on unity and mission of the church). Hong Kong: Hong Kong Christian Institute, 1993.

Hong Kong Braves 1997. Hong Kong: Hong Kong Christian Institute, 1994.

Zaizhihua bianyuan de Xianggang (Hong Kong on the brink of recolonisation). Hong Kong: Hong Kong Christian Institute, 1996.

1997: Hongkong's Struggle for Selfhood. Hong Kong: Hong Kong Christian Institute, 1996.

Renxing de huhuan: Xianggang jiaohui shiming de quanshi (Call to humanness: an interpretation of the mission of the church in Hong Kong). Hong Kong: Hong Kong Christian Institute, 1997.

A Church in Transition. Hong Kong: Hong Kong Christian Institute, 1997.

Guanshe shenxue chu tan (Theology of social concern). Hong Kong: Hong Kong Christian Institute, 1998.

Hong Kong after 1997: the first 1000 days. Hong Kong: Hong Kong Christian Institute; Asian Human Rights Commission, 2000.

Gengxin difang jiaohui de celue (Local church renewal strategies). Hong Kong: Hong Kong Christian Institute, 2000.

—, et al. *Xianggang jiaohui yu shehui yundong: 80 niandai de fansi.* (Social movements and the Christian Church in Hong Kong - Reflections on the 1980s). Hong Kong: Hong Kong Christian Institute, 1994.

3.4.6. Raymond Fung (ca 1940-)

Fung has been a lay theologian and organiser who largely developed the many-sided activities of the CIC (see 3.3.5.). He has also been a leader in many social causes and civic campaigns, as well as in regional urban mission training and programmes of action, theologies of mission, social action and new patterns of church life. In Monthly *Memo*, a socio-theological diary, he presented (often along with Hans Lutz) a range of people stories, theological reflections on incidents, campaign issues, courses and conferences; outlined the principles of urban and justice ministries, of labour evangelism and of worker Christian fellowships, and included inter-staff reflections, social criticism, case studies, and personal theological and devotional reflection.

Writing on the Kingdom of God, Fung suggests that mission should take the form of building a community where God's rule of justice, peace and love concretely operates, so that mission holds an open invitation for all to enter the community ("church") which is rooted in the world, offers sharing and solidarity, and joins pastoral nurture with political involvement, personal devotion with public witness, evangelism with social action. In labour evangelism he writes, the trustworthiness of the Christian message depends on the trustworthiness of the evangelists, which in turn depends on a long-term and high priority commitment to workers ("the sinned against") and their concerns, and on the evangelists' ability to create a community, which recognises the worker's identity and articulates its faith in Jesus Christ. Here there are no readymade answers, and growing awareness of institutional sin awakens and deepens the sense of personal sin. But for him the appeal of the Christian message begins with a call to new life (rather than a call to mend past broken life), and to reconciliation with God and man/woman i.e. fellow-workers in a common struggle for justice and dignity.

Selected References
Works by Raymond Fung
> *The Isaiah Vision: An Ecumenical Strategy for Congregational Evangelism.* Risk Book Series 52. Geneva: WCC, 1992.
> *Letters to Chi Cheung.* Hong Kong: Chinese Christian Literature Council, 1995.
> *Monthly Memo.* A monthly description of the 'environment' in which the staff of the CIC think and work. (1974-1983).

Households of God on China's Soil, compiled and translated by
    Raymond Fung. WCC Mission Series 2. Geneva: WCC,1982.
—, et al. *Shidai langchao zhong de fansi* (Reflection in our times).
    Hong Kong: Hong Kong Christian Institute, 1997.
"A Bystander Looks at his Own." *Ching Feng* 16.1 (1973).
"A Spirituality and Strategy for Industrial Mission." *Change* 43
    (1978).
"Involvement with the Poor in the Process of Theologising." *Ching
    Feng* 2.1 (1979).
"Human Sinned-Against." *International Review of Mission* (1980).
"Evangelism in China." *China Study Project* 23 (1983).
"Mission in Christ's Way." *International Review of Mission* 78.309
    (1989).

3.4.7. Joseph Kaung Tai-wai (Jiang Dahui, 1949-)

Kaung received his MTh at the Perkins School of Theology, Southern Methodist University, and has been on the faculty of the Theology Division, Chung Chi College, Chinese University of Hong Kong for over 20 years. He is also one of the earliest of local theologians to become involved in the Asian theological movement. Some of his chief theological concerns have been in the areas of social and political ethics, church-state relations and the indigenous rethinking of theology. He has contributed to many ecumenical symposia both nationally through the HKCC (see 3.3.1.) and regionally through such bodies as the CCA and PTCA. Apart from articles in a number of local and overseas journals, he has also edited volumes in the Tolo and Chung Chi College series.

Selected References

Works by Joseph Kaung Tai-wai (Jiang Dahui)

Jiji yu weiji. (To be and not to be). Hong Kong: Hong Kong Christian
    Institute, 1996.
"A Hong Kong Response to Chhu-Thau-Thi Theology". *Ching Feng*
    39.2 (1996).
—, ed. *Jidutu yu zhengzhi* (Christians and politics in the Hong
    Kong context). Tolo Series. Hong Kong: Chung Chi College
    Theology Division, 1985.
—, and Kwok Pui-lan, eds. *Fengcheng de fuyin: Cong "jiuqi" suo
    yinfa de fanxing* (The Fullness of the Gospel: Reflections on

1997). Hong Kong: Chung Chi College Theology Division, 1984.

—, and Ina Lau. *Death and the Meaning of Life*. Tolo Theological Series 5. Hong Kong: Chung Chi College Theology Division, 1987.

3.4.8. Archie Lee Chi-chung (Li Zhiiang, 1950-)

Lee is an ordained minister of the Hong Kong Council of the Church of Christ in China. Following study at Chung Chi College, the Chinese University of Hong Kong, he obtained his doctoral degree in Hebrew and Old Testament studies from the University of Edinburgh. He has taught theology at Chung Chi, and is currently the head of the religion department at the Chinese University of Hong Kong. One of the original resource persons for the Programme for Theology and Cultures in Asia (see Vol. 1, chap.3), he became its dean (1994-2000) and he has been director of the Christianity in Asia Project (Cambridge University, U.K.).

Lee has given most attention in his research and writing to theological reflection upon major Chinese cultural texts, which are read simultaneously with the biblical text, as a "doing of theology with Asian resources". In order to take seriously both the faith and life of our forbears and the central truths of the Bible he proposes a "cross-textual" hermeneutical approach that focuses on "what claims your life" in the multiple texts of both Asian culture and of the Bible. This is a method, he affirms, that is necessary in order to discover the full significance of both our cultural identity and our Christian faith and also to "provide adequate space to assess the creative interaction between the Bible and the Asian text". He has therefore written extensively on biblical interpretation in Asian perspectives, on prophetic and sapiential hermeneutics and on the theological bases for cross-textual hermeneutic. Much of his writing also appears in a series of cross-textual studies, including the interaction and mutual criticism in various texts, concerning lamentation and death, the understanding of creation, recitation of the past, the "aniconic God" and iconolatry, humanism and humanisation, and socio-political concerns. His hermeneutic approach is therefore deeply historical and multi-scriptural, and utilises Chinese, western and biblical paradigms in order to respond to particular events and life situations. This is further to be seen in his papers on feminist critique, on the implications of Hong Kong's return to China, and on the responsibility of Christian universities in Hong Kong.

Selected References
Works by Archie Lee Chi-chung (Li Zhiqiang)
> *The Old Testament in Context.* Tolo Theological Series 2. Hong Kong: Theology Division, CUHK, 1988.
> "The 'Aniconic God' and Chinese Iconolatry." *ATESEA Occasional Papers* 4 (1987).
> "Prophetic and Sapiential Hermeneutics in Asian Ways of Doing Theology." *ATESEA Occasional Papers* 13 (1993).
> "Exile and Return in the Perspective of 1997." In *Reading from this Place. Vol. 2, Social Location and Biblical Interpretation in Global Perspective*, edited by Fernando Segovia and Mary Ann Talbot. Minneapolis: Fortress Press, 1995.
> "The Recitation of the Past: A Cross-Textual Reading of Ps.78 and the Odes." *Ching Feng* 39.3 (1996).
> "Cross Textual Hermeneutics on Gospel and Culture." *Asia Journal of Theology* 10.1 (1996).
> "Perspectives in Reading the Bible through Asian Eyes." In *The Bible Through Asian Eyes.* Hong Kong: Christian Conference of Asia, 1998: 3-10.
> "Cross-textual Interpretation and its Implications for Biblical Studies." In *Teaching the Bible: Discourses and Politics of Biblical Pedagogy*, edited by Fernando F. Segovia and Mary Ann Tolbert, 247-54. Maryknoll, NY: Orbis Books, 1998.
> "Lamentation in the Hebrew Psalter and the Chinese Shijing: A Cross-textual Reading." *Ching Feng* 41 (1998).
> "Returning to China: Biblical Interpretation in Postcolonial Hong Kong." *Biblical Interpretation* 7 (1999).
> "Identity, Reading Strategy and Doing Theology." *Biblical Interpretation* 7 (1999).

3.4.9. Lo Lung-kwong (Lu Longguang, 1951-)

Lo was ordained as a Methodist minister in 1979 and is known in Hong Kong as a Christian social activist and theological educator. He obtained his MDiv from the Theology Division, Ching Chi College, Chinese University of Hong Kong, in 1976, and his doctoral degree in New Testament studies from the University of Durham. He has been the head of the Theology Division, Chung Chi College, Chinese University of Hong Kong since 1995. He is also ecumenically active, has served on the boards of the Industrial Evangelistic Fellowship, the Fellowship of Evangelical Students and the China Graduate School of Theology, as well as on the Executive Committee of the Hong Kong Christian Council (HKCC) where he has also been chairperson of the Social Concern Committee of the HKCC since 1990.

Lo is known for his theological reflection on the role of Christians and the Christian Church in society, which has arisen out of many direct involvements in social and political movements. Biblical studies have been particularly important for him in this. His leadership in Christian social involvement and in theological training is apparent also in his shorter writings which have appeared in Hong Kong Christian periodicals, and in two volumes (below).

Selected References
Works by Lo Lung-kwong (Lu Longguang)

Paul's Purpose in Writing Romans: The Upbuilding of a Jewish and Gentile Christian Community in Rome. Jian Dao Dissertation Series 6. Hong Kong: Alliance Bible Seminary, 1998.

—, et al. *Shidai langchao zhong de fansi* (Reflection in our times). Hong Kong: Hong Kong Christian Institute, 1997.

3.4.10. Liu Xiaofeng (1956-)

Liu was born in mainland China, and experienced the Cultural Revolution at first-hand. He received his doctoral degree from the University of Basel. Liu is known for his promotion of what he calls "Sino-Christian theology". Highly critical about past efforts at theological indigenisation, Liu contends that the indigenous language should be the carrier of theology. He is now the director of the Institute of Sino-Christian Studies (1995). This institute is a continuation of the former department of academic studies of the reconstituted Tao Fong Shan Christian Institute (1988) which publishes the *Areopagos* magazine. Stated aims of the institute are the promotion of the contextualisation of Christian theology in

Chinese culture and furtherance of the dialogue between Chinese culture and other religions. It also aims to invite and mobilise academicians and scholars from China and across the world, both church and non-church affiliated, to undertake a joint exploration and construction of a theology of contextualisation that is deeply rooted in the Chinese soil as a living embodiment of Chinese culture and thought. A major project in recent years however has been the publication of western theological texts in Chinese translation.

Selected References
Works by Lui Xiaofeng

> *Zhengjiu yu xiaoyao: Zhong xi fang shiren dui shijie de butong taidu* (Salvation and freedom). Shanghai: Shanghai renmin chubanshe, 1988.
> *Towards the Truth of the Cross* (in Chinese.) Hong Kong: Joint Publishing, 1990.
> *Zhe yi dai ren de pa huo ai* (Fear and love of this generation). Hong Kong: Excellence Book House, 1993.
> *Xiandai xing shehui lilun xulun: Xiandai xing yu xiandai zhongguo* (An Exordium on social theories of modernity). Shanghai: Shanghai sanlian shuju, 1998.
> *Hanyu shenxue yu lishi zhexue* (Sino-Christian theology and the philosophy of history). Hong Kong: Institute of Sino-Christian Studies, 2000.
> "A Theological and Socio-Cultural Commentary on 'The Way' and 'The Word'." *China Study Journal* 7.3 (1992).

3.4.11. Kwok Pui-lan (Guo Peilan)

Kwok is one of the few feminist theologians born in Hong Kong. She received her doctorate at the Harvard Divinity School, and was formerly a lecturer at the Theology Division, Chung Chi College, the Chinese University of Hong Kong. She is now on the faculty of the Episcopal Divinity School in Cambridge, U.S.A.

Following publication of her doctoral work on "Chinese Women and Christianity 1860-1927" (1992), Kwok has drawn on Chinese, Indian and biblical sources to outline an interpretation of the Bible in the non-biblical world (1995). Oral theology, Asian women's theology and social biography are used to explicate the unique Asian context for biblical understanding and the challenge this brings to western traditions of interpretation. This is particularly to be found in the oral hermeneutics of Asian women. Kwok presents this and other aspects of Asian women's theology in *Introducing Asian Feminist Theology* (2000) in which she traces the emergence of feminist consciousness in the actual contexts of Asian women's experience. Here she presents images of God as the "creative power of life", and of Jesus as a "priest of Han", and "embodiment of feminine principle." These yield, for her, both an organic christology and a holistic view of spirituality and sexuality. Despite the oppressions of dualisms, economic greed and patriarchy, women offer in their theology a union of compassion and justice, of social action and spirituality.

Selected References

Works by Kwok Pui-lan (Guo Peilan)

Chinese Women and Christianity 1860-1927. Atlanta: Scholars' Press, 1992.

Xingbie xue yu funu yanjiu: Huaren shehui de tansuo (Gender and women studies in Chinese societies). Hong Kong: CUHK, 1995.

Discovering the Bible in the Non-Biblical World. Maryknoll, NY.: Orbis Books, 1995.

Introducing Asian Feminist Theology. Introductions in Feminist Theology 4. Sheffield: Sheffield Academic Press, 2000.

"God Weeps with our Pain." *East Asia Journal of Theology* 2.2 (1984).

"The Feminist Hermeneutics of Elizabeth S. Fiorenza: An Asian Feminist Response." *East Asia Journal of Theology* 3.2 (1985).

"Chinese Non-Christian Perceptions of Christ." *Concilium* 2 (1993).

"Ecology and Christology." *Feminist Theology* 115 (1997).

"Jesus the Native: Biblical Studies from a Post-colonial Perspective." In *Teaching the Bible: Discourses and Politics of Biblical Pedagogy*, edited by Fernando F. Segovia and Mary Ann Tolbert. Maryknoll, NY: Orbis Books, 1998.

—, ed. *1997 and the Theology of Hong Kong*. Tolo Theological Series 1. Hong Kong: Theology Division, CUHK, 1983.

—, and Kaung, Joseph Tai-wai, eds. *Fengcheng de fuyin: Cong "jiuqi" suo yinfa de fanxing* (Fullness of the Gospel: Reflections on 1997). Tolo Theological Series 2. Hong Kong: Theology Division, CUHK, 1984.

3.4.12. Angela Wong Wai-ching (Huang Huizhen)

Wong is a widely-known young woman theologian, currently assistant professor at the Theology Division, Chung Chi College, Chinese University of Hong Kong. She earned her doctoral degree in Old Testament Studies and feminist theology from the University of Chicago. She has also been an active participant in the Asian ecumenical movement - assisting to restore the Hong Kong Student Christian Movement in the 1980s, serving as Secretary for the WSCF (Asia-Pacific) and later (1995-1999) becoming chairperson of the World Student Christian Federation. She was elected into the Presidium of the Christian Conference of Asia in 2000.

Wong has written on many aspects of post-colonial identity and 'hybridisation', the post-coloniality of Asian theology as post-colonial theory, women's consciousness and theology, and biblical interpretation in Asia. Writing in both Chinese and English, her main theological writings include studies of the changing selfhood of Asian theologians, of gender consciousness and biblical interpretation, and on issues of theological methodology. She has also written on feminist perspectives in the study of systematic theology, Asian women theologians "between colonialism and nationalism", sexual politics and textual politics, and on the particular issues faced by people in Hong Kong amidst major political and social changes. Her current research focuses upon such areas as Chinese identity and change in Christian community in colonial Hong Kong before 1949, the place of women in church and society in contemporary Hong Kong, and the relation of Christianity to women's political development in Hong Kong in the 1980s. In a recent address to regional audiences, Wong has recalled Asian Christians to biblical (and Asian) approaches to theology - as seen for example in apocalyptic literature - whereby enlightenment and the gift of the Spirit comes through aspects "of reality not available to rational consciousness" or to logical consistency. To "discern God's presence" in our midst and respond to this, we must recover vision and myth, she believes, in the encounter and critique between our faith and our culture, and within the historical processes of post-colonisation and globalisation.

Selected references
Works by Angela Wong Wai-ching (Huang Huizhen)
Xingbie yizhi yu sheng jing quan shi (Gender consciousness and biblical interpretation). Hong Kong: Hong Kong Christian Institute, 2000.
"The Poor Woman": A Critical Analysis of Asian Theology and Contemporary Chinese Women's Stories. Asian Thought and Culture Series 42. New York: Peter Lang, 2000.
"Asian Theologians between East and West: A Postcolonial Self-understanding." *Jian Dao: A Journal of Bible and Theology* 8 (1997).
"Asian Theology in a Changing Asia: Towards an Asian Theological Agenda for the 21st Century." *CTC Bulletin: Special Supplement* 1 (1997).
"History, Identity and the Story of Hesed: Reading the Book of Ruth in the Context of Asia." Presented at the Society of Biblical Literature, Boston, November 20-23, 1999.
"Asian Women's Lamentation and Celebration: Doing Feminist Theology in Asia." *PTCA Bulletin* 12.1-2 (1999).
"Cong xifang funu zongjiao jingshen yundong dao yazhou funu shenxue de fanxing" (From the feminist spirituality movement in the West to a reflection on Asian feminist theology). *Logos & pneuma: Chinese Journal of Theology* 10 (1999).
"Postcolonialism." In *Dictionary of Third World Theologies,* edited by Virginia Fabella and R.S. Sugirtharajah. Maryknoll, NY: Orbis Books, 2000.
"Negotiating for a Postcolonial Identity: Theology of 'The Poor Woman' in Asia." *Journal of Feminist Studies of Religion* 16.2 (2000).

3.4.13. Other Writers/Animateurs of Contextual Theology

Apart from those mentioned in entries above many others have contributed to contextualising theology in Hong Kong in recent decades. Amongst these are Heyward Wong of the Chinese Christian Literature Council, Ralph Lee of Ward Memorial Church (formerly of the Student Christian Centre and the HKCC), Milton Wan Wai-yiu, and Kung Lap-yan (Theology Division, Chung Chi College), Lam Wing-hung and Carver Yu (see below) of the China Graduate School of Theology, Leung Ka-ling and Ying Fuk-tsang of the Alliance Seminary, Fung Chi-wood of *Mount Olive* (weekly

Contextual Theology in Hong Kong

public meetings on Christian faith and society), and Chan Ka-wai of the Christian Industrial Committee; along with Enoch Choi, Jane Chui, Gong Liren, Arnold Yang Mugu; and Guan Ruiwen, Wan Weiyao and Rose Wu (for these see below). Expatriates who since the 1960s have also assisted in the development of contextual theology in Hong Kong include Denis Rogers of Hong Kong Union Church, Paul Webb, Tom Lung and Hans Lutz of the Hong Kong Christian Council, Manfred Berndt of Concordia Lutheran Seminary, Dorothy Jones of the Chinese Christian Literature Council, Loren Noren and Lennart Hamark of the Christian Study Centre, Richard Deutsch and Paul Clasper of Chung Chi College, and Anders Hansen of the Evangelical Lutheran Theological Seminary.

Other centres or institutes which have contributed include the (Catholic) Centre for the Progress of Peoples and the Holy Spirit Study Centre (4.2.5.2.: 4.2.5.1.), the China Church Research Centre, the Institute of Sino-Christian Studies, and the Centre for Asian Studies, University of Hong Kong.

Jane Chui (1954-) studied at the Chinese University and has been active in ecumenical movements for students, for women, and for contextual theology. These have included the SCM, the CCA, the AWRCCT and PTCA. Her writings on women's theology, theology of the Reign of God and on the issues of 1997 have appeared in *In God's Image*, *PTCA Bulletin* and in publications of the HKCI and CCA.

Kwan Sui-man (Guan Ruiwen, 1963-) is currently assistant professor at the Theology Division, Chung Chi College, teaching Asian theologies and contextual theologies. He is one of the few Asian theologians in Hong Kong as Programme Coordinator of an Asian theological movement, the Programme for Theology and Cultures in Asia. Moreover, and editor of the *Journal for Theologies and Cultures in Asia*.

Kung Lap-yan (Gong Liren) is currently associate professor at the Theology Division, Chung Chi College, teaching systematic theology, liberation theology and Christian ethics. He is among the writers who write in the local language.

Lam Wing-hung (Lin Ronghong) completed his doctorate at Princeton Theological Seminary (1978) and has taught at the China Graduate School of Theology in Hong Kong and at other colleges. His earlier studies on the emergence of a Protestant Christian apologetics in the Chinese Church during the anti-Christian movement in the 1920s, led to the volume *Chinese Theology in Construction* (1980) and writings on both Chinese theological patterns and the encounter between Christianity and Chinese culture.

Milton Wan Wai-yiu (Wen Weiyao, 1952-) is now on the faculty of the Theology Division, Chung Chi College, Chinese University of Hong Kong. He was trained as a scientist as well as a philosopher in his earlier years, and later entered into the field of theology. He earned his first doctoral degree in Chinese philosophy from the Chinese University of Hong Kong, and the second from Oxford University.

Rose Wu is a local feminist theologian and now is director of the Hong Kong Christian Institute. She is one of the founding members and was the general secretary of the Hong Kong Women Christian Council. She received her theological education at Chung Chi College, Chinese University of Hong Kong, from 1983 to 1988 and her Doctor of Ministry from the Episcopal Divinity School in Boston (2000).

Arnold Mugu Yang is a prolific writer, who has written a systematic theology for Hong Kong, *Theology of Reconciliation* (1987). Yang received his BD from the University of Edinburgh, and his doctoral degree from the University of Cambridge (1981). He taught systematic theology at the Theology Division, The Chinese University of Hong Kong, from 1981 to 1987 and is now a full-time free-lance writer.

Carver T. Yu has taught systematic and historical theology at the China Graduate School of Theology and philosophy and theology at the Hong Kong Baptist University. Along with many theological articles, he has frequently written on European literature. A major work has been a "theological critique of western dualism and individualism" (1987). In this he presents an alternative ontological model by which cultural reconstruction can come through the recovery of "being as being-in-communion in the biblical tradition."

Selected References

Berndt, Manfred H. *The Diakonia Function of the Church in Hong Kong.* St Louis: n.p., 1970.

Chui, Jane C.L. "Seeing a Vision of a New Earth". In *Peoples of Asia, People of God,* edited by Salvador Martinez. Osaka: CCA, 1990.

——. *Huiying jiuqi: Jidutu qunti de jianzheng* (Some Christian responses to 1997 issues). Hong Kong: Hong Kong Christian Institute, 1992.

Chong, Eric. "Fellow Pilgrims on the Road to Truth". In *Turn Around. Called to Witness Together Amidst Asian Plurality.* Hong Kong: CCA, 1994.

Deutsch, Richard. "Cultural Heritage Versus the Old Testament?" *Ching Feng* 29.1 (1971).

Kung Lap-yan. *Jiefang shenxue yu Xianggang kunjing* (Liberation theology and Hong Kong's predicament). Hong Kong: Hong Kong Christian Institute, 1999.

——. *Renji shehui de jian li: Jidu jiao shehui lunli* (Building a relational society : a proposal for Christian social ethics). Hong Kong: Hong Kong Christian Institute, 1999.

Kwan Shui-man, Guan Ruiwen et al. *Heaven and Earth.* Hong Kong: Hong Kong Christian Institute, 1994. (Co-authored with Hay Wing Pong, et al.)

——. "Collaboration as an Alternative Mode of Anti-colonialist resistance: a Postcolonial Rethinking of the Asia-West Binarism inscribed in the Asian Theological Movement." Ph.D. diss., Chinese University of Hong Kong, 1999. Forthcoming.

Lam Wing-hung. *Chinese Theology in Construction.* Pasadena: William Carey Books, 1983. (In Chinese: Hong Kong: Tien Dao, 1980.)

——. "Patterns of Chinese Theology." *Evangelical Review of Theology* 6.2 (1982).

Liu Xiaofeng. *The Sino-Christian Theology and Philosophy of History.* Institute of Sino-Christian Studies Monographs. Hong Kong: ISCS, 2000.

Wan, Milton Wai-yiu. *A Christian Introduction to Communism.* Hong Kong: Tien Dao Publishing House, 1979.

Wen Weiyao. *Gongchan zhuyi yu jidu jiao* (Communism and Christianity). Hong Kong: Tien Dao, 1979.

—. *Chengsheng zhi dao: bei Song er Cheng xiuyang gongfu lun zhi yanjiu* (The way to sanctification). Taipei: Wen shi zhe, 1996.

—, and Lam Wing-hung. *Jidu jiao yu Zhongguo wenhua de xiangyu* (Encounter between Christianity and Chinese culture), edited by Lo Lung Kwong. Hong Kong: Chung Chi College Theology Division. Forthcoming.

Wu, Rose. "Political Participation and Hong Kong Women." In *Uncertain Times: Hong Kong Women Facing 1997*, edited by Susan Romaniuk and Denise Tong Ka-wing. Hong Kong: HK Women Christian Council, 1995.

—. "Liberating Theology to Liberate Women." *In God's Image* 17.1 (1998).

—. *Liberating the Church from Fear: the Story of Hong Kong's Sexual Minorities.* Hong Kong: Hong Kong Women Christian Council, 2000.

Yang, Arnold Mugu. *Fuhuo shenxue yu jiaohui gengxin* (Theology of reconciliation and church renewal). Hong Kong: Seed, 1987.

—. *Jiushi niandai jiaohui weiji yu tiaozhan* (Crisis and challenge facing the church in 1990s). Hong Kong: Tian Dao, 1989.

—. *Jiuqi de yingxu* (The Promise of 1997). Hong Kong: Logos, 1993.

Yeung, Daniel, ed. *Preliminary Studies on Chinese Theology.* Institute of Sino-Christian Studies Monographs Series 6. Hong Kong: ISCS, 2000.

Yu, Carver T. *Being and Relation. A Theological Critique of Western Dualism and Individualism.* Edinburgh: Scottish Academic Press, 1987.

4 Catholic Contextual Theology
4.1 Introduction

The Hong Kong Roman Catholic Mission was established as a prefecture in 1841 with the first seminary established for teaching in Chinese and Latin in 1843. By 1865 there were two seminaries in operation. In 1850, the Milan Foreign Mission - an association of secular priests - arrived, being assigned responsibility for Hong Kong in 1858. The Sisters of Paul de Chartres entered upon work here in 1848, and many other congregations would follow in coming decades. Despite controversy concerning a Marriage Ordinance in the 1870s (Bp Raimondi threatening civil disobedience over certain clauses), and also concerning support for Christian schools, Catholic mission activity grew rapidly. In 1880 the first All China Catholic Synod was held in Hong Kong, and amongst other decisions maintained missionary control over Chinese priests, of which there were 12 (out of a total of 29 priests) in Hong Kong by 1913. This situation would not be significantly changed until the late 1920s. A wide range of educational, medical, welfare and laity organisations developed, with St Joseph's College being formed in 1918 and a regional seminary in Aberdeen (1931).

In 1877 the first Catholic weekly, *Hong Kong Catholic Register,* appeared, and in 1888 the cathedral was consecrated. By 1890, the Paris Foreign Missions (MEP) had established a printing press in Hong Kong with many of its early productions being *Acta* and *Decreta* of the Congregatio de Propaganda Fide. In the following decades this would become a major publishing house for the Catholic Church throughout China for historical, doctrinal and catechetical books or booklets. By 1949 it was operating three printing presses, although few publications showed concern for localised theological reflection. In 1928 the first Chinese Catholic weekly, *Kung Kau Po,* commenced publication. However, a full study of publications of the Catholic Truth Society, and of early periodicals such as the *Mission Bulletin*, the *Hong Kong Catholic Register, Kung Kau Po* and the later *Hong Kong Catholic Directory and Year Book* is yet to be undertaken.

Under the leadership of Bishops Henry Valtorta (1926-1951) and Lawrence Bianchi (1952-1969), a further range of educational, welfare and pastoral organisations developed, especially in response to the great increases in refugee numbers. The Catholic Centre was established in 1946, when the *Sunday Examiner* was also begun, chapels and welfare centres multiplied and Caritas Hong Kong was fully formed in 1961. The first Chinese bishop, Francis Hsu Chen-ping was consecrated in 1969, and in 1975, John Baptist Wu Cheng-chung became bishop. By the 1970s, the earlier order of priorities in Catholic mission activity - educational, welfare and pastoral - were being restored; the former two again with extensive government subsidies. This led, as with other churches, to the close association of many Catholics with government policies, with a consequent emphasis upon being "service providers" rather than roles as advocators or animateurs.

By the 1980s, however, there were progressive groups amongst younger priests and sisters, student leaders, worker groups, lay intellectuals, in the New Youth Workers' Night School, the Centre for the Progress of Peoples (4.2.5.2.) and in sometimes short-lived diocesan commissions for human development, social justice and peace-making. Clergy and laity in these programmes also frequently worked closely with Protestant networks of students, workers, study centres, theologians and activists. Other priests and lay people actively concerned for creative living of the faith in Hong Kong society included Cynnec Cheng, Jack Clancy and team members of the Federation of Catholic Students and IMCS; Dominic Cheung and colleagues of the Lay Apostolate; Joan Delaney and sisters of the Maryknoll Convent; parish priests such as James Hurley, Stephen Tam, P. Elsinger, John Collins and Franco Mella; along with Bartolomeo Tsui of the Chinese University; and staff-members of Holy Spirit Seminary and Study Centre (4.2.5.1.). Writings from many of these appear in the journals presented below (4.2.1.; 4.2.2.; 4.2.3.).

In the last decade, the publication of Catholic theological reflection has greatly expanded to include many contextual writings on missiology, ecclesiology, theology, social ethics, spirituality and even ideology. These can be found in such periodicals as *Tripod, Theology Annual, Spirit, Yi* (Yik, China Message) and the *Examiner.*

Selected References
(See also supplementary Bibliography)
>Barry, Peter. "Political Reform in Hong Kong: A Commentary." *Tripod* 40 (1987).
>*Catholic Hong Kong: a Hundred Years of Missionary Activity: On the Occasion of the Centenary Year of the Arrival in Hong Kong of the Pontifical Foreign Missions Institute.* Hong Kong: Catholic Press Bureau, 1958.

Chau, Edward. "A New Leaf in History - the Origins of the Hong Kong Union of Six Major Religions and Reflection on its Current Situation." *Spirit* 27 (1995).

Cheung Ka-hing. "A Reflection on Society and the Catholic Church 1950-1980s". *Tripod* 42 (1987).

Hurley, James. "Reflection of the Church in Hong Kong on Democracy." *Spirit* 9 (1991).

Kwong Ha-siong, Louis. "The Foundation of the Catholic Mission in Hong Kong, 1841-1894." PhD diss., University of Hong Kong, 1998.

Leung, Beatrice. "Hong Kong Roman Catholic Church in 1997: Church and State." *Tripod* 49 (1989).

Maheu, Betty Ann. "Hong Kong Returns to the Dragon." *Tripod* 113 (1999).

Malek, Roman, ed. *Hongkong: Kirche und Gesellschaft im Übergang: Materialien und Dokumente*. Sankt Augustin: China-Zentrum; Nettetal: Steyler, 1997.

Ticozzi, Sergio, pime. "Old and New Challenges for the Hong Kong Catholic Church." *Tripod* 97 (1997).

Tse, Christine. "Hong Kong Roman Catholic Church in 1997: Church and Society." *Tripod* 49 (1989).

Yuen, Mary M.Y. "The Catholic Church in Political Transition." In *The Other Hong Kong Report 1997*, edited by Cheng Yüshuo. Hong Kong series. Hong Kong: Chinese University Press, c1997.

4.2 Contextual Theological Concerns

Most Catholic theological reflection in Hong Kong appears in one or other of the three journals *Tripod, Theology Annual,* and *Spirit.* Along with writings on church history, pastoral theology or Confucianism and Taoism, there have also appeared studies of the just society, ecology, secularisation and indigenisation, religious freedom, Marxism, democratic reform, women's theological reflection, Chinese culture and Christianity, the history and present ecclesiological issues for the church in China, Sino-Vatican relations, human rights, new ways of being church in Chinese societies, religious and cultural dialogue, social justice and social ministries, the Eucharist, and theological method. Particular debates have ensued on whether Catholicism is anti-communist, and on Catholic attitudes to the socio-political and religious changes before, during and following reversion of Hong Kong to China (1997). Continuing discussions concern Vatican II teachings and the Synod of Asian Bishops (1998), democracy and discipleship in Hong Kong and the relevance of Jubilee to present mission (see 4.2.1.-3 below).

4.2.1. *Tripod* (since 1981)

Tripod was established as a bi-monthly, to foster "harmony through wisdom and understanding". It therefore aims to "encourage dialogue and a free expression of views, to provide a medium of expression for scholars ..., and to communicate developments taking place in the Chinese church and Chinese society." More than 200 authors throughout Asia (including China and beyond) have assisted in articles on missiology, church history, ecclesiology, theology, interchange and dialogue, church and state, education and formation, patriotism and Marxism, Protestant churches, discernment and prayer, and China study centres - many of these being studied not only for Hong Kong, but also Macau and mainland China.

Those writing frequently in these areas have included John Tong, Maria Goretti Lau, Beatrice Leung, Anthony Lam, Christine Tse, Jack Clancy, Peter Barry (for all these see below); along with Betty Ann Maheu, Peter Lee King-hung, Li Shen, Bernard Hung-kay Luk, Mary Louise Martin, Jean Charbonnier, Elmer Wurth, John Cioppa, John Young, Angelo Lazerotto, Gianni Criveller, Michael Sloboda, Sergio Ticozzi, Aloysius Chang and Mark Fang (see this volume, chap.10 "Taiwan"). Many articles and reports have been prepared cooperatively by the staff of Holy Spirit Study Centre and amongst the writings for mainland China many have remained anonymous.

Selected References

Angelo Lazzarotto pime. "Searching for a Meaningful Dialogue." *Tripod* 28 (1985).

—. "The Church in China: A Fifteen Year Review." *Tripod* 90 (1995).

Chan, Joanna, mm. "A Few Words to our Western Missionaries." *Tripod* 4 (1981).

Chao, Paul. "Response to Chinese Culture and Christianity." *Tripod* 71 (1992).
Clancy, Jack. "Theological Reflections on Yin Yang and Human rights." *Tripod* 96 (1996).
Lee, King-hung Peter. "Chinese Sages Come to Worship Jesus." *Tripod* 96 (1996).
Li Shen. "Science and Religion." *Tripod* 111 (1999).
Liu, Monica. "Inculturating Religious Art." *Tripod* 106 (1998).
Maheu, Betty Ann. "The Chinese Woman in Church and Society." *Tripod* 87 (1995).
—. " Hong Kong Returns to the Dragon." *Tripod* 113 (1999).
Masson, Michel, sj. "Chinese Culture and Christianity: Assessing the Agendas." *Tripod* 71 (1992).
Goodstadt, Leo "Atheism and the Communist Party after Mao Zedong." *Tripod* 3 (1981).
—. "Karl Marx: China's Foreign Philosopher." *Tripod* 18 (1983).
Sloboda, Michael, mm. "China and Human Rights." *Tripod* 92 (1996).
Ticozzi, Sergio, pime. "Old and New Challenges for the Hong Kong Catholic Church." *Tripod* 97 (1997).
Tse, Christine. "Hong Kong Roman Catholic Church in 1997: Church and Society." *Tripod* 49 (1989).
Wurth, Elmer. "Reconciliation in China - A Holy and Urgent Task." *Tripod* 14 (1983).
Young, John D. "Christianity and its Dilemma in Contemporary China." *Tripod* 7 (1982).

4.2.2. Theology Annual (since 1986)

Editors of the *Annual* aim to assist the "Word of the Gospel [to] sink itself deeply into our Chinese culture" and to "grasp our Christian sources more fully", while also recognising what "others elsewhere are thinking and talking about". Here theology is to be selective in receiving outside influences and for a religious minority in Asia, is to give priority to the questions there. This is to be in "a spirit of incarnation, not simply of translation or adaptation". Subjects dealt with have included Christology, the Rites controversy, global church history, Buddhist-Christian dialogue, Christian ethics, pastoral and sacramental theology, pneumatology and life, post-Vatican II ecclesiology, the inter-relationship between the Kingdom of God and a just society, challenges of internet culture, the Jubilee and recent encyclicals. Discussion is sometimes in relation to the Hong Kong situation.

Those writing on such topics - apart from those given separate entries below - have included Bernard Hung-kay Luk, John J. Casey mm, Joseph Wong, Hong Tui-kit, Benedict Lam, Vincent Shen, Henry Ng, Savio Hon, Lanfranco Fedrigotti, Benjamin Leong, Lionel Goh, Anselm Lam, Lee Gong and William Ho. Recent Special Issues have considered Jubilee and its "orientation towards joy, mutual dialogue ...reconciliation and harmony" (20); and inculturation (21, 2000). Included also have been articles on "the story of the Chinese people in the economy of grace"; a theology of beauty; personal life experience in Chinese culture; the structure of Chinese thought as place for interchange of inculturation of theology and philosophy; and inculturation in liturgy and hermeneutics.

Selected References

Chan, Anna. "The Transmission and Reception of Faith and Theological Method." *Theology Annual* 19 (1998).
Chau, Edward. "Religious Dialogue - A Breakthrough of Thinking." *Theology Annual* 17 (1996).
—. "Preserving and Fostering Our Common Heritage." *Theology Annual* 19 (1998).
Goodstadt, Leo. "Religion in Contemporary Chinese Politics." *Theology Annual* 3 (1988).
Goretti-Lau, Maria. "The Kingdom Promised by Marxism." *Theology Annual* 4 (1980).
Hong Tui-kit. "Religion and Chinese Culture." *Theology Annual* 13 (1991-1992).
Kwong, Maria. "Theology of Beauty." *Theology Annual* 21 (2000).
Lee Gong. "Life and Death in Taoism." *Theology Annual* 15 (1996).
Liu, Andrew C.C. "Vincent Lebbe and Matteo Ricci." *Theology Annual* 7 (1983).
Luk, Bernard. "From Ancient Heresies to Medieval Religions: A Guide to the Study of Nestorianism and Manichaeism." *Theology Annual* 5 (1981).
Ng, Robert. "Method in Moral Theology." *Theology Annual* 9-10 (1985-1986).
Shen, Vincent. "Dialogue between Buddhist and Christian." *Theology Annual* 17 (1996).

4.2.3. Spirit (since 1989)

Spirit, A Review of Theology and Spirituality (called "*Shen Si*" in Chinese) is produced by the Society of Jesus, Hong Kong, but publishes the writings of not only regular and secular clergy or religious, but also of lay women and men. Principal subjects have included theology of community and communities, inculturation, Chinese and Christian spirituality, christology, Christian marriage and vocation, the mystery of the incarnation, the Church and democracy in Hong Kong, the Christian role in social involvement, catechetics, the Church's social teaching, justice, peace and the environment, spirituality of work for justice, charismatic movements, sacramental theology, spirituality and ecology, spiritual direction, the internet and evangelisation, and Jubilee tradition and reconciliation. Writers have included John Tan, Edward Collins, Peter Choy, Andrew C.C. Liu, Thomas Leung, Dominic Chan, Joseph Wong, James Hurley sj, Stephen Chan ofm, William Yip, Louis Lee, Ou Jifu, Bernard Shields sj, Lam Hong-ching, Thomas Kwan Chun-tong, Ho Chuk-ping, Carlo Kwan, Joseph Ha ofm, and Li Chen.

Special issues of *Spirit* have been issued on, for example, "Spirituality in the Chinese Context" (3, 1989); "Interreligious Dialogue" (27, 1995); Women's concerns - their dignity, status, discipleship and mission (24, 1995 and 31, 1996); the Asian Synod (40, 1999); Jubilee (44 and 45, 2000); and inculturation: principles for inculturation of theology, 19th century missionaries in Hong Kong and difficulties and prospects for the inculturation of theology (47, 2000).

Selected References

Chang, Anthony. "Inculturation of the Church." *Spirit* 40 (1999).
Ha, Joseph ofm. "New Trends in Contemporary Catholic Spirituality." *Spirit* 41 (1999).
Ho Chuk-ping. "Contact and Dialogue with Other Religions According to the Spirit of Confucianism." *Spirit* 27 (1995).
Ho Ka-hing. "New Evangelisation in the New Millennium." *Spirit* 40 (1999).
Hurley, James. "Reflection of the Church in Hong Kong on Democracy." *Spirit* 9 (1991).

Kwan, Carlo. "Theology as the Mediator between Religion and Culture." *Spirit* 29 (1996).

Lai, Francis. "Reflection on the Technology of Replicating Human Life." Spirit 38 (1998).

Lam Hong-ching. "Lay Pastoral Ministry in the Church after Vatican II." *Spirit* 18 (1993).

Lee, Agnes. "Chinese Spirituality - Another View." *Spirit* 3 (1989).

Li Chen. "Reflection on Science, Philosophy and Faith." *Spirit* 43 (1999).

Lok Shung-fai. "Inter-religious Dialogue as Common Understanding and Co-operation." *Spirit* 27 (1995).

Naylor, Harold sj. "Green Spirituality." *Spirit* 17 (1993).

Tsui, Luke. "Chinese Culture and the Green Idea." *Spirit* 17 (1993).

Wong, Teresa. "Jubilee of the Poor." *Spirit* 44 (2000).

4.2.4. Women Doing Theology

The story for Catholic women's theological reflection in Hong Kong over the last century or more has yet to be written, yet their role in the life and mission of the church since arrival of the first missionary sisters in 1848 has been central. Only scattered letters, reports or biographical notes have as yet been discovered for this study and much more research is to be done. In particular the lived theology of women's devoted apostolates - both religious and lay - requires recognition and study. The last few decades have, however, seen a rich development in opportunities for Catholic women to have their writings and studies published. More detailed entries are given below for such theologians and scholars as Maria Goretti Lau (4.2.6.2.), Madeleine Kwong Lay-kuen (4.2.6.3.), Beatrice Leung (4.2.6.6.), Judith Xu Chan (4.2.6.6.), and Betty Ann Maheu (4.2.6.6.), along with Christine Tse, Mary Yuen and Cecilia Tse Kam Fong fma. But many more lay and religious women have published theological reflection, since 1980 in particular. Apart from diocesan and Congregation newsletters, chronicles or newspapers, the three journals *Tripod, Theology Annual,* and *Spirit* (4.2.1.; 4.2.2.; 4.2.3.), are again the fullest sources for these writings.

In *Tripod* are found articles by, for example, Lucia Lee, Grace Lee, Iris Tsang, Emily Wong, Margaret Farley, Monica Liu, Edith Wong Hee-kam, Eva Man Kit-wah, Joanna Chan mm, Dominica Cheng spb, Jessica Ho, Teresa Yeung, Joyce Chang, Phyllis Wong,

Therese Howard mm and Josephine Fung-ming Leo. Subjects of their writings include Hong Kong interpretations of feminism and the Chinese church, sister formation and lay apostolate, inculturation, religious freedom, Confucianism and inter-faith dialogue, along with aspects of church history, ecclesiology and christology.

In the *Theology Annual*, writers include Maria Ko, Ophelia Lui, Vivian Cheung, Agatha Ho, Anna Chan Kai-yung, Louise Wong, Maria Kwong, Esther Ling fdcc, Teresa Wong, Emily Wong, Maria Kou fma, and Veronica Soong. Their concerns include biblical theology, christology, the mission of the church in Hong Kong, theological method and scriptural hermeneutics, classical and contemporary spirituality, sexual and spiritual love, a theology of beauty, the Nestorians' different names for God and indigenisation, catechetics and pastoral theology.

In *Spirit*, we find articles by many women, most of them Catholic: Madeleine Kwong Lay-kuen, Emily Wong fmm, Teresa Wong fdcc, Agnes Ho spb, Jessica Ho, Maria Kou fma, Clare Lai, Andrina Lee fmm, Maria Lau Lai-kwan, Teresa Yuen fmm, Anna Chan, Agnes Lee smic, Louise Wong, Pauline Yuen mic, Margherita Chan fma, Catherine Liu spb, Anna Maria Kwan fdcc, Pauline Cheng, Cecila Lai, Tsui Shan-shen, Clara Chiang mmb, and Catherine Wan. Their concerns range widely to include contemporary christology (western and Asian), contemporary mission, non-violence, Chinese and Christian spirituality, New Testament exegesis, incarnation and resurrection, family life, spiritual direction, suffering and hope, the kingdom of God, Mary and women and church, the sacrament of reconciliation, the beauty of male and female, and Jubilee and the poor.

Selected References

Barry, Peter. "The Chinese Woman in Church and Society." *Tripod* 87 (1995).

Chan, Anna. "The Transmission and Reception of Faith and Theological Method." *Theology Annual* 19 (1998).

Chan, Joanna mm. "A Few Words to our Western Missionaries." *Tripod* 4 (1981).

Chen, Pauline. "An Approach to Using the Catechism of the Catholic Church in Writing Local Catechetical Material." *Spirit* 33 (1997).

Cheng, Dominica spb. "My Ten Years in Sister Formation." *Tripod* 51 (1989).

Farley, Margaret rsm. "A New Form of Communion: Feminism and the Chinese Church." *Tripod* 77 (1993).

Ho, Jessica. "My Experience as a Lay Missioner." *Tripod* 42 (1987).

—, and Peter Lo. "Reflections on Lay Participation in the Church's Ministry in Hong Kong." *Tripod* 42 (1987).

Ko, Maria fma. "The Asian Synod: A Look at the Prospects of the Church in Asia." *Spirit* 40 (1999).

Kwong, Maria. "Theology of Beauty." *Theology Annual* 21 (2000).

Lee, Agnes. "Chinese Spirituality - Another View." *Spirit* 3 (1989).

Liu, Monica. "Inculturating Religious Art." *Tripod* 106 (1998).

Tsang, Iris. "Religious Freedom and the Basic Law." *Tripod* 38 (1987).

Wan, Catherine. "The Cross: the Focal Point of the World." *Spirit* 31 (1996).

Wong, Emily fmm. "All Things to All People." *Tripod* 45 (1988).

Wong, Teresa. "Jubilee of the Poor." *Spirit* 44 (2000).

Yuen, Mary. "Hong Kong Catholics' Recent Participation in Social Movements." In *Hong Kong's Social Movements: Voices from the Margins*, edited by Sophia Woodman. Hong Kong: July 1 Link and Hong Kong Women Christian Council, 1997.

4.2.5. Centres and Movements

In recent decades centres and movements from which Catholic contextual theological reflection has arisen include progressive groups amongst younger priests and sisters, student leaders, worker groups and lay intellectuals, the New Youth Workers' Night School, ecumenical social programmes, China study groups, the Holy Spirit Study Centre and the Centre for the Progress of Peoples. The last two in particular have published a number of periodicals and monographs.

4.2.5.1. Holy Spirit Study Centre (1981)

The Centre is "an organ of the Diocese of Hong Kong established .....as an expression of pastoral concern for China and the Church in China. It is a research institute whose primary practical task has been to gather, store and analyse pertinent data about China that will serve to broaden understanding of, and effect appropriate Christian responses to, the mainland's rapidly changing situation."

Primary aims of the Centre have been to study church life, history and theology in mainland China; Chinese culture and religion; social order in Hong Kong and China; the work of Chinese intellectuals; as well as the mission of the church in Hong Kong, the inculturation of the faith, inter-religious and ecumenical dialogue. By the 1990s the Centre was also assisting in the development of theological education in mainland China. Key figures in the work of the Centre and its publications have included John Tong, Maria Goretti Lau, Peter Barry, Anthony Lam (for these see 4.2.6.5.; 4.2.6.2.; 4.2.6.6.), Betty Ann Maheu, Teresa Yeung, Elmer Wurth, Michael Sloboda and Sergio Ticozzi.

The Centre has a library with archives for collected documentation from over 100 Chinese and other language periodicals and 10 daily newspapers. Its principle periodicals are *Tripod Magazine* (4.2.1.), *China Bridge* and *Vox Mundi*. *Tripod* is the Centre's quarterly, bi-lingual publication. Concerned with Christianity in China, it is Christian, ecumenical, and catholic in style and content, encouraging an open dialogue and free exchange of views. *China Bridge* is a monthly insert in the Hong Kong Diocesan English weekly *Sunday Examiner*. *China Bridge* carries up-to-date information on the Catholic Church in China, as well as analytical articles. *Vox Mundi* is a Catholic newsletter published in Chinese on a monthly basis. The newsletter aims at providing information about the Universal Church to those in China, especially bishops and priests interested in following events in the broader Church.

The Centre also publishes articles about religion directed at an audience living in a socialist society, presenting aspects of religious faith which may be overlooked by Marxist scholars of religion. In this way the Centre's staff hopes to build up a dialogic exchange regarding religion with these scholars.

Selected References
Amongst books published or facilitated by the Centre are:

> Lazzarotto, Angelo S. *The Catholic Church in Post-Mao China*. Hong Kong: Holy Spirit Study Centre, 1982.
>
> Zhang, Heqin. *Can Mainland China's 'Official' Church still be Called "Catholic'?: Some Theological Reflections about the Structural-institutional Aspect of the 'Official' Catholic Church in Mainland China.* Hong Kong: Holy Spirit Study Centre, 1995.
>
> Lam, Anthony S.K. *The Catholic Church in Present-Day China. Through Darkness and Light.* Leuven: Ferd Verbiest Foundation; Hong Kong: Holy Spirit Study Centre, 1994.
>
> For articles by staff and associates of the Centre see above 4.2.1 and 4.2.4.

4.2.5.2. The Asian Centre for the Progress of Peoples (ACPP)

The ACPP (formerly CCP) was established with the aim of furthering Pope John 23rd 's concerns for the full development of peoples, whose struggles and aspirations he declared were "the signs of the times." Activities and publications have therefore focused on such concerns as social justice, human rights, the future of Catholic social thought, women's concerns, migrant workers and prisoners, adequate government welfare assistance, relief for boat-people, improved wages and working conditions, prayer manuals for workers, and human rights issues in both HK and neighbouring countries. A number of the Centre's seminars and writings focus upon aspects of contextual and social theology, drawing on local theologians as well as regional figures such as C.S. Song, Michael Amaladoss and Julio Labayen.

Amongst those who have led in research, education and animation have been Cynnec Cheng (d.1979), Eugene Thalman mm, Jack Clancy, Edith To, James Hurley, Virginia Unsworth mm, Christine Tse and Cheung Ka-hing.

ACPP supports a publishing arm, Plough Publications, and a newsletter, *Hotline*. A full range of related publications include the following volumes:

Contextual Theology in Hong Kong

Selected References

Anzorena, Jorge. *A Time to Build: People's Housing in Asia.* Hong Kong. Plough Publications 1985.

Cheng Cynnec. "The True Revolutionary." Mimeo'd. 1978.

Cheung Ka-hing. "A Reflection on Society and the Catholic Church 1950-1980s". *Tripod* 42 (1987).

Clancy, Jack. *God Hear Our Prayer: A Prayer Book for Workers.* 3 vols. Hong Kong: Asian Centre for the Progress of Peoples, 1991.

—. "Hong Kong 1997: Church and Society." *Tripod* 99 (1997).

—. "Theological Reflections on Yin Yang and Human rights." *Tripod* 96 (1996).

—, and John Ma. eds. *Theological Reflection on Asia's Struggle for Full Humanity.* Hong Kong: Plough Publications, 1982.

Hurley, James. "Social Involvement. The Experience of One Parish." *Tripod* 74 (1993).

Karunan, Victor P. *"If the Land Could Speak, it Would Speak for Us."* Hong Kong: Plough Publications, 1984.

Thalman, Eugene. *Let Your Heart be Bold - A Study on Church and National Security in Korea, Philippines and Taiwan.* 3 vols. Hong Kong: Centre for the Progress of Peoples, 1985.

Moon, Cyris H.S. *A Korean Minjung Theology: An Old Testament Perspective.* Hong Kong: Plough Publications; Maryknoll, NY: Orbis Books, 1985.

Tse, Christine. "New Ways of Being Church: A Catholic Perspective." In *We Dare to Dream,* edited by Virginia Fabella and Sun Ai Lee Park. Hong Kong: AWRCCT, 1989. Also in *Spirit* 9 (1991).

—. "Hong Kong Roman Catholic Church in 1997: Church and Society." *Tripod* 49 (1989).

4.2.6. A Selection of Theologians
4.2.6.1. Edward Chau

Fr. Edward Chau is dean of philosophy, Holy Spirit Seminary College, chairs the diocesan Commission for Inter-Faith Dialogue, and has been Editor of *Theology Annual.* He also exercises a parish ministry and has written extensively on inter-religious and inter-philosophical encounter and dialogue. Subjects for his writings have included Chinese humanism, spirituality, Christian response to the heritage of Chinese culture, the wisdom traditions in both

Chinese and Jewish traditions, Confucianism, Taoism and the Christian understanding of death. He has also written on the "glory of God" in western philosophy, the experience of God as love, and on the common heritage of China, Hong Kong and Macau, along with Hong Kong's role in nurturing a "common awareness and a cogent methodology".

On the spirit of Chinese humanism, Chau writes of developing this in Chinese Christians in the new century. He examines the relationship between humanism and education, and emphasises a "holistic human development". He also suggests that the concepts of "goodness", "love", "harmony between heaven and earth", as seen from the perspective of Chinese culture, fit in with the spirit of renewal in Christian faith. This allows Chinese Christians to make an authentic affirmation of the human person, of God, and of every culture. Chinese Christians can therefore live out the love and compassion of Christ in the context of their own culture. On traditions of wisdom in ancient Chinese and Jewish traditions he focuses in particular upon friendship as this is presented in these traditions, and which is ultimately "essential to the enrichment of the spiritual life and of compassionate love". Writing from his continuing experience of inter-religious dialogue he presents this as a "break-through" in both philosophy and praxis, for he believes that practical co-operation is the most effective means by which inter-faith dialogue can take place (See also Vincent Shen in *Theology Annual* 17, 1996). He also draws on Confucian and Taoist thought in portraying the harmony - personally and nationally - which can be fostered in the face of a confused world.

Selected References
Works by Edward Chau
"The Cultivation of Illustrious Virtue." *Spirit* 3 (1989).
"Harmony: An Investigation into Uniting Chinese Cultural Ideals of Life." *Spirit* 14 (1992).
"Religious Awareness in Laozi." *Tripod* 68 (1992).
"A New Leaf in History - the origins of the Hong Kong Union of Six Major Religions and Reflection on its Current Situation." *Spirit* 27 (1995).

"Religious Dialogue - A Breakthrough of Thinking". *Theology Annual* 17 (1996).

"The Glorious Reality of the Friendship and Dialogue Produced by Hong Kong's Religious History - The Vital Cooperation between the Six Religions." *Theology Annual* 19 (1998).

"Preserving and Fostering Our Common Heritage." *Theology Annual* 19 (1998).

4.2.6.2. Maria Goretti Lau (Lau Choi-mei) spb

Maria Goretti Lau, was born in China and became a religious in Hong Kong in the 1960s. Following doctoral study at Leuven she taught theology at the Holy Spirit Seminary College, Hong Kong. She is a member of the Catholic Board of Education, and has been chief editor of *Theology Annual* and chairperson of the Association of Major Superiors of Religious Women in Hong Kong. Her writings have been published in many journals and often deal with issues for indigenous Chinese theology, both Protestant and Catholic, biblical theology, ecclesiology, incarnational and Trinitarian theology, charismatic movements, Teilhard de Chardin's evolutionary theology, Asian Catholic literature, Third World theology, inter-faith dialogue and Marxism.

Regarding Christology, Goretti Lau envisages a theology for which the incarnated and resurrected Jesus Christ is the centre of the circle and human society is the circumference. She studies the incarnation in the light of the mystery of the Trinity, and employs symbolic theology in order to clarify their relationship. Drawing on insights from C.S. Song, her christology is one of the "Resurrected-Suffering Jesus", known within the suffering of men and women and incarnated there. Writing of the local church, she stresses the uniqueness of Chinese experience and proposes a "praxical ecclesiology", in which "local church" and "universal church" are not opposed but are rather integrated and complementary, as are the local and universal aspects of Jesus Christ. Regarding the Kingdom of God, Goretti Lau reflects theologically "on the similarities and differences between the 'classless kingdom' in Marxist philosophy and 'the Kingdom of Heaven' and suggests directions by which theology preserves the communitarian and just-making aspects of the Gospel in facing the currents of present-day socialism. Other writings include aspects of church history relevant to today's Hong Kong, Matteo Ricci's eschatology, and Mary as the Type and Mother of the Church.

Selected References
Works by Maria Goretti Lau (Lau, Choi-mei)
"The Kingdom Promised by Marxism." *Theology Annual* 4 (1980).
"The Possibility of a Praxical Ecclesiology." *Tripod* 5 (1981).
"An Emerging Hope - A Theological Response to Professor Chen Ze-min's Talk on 'Some Theological Insights in the Chinese Church'." *Tripod* 6 (1981).
"The Theological Implications of Human Suffering." *Tripod* 8 (1982).
"An Introduction to Third World Theologians (1): The Theology of Liberation." (2)"The Religious Situation of Korea and its Theological Trends." *Tripod* 10 and 11 (1982).
"A Brief Analysis of the Instruction on Certain Aspects of the Theology of Liberation." *Tripod* 24 (1984).
"A Reflection on 'Particular Church': Based on the Experience of the Chinese Church." *Tripod* 19 (1984).
"The Dawn of Salvation History - Mary the Mother of Faith." *Tripod* 43 (1988).
"Toward a Theology of the Local Church (in the Present Situation of the Catholic Church in China)." PhD diss., Leuven, Katholieke Universiteit, 1989.
"The Incarnation seen from the Mystery of the Trinity." *Spirit* 7 (1990).
"Small Faith Communities: A Preliminary Theological Enquiry." *Tripod* 55 (1990).
"A Theological Reflection on the Charismatic Movement." *Spirit* 15 (1992).
"The Church Local and Universal: From the Faith Experience of the Early Church." *Spirit* 18 (1993).

4.2.6.3. Kwong Lay-kuen, Madeleine (Magdalena) spb

Kwong Lay-kuen studied at the Catholic University of Fujen, Taipei, and later gained her doctorate in theology at the Sevres Centre, Paris. She now staffs the Precious Blood Wah Fu Community in Hong Kong and teaches dogmatic theology at the Seminary of the Holy Spirit. Her major work, *Chinese Qi and*

Christian Anthropology, brings together study of *qigong* (Chinese traditions of breathing exercises), the understanding of Holy Spirit in the Bible and church history, contemporary pneumatology, and the expression of creative *qi* in literature, the arts, medicine and morality.

In Chinese culture, Kwong writes, the spiritual inspiration in all these activities is *qi*. It is therefore not only a cosmological principle but sheds light on the entire ethical, social and spiritual order. In Chinese thought the fulfilled human being is inseparable from the world of nature; the deepest desire is to live in harmony with all creatures and all people. And this can only be through harmonious communication between 'heaven' and earth which *qi* makes possible. *Ruah, pneuma* and *qi* all serve to designate the all-creating Spirit of God, fully present in Jesus Christ. In him also is the full harmony between 'heaven' and earth, and complete response in answer (*ganying*) to the infinite wisdom of God. *Qi* provides the dynamic for this reception-and-answer between God and all humanity, nourishing and incarnating the Cosmic Christ and the universal Body of Christ within our history. Kwong concludes that human life is "a life of Qi" where moral sensibility, ethical action and spirituality are united.

Selected References
Works by Madeleine Kwong Lay-kuen
Chinese Qi and Christian Anthropology. Paris: Harmattan, 2000.
"Christian and Lay Formation Ideals." *Spirit* 1 (1989).
"Spirituality in the Chinese 'Anonymous Christian'." *Spirit* 3 (1989).
"A Spirit-originated Feminist Spirituality." Spirit 36 (1998).
Holy Spirit Study Centre. "The Chinese *Qi."* China Bridge (Dec. 2000).
Zhonglian Centre. "Chinese Qi and Christian Anthropology". *Les Revues des MEP*. Forthcoming.

4.2.6.4. Robert Ng Chi-fun sj

Ng Chi-fun is professor of moral theology at the Holy Spirit Seminary College, Hong Kong and warden of Ricci Hall, University of Hong Kong. He has written regularly for both the *Theology Annual* and *Spirit*. Many of his writings deal with such subjects as the comparative study of moral theologies, natural law ethics, the relation of Scriptures to moral theology, euthanasia, sexuality, marriage and family, the morality of Papal infallibility, the relationship between Chinese "orthodoxy" and law, and media ethics. In a major article regarding inculturation, however (2000), he affirms that an inculturated Chinese theology must come from Chinese theologians, express their religious experience and be expressed in elegant Chinese. It must respond to the question of the identity of modern Chinese and respect the tradition of Chinese ethical morality. Such an inculturated theology will not destroy the universality of theology but in Ng's view, "rather integrates with it to allow a universal theology to reside within the inculturated theology". He has also written on *lectio divina,* and on the new Catholic catechism.

Selected References
Works by Ng Chi-fun
"The Characteristics of Christian Ethics." *Theology Annual* 6 (1982).
"Method in Moral Theology." *Theology Annual* 9-10 (1985-1986).
"The Problem of the Interpretation of Law from the Perspective of the Chinese 'Concept of 'Orthodoxy'." *Theology Annual* 13 (1991-1992).
"The Eucharist and the Moral Life." *Spirit* 12 (1992).
"Trends in Moral Theology since Vatican II." *Spirit* 41 (1999).
"Principles for Inculturation of Theology." *Spirit* 47 (2000).

4.2.6.5. John Tong

John Tong has been director of Holy Spirit Study Centre from its inception in 1981, lecturer in theology at Holy Spirit Seminary and is now assistant bishop in Hong Kong. He has exercised a key role in developing the study and publication in Hong Kong of writings upon contemporary issues facing the church in Hong Kong and China. In his own study and writing special interests have included missiology, pastoral and eucharistic theology, Confucian-Catholic dialogue (including historical studies), the collegiality of bishops, Protestant theology in China and religious freedom. Tong's articles in *Theology Annual* (4.2.2.), have considered, for example, the ideas of "secularization" latent in the works of Thomas Aquinas and Immanuel Kant, comparing these with the tendencies of Confucian intellectualism of the same period (*Theology Annual* 2); and with Sister Joanna Chan he analyses Bishop Ting's speeches in accordance with the thought structure of today's Chinese Communism. (*Theology Annual* 4). He has written text-books for Chinese theology (in Chinese) and also "Annual Reviews" for the Holy Spirit Study Centre since 1981 (See *Tripod*).

Selected References
Works by John Tong
    Theology of Creation. Chinese Theology Textbook 1 (In Chinese). Hong Kong: Catholic Truth Society, 1993.
    Challenges and Hopes. Stories from the Catholic Church in China. Taipei: Wisdom Press, 1999.
    "Mission, Indigenization, Dialogue." *Tripod* 21 (1984).
    "Modernization and the Beijing Student Movement." *Tripod* 51 (1989).
    "Hong Kong Diocese in the 1980s: A Bridge."*Tripod* 81 (1989).
    "The Presence of Christ in the Eucharist." *Spirit* 12 (1992).
    "Confucian-Catholic Dialogue in Historical Perspective." *Tripod* 68 (1992).
    "Between Pessimism and Optimism." *Tripod* 99 (1997).
    "Society and the Catholic Church of Hong Kong Toward 1997." *Verbum SVD* 34.4 (1997).

4.2.6.6. Other Catholic Writers of Contextual Theology

Amongst other writers, teachers and scholars must be mentioned the following:

Peter Barry mm has been a staff member of Holy Spirit Study Centre, an editor/contributor/translator for *Tripod* and *Bridge* and a member of many ecumenical work-groups and study-tours concerned for Christian and Catholic studies in China and Hong Kong. His regular contributions to *Tripod* include studies of Catholic history and theology in China, spiritual civilisation and politics and ideology in Hong Kong and China, the role of women, profiles of Catholic leaders and provincial church studies.

Gianni Criveller pime is a researcher at the Holy Spirit Study Centre and professor at the Holy Spirit Seminary. He also lectures at the Institute of Sino-Christian Studies. He writes on Christology in Chinese history and in Chinese culture, Christology as basis for mission and also on the encounter of the Gospel with postmodernism.

Hon Tai-fai, Savio, sdb is professor of theology and philosophy at Holy Spirit Seminary, and editor of the Chinese Theology Textbook Series. He is also an academic member of the Office of Theological Concerns of the Federation of Asian Bishops' Conferences. He has particular interest in Christology, sacramentology, philosophy and culture and has written in both English and Chinese in these areas, including chapters and articles on Christianity and culture, and on dialogue with Confucian classics. His Chinese translation of *Catechism of the Catholic Church and Cultural Adaptation* is forthcoming from Chinazentrum and the Institute of Sino-Christian Studies, and "Dialogue with Confucian Classics from a Christian Perspective" will appear in the journal *Path*.

Anthony S.K. Lam has been staff member, editor and writer for the Holy Spirit Study Centre with particular interests in the history and role of Catholic bishops in China, and the work of the Catholic Bishop's Conference there. He has also studied changing structures of the family in China and the work of peace committees there. In his volume on *The Catholic Church in Present-Day China* (1994), he gives special attention to theological education, the recovery of the 'Open church', the rise and development of the 'Underground Church', the Communist Party's policy towards religion and the spirit of Vatican II and the Church in China.

Beatrice Leung completed doctoral study at London University and has taught and done research at the University of Hong Kong. She has also contributed to many national and international symposia, also editing a number of their papers. Her own writing and study has centred largely upon Sino-Vatican Relations, and Church-State relations in Hong Kong, China and throughout Asia.

Betty Ann Maheu mm is on the staff of the Holy Spirit Study Centre, with special responsibility for the editing of *Tripod*. Her writings, often in collaboration, are chiefly concerned with the roles of Chinese Catholic women and the policies and practices regarding religion in China.

Judith Xu Chan did her doctoral studies for her degree in theology in the department of theology at Fordham University, New York City. She also did studies in Zen Buddhism, Tibetan Buddhism and Chinese religious traditions at the Graduate Theological Union at Berkeley, CA. Her research and writing are focussed upon study of Confucianism and Buddhism in relation to Catholic tradition.

Selected References

Barry, Peter. "The Chinese Rites Controversy." *Tripod* 12 (1982).
—. "Is There a Marxist Humanism?" *Tripod* 16 (1983).
—. "Political Reform in Hong Kong: A Commentary." *Tripod* 40 (1987).
—. "A Discussion on Separation of Church and State in Hong Kong after 1997." *Tripod* 38 (1987).
—. "The Chinese Woman in Church and Society." *Tripod* 87 (1995).
—. "Building up a Spiritual Civilization." *Tripod* 91 (1996).
—. "Their Voice Should be Heard." *Tripod* 110 (1999).
—. "Macau: Center for Cultural Exchange." *Tripod* 114 (1999).
Criveller, Gianni. "Christ in Late Ming China." *Tripod* 102 (1997); 104 (1998).
—. "Dialogues on Jesus in China." *Tripod* 108 (1998); 115-120 (2000).
—."Trinitarian and Christological Bases for a Christian Theology of Interreligious Dialogue." *Theology Annual* (1998); *Zongjiao Wenhua* (Religion and Culture) Beijing (2000).
Hon Tai-fai, Savio. *Covenant and Rendezvous with Christ. From Celebration to Mystery.* Holy Spirit Seminary College of Theology and Philosophy Chinese Theology Textbook Series 3. Hong Kong: Catholic Truth Society, 1995. Chap. 17.
—. "On Gospel and Culture" (in Chinese). In Preliminary Studies on Chinese Theology, edited by Daniel Yeung. Hong Kong: Institute of Sino-Christian Studies 1999.
—. "The Synod of Bishops in Asia" (in Chinese). *Spirit* 40 (1999).
—. "Christ in Contemporary Christologies" (in Chinese). *Spirit* 41 (1999).
—. "The Church in China: Signs of Hope in the Third Millennium." *Tripod* (Christianity and Chinese Culture) 120 (2000).

—. "Liturgical Celebration as Trigger of Inculturation of Gospel" (in Chinese). *Theology Annual* 21 (forthcoming).
Lam, Anthony. *The Catholic Church in Present-Day China. Through Darkness and Light*. Leuven: Ferd. Verbiest Foundation; Hong Kong: Holy Spirit Study Centre, 1994.
—. "Bishops of the Chinese Patriotic Association, 1959-1963." *Tripod* 52 (1989).
—. "The Chinese Bishops' Conference in Beijing." *Tripod* 56 (1990).
—. "The Chinese Bishops' Conference: A Proposal." *Tripod* 79 (1994).
—. "A Response to the Pastoral Letter of the China Catholic Bishops' Conference." *Tripod* 116 (2000).
—. "The Catholic Church in China: Conflicting Attitudes." *Tripod* 115 (2000).
Leung, Beatrice. *Sino-Vatican Relations: Problems in Conflicting Authority 1976-1986*. London School of Economics and Political Science Monographs in International Studies. London: Cambridge University Press, 1992.
—. "Hong Kong Roman Catholic Church in 1997: Church and State." *Tripod* 49 (1989).
—. "The Mystery behind the Chinese Response to the Pope's Address." *Tripod* 97 (1997).
—, ed. *Church and State Relations in the 21st Century*. Hong Kong: University of Hong Kong Press, 1996.
—, and John D. Young, eds. *Christianity in China: Foundations for Dialogue*. Centre of Asian Studies occasional papers and monographs, Papers from a conference held at the University of Hong Kong from May 29-30, 1992. Hong Kong: Centre of Asian Studies, University of Hong Kong Press, 1993.
Maheu, Betty Ann. "The Chinese Woman in Church and Society." *Tripod* 87 (1995).
—. "Models of Faith and Love." *Tripod* 108 (1998).
—. "China's Religious Policy, 1981-1999." *Tripod* 113 (1999).
—. "Hong Kong Returns to the Dragon." *Tripod* 113 (1999).
Xu-chan, Judith. "Confucian View of Human Nature: Its Relevance to the Contemporary Chinese." *Tripod* 86 (1995).
—. "Zen and the Forms of Knowing." *Tripod* 101 (1997).

5 Supplementary Bibliography
5.1 Book Titles

1997 The Church at a Crossroads: Worship Resources for Hong Kong. Hong Kong: July 1 Link, 1996.

Astorino, Robert F., ed. *A Survey of Catholic Publications in Asia: Presented to the 12th Catholic World Congress of the Press, Rome, 22-26 September 1980*. Hong Kong: International Catholic Union of the Press, 198-?

Aymer, Goran and Virgil K.Y. Ho. *Cantonese Society at a Time of Change*. Hong Kong: Chinese University, 1998.

Ball, James Dyer. *Is Buddhism a Preparation or a Hindrance to Christianity in China?* Hong Kong: St Paul's College, 1907.

Bray, Mark and Ramsey Koo, eds. *Education and Society in Hong Kong and Macau: Comparative Perspectives on Continuity and Change*. Hong Kong: Comparative Education Research Centre, Hong Kong University Press, 1999.

Catholic Church. Congregatio de Propaganda Fide. *Collectanea constitutionum, decretorum* ... Hong Kong: Typis Societatis Missionum ad Exteros, 1905.

Chao, Jonathan, comp. *A History of the Church in China since 1949. A Reader and Expanded Study Guide*. Grand Rapids: Institute of Theological Studies, 1995.

Cheung, Anthony B.L. "Tiananmen Revisited." *Tripod* 81 (1994).

"Chinese Theology and Hong Kong." *Yi* 23 (1982).

Chung Chi Theology Division. Tolo Theological Series (in Chinese). Hong Kong: Chinese University of Hong Kong, 1983-88.

Catholic Institute for International Relations. *Hong Kong Comment*. London: CIIR, 1990.

Cioppa, John mm. "The Catholic Church in China: Between Death and Resurrection." *Tripod* 76 (1993).

Constable, Nicole. *Christian Souls and Chinese Spirits: a Hakka Community in Hong Kong*. Berkeley: University of California Press, c1994.

Deng Zhaoming. *The Vicissitudes of the Three-Self Patriotic Movement in the 1950's and its Predicament Today* (in Chinese.) Hong Kong: Christian Study Centre on Chinese Religion and Culture, 1997.

Evans, Grant, and Maria Tam Sui-mi, eds. *Hong Kong: The Anthropology of a Chinese Metropolis*. Surrey: Curzon Press, 1997.

Zhao Zhilian. "Explore Theological Theory suited to the Thinking and Sentiments of One's Own Nation." *Yi* 32 (1982).

Franklin, J. "Christian presence in a refugee-commercial-urban-industrial society: Towards a Christian Witness in Hong Kong." MTh. Thesis, San Francisco Theological Seminary, 1965.

Gheddo, Piero. *Lorenzo Bianchi di Hong Kong*. Novara: Istituto Geografico de Agostini, c1988.

Ho, Samuel Sung-him, ed. *Faith and Practice. Liturgical Renewal in Chinese Churches*. LWF China Study Series 4. Hong Kong: Lutheran World Federation and Lutheran Theological Seminary, 1998.

Hong Kong Central Council of Catholic Laity. "Hong Kong Central Council of Catholic Laity and the Work of Evangelization." *Spirit* 28 (1996).

International Movement of Catholic Students. *Students' Response to the Struggle for a New Asia: IXth and Xth Pan Asia Assembly IMCS Asia*. Hong Kong: Asian Secretariat International Movement of Catholic Students, 1982.

Lam Wing-hung. *The Life and Thought of T.C. Chao* (in Chinese.) Hong Kong: China Alliance Press, 1994.

Law Gwok-fai, Thomas. "The Chinese Liturgy Yesterday, Today and Tomorrow." *Tripod* 73 (1993).

Lee, Peter K. H., ed. Confucian-Christian Encounters in Historical and Contemporary Perspective.. New York: The Edwin Mellen Press, 1991.

Lee Kit-man. "Hong Kong Catholic Chinese: Their Identity as Hong Kong Citizens and Christians." *Tripod* 97 (1997).

Lo Ping-cheung. *Christian Ethics: Principles and Applications*. Hong Kong: China Alliance Press, 1992.

Lo, William and Henry Ng. "A Critique of Some Concepts in the True Idea of God of Matteo Ricci." *Theology Annual* 3 (1979).

Meyer, Bernard. *Like to Leaven*. Hong Kong: Catholic Truth Society, 1950.

Ng, Peter and Daniel Wong. *Citizenship and Civic Education - From the Perspective of Christian Faith and Practice*. Tolo Theological Series 4. Hong Kong: Chung Chi College, 1987.

Rear, John. *Workers, Know Your Rights!* Kowloon, HK: Hong Kong Christian Industrial Committee, c1972.

Rogers, Anthony. "Constitution and Religious Freedom - An Overview of Hong Kong in Historical Perspective." *Tripod* 38 (1987).

Roy, Andrew Tod. *Risk and Hope: the Hong Kong Story.* New York: Board of Foreign Missions of the Presbyterian Church in the USA, 1956.

Shao Yidan. "Challenge and Response: Hong Kong Roman Catholic Church and the Retrocession in 1997." *China Study Journal* 11 (1996).

Shen, Philip. *Thirty Years of Sense and Sensibility.* Faith and Life series 2. Hong Kong: Christian Institute, 1992.

Sheng ko hsüan chi (Catholic Hymnal: with accompaniment). Hong Kong: 1969.

Shields, Bernard J., sj "In Print: A Bibliographic Sketch of the Regional Seminary, Hong Kong (1931-1964)." *Theology Annual* 5 (1981).

Sovik, Ruth, Aagoth Fosmark and Clara Peterson. *Mission in Formosa and Hongkong: Studies in the Beginning and Development of the Indigenous Lutheran Church in Formosa and Hongkong.* Minneapolis, MN: Augsburg Publishing House, 1957.

Surface, William and Jim Hart. *Freedom Bridge; Maryknoll in Hong Kong.* New York, Coward-McCann, 1963.

Tan Xing. "Culture Christianity in Mainland China." *Tripod* 60 (1990).

Tang, Edmund and Jean-Paul Wiest, eds. *The Catholic Church in Modern China: Perspectives.* Maryknoll, NY: Orbis Books, 1993.

Tang, Samuel T.C. *Jiaohui zai houxiandai de shengsi* (Reflections of the Church in the post-modern period). Hong Kong: Excellence Book House, 1993.

Wong Man-kong. *James Legge: A Pioneer at Crossroads of East and West.* Hong Kong: Hong Kong Educational Publication Co., 1996.

Wong Kai-shing and others. *Human Rights Issues Prior to 1997.* Hong Kong: Asian Human Rights Commission, 1992.

Ying Fuk-tsang. *Wenhua shiying yu zhongguo jidutu (1860-1911)* (Cultural accommodation and Chinese Christians 1860-1911). Hong Kong: Alliance Bible Seminary, 1995.

—, and Leung Ka-lun. *Wushi niandai sanzi yundong de yanjiu* (Studies on the Three-Self Patriotic Movement in the 1950s). Hong Kong: Alliance Bible Seminary, 1996.

Yip, Francis. *Chinese Theology and State-Church Context: A Preliminary Study.* Hong Kong: Christian Study Centre on Chinese Religion and Culture, 1997.

5.2 Periodicals

Selected Hong Kong journals for research would include:

Areopagos (TFS Institute); *Asia Bulletin* (formerly *Mission Bulletin*); *Asia Focus* and *Union of Catholic Asian News; Breakthrough; Asian Exchange* (Arena); *Bridge. Church Life in China Today.* (Tao Fong Shan Ecumenical Centre); *Change* and *News and Views* (HK Christian Council); *China Missionary Bulletin* (Catholic Truth Society, Hong Kong); *China and the Church Today* (China Church Research Centre); *Ching Feng* (Christian Study Centre on Chinese Religion and Culture); *Chung Chi Journal* (Chung Chi College); *FABC Papers* (FABC); *Hong Kong Catholic Register*; *Hong Kong Journal of Religious Education* (HK Assoc. for Religious Education); *Institute of Sino-Christian Studies Newsletter* (TFS Institute); *Interflow* (IMCS); *Jian Dao: A Journal of Bible and Theology*; *Journal of the History of Christianity in China* (Hong Kong Baptist University); *Logos & Pneuma: Chinese Journal of Theology; Mission Bulletin* (continued *Serloc*); *Reflection* (Hong Kong Christian Institute); *Spirit* (Society of Jesus) *Sunday Examiner* (Catholic Diocese); *Theology and Life* (Lutheran Theological Seminary); *Theology Journal* (Holy Spirit Seminary); *Tripod* (Holy Spirit Study Centre); *Yi* (China Message).

— KSM and JCE

5 A Note on Inner Asia

See also

1 Introduction

Only a little study has yet been given to the sources for contextual theology from the countries of Inner Asia ("Central Asia"), but there is a long history of Christian presence throughout these regions and extensive documentation from this. Christian reflection has here often been closely related to ancient trading patterns, to travel or geographical exploration, to colonial ventures, as well as to missionary endeavours. To take seriously the experience and reflection of Christians in such diverse cultural and ethnic contexts, many different sources are to be studied, and many are still to be unearthed. It is only possible here to outline some of the chief materials that could be included in such study.

Many countries of Inner Asia possessed numerous Christian communities between the 5th and 15th centuries. This was so for Afghanistan, Tibet, Mongolia, Siberia and much of what was formerly east and west Turkestan and southern Russia; now northwest China, Kazakhstan, Kyrgyzstan, Tajikistan, Turkmenistan, Uzbekistan and the east Russian Federation. Theological writings from this period are outlined in volume 1, chapter 1.[See also Moffatt (1992), England (1998), Philip (1998) and Gillman and Klimkeit (1999)]. For most of these territories, we also have records of Christian presence of longer or shorter periods from the 17th century onwards, along with scattered and often fragmentary writings containing Christian reflection. Much fuller research is necessary for any adequate presentation of such theology-in-process and for our purposes here the note following is limited to a brief survey for Afghanistan and Mongolia with references for Tibet also.

2 Afghanistan

Christian presence in Afghanistan includes, for example, Georgian Christians in Kandahar, Kabul and elsewhere from the early 1700s; Armenian Christians in various places in the 1830s, 1840s and 1880s; Roman Catholic priests in the 1880s, and later; and Protestant missionaries in the 1830s/1840s, and the early 1900s. Some families have been known as being Christian over some centuries and they have sometimes been relatively free of harassment. More recently have been the movements from 1949 on, some of which developed the Community Christian Church in Kabul until its closure in 1973. In the troubled years since, Christian presence has continued through scattered "house churches" and agency staff groups, although new converts have risked imprisonment and sometimes death.

Extant letters and records for the earlier periods include those of 'Mullah' Joseph Wolff, Sultan Mohammad Paul, G.A.M.R. Browne and his fellow Mill Hill Missionaries, Theodore Pennell, Flora Davidson of Kohat and William McElwe Miller, and a number of visiting physicians and missioners. Recent writings include those of Dilawar Khan, Christy Wilson, Zia Nodrat and a number of writers of lyrics and testimonies. Christians of many denominations have been active since 1965 in aid, welfare and development programmes in Afghanistan, including Christian agencies. These include ACT (WCC) networks, Catholic Relief, ecumenical Church World Service, Quaker, Reformed and United Methodist agencies, the International Assistance Mission (IAM, formerly the International Afghan Mission) and World Vision. Staff members of these have often worked with Afghan Christians to foster house churches in many localities. They have also sometimes included theological reflection in letters, sermons or poetry which is fully shaped by Afghan issues and heritage (see e.g. Arley Loewen below).

A small number only of Christian writings from recent decades are yet accessible but among them are hymns, songs, life-stories, biblical studies and testimonies. A notable writer was Zia Nodrat (1950 -?1988), who although blind, studied both Islamic law at the University of Kabul, along with Christian theology, and translated the New Testament from Persian into his own Afghan Dari dialect in the early 1970s. (Its third edition was published by the Cambridge University Press 1989). He also wrote a book on the New Testament, directed the Kabul Institute of the Blind and later went as a missionary to Pakistan, where still later, he was martryred.

Amongst writers of hymns and songs in Afghan dialects are Nazira Shaeq, Khalilullah, Wahid Khan, Rakhel (Rachel), and Hussain Andaryas. Most of their songs are devotional lyrics with strong emphasis upon Jesus Christ as shepherd, shield and saviour. Testimonies which are valued by many Afghan Christians include those of former Haji Sultan Mohammad Paul (early 19th century) and Hussain Andaryas Khan (b.1965). A vehicle for these writings is now the quarterly 16-page bulletin called *Wheat* which has been commenced by Afghan Christians overseas. This includes poetry, devotional and pastoral articles and biblical studies. Another source of Afghan Christian writing and reflection is found in several websites now established by and for Afghan Christians.

Little is known of any writings by Christian women, but much of the shared struggle for women in Afghanistan has been undertaken by RAWA, the Revolutionary Association of Women of Afghanistan. Despite all obstacles RAWA has in recent years striven for human rights, and for equal access to education and employment. It has also strongly opposed all militarism and fundamentalism, and is critical of the ways in which both Russia and the US have intervened (since the 1970s). The Afghan Women's Mission, led by such scholars as Sonali Kolhatkar, is in full solidarity with RAWA.

Selected References
History
    Adamec, Ludwig Warran. *Historical Dictionary of Afghanistan*. Asian Historical Dictionaries no. 5. Metuchen, NJ; London: Scarecrow, 1991.

    Barakat, Sultan, Mohammed Ehsan and Arne Strand. *NGOs and Peace-building in Afghanistan : workshop report 3-7 April 1994*. York: University of York, c1994.

Brodsky, Anne E. with All Our Strength. The Revolutionary Assoc. of Women of Afghanistan. RAWA, forthcoming.

Duprée, Louis. *Afghanistan*. Series: Oxford Pakistan paperbacks. Karachi; Oxford: Oxford University Press, 1997.

Ellis, Deborah. *Women of the Afghan War.* Westport, CT: Praeger, 2000.

Fraser-Tytler, William Kerr. *Afghanistan : a Study of Political Developments in Central and Southern Asia*. 2nd ed. London; New York: Oxford University Press, 1953.

Giustozzi, Antonio. *War, politics and society in Afghanistan, 1978-1992*. Washington, DC: Georgetown University Press, c2000.

Kohatkar, Sonali. "The Impact of US Intervention on Afghan Women's Rights." *Berkeley Women's Law Journal*. Forthcoming.

Marsden, Peter. *The Taliban: War, Religion and the New Order in Afghanistan*. Series: Politics in Contemporary Asia . Karachi: Oxford University Press; London: Zed, 1998.

Rubin, Barnett R. *The Fragmentation of Afghanistan : State Formation and Collapse in the International System*. New Haven; London: Yale University Press, c1995.

Weinbaum, Marvin G. *Pakistan and Afghanistan: Resistance and Reconstruction*. Boulder: Westview Press; Lahore: Pak Book Corp., 1994.

Christian Presence and Writing

Camps, Arnulf. *Studies in Asian Mission History (1956-1998)*. Leiden: Brill, 2000.

Clark, Robert. *Dilawar Khan*. London: Church Missionary Society, n.d.

Curry, Dayna and Heather Mercer with Stacy Mattingly. *Prisoners of hope : the Story of our Captivity and Freedom in Afghanistan*. New York : Doubleday, Forthcoming.

Davidson, Flora M. *Hidden Highway*. New York: Fleming H. Revell, 1948.

— *Wild Frontier*. London : Christian Literature Crusade, 1957.

England, J.C. *The Hidden History of Christianity in Asia: The Churches of the East before the Year 1500*. Delhi: ISPCK; Hong Kong: CCA, 1998.

Gillman, Ian and Hans-Joachim Klimkeit. *Christians in Asian before 1500*. Richmond: Curzon, 1999.

Lee, Jonathan. "The Armenians of Kabul and Afghanistan." In *Cairo to Kabul. Afghan and Islamic Studies presented to Ralph Pinder-Wilson.* London: Melisande. Forthcoming.
Levi, Peter. *The Light Garden of the Angel King.* London: Collins, 1972.
Loewen, Arley. "The Walls of Darkness and God's Light." (A sermon to Christian NGO workers in Afghanistan). Kabul: Mimeo'd, 1999.
Miller, William McElwe. *My Persian Pilgimage.* Pasadena: William Carey, 1995.
Moffatt, Samuel H. *A History of Christianity in Asia. Vol.1: Beginnings to 1500.* San Francisco: Harper, 1992.
Pennell, Theodore. *Among the Wild Tribes of the Afghan Frontier.* London: Seeley Service, 1909.
Philip, T.V. *East of the Euphrates: Early Christianity in Asia.* Delhi: ISPCK; Tiruvalla: Christian Sahitya Samithy, 1998.
Wilson, J. Christy, Jr. *Afghanistan: The Forbidden Harvest.* Elgin, IL; Weston, Ont: David C. Cook Publishing, 1981.
Wolff, Joseph. *Researches and Missionary Labours among Jews, Mohammedans, and Other Sects.* London: 1835.
"The Story of Zia Nodrat" has been published by the Fellowship of Faith, Toronto, Canada, and can be found on www.leaderu.com/wri/pages/zia.html.

3 Mongolia

In order to study the Christian writings and reflection from Mongolia it would be necessary to consider first a long history of Christian presence. This includes Nestorian communities from at least the 8th century and Roman Catholic presence from the 12th century (see vol. 1, chap. 1, 2.6, 2.7). In the 17th-19th centuries came a series of Protestant and Roman Catholic missionaries. These included the Moravians Isaak Jakob Schmidt (1779-1847), Edward Pagell (d.1883) and Heny A. Jaeske (1817-1883); along with members of the LMS, including Edward Stallybrass (1793-1884), William Swan (1791-1866) and John Abercrombie (1800-c.1870), and James Gilmour (1843-1891). Catholic missionaries included the Lazarists Evariste Régis Huc (1813-1860) and Joseph Gabet (1808-1853); the CICM fathers Théophile Verbist and Antoine Mostaert (these present after 1864), and the Episcopalian and linguist Samuel Isaac Joseph Schereschewsky (1831-1906). Writings are extant by or about all these expatriates working in Mongolia for varying lengths of time, and some provide part of the groundwork for contextual reflection in Mongolia (see below).

Although the CICM (Scheut Fathers) officially returned to Mongolia in 1922, their presence would be only sporadic during the rule of the Mongolian People's Revolutionary Party. CICM staff were appointed in 1990, when the newly democratic government allowed the entry of missionaries. A papal embassy and mission was established in Ulan Bator and the Catholic Centre was opened there in 1996. The Khalka translation of the New Testament had been published by the United Bible Societies in 1990, from when permanent Protestant presence also dates. By 1994 the number of Christians was estimated to be 3000, and by the year 2000, ten times that number, with some form of Christian church now in every province. Protestant activities centre largely upon church-planting and leadership development, with some congregations under sole Mongolian leadership.

A selection of those in the 20th century whose writings are to be studied would include: John Sheepshanks (fl.1890), Reginald Sturt (1881-1948), the 'Mongol Duke' Frans Larsen (in Mongolia 1894-1923), Stuart and Margaret Gunzel (1905-1995); along with J. Leyssen, J. van Hecken, Wenceslao Padilla, Robert Goessens, Jacqueline Thevenet and Hugh Kemp (see below). There are in addition occasional writings by other Scheut Fathers, and Les sœurs de Saint-Paul de Chartre and Les sœurs de mère Teresa. Understandably, very little is yet available of published writings by nationals, considering that the contemporary Mongolian church entered upon a quite new phase following the major political changes of 1990 -1993. However the liturgies of the Catholic Church are now bilingual, and some Mongol chants and texts have been introduced there.

It is hoped that future Christian writers may come from Christian student groups now formed at the Mongolian State University of Ulan Bator. Other aspects of Christian mission in Mongolia from which theological reflection can be expected include humanitarian work, especially with street children, activities of youth formation, the work of national writers in journalism, language teaching in association with the University of Ulan Bator, and various pastoral ministries. There is also a developing ecumenical co-operation between Episcopal, Roman Catholic, Lutheran and Anglican churches, along with the establishment of the Mongolian Evangelical Coalition. Inter-faith dialogue has also been initiated with meetings between Buddhist leaders and monks of the Gandan (Catholic) monastery. Local Christian reflection will also be much nourished through the thorough revision, commenced in 1999, of the earlier translations of the Bible in Mongolian.

Selected References
History and Religion

    Bawden, C.R. *The Modern History of Mongolia.* London: Weidenfeld and Nicholson, 1969 et. seq.

    Christian, David. *A History of Russia, Central Asia and Mongolia.* London: Blackwell Publishers,1998.

    Eliade, Mircea. *Shamanism. Ancient techniques of ecstasy.* Princeton University Press, 1974.

    Heissig, Walther. *The Religions of Mongolia.* Berkeley: University of California Press, c1980.

    Howerth, H.H. *History of the Mongols from the Ninth to the Nineteenth centuries.* London: Franklin, 1876.

    Jagchid, Sechin and Paul Hyer. *Mongolia's Culture and Society.* Boulder: Westview Press, 1979.

    Morgan, David. *The Mongols.* London: Blackwells, 1986.

    Sinor, Denis, ed. *The Cambridge History of Early Inner Asia.* Cambridge University Press, 1990.

    Szamuely, Tibor. *The Russian Tradition.* London: Secker & Warburg, 1974. (Chap. 2, The Mongol Heritage).

    Trubetzkoy, Nikolaj Sergeevich. *The Legacy of Genghis Khan.* Ann Arbor: Michigan Slavic Publications, 1991.

    Vernadsky, George. *The Mongols and Russia.* New Haven: Yale University Press, 1953.

Christian Presence and Writing

    Aubin, Françoise. "Une colonie étrangère d'un type nouveau à Oulan-Bator et dans les environs: les prêtres et religieuses catholiques" (Part 1). *Anda* 32 (1999).

Cable, Mildred and Francesca French. *The Gobi Desert*. London : Hodder, 1942.

Dawson, Christopher. *Mission to Asia* . Toronto: University of Toronto Press in association with the Medieval Academy of America, c1980. (Originally published as: *The Mongol Mission*. London: Sheed and Ward, 1955).

French, Francesca. *Thomas Cochrane: Pioneer and Missionary statesman*. London: Hodder and Stoughton, 1956.

Goessens, Robert. "La Mission catholique d'Oulan-Bator: propos recueillis par J. Thevenet ." *Anda* 27 (1997).

Heyndrickx, Jeroom, cicm. "A New C.I.C.M. Mission to Mongolia: a Report on a Visit to Mongolia, Oct 12-25." Mimeo'd, 1991.

Jagchid, Sechen, and Hyer, Paul. *Mongolia's Culture and Society*. Boulder: Westview Press, Inc. 1979.

James Gilmour of Mongolia: his Diaries, Letters, and Reports. Edited and arranged by Richard Lovett. London: Religious Tract Society, 1892.

Larson, Frans August. *Larsen Duke of Mongolia*. Boston: Little, Brown and Company, 1930. Autobiography of Larson, who went to Mongolia in 1893 and lived with the Mongolians.

"Lettre circulaire de Wens Padilla." Ulaanbaatar: Mimeo'd, December 18, 1999.

Leyssen, J., *Formatio cleri in Mongolia*. Pekin: Ex Typographia Lazaristarum, 1940.

Kemp, Hugh P. *Steppe by Step: Mongolia's Christians - from Ancient Roots to Vibrant Young Church*. London: Monarch Books, 2000.

Kasemuana, Pierre. "Premiers pas dans les steppes : en Mongolie." *Spiritus* 151 (1998).

Melckebeke, Carlo van. *Service social de l'Eglise en Mongolie*. Bruxelles: Editions de Scheut, 1968.

Morel, Luigi. *Glieroi delle missioni di Scheut in Mongolia*. *Roma* : Procura delle Missioni di Scheut, 1962.

Sheepshanks, John. *My life in Mongolia and Siberia from the Great Wall of China to the Ural Mountains*. London, Society for Promoting Christian Knowledge, 1903.

Status missionum Congregationis Imm. Cord. B.M.V. (Sheut) in Sina et in Mongolia. Zi-ka-wei : [s.n.] (ex typographia Missionis catholicae), 1925-1927.

Thevenet, Jacqueline. "The Catholic Church in Mongolia since 1992." *UCAN* 10 (Nov. 2000).

Vladimir, Archbishop of the Orthodox Diocese of Bisjkek and All Central Asia. "Christianity and Islam in Central Asia." In *Islam and Central Asia: an enduring legacy or an evolving threat?*, edited by Roald Sagdeev and Susan Eisenhower. Washington, DC: Center for Political and Strategic Studies, c2000.

van den Berg, Leo. "The Mongolian Territory and the Christian Encounter." *Tripod* 1 (1981); 10 (1982)

van Hecken, J. "La Littérature Mongole Chrétienne." *Neue Zeitschrift fur Missionswissenschaft,* 1947. Eng. trans. (unpublished) by Anne Windsor.

A Basic Selection for Tibet

Caraman, Philip. *Tibet: The Jesuit Century.* St. Louis: Institute of Jesuit Sources, 1997.

Dauvillier, Jean. *Histoire et institutions des Eglises orientales au Moyen Age.* London: Variorum Reprints, 1983.

Desideri, Ippolito, sj. *An Account of Tibet: The Travels of Ippolito Desideri of Pistoia, S.J., 1712-1727.* London: George Routledge & Sons, 1984.

Ekvall, Robert B. *Tibetan Sky Lines.* New York: Farrar, Straus and Young, 1952.

Hale, Thomas. *A Light shines in Central Asia : a Journey into the Tibetan Buddhist World.* Pasadena, Calif. : William Carey Library, c2000.

Le Lacheur, D.W. *The Land of the Lamas, or, The Opening of Thibet to the Gospel.* South Nyack, N.Y. : Christian Alliance Pub. Co., 1898?

Lowe, Robson. *From China and Tibet a commentary on letters written by missionaries working in the interior, 1844-1865.* London : Pall Mall Stamp Co. 1981.

Plymire, David V. High Adventure in Tibet. Springfield: Gospel Publishing, 1959.

Simonnet, Christian. *Thibet. Voyage au bout de la Chrétienté.* Paris : Éditions du Monde Nouveau, 1949.

6 Contextual Theology in Japan

1 **Contextual Theology in Japan 1800-1945**
  1.1 Introduction
     1.1.1. The Setting; **1.1.2.** Christian Presence
  1.2 Roman Catholic Continuities
     1.2.1. Kakure Kirishitan; **1.2.2.** Lay Scholars
         1.2.2.1. Sadakata Ryosuke, penname Kisei Chishi (fl. 1865); **1.2.2.2.** Hirata Atsutane (1776-1843)
  1.3. Seed-beds for Japanese Protestant Theology
     1.3.1. Preaching Bands, Colleges, Churches; **1.3.2.** Niijima Jo (Joseph Hardy Neesima, 1843-1890; **1.3.3.** Paul Sawayama (1852-1887) and Naruse Jinzo (d.1919); **1.3.4.** Expatriate Scholars and Writers: 1
  1.4 Pioneer Theologians
     1.4.1. Kozaki Hiromichi (1856-1928); **1.4.2.** Uemura Masahisa (1861-1925); **1.4.3.** Uchimura Kanzo (1861-1930); **1.4.4.** Ebina Danjo (1866-1937); **1.4.5.** Iwashita Soichi (1889-1940); **1.4.6.** Yoshimitsu Yoshihiko (1904-1945)
  1.5 Theology of Independent Scholars and Writers
     1.5.1. Arai Osui (1846-1922); **1.5.2.** Yokoi Tokio (1857-1937); **1.5.3.** Nitobe Inazo (1862-1933); **1.5.4.** Iha Fuyu (1876-1947)
  1.6 Buddhist-Christian Studies 1
     1.6.1. Takahashi Goro (1856-1935); **1.6.2.** Aimé Villion mep (1843-1932)
  1.7 Christianity, Society and Nationalism
     1.7.1. Theologians, Writers and Social Reform; **1.7.2.** Ecumenical Movements and Writings; **1.7.3.** Tanaka Shozo (1842- 1913); **1.7.4.** Tokutomi Soho (1863-1957); **1.7.5.** Yamaji Aizan (1864-1917); **1.7.6.** Hatano Seichi 1877-1950

1.8 Women Doing Theology: Thought and Movements 1
  1.8.1. Context and Education; **1.8.2.** Kawai Michi (1877-c.1952); **1.8.3.** Yamada Waka, (1879-1957)
1.9 Expatriate Scholars and Writers 2
1.10 Theologians Furthering Contextual Theology
  1.10.1. Ishihara Ken, 1882-1976; **1.10.2.** Kagawa Toyohiko (1888-1960); **1.10.3.** Nakajima Shigeru 1888-1946; **1.10.4.** Kan Enkichi 1895-1972; **1.10.5.** Otsuka Setsuji (1887-)
1.11 Systematic and Historical Theologians
1.12 Supplementary Bibliography I

2 **Contextual Theology in Japan 1945 -2000**
2.1 Introduction
  2.1.1. Theological Context; **2.1.2.** Roman Catholic Background; **2.1.3.** Protestant Background
2.2 Women Doing Theology: Thought and Movements 2
2.3 Theology, Culture and Society
2.4 Inter-faith Encounter and Reflection
  2.4.1. Catholic Writings; **2.4.2.** Ecumenical Writings
2.5 Contextualising Theologians
  2.5.1. Hugo Enomiya-Lassalle sj (Enomiya Makibi, 1898-1990); **2.5.2.** Akaiwa Sakai (1903-1966); **2.5.3.** Takizawa Katsumi (1906-1984); **2.5.4.** Doi Masatoshi (1907-); **2.5.5.** Suzuki Masahisa (1912-1969); **2.5.6.** Joseph John Spae cicm (1913-1989); **2.5.7.** Sumiya Mikio (1916-); **2.5.8.** Kitamori Kazoh (1916-); **2.5.9.** Takeda Cho Kiyoko (1917-); **2.5.10.** Takenaka Masao (1925-); **2.5.11.** Furuya Yasuo (1926-); **2.5.12.** Kadowaki Kakichi, Johannes sj (1926-); **2.5.13.** Inoue Yoji (1927-); **2.5.14.** Jan Van Bragt (1928-); **2.5.15.** Isshiki Yoshiko (1928-); **2.5.16.** Kumazawa Yoshinobu (1929-); **2.5.17.** Koyama Kosuke (1929-); **2.5.18.** Arai Sasagu (1930-); **2.5.19.** Takayanagi Shunichi sj (1932-); **2.5.20.** Yagi Seiichi (1932-); **2.5.21.** Aiko Carter; **2.5.22.** Tagawa Kenzo (1935-); **2.5.23.** Yamada Keizo sj (1936-); **2.5.24.** Momose Fumiaki sj (1940-); **2.5.25.** Nobuhara Tokiyuki (1937-); **2.5.26.** Kinukawa Hisako (1938-); **2.5.27.** Honda Testuro (1942-); **2.5.28.** Kuribayashi Teruo (1948-); **2.5.29.** Iwashima Tadahiko sj

(1943-); **2.5.30.** Watanabe Hidetoshi; **2.5.31.** Yamano Shigeko; **2.5.32.** Oda Takehiko (1953-); **2.5.33.** Yamashita Akiko; **2.5.34.** Kawamura Shinzo sj (1958-); **2.5.35.** Kohara Katsuhiro

2.6 Other Sources for Contextual Theology

2.6.1. In Selected Catholic Periodicals; **2.6.2.** Other Socio-Theologians Working Since the 1960s; **2.6.3.** Other Protestant Theologians Contributing to Contextual Theology; **2.6.4.** Other Catholic Scholars and Writers **2.6.5.** Other Texts in Prophetic Theology - 1980-2000

2.6.5.1. The Period 1980 - 1990; **2.6.5.2.** The Period 1990 - 2000

2.6.6. Institutes, Movements, Associations

2.6.6.1. Catholic Bishops' Conference; **2.6.6.2.** Ecumenical and Scholarly Institutes; **2.6.6.3.** National Christian Council in Japan (NCCJ); **2.6.6.4.** The Tomisaka Christian Center; **2.6.6.5.** The Hyakunincho Church, Nippon Kiristo Kyodan (UCCJ)

2.7 Philosophical Theologians

2.8 Supplementary Bibliography II

1 Contextual Theology in Japan 1800-1945
For the pre-1800 period see chapter 2 above
1.1 Introduction
1.1.1. The Setting
Japanese peoples were early enriched by various ethnic strands from northern and southern Asia, as well as those indigenous to the Japanese islands. A largely centralised state had emerged by the 5th century and culture and society developed under strong influences from both China and Korea. In the following centuries, arts, letters and religious traditions flourished along with sophisticated social life for some classes, in "an age" writes G.B. Sansom, "of intellectual ferment, of spiritual fervour, and of artistic excitement." The cosmic 'shamanism' of indigenous Shinto traditions had long shaped Japanese religiosity, but from the 4th century onwards, Chinese-Korean Buddhism, fused with Confucian morality, became increasingly influential. The Nara (710-781),

Contextual Theology in Japan

Heian (781-1191) and Kamakura (1192-1333) periods were notable for creative developments in all these cultural and religious traditions. The first missionary, Francis Xavier sj, landed in Kagoshima in 1549. From 1603 until 1868, the Tokugawa Shogunate continued to rule an isolated and feudally structured Japan, nominally on behalf of the Emperor. Society was meticulously stratified, with all classes - from the Daimyo (nobles) and Samurai (warrior class) to farmers, merchants, artisan, Eta and Hinin (people of the discriminated-against "Buraku") - subject to strict social control. By mid-19th century, however, Japanese society was becoming fragmented because of clan conflict, opposition to the Shogunate, growing economic grievances and external pressures to end Japanese isolation.

It was in this context that the enforced opening of Japanese ports to foreign trade (1854), and the restoration of the Meiji Emperor (1868), brought continuing major political, social and religious changes over the next half century. In quick succession would come the abolition of feudal fiefs - although not of class structures; acceptance by many of western thought and education; and rapid industrialisation "on the backs of the peasantry". Following serious rebellions and social disruption which particularly affected the Samurai class, military and imperial aims led to war with China (1894-95) and Russia (1904-05), and to the annexation of Korea (1910). The roots were thus sown in the Meiji period (1868-1912) for the developments of the Taisho and Early Showa periods (1912-1945). These included the extension of such aims - in the Sino-Japanese war (from 1931) and the Pacific War from (1941) - and for the growth of many socialist, pacifist and cultural movements dedicated to peace, economic justice and the creative arts. Imperial policies would lead also to the traumatic experiences of Hiroshima and Nagasaki, to national surrender and the emperor's formal rejection of divinity; and to the Allied occupation (until 1952) and promulgation of a democratic constitution.

In 1956 Japan became member of the United Nations, in 1960 it entered into controversial security agreements with the USA, and in 1972 it normalized relations with China. During these and following years the Japanese economy reached high levels of productivity and wealth, while Japanese scholarship, education and artistic endeavour made widely influential contributions in many fields. Yet the legacies of wartime and economic divisions, and of civil disturbance (especially severe in the years 1968-72) would remain to divide society and those of all religious persuasion in the ensuing decades. By the start of the Heisei period (1989) further major changes led to periodic political, international and economic reversals. Japan's role, however, in international development and aid, both governmental and non-governmental, has remained strong. Japan remains a constitutional monarchy, with strong faction leadership in the legislature (Diet) and a central role for the bureaucracy. The population numbers approximately 126 million with a density of 350 persons per square kilometre although effective population density is much higher because 80% of the country is mountainous.

Religious affiliation is given as follows: Buddhism: 89,828,500 persons (72%); Shinto: 117,378,185 (94%); Christianity: 1,519,396 (1.2 % - formally registered only) - comprised of Catholic: 447,639; Protestant: 527,408, Undifferentiated: 544,349; other religions: 11,112,595 (8.9 %). It is to be noted that these figures total 176%, largely because of the dual allegiance of most Japanese to both Buddhism and Shintoism.

Selected References

Allinson, Gary D. *Columbia Guide to Modern Japanese History*. New York: Columbia University Press, c1999.

Anesaki Masaharu. *History of Japanese Religion: with Special Reference to the Social and Moral Life of the Nation*. Rutland, Vt.; Tokyo: Tuttle, 1963.

Beasley, W. G. *The Modern History of Japan*. 3rd ed. London: Weidenfeld and Nicolson, 1981.

Best, Ernest E. *Christian Faith and Cultural Crisis: the Japanese Case*. Leiden: Brill, 1966.

Fukutake Tadashi. *Japan Social Structure 1870-1980*. Tokyo: University of Tokyo; New York: Columbia University Press, ?1981.

Halloran, Richard. *Japan. Images and Realities*. Tokyo: Tuttle, 1970.

Hane Mikiso. *Peasants, Rebels, & Outcasts: The Underside of Modern Japan*. New York: Pantheon, 1982.
Mason, R.H.P. and J.G. Caiger. *A History of Japan*. Rev. ed. Rutland, Vt.: Tuttle, c1997 (1972).
Reader, Ian, Esben Andreasen and Finn Stefánsson. *Japanese Religions: Past and Present*. Honolulu: University of Hawaii Press, c1993.
Sansom, George. *A History of Japan*. 3 vols. Folkstone: Dawson, 1978.
Tamaru Noriyoshi and David Reid. *Religion in Japanese Culture*. Tokyo: Kodansha International, 1996.
Tsunoda Ryusaku, Wm. Theodore de Bary and Donald Keene. *Sources of Japanese Tradition*. 2 vols. New York and London: Columbia University Press, 1958.
Varley, H. Paul. *Japanese Culture*. 3rd ed. Tokyo: Tuttle, 1986.

1.1.2. Christian Presence

For the first half of the 19th century Christianity was still proscribed and subject to persecution in Japan, as it had been since 1614. Communities of "hidden Christians" (*Kakure Kirishitan*) had, however, maintained Christian practices in some districts, and would partly emerge to surprise returning Roman Catholic missionaries in 1865. Much of their Christian literature, liturgies and art-forms has survived and contain creative theological insights (See 1.2.1.). Persecution continued, however, in the next decade, and although in 1873 the Meiji government withdrew religious sanctions, freedom of religion was not fully granted until 1945. By 1900, however, a number of Catholic periodicals were being regularly published, including *Kokyo Banpo* (Universal Church Monitor), *Nippon Kokyo Zasshi* (a cultural magazine), *Tenchijin* (Universe) and *Koe* (Voice; First published in 1891, *Koe*'s 475th issue will appear in December 2002). By 1914, 45 orders of men and women had arrived to join the Missions Etrangères de Paris missioners.

Protestantism in Japan dates only from the mid-19th century, but grew rapidly in the period of social fragmentation which followed the restoration of the Meiji Emperor (1868). Early leaders included many disaffected Samurai who, along with exceptional expatriates, led in the formation of Christian educational foundations which played a central role in such growth. Aoyama Gakuin (now Aoyama Gakuin University) and St Paul's School (now Rikkyo University) in Tokyo, were founded in 1874; and English School (now Doshisha University) was founded in Kyoto in 1875. These were later followed by Catholic colleges: Sophia University (Jochi Diagaku), Tokyo, 1913; Sacred Heart College (Seishin Joshi Daigaku), 1915; and Nanzan University in Nagoya, 1916. By 1908 there were also an estimated 1,300 missionaries in Japan. In 1910 the first Catholic full translation of the New Testament was complete and in 1917, the revised Protestant translation of the New Testament.

Prolific writings, dating from the 1880s on, are extant from Samurai converts, expatriate teachers, and the growing body of Japanese theologians. The writings of western, particularly German, theologians were rapidly assimilated by Protestant writers and their major themes would be extensively reproduced and debated throughout the whole of this period. Yet in only a few of these theologies was there any recognition of the particular cultural, religious and social context of Japanese Christian life. Before the end of this period these theological trends would allow the growth of political quietism and individualist piety in many churches. There were also, however, pastors and theologians, sometimes from independent Christian communities such as the *Mukyokai* ("Non-Church"), who were critical of many features of western Christianity and theology, and who, along with others, developed more contextual writings by the turn of the century. Amidst the tensions of social reconstruction, growing nationalism, inter-faith encounter and social struggle, some theologians and writers in the early decades of the 20th century also articulated a faith directly shaped by the experience of impoverished classes, of women, of minorities and of movements for social justice.

At the beginning of the 20th century Christians were fully involved in the foundation of socialist and trade union movements in the face of severe social problems caused by rapid industrialisation. Many of the founding members of the Social Democratic Party were active Christians. Suzuki Bunji founded the *Yuikai* or Friendship Foundation in 1912 (later the *Nihon Rodo*

Sodomei or Japan Federation of Labor). The *Nihon Nomin Kumiai* (Japan Farmers Union) was founded in 1922 by two Christian Socialists. In following years many of these movements were split by disputes and much of the initial Christian influence was weakened or lost. The churches continued, however, their wide range of involvements in social and medical projects, hospitals, sanatoriums, leprosariums, orphanages and social work centres. Many of these programmes, and the reflection arising from such ministries, would be developed further by ecumenical and women's movements such as the *Fujin Kyofukai* (Society for the Reform of Manners, or Women's Christian Temperance Union), by the National Christian Council, by the "Social Christianity Movement" and by "the Kingdom of God Movement". By the 1930s such movements, along with other reforming or dissenting groups, and the writings arising from them, were subject to increasing surveillance and harassment. Resistance on theological grounds would come from a few only, such as Murao Moses Shoichi, Yanaihara Tadao of the Mukyokai and the Reformed pastor Onomura Rinzo.

Milestones at this time in the development of Catholic churches included the first edition of *Kokyo Seinen-Kai Kaiho* (Catholic Youth Society Bulletin) published in 1921 and the revision of the *Catholic Prayer Book* and *Catholic Catechism* in 1935 and 1940 (first published 1896). *The Kokyo Seinen Jiho* becomes *The Catholic Times* (later *The Japan Catholic Newspaper,* 1923, with a weekly edition in 1931), but was closed by government in 1938. The First National Catholic Lay Conference was held and the Association of Catholic Laity launched (1924) and in October, 1929, the Major Seminary in Tokyo was opened. The growing influence of militarist and nationalist movements directly affected Catholic communities as well, leading to Catholic involvement also in democratic and peace movements. Students of Sophia University refused to offer reverence at Yasukuni Shrine (May 1932), although three years later the Japanese hierarchy decided, in the light of statements by the Ministry of Education, that such reverence is merely an expression of patriotism and loyalty and that Christians may show reverence at Shinto shrines.

Following the end of the Pacific War, Roman Catholic and Protestant churches would greatly increase in strength for a period, despite continuing divisions that arose from differing responses to state control during the war years. Herein lay the cause of fragmentation in the *Nihon Kirisuto Kyodan*, or United Church of Christ in Japan, which under government pressure had earlier included some 30 Protestant churches. Many members of both Catholic and Protestant churches would, however, become active in the movements for social and political reform which now multiplied. Amongst these would be teachers and students, social workers and priests or ministers, activists and theologians - both women and men - who from their experience and studies came to work for social justice, for holistic peace and for theological renewal.

Selected References

See Annotated Bibliography of *Christian Writings 16th-18th centuries* (chap. 2, above).

> Aoyama G. "Catholic Mission Activity in Japan at the End of the Tokugawa Period." *Katorikku Kenkyu* 18.35 (1979).
>
> Bamba Nobuya and John F. Howes, eds. *Pacifism in Japan: The Christian and Socialist Tradition*. Vancouver: University of British Columbia Press, 1978.
>
> Cary, Otis. *A History of Christianity in Japan: Roman Catholic, Greek Orthodox, and Protestant Missions*. Two volumes in one. Rutland, Vt.; Tokyo: Tuttle, 1976.
>
> Dohi Akio "Theological Trends in the Early Period of Modern Japan." *Japan Christian Quarterly* 50.1; 50.2 (1989).
>
> Drummond, Richard H. *A History of Christianity in Japan*. Grand Rapids: Eerdmans, 1971.
>
> Ikado Fujio, and James R. McGovern. *A Bibliography of Christianity in Japan: Protestantism in English Sources (1859-1959)*. Tokyo: Committee on Asian Cultural Studies, International Christian University, 1966.
>
> Iglehart, Charles W. *A Century of Protestant Christianity in Japan*. Rutland, Vt.; Tokyo: Tuttle: 1959.
>
> Jennes, Joseph. *A History of the Catholic Church in Japan from its Beginnings to the Early Meiji Era*. Tokyo: Oriens Institute for Religious Research, 1973.

Lande, Aasulv. *Meiji Protestantism in History and Historiography.* Studia Missionalia Upsaliensia. Uppsala: Uppsala University, 1988.

Laures, J. *Kirishitan Bunko: A Manual of Books and Documents on the Early Christian Mission in Japan...* Tokyo: Sophia University, 1957.

Scheiner, Irwin. *Christian Converts and Social Protest in Meiji Japan.* Berkeley and Los Angeles: University of California Press, 1970.

Stauffer, Milton, ed. *Japan Speaks for Herself: Chapters by a Group of Nationals Interpreting the Christian Movement.* New York: Student Volunteer Movement for Foreign Missions and the Missionary Education Movement, c1927.

Sumiya Mikio. *Kindai Nihon no keisei to kirisutokyo* (The formation of modern Japan and Christianity). Tokyo: Shinkyo Shuppan, 1961.

Terao Kazuyoshi, comp. *Annotated Bibliography of Christianity in Japan.* Nagoya: Nanzan Shukyo Bunka Kenkyujo, 2000.

Uoki Tadakazu. *Nippon Kirisutokyo no seishinteki dento* (The spiritual tradition of Japanese Christianity). Tokyo: Kirisutokyo Shiso sosho Kankokai, 1941. (Reprinted Tokyo: Ozorasha, 1996).

1.2 Roman Catholic Continuities

1.2.1. Kakure Kirishitan (see also chapter 2 above - Japan)

Collections of often anonymous documents of the 'Hidden Christians' dating from the 18th century continued in use during the 19th century and later. These preserved key elements of Roman Catholic belief but in the *Tenchi Hajimari*, for example, include them in a "folk Gospel" which relates events in the four Gospels - especially the suffering of Jesus - directly to the experience of Japanese Christians. It makes each incident the subject of particular *orashio* (prayers), employs the imagery of rural life in Japan, and presents the Buddha also as close partner with the Creator God. This and other sources for the life and faith of the Kakure Kirishitan have been the subject of renewed research and writing in the last decade, of which a selection is given below.

Among the most important documents are:

Tenchi Hajimari no Koto (Origin of the universe) - Compiled and circulated throughout the 18th century - brought to Fr. Petitjean at Nagasaki, 1865; reprinted by Tagita 1954. Differing manuscripts are extant from Urakami, Sotome and Ikitsuki. (See also Harrington 1993: chap 4, and Whelan 1996.)

Yasokyo Sosho (Collection of Catholic books). Fourteen manuscripts from Urakami, 1790-1794. Printed and annotated by Anesaki, who later (1931) abridged them.

Kirishitan Nagasaki ni Kansuru Utsushi (Copies of notes on Christianity in Nagasaki c.1760), *Nagasaki Kirishitan Monjo* (Christian documents of Nagasaki) c.1750, and *Kirishitan Shiryo* (Christian documents) 1781-1800; all listed in Ebisawa (1960).

Orasa no Mitsuji (Mysterious prayers) a manuscript (c.1794) printed and annotated by Ebisawa. Tokyo: 1953.

Prayers for the Dying, Doctrine in Ten Articles, Kereto (the Creed) and other prayers composed and used over many decades, were brought in manuscript or recited from memory, to the French missionaries in 1865. (Jennes 1973).

Mi Kurusu Michiyuki no Orashio (Prayers for the way of the cross). Ancient manuscript from Urakami in a lithographic print, published at Shanghai,1869. (Laures 1957).

Konchiristan no Ryaku (An abridgement of contrition). Five articles concerning contrition, reproduced by Petitjean from manuscript copy of book originally printed in 1603. Lithographed in Sanghai, 1869. (Laures 1957).

Selected References:

Anesaki Masaharu. *History of Japanese Religion: with Special Reference to the Social and Moral Life of the Nation*. Rutland, Vt.; Tokyo: Tuttle, 1963.

Cary, Otis. *A History of Christianity in Japan: Roman Catholic, Greek Orthodox, and Protestant Missions*, 242ff. Two volumes in one. Rutland, Vt.; Tokyo: Tuttle, 1976.

Harrington, Ann M. *Japan's Hidden Christians*. Chicago: Loyola University Press, 1993.

Jennes, Joseph. *A History of the Catholic Church in Japan from its Beginnings to the Early Meiji Era*, 204f. Tokyo: Oriens Institute for Religious Research, 1973.

Laures, J. *Kirishitan Bunko: A Manual of Books and Documents on the Early Christian Mission in Japan ...*, 139f. Tokyo: Sophia University, 1957.

Marnas, Francisque. *La Religion de Jésus (Yasa ja-Kyo) ressuscitée au japon dans la seconde moitié du XIXe siècle*. Paris: Séminaire des Missions Etrangères, 1931. First published in 1896.

Nosco, Peter. "Secrecy and the Transmission of Tradition, Issues in the Study of the 'Underground Christians'." *Japanese Journal of Religious Studies* 20.1 (1993).

Tagita Koya Paul-M. *Acculturation among the Secret Christians of Japan*. Tokyo: Tagita, ?1967.

Turnbull, Stephen R. *The Kakure Kirishtan of Japan: a Study of their Development, Belief and Rituals to the Present Day*. Richmond, Surrey: Japan Library, 1998.

—, ed. *Japan's Hidden Christians 1549-1999*. Richmond: Curzon, 2000.

Whelan, Christal. *The Beginning of Heaven and Earth: The Sacred Book of Japan's Hidden Christians*. Honolulu: University of Hawaii Press, 1996.

van Hecken, Joseph Leonard. *The Catholic Church in Japan since 1859*. Trans. and rev. by John Van Hoydonck. Tokyo: Herder, 1963. Trans. of: *Un siècle de la vie catholique au Japon*.

1.2.2. Lay Scholars

Following the return of Roman Catholic missions, notably the MEP and the sisters of St Maur, students of the re-established seminaries (Tokyo 1873; Nagasaki 1875) emerged as assistants to Bishop Petitjean, Fr Joseph Laucaigne and Bishop Peter Osouf. In apostolic activity MEP missionaries were guided by the principles of the *Monita ad Missionarios*, of the Sacred Congregation for the Propagation of the Faith, and catechetical or apologetic writing depended almost wholly upon European originals. Other educated lay people produced manuals, apologetic and historical or biblical works. Contextual elements are discernible only in the choice of imagery and of Japanese terminology, which largely remained that of the Kakure Kirishitan. Writings by missionary or catechist also often attempted to recognise, in language and example, the "more modern and intellectual way of life" of non-Christian Japanese (Drummond 1971: 310). Amongst writings by scholars sympathetic to Christian teaching, some placed this within the framework of Japan's religious traditions. Amongst these were:

1.2.2.1. Sadakata Ryosuke (fl.1865, penname Kisei Chishi)

Sadakata was an educated neophyte and Chinese interpreter. He also edited many books with Petitjean and wrote apologetic works in Japanese context, such as *Musei Shinron. Meiji ni saiji kishi kishun sosei shincho* (A Treatise on truth. Sequel to an awakening from delusion.) Newly published in the second year of Meiji, ?Shanghai, 1869.

Compare Kokyo Shoryaku. *Zesusu kosei sen happyaku hachi-ju nen shichi-gatsu* (Summary of Catholic apologetics) edited by Franciso, a Catholic, 1880; and Kojima Junji (fl. 1875), catechist and editor whose *Kyushin ryoyaku Seishoden* (History of the Old and New Testaments) presented a biblical history edited from Chinese, German and French versions. (Nagasaki: 1979).

1.2.2.2. The scholar and reformer Hirata Atsutane (1776-1843)

Though a student of writings from China by Ricci and colleagues, Hirata became an ardent and sometimes extreme nationalist and Shinto theologian. He accepted, however, a monotheistic creator, a heavenly Lord who rules over the universe and the immortality of the human soul. In *Honkyo Gehen* (Introductory notes on Shinto, 1806) he draws on Giulio Aleni's *Doctrine of the Three Mountains* and Ricci's *Ten Paradoxes* to refute Confucianism in order to outline a version of Shinto.

[See other lay scholars below: 1.3.2. Niijima Jo; 1.3.3. Naruse Jinzo; 1.4.6. Yoshimitsu Yoshihiko; 1.5.1. Arai Osui; 1.5.2. Yokoi Tokio; 1.5.3. Nitobe, Izano; 1.6.1. Takahashi Goro; 1.7.3. Tanaka Shozo; 1.7.4. Tokutomi Soho; 1.7.5. Yamaji Aizan; 1.7.6. Hatano Seichi; 1.8.2. Kawai Michi; 1.8.3. Yamada Waka; 1.10.1. Ishihara Ken; 1.10.2. Kagawa Toyohiko; 1.10.3. Nakajima Shigeru; 1.10.4. Kan Enkichi.]

Selected References

Drummond, Richard H. *A History of Christianity in Japan*, 309ff. Grand Rapids: Eerdmans, 1971.

Jennes, Joseph. *A History of the Catholic Church in Japan from its Beginnings to the Early Meiji Era*, 188f; 221ff. Tokyo: Oriens Institute for Religious Research, 1973.

Laures, J. *Kirishitan Bunko: A Manual of Books and Documents on the Early Christian Mission in Japan ...* Tokyo: Sophia University, 1957: 138, 162, 165.

Okada Norio. *Nihon no dento shiso to Kirisutokyo: sono setten ni okeru ningen keiseiron* (Christianity and intellectual life-1868-1912). Tokyo: Kyobunkwan, 1995.

Ryusaku Tsunoda, Wm. Theodore de Bary and Donald Keene, comps. *Sources of Japanese Tradition*, 35-46. New York: Columbia University Press, 1958.

Tawara Tsuguo. *Hirata Atsutane.* Tokyo: 1963.

Terao Kazuyoshi, comp. *Annotated Bibliography of Christianity in Japan.* Nagoya: Nanzan Shukyo Bunka Kenkyujo, 2000.

1.3 Seed-beds for Japanese Protestant Theology
1.3.1. Preaching Bands, Colleges, Churches

Western Protestant missionaries entered Japan from 1859, but Christian communities grew rapidly only after 1873 when official harassment ended. From 1872 came the formation of Bands for Bible Study, of young men with "high intellectual quality and spiritual vitality", drawn from a variety of samurai clans. These were the Yokohama Band of Dr Brown, the Kumamoto Band (Kyushu) of Capt L.L. Janes and the Sapporo Band of William Clark. Distinctions in emphasis can be seen between the Yokohama group, led by a missionary with more formal theological concern, and the Kumamoto and Sapporo Bands where lay leadership had a greater role. This early influence can still be seen in indigenous Christian movements in Japan, where "experiential orientation" has often shaped theology to a greater extent than in the mission-founded churches.

From Yokohama, would come Uemura Masahisa and Honda Yoichi; from Kyushu, Kozaki Hiromichi, Yokoi Tokio, Ebina Danjo and Kanamori Tsurin; from Sapporo, Sato Shosuke, Nitobe Inazo, Uchimura Kanzo, Miyabe Kinga and Ito Katsutake. The majority of Band members would come to play leading roles in the colleges and churches of Japan in the following decades. In particular, Uemura, Kozaki, Yokoi, Ebina, Nitobe and Uchimura would leave seminal Christian writings and provide the foundations for much later theological endeavour in Japan (See sections 1.4 and 1.5).

The foundation of Aoyama Gakuin (now Aoyama Gakuin University) and St Paul's School (now Rikkyo University) in Tokyo (1874), and of Doshisha English School (now Doshisha University) in Kyoto (1875), nurtured many of Japan's first Protestant theologians. Niijima Jo (Joseph Hardy Neesima, 1843-1890) received members of the Kumamoto Band 1876 to help form the School of Theology at Doshisha, and Kozaki Hiromichi would succeed him as president there. Many of Japan's later contextual theologians would also be trained in these universities and in the traditions first developed in the "Bands".

Selected References

Cary, Otis. *A History of Christianity in Japan: Roman Catholic, Greek Orthodox, and Protestant Missions*, 123ff. Two volumes in one. Rutland, Vt.; Tokyo: Tuttle, 1976.

Dohi Akio. "Theological Trends in the Early Period of Modern Japan." *Kirisuyokyo Kenkyu* 50.1; 50.2 (1989).

Ebizawa Norimichi. *Japanese Witnesses for Christ*. World Christian Books 20. London: Lutterworth Press, 1957.

Drummond, Richard H. *A History of Christianity in Japan*, 166ff. Grand Rapids: Eerdmans, 1971.

Hardy, Arthur Sherburne. *Life and Letters of Joseph Hardy Neesima*. Kyoto: Doshisha University Press, 1980.

Iglehart, Charles W. *A Century of Protestant Christianity in Japan*. Rutland, Vt.; Tokyo, Tuttle: 1959.

Jennings, Nelson. "The Socio-political Context of the Christian Church in Meiji Japan (1868-1912)." *Premise* 4.1 (1997).

Kosaka Masaaki, ed. *Japanese Thought in the Meiji Era*. Trans. by David Abosch. Tokyo: Pan Pacific Press, 1958.

Kozaki Hiromichi. *Remembrances of 70 Years*. Tokyo: Kyobunkwan, 1933.

Lande, Aasulv. *Meiji Protestantism in History and Historiography*. Studia Missionalia Upsaliensia. Uppsala: Uppsala University, 1988.

Mullins, Mark R. *Christianity Made in Japan: A Study of Indigenous Movements*. Honolulu: University of Hawaii Press, 1998.

Okada Tetsuzo. *A Biography of Yoichi Honda*. Tokyo: 1918.

Scheiner, Irwin. *Christian Converts and Social Protest in Meiji Japan*, 83ff. Berkeley and Los Angeles: University of California Press, 1970.

Shinoda Kazuto. *Kumamoto bando kenkyu: Nihon Purotesutantizumu no ichi genryu to tenkai. Doshisha Daigaku Jinbun Kagaku Kenkyujo Kirisutokyo Shakai Mondai Kenkyukai hen.* Tokyo: Misuzu Shobo, 1965.

Thomas, Winburn T. *Protestant Beginnings in Japan: The First Three Decades 1859-1889.* Philadelphia: Presbyterian and Reformed Pub. Co., 1961. (1959).

Uchimura Kanzo. *How I Became a Christian: Out of My Diary.* In *Uchimura Kanzo Zenshu,* vol. 3. Tokyo: Iwanami Shoten, 1980-1984.

1.3.2. Niijima Jo (Joseph Hardy Neesima, 1843-1890)

Bred in the samurai domain of Annaka (Gumma prefecture), Niijima escaped to the USA in 1864 in quest of "social and moral transformation". Studying at Amherst and Andover, he discovered his mission as a Christian Educator, to teach "what is love of nation, benevolence for the people and the morals to allow oneself to be true to one's conscience". In response to this calling, he returned to Japan in 1874 to found a Christian school (later Doshisha University). Doshisha School of Theology was established in 1876.

Niijima saw hope for a broken social order only in the enlightenment that true education can bring. To cultivate the individual's moral sense was for him the key to Japan's social reformation and Christians are required to make society according to the rulings of conscience. The spiritual growth of the individual was in Niijima's thought inextricably linked with the growth of a reformed state, and both forms of growth were only possible through Christianity, in both prayer and social action. "[Those] who will be activists," he wrote later, "love truth and freedom, [and] respect morality and true principle ... [and] will devote themselves to our nation Japan. ... You must dare to take the responsibility of managing the world ... you must die for the sake of the world."

Selected References

Hardy, Arthur Sherburne. *Life and Letters of Joseph Hardy Neesima.* Kyoto: Doshisha University Press, 1980.

Otsuka Setsuji. *Niijima Jo shokanshu* (Selected letters of Niijima Jo). Tokyo: Showa 29.

Scheiner, Irwin. *Christian Converts and Social Protest in Meiji Japan*, chaps. 6 and 7. Berkeley and Los Angeles: University of California Press, 1970.

Watanabe Minoru. *Niijima Jo*. Tokyo: Yoshikawa Kohbundo, 1959.

Yahiko Ito. *Nobiyakani Kataru Niijima Jo to Meiji no Syosei*. Tokyo: Koyo Syobo, 1999.

1.3.3. Paul Sawayama (1852-1887), and Naruse Jinzo (d.1919)

Of the samurai class, and the first minister to be ordained in Japan, Sawayama was a pioneer of "self-supporting missions". Following study in Japan and America, he rejected dependence upon foreign leadership and finance, and "declared the necessity of spiritual freedom". The aim was to have a living Japanese church with its own independent growth and power expressed in every facet of its own religious life. He established a small independent church in Osaka where faith could freely and spontaneously grow of itself, living out his theology of selfhood, independence in poverty and self-sacrifice.

"The principle of self-support (*Kyokaihi-jik yu-ron*) is the one thing that is instrumental in making each believer mindful of the Lord's grace", he declared in his address to the 1883 Osaka Conference. "... if from the commencement people be urged to give money to the support of the work of God, ... Christians will look upon their churches as their own and will show great diligence in spreading the Gospel". The spirit of his thought and life can also be seen in, for example, his sermons and the verses for his dying wife, as well as in the continuance of his pioneer work for the education of women.

His work in this area was continued by his biographer, Naruse Jinzo who founded the Japan Women's College (1900), in succession to Sawayama's girls' high schools in Osaka and Niigata. Naruse studied abroad and became a pioneer in the field of higher education for women in Japan, and gained many friends among the foremost philosophers and educators of the world. He founded Japan Women's College as a non-sectarian institution, stressing independence and freedom of thought. Although he remained independent of institutional churches, Naruse advocated a life of faith, love and prayer and continued Sawayama's teaching of a life of self-support and independence in the spiritual life. Naruse summed this up as "faith penetrating the innermost depth (of soul); a life of mutual service, spontaneity and creativeness."

Selected References

> Anesaki Masaharu. *History of Japanese Religion: with Special Reference to the Social and Moral Life of the Nation*, 343f. Rutland, Vt.; Tokyo: Tuttle, 1963.
>
> Naruse Jinzo. *A Modern Paul in Japan: An Account of the Life and Work of the Rev. Paul Sawayama*. Tokyo: Keiseisha, 1893 (1910).
>
> Spae, Joseph J. *Christianity Encounters Japan*, 184f. Tokyo: Oriens Institute for Religious Research, 1968.
>
> Speer, Robert. *Studies in Missionary Leadership*. Philadelphia: Westminster Press, 1914.

1.3.4. Expatriate Scholars and Writers: 1

Amongst the many expatriates who produced historical or religious works during this period - almost all members of the Missions Etrangères de Paris - a number produced works that are significant for contextual Japanese theology. The following should be mentioned for writings which took seriously the particular context of Japanese Christianity, sought to present its key elements, or reflected theologically upon such a Christian witness.

Louis-Théodore Furet (1816-1900): "Relations," in *Annales de la Propagation de la Foi*. (Lyon: Chez l'éditeur des Annales, 1896); *Les Lies Lou-tech* (1859); and *Manuel de philosophy japonaise* (1858).

Pierre Mounicou (1825-1871): *Mythologie japonaise* (1863); *Autour de l'impénétrable Japon* (1856-1864); and *Seikyo Yori Mondo* (1865).

Eugène-Immanuel Mermet-Cachon (1828-1871): *Les Ainos, Origine Langue, Moeurs, Religion* (1863).

M.M. de Rotz (1840-1914): *Chie Ake no Michi* (On the way that leads to wisdom); and *Kofuku Kyodo* (A doctrine which leads to happiness). Nagasaki: 1877.

Bernard-Thadée Petitjean (1829-1884): Amongst many writings in which he preserves the terminology of the *Kakure Kirishitan*, are *Seikyo Shogaku Yori (1868); Rozario Kiriku* (1869); booklets on *Way of the Cross* (1873); *The Holy Passion* (1873); *Christian Calendar* (1874); and *Prayer Collections* (1872, 1876).

1.4 Pioneer Theologians
1.4.1. Kozaki Hiromichi (1856-1928)

Educated in Confucianism and a member, after long questioning, of the Kumamoto Band, Kozaki studied at Doshisha, succeeding Niijima as president there. He was later co-founder of the YMCA and chair of the National Christian Council of Japan. In all these callings, and although often aligned with both "liberal' and "non-liberal" colleagues, Kozaki took an independent, though devotedly Christian, approach. For him, Doshisha was not a school for the purposes of (western) missionaries but one for the moulding of ordinary Japanese citizens.

As with his mentor, Capt L.L. Janes, Kozaki's approach to the Bible was critical and historical, rejecting verbal infallibility, but affirming its central testimony to Jesus Christ. Accepting the "logic of evolution" he applied this to the immanence of God in creation and to the doctrine of the Holy Spirit. He believed that statements of belief, or church polity, must be of the simplest form, and firmly advocated an independent and self-supporting church. He also accepted many socialist principles and strongly opposed the invasion of Formosa (1874), worship of the Emperor and the Imperial Rescript on Education (1890). The real import of Confucianism, through which he had come to Christianity, he believed, was extended and fulfilled in the Gospel teaching of salvation, and the universal and egalitarian Kingdom of God. In all these areas Kozaki often firmly opposed the policies of overseas missionaries, and sometimes also those of his Japanese colleagues. Yet during half a century he was a central figure in many pioneer Christian initiatives, and in many religious and political movements.

Many of his writings are found in *Rikugo Zasshi* (Cosmos); later *Kirisutokyo Sekai* (Christian World), of which he was a founder (1886); in *Fukuin Shimpo* (Gospel News, formerly *Shichi ichi Zappo*), edited by Kozaki Hiromichi, Uemura and Ukita Kazutami; in *Shinseiki* (New Century - later incorporated in *Seinen*, Young

Men); and in *Kirisutokyo Shimbun* (Christian News, later *Tokyo Weekly Record*). In addition he published 12 volumes on subjects which included central Christian beliefs, political and religious studies. In all his writing and teaching, as well as in evangelistic tours, Kozaki argues for a "fuller" Christianity, centred in Jesus Christ, yet committed to social and political concern and sympathetic to other faiths.

Selected References
Works by Kozaki Hiromichi
>*Seikyo Shinron* (New essays on politics and religion). Tokyo: Keiseisha, 1886.
>*Kirisutokyo no Honshitsu* (The essence of Christianity). Tokyo: 1911.
>*Kirisutokyo to Waga Kokutai* (Christianity and the Constitution). Tokyo: 1911.
>*Reminiscences of Seventy Years*. Tokyo: Kyo Bun Kwan, 1933 (1926).
>Dohi Akio. "The First Generation: Christian Leaders in the First Period." In *A History of Japanese Theology*, edited by Yasuo Furuya. Grand Rapids: Eerdmans, 1997.
>Moore, George Eagleton. *Kozaki Hiromichi and the Kumamoto Band: a Study in Samurai Reaction to the West*. Ann Arbor: Michigan University, Microfilms International, 1985, (c1967).

1.4.2. Uemura Masahisa (1861-1925)
Son of a feudal vassal of the shogunate, Uemura accepted Christianity while studying at a mission school in Yokohama, "stormed by the wonderful faith in the one, true God". He later worked closely with Kozaki and Uchimura in education, the YMCA and in publishing ventures, became a dominant leader in the *Kirisuto Kyokai* (Church of Christ in Japan), edited *Nippon Hyoron* and founded Tokyo Theological Seminary in a corner of his church building (1904). He also assisted in the translation of the New Testament, wrote vigorous apologetics and influenced generations of scholars of the Reformed tradition.

Uemura knew in Bushido a commitment to social justice and human dignity, but now found this enriched and purified by Christianity. He accepted the findings of biblical criticism and comparative religious study, but came to affirm - over against more "liberal" colleagues like Ebina and Kanamori - the deity, Saviourhood and immanence of Christ, and the divine origin of Christian revelation in the Bible and in Christian history. He wished to assert that Christianity is an "absolute religion", unchangeable in its central beliefs, and needing no dialogue with other faiths. Regarding social concerns, he was critical of many Christian involvements in social reform and avoided any overt stand on national issues. On these he advocated that Christians as Japanese should comply with the formal obligations of citizenship but at the same time "... believe in the obligation to God". In the life of the church and its faith, Japanese could find an ethical alternative to state and family. His major books and articles therefore concentrated upon matters of faith and church policy, and drew largely upon western writings in doing this. Nevertheless he agreed with Kozaki that Christianity provided the basis for social order, and for work for social justice. He defended resistance to the emperor and the Meiji government, and found in conscience - "the image of God" - the power to recognise "justice ... and know goodness" and the source of social, as well as of moral, values. He was also remarkable in his unique respect and advocacy for women and their concerns, both in personal and public life.

Selected References
Works by Uemura Masahisa
> *Uemura chosaku* (Selected writings of Uemura). 8 vols. Tokyo: Kyo Bun Kwan, 1955. Includes *Shinri Ippan* (The outline of truth, 1884) and *Fukuin no Michishirube* (A guidepost to the Gospel, 1885).
> Aoyoshi Katsuhisa. *Uemura Masahisa den*. Tokyo: Kyobunkan, 1935.
> Furuya Yasuo, ed. *A History of Japanese Theology*. Grand Rapids: Eerdmans, 1997.
> Germany, Charles H. *Protestant Theologies in Modern Japan: A History of Dominant Theological Currents from 1920-1960.* Tokyo: IISR Press, 1965.
> Sawa Wataru and Ozawa Saburo. *Uemura Masahisa to sono jidai* (Masahisa Uemura and his age). 7 vols. Tokyo: Kyo Bun Kwan, 1966-1967.

Scheiner, Irwin. *Christian Converts and Social Protest in Meiji Japan.* Berkeley and Los Angeles: University of California Press, 1970.

1.4.3. Uchimura Kanzo (1861-1930)

Like Uemura, Uchimura was also shaped by Confucian morality and Bushido, being the son of an Edo warrior. Studying at Sapporo Agricultural School he came to see "his life's work as explaining the relation between Christian theism and the doctrine of evolution" (Dohi 1997: 18). Following study, and work overseas, he worked in Japan first as a journalist and then as an independent evangelist. His deep commitment to follow Christ, as a Japanese, led to the formation of congregations which eventually he named *Mu kyokai* (non-church). This was not to reject the Christian concept of church, but from his desire to recover the essential nature of the church, freed of institutional structures, in a form indigenous to Japan; a "brotherly community like a family".

Here Uchimura believed, would grow a truly Japanese Christianity. Such a Christianity would be grafted onto Bushido and the deeply religious nature of the Japanese, would be centred upon faith rather than "church", and would be nondenominational, free from the domination of missionary or institution. For him sacraments, clergy, or special buildings are not essential, but may be means of receiving faith, hope and love. The Non-Church has all of nature for its church, and God is its preacher in the Bible faithfully studied. The Christian faith arose in Asia, and for Uchimura, it had special affinities with the Japanese race; in respect for nature, in community fellowship and in the spirituality of their indigenous religions. His Mu kyokai has maintained its life throughout the 20th century, notably in costly witness against militarism, in lay leadership and in social witness. His many writings first appeared in magazines such as *The Study of the Bible* (his own monthly), *Seisho no kenkyu*, *Kokumin no Tomo*, *Yorozu choho* and the *Japan Christian Intelligencer*. The full body of his writings was published in 40 volumes in 1984. Later Non-Church theologians included Tsukamoto Toraji and Kurosaki Kokichi.

Selected References

Works by Uchimura Kanzo

Uchimura Kanzo Zenshu (The Complete works of Kanzo Uchimura). 40 vols. Tokyo: Iwanomi Shoten, 1980-1984.

How I Became a Christian: Out of My Diary. In *Uchimura Kanzo Zenshu,* vol. 3. Tokyo: Iwanami Shoten, 1980-1984.

Chung Jun Ki. *Social criticism of Uchimura Kanzo and Kim Kyoshin.* Seoul: UBF Press, 1988.

Dohi Akio. "The First Generation: Christian Leaders in the First Period." In *A History of Japanese Theology*, edited by Yasuo Furuya. Grand Rapids: Eerdmans, 1997.

Jennings, R.P. *Jesus, Japan and Kanzo Uchimura.* Tokyo: Kyo Bun Kwan, 1958.

Kawashima Masayoshi. *Uchimura Kanzo and Non churchism.* Ann Arbor, Mich.: University Microfilms International, 1978.

Kimura-Andres, Hannelore. *Mukyokai: Fortsetzung der Evangeliumsgeschichte.* Erlanger Monographien aus Mission und Okumene. Erlangen: Verlag der Ev.-Luth. Mission, c1984.

Masaike Hitoshi. *Uchimura Kanzo Den* (The life of Kanzo Uchimura). Tokyo: Kyobunkwan, 1977.

Miura Hiroshi. *The Life and Thought of Kanzo Uchimura.* Grand Rapids: Eerdmans, 1996.

1.4.4. Ebina Danjo (1866-1937)

Ebina came from a samurai family in Kyushu and, like Kozaki, studied in the Kumamoto Western School there under Leroy Lansing Janes. A Confucian and nationalist upbringing gave him a strong sense of independence which was enhanced by his own religious experience. Studying further at Doshisha School, he came to describe the Christian's relationship to God as *Fushi Ushin* (ethic of father-son relationship), closely analogous to Confucian moral precepts. This was the basis of his "theology of experience" which also sought to integrate the insights both of Japan's own religious traditions and of modern science. He held influential pastorates in Gumma Prefecture, in Tokyo, Kumamoto and Kyoto; was chancellor of Doshisha University and undertook preaching tours in Manchuria and Korea.

Although he never wrote a systematic statement of his theology, his teachings on the Trinity, the Incarnation and the Atonement aroused great interest and controversy and are perhaps his most distinctive contributions. Questioning the Greek thought-forms traditionally used in Trinitarian doctrine, Ebina saw Jesus of Nazareth, rather than being himself God, as participating in a full ethical and loving union with God but also sharing in heightened degree the nature of God possessed by all humanity. However, "I believe in the divinity of Christ," he said, "... and I also believe the doctrine of the Trinity contains profound religious truth". Regarding sin and forgiveness, "only the life and death of Christ are unlimited in effective power. Possessing fullest love and holiness and for the purpose of the fullest holiness for all mankind, in the fullness of time he shed his blood. This alone has supreme inspirational power." Although not affirming that God became man in Jesus, he could write that "He is man towards God and God towards man (sic.)". His disciple Imanaka believed that in relating the Christian teaching to the real social and religious world of Japan, Ebina had "developed the gospel to a position of cultural significance". He would have continuing significance for many later theologians.

Selected References
Works by Ebina Danjo
> Articles in *Shinjin* (New Man), *Rikugo Zasshi* (Cosmos) and *Kirisutokyo Kenkyu*.
> *Kirisutokyo Shinron* (A new theory of Christianity). Tokyo: 1918.
> *Kirisutokyo Daikan* (A comprehensive view of Christianity). Tokyo: 1930.
> Furuya Yasuo, ed. *A History of Japanese Theology*. Grand Rapids: Eerdmans, 1997.
> Germany, Charles H. *Protestant Theologies in Modern Japan: A History of Dominant Theological Currents from 1920-1960*. Tokyo: IISR Press, 1965.
> Tsunekichi Watase. *Ebina Danjo Sensei*. Tokyo: Ryugin Sha, 1938.
> Otsuka Setsuji. "Ebina Danjo Sensei to Shokuzairon." *Kirisutokyo Ningengaku*. Tokyo: Zenkoku Shobo, 1948.

1.4.5. Iwashita Soichi (1889-1940)
Following studies in Tokyo, Louvain, Oxford and Rome, Iwashita was ordained priest in 1925, and returned, not to teaching or parish ministry, but to direct a leper hospital, where he remained until his

death. He also founded the Tokyo Catholic student center, Veritas Vita House, in the 1930s (later re-organised by Sawada Kazuo). However, he continued vigorous and wide-ranging studies and writing throughout his life, not only in medieval Catholic history which he had early studied, but also in Luther studies and in modern thought. He was influenced in these by von Koeber, von Hugel and others.

His particular theological concern was to demonstrate, both in theology and in practice, "the vital truth of Christ within the historical reality of the religious life" (Sato Toshio, 1997). For him, the vital historical traditions of Catholic theology were to be now renewed and also embodied in the vocation and lifestyle of believers, and especially 'theologians'. His dedicated work in the leper hospital, blended with a life of prayer, academic study and writing, itself mirrored this vision and had therefore a wide impact on the thought and outreach of the Catholic Church in Japan. This would be furthered by disciples such as Yoshimitsu Yoshihiko (1.4.6.).

Selected References
Works by Iwashita Soichi

> *Chusei Shicho* (Medieval current of thought). Tokyo: Chuo Shuppansha, 1928. Reprinted in 1962.
> *Shin Sukora Tetsugaku* (Neo-Scholastic philosophy). Tokyo: Iwanami Shoten, 1932.
> *Kami no Kuni* (City of God). Tokyo: Iwanami Shoten, 1935.
> *Shinko no Isan* (The deposit of faith). Tokyo: Iwanami Shoten, 1941.
> *Iwashita Soichi Zenshu* (Collected works). 9 vols. Tokyo: Chuo Shuppansha. Vols. 1-3: Introduction of Theology (*Shingaku nyumon*), 1961; Vol. 4: Legacy of Faith (*Shinko no isan*), 1962; Vol. 5: Studies on Fathers (*Kyofu kenkyu*), 1962; Vol. 6: Thought of the Middle Ages (*Chusei shiso*), 1962; Vol. 7: Articles on Philosophy (*Tetsugaku ronshu*), 1962; Vol. 8: The History of Struggling with the Relief of Leprosy for 50 Years (*Kyurai 50 nen kutoushi*), 1962; Vol. 9: Kobayashi Yoshio Life Story of Fr. Iwashita (*Iwashita shinpu no shogai*), 1961.

Ikkan Senshu (Addresses, essays, lectures). Tokyo: Iwanami Shoten, n.d.

Kobayashi Yoshio gives an appreciation of Iwashita Soichi's theological work in *Nihon no Shingaku* I, 1962.

Sato Toshio. "The Second Generation." In *A History of Japanese Theology*, edited by Yasuo Furuya. Grand Rapids: Eerdmans, 1997.

1.4.6. Yoshimitsu Yoshihiko (1904-1945)

After studies in Japan, in which he was greatly influenced by Iwashita Soichi, and France, where he studied under Jacques Maritain, Yoshimitsu taught at Sophia University and at the Catholic Seminary in Tokyo. His wife died not long after their marriage, and he himself died after only ten years lecturing in ethics at Tokyo Imperial University. He had been, however, a leader in the Catholic student movement, and a close collaborator with Iwashita in Catholic intellectual life. In his writing he explored neo-Thomist answers to what he saw as the crisis of modern thought in Japan and Europe, studying the work of Pascal, Kierkegaard, Nietzche, Newman, Dostoevsky and Péguy.

Yoshimitsu also accepted and worked for Iwashita's ideal of the union of a renewed Catholic theology with a lifestyle which would demonstrate this. He was therefore deeply concerned for a union of spirituality, ethics and culture. He is chiefly remembered for his writings on the relationship of culture to religion, on cultural ethics, and on poetry and philosophy.

Selected References
Works by Yoshimitsu Yoshihiko

The Basic Problems of Cultural Ethics (Bunka rinri no konponmondai). Tokyo: Misuzushobo, 1936.

The God of the Philosopher (Tetsugakusha no kami). Tokyo: Misuzushobo 1947.

The Idea of Culture and Religion (Bunka to shukyo no rinen). Tokyo: Kodansha, 1947.

Mysticism and the Modern Age (Shinpishugi to gendai). Tokyo: Misuzushobo, 1952.

Poetry and Love and Existence (Shi to ai to jitsuzon). Tokyo: Kadokawashoten, 1940; Kodansha 1985.

A Study of History of Modern Philosophy (Kinsei tetsugakushi kenkyu). Tokyo: Kodansha, 1949.

1.5 Theology of Independent Scholars and Writers

See also: Kimura Takataro, 1870-1931. *Yasokyo konin kahiron* (Christianity, religion and culture). Tokyo: Shoeido Shoten, 1899.

Murao Moses Shoichi and W. H. Murray Walton. *Japan and Christ: a Study in Religious Issues*. London: Church Missionary Society, 1928.

Fujii Takeshi. *Seisho yori mitaru Nihon* (Japan as seen from a biblical point of view). Tokyo: Iwanami Shoten, Showa 4 [1929].

Hino Masumi. *Izaya Kogi* (Lecture on Isaiah). Osaka: Kirisutokyo Sekaisha; Tokyo: Keiseisha Shoten, 1908.

—. *Kirisutokyo no Konpongi* (The basic justice of Christianity). Tokyo: Daito Shuppansha, 1933.

And works by such writers as Miura Toru, Chiba Yuguro, Matsumoto Takuo, Shirato Hachiro, Ibuka Kajinosuke, and Kanamori Tsurin.

1.5.1. Arai Osui (1846-1922)

Of samurai family, Arai was first a student of Fr (later Bishop) Nicolai (1861-1912), the founder of Russian Orthodox communities in Japan, and his assistant Sawabe. With colleagues of the Sendai clan, Arai saw in Christianity the means of building a united and reformed society "for the good of their country". He later studied in America (1870-1875) and for 24 years shared the study, labor and worship of the Fountaingrove community at Santa Rosa (CA). Back in Japan, he established an informal house of study in Sugamo, Tokyo, maintaining a simple lifestyle as teacher and writer.

Arai's many writings were assembled and compiled by Nagashima Tadashige (1871-1938) who found in Arai's message "the unalloyed teachings of Christ". In these Arai meditates upon - amongst other subjects - the self-knowledge that leads to self-renunciation and "re-evolution"; on "true education" for man and woman through which the "one family" of the "one whole man" emerges; and on "integral sincerity" by which we attain the "human-divine nature" of the "most gracious and merciful Mother-Father,

Lord-Lady, Savior-Savioress ...". In such language Arai pictures the One, all-embracing Saviour of all - Christus/Christa - who transforms us by His/Her Spirit. This is the twain-in-one who is known in Christ as worker, restorer of right and rebuilder of the universe. His thought therefore anticipated many later developments.

In Arai's thought insights are brought together from mystical theology of the Eastern Church, from Confucianism, communitarian socialism and Methodist evangelicalism. In meditations sometimes resembling Sufi utterances, Arai affirms that "to serve humanity is to serve God ... loving the Lord-Lady in them ... inbrothering and insistering" all people; such a Christianity being the goal of all doctrines, all quests.

Selected References
Works by Arai Osui
> A full collection of Arai's works are held at Waseda University, Tokyo (17 vols. in Japanese).
> *Inward Prayer and Fragments*. (1893-1896). Kyoto: Horii Printing House, 1941.
> Cary, Otis. *A History of Christianity in Japan: Roman Catholic, Greek Orthodox, and Protestant Missions*, I, 384ff. Two volumes in one. Rutland, Vt.; Tokyo: Tuttle, 1976.
> Ericson, Jack T., ed. *Thomas Lake Harris and the Brotherhood of the New Life: Books, Pamphlets, Serials and Manuscripts 1854-1942. A Guide to the Microfilm Collection*. Ann Arbor MI: UMI, n.d.
> cf. Miyazaki Toranosuke. *My New Gospel*. Translated by Takahashi Goro. Tokyo: New Gospel Society, 1908.

1.5.2. Yokoi Tokio (1857-1937)

A member of the Kumamoto Band, a pastor and journalist, Yokoi was a regular contributor to *Rikugo Zasshi* and active - with Honda, Uemura, Uchimura, Onishi Hajime and Takahashi Goro - in the debate concerning education and religion following the Imperial Rescript on Education (1890s). Yokoi shared the concerns of those studying liberal theology and western philosophy - including Ebina Danjo, Onishi Hajime, and Kanamori Tsurin - to develop a theology and forms of church life which would be fully Japanese, and also closer to the original apostolic faith. "We should believe in Christianity as Japanese", he wrote in *Rikugo Zasshi* in 1890, "study theology as Japanese, and propagate Christianity as Japanese."

Christianity, he believed, should stand on the indigenous traditions of a (reformed) Confucianism and Buddhism, inheriting and fulfilling their best elements, yet "the teachings of the church must be the teachings of Christ himself", who is "the manifestation of God". This would involve "both an assimilation of national traditions and a rejection of the evil elements in religious practice and traditional theology" (Thelle, 1987: 179), along with the construction of a new theology; concerns he shared in the first Buddhist-Christian Conference (1896). (The scholar of religion, Kishimoto Nobuta (1866-1928) later advocated a similar relationship between living religions.)

One of the most prominent pastors in this period, Yokoi retained a close relationship with those like Uemura and Uchimura who shared few of his more liberal views. His last book repudiated traditional Christian orthodoxy, and later he worked outside the institutional church. His writings however were central to the "new theology" movement and have had continuing influence.

Selected References
Works by Yokoi Tokio

    Kirisutokro shinron (A new treatise on Christianity). Tokyo: Keiseisha, 1891.

    Christianity - What is it? A question in the Far East. Yokohama: Japan Mail Office, 1893.

    Waga kuni no Kirisutokyo mondai (The problem of Christianity in our country). Tokyo: Keiseisha, 1994.

    Lande, Aasulv. *Meiji Protestantism in History and Historiography.* Studia Missionalia Upsaliensia. Uppsala: Uppsala University, 1988.

    Thelle, Notto R. *Buddhism and Christianity in Japan: From Conflict to Dialogue, 1854-1899.* Honolulu: University of Hawaii Press, 1987.

1.5.3. Nitobe Inazo (1862-1933)

Nitobe was a member of the Sapporo Band, a prolific writer, educator, and honorary president of Tokyo Women's Christian College. He concluded his diplomatic career as under-secretary general to the League of Nations. Nitobe wrote extensively upon Japanese character and society, and upon issues of national development and international relations.

Deeply Christian, Nitobe held with Ebina, Kozaki, Uemura, Yokoi and others that Japan's indigenous religious and ethical traditions provided preparation and insight for the Christian faith in Japan. He described Christianity as the fulfilment of Bushido spirituality, which in comparison is only "a dimly-burning wick". Nevertheless it provides a persisting social ethic and, along with the best of other religious faiths, could be seen as a second "old testament". He has been sometimes criticised as idealising the traditions of Bushido, but a wholly contextualised assessment is yet to be made of his work. His influence in education (Christian and 'secular'), in cultural studies, and even upon Buddhist socialist leaders has been considerable (See 1.6).

Selected References
Works by Nitobe Inazo
> *Bushido - The Soul of Japan.* New York: Putnam, 1905.
> *Lectures on Japan: an Outline of the Development of the Japanese People and Culture.* Tokyo: Kenkyusha, 1936.
> *The Complete Works.* 23 vols. Tokyo: Kyo Bun Kwan, 1994. (Vols. 12-16, 23 in English).
> *Japan's Bridge Across the Pacific,* edited by John F. Howes. Boulder: Westview Press, 1995.
> Kitasawa Sukeo. *The Life of Dr. Nitobe.* Tokyo: Hokuseido Press, 1953.
> Okakura Kakuzo. *Japan's Innate Virility: Selections from Okakura and Nitobe.* Tokyo: Hokuseido Press, ?1943.
> Uchikawa Eiichiro. *Nitobe Inazo: the Twilight Years.* Tokyo: Kyo Bun Kwan, 1985.

1.5.4. Iha Fuyu (1876-1947)
Iha was a noted folklorist, literary scholar and linguist, historian and librarian, as well as being an ardent Okinawan and a Christian.

Following studies at Kyoto and Tokyo Imperial University, he returned to Okinawa to research and collect Okinawan literature and archives. He was active in temperance and socialist movements and in the education of Okinawan youth, lectured on history, literature and eugenics, and worked with Henry B. Schwartz in the translation of Christian materials.

In books and articles Iha supported the revival of Okinawan culture and history, and of Okinawan identity and self-confidence. Along with his colleague Higa Shuncho, he was strongly influenced by study of Tolstoy, and both came to be critical of conservative practices in the churches. Using the Ryukyu dialect (despite official disapproval) Iha initiated a range of educational programmes in order to develop for Okinawans individual character and social responsibility through Bible teaching, use of world literature, Okinawan cultural resources, and later, through Marxist-socialism.

Selected References
Works by Iha Fuyu

 Ko Ryukyu no seiji (On the Ryukyu Islands). Tokyo: Kenkyusha, 1922.
 Ryukyu bungaku (Ryukyuan literature). Tokyo: Iwanami Shoten, 1931.
 Ryukyu no hogen (Ryukyuan language). Tokyo: Meiji Shoin, 1933.
 KoRyukyu (Ancient Ryukyu). Rev. ed. Naha: Ryukyu Shinpo, 1965.
 Iha Fuyu Centennial Committee. *Iha Fuyu 1876-1947*. Naha: Kyobundo, 1976.
 Bollinger, Edward E. *The Cross and the Floating Dragon: The Gospel in Ryukyu*. Pasadena: William Carey Library, 1983.
 Higa Seijin. Okinawa Kiristokyo Shiryo (Okinawan Christian historical materials). Tokyo: Word of Life Press, 1972.
 Higa Shuncho. Higa Shuncho Zenshu (Complete works of Higa Shuncho). 4 vols. Naha: Okinawa Times, 1971.
 Schwartz, Henry B. *The Loo Choo Islands: A Chapter of Missionary History*. Nagasaki: Nagasaki Press Office, ?1910.

1.6 Buddhist-Christian Studies 1

 Compare also Ebina Danjo (1.4.4.), Nitobe Inazo (1.5.3.), Yokoi Tokio (1.5.2.), Arai Osui (1.5.1.); and also

2.4. (below). Amongst others working on Buddhist-Christian relations before 1900, were Matsumura Kaiseki, Togawa Yasuie, Hoshino Tenchi, Sajo Jitsunen and Kishimoto Nobuta. (For these see Thelle, Notto R. *Buddhism and Christianity in Japan: From Conflict to Dialogue, 1854-1899*. Honolulu: University of Hawaii Press, 1987.)

1.6.1. Takahashi Goro (1856-1935)

Born into a samurai family in Niigata, Takahashi studied at Yokohama and met Uemura there. He was a talented linguist and co-operated in the translation of the Japanese Bible. His particular study, however, was Buddhism and he became "the leading Christian expert on Buddhism in the 1880s". In *Rikugo Zasshi* and *Nihon Hroron*, the writings of prominent Christians like Ibuka Kajinosuke, Hiraiwa Yoshiyasu, Uemura Masahisa and Kozaki Hiromichi also showed a deep concern for Buddhism.

Takahashi himself took most seriously the contrast between Christian "monotheism" and Buddhist "atheism" and at the 1896 Buddhist-Christian Conference argued against "compromise". Many articles appeared in *Rikugo Zasshi* over his name, and he then published four volumes on Japanese religion. These had an apologetic purpose, and while he remained largely negative in his judgments of Buddhism, he nevertheless argued for an unbiased search for truth in all religious study. "Leave prejudice", he wrote in *Rikugo Zasshi*, "forget the conventional criticism, open your minds and empty your hearts and consider thoroughly what I have written about Buddhism ... and make your own impartial judgement."

Selected References
Works by Takahashi Goro

> *Bukkyo Shinkai* (New interpretation of Buddhism). Tokyo: 1883.
> *Hai gitetsugakuron* (Refutation of the false philosophy). Tokyo: Minyusha, 1893.
> *Sekai sanseiron* (The three sages of the world). Tokyo: Bun'eikaku, 1903.
> Thelle, Notto R. *Buddhism and Christianity in Japan: From Conflict to Dialogue, 1854-1899*. Honolulu: University of Hawaii Press, 1987.

Shinoura Takanori. "Relation between Philosophy (Science) and Religion (Christianity) as Discussed in Early Meiji Periods - With Special Respect to Takahashi Goro's *Religion and Philosophy*." Thesis. Tokyo: International Christian University, 1990.

1.6.2. Aimé Villion mep (1843-1932)

Villion came to Japan in 1868, working there until his death in 1932. He dedicated himself to the study of Buddhism, preferring to rely directly upon Japanese Buddhist scholars for instruction, rather than using western texts. Over many years he studied in particular at the centres of the Jodo, Hosso, Shingon and Shin-shu sects.

Although describing Buddhism as "a magnificent pantheism", and regarding the Mahayana as a "deformation" resulting from Nestorian influence, he found in Shin Buddhism profound and devout religious qualities, characterising it as a "Protestant Buddhism". He also noted close outward similarities between Shin Buddhism and Catholic practices. Villion was a prolific author and his many articles and treatises appeared in *Missions Catholique* and *Bulletin des Missions-Etrangères de Paris*. He also co-operated closely with Buddhist scholars in Tokyo in preparing a major work on Japanese Buddhism. Volumes include historical and religious works, including a 13-volume work on Buddhism.

By comparison, in the same period, the Roman Catholic magazine *Koe* (Voice) was almost entirely polemical and didactic in its response to "the influence of heretics". This was, however, itself in contrast to the later skilled writing of for example, Sauveur Candeau mep, director from 1931 of the Catholic Bureau of Publication. He maintained a genial and winsome apologetic with those of other beliefs, in publications and through a daily column in metropolitan newspapers.

Selected References

Works by Aimé Villion

    Shinkyo no mezamashi (Awakening of Protestantism). Kyoto: 1887.
    Baramon kyoron (Study of Brahmanism). Kyoto: 1889.

Cinquante ans d'Apostolat au Japon. Hong Kong: Société des Missions-Etrangères, 1923.
Pourquoi j'aime les Japonais? Louvain: 1929.
Le Bouddhisme au Japon. 13 vols. MSS. Tokyo: Oriens Institute, c.1930.
Caneau, Sauver. "Apostolate among the Japanese Intellectuals." *Japan Missionary Bulletin* 18.4-5 (1964).
Thelle, Notto R. *Buddhism and Christianity in Japan: From Conflict to Dialogue, 1854-1899.* Honolulu: University of Hawaii Press, 1987.
Verwilgen, Albert Felix. "The Buddhist Studies of Father A. Villion". *Japan Missionary Bulletin* 25 (1971).

1.7 Christianity, Society and Nationalism
1.7.1. Theologians, Writers and Social Reform

Widespread debate of religious and social issues in the 1870s and 1880s arose from the encounter of Christian, Confucian and Buddhist thought, the close association of Christianity with the processes of modernisation, the foundation of Christian schools and colleges directed to social witness, and the social teaching of western missionaries. There was also a rapid growth of periodicals - many of them Christian, such as *Rikugo Zasshi* - devoted to such issues. In the 1880s, public debates on a wide range of religious, scientific and patriotic questions were organised by the newly formed YMCA, led by Kozaki, Uemura and Kanda.

By 1896, many informal encounters between Buddhists and Christians resulted in the first Buddhist-Christian Conference, held in Tokyo, where central concerns included those of national morality and religious unification for the renewal of the nation (Thelle 1987: 225ff). Confucian scholars also gathered to discuss issues of national reform and morality, and Confucian teachings on the state were critically utilised by Ebina, Kozaki, Uemura, Nakamura Masanao and Motoda Sakunoshin in their writings. In this period also the pioneer Christian pacifist Kitamura Tokoku (1868-1894) wrote in essays, poetry, novels and plays on themes of peace, individual freedom, the inner life and universalism, "exploring seriously the nature and the possibilities of the self". He saw no conflict between Christianity and Buddhism, utilising Buddhist terminology and ideas and rejecting much western influence. Yet he affirmed that Christ alone was the true life of the believer and that "love resides at the core of human existence".

In the Taisho period also, Yoshino Sakuzo and Imanaka Tsugumaru proposed in their writings and teaching, political measures based on Christian principles. Socialists and dissenters, whether Christian or of other faiths, were deeply critical of the Japanese social system, and for many Christian converts it was the promise of Christian social ethics for a society in renewal which proved a powerful attraction. Younger Christian Socialists at this time, who were pacifist also, included Abe Iso (1865-1949), Kinoshita Naoe (1869-1937), and Sakai Toshihiko (1871-1933). Katayama Sen was a pioneer socialist and labor organiser, later moving outside the institutional Church and Togawa Zanka (d.1924) was both Christian activist and writer. Yanaihara Tadao, whose criticism of government policy led to his dismissal from Tokyo Imperial University in 1936, was, however critical of both Marxist theory and institutionalised Christianity in his writings. In a more activist and evangelical vein, Yamamuro Gumpei wrote out of experience in his prominent work to liberate women from prostitution and in order to expound the Christian message for those of limited education. "Social work" was, however, pictured by him as primarily a means to evangelism.

Abe, a Unitarian and professor at Waseda University with a fuller theology of society, gave sustained commitment to movements for social reform, was instrumental in organising a Society for forming labour unions, and the Association for the Study of Socialism, and later assisted Suzuki Bunji in the Friendly Aid Association, Tokyo, from 1912. Kinoshita was a journalist and novelist highly critical of social injustice and militarism, and with Ishikawa Sanshiro, edited *Shin Kigen* (1905-). Sakai worked with Uchimura and Kotoku Shusui (1871-1911) on the newspaper *Yorozu choho*, later publishing the paper *Heimin Shimbun* and *Kyosanto Sengen* (the Communist Manifesto). Studies, discussions and programmes of social action were initiated at Doshisha University through the leadership of Otsuka Setsuji (see 1.10.5.), Nakajima

Shigeru (see 1.10.3.), Kagawa Toyohiko (see 1.10.2.), and Takenaka Katsuo.

Of those above named, the most extensive writings which include contextual reflection are those extant for Abe Iso, Kitamura Tokoku, Katayama Sen, Yamamuro Gumpei and Yanaihara Tadao. See Selected References below, also 1.7.2. and 2.3, and entries for Kan Enkichi (1.10.4.) and Sumiya Mikio (2.5.7.).

Women like Yajima Kajiko, Miura Riu and Hattori Chiyo were also active in social reform, and in the formation of the *Fujin Kyofukai* (Women's Christian Temperance Union (1886). (See also 1.8 below.)

Selected References

Abe Iso. *Riso no hito* (The ideal man). Tokyo: Meiji 39.
—. *Shakaishugisha to noru made* (Until I became a socialist). Tokyo: Showa 7.
Bamba Nobuya, and John F. Howes, eds. *Pacifism in Japan: The Christian and Socialist Tradition*. Vancouver: University of British Columbia Press, 1978.
Dohi Akio. "Christianity and Politics in the Taisho Period of Democracy." *Japanese Religions* 5.4 (1969); 7.3 (1972).
Hane Mikiso. *Peasants, Rebels, & Outcasts: The Underside of Modern Japan*. New York: Pantheon, 1982.
Iwata Tokuji. *Shakai Kairyo ron* (An essay on social reform). Tokyo: 1988.
Kitamura Tokoku. *Tokoku Zenshu* (Complete works of Kitamura Tokoku). Tokyo: Iwanami Shoten, 1970.
Scheiner, Irwin. *Christian Converts and Social Protest in Meiji Japan*. Berkeley and Los Angeles: University of California Press, 1970.
Katayama Sen. *The Labour Movement in Japan*. Chicago: Charles H. Kerr & Co., 1918.
Sumiya Etsuji. "Kirisutokyoto no shakai kairyo to jissen" (The thinking and practice of Christian social reformers). *Doshisha University Economic Review* 7.6 (1958).
Takenaka Masao. *Reconciliation and Renewal in Japan*, chap. 3. New York: Friendship Press, 1957 (1967).
Williams, M. "Meiji Intellectuals and the Spirituality of the West." *Japan Christian Quarterly* 54.4 (1988).

Yamaji Aizan. *Essays on the Modern Japanese Church: Christianity in Meiji Japan.* Ann Arbor: University of Michigan, 1906 (1999).

Yamamuro Gumpei. *Heimin no Fukuin.* Tokyo: Kyuseigun Shuppan Kyokyubu, 1954. See also *Japan Christian Quarterly* 29.4 (1962).

1.7.2. Ecumenical Movements and Writings

By the turn of the century many initiatives for Christian collaboration were reaching fruition, in literature production, relief work, social concern and study. The YMCA had been founded in 1880, and commenced publication of *Rikugo Zasshi* (The Cosmos Magazine) reflecting many levels of theology for church and society (See 1.7.1 above). In the 1920s the YMCA's *Kaitakusha* (The Pioneer) would play a similar role. The *Japan Christian Yearbook* began regular publication on issues of common concern to the Churches in 1903 and would continue until 1942 (resumed later), including a wide range of articles and surveys on education, evangelism, social concerns and theology.

The *Nihon Kirisuto Kyokai Domei* (Japan Federation of Christian Churches) had been formed in 1911, becoming the National Christian Council in 1922, later to be re-organised in 1948. Along with fostering inter-church co-operation, the *Domei* also monitored social and political concerns, and published statements such as that in 1920 which was a *Manifesto* on current issues that included the alleged torture of Korean prisoners as well as conditions of labour for all unskilled workers. Exhaustive preparatory studies for the Jerusalem Conference of the International Missionary Council (1928) were also prepared by the NCC. Staff of the YMCA, like Kenji Nakahara and Kakehi Mitsuaki, and professors such as Kan Enkichi (1.10.4.) Sugiyama Kenji and Nakajima Shigeru (1.10.3.), led in the formation of the *Nihon Gakusai Kirisutokyo Undo* (SCM), and in the formulation of an emerging social theology.

From the work of Kagawa Toyohiko (1.10.2.) in Kobe slums, and with his colleagues in movements such as the Japan Peasants' Union (1922) and the Kingdom of God Movement, would come a series of volumes by Kagawa and others developing a theology

Contextual Theology in Japan

which was both missional and socio-theological. The YWCA and WCTU were active in programmes of education and advocacy for women in particular, and the WCTU published a *Social Creed* (1928) which covered the issues of labour, family life, co-operatives, armaments and women's concerns (See 1.8 below). The NCC Commission on Christian Education, which also fostered publication, was formed in 1931, and reflective articles by some YMCA leaders like Saito Soichi (b.1886) were published in, for example, the *International Review of Mission*.

A number of Christians were active in groups working for reconciliation and peace in the 1930s and 1940s, some becoming conscientious objectors, and significant writings from them are extant. In the context of political turbulence, increasing militarisation and later war, such actions and writings would become hazardous undertakings and, for some, bring imprisonment by the end of World War II (See also 2.1, 2.3, 2.6).

Selected References

Bamba Nobuya and John F. Howes, eds. *Pacifism in Japan: The Christian and Socialist Tradition*. Vancouver: University of British Columbia Press, 1978.

Davidann, Jon Thares. *A World of Crisis and Progress: the American YMCA in Japan, 1890-1930*. Bethlehem: Lehigh University Press; London: Associated University Presses, c1998.

Francis, Carolyn Bowen and John Masaaki Nakajima. *Christianity in Japan*. New York: Friendship Press, 1991.

Germany, Charles H., ed. *The Response of the Church in Changing Japan*. New York: Friendship Press, 1967.

Gulick, Sidney L. *Working Women of Japan*. New York: Missionary Education Movement, 1915.

Howes, John F. "Internationalism and Protestant Christianity in Japan before World War II." *Japan Christian Review* 62 (1996).

Iglehart, Charles W. *A Century of Protestant Christianity in Japan*. Rutland, Vt.; Tokyo: Tuttle, 1959.

Inagaki Masami. *Japanese Conscientious Objectors*. Tokyo: Iwanomi Shoten, 1972.

Nihon Kirisutokyo Kyogikai. *The Work of the National Christian Council; a Liaison Organ of Christianity in Japan*. Tokyo: National Christian Council [n.d.]

Owada Yasuyuki. "The Japanese Christian Conscience During the Pacific War." *Japan Christian Quarterly* (1958).

Weber, Hans-Ruedi. *Asia and the Ecumenical Movement 1895-1961*. London: SCM Press, 1966.

1.7.3. Tanaka Shozo (1842- 1913)

Tanaka grew up in Tochiji Prefecture, son of the *nanushi* (village master), as he also would later become. Although falsely imprisoned four times, for exposing corruption and opposing high officials, Tanaka dedicated his life to the championing and protection of rural people. From boyhood on, he studied Confucian ethics and the life of the Buddha, becoming Christian later in life under the influence of Arai Osui (See 1.5.1.), when in prison (1902). He became a member of the regional parliament (1880-1884) and of the National Diet, and "one of the pioneers of the people's movement in modern Japan". Throughout his life he worked to sustain the livelihood and safety, the land and villages of peasant farmers, which were being destroyed by mining, pollution and confiscation.

Tanaka's ethics were based on the joy and responsibility inherent in nature and the land, in neighbourhood and community. "God is working among us", he wrote in his diary, "... if we search nearby we can find him ... God exists not only ... in the pure place, but also in the bad place and the dirty place". He also recognised human responsibility to the state and to political process, declaring that "Japan is a constitutional monarchy and a robber state, all at the same time ... For me, Japan is a family". Though not a member of any church, Tanaka was deeply Christian and found in the Bible "the Heavenly way"; of love and justice, peace and disarmament, of care for nature and for neighbour. He found in Jesus Christ a full humanity "without losing the quality of holiness", the courage to stand unwaveringly for truth, and as Arai did, he also found there "the reality of resurrection continuously occurring in the midst of cosmic life" (Takenaka 1984: 202). From this came the strength to continue his campaigns, identified fully with the cause and living conditions of Yanaka peasants, and recognising their wisdom. "Learning from the people of the bottom fits in the heavenly way", he declared. One year before his death he testified at the local court that: "The hope of Shozo Tanaka, a resident of Yanaka, is the resurrection of self-government of people".

Selected References
Works by Tanaka Shozo
> Shozo Tanaka Zenshu. Complete Works in 19 vols. Tokyo: 1979-1980. (Includes autobiography, articles, Diet speeches and records, diary and letters).
> Kinoshita Naoe. *Kinoshita Naoe chosaku shu* (Collected works). Tokyo: Meiji Bunken: 1969-1972. (Articles on Tanaka between 1907 and 1934).
> Strong, Kenneth. *Ox against the Storm. A Biography of Tanaka Shozo, Japan's Conservationist Pioneer*. Tenterden, UK: Paul Norbury Publications, 1977.
> Takenaka Masao. "Ethics of Betweenness - from a Case Study on Shozo Tanaka (1841-1913)." *East Asia Journal of Theology* 2.2 (1984).

1.7.4. Tokutomi Soho (1863-1957)

A member of the Kumamoto Band, Tokutomi became a leading social critic, and later editor of the influential journal *Kokumin no Tomo* (The Nation's Friend). He found in Niijima "a true teacher ... a great model for Japan's man" and through him came "close to Christ and to God". But Tokutomi challenged all conventional sentiments, feudal social structure and inherited authority. He accepted the ideas of Herbert Spencer, which depicted a "universal process of human development" and advocated acceptance of Christianity as "the internal spiritual phenomena" which would offer Japan the "blessings of God" in "progressive politics, society, religion and customs". *Kokumin no Tomo* became widely known for these affirmations and attracted scholars and writers like Ukita Kazutami and Yamaji Aizan (see 1.7.5.).

Compare the many writings of the Christian novelist Shimazaki Toson which vividly depict the social realities of Japan at that time, and most notably in *The Broken Commandment* (University of Tokyo, 1974), the sufferings of those at the bottom of society, the *burakumin*.

Selected References
Works by Tokutomi Soho
The Future Japan, translated and edited by Vinh Sinh, et al. Calgary: University of Alberta Press, 1989.
Pierson, J. D. *Tokutomi Soho, 18631957: a journalist for Modern Japan*. Princeton: Princeton University Press, 1980.
Scheiner, Irwin. *Christian Converts and Social Protest in Meiji Japan*. Berkeley: University of California Press, 1970.
Shimazaki Toson. *The Family* (translated and with an introduction by Cecilia Segawa Seigle. Tokyo: University of Tokyo Press, c1976.
—. *Before the Dawn* (translated by William E. Naff). Honolulu: University of Hawaii Press, c1987.
Uete, Michihari. "Nihon no shiso zasshi" (Japanese thought magazines). *Shiso* (Thought) (1962).
Vinh Sinh. *Tokutomi Soho (18631957): the Later Career*. Toronto: University of Toronto; York University, Joint Centre on Modern East Asia, 1986.
Yamaji Aizan. *Essays on the Modern Japanese Church: Christianity in Meiji Japan*. Ann Arbor: University of Michigan, 1999.

1.7.5. Yamaji Aizan (1864-1917)

Of samurai family, Yamaji was a lay pastor, a journalist and a scholar. Deeply concerned at growing social inequalities, he became a strong critic of the Meiji government, and also of many western missionaries who neglected the issue of Japanese culture and society. He worked with Tokutomi at the *Min'yusha* and the *Kokumin no tomo*, founding his own journal, *Dokuritsu hyoron* (Independent Review) in 1903.

Yamaji affirms a distinction between the 'spiritual' and 'material' worlds and finds spiritual reality in the capacity of people to change the 'material'. He favours an active, though flexible role for the state, and the independence of scholarship which nurtures a spirit of freedom and human rights in Japan. He is critical of much of the "new theology", but demands with Kozaki, Yokoi and others that Christianity be relevant to modern study, theology and understanding of the self. Religion, he insists is not however limited to historical or philosophical categories; it is the heart's experience, it is poetry, and faith. His many writings include journal articles,

Contextual Theology in Japan

biographies, autobiographical novels and works in history and social theory. His volume of collected essays upon the Church in the Meiji era, recently translated into English, was the first Japanese-language book on the subject, and provides a classic study of Christian thought and intellectual history in Japan.

Selected References
Works by Yamaji Aizan
  Shakaishugi kanken (A personal view of socialism). Tokyo: 1906.
  Essays on the Modern Japanese Church: Christianity in Meiji Japan. (Gendai Nihon kyokai shiron). Michigan monograph series in Japanese studies 27. Ann Arbor, MI: Center for Japanese Studies, University of Michigan, 1999.
  Dokuritsu Hyoron (Independent Review) 1-7. Tokyo: 1903-1910. Reprint, Tokyo: Misuzu Shobo, 1987.
  Yamaji Aizan denki senshu (Collected writings). 10 vols. Reprint, Tokyo: Nihon Zusho Sentaa, 1998.

1.7.6. Hatano Seichi 1877-1950

Studies in Tokyo, Berlin and Heidelberg were followed by teaching appointments in state universities, at Tokyo (from 1906) - in primitive Christianity, and at Kyoto (1917-1937) - in the philosophy of religion and in Christian studies. Influences upon him included Uemura Masahisa and Nishida Kitaro, and he is sometimes seen as a leader, with Nishida, Tanabe Hajime and Nishitani Keiji, of the Kyoto school of Japanese philosophy. From early writings in western philosophy he came to focus upon the philosophy of religion, and in later years particularly on the psychology and phenomenology of religion as: "the theoretical retrospection of religious experience and the reflective understanding of it". Personalism has been taken as his central philosophical position, but a personalism that moves from a self-centred "natural" life, to a neutrally related "cultural", and finally to a "religious" life, which here includes a personal relationship with God.

His last, and possibly most well-known book, *Time and Eternity*, works out these ideas in relation to life which is both real and inter-subjective. Rejecting Barth and Brunner as "philosophically inadequate", he replaces "natural" and "supernatural" categories with those of time and eternity, emphasising throughout, human life in history. Religious life, which is only to be understood through a living body of experience, he portrays as the "time of agape" which is a manifestation of eternity; God's holy presence; the fellowship between the present and the future. Death is therefore to be solved within time, not by a mere self-fulfilment, but by the gifts of grace and agape. Described as sophisticated and subtle apologetic and metaphysic, Hatano's work remains a most significant body of Japanese "philosophy of religion". His collected works include articles and volumes on the above topics, along with selections of essays, letters, introductions and bibliographies.

Selected References
Works by Hatano Seiichi

> *Seiyo Tetsugakushi Yo* (The essence of western philosophy). Tokyo: Dai Nihon Tosho, 1901,1907; Tokyo: Tamagawa Daigaku Shuppanbu, 1977.
> *Kirisutokyo no Kigen* (The origin of Christianity). Tokyo: Keiseisha, 1908; Tokyo: Iwanami, 1976.
> *Seiyo Shukyo Shishoshi* (History of religious thought in the West). Tokyo: Iwanami, 1921, 1925.
> *Shukyo Tetsugaku no Honshitsu Oyobi Sono Konpon Mondai* (The essence and basic problems of philosophy of religion). Tokyo: Iwanami, 1926.
> *Shukyotetsugaku* (Philosophy of religion). Tokyo: Iwanami, 1935.
> *Hatano Seiichi Zenshu* (The collected works of Hatano Seiichi 1). 5 vols. Tokyo: Iwanami, 1949.
> *Genshi Kirisutokyo* (The primary Christianity). Tokyo: Iwanami: 1950.
> *Hatano Seiichi Zenshu* (The collected works of Hatano Seiichi, 2). 6 vols. Iwanami: Tokyo, 1968-69.
> *Time and Eternity* (translated by Ichiro Suzuki). Classics of modern Japanese thought and culture: Vol. 4. Tokyo: Yushodo, 1988, (1943, 1949, 1963).
> Michaelson, Carl. *Japanese Contributions to Christian Theology*. Philadelphia: Westminster Press, 1960.

1.8 Women Doing Theology: Thought and Movements 1
1.8.1. Context and Education

Uemura Masahisa was perhaps unique among Christian leaders of his time in his lifelong efforts to raise the status and recognition of women. Through his and others' work, there were by 1883 fifteen schools and seminaries, offering up to eight years' education for girls and women. Particular missions established training centres for women, initially to be employed as Bible women, and from these, as well from the women's seminaries, came lay leaders, teachers, evangelists and, in some cases, writers from whom we have theological reflections from life. From 1877, periodicals like *Yorokobi no Otozure* (Good Tidings) were established particularly for women. The *Fujin Kyofukai* (WCTU), co-founded in 1886 by (Ms) Yajima Kajiko, established its own periodical, *Fujin Kyofukai*, of which the first editor was (Mrs) Sasaki Toyoji, followed by (Mrs) Takeo Tadao and (Mrs) Takeoshi Yasaburo. Following suspension by the government in 1895, a new monthly magazine, the *Fujin Shinpo*, was founded by *Kyofukai,* and is still in publication. In this, and in *Memorials* to government, WCTU advocated social and moral reforms in such areas as prostitution, franchise, intemperance and concubinage. Reports and reflections also appear in periodicals such as *Yokohama Temperance Magazine* and *The Union Signal*.

From the 1890s on, a wide variety of Japanese women found in the WCTU and related movements such as *Seito* Society, with its journal *Seito Magazine* (see 1.8.3.), and *Jogaku Zasshi* (Journal of Women's Learning), the means to both education and to potentially radical activism on urgent social issues. In 1904, the YWCA was founded, with Michi Kawai (see 1.8.2.) and Caroline Macdonald as leaders, and undertook a broad range of educational and welfare programmes for both students and urban workers. In later decades, Kubushiro Ochimi led the WCTU in women's campaigns and was a leader in women's liberation from prostitution. A number of other informal centres and training courses for women developed early in the century, directed to raising the consciousness and abilities of women amidst major social transitions. A notable example is the network of programmes fostered after 1906 by

Yamada Waka in Tokyo (see 1.8.3.), from which we have many writings. However, rising nationalism and the backlash against rapid modernisation in the later Meiji period imposed increasing restrictions on women.

Other women to be noted include pastors and teachers such as Tsuda Umiko, Yasui Tetso, Uenura Tamaki, Hayashi Utako, Yajima Kajiko, and Omurasan. For some activist women such as Kanno Sugako, related to Christian associations like the *Kyofukai*, prison and even death would follow their more revolutionary actions, but for them also writings are extant (see Hane Mikiso 1988).

Selected References

Furuki Yoshiko. *The White Plum: A Biography of Ume Tsuda*. New York: Weatherhill, 1991.

Hane Mikiso. *Reflections on the Way to the Gallows*. Berkeley: University of California, 1988.

Husted, Edith E. *Gift to Japan: A Teacher's Perceptions in an Erupting Decade 1931 to 1939, Letters from Edith E. Husted, American Missionary to Japan*. With background notes by Jeanne D. Wandersleben. Alliance, Ohio: Pacem Press, 1996.

Iglehart, Charles W. *A Century of Protestant Christianity in Japan*. Rutland, Vt.; Tokyo: Tuttle, 1959.

Kawai Michi. "The Place of the Young Women's Christian Association in the Missionary Awakening." *YWCA Berlin*. Geneva (1910).

Kubushiro Ochimi. *Anata wa Dare* (Who are you?: Biography of Hayashi Utako). Tokyo: Ozorasha, 1989.

—. *Yajima Kajiko Den* (Biography of Yajima Kajiko). Tokyo: Ozorasha, 1988.

Nihon Kirisutokyo Fujin Kofukai 100 nenshi (History of 100 years of Japan Woman's Christian Temperance Union). Tokyo: *Fujin Kyofukai*, 1986.

Prang, Margaret. *Heart at Leisure from Itself: Caroline Macdonald of Japan*. Vancouver: UBC Press, c1995.

Schneder, Anna M. *Omurasan*. Philadelphia: Board of Foreign Missions Reformed Church, 1905.

Tanaka Sumiko, ed. *Jyosei Kaiho no Shiso to Kodo* (Thought and behaviour in the emancipation of women). Tokyo: Jiji Tsushinsha, 1975.

Thomas, Winburn T. *Protestant Beginnings in Japan: The First Three Decades*. Rutland, Vt.; Tokyo: Tuttle, 1959.

Yamada Waka. *Fujin no kaiho to seiteki kyoiku* (Collected essays). Tokyo: Toyo shuppansha, 1920.

—. *The social status of Japanese women*. Tokyo: Kokusai Bunka Shinkokai (The Society for International Cultural Relations), 1935.

Yasutake Rumi. *Transnational Women's Activism: the Woman's Christian Temperance Union in Japan and beyond 1858-1920*. [microform - Yale University] 1998.

1.8.2. Kawai Michi (1877-c.1952)

Educated at Sapporo, Michi Kawai was persuaded by Nitobe and his wife to undertake study overseas. From this she returned in 1904, and with Caroline MacDonald founded the Japan YWCA in 1904 and became active also in the SCM, from 1911-1922 as an official in the WSCF. By then she had developed special courses for women emigrants, helped to establish the YWCA in Korea independent of Japan, and completed, along with YMCA colleagues, a series of important studies of Japanese society. Deeply concerned to foster women's self awareness, and also international and inter-racial relations, she devoted her energies from 1925 to the formation of a school where girls of many nations, from city and country, "could learn together how to live in the fullness of life". The *Keisen Jogaku-en* (Fountain of Blessings Girls' Learning Garden) was to be grounded in Christian faith, but also specifically included courses in horticulture and international relations. In these three aims, Nitobe's influence is also clearly seen.

Apart from many reports and documents prepared for the YWCA, WSCF and for the *Jogaku-en*, Michi Kawai's writings appeared in *Student World*, and YWCA periodicals and in two volumes of autobiography. In these and in addresses at ecumenical conferences (from Tokyo 1907 to Tambaram 1938), Kawai presented a life centred upon Jesus Christ "the greatest volunteer worker" of all, which is freely offered for the most needy, works unceasingly for international and inter-racial reconciliation and peace, and 'evangelises' through the demonstration of full human community. In this, she affirmed, the selfhood and capacities of women of faith and global vision are key ingredients.

Selected References
Works by Kawai Michi
Letters in *World's YWCA Archives*, Geneva.
My Lantern. Tokyo: Kyo Bun Kwan, 1939.
Sliding Doors. Tokyo: Keisen Jo-Gaku-En, 1950.
"The Place of the Young Women's Christian Association in the Missionary Awakening." *YWCA Berlin*. Geneva (1910).
"The Real Objective of Christian Schools." *Japan Christian Yearbook*, 37 (1939): 139-145.
—, and Ochimi Kubushiro. *Japanese Women Speak: A Message from the Christian Women of Japan to the Christian Women of America*. Boston: the Central Committee on the United Study of Foreign Missions, 1934.
Isshiki Yoshiko. *Ai no hito*. (Kawai Michiko Sensei.) Tokyo, Sogensha, Showa 28 i.e. 1953.
Thomas, Winburn T. *Protestant Beginnings in Japan: The First Three Decades*. Rutland, Vt.; Tokyo: Tuttle, 1959.
Walton, W.H. Murray. *A Torch in Japan: the Story of Michi Kawai*. London: SCM Press, 1949.

1.8.3. Yamada Waka, (1879-1957)

A former migrant and prostitute, Yamada began with her husband, Kakichi, a language and literature school in Tokyo in 1905, which soon became a centre for students, socialists and intellectuals. She joined the *Seito Society* (Bluestocking Women's Literature Club), which had been founded in 1914 to raise the consciousness of women, and became a regular contributor to *Seito Magazine*. Yamada also wrote for other journals and became a skilful translator. The Yamadas maintained a frugal lifestyle, but developed a large library of Japanese and western books; their house becoming a shelter, a hostel and an educational salon. In later years she also lectured in North America and in 1937 established in Tokyo the Hatagaya Rehabilitation School for women and girls.

Through discussion groups, seminars and writings - especially in the magazine she founded (*Women and the New Society*) - Yamada came to play a central role in emerging women's movements and in expressing a practical theology in their activities and concerns. Her writings, which also appeared regularly in the *Asahi Shimbun* (from 1931) and in the magazine *Shufunotomo*, address many social issues, including women's education, labour unions, free love, abortion, voting rights, love and marriage, and new trends in women's thinking. Her collected essays were published in 1920, including the widely-read "Love and Society", "Society and Family" and "Women Bow Down to Society" (on prostitution). Although strongly critical of aspects of Japanese society, Yamada persistently advocated social co-operation and volunteer service at every level of national life. Her approach to the dilemmas of women, in particular, was extremely simple and personal and her writings had wide impact, because for her, Christian faith, practical service and social criticism were one. Reprints of her volumes have been issued in 1982, 1986 and 1992.

Selected References
Works by Yamada Waka

See the Special Collection of Yamada's writings, held in the library of Waseda University, Tokyo.

Fujin no kaiho to seiteki kyoiku (Collected essays). Tokyo: Toyo Shuppansha, 1920.

Gensai Fujin no Shisho to Sono Seikatsu (Modern women's thought and life). Kindai fujin mondai meicho senshu, dai 8 kan (Selection of famous books on modern women's problems no. 8). Tokyo: Bunkyo Shoin, 1928. Reprinted Nihon Tosho Senta, 1982.

The Social Status of Japanese Women. Tokyo: Kokusai Bunka Shinkokai (The Society for International Cultural Relations), 1935.

On'na Hito Haha (Woman, human flower). Sosho seito no on'natachi. Tokyo: Fiji Shuppan, 1986.

Senka no Sekai Isshuki. Kindai Josei Bunken Shiryo Sosho (Documents and materials on modern women). Tokyo: Ozorasha, 1992.

Weber, Hans-Ruedi. *Asia and the Ecumenical Movement 1895-1961*, Part 4. London: SCM Press, 1966.

Yamazaki Tomoko. *The Story of Yamada Waka: From Prostitute to Feminist Pioneer*. Tokyo: Kodansha International, 1985.

1.9 Expatriate Scholars and Writers 2

Expatriate writers produced a wide range of tracts on Catholic and Protestant belief and practice from 1864 on, and by 1889 there were over 800 titles of Christian books and booklets published. These included commentaries, translations, and works of apologetic or of devotion. Along with many national colleagues, writers and editors having contextual concerns are included J.D. Davis, O.H. Gullick, (Miss) M.B. McNeal, (Mrs) L.H. Pierson and George Allchin. In 1910 the Committee on Christian Literature, through the work of Samuel Wainwright and E.L. Walne, established the Christian Literature Societies (CLS - later *Kyo Bun Kwan*), fostering collaboration by almost a score of publishers, many of which developed lists of Japanese Protestant theological works. The *Pastoral Letters* of Archbishop Nicolai (Ivan Kasatkin) were important both within and beyond Orthodox communities and stressed above all the training of national workers and the indigenisation of the Church.

Expatriate scholars included the church historians for Japan: Otis Cary, Henry Tucker, Johannes Laures sj, Francisque Marnas mep, Winburn Thomas, Pierre Humbertclaude and Hubert Cieslik sj. Sympathetic writers on Buddhism included A.K. Reischauer, Arthur Lloyd, Hans Haas, Robert C. Armstrong, Aimé Villion (see 1.6.2.) and John Hyde DeForest. Amongst other expatriates active in ecumenical and literary endeavours in the early decades of the 20th century are Frank L. Brown of the YMCA, William Axling of *Misaki Kaikan* in Tokyo, Anna M. Schneder of Sendai, Allen K. Faust, and Thomas McNair of *Meiji Gakuin*. Women for whom extensive papers are extant include Constance Buell, Abbe Sanderson, Mary McMillan, Charlotte DeForest, Caroline MacDonald and Azalia Emma Peet.

In 1925, the *Japan Evangelist*, founded in 1894, became the *Japan Christian Quarterly*, which would continue - largely under expatriate leadership - to publish pastoral, historical and theological papers in various formats until 1991. By 1930, there would be over 200 Christian periodicals in print. Although the enforced union of Christian publishers in the *Shinkyo Shupannsha* (1942) would

Contextual Theology in Japan 351

produce few writings, the Organisation of Christian Publishers in 1946 led to a steady growth of publications of writings by both expatriates and nationals in the following period.

Selected References

Faust, Allen Klein. *Christianity as a Social Factor in Modern Japan*. Lancaster, PA: Steinman and Foltz, 1909.

Greene, D.C., ed. *The Christian Movement in Japan: Fifth Annual Issue, Published for the Standing Committee of Co-operating Christian Missions*. Tokyo: Methodist Publishing House, 1907.

Haas, Hans. *Japans Zukunftsreligion*. Berlin: Verlag von Karl Kurtius, 1907.

Humbertclaude, Pierre. "Littérature chrétienne il y a trois cents ans." Reprinted from *Bulletin de las Maison Franco-Japonaise* 8.2-4 (Tokyo 1936).

Iglehart, Charles W. *A Century of Protestant Christianity in Japan*. Rutland, Vt.; Tokyo: Tuttle, 1959.

Laures, J. *Kirishitan Bunko: A Manual of Books and Documents on the Early Christian Mission in Japan* ... Tokyo: Sophia University, 1957.

Lloyd, Arthur. *Shinran and His Work: Studies in Shinshu Theology*. Tokyo: Kyo Bun Kwan, 1910.

Proceedings of the General Conference of Protestant Missionaries in Japan, held in Tokyo October 24-31, 1900, with extensive supplements. Tokyo: Methodist Publishing House, 1901.

Reischaur, A.K. *Studies in Japanese Buddhism*. New York: McMillan, 1925.

Spae, Joseph J. *Christianity Encounters Japan*, 143ff. Tokyo: Oriens Institute for Religious Research, 1968.

Sumiya Mikio. *Kindai Nihon no kisei to kirisutokyo* (Christianity and the establishment of modern Japan). Tokyo: 1950.

Thomas, Winburn T. *Protestant Beginnings in Japan: The First Three Decades*, 123. Rutland, Vermont & Tokyo: Tuttle, 1959.

Yamamoto H. *History of Christianity in Japan*. 2 vols. Tokyo: n.p., 1918.

1.10 Theologians Furthering Contextual Theology
1.10.1. Ishihara Ken, 1882-1976

Following studies in Tokyo and Heidelberg, the church historian and theologian Ishihara Ken served as a professor at Tohoku

University and at Aoyama Gakuin University as well as president of Tokyo Women's College. Although his first specialisation was in Reformation studies, he came to write widely on Christian history and particularly that of Japan, giving particular attention to the place of Japanese theological movements. Ishihara's studies introduce themes which would long remain central to the study of Christian history in Japan, focusing especially on Protestantism. In his major work he presents this, including the theology of the United Church of Christ in Japan (*Nippon Kirisuto Kyodan*), in the larger context of earlier events leading up to the reintroduction of Christianity to Japan in the mid-19th century. He also includes here treatment of the theological motives which brought Protestant missions to China earlier in the century. His writings deal with the theology behind the formation and character of church institutions in Japan and the ecumenical principles of *kokaishugi* (indigenous non-denominationalism). He also considers the Christian idea of personal salvation within the Japanese context and examines the post-war problems and development of Christianity in Japan.

Selected References

Works by Ishihara Ken

    Philosophy of Religion (Shukyo Tetsugaku). Tokyo: 1915.

    Shingakushi (History of theology). Vols.1 & 2. Tokyo: Iwanami Shoten, 1933.

    History of Christianity (Kirisutokyoshi). Tokyo: Iwanami Shoten, 1934, 1951.

    Nippon Kirisuto Kyoshiron (Historiography of Christianity in Japan). Tokyo: Shinkyo Shuppansha, 1967.

    Kirisutokyo to Nippon: Kaiko to Tenbo (Christianity and Japan: reflection and development). Tokyo: Nihon Kisituokyodan Shuppankyoku, n.d.

    The Development of Christianity (Kirisutokyo no Tenkai). Tokyo: Iwanami Shoten, 1972.

    —, and others. *Shukyo to Tetsugaku no Konpon ni Arumono - Hata no Seiichi Hakase no Gakugyo ni tsuite* (The foundation between religion and philosophy - achievements of Dr. Hatano Seiichi). Tokyo: Iwanomi Shoten, 1954.

    Philips, James M. *From the Rising of the Sun: Christians and Society in Contemporary Japan*. Maryknoll, NY: Orbis Books, 1981.

1.10.2. Kagawa Toyohiko (1888-1960)

Kagawa has been recognised as prophet, theologian and evangelist, as poet, mystic and early advocate of non-violence, as labour leader, social scientist and civic welfare administrator. He is described by Drummond as the "dynamic initiator of almost every movement for constructive social reform in Japan for more than 40 years", who played a seminal role in informing the conscience of large numbers of Japanese over that period. Believing that he had been called to serve the poor, he declared that God dwells in the lowliest of men and women, and both in his many campaigns and writings this shaped his lifestyle, his evangelistic programmes and socio-political education, as well as his theology. For these he drew on a very wide range of resources in literature, the social sciences, church history, and the Bible, making simultaneous use in his writings of the terms of evangelical thought and of scientific knowledge.

In his many writings, which date from 1906, Jesus is presented as the incarnation of the God who so desires reconciliation with men and women that a total self-sacrifice is made in Jesus Christ for human redemption. But this Jesus is "seen through Japanese eyes" and is known directly in the daily life of Japanese, demonstrating the redemptive love which is received and experienced as one moves into society to live that same life of redemptive love for others. "The Christian life", Kagawa wrote, is "born when one takes the failure of another upon oneself as one's own failure". In this outgoing life lies the possibility of the Kingdom of God being realised in history, in "the co-operative society" of all. This was because, in his thought, the Gospel brings a "full-rounded emancipation" of the whole person and the transformation of all life. This was Kagawa's Christian socialism, grounded in a theology of society and peace which inspired countless Japanese along with many of his theological contemporaries. It was to be the heart of the Kingdom of God movement. Whatever utopianism Kagawa expressed, it demanded, he believed, rational planning and direct social action which was to be modelled on the life of Jesus. His theology is therefore to be found in the continuing dialogue between his mysticism, his politics and his discipleship with others.

Selected References

Works by Kagawa Toyohiko

Kagawa Toyohiko Zenshu (Collected works). 24 vols. edited by Muto Tomio. Tokyo: Kirisuto Shimbunsha, 1963-64.

Love: the law of life. Translated by J. Fullerton Gressitt; Memoir by Eleanor M. Hinder and Helen F. Topping. Philadelphia: The J.C. Winston, [c1929].

The Religion of Jesus and *Love, the law of life.* Both translated by Helen F. Topping and J. Fullerton Gressitt. Biographical sketches. Philadelphia: J.C. Winston, c1931.

A Grain of Wheat. Translated by Marion R. Draper. London: Hodder & Stoughton, 1933.

Christ and Japan. Translated by William Axling. New York: Friendship Press, 1934.

Jesus through Japanese eyes: a study of the daily life of Jesus. Translated by Helen F. Topping and Marion Draper. London: Lutterworth Press, 1934.

Meditations on the cross. Translated by Helen F. Topping and Marion R. Draper. Chicago: Willet, 1935.

*Songs from the slums (*Hinminkutsu nite utau). Poems by Toyohiko Kagawa; interpretation by Lois J. Erickson. Nashville, TN: Cokesbury Press, [c1935]

Behold the Man, edited by Maxine Shore and M.M. Oblinger. New York: Harper, c1941. Also published as: *The Two Kingdoms.* London: Lutterworth Press, 1941.

Meditations. Translated and edited by Jiro Takenaka. Westport, Conn.: Greenwood Press, 1979 (c1950).

Bikle, George B. *The New Jerusalem: Aspects of Utopianism in the Thought of Kagawa Toyohiko.* The Association for Asian Studies 30. Tucson: The University of Arizona Press, 1976. Includes full bibliography of Kagawa's works.

Germany, Charles H. *Protestant Theologies in Modern Japan: A History of Dominant Theological Currents from 1920-1960.* Tokyo: IISR Press, 1965.

Sumiya Mikio. *Kagawa Toyohiko, Jin to Shiso Shirizu* (Kagawa Toyohiko, the man and the sequence of his thought). Tokyo: Nihon Kirisuto Kyodan Shuppanbu, 1966.

van Drey, Carl. *Toyohiko Kagawa: ein Samurai Jesu Christi.* Stuttgart: Evangelischer Missionsverlag im Christlichen Verlagshaus, c1988.
Yokohama Hariuchi. *Kagawa Toyohiko Den* (A biography of Kagawa Toyohiko). Tokyo: Kirisuto Shimbunsha, 1951.

1.10.3. Nakajima Shigeru 1888-1946

Nakajima taught law at Doshisha University and Kansei Gakuin University, and was influenced by Ebina Danjo and Kagawa Toyohiko. He became secretary of the *Doshisha Rodosha* (Labour) Mission (1928), was active along with Kan Enkichi in the SCM, and became the central figure of the National Alliance of Social Christianity and publisher of their magazine *Social Christianity*.

With Kan, Nakajima viewed God as the creative life-force immanent in human beings and in the world; the socialising or unifying element that was inherent to all human society. This creative spirit was the aspect of God immanent in the world - the "Immanent Christ" in Nakajima's terms - for Jesus of Nazareth is the concrete revelation of God's "socialising love". The Gospel, therefore, had primarily to do with receiving the grace of God in order to build God's kingdom; the community of men and women in union and solidarity with God's immanent Spirit. But to fully present such a theology he believed that the immanent God of Oriental faith was necessary, along with a direct understanding of the human issues of today in Japan. Although he was deeply sensitive to questions of social justice, Christianity was not just for one class, the "proletariat", nor was it merely a "social gospel". He remained critical of many aspects of Marxism and affirmed that redemption from sin (of egoistic and anti-social actions), whereby Christ is resurrected within, remained necessary. To experience salvation is to be "socialised" by dying to self and practising redemptive love. For Nakajima, this is why he would say that "social theology is the whole of systematic theology".

Selected References
Works by Nakajima Shigeru
God and Community (Kami to kyodoshakai). Tokyo: 1929.

Shakaiteki Kirisutokyo to Atarashiki Kami no Taiken (Social Christianity and the new experience of God). Tokyo: Kaitakusha, 1931.

The Essence of Social Christianity: The Religion of Redemptive Love (Shakaiteki kirisutokyo no honshitsu: shokuzai ai no shukyo). Tokyo: 1937.

Biblical Jesus and Modern Thinking (Seisho no Iesu to gendai no shii). Tokyo:1965.

Germany, Charles H. *Protestant Theologies in Modern Japan: A History of Dominant Theological Currents from 1920-1960.* Tokyo: IISR Press, 1965.

Imanaka Tsugimaro. *Iesu no Shukyo Marukishizumu* (The religion of Jesus and Marxism). Tokyo: Tamagawa Gakuin Shuppanbu, 1929.

Sato Toshio. "The Second Generation." In *A History of Japanese Theology*, edited by Yasuo Furuya. Grand Rapids: Eerdmans, 1997.

1.10.4. Kan Enkichi 1895-1972

After studies in Kyoto and Harvard, Kan took up a long life of teaching at Rikkyo University. Influenced by Hatano Seichi, Charles Gore and Ernst Troeltsch, he became active with Nakajima Shigeru in the Social Christian movement and argued strongly for the socialisation of Christianity. With others in the SCM and related groups, Kan was convinced of the sickness of post-war (World War I) economic structures, declaring in 1930 that "rather than the transformation of society through the reformation of the individual, we have come to the time to emphasise the transformation of the individual through the reform of society."

For Kan, salvation meant participating in the building of the Kingdom of God on earth: "the God-centred society as begun by Jesus". The Spirit of God was immanent in all human life and so there was also continuity between Christianity and culture. Although he went on to concentrate upon other theological areas, the socio-theology articulated by Kan and his colleagues, and in different form by Kagawa Toyohiko, would later be developed in new ways by ecumenical theologians and social ethicists from the 1960s on.

Contextual Theology in Japan 357

Kan Enkichi was later influenced by Barth, and also Brunner, and wrote on dialectical theology, as well as on Tillich and Berdyaev. In his major later writing, *Risei to Keiji*, he recognised the limits of philosophy and called for a "theological" philosophy of religion, and for a theology which is both "thinking in prayer" and a critical self-examination.

Selected References
Works by Kan Enkichi
> *Kirisutoky no Tenko to Sono Genri* (The turning of Christianity and its principles). Tokyo: Kaitakusha, 1930.
> *Kirisutokyo Shakaika no Riron* (The theory of the socialisation of Christianity). Tokyo: Kirisutosha Gakusai Undo Shuppanbu, 1932.
> *Gendai no Shukyotetsugaku* (Modern philosophy of religion). Tokyo: Nihon Hyoronsha, 1934.
> *Shukyo Fukko* (Religious revival). Tokyo: Nihon Hyoronsha, 1934.
> *Risei to Keiji* (Reason and revelation). Tokyo: Yoshobo, 1953.
> "Kami no Mondai" (Problem of God), edited by Kishimoto Hideo. *Shukyo Ronshu* (Bulletin of Religion) 1 (1948).
> Germany, Charles H. *Protestant Theologies in Modern Japan: A History of Dominant Theological Currents from 1920-1960*. Tokyo: IISR Press, 1965.
> Philips, James M. *From the Rising of the Sun: Christians and Society in Contemporary Japan*. Maryknoll, NY: Orbis Books, 1981: 254.
> Sato Toshio. "The Second Generation." In *A History of Japanese Theology*, edited by Yasuo Furuya. Grand Rapids: Eerdmans, 1997.

1.10.5. Otsuka Setsuji (1887-)
Following studies of Ritschl, and John Dewey, and later, of dialectical theology and Kagawa Toyohiko, Otsuka Setsuji came to defend the independence of faith over against philosophy and history, as the true existence of man and woman and the criterion for all thought. He was instrumental in publishing in 1923, the periodical *Kirisutokyo Kenkyu* (Studies in the Christian Religion) of the Doshisha Theological Department, which presented for many decades the creative involvement of Christianity with society. With

Kagawa, Sugiyama Motojiro and Namae Takayuki, he also shaped the social-ethical programme of the seminary to establish effective encounter with Japanese civilisation, a theological openness to new insight, hermeneutic principles which were historical rather than dogmatic, and involvement in practical social concerns.

Otsuka's consistent theme is the social relevance of Christian faith, and the social responsibility of all Christian workers in reclaiming the purpose of God within human history. For him this is only possible by so restoring the power of the Spirit in the Church that it can exercise leadership in society, and his theology thus held together social ethics and ecclesiology. Although other theologians were also strongly influenced by "crisis theology" (see 1.11), Otsuka's own position was one of "modified dialectical theology" along with a critical liberalism which included a "Christian ethic relevant to culture and society". While affirming that "faith is a gift of grace" which is necessary to transform human incapacity, Otsuka emphasises the revitalisation of human reason and experience which comes through grace, making possible the Church's engagement in the world and contributing to the purpose of God within history, where there is no complete contradiction between time and eternity. His work at Doshisha influenced students and colleagues in later decades and concerns for a theology of social action were continued there later by teachers such as Shimada Keiichiro and Takenaka Masao.

Selected References
Works by Otsuka Setsuji

    Shinko no Dokujisei (The independence of faith). Osaka: Nihon Kumiai Kirisuto Kyokai Hombu, 1929.

    Kirisutokyo Rinrigaku Josetsu (Introduction to Christian ethics). Tokyo: Kirisutokyo Shiso Sosho Kankokai, 1935.

    Kirisutokyo Ningengaku (Concept of humanity within Christianity). Kyoto: Zenkoku Shobo, 1948.

    Nihonkoku kempo to Kirisutokyo (The constitution of Japan and Christianity). Kyoto: Doshisha, 1960.

    Outline of Christianity (Kirisutokyo gaiyo). 1971.

    Kaiko shichijushichine (Look back on 77 years). Kyoto: Dohosha, 1977.

"The Academic Tradition of the School of Theology, Doshisha University." *Kirisutokyo Kenkyu* (1958).

Furuya Yasuo, ed. *A History of Japanese Theology*. Grand Rapids: Eerdmans, 1997.

Germany, Charles H. *Protestant Theologies in Modern Japan: A History of Dominant Theological Currents from 1920-1960*. Tokyo: IISR Press, 1965

1.11 Systematic and Historical Theologians

Many systematic and historical theologians did not in this period give priority to the search for, or formulation of, a contextualising theology for which Japanese life and history provided essential sources. Rather, their attention was largely given to questions of orthodox doctrine, to exposition of western theologies and to the historical and philosophical issues these raised. Many were strongly influenced by the early writings of Barth and their approach therefore to Japanese culture, religion and social reality was often unsympathetic. Amongst these was Takakura Tokutaro (1885-1934), who in the name of "evangelical" Christianity opposed what he saw to be liberal or humanistic theology. Kuwata Hidenobu (1895-1975) similarly rejected liberal theology, followed Barth in holding that theology was a science of the church and of revelation, and led in the introduction of dialectical theology to Japan. In his last years, however, he supported the movement for Christian social action. Kumano Yoshitaka (b.1899) was also heavily westernized in his approach, was active in the introduction of dialectical theology and produced one of the few fully systematic - in the western sense -works of dogmatics. Only in the third volume does Kumano show that he has been influenced in part by the Japanese philosophers Nishida and Tanabe, and Mukyokai theologians like Uchimura and Sekine.

Others who were strongly influenced by dialectical theology included Yamamoto Kano (b.1909), the later Kan Enkichi (1.10.4.), Ogawa Keiji (b.1927), Watanabe Zenda (1885-1978), Kishi Chitose (b. 1898) and also the early Furuya Yasuo (2.5.11.). Critical reflection upon the role of Barthianism, and of much western philosophy, in Japan would see in it a cause for the isolation, over some decades, of much Japanese theology from the living issues of the Japanese people. Certainly those most influenced by these traditions gave much less attention to the study of Japanese history or culture or to the articulation of uniquely Japanese theological insights and imagery.

Selected References

Takakura Tokutaro. *Oncho to Shinjitsu* (Grace and faithfulness). Tokyo: Kozumosu Shoin, 1925.

—. *Oncho no Okoku* (The kingdom of grace). Kamakuracho (Kanagawa Ken): Seisho Kensansha, 1922; Tokyo: Nagasaki Shoten, 1927.

Kuwada Hidenobu. *Kuwada Hidenobu Zenshu* (The collected works of Kuwada Hidenobu). 7 vols. Tokyo: Kirisuto Shinbunsha, 1974-1976.

—. *Shingaku no Rikai* (Understanding of theology). Tokyo: Nagasaki Shoten, 1939.

Kumano Yoshitaka. *Kiki Shingaku* (Theology of the turning point). Tokyo: Toho Shoin, 1934.

—. *Shinko to Genjitsu* (Faith and reality). Tokyo: Sinseido, 1939.

—. *Kyokai to Bunka* (Church and culture). Tokyo: Shinseido, 1943.

—. *Kirisutokyo Rinri NyUmon* (Introduction to Christian ethics). Tokyo: Shinkyo Shuppansha, 1960.

—. *Nihon Kirisutokyo Shingaku Shisoshi* (History of Japanese Christian theological thought). Tokyo: Shinkyo Shuppansha, 1968.

1.12 Supplementary Bibliography

Ariga Tetsutaro, with Tadakazu Uoki. *Gaisetsu Kirisutokyo Shisoshi* (An outline of the history of Christian thought). Tokyo:1934.

—. "From Confucius to Christ: A Feature of Early Protestantism in Japan." *Japanese Religions* 2/2-3 (1961).

Catholic Weekly (formerly *The Japan Catholic Newspaper*). Inter-Diocesan Conference of the Japanese Hierarchy.

Clement, Ernest Wilson. *Christianity in Modern Japan*. Philadelphia: American Baptist Publication Society, 1905. ATLA Monograph Preservation Program (Phase II, 1986).

Dohi Asao. *Nippon Purotesutanto Kirisuto Kyoshi* (History of Protestant Christianity in Japan). Tokyo: Shinkyo Shuppansha, 1927 (1980).

Ebisawa Arimichi. *Christianity in Japan; a Bibliography of Japanese and Chinese Sources*. Tokyo: Committee on Asian Cultural Studies, International Christian University, 1960- .

—, and Ouchi Saburo. *Nippon Kirisuto Kyoshi* (The history of Christianity in Japan). Tokyo: Nippon Kirisuto Kyodan Shuppan Kyoku, 1990 (1970).

Gino K. *Recent Japanese Philosophical Thought 1862-1962: A Survey*. Tokyo: Enderle, 1963.

Hino Masumi. *History of Christian Doctrine* (Kirisutokyo kyorishi). Tokyo: 1917.

Honda Yoichi Sensei (Bishop Yoichi Honda; life, sermons, addresses). Compiled by Aoyama Gakuin. Tokyo: Nihon Kirisutokyo Kobun Kyokai, Taisho 7 (1918).

Imai Toshimichi. *Old Testament Theology* (Kyuyaku seisho shingaku). Tokyo: 1911.

Inoue Yoji, and Yamane Michihiro. *Kaze no naka no omoi: Kirisutokyo no bunkanai kaika no kokoromi* (Yagi Jukichi, 1989-1927 - Criticism and interpretation.) Tokyo: Nihon Kirisuto Kyodan Shuppankyoku, 1989.

Ishizaka Masanobu. "Christianity in Japan, 1859-1883." PhD diss. John Hopkins University, 1895.

The Japan Christian Yearbook

    1903-05 *The Christian Movement in its Relation to the New Life in Japan*. Japan Missionary Federation.

    1906-14 *The Christian Movement in Japan*. Tokyo: Methodist Publishing House, and Kyo Bun Kwan.

    1915-20 *The Christian Movement in the Japanese Empire, Including Korea and Formosa*. Tokyo: Kyobunkwan.

    1921-26 *The Christian Movement in Japan, Korea & Formosa*. Tokyo: Kyobunkwan.

    1927-31 *Japan Mission Year Book: The Christian Movement in Japan & Formosa*. Tokyo: Kyobunkwan.

    1932-41 *The Japan Christian Yearbook*. Tokyo: Kyobunkwan.

Kashiwai En. *History of Christianity* (Kirisutokyoshi). Tokyo: Shinkyo Shuppansha, 1924, 1956, 1965.

—. *Kashiwai Zenshu* (Kashiwai En, the collected works): Vols. 1-6. Tokyo: Keiseisha Shoten, 1922-1927.

Kishimoto Hideo, ed. *Japanese Religion in the Meiji Era,* translated and adapted by John F. Howes. Tokyo: Obunsha, 1956.

Kokusai Kirisutokyo Daigaku. *Ajia Bunka Kenkyu Iinkai Nihon Kirisutokyo bunken mokuroku.* Part I. *Christianity in Japan - A Bibliography of Japanese and Chinese sources (1543-1912).* Tokyo: Kokusai Kirisutokyo Daigaku, 1960.

Kuwada Hidenobu. *Christian Theology in Outline* (Kirisutokyo shingaku gairon). Tokyo: 1941.

—. *The Essence of Christianity* (Kirisutokyo no honshitsu). 1932.

Lee Kun Sam. "The Christian confrontation with Shinto nationalism: a Historical and Critical Study of the Conflict of Christianity and Shinto in Japan ... 1865-1945." PhD diss. Vrije Universiteit, Amsterdam: Soest, 1962.

Morioka Kiyomi. *Nihon no kindaishakai to kirisutokyo* (Japan's modern society and Christianity). Tokyo: Hyoronsha, 1976.

Nihon kirisutokyo bunken mokuroku, Meiji (Guide to Meiji Christian literature). Tokyo: Asian Cultural Research Committee, 1965.

Nishitani Keiji et al. *Sengo Nihon seishinshi* (Christianity and intellectual life in Japan). Nishinomiya: Kirisutokyo Gakuto Kyodaidan: Sobunsha, 1951.

Nolan, Liam. *Small Man of Nanataki* (Kyoshi Watambe). New York: Dutton, 1966.

Omura Haruo. *Nippon Purotesutanto Shoshi* (Concise history of Protestantism in Japan). Tokyo: Inochi no Kotoba, 1993.

Rimer, Thomas J., ed. *Culture and Identity: Japanese Intellectuals during the Interwar Years.* Princeton: Princeton University Press, c1990.

Shizuo Kawa. *Arishima Takeo to Kirisutokyo narabini sono shuhen.* Tokyo: Kasama Shoin, 1998. (Writings of Arishima Takeo 1878-1923).

Takagi Mizutaro. *Kirisutokyo Daijiten* (Great dictionary of Christianity). Tokyo: Keiseisha, 1911.

Takeno Keisaku. *Shizen rinri to Kirisutokyo rinri* (Nature and Christianity). Tokyo: Chuo Shuppansha, Showa 22 (1947).

Tominaga Tokumaro. *A New Interpretation of Christianity* (Kirisutokyo shinkai). Tokyo: 1909.

Watanabe Zenda. *Seisho Kaishakuron* (Interpretation of the Bible). Tokyo: Shinkyo Shuppansha, 1954.

—. *Seisho Shingakuron* (Theology of the Bible). Tokyo: Shinkyo Shuppansha, 1963.

Yanagita Tomonobu. *Japan Christian Literature Review; a Comprehensive Subject Listing of Protestant and Catholic Books with over 600 Analytical Reviews*. Sendai, Seisho Tosho Kankokai, c1958.

2 Contextual Theology in Japan 1945 -2000
2.1 Introduction
2.1.1. Theological Context

According to the *Religious Yearbook* issued by the Agency for Cultural Affairs every four years, Christianity in Japan is always counted as one of the major three Japanese religions together with Shinto and Buddhism. But, considering the number of Christians in Japan, this is a singular phenomenon, for only 1.4% of the net population are recorded as church members. The number of actual adherents, however, almost triples this number, and despite its comparatively small proportion, Christianity is considered as one of the major religions, signifying a popular appreciation of the spiritual and cultural contribution of Christianity to Japanese society. Nor is this just because of its relationship to other westernizing influences; at least in part, it recognises major Christian contributions in the fields of education, scholarship, literature, social welfare and non-government organizations.

To be sure, since Japan's modernisation in the Meiji Era, Christian thinking in Japan has been greatly nurtured by means of translated works of western thinkers as well as by other social and cultural influences in both East and West. (See above for the period 1800-1945.) This general trend has continued after World War II also. The influence of European theologians such as Karl Barth and Dietrich Bonhoeffer, John Bennet, Paul Tillich, and others was extensive, especially in the 1950s and 1960s. More recently, along with the documents of Vatican II and of the World Council of Churches, theologians like Karl Rahner and Hans Urs v. Balthasar, Jurgen Moltman and Edward Schillebeeckx have had wide influence. But along with these, liberation theologies, Asian theologies and feminist theologies have made an immeasurable impact upon Christian thinking even though the general concern of Christians within the church has remained largely conservative. More widely in Japanese society, thought and piety is often highly westernised, whereas inner spirituality remains deeply influenced by traditional Japanese thought-forms. Westernised intellectuals, including many theologians, have often failed to address such traditions, or to locate their reflection within the particular problems and potentials of Japanese society, culture and religion.

But even in a situation of 'intellectual (and industrial) westernization', and within a complex of widely diverse social and political forces, creative minorities within the churches and related movements have long reflected and written on the concrete issues of social life, spirituality and Christian faith in Japan. (See 1 above, Contextual Theology in Japan 1800-1945.) There has been indigenous response to Christian teaching, careful study of religious and cultural tradition, and reflection upon struggle, suffering and aspirations in Japanese life. The questions addressed by many Japanese theologians of the late 19th and early 20th centuries, and their often pioneering insights, remain central to much contemporary work now, although the thought of some - along with that of earlier writers - is yet to be adequately assimilated. In the last half century genuine attempts to do theology 'on our own ground' have multiplied, drawing on our own resources and encouraged by various contextual theologies in Asia and the Two-Thirds World.

Key themes for Japanese Christians in their reflection and commitments remain the transcendence of God, the lordship of Christ, a theology of the Cross and the local and universal Church. But these have been influenced by a growing sense of selfhood for Japanese churches since the 1970s and by the fuller articulation of contextual and life-oriented theologies. The contributions especially of those engaged in frontier ministries, study centres and lay movements, along with that of a growing number of women theologians, have made possible renewed and re-oriented approaches within Japanese theology - in methodology and locus, as well as in content and sources. This has greatly diversified the forms and direction of theological endeavour in Japan, and its role within churches and communities, and has also stimulated a wide variety of writing and publication in a plurality of theologies.

Selected References

Dohi Akio. "The Christian Mission and the Role of Christian Church in Postwar Japan." In *1999 Graduate Students' Conference on North East Asia Church History: Korea.* Edited by the Korea Academy of Church History, 34-50. Seoul: 1999.

Fujii Takao. "The Church and the World." *Kwansei Gakuin University Annual Studies* 11 (1962).

Furuya Yasuo. *A History of Japanese Theology.* Grand Rapids, Mich.: Eerdmans, 1997.

Germany, Charles H. *Protestant Theologies in Modern Japan.* Tokyo: IISR Press, 1965. Note Bibliography.

Hori Mitsuo. "A Historical Survey of Radicalism in Japan." *Japan Christian Quarterly* 37.3 (1971).

Ishii Masami. "Systematic Theology in Japan." In *Christian Presence in Japan: Essays in Honor of William J. Danker*, edited by Wi Jo Kang and Masaru Mori, 137-158. Tokyo: Seibusha, 1981.

Kumano Yoshitaka. "Social Christianity in Japan." *NEAJOT* 8.1 (1972).

Kumuzawa Yoshinobu and David Swain, eds. *Christianity in Japan 1971-1990.* Tokyo: Kyo Bun Kwan; Cincinnati: Friendship Press, 1991.

Morioka Iwao. "Japanese Churches and World War II." *Japan Christian Quarterly* 34.2 (1968).

Phillips, James M. *From the Rising of the Sun: Christians and Society in Contemporary Japan*, especially chaps. 8 and 9. American Society of Missiology Series 3. Maryknoll, NY: Orbis Books, 1981.

Reid, David. *New Wine: The Cultural Shaping of Japanese Christianity.* Nanzan Studies in Asian Religions. Berkeley, CA: Asian Humanities Press, 1991.

Swain, David. "Japanese Society Today - Some Conceptual Maps." *Japan Christian Review* 58 (1992).

Yamamoto Kano. "Theology in Japan: Main Trends of Our Time." *Japan Christian Quarterly* 32.1 (1966).

2.1.2. Roman Catholic Background (See also 1.2 above)

In the first decades of this period, the Catholic Church in Japan faced immense tasks of reconstruction: in such areas as the re-establishment of churches and welfare programmes, diocesan and national organizations, religious orders, schools and colleges, as well as for four major seminaries and Catholic lay movements such as Catholic Action and Young Christian Workers (JOC). By 1960, however, there were many Catholic publications in the fields of philosophy, apologetics, law, history, education and literature. Study and implementation of the renewal of Vatican II was a major task also from the late 1960s (to the present), leading to a new stress on vernacular liturgy, Bible study and hymnology; re-education of laity, clergy and religious; promotion of unity among Christians; co-operation with those of other faiths; along with new ministries in social concern, justice and peace. Japanese scholars in scholastic studies of theology and philosophy were often, however, critical of traditional Japanese thought, and amongst these were Matsumoto Masao (b.1910), Takahashi Wataru (b.1909), Imamichi Tomonobu (b.1922) and Yamada Akira (b. 1922).

In 1970, following studies of Catholic social teachings, the Bishops' Conference of Japan set up the Japan Catholic Council for Justice and Peace as a conference of the various Catholic groups and as the main vehicle for increased co-operation with the National Christian Council on such issues as the Yasukuni Shrine, the imperial enthronement ceremonies, release of South Korean political prisoners, and revision of the Alien Registration Law. From the 1970s, a growing interest in other faiths led to acceptance by many of insights and methods of meditation from Zen and Pure Land Buddhism, although study of Shinto would only seriously begin in the 1990s. From 1980 on, however, many became more conscious of their self identity as the Church in Japan, with a stronger sense of responsibility for peace and justice, and for evangelization.

In 1984 "The Missionary and Pastoral Center" was renamed "The Japan Catholic Research Institute for Evangelisation" and extended its activities. Actions by the Bishops' Conference and related movements - often in co-operation with Protestant movements - would, in the next 20 years, address a wide range of issues, including appeals and education for peace, refugees and "Boat People"; the influx of migrant workers and solidarity with Asian women in Japan; Japanese responsibility for atrocities in World War II and the inclusion of this in school textbooks; the discrimination suffered by Buraku minorities and by Korean residents in Japan; and the treatment of foreign prisoners in Japan today.

In publication and literature, apart from official publications of the hierarchy, other journals were also established or re-appeared. By 1960, the Catholic Study Center on Social Problems was publishing *Shakai Kankei to Ningen* (People and Social Relationships), and in 1961 the *Japan Missionary Bulletin* (now *Japan Mission Journal*) became an independent journal produced by the Oriens Institute for Religious Research, Tokyo. Revised liturgies for almost all sacraments and for the Mass itself appeared between 1971 and 1978; and many writings came from both Catholic centres, such as Oriens, Sophia University and Nanzan Institute, and from increasing ecumenical and interreligious exchanges (see 2.4. below). A "New Interconfessional Translation" of the Bible was issued by the Japan Bible Society in September 1987 and a series of catechetical studies of the Scriptures appeared, often outlining the steps of *pre-catechesis*, *kerugma* and *catechesis* proper. In 1989, the first national assembly of priests was held in Osaka on the subject of "The Joy and Pain of Working to Build an Open Church". From the Conference of Catholic Bishops and their organs, came a flow of pastoral letters and statements (2.6.6.1.), and journals such as *Katorikku Kenkyu, Japan Mission Journal, Monumenta Nipponica* and *Japanese Journal of Religious Studies* have enlarged and developed their contents and influence.

More than 70 Catholic presses have become active in the period, although only a small number include works of contextualising theology in their lists. More prominent in the 1960s and 1970s were studies of medieval theologians or Neo-Thomist studies by scholars such as Tanaka Kotaro, Matsumoto Masao and Joseph

Roggendorf. Although writings of more inculturating intention have earlier sometimes seen Japanese religion and culture as belonging to a "pre-catechetical" stage in the development of Japanese theology, since 1970 a growing number of Japanese theologians, whether clergy or lay, have concentrated upon the inculturation and contextualisation of Christian faith in the unique milieu of Japan. They have therefore focused their theological reflection upon, for example, the image of Jesus in Japan, how to incarnate the spirit of the Vatican Council in the life of contemporary Japan, Christian unity, dialogue and collaboration with those of other faiths, the growth of a people's church, and in response to issues of peace, human rights and social justice. In recent decades the context for such theologising has included a growing domestic and international insecurity for the Japanese people, apparently growing forces of ethno - centrism and reaction in Japanese society, along with persisting theological assumptions in the church which are both strongly conservative and westernising. To this the Conference of Bishops, along with a number of individual theologians, are significant exceptions in recent publications.

Selected References

The Bishops' Conference. *Cathopedia '92*. Tokyo: Catholic Bishops' Conference, 1992. (Replaces *Japan Catholic Directory*).

Drummond, Richard H. *A History of Christianity in Japan*. Grand Rapids, MI: Eerdmans, 1971.

Ebisawa Arimichi. *Christianity in Japan; a Bibliography of Japanese and Chinese sources, 1910-* . Tokyo: Committee on Asian Cultural Studies, International Christian University, 1960.

Saburo Matsumoto. "The Roman Catholic Church in Japan." In *Christianity in Japan 1971-1990*, edited by Kumuzawa Yoshinobu and David L. Swain. Tokyo: Kyo Bun Kwan, 1991.

Oda Takehiko. "Response to the Holy Spirit: Lay Christian Movements Today." *Japan Missionary Bulletin* 46.3 (1992).

Phillips, James M. *From the Rising of the Sun: Christians and Society in Contemporary Japan*, especially chaps 8 and 9. American Society of Missiology 3. Maryknoll, NY: Orbis Books, 1981.

Spae, Joseph J. *Christian Corridors to Japan*. Tokyo: Oriens Institute, 1965.
—. *Christianity Encounters Japan*. Tokyo: Oriens Institute, 1968.
Suzuki Norihasa and Joseph J. Spae. *Nihonjin no Mita Kirisutokyo*. Tokyo: Oriens Institute, 1968.
Tokuoka Takao. "Catholic Publications in Japan - Inculturation of the Church." *Japan Missionary Bulletin* 34.10 (1980).
Van Hecken, Joseph L. *The Catholic Church in Japan since 1859*. Tokyo: Herder, 1963.

2.1.3. Protestant Background (See also 1.3 above)

Many of the factors mentioned above regarding the context for Catholic theologising also apply to Protestant theological reflection, although from the Meiji period onwards, larger numbers of theologians of Protestant background have undertaken extensive study and writing in the articulation of Japanese contextual theology. In the period following 1950, there have been diverse factors influencing these endeavours. Earlier theologies of salvation, of society and of religion have been questioned or recast in the context of both vast social and political changes, and of creative theological movements grounded in Japanese culture and society. The influence of such European theologians as Barth and Brunner - and especially the long-running debates regarding natural theology - began to wane from 1948 onwards and the role of "post-Barthians" emerged more fully. (See for example Akaiwa Sakae and Suzuki Masahisa, 2.5.2. and 2.5.5.) Movements of social concern and thought, both within and beyond Japan, brought increasing awareness of issues of social justice, human rights and war-guilt, which raised major theological questions and strongly influenced methodology and hermeneutic for the doing of theology in Japan.

The formation of the Kyodan (United Church of Christ) and continuing debates over its origin, its statements of faith and its social witness, stimulated much theological controversy and writing. The Kyodan Confession of Faith (see Kitamori Kazoh and Kumuzawa Yoshinobu, 2.5.8. and 2.5.16.) was forged after considerable struggle, to declare that the Kyodan "commits itself to ethical activities 'in works of love' in order to overcome serious social contradictions". One early consequence was the Confession of War Guilt (see Suzuki Masahisa 2.5.5.), which was also highly controversial. This, along with the silence of some other denominations, was, however, still an inadequate response in the eyes of many who were concerned for more indigenous patterns of theology, and especially for a theological response to the issues raised by the Mutual Security Treaty (with the USA), the role of the Emperor and the Yasukuni Shrine, social injustice and discrimination, and the Expo 70 Pavilion. These and related issues have continued to provoke lively theological discussion and publication, which has been closely linked to specific programmes of laity formation, urban industrial mission and advocacy for social justice and human rights; along with movements such as the YWCA, the WCTU, the Japan Christian Academies, Korean/Buraku Centres and other Study Centres, the YMCA and the many ecumenical networks related to the NCCJ (see also 2.2, 2.3, 2.6.5.).

More specifically christological issues have also often arisen within the above contexts, as well as in the settings of New Testament Studies and of inter-religious encounter and dialogue. The presence of the Christ within Japan's social and religious movements, and deep within the Japanese consciousness and religiosity, informs the work of many of Japan's theologians in recent decades and has frequently emerged as much from detailed textual criticism of the Gospels (see, for example, Arai Sasagu, Tagawa Kenzo and Kinukawa Hisako, 2.5.18., 2.5.22. and 2.5.26.) as it has from careful reflection upon major doctrines of Mahayana Buddhism (see Doi Masatoshi, Yagi Seiichi and Takizawa Katsumi, 2.5.4., 2.5.20. and 2.5.3.). A central portrayal of Jesus in many of these scholars is that of a fully human person in his time, but also as a universal "principle of Emmanuel" - God with us.

The work of women theologians and animateurs has greatly increased in influence in this period, with both individual scholars and women's movements making major contributions to a range of creative theologies - in biblical, religious, societal and cultural studies, international relations and conscientisation (see for example Aiko Carter, Watanabe Mine, Kim Young [Sawa] and Yuasa Yuko, 2.5.21. and 2.2.). And this is despite continuing restraints upon their full role in theological teaching and in church leadership.

Particular networks such as the ecumenical Women Doing Theology Group (linked to the NCCJ), along with groups of the YWCA, Tomisaka Center and the Kyodan, have published series of reports from seminars and other programmes. Women, along with other scholars such as Sumiya Mikio (see 2.5.7. below) and Hane Mikiso, have also contributed to wide-reaching studies of the Japanese historical and religious context for doing theology in Japan. (See for example, Takeda Cho Kiyoko 2.5.9., Matsui Yayori 2.2.; 2.6.2. and Yamano Shigeko 2.5.31.)

Selected References

Amemiya Eiichi. *Ecclesiology of the United Church of Christ in Japan*. Tokyo: Shinkyo Shuppansha, 1981.

Dohi Akio. *Nippon Purotesutanto Kirisuto Kyoshi* (The history of Protestant Christianity in Japan). Tokyo: Shinkyo Shuppansha, 1927 (1980).

Furuya Yasuo. *A History of Japanese Theology*. Grand Rapids, Mich.: Eerdmans, 1997.

Germany, Charles H. *Protestant Theologies in Modern Japan*. Tokyo: IISRR Press, 1965. Note Bibliography.

Ishii Masami. "Systematic Theology in Japan." In *Christian Presence in Japan: Essays in Honor of William J. Danker*, edited by Wi Jo Kang and Masaru Mori. Tokyo: Seibusha, 1981.

Kumuzawa Yoshinobu and David Swain, eds. *Christianity in Japan 1971-1990*. Tokyo: Kyo Bun Kwan; Cincinnati: Friendship Press, 1991.

Morioka Iwao. "Japanese Churches and World War II." *Japan Christian Quarterly* 34.2 (1968).

Ookura Ichiro. *Kawara no kyoukai nite, Sensou sekininn kokuhaku no jisshitsuka wo motometsudukete* (At the Riverside Church - Searching for realizing confession on war responsibility). Tokyo: Shinkyo Publishing, 2000.

Phillips, James M. *From the Rising of the Sun: Christians and Society in Contemporary Japan*, especially chaps. 8 and 9. American Society of Missiology Series 3. Maryknoll, NY: Orbis Books, 1981.

Reid, David. *New Wine: The Cultural Shaping of Japanese Christianity*. Nanzan Studies in Asian Religions. Berkeley, CA: Asian Humanities Press, 1991.

Terao Kazuyoshi, comp. *Annotated bibliography of Christianity in Japan*. Nagoya: Nanzan Shukyo Bunka Kenkyujo, 2000.

2.2 Women Doing Theology: Thought and Movements 2

A number of Christian women in Japan have been at the cutting edge of action and reflection upon social and community issues since the 1950s, being "impelled by their faith" to participate in movements for peace and human rights, for social justice and religious freedom. Women scholars such as Takeda Cho Kiyoko (2.5.9.) had from the late 1950s also pioneered in studies of Christianity within Japanese culture and society. Members of the YWCA had affirmed strong opposition to nuclear power or weapons since the early 1960s, and in 1970 affirmed that 'nuclear' was for them a symbol for the whole of "misdirected modern civilization". For them this was to be countered by the "choice of life over death" and required a reassessment of lifestyle and an emphasis upon peace-making, community-building, on organic farming and natural foods. The National Federation of Kyodan Women's Societies formed, in 1973, a study-group on the issues for Koreans in Japan and published booklets on these. The KCCJ (Korean Christian Church in Japan) Women's Association also published six collections of Mothers' Stories between 1975 and 1978 (reprinted in 1985). The WCTU, which also worked with the YWCA in opposition to sexual exploitation and particularly 'sex tours', recognised the problems faced by women migrant workers and continued their long tradition by establishing the Asian Women's Shelter (HELP: House of Emergency Love and Peace) in 1986.

The National Federation of Kyodan Women's Societies had initiated, since 1968, a wide range of action committees, study programmes and conventions where Bible study, social issues and education have been central concerns. From 1972, Nakaya Yasuko, widow of a Self-Defense Forces soldier, maintained a long campaign for freedom of religious expression and for the Christian burial of her husband, as an expression of her Christian faith. This also became the focus for many writings of life-centred theology. Since the 1970s, more church women in Japan became further conscientised by new waves of feminist theology, some of which came from the West. Gatherings of these women from many denominations, who were interested in transforming traditional churches from the women's perspective, were organised from 1984

Contextual Theology in Japan

by Aiko Carter (2.5.21.), then working as the NCCJ Women's Desk. Bible studies, story-telling, discussions and seminars on a range of theological and social concerns later led to the formation of the Women Doing Theology Group in 1987. The key task for them was to "rethink theology" as shared faith-reflection upon human life, in which both women and men view their "own liberation in relation to the liberation of [their] sisters in the Third World" (Watanabe, 1991). Some like Yamano Shigeko (2.5.31.) became active in the Asian Women Workers' Fellowship and later pursued alternative theologies in centres such as that for Christian Response to Asian Issues or the Tomisaka Christian Center (2.6.6.4.). The women clergy's caucus of the Kyodan established, in 1988, a committee on gender discrimination issues and commenced publishing their newsletter *Josei to Jinken* (Women and Human Rights). The Anglican group "Women Thinking about Church" submitted in 1988 an agenda to the General Assembly to make concrete efforts toward women's participation. Studies in feminist theology overseas brought to theologians like Isshiki Yoshiko (2.5.15.), Yamaguchi Satoko and Kinukawa Hisako (2.5.26.) awareness of the importance of doing feminist theology from their own contextual perspective.

In the 1980s, two more associations were formed. The Japan-Korean Resident Women's Theologies Forum first met in Seoul, and was led by Chung Sook-ja, and Christian women of the three groups met together, to face the issue of the guilt of the Japanese Military during the Second World War and to begin formulating a theology of reconciliation. Other meetings followed. The second association was the national and ecumenical Church Women's Congress, begun spontaneously by church women involved in a variety of social issues for mutual empowerment, reflection, and to deepen solidarity. In addition the VAWW-NET (a worldwide network on 'Violence Against Women in War') led by Matsui Yayori, has been working since 1997 to hold the Women's International War Crimes Tribunal on Japan's Military Sexual Slavery.

These associations have also worked cooperatively with regional groups of the YWCA and the WCTU and other theological and grassroots movement and groups. A major issue dealt with over the last two decades is that of "Comfort Women" (sexual slavery by Japanese military during the Second World War), exposed initially by Korean women survivors and Korean women theologians. The struggle within Japan has now spread beyond the Christian churches into wider grassroots movements, involving more women and men seeking for justice and peace for the women forced to become military slaves; not only those in Korea, but also in China, Taiwan, the Philippines, Indonesia, Malaysia and elsewhere.

In 1993, Kinukawa Hisako (2.5.26.) and Chung Sook Ja succeeded in giving birth to a Doctorate of Ministry programme with initially 14 women from Korea, Japan and the Philippines, at the International Christian University, Tokyo. Yuasa Yuko wrote her dissertation, *Noh Drama and Christian Faith: A Hermeneutical Tool in Japanese Context,* and published her book on the Bible and Noh Drama (2000). Mayumi Mori wrote her dissertation, *Sharing the Pain and Hope in Women's Struggle against Domestic Violence in Japan*, which was also published in Japanese in 1999. Also in 1999, Kinukawa edited a collection of writings by Japanese women for the journal *In God's Image* which included contextual reflection by, for example, Kuroda Nobue, Eunja Lee, Yuasa Yuko, Kuwahara Shinobu and Yamaguchi Satoko. The Center for Feminist Theology and Ministry in Japan was established in February, 2000 as an ecumenical institution, more than ten years after its conception. Activities include regular seminars and newsletters in both Japanese and English. In 2000 also, a collection of theological and autobiographical papers were edited by Chun Kwang-Rye, Isshiki Yoshiko, Kinukawa Hisako and Yamaguchi Satoko.

Catholic women who were by now writing theology included Misako Maria Takeda, Mori Setsuko, Yugichi Yuriko, Grace Mary Kuji, Arai Sayoko, Iyori Naoko, Yuasa Makoto and Sr M. Shimamoto. Other women scholars and writers on issues of contextual theology include Minato Akiko of Tokyo Christian University, Horiguchi Ikiko of the University of the Sacred Heart in Tokyo, Arai Eiko and Yoshida Megumi of Tomisaka Center, Ogoshi Aiko of Kinki University, Carolyn Francis of HELP center,

Cheryl Allam mm and Mizuno Kayano of *Japan Christian Review* (1992-98), and Okano Haruko of Jissen Women's University in Tokyo. Writers of both books and of papers in national or international journals include Kim Young, Yamaguchi Satoko, Kurihara Sadako, Livia Kohn, Isshiki Yoshiko and Yamashita Akiko (2.5.33.).

Selected References

Chun Kwang-rye et al. *Women Moving Mountains. Feminist Theology in Japan*. Kuala Lumpur: Asian Women's Resource Centre for Culture and Theology, 2000.

Francis, Carolyn B. and John Masaaki Nakajima. *Christians in Japan*, 87-93, "Women". New York: Friendship Press, 1991.

Hirota Filo. "The Church in Japan is a Women's Church?" *In God's Image* (Dec. 1985/Feb. 1986).

Horiguchi Ikiko. "Metaphors of the Divine." *Japan Christian Review* 59 (1993).

Kinukawa Hisako, ed. *Quilting Voices of Diverse Lives in Japan*. Special Issue. *In God's Image* 18.4 (1999).

Lebra, Takie Sugiyama. *Japanese Women: Constraint and Fulfilment*. Honolulu: University of Hawaii Press, 1984.

Matsui Yayori. *Women's Asia*. London: Zed Books, 1989.

—. *Women in the New Asia*. London: Zed Books; Bangkok: White Lotus; Victoria: Spinifex, 1996.

Minato Akiko. "Women's *Jiritsu* and Christian Feminism in Japan." *Japan Christian Review* 59 (1993).

National Federation of Kyodan (UCCJ) Women's Societies. *Thinking of a Human Being in Relation to Discrimination*. Tokyo: Shinkyo Shuppansha, 1994.

Ohshima Shizuko, and Carolyn Francis. *Japan Through the Eyes of Women Migrant Workers*. Tokyo: Women's Christian Temperance Union, 1989.

Okuda Akiko. "Women's Liberation in Japan and Japanese Christianity." *Modern Churchman* 28.4 (1986).

Suggate, Alan, with Yamano Shigeko. *Japanese Christians and Society*. Berne: Peter Lang, 1996.

Watanabe Mine. "Women's Issues." In *Christianity in Japan 1971-1990*, edited by Kumuzawa Yoshinobu and David L.Swain. Tokyo: Kyo Bun Kwan, 1991.

—. "Expectations Concerning the Laity in Contemporary Japan." *Japan Christian Review* 64 (1998).

Yamamoto Kikuko, and Barbara Dunn Mensendiek, eds. *Grace Abounding: a History of the Ordination of Women in Japan*. Claremont, Calif.: Society of Women Clergy for Theological Studies in Japan, 1999.

Yuasa Yuko. *Wings of Love: A Dialogue between the Bible and Noh Drama*. Kyoto: Koko-do, 2000.

Yoshida Megumi. "Professor Yang's Great Achievements Illuminate Indigenous Christianity in East Asia." in *Handbook of the Symposium on Humanity, Art and Technology*. Taipei: International Conference on the Art of Yu-yu Yang, 2000.

2.3 Theology, Culture and Society

In addition to such theologians as Akaiwa Sakae, Kagawa Toyohiko, Sumiya Mikio, Suzuki Masahisa and Tagawa Kenzo (2.5.2., 1.10.2., 2.5.7., 2.5.5. and 2.5.22.), a number of lively networks of lay and professional theologians have worked to relate theology more directly to social developments and the actual lives of Japanese people. Amongst these have been both women and men, including staff members of state universities as well as some at theological schools, writers and journalists, socialists and pacifists, student leaders and pastors. (See also the period 1800-1945 above: 1.7.1.-1.7.6., 1.8.3, 1.10.1-1.10.5, and also: "Prophetic Theology" 2.6.5. and "Women's Theologies" 2.2.)

The theology of contemporary Japanese Christians is essentially done in and through the issues that are thrown up by Japanese Society, for doctrine and tradition need constantly to be reappropriated by engagement with today's issues, if they are to be living, affirms Kajiwara Higashi. "Japanese Christianity has always confronted Jesus' questioning: 'You are the salt of the earth; but if salt has lost its taste, how shall its saltiness be restored?' It may be fairly said that the social and cultural raison d'être of Japanese Christianity lies in its prophetic utterance and action as a minority. However, in spite of its unexpectedly high evaluation from the general public, the prevalent trend within Christian churches is not always prophetic enough. Rather it often conforms to the dominant political and social trend of our society. So the way of going forward as a true witness to the prophets of the Old Testament and to our Savior Jesus Christ in this country, is that followed only by a

Contextual Theology in Japan

minority of the overall Christian minority." But from these a rich variety of theological writings are available, from a wide range of social commitments.

Socio-political crises such as the 1960 Security Treaty (with the USA) led to more critical responses to western influence, both in society and in Christian thought. New social needs were also being recognised, with increased opportunities within Japanese cultural forms for co-operative responses by non-governmental and religious groupings. Amongst those who provided contextual analysis and theological reflection in this period were Iisaka Yoshiaki, Sumiya Mikio, Shiozuki Kentaro, Takenaka Masao and Yamaguchi Kosaku. On the basis of earlier movements such as Kagawa's for the "Kingdom of God", many coalitions to relate theology more directly to the issues of Japanese life and society had developed further from the 1950s on, including YMCA and student groups; the All Japan Socialist Christians' Frontier Union; occupational and urban evangelism networks such as that in the Kansai area; the Christian Peace Fellowship; programmes of the WCTU and the YWCA, and the Nippon Christian Academies. The periodical *Church Labor Letter* (1954-?1986) grew from concerns to support Christian witness in Asia's industrial society, and addressed the issues and theology of urban-industrial mission both within Japan and, especially from 1970 on, throughout the Asian region. Key figures here were Henry Jones, Takenaka Masao (see 2.5.10.) and members of the Kansai UIM.

Many individual Christians in Japan also undertook political action in national or local structures or for particular causes such as peace-education, recognition of minorities, opposition to state-Shintoism, pollution control, and issues of human rights (including those in Korea). Writers of fiction or biography who have also reflected on Christian faith within Japanese society include, in particular, Shiina Rinzo (1911-1973) who was baptised by Akaiwa Sakae and has left many novels and stories (see *The Go-Between and Other Stories,* Valley Forge: Judson Press, 1970). Others include Abe Mitsuko (1912-), Mori Arimasa (1912-1976), Ishihara Yoshiro (1915-1977), Fukunaga Takehiko (1918-1979), Miura

Ayako (1922-1999), Sakata Hiro (1924-), Tanaka Komimasa (1925-), Mori Reiko (1928-), and Shigekane Yoshiko (1927-).
See also 2.6.6.4.; 2.2.6.6.5. below.

Selected References
> Takenaka Masao. *Reconciliation and Renewal in Japan*. Rev. ed. New York: Friendship Press, 1967.
> Germany, Charles, ed. *The Response of the Church in Changing Japan*, chaps. 2 and 4. New York: Friendship Press, 1967.
> Ishida Manabu. "Doing Theology in Japan: The Alternative Way of Reading the Scriptures As the Book of Sacred Drama in Dialogue with Minjung Theology." *Missiology* 22 (1994).
> Kumazawa Yoshinobu. "Asian Theological Reflections on Liberation." *Occasional Bulletin from the Missionary Research Library* 24:4 (1974).
> Kumuzawa Yoshinobu and David Swain, eds. *Christianity in Japan 1971-1990*. Tokyo: Kyo Bun Kwan; Cincinnati: Friendship Press, 1991.
> Ninomiya Akiie. "Christianity and the Postwar Changes in the Welfare System." *Japan Christian Review* 64 (1998).
> Phillips, James M. *From the Rising of the Sun, Christians and Society in Contemporary Japan*. Maryknoll, NY: Orbis Books,1981.
> Osamu Tsukada. "The Church, Theology and the Emperor System." *The Japan Christian Quarterly* 49:2 (1983).
> Sawa Masahiko. "Christian Identity in Japan: Self-Discovery through Encounter." *The Japan Christian Quarterly* 44:2 (1978).
> Shiozuki Kentaro. "Our Calling to Service in Asia Today." *Student World* 55.3 (1962).
> Suggate, Alan, with Yamano Shigeko. *Japanese Christians and Society*. Bern: Peter Lang, 1996.

2.4 Inter-faith Encounter and Reflection
2.4.1. Catholic Writings
Study of Buddhism and Shintoism has long been a central task for many creative Catholic scholars and believers in Japan, and an essential element in all approaches to the inculturation and contextualising of Christian life and faith. Amongst significant leaders here were Hugo Makibi Enomiya-Lassalle (1898-1990 - see 2.5.1.), Heinrich Dumoulin (1905-1995), Joseph Spae (1913-

1989 - see 2.5.6.), Onodera Isao (b.1922), Oshida Shigeto (1922-), Okumura Ichiro (1923-), Jan Van Bragt (1928- see 2.5.14.) and William Johnston (1925-).

Heinrich Dumoulin taught the philosophy and history of religion for many years at Sophia University, founded its Institute for Oriental Religions, and was first director of what became the Nanzan Insitute (1975-76). One of the world's foremost Zen scholars, he has left a score of major works, of which the two volumes of *Zen Buddhism - A History*, first published in the mid-1950s, are regarded as his magnum opus. Amongst others, his *Buddhism in the Modern World* (1970) has also been widely influential. The Catholic philosopher Onodera Isao has worked closely with Dumoulin and others at the Nanzan Insitute, has made careful studies of the Kyoto School of Japanese philosophy, and written on Nishida, and on anthropological and ecological dimensions of religious dialogue. William Johnston has been professor of religious studies at Sophia University, Tokyo, and a student of both Zen Buddhism and the later medieval English mystics. He has written extensively upon the convergences between Christianity and Zen, in both mystical and ethical practice, as well as in the narratives of their greatest practitioners. Central works include *The Still Point, The Mirror Mind* and *Christian Zen*.

Oriens Institute of Religious Research in Tokyo, based on the centre founded in 1959 by Joseph Spae, included inter-religious studies in its programme, along with wide-ranging pastoral research and teaching. Much of this has been included in their quarterly the *Japan Mission Journal* (formerly the *Japan Missionary Bulletin*). The institute has also published a variety of monographs and collections (see under various entries below). Amongst their scholars and writers on cultural and inter-faith concerns have been Jan Swyngedouw, Fujiwara Takanori, Thomas Imoos, Ernest D. Piryns and John A.Raymaker.

Nanzan Institute (1979) along with associated institutes, ecumenical as well as Catholic (see 2.6.6.), has been the centre for much of the serious inter-religious encounter and study in Japan during the last 25 years, along with the promotion of mutual understanding between Christians and those of other faiths. As well as those mentioned above, key figures in the Institute's work have included Kadowaki Kakichi (see 2.5.12.), Nagasaka Genichiro, Nagakura Hisako, Aoyama Gen, Ishiwaki Yoshifusa, Okuyama Michiaki and Watanabe Manabu. James Heisig's principal concerns (director 1991-2000), have been to "pry open the western philosophical tradition to the contributions of the east, and in this way to create for the first time a properly 'world philosophical forum'; and to bring to the fore elements hidden or forgotten in the Christian tradition as our birthright: the riches of the scriptures, practices, and ideas of religions of the east." Paul Swanson (current director) is particularly interested in "the relationship between one's academic work, study of religion and one's own personal faith ... and in scholars of religion who specialize in a religion other than their own." Both scholars have worked extensively in Buddhist translation and research for a number of Mahayana Buddhist texts.

In addition to its annual bulletins and the *Japanese Journal of Religious Studies*, the Nanzan Institute has published several series of monographs, as well as numerous independent titles. The 18 volumes of *Nanzan Studies in Religion and Culture* include those by Heinrich Dumoulin, Frederick Franck, Paul Mommaers and Jan Van Bragt, Nishitani Keiji, Takeuchi Yoshinori, Tanabe Hajime and Taitetsu Unno.

Along with the NCC Center for the Study of Japanese Religions (see 2.4.2.), Nanzan is associated with the Oriens Institute, Tokyo, and the Japan Society for Buddhist-Christian Studies founded in 1982 with the aim, as the Japan Chapter of the broader "East-West Religions Project", of promoting inter-cultural, and inter-religious dialogue at the doctrinal, philosophical and theological levels. Associated in these programmes have been the staff of the NCC Center - including Doi Masatoshi, Notto Thelle, Yuki Hideo, Martin Repp, as well as Catholic scholars such as Oshida Shigeto, Ruben L. Habito, Torisu Yoshifumi and Hisamatsu Eiji.

Selected References

Dumoulin, Heinrich. *Zen Buddhism - A History.* Translation by James Heisig and Paul Knitter. New York: Macmillan, 1988.

—. *Buddhism in the Modern World.* New York and London: Collier Books, 1976.

—. *Zen Enlightenment: Origins and Meanings.* Tokyo: Weatherhill, 1979.

Habito, Ruben. *Shinran ti kirisutokyo no Deai Kara - Nihonteki Kaiho no Reisi* (From the encounter between Shinran and Christianity - A Japanese spirituality of liberation). Tokyo: Akashi Shoten, 1989.

—. *Healing Breath - Zen Spirituality for a Wounded Earth.* Maryknoll NY: Orbis Books, 1993.

—, and Yamada Keizo. *Kaiho no Shingaku yo Nippon* (Liberation theology in Japan). Tokyo: Akashi Shoten, 1985.

Heisig, James. "Converting Buddhism to Christianity; Christianity to Buddhism." *Japanese Religions* 22 (1997).

—. "Philosophy as Spirituality: The Way of the Kyoto School." in *Buddhist Spirituality. Volume 2: Later China, Korea, Japan, and the Modern World*, edited by Takeuchi Yoshinori. New York: Crossroad, 1999.

—. "What Time is it for Christianity?" *Metanoia* 8:3/4 (1998).

Johnston, William. *The Still Point: Reflections on Zen and Christian Mysticism.* New York: Fordham University Press, 1970.

—. *Christian Zen. A Way of Meditation.* Dublin: Gill and Macmillan, 1977.

—. *The Mirror Mind. Zen-Christian Dialogue.* New York: Fordham University Press, 1990 (1981).

Nazan Institute, eds. *What Can Christianity Learn from Buddhism?* Tokyo: Houzou-Kan, 1999.

Onodera Isao. *Daichi no tetsugaku* (Philosophy of the earth). Tokyo: San'ichi Shobo, 1983.

—. "Holy Spirit and Basho: Foundation for a Theology of the Holy Spirit." In *What does Christianity have to Learn from Buddhism?* edited by Nanzan Institute of Religion and Culture. Tokyo: Hôzôkan, 1999.

Oshida Shigeto. "The Mystery of the Word and the Reality." *East Asia Pastoral Review* 18.1 (1981).

Piryns, E. *Japan en het Christendom : naar de overstijging van een dilemma.* Tielt: Lannoo, 1971.

Raymaker, John A. "The Dilemma Created by the Vatican Letter on Christian Meditation." *East Asia Pastoral Review* 27 (1990).

Swanson, Paul. *Foundations of T'ien-t'ai Philosophy: The Flowering of the Two Truths Theory in Chinese Buddhism.* Berkeley: Asian Humanities Press, 1989.

—. "Dry Dust, Hazy Images, and Missing Pieces. Reflections on Translating Religious Texts." *Bulletin of the Nanzan Institute for Religion and Culture* 23.29-43 (1998).

—, and Jamie Hubbard. *Pruning the Bodhi Tree: The Storm over Critical Buddhism*. Honolulu, University of Hawaii Press, 1997.

Swyngedouw, Jan. "In Search of a Church with a Japanese Face." *Japan Missionary Bulletin*, from 37.1&2 (1983).

Watanabe Manabu. *The Psyche and the Experiential World*. Tokyo: Shunjûsha, 1991.

2.4.2. Ecumenical Writings

Along with the theologians Doi Masatoshi (2.5.4.), Takizawa Katsumi (2.5.3.) and Yagi Seiichi (4.5.20.), and with Catholic scholars, treated above (2.4.1.), and below (2.6.1, 2.6.4.), a number of others have been active in study, dialogue, education and writing. Apart from the International Institute for the Study of Religion established in Tokyo by Kishimoto Hideo and William Woodard, and the Japan Society for Buddhist-Christian Studies, a key centre for such work has been the NCCJ Center for the Study of Japanese Religions. With Doi Masatoshi must be mentioned his colleague Notto R. Thelle (1941-), whose involvement on many levels with Buddhists in Japan bore fruit in many articles, and his major book *Buddhism and Christianity In Japan*, in which he traces the history of encounters and growing understanding between Christians and Buddhists as context and source for contemporary dialogue. For him, both this century-long history in Japan and present experience of such encounter must be taken to the heart of the church; as much for the missiological quest of the church as for its own radical reshaping.

Doi's successor at the Study Center was Yuki Hideo (1926-), who was professor of religion at Doshisha University from 1965. As well as lecturing and writing on Christianity in Japan, on peace-making, utopian thought and Christian socialism, he has special interests in Japanese religiosity and its expressions and has made specialised studies of Shintoism. Critical of the role of state Shinto and the role of such institutions as the Yasukuni Shrine, Yuki, however, finds levels of truth in the tradition and parallels with Christianity regarding understandings of universality and particularity, and of indigenous selfhood. He has written on the call for the church to be fully Japanese; being Christian he affirms, enables Japanese to become more not less, Japanese in all creative ways. A colleague of Yuki (since 1988) is Martin Repp (1953-), who has similarly participated widely in inter-faith encounter and reflection, and has specialised in studies of Pure Land Buddhism, of New Religions in Japan, and in the early history of Christianity in Japan. Repp has recently written fully on Aum Shinrikyo, seeking to understand the movement from the inside as both authentic and distorted religiosity.

Other staff members and colleagues working with or writing for the NCC Study Center since the 1980s include Yamashita Akiko (2.5.33.), Haakon Elert, Eto Naozumi, Fredrik Spier, Muto Kazuo, Brian McVeigh, Livia Kohn and Nobuhara Tokiyuki (2.5.25). The Center's journals are the quarterlies *Japanese Religions* and *Deai - Kirisutokyo to Shoshukyo*. Along with these, other journals publishing studies in inter-faith dialogue and the study of Japanese religions include *Process Thoughts* (Proceedings of the Japan Society for Process Studies - since 1984) and the *Japanese Journal of Religious Studies* (since 1974). A network of scholars have contributed to Christian reflection in the *Japanese Journal of Religious Studies* (see above 3.2.4.), including David Reid, Yanagawa Keiichi, Michael Pye, Mark Mullins, Ota Yuzo, Abe Yoshiya, Richard Fox Young, Daniel Metraux, along with a number of the Catholic writers already mentioned such as James Heisig, Watanabe Manabu, Jan Van Bragt, Paul Swanson, and Ruben Habito.

Selected References

    Doi Masatoshi. *Theology of Meaning* (Imi no shingaku). Tokyo: Kyo Bun Kwan, 1963.

    —. "A Methodological Reflection on the Theology of Mission." *Japanese Religions* 4.3 (1966).

    —. "Confessing the Faith in Asia Today." *Japanese Religions* 4.4 (1966).

    —. "Dialogue between Living Faiths in Japan." *Japanese Religions* 6.3 (1970).

—. *Search for Meaning Through Interfaith Dialogue*. Tokyo: Kyo Bun Kwan, 1976 (1962).
Eto Naozumi. "Japanese Civil Religion and the Yasukuni Shrine." *Japanese Religions* 2 (1986).
Repp, Martin. "NCC Center for the Study of Japanese Religions in Kyoto." *Inter-Religio* 27 (1995).
—. *Aum Shinrikyo. A Section of Criminal Religion History*. Religion-scientific series Bd. 9. Marburg: diagonal-Verlag, 1997.
—. "Millennial Movements in East and Southeast Asia - An Introduction." *Japanese Religions* 1 & 2 (1998).
Thelle, Notto R. "Theological Implications of Inter-Faith Dialogue." *Japanese Religions* 4 (1977).
—. "Jesus in Japanese Religions." *Japan Christian Quarterly* 49 (1983).
—. "Doing Theology in a Buddhist Environment." *Japanese Religions* 12.4 and 13.1 (1983).
—. *Buddhism and Christianity in Japan. From Conflict to Dialogue 1854-1899*. Honolulu: University of Hawaii, 1987.
Yamashita Akiko. "Tenrin-O and Henjo-Nanshi: Two Women Founders of New Religions." *Japanese Religions* 2 (1990).
—. "The 'Eschatology' of Japanese New, and New New Religions." *Japanese Religions* 1 & 2 (1998).
Yuki Hideo. "A Shinto-Christian Dialogue." *Inter-Religio* 3 (1983).
—. "Tashukyo to Taiwa." In *Jissen Shingaku Sosetsu* (Practical theology: a general survey), edited by Kanda Kanji, Sekita Hiroo and Morino Zenemono. Vol. II. Tokyo: Kyodan Shuppansha, 1993.
—. "Problems with the Revisions to the Religious Corporations Law." *Japanese Religions* 1 (1997).
—. The Religion of the Japanese People. *Kirisuyokyo Kenkyu* 49.2(1988).

2.5 Contextuallising Theologians
2.5.1. Hugo Enomiya-Lassalle sj (Makibi Enomiya) 1898-1990
Accepting Japan as his homeland in 1929, Hugo Enomiya-Lassalle entered upon his life-work of inculturating Christianity within Japanese culture, both through immersion in Zen Buddhism and in dedicated social service. While assisting in the reconstruction of Sophia University, he also established a social welfare and medical organisation for slum-dwellers in Tokyo (1931), and began studies

of Zen, later studying with Harada Sogaku Roshi, Yasutani Roshi and Yamada Roshi. He undertook extensive teaching journeys, sometimes in company with Zen monks with whom he recognised a common ethical impulse. His partnership with Yamada Roshi, especially, is an outstanding example of inter-faith co-operation: Lasalle established centres and movements, particularly for laypeople, through which he " wished to lead Christians, by the integration of the Zen, back to their own sources of mysticism, while it was Yamada's intention to approach Catholicism with the help of Lasalle's understanding of Zen". At the same time, Lasalle campaigned for the use of Japanese in the liturgy, received Japanese citizenship and as a survivor of the Hiroshima bombing, and was active in promoting the establishment of the Peace Church there. He was also deeply concerned for Catholic presence in rural areas where he believed a deep understanding of Buddhism was necessary.

In Zen thought Enomiya-Lasalle found parallels with Thomist thought and with traditions of Christian mysticism, but also discerned in Zen practices which offered great spiritual enrichment to Christians in Japan in the post-war years. He had also come to see close relationship between the experience of illumination in Catholicism and in Zen, and between the Exercises and Zazen, and despite censure and criticism, he would devote much of his future teaching, and writing in scores of articles, to expounding this. In these he considers many aspects of Zen in particular, in relation to Christian meditation, liturgy and the Eucharist, to Christian mystical and prayer traditions. Along with Heinrich Dumoulin, he co-operated closely with Zen monk colleagues, but also drew on the insights of Theravada Buddhism, Hinduism and Eastern Orthodoxy, while continuing in active social concerns as well. An "object-free" meditation practice, he believed, could be a major new step towards the future evolution of humankind. He is remembered for his humility and simplicity, the brevity of his teaching, the depth of his learning and the ways in which in him were merged prayer and ethical practice, Eucharist and Zazen, Christianity and Zen Buddhism. His key work is probably *Zen - Way of Enlightenment*, written in 1959.

Selected References
Works by Hugo Enomiya-Lassalle
Zen-Meditation for Christians. Illinois: University of Notre Dame, 1974.
Leben im neuen Bewußtsein (Life in new consciousness), edited by R. Ropers. München: Herder, 1985.
Zen und christliche Mystik. München: Herder, 1986.
Zen - Way of Enlightenment. London: Burns & Oates, 1967 (1960). Vienna and Freiburg, 1987.
Die Übung der Kontemplation-Christen gehen den Zen-Weg, edited by G. Stachel. Mainz: 1988.
Mein Weg zum Zen (My way with Zen), edited by R. Ropers and B. Snela. München: Herder, 1988.
Kraft aus dem Schweigen - Einübung in die Zen-Meditation. Freiburg: 1990.
"A Few Thoughts on Zazen as Christian Meditation." *Ars et Mystica* 16 (1967).
"The Spirituality of Non-Christian Monasticism in Japan." In *New Charter for Monasticism*, edited by J. Moffitt. Illinois: Notre Dame, 1970.
"Zen and Christianity." *The Asiatic Society in Japan Bulletin* 4 - Special Issue (1972).
"Verändert die Praxis des Zen das religiöse Bewußtsein?" In *Stille Fluchten,* edited by K. Walf. München: Herder, 1984.
Luhmer, K., sj. "Pioneer of Zen Meditation for Christians Fr. H. M. Enomiya-Lassalle." *Japan Mission Bulletin* (1990).

2.5.2. Akaiwa Sakai (1903-1966)

Akaiwa Sakai studied in Tokyo and was ordained pastor in 1932. Influenced by Barth, Bultman and also Marx, he came to reject the absolutising developments in the doctrine and institutions of the church which were in contrast to the life and commitments of Jesus. He therefore distinguished between the person of the historical Jesus and the "principle" of Christ in human history, taking further Odagiri's distinction between the concept of God and the Son of God. His support for communist policies, while continuing to pastor a Kyodan congregation, provoked controversy, but also strongly influenced socialist Christians as well as the widely-read author Shiina Rinzo (1911-1973), whom he baptised. Akaiwa's church ("The Meeting") became also a centre for political education and action, and for the publication of the journal *Yubi*, which he edited. He also compiled devotional manuals.

Although dramatically selling his collection of Barth's *Church Dogmatics* (1959) to show his move from Barthianism over the previous ten years, Akaiwa's teaching retained central affirmations of the Christian faith, in particular a personal relationship with Jesus, on which was based his social passion. He stressed that a full personal relationship to God was also a full relationship to neighbours and full membership of human society. When that society held such suffering and inequalities as he observed about him, radical change was the task of Christians. He rejected, however, the way that Marxism made absolute the economic functions of life, its determinism and its use of violence. In his controversial book *Exodus from Christianity* he accepted many of the positions of radical New Testament criticism of the time, showed a strong sympathy for aspects of Buddhism, and rejected much of traditional Christianity in the name of the radical humanism of Jesus and an understanding of God that was often close to the Buddhist *sunyata*.

Selected References
Works by Akaiwa Sakai

Kami o tazunete (On God and faith). Tokyo: Kobundo, 1949.
Kirisutokyo to kyosan shugi (Communism and Christianity). Kyoto: San'ichi Shobo, 1949.
Watakushi wa ima mo Iesu o ou (Person and work of Jesus Christ). Tokyo: Kadokawa Shoten, 1949.
Kirisutokyo Dasshutsuki (Exodus from Christianity). Tokyo: 1964.
Akaiwa Sakae chosak shu (Collected works). 10 vols. Tokyo: Kyo Bun Kwan, 1970-72.
—, and Takakuwa Sumio. *Tetsugaku no tankyu* (Christianity, existentialism, dialectical materialism). Tokyo: 1948.
See also articles by Takao Toshikazu. "An Alliance of Egoists." *Risk* 6.1 (1970); "Representative Critical Approaches to the Contemporary Japanese Situation." *Japan Christian Quarterly* and 43.1 (1973); and Yamamoto Kano, "Theology in Japan: Main Trends of our Time." *Japan Christian Quarterly* 32.1 (1966).

2.5.3. Takizawa Katsumi (1906-1984)

Takizawa Katsumi first studied law, then moved to the extensive study of European philosophy, the works of the Kyoto philosopher Nishida Kitaro (1870-1945), and those of Karl Barth. He later taught religious philosophy and systematic theology in Kyushu University and regularly in Germany. His early writings gave interpretations of Nishida and Hisamatsu Shin-ichi, the philosophy of religion, student movements in Japan, Karl Barth, Marxian economics, and dialectical materialism. Later he would write books specifically on Jesus Christ (1972), on Jodo Shishu (1974), the philosophy of religion, on prominent Japanese literary figures, and many on the relationship of Christianity to Buddhism and contemporary thought. Collections or studies of Takizawa's writings appeared in 1973, 1984, 1987 and in 1989, and include those in the fields of Christology, anthropology and soteriology, as well as inter-faith dialogue.

Takizawa's most seminal work was that on the thought of the Zen master Hisamatsu (1889-1980) in *Buddhism and Christianity* (1964, second volume in 1979). This was sympathetic but also critical of the fusion of Buddha as the ultimate with the Buddha open to human realisation. Parallel to this was Takizawa's contention that there are primary and secondary meetings of God with the human being: the first is the unconditional presence of God with every person Christian or not - Immanuel. The awakening to this is primary, whereas faith realised within oneself is the secondary contact. Bringing together the insights of both Barth and Nishida, Takizawa declares that Japanese theologians have yet to recognize the "original fact of Immanuel" - as when Buddhists make the experience of enlightenment the judge of all - but must also make a distinction between God's "irreversible ... primary contact" with all humanity, and the Jesus who fully realized this in his life with others.

Widely read as this work was, it would be fundamental to much of Takizawa's future thought and writing. This was not least because it led to extensive exchanges, with both Buddhist scholars such as Akizuki Ryomin and Abe Masao, and Christians such as Honda Masaaki and Yagi Seiichi. With the latter the debate would continue for two decades and be the catalyst for many wider discussions by theologians in Japan and elsewhere. In Christology Takizawa was affirming the contemporaneity of Jesus and the Christ: rather than a temporal movement from the historic Jesus to the preached Christ, thus making Christian faith intelligible to all, without fully exclusive claims. His acceptance of Buddhism as a genuine religion, which witnessed also to a fundamental aspect of Christian faith - the presence of "God" in all - laid the basis for future creative dialogue. His conclusion also that the presence of "Immanuel" requires political and theological commitments, along with his sympathy for both protest movements and for discriminated-against minorities such as the Burakumin, added a vital dimension to theological endeavours.

Selected References
Works by Takizawa Katsumi
> *Buddhism and Christianity* (Bukkyo to Kirisutokyo). Kyoto: Hozokan, 1964, 1979.
> *Zoku Bukkyo to Christ-kyo* (Buddhism and Christianity - A continuation). Kyoto: Hozokan, 1979.
> *Gendai ni okeru ningen no mondai* (Contemporary human issues). Tokyo: San'ichi Shobo, 1984.
> *Junsui shinjingaku josetsu: mono to hito to* (Introduction to pure God-humanics: with substance and humans). Fukuoka: Sogensha, 1988.
> *Gendai no iryo to shukyo: shinshinron o megutte* (Current medical treatment and religions: about the theory of psychosomatic). Fukuoka: Sogensha, 1991.
> "On the Primary and Secondary Contacts between God and Man." *Buddhist Christian Studies* (1983).
> *Reflexionen über die universale Grundlage in Buddhismus und Christentum.* Studien zur interkulturellen Geschichte des Christentums. Frankfurt a.M.; Bern; Cirencester, U.K.: Lang, 1980. Bibliography of works by Katsumi Takizawa: 180-181.
> —, and Kasahara Hatsuji. *Naze Shinran na no ka: Kasahara Hatsuji ikoshu* (Why Shinran now?). Kyoto: Hozokan, 1984.
> Sakaguchi Hiroshi. *Takizawa Katsumi chosaku nenpu.* Fukuoka: Sogensha, 1989.
> Sundermeier, Th., ed. *Das Heil in Heute - Texte einer Japanische Theologie.* Gottingen: Vandenhoeck und Reprecht, 1987.

2.5.4. Doi Masatoshi (1907-)

Doi Masatoshi was professor of systematic theology and the history of Christian thought at Doshisha University (1956-) and later concurrently director of the NCC Center for the Study of Japanese Religions (1965-). He has played a leading role in the development of Christian study of Asian religion and of programmes of encounter and publication in inter-religious dialogue. Doi was the principal initiator in the formation of the Japan Society for Buddhist-Christian Studies (1982) and prominent in the East-West Religions Project at the University of Hawaii. He was also a Protestant observer at Vatican Council II and active in the Faith and Order movement of the WCC.

Along with studies of the place of meaning in theological enquiry, and its place in inter-faith encounter, Doi has been deeply concerned for the indigenisation of Christianity in Japan, affirming that human intention, from which all meaning comes, is always deeply rooted in one's own culture. *Theology of Meaning* is one of his central works in which he treats of the methodology and sources of a theology of meaning as being vital to any 'systematic' theology and as part of the theology of mission. Influences from Bultmann, Ebeling, Brunner, Ferré, Tillich and John Baillie can be discerned, but for Doi, the "ultimately meaningful" event occurs not only in relation to the personal subject but also to the cultural identity, thought-forms and existential circumstance of a people. In Japan and in the light of Buddhism's indigenisation there he suggests, this will require "a Japanese-Christian pattern of respect for the deceased"; theological expression of "a closer relationship between Christianity and nature"; the use of Japanese symbolism in architecture, art and liturgy; and a simplification of doctrine through the "deep personal experience [of] great souls" within the Christian community. In articles and books Doi further elaborates on these proposals.

Selected References
Works by Doi Masatoshi
> *Search for Meaning through Interfaith Dialogue.* Tokyo: Kyo Bun Kwan, 1976 (1962).

Theology of Meaning (Imi no shingaku). Tokyo: Kyo Bun Kwan, 1963.
Religion and Nature. Japanese and Christian Views. Tokyo: Kyo Bun Kwan, 1970.
Gendai ni okeru shukyo no ningenkan. (The modern man's search for meaning). Kyoto: Hozokan, 1983 (1971).
Kirisutokyo to Bukkyo: Doi Masatoshi shukyo ronshu. (Christianity and Buddhism). Kyoto: Hozokan, 1989.
Shinran to Kirisutokyo. (Shinran and Christianity). Kyoto: Hozokan, 1990.
"A Methodological Reflection on the Theology of Mission." *Japanese Religions* 4.3 (1966).
"Confessing the Faith in Asia Today." *Japanese Religions* 4.4 (1966).
"Dialogue between Living Faiths in Japan." *Japanese Religions* 6.3 (1970).
"On Meaning." *Mahayana Zen Buddhism* 769 (1988).
Spier, Fredrik. "'Dialogue is Between Fully Committed Persons': A Portrait of Doi Masatoshi." *Japanese Religions* 13.2 (1984).

2.5.5. Suzuki Masahisa (1912-1969)

Suzuki Masahisa was a pastor and church leader of high personal character and qualities of leadership, now chiefly remembered for his role in carrying through the *Confession of War Guilt* by the Kyodan (1967). However he was also one of the first to translate and edit Barth's ethical writings, as well as being one of a group - along with Inoue Yoshio - who in their ethical studies drew on Marxist insights for their social concern. Despite heavy duties in church and community, he was able in many articles, books and sermons to present the theology by which he lived and acted. He had found in Christianity - through his family life and his theological training - a deep moral discernment believing that "a spiritual revolution of sufficient depth has the power to encompass and change the world". For him, God's action in the Exodus and in Jesus and the cross achieves liberation for humanity, and also makes it possible for human beings to follow the way of Jesus: *Odo*, "the way of the king". This meant for him responsibility for the church to achieve self-reliance and autonomy; for his people in facing their past history; and for the individual in exercising moral courage and faith in the face of injustice and evil "in spite of the status quo".

His theology of church and mission had early led him to dissociate himself from missionaries and agencies that encouraged dependence, maintaining that Japanese churches are equal partners with those elsewhere and so carry equal responsibility for all aspects of their life. He led the Kyodan in specific policies to achieve this - in "self-reliance ... consolidation ... advance". (1966). This was for him also a step in what he termed "eschatological indigenization". Regarding suffering, both for persons and society, he saw this as often the result, in God's moral universe, of injustice and war, yet also found in this - and in his own personal suffering - the possibilities of redemptive power. Following a meaningless war, he believed, a new world would come through the deepened moral commitment of those who are left. In this way sure hope in the cross and resurrection of Jesus would be seen in love and service to overcome death and make possible a new world. On the basis of this theology of experience Suzuki came to write the church's *Confession of War Guilt* (1967), and in his last months summarised it in words his lost colleagues had wanted to say, but now could not: "Japan did wrong and the Church did wrong. We ask God and our neighbours to forgive us. The church must become new so it can build a new society ..." (*Odo*, 1969). The church stands by grace alone, and in her actions must proclaim grace. It was a noble example that would be followed by successive moderators of the Kyodan such as Ii Kyoshi.

Selected References
Works by Suzuki Masahisa
>*The Present-Day Mission of Christianity.* Tokyo: Shinkyo Shuppansha, 1969.
>*The Coming of God's Kingdom.* Tokyo: Shinkyo Shuppansha, 1969.
>*Odo* (The way of the king). Tokyo: Kyodan, c.1970. (English translation, *Japan Christian Quarterly* vols. 50 and 60 (Spring 1984 - Spring 1986).
>*Collected Sermons of Masahisa Suzuki.* Tokyo: Nihon Kirisuto Kyodan Shuppansha, 1973.
>*Suzuki Masahisa chosakushu* (Selected works of Susuki Masahisa). 4 vols. Tokyo: Shinkyo Shuppansha, 1980.

"The Kyodan of Tomorrow." Mimeo'd. Address delivered at the Kyodan's General Assembly at Osaka, Oct.23, 1966.

"Notes on Present-day Secularization." *Japan Christian Quarterly* 33.3 (1967).

"The Problem of Church Renewal Today in Japan." *NEAJOT* 3.1 (1968).

ed. and trans. *Karl Barth, Kirisutokyo Rinri* (Christian ethics). 4 vols. Tokyo: Shinkyo Shuppansha, 1954-1955.

Shin Murakami. "Bonnhoeffer and Suzuki on Death." *Japan Christian Quarterly Summer* (1986).

2.5.6. Joseph John Spae cicm (1913-1989)

Following ordination in 1936, Spae studied Buddhism under Etienne Lamotte at Louvain, and after a brief period in China, under Yamaguchi Susumu and others at Kyoto (from 1938). Studies in Japanese Confucianism of the 17th century led to a doctoral thesis at Columbia University in 1947. In the 1950s he founded what became the Oriens Institute of Religious Research in Tokyo in 1959. He wrote extensively on Christianity and Japanese culture and religion, and his regular articles in the *Japanese Missionary Bulletin* - of which he was for some years editor - were later collected and published in a series of volumes. These provided what were at the time unique introductions to Christianity within the religious and social context of Japan, as well as to important features of Japanese religiosity. He later became co-director of SODEPAX, Geneva, consultor to the Vatican Secretariat for Non-Christians, and was the co-director of the Chicago Institute of Theology and Culture. In his last years he returned to research on China and edited and published *China Update*.

Using primary resource materials and an interdisciplinary method, Spae's three main works - *Christian Corridors to Japan*, *Christianity Encounters Japan,* and *Religiosity, Japanese and Christian* - explore "the conditions for a fruitful meeting of Christianity with Japan". Questions of missionary methodology and cultural analysis addressed in the first volume, are followed by a "closer examination of the sociological, psychological and theological dimensions of the encounter in the second, and a treatment in the third of the ethical dimensions involved. He concludes that the Christian encounter with Japan is a mystery of love, that can never be limited to the observable or measurable, but which will always include, as in the stories of Akutagawa Ryonosuke, both the Japanese way of cultural and spiritual integration, and the mystic attraction to the divine that grips the imagination of Japanese people.

Selected References
Works by Joseph John Spae
> *Ito Jinsai, a Philosopher, Educator and Sinologist of the Tokugawa Period.* Peiping: Monumenta Serica, Monograph Series, 1948. New York: Paragon Books, 1967.
> *The Neighbourhood Associations. A Catholic Way for Japan.* Himeji Committee of the Apostolate, 1956.
> *Catholicism in Japan: a Sociological Study.* 2nd rev. ed. Tokyo: ISR Press, 1964.
> *Catholicism in Japan.* Tokyo: International Institute for the Study of Religions, 1964.
> *Christian Corridors to Japan.* Tokyo: Oriens Institute, 1965.
> *Christianity Encounters Japan.* Tokyo: Oriens Institute, 1968.
> *Japanese Religiosity.* Tokyo: Oriens Institute, 1970.
> *Buddhist-Christian Empathy.* Chicago: Chicago Institute of Theology and Culture; Tokyo: Oriens Institute for Religious Research, 1980.
> "Redemption, Japanese and Christian - An Essay in Comparative Theology." *Japanese Religions* 14.3 (1966).
> Raymaker, John. *In Memoriam: Joseph J. Spae (1913-1989). Inter-Religio* 16 (1989).

2.5.7. Sumiya Mikio (1916-)

Professor of economics at Tokyo University, Sumiya Mikio was both a theologian and social scientist who taught labor economics and produced over many years a series of impressive writings on the history and sociology of Christianity in Japan. He was active in resourcing many ecumenical groups and programmes, chaired the CCRAI of the National Council of Churches in Japan, and with NCC colleagues, undertook responsibilities for reconciliation endeavours in North Korea. He was also a member, with Sakaibara Gan, Miyamoto Takenosuke, (Mrs) Yamamoto Chiyo, Yamamoto

Kano, Kawakami Jotaro and Samuel Franklin, of the All Japan Socialist Christians' Frontier Union, which worked for the renewal of Japanese society. Marx, Weber and Reinhold Niebuhr were important for Sumiya's approach to a theology of society, in linking socialist insights with a Christian sociology, in the face of immense social and political change. In addition Sumiya learned, from the Christian economist Otsuka Hisao, to take very seriously the human rather than materialist dimension of social history, and so came to specialise in industrial problems and labor relations, challenging his fellow social scientists to "appropriate the human element within the concepts of social science". He also participated in, and wrote on, programmes of Urban Industrial Mission in Japan.

In his historical studies which have been widely influential, Sumiya values the approach of Meiji Christianity of the earliest years in critiquing the institutions of family, emperor and feudal systems in Japan, and thus presenting the alternative of a more just and equitable society. In analysing later periods, however, he finds causes for the dilution of such challenges in the neglect by the largely middle-class churches, of laborers, farmers and rural communities, as well as of the leaders of Japanese society. Nor did Christians actively challenge the industrial system which only increased many of the injustices of feudal structures, so that any recognition of, or ministry to, the new classes of industrial workers and marginalised groups, was again largely abandoned. The "underside experience", felt so deeply by such Christian critics as Abe Isoo, Kinoshita Naoe, Sakai Toshihiko and Kagawa Toyohiko (1.10.2.), was therefore now ignored by the church. His analysis of the church as a social phenomenon was directed, however, to clarifying the issues and problems faced by the church and to making concrete suggestions for possible solutions.

Selected References
Works by Sumiya Mikio
> *Kindai Nihon no keisei to Kirisutokyo* (The formation of modern Japan and Christianity 1868-1945). Tokyo: Shinkyo Shuppansha, 1950.

Nihon shakai to Kirisutokyo (Japanese society and Christianity). Tokyo: Tokyo Daigaku Shuppankai, 1954.
Gendai Nihon to Kirisutokyo (Christianity and contemporary Japan). Tokyo: Shinkyo Shuppansha, 1962.
Nihon shihon shugi to Kirisutokyo (Church and social problems). Tokyo: Daigaku Shuppankai, 1962.
Nihon Shakaishiso no Zahyojiku (The co-ordinate axis of Japanese social thought). Tokyo: Tokyo University Press, 1983.
Ajia no kaihatsu to Minshu (People and development in Asia). *Tokyo: Japan YMCA Press,* 1994.
Okinawa no toikake, Kunan no Rekishi to Kyosei no Negai. (Challenge of Okinawa - history of suffering and search for living together). Tokyo: Yotsuya Round, 1998.
Hendo no Jidai ni Ikite - hakai Kagakusha no Kaiso (Living in the period of radical change - retrospect of a social scientist). Tokyo: Iwanomi Shoten, 2000.
"Christianity and Social Science in Japan." *Student World* 44.1 (1951).
"A Responsible Church in Japan." *Japan Christian Quarterly* 21.1 (1955).
"The Social Scientist as Christian." In *The Relevance of the Social Sciences in Contemporary Asia - University Teachers in Dialogue*, edited by Shiozuki Kentaro. Tokyo: World Student Christian Federation, 1968.

2.5.8. Kitamori Kazoh (1916-)

Deeply influenced by Tanabe Hajime of the Kyoto School of philosophers, and also by Luther, Hegel, and Barth, Kitamori was professor of systematic theology at Tokyo Union Seminary. Although a Lutheran, he served also as pastor in the *Kyodan*. His independent stance included sympathy with aspects of Buddhist tradition when this was largely scorned by theologians, and forthright criticism of Barth when Barthianism was very influential.

Although he wrote over 20 volumes, he is chiefly remembered for his *Theology of the Pain of God* (1946). In this he presents "the pain of God" as the key to understanding both the biblical faith and the history of Christianity, for such pain is the means by which the "wrath of God" is reconciled with the Love of God towards sinful humanity. Theology of the Cross, rather than of glory becomes central, theology becomes the "science of "the pain of God" - which cannot be carried out through merely philosophical reasoning. It proceeds by use of an *"anologia doloris* in contrast to other types of analogy": the suffering of humankind is a symbol of the suffering which God himself accepts in the process of redemption. This makes possible for him a middle path between over-emphasis on either God's love or upon God as "wholly other". It also enabled him and his colleagues to prepare a Confession of Faith for the *Kyodan* (1954) which aimed to embrace diverse Christian traditions in a united church.

Although widely read by both Christians and non-Christians in the post-war years, Kitamori was often misunderstood as declaring in his theology that God suffered with people in their pain. He was, however, saying rather that the "transcendent pain of God is immanent in the painful reality of the world": through human pain we can be united with God, for it symbolizes, not punishment, but instead the pain of God's reconciliation of sin. Such pain can be symbolised also in the voluntary acceptance of suffering and in a strongly disciplined lifestyle. Kitamori draws on his own experience and that of Japan during the recent war to shape both his theology and lifestyle, and finds parallels to "suffering in God" in Japanese Buddhist tradition, notably in the concept of *tsurasa* - the suffering imposed on oneself to save others whom one loves. Yet although Japanese reality is included in God's universal concern, through the pain of God's reconciling love, and although love for neighbor involves feeling another's suffering as one's own, Kitamori spends little time on the concrete implications of such a theology for Japanese in the context of their actual struggles and suffering. The Christian attitude to social need, he believed, was deeper than the Marxist attitude, for it places devotion to Christ first, before action to meet human needs. Despite serious reflection in his theology on the human situation, therefore, Kitamori refrained from integrating actual human suffering into his metaphysic of suffering.

Selected References
Works by Kitamori Kazuo
>*Theology of the Pain of God.* Richmond, Va.: John Knox, 1965 (1946).

Fukuin no Seikaku (The character of the gospel). Kyoto: Nishimura Shoten, 1948.
Konnichi no Shingaku (Theology today). Tokyo: Sogensha, 1950.
Kyusai no ronri (The logic of salvation). Tokyo: Sogensha, 1953.
Pauro shokan kowa (Paul, the apostle). Tokyo: Kawade Shobo, 1957.
Bungaku to kami. (Literature of God) Tokyo: Nihon no Bara Shuppansha, 1983.
"Is 'Japanese Theology' Possible?" *NEAJOT* 3 (1969).
Muto Kazuo and Matsuda Tomoo. *Kirisutosha no jitsuzon: Marukusu shugi hihan* (Communism and Christianity). Tokyo: Shinkyo Shuppansha, 1950.
Michaelson, Carl. *Japanese Contributions to Christian Theology.* Philadelphia: Westminster Press, 1960.

2.5.9. Takeda Cho Kiyoko (1917-)

Takeda Cho was professor of Christian ethics at International Christian University, Tokyo (1961-1988), and director of the Institute for Asian Cultural Studies there, working closely with Yuasa Hachiro, Ishihara Ken, Roy Miller, Ebisawa Arimichi and Yamamoto Sumiko. She was the author of books on Christianity and culture, on the indigenisation of Christianity in Japan, on politics and government, on the emperor system in Japan, on Japanese intellectual history and the ethics of labor.

Takeda Cho was influenced by Japanese scholars of culture such as Nitobe Inazao (1.5.3.), and with Iisaka Yoshiaki, also introduced Niebuhr's writings to Japan, herself translating three of Niebuhr's key works. The place of Christianity in Japanese history and the responses of Christians to that history have been a particular interest in her studies, as have been the complex symbols and myths shaping traditional value systems in Japan and Asia. The long Christian dialogue with Japanese culture, in ideology, religious encounter, moral education, and in movements of nationalism and modernisation, has, therefore, been central to her writing and teaching. From this, too, comes her particular concern for the processes of indigenisation, and for analyses of the functioning of patriarchy, norms of belief and cultural energies.

In writing of indigenization, Takeda Cho distinguishes five types of process: the buried (where truth is lost through compromise), the isolation type (where compromise is completely refused), the confrontation type (of ongoing conflict), the grafting type (where there is both fusion and a background confrontation), and apostasy (where conscious denial becomes a means of indigenisation). Of these she chooses the grafting model by which Christianity buries itself in Japanese soil while still also confronting Japanese indigenous culture. For the Humanum Studies of the World Council of Churches, Takeda Cho compiled a pioneering report on indigenous cultural energies which provides significant resources for any contextualising theology. She includes in particular the energies of despair and anguish - for greater justice and freedom; the energies of traditional religious and philosophical values; and the energies of all women, in their unique potentialities. She also recognised in such energies both the roots of the mystery of evil - in for example an absolutist nationalism or idolatry - and the hidden blessing of indigenous energies in their imminent potential for more universal truth. Since retiring from ICU and the Institute, Takeda Cho has continued writing on politics and government, democracy in Japan, and Christian history in Japan.

Selected References
Works by Takedo Cho Kiyoko

Conflict in the Concept of Man in Modern Japan. Tokyo: Kobundo, 1959.

Dochaku to haikyo: dentoteki Etosu to Purotesutanto (Indigenousness and apostasy: traditional ethos and Protestantism). Tokyo: Meiji Tosho Shuppan, 1963.

Gendai Nihon to Kirisutokyo (Christianity in modern Japan). Gendai Nihon shiso taikei. Series of Modern Japanese Thoughts 6. Tokyo: Chikuma Shobo, 1964.

Indigenization and Compromise. Tokyo: Shinkyo Shuppansha, 1967.

Haikyosha no keifu: Nihonjin to Kirisutokyo (A genealogy of apostates. Japanese and Christianity). Tokyo: Iwanami Shoten, 1973.

Seitu to Itan no Aida (Between orthodoxy and heterodoxy - A study of the intellectual history of Japan). Tokyo: University of Tokyo Press, 1976.

The Image of Christianity in Japan. English version edited by James P. Colligan. Tokyo: Institute of Christian Culture, Sophia University, c1980.
The Milestones for Women's Liberation in Modern Japan. Tokyo: Domes Publishing, 1985.
The Dual Image of the Japanese Emperor - Before and After 1945. London: Macmillan, 1988 (1978).
Sengo demokurashi no genryu (The origin of postwar democracy). Tokyo: Iwanami Shoten, 1995.
"State Religion and Ideologies in Japan." In *Religion, State and Ideologies in East Asia,* edited by M.M. Thomas and M. Abel. East Asia Christian Conference, 1965.
"Christian Dialogue with Traditional Japanese Culture." *Japan Christian Quarterly* 44.1 (Winter 1978).
"The Continuity of Old Symbols and the Innovation of Traditional Value Systems in Asia." *Asian Cultural Studies* 12 (1981).

2.5.10. Takenaka Masao (1925-)

Born in Northeast China, Takenaka Masao studied ecomonics and theology at Kyoto and social ethics at Yale University. Since 1955 he has taught Christian ethics and the sociology of religion at Doshisha University. Since the late 1950s he has also been prominent in the Japan Christian Academy movement, and programmes of urban mission in Japan. Throughout Asia and beyond he has been active in a wide range of ecumenical programmes, with the EACC/CCA, the WCC, the Asian Christian Art Association and the Programme for Theology and Cultures in Asia.

Much of his writing has arisen from long-held concerns for Christian ethics in Japan, for urban mission and laity formation, for recording the life and work of significant Japanese Christians, and for the place of Christianity within Asian cultures and for Asian Christian Art. The entire secular world is for Takenaka, the arena for God's activity and he draws on the resources of Japanese Christian biography, history and art, Asian culture and folk music, social analysis and biblical study in his writings. But his life has also been marked by close involvement in people movements for social justice, theological reflection and creative art. His own reflection has been nourished by these involvements and by his conviction that the heart of Christian ethics is "based upon an 'agonistic' way of life" in the midst of secular engagement. There he finds the "A-ha!" experience of God's always unexpected yet sustaining presence in hope and courage, solidarity and beauty. Hope for God's future is found in koinonia in the midst of people's struggle, in the prophetic role of artistic expression, and in Asian cultural reformation and renaissance.

Selected References
Works by Takenaka Masao
- *Reconciliations and Renewal in Japan.* New York: Friendship Press, 1957.
- *Shinjin no Kyodotai* (Community of true humanity). Tokyo: Shinkyo Shuppansha, 1962.
- *Christian Art in Asia.* Tokyo: Kyo Bun Kwan and Singapore: CCA, 1975.
- *Searching for an Image of the Working Person: Kansai Labor Evangelism Fellowship Notes - Its Last 20 Years.* Tokyo: Shinkyo Shuppansha, 1978.
- *Tencho no Tabibito* (A heavenly pilgrim - The life and works of Yoshihei Miya). Tokyo: YMCA Shuppan, 1979.
- *God is Rice.* Risk Book series. Geneva: WCC, 1988.
- *Cross and Circle.* URM Series 1. Hong Kong: CCA - URM, 1990.
- *Wafuku no Kirisutosha* (A Christian in Japanese kimono - life of Sentaro Nanba 1865-1945). Tokyo: Nihon Kirisuto Kyodan Shuppan Kyoku, 1992.
- *Ryokan to Kirisuto* (Ryokan and Christ - life of Suesada Omiya 1866-1944). Tokyo: Kokodo, 1996. See also "Ryokan and Christians in Japan." *Japanese Religions* 21.2 (1996).
- *Katsuokaishu Neeshima Jyo.* (Kaishu Katsu and Jo Neeshima). Kyoto: Doshisha University, 1999.
- "First-fruits of the New Humanity." In *Christ's Ministry and Ours*, edited by John R. Fleming. Singapore: EACC, 1962.
- —, and Ron O'Grady. *The Bible Through Asian Eyes.* Auckland: Pace Publishing, 1991.

2.5.11. Furuya Yasuo (1926-)
Furuya has been chaplain and professor of theology and religion at International Christian University, Tokyo. Amongst his principal theological concerns have been the history of Christianity in Japan,

the theology of religions and inter-faith dialogue, the possibility of a "Japanese theology", and the secularization of the Christian university.

He finds in the history of Christianity in Japan frequent conflict with a spiritual core of Shintoist nationalism, yet sees the task of theology in Japan as one of clarifying "Japan's mission as a nation [and helping] nationalism to achieve its purpose". Furuya presents a theology of religions which seeks reality and truth in other religions yet retains the uniqueness of Jesus Christ. "The exclusiveness of Revelation in Christ is not inconsistent with its comprehensiveness", he maintains, "and the uniqueness of Christ is not inconsistent with his universality". For him, therefore, uniqueness and universality are not in conflict, even though this may be beyond a completely logical - in the western sense - resolution. But then in Jesus Christ there is "the judgment and grace of God on all religions and civilizations of both east and west, including Christianity and western civilization". In writing of inter-faith dialogue Furuya also contrasts the approaches often taken by western scholars which, be believes, misunderstand the realities of inter-faith encounter in Asia, and appeals to them to "also have dialogue with your fellow Christians and theologians in Asia".

Regarding the task of theology in Japan, Furuya, along with Ohki Hideo, has declared that this cannot be a Japanese theology as such, although it may include Japan's participation in the formation of theology, but is rather a theology which totally questions Japan from a theological - that is "God's" - point of view. This position is partly in response to "the myth of the so-called uniqueness of Japanese culture" which has led to extremes of nationalism in the past, but Furuya finally leaves open the question as to whether a specifically Japanese culture exists or not (see Ohki 2.7.).

Selected References
Works by Furuya Yasuo
   Gendai Kirisutokyo to shorai (Today's Christianity and the prospects). Tokyo: Shinchi Shobo, 1984.

Shukyo no shingaku: sono keisei to kadai (Theology of religions). Tokyo: Yorudansha, 1985, 1987.

Nihon dendoron. Tokyo: Kyobunkan, 1995. Subjects: Missions—Japan.

"The Challenge of Asian Christianity." *Pacific Theological Review* (1977); *Theology Today* 35.1 (1978).

—, ed. *A History of Japanese Theology.* Grand Rapids, Mich.: Eerdmans, c1997.

—, and Oki Hideo *Nihon no shingaku* (Theology of Japan). Tokyo: Yorudansha, 1989.

—, and Kuramatsu Isao, Namiki Koichi, Kondo Katsuhiko. *Chi to shin to daigaku: Furuya Yasuo koki kinen ronbunshu.* Tokyo: Yorudansha, 1996. List of works by Yasuo Furuya: 477-481.

2.5.12. Kadowaki Kakichi, Johannes, sj (1926-)

Kadowaki Kakichi graduated from Tokyo University, studied in Rome, New York and Regensburg, and taught the philosophy of religion at Sophia University in Tokyo until his recent retirement. He has also participated fully in the programmes and studies of the Nanzan Institute for Religion and Culture, Nagoya. His major philosophical work has focused upon a philosophy of "the way" - *Michino Keijijyogaku* (Metaphysics of the Way), and of "the body" - *Karadano Keijijyogaku* (Metaphysics of the Body). Kadowaki established with Aoki Hiroyuki the Society for Mind-Body Science (*Jintai-kagaku-kai*) in Tokyo (1991), in pursuance of these concerns. He has studied Buddhism fully and, an accredited Zen teacher, promoted inter-faith dialogue with Zen both in personal engagement and in his writing. He also played a key role in making possible the unique series of meetings called "East-West Spiritual Exchange" (1979), in which Zen and Catholic monks shared ideas that went beyond cultural or racial differences.

Kadowaki believes that in one chief matter "the teachings of Nichiren and Jesus are similar in that both tell us we can only realize the loving vow for salvation of God and the Buddha when we are willing to risk our very lives". For Kadowaki and his colleagues this is both a theological and a pastoral concern within the context of Japan's religious and social life. He has also written on Basho, Dogen and Taoism, on the relationship of Noh Drama to the Mass, as well as on the issues of suffering and of death as these are understood in major religious traditions.

Selected References
Works by Kadowaki Kakichi

Koan to Seisho no Shindoku - Kirisutosha no Sanzen Taiken. (Koan - catechetical question for meditation and bodily reading of the Bible. A Christian participation in Zen experience). Tokyo: Shunjyusha, 1977.

Zen and the Bible. A Priest's Experience, translated by Joan Rieck. London: Routledge and Kegan Paul.1980.

Nihon no Shukyo to Kirisuto no Michi (Japanese religions and the Christian way). Tokyo: Iwanami Shoten, 1997.

"Ways of Knowing: A Buddhist-Thomist Dialogue." *International Philosophical Quarterly* 6.4 (1966).

"Kõan and New Biblical Hermeneutics." In *Religious Experience and Language: A Buddhist-Christian Dialogue,* edited by Nanzan Institute for Religion and Culture. Tokyo: Kinokuniya, 1978.

"From Chuang-tzu's Way to Jesus Christ as the Way." *Inter-Religio* 15 (1989).

"Christianity and Shintoism." *Japan Mission Journal* 47.2 (1993).

ed. *Gendai no Kunoto Shukyo* (Contemporary agony and religion). Tokyo: Sogensha, 1976.

ed. *Mikkyo to Kirisutokyo* (Esoteric Buddhism and Christianity). Tokyo: Sogensha, 1977.

ed. *Shino Kanata ni - Shukyoteki Shiseikan* (Beyond death - the understanding of life and death in religions). Tokyo: Nansosha, 1985.

Åmell, Katrin. *Contemplation and dialogue. Some examples of dialogue between spiritualities after the council Vatican II.* Uppsala, 1998.

2.5.13. Inoue Yoji (1927-)

Following study at the University of Tokyo, Inoue Yoji entered a Carmelite monastery in France and taught theology at the Universities of Lyon and Lille. Returning to Japan in 1958 he immersed himself in Japanese culture, became a priest in Tokyo, and taught at the Asahi Culture Center. He has collaborated in studies of Japanese Christian literature and also written biographies of Japanese clergy. His principal writings, however, have been on the relationship between Christianity and Japanese culture and these are acknowledged to be major contributions to contextual Japanese theology.

In these he seeks to discover, in contrast to traditional images held of Christianity in Japan, and as the fruit of his own experience, the authentic image of Jesus within the life and culture of Japanese people. Believing there can never be a Christianity which does not exist as a complex of a certain culture, he understands his calling to be that of expressing Jesus' teachings - something that is universal for humankind - "within the sensibility of Japanese everyday life". This involves the recognition that whereas "substance" is the basis for western ways of thinking, the foundation for Japanese thought is "the field which envelops substances" which is God, and which embraces both subject and object. Christianity must therefore undergo restoration as a religion of "field" - where God transcends the distinctions between Christianity and non-Christianity, being and non-being, in the self-negation of Jesus' life and death.

Although Inoue affirms the uniqueness of Jesus as understood by Japanese, he also takes very seriously the historic life of Jesus within a particular place and culture and on this he has written extensively. But he uses also such images as those from the *Kojiki* chronicle, the poetry of *Basho* and *Ryokan*, from Japanese gardens and temples, from *Amitabha* of the Pure Land and the road-side statues of *Ojizo-sama*, to explore the realities of Jesus' life in the life and local situations of Japan. The Divine here becomes "unobjectified [as] a deep fountainhead of life-force ... the holy Mu (No-thingness)"; Jesus' life and teaching is the means to make us experience this quiet and fecund spaciousness "as the great life which makes us fully alive"; and the presence of Jesus for us is found as the "heart of a cloud" - a compassion received and lived in nature and society, and a response of "unlimited agape" in the all-embracing field of eternal life. The love which Jesus offers makes one give "co-suffering hands to those who are valueless ... and are suffering, like the sun shining upon all living things without an exception".

Selected References
Works by Inoue Yoji

The Face of Jesus in Japan (Nihon to Iesu no Kao). Tokyo: Shuppankyoku, 1976. Translated by Hisako Akamatsu. Tokyo: Kindai-Bungeisha, 1994.

Watakushi no Naka no Kirisuto (Christ within me). Tokyo: Shufunotomo, 1978.

Kirisuto o hakonda otoko Paul (Epistles of Paul). Tokyo: Kodansha, 1987.

Nihon to Iesu no kao (The Face of Jesus in Japan). Tokyo: Nihon Kirisuto Kyodan Shuppankyoku, 1990.

"Western Christianity and Japan." *Japan Missionary Bulletin* 35 (1981).

"From a 'Theology of the Individual Person' towards a 'Theology of the Local Situation'." *Japan Missionary Bulletin* 37.7 (1983).

"As the Wind Blows. Interview with Fr. Inoue Yoji." *Japan Mission Journal* 52.2 (1998).

—, and Yamane Michihiro. *Kaze no naka no omoi: Kirisutokyo no bunkanai kaika no kokoromi* (on Yagi, Jukichi, 1889-1927 and Christianity and culture). Tokyo: Nihon Kirisuto Kyodan Shuppankyoku, 1989.

—, and Yasuoka Shotaro. *Warera naze Kirisuto kyoto to narishi ka.* Tokyo: Kobunsha, 1999.

2.5.14. Jan Van Bragt (1928-)

Jan Van Bragt is research fellow (1976-1996) and director of the Nanzan Institute for Religion and Culture (1976-1991), Professor Emeritus, Nanzan University and lecturer at Otani and Ryukoku Universities. His chief theological concerns have been: how to fully recognise the other religions, while recognising Jesus Christ as Son of God in a unique sense and as universal Saviour, and how to learn from Buddhism for Christian theology. Jan Van Bragt has tried to solve the koan, "How can such a natural affinity in religiosity [between Buddhism and Christianity] result in such an incurable disjunction in doctrine?" He believes that mysticism is "the true factor of salvation [in Buddhism], while in Christianity salvation is a question of faith". By this he does not mean that faith is absent in, or unimportant for, Buddhism, but finds this most significant in such traditions as Pure Land Buddhism in particular. The tendency to Oneness, which is regarded as a key element in what is called mysticism, he sees to be more native to Buddhism than to Christianity, with its insistence on a transcendent Other called God.

In recent writings Jan Van Bragt has expounded the trends in Japanese theology which have been influenced by Buddhism, and which incorporate basic Buddhist concepts in their theologising. Here he feels that the contributions of such writers as Hatano, Takizawa, Ariga, Doi, Muto, and Inoue are important for Japanese theology as a whole and not only for Buddhist-Christian dialogue; especially in their hopes for an intellectual underpinning for faith. This would then be freed from graeco-latin influence and become more truly Japanese. Christian theology, Van Bragt believes, is learning again from Buddhism, the role in spirituality of meditation, "wisdom" and "attention", in place of widespread neglect by Christians of the spiritual path; a freedom and scepticism regarding laws, rituals and institutionalisation; a rejection of the self-sufficient "person", and mutual indwelling of all things; along with inwardly religious philosophy of 'self-emptying' which can embrace all the negatives of life. His picture of a world religion, therefore, is one which is a religion of and by lay people; in which social responsibility is central; which has the capacity to appreciate other religions in terms of its own religiosity; and which is humanist and compassionate, non-patriarchal and liberative, communitarian and mystical.

Selected References
Works by Jan Van Bragt

"Notulae on Emptiness and Dialogue - Reading Professor Nishitani's What is Religion?" *Japanese Religion* 4.4 (1966).

"Toward a Theology of Religions." Article series. *Japan Missionary Bulletin*, from 38.1 (1984) and *Oriens Studies* 17. Tokyo: Oriens Institute for Religious Research, 1984.

"Salvation and Enlightenment: Pure Land Buddhism and Christianity." *Nanzan Bulletin* 14 (1990).

"Liberative Elements in Pure Land Buddhism." *Inter-Religio* 18 (1990).

"The Way of Devotion: Pure Land Buddhism." *Japan Missionary Bulletin* 47.4 (1993).
"Buddhism-Jodo Shinshu-Christianity, Does Jodo Shinshu Form a Bridge Between Buddhism and Christianity?" *Japanese Religions* 8.1 (1993).
"World Religion: Its Conditions and Tasks." *Nanzan Bulletin* 18 (1994).
"Christian Theology Learning from Buddhism." *Nanzan Bulletin* 21 (1997).
"Apocalyptic Thought in Christianity and Buddhism." *Japan Mission Journal* 52.3 (1998).
"Inculturation of the Gospel in Buddhist Countries." *Japan Missionary Bulletin* 52.4 (1998).
"Contributions of Buddhism to Christianity." *Nanzan Bulletin* 23 (1999).
—, and Paul Mommaers. *Mysticism Buddhist and Christian: Encounters with Jan van Ruusbroec*. Nanzan Studies in Religion and Culture. New York: Crossroad, 1995.
Keiji Nishitani. *Religion and Nothingness,* edited and translated by Jan Van Bragt. Berkeley: University of California Press, 1982.

2.5.15. Isshiki Yoshiko (1928-)

Isshiki Yoshiko, an ordained minister in the United Church of Christ in Japan, was the first woman to serve as secretary of her church's National General Assembly and has been president of *Kyofukai,* the oldest Japanese Christian women's organisation, founded in 1886. Her particular concerns have included problems of discrimination - especially against Koreans - in Japan, along with the range of issues involved in the struggles within the church for women to gain recognition and participation in leadership, and in the development of feminist theology in Japan.

In early writings Isshiki presented the work and thought of Kawai Michi (1.8.2.) and later developed her thought in relation to issues of patriarchy, ecology, social justice and personal spiritual life. In biblical studies she has directly applied accounts of Jesus' dealings with women to the circumstances of women in Japan and to the distortions of paternalistic societies. The development of feminist theologies she sees as "an expression of the very personal experience of acceptance and empowerment through the encounter

Contextual Theology in Japan 409

with Jesus." She describes eco-feminism as the establishment of "solidarity among the inhabitants of the oikos ... a movement for sharing and caring for others ... women's way of living as in sharing their bodies for babies to grow in their wombs".

Selected References
Works by Isshiki Yoshiko
- *Hikari no ko* (Children of light). Tokyo: Shinkyo Shuppansha, 1947.
- *Ai no hito* (Kawai Michiko Sensei person of love). Tokyo, Sogensha, Showa 28 (i.e. 1953).
- *Mizu ga me o oite: Iesu to deatta joseitachi* (Putting down the water jar: the women who met Jesus). Tokyo: Kirisuto Shinbunsha, 1996.
- —, et al. *Kaiho no shingaku: josei kara no shiten* (Liberation theology: a women's perspective). Tokyo: San'yo Shuppansha, 199
- —, et al. *Women Moving Mountains. Feminist Theology in Japan*. Kuala Lumpur: Asian Women's Resource Centre for Culture and Theology, 2000.
- "The Woman Who was about to be Stoned." *Japan Christian Review* 64 (1998).
- "Eco-Feminism in the 21st Century." *In God's Image* 19.3 (2000).

2.5.16. Kumazawa Yoshinobu (1929-)

Kumazawa Yoshinobu studied in Tokyo and Heidelberg. He wrote his doctoral thesis on hermeneutics, acknowledging the influence of Brunner and Bultmann. He then taught systematic theology for many years at Tokyo Union Theological Seminary and led in the Asian Ecumenical Institute there. He was active in the National Council of Churches, in national religious television programmes and in movements for urban mission and for the disabled and handicapped. He has also been committed to international theological ministries through the EACC/CCA, in the Northeast Asia Association of Theological Schools, and through both the Asian Ecumenical Institute and the Center for Christian Response for Asian Issues. He stands out as a professional theologian who has done much of his most creative writing out of direct experience within the concrete situations of local communities.

Amongst his writings, *Burutoman* (Bultmann, 1962) was pioneering work in hermeneutic study for Japan. He had supported the placing of a Christian pavilion at the Osaka Expo 1970 as a symbol of God's presence (even) there, and would subsequently give much attention in his writings to the theology of *missio Dei* within the Japanese context. His treatment of this, and of the *promissio dei* - the response of Christ and of ourselves - is always firmly christocentric and trinitarian. A collection of his articles published in 1974, chiefly missiological, included reflections on secularisation, changing ecclesial structures, and urban movements, from his experience in downtown Tokyo. The particular issues to be faced in contextualising theology in Japan occur regularly in his articles and books, and he has also written on christology, Christianity's "modern discourse", mass media and communication, and as a major concern, theology of the handicapped. From experience at a center for the disabled, he here wrestles with the dilemmas of those who cannot "confess faith" because of their disability, affirming that faith is "confessed" not only by word but by the "being" of the people themselves. This also applies to the whole people of God he believes, and raises sharp issues for the priestly role of the church in society.

Selected References
Works by Kumazawa Yoshinobu

> *Asuno Shingaku to Kyokai* (Theology and Church for tomorrow). Tokyo: Kyodan Shuppankyo, 1974.
> "A Theologian looks at Urban Mission." *Breakthrough* 12 (1968).
> "Salvation Today: a Missiological Approach." In *Mission Trends*, edited by T. Stransky and G.H. Anderson. New York: Paulist; Grand Rapids: Eerdmans, 1974
> "Asian Theological Reflections on Liberation." *NEAJOT* 14 (1974).
> "Seeking to Integrate Text and Context." In *Asian Voices in Christian Theology*, edited by G.H. Anderson. Maryknoll, NY: Orbis Books, 1976. (Also as "Kirche und Theologie unter der missio Dei." In *Brennpunkte in Kirche und Theologie Japans*, edited by Terazono Yoshiki and Heyo E. Hamer. Beiträge und Dokumente. Neukirchen-Vluyn: Neukirchener Verlag, 1988.

"Confessing Christ in the Context of Japanese Culture." *NEAJOT* 22/23 (1979).

"Non-Christian Context as Post-Christian Context: The Hermeneutic Task ... in the Japanese Context." *NEAJOT* 24/25 (1980).

—, and Paul Pfister. *Eyes and Hands; The Discovery of Humanity; The Christian Pavilion at Expo '70.* Tokyo: Enderle, 1970.

—, and David Swain, eds. *Christianity in Japan 1971-1990.* Tokyo: Kyo Bun Kwan; Cincinnati: Friendship Press, 1991.

2.5.17. Koyama Kosuke (1929-)

Koyama Kosuke is widely known for his writings in contextual theology, and although much of his teaching and writing has been done outside Japan, his significance for Asian theologies is no less important for Japanese contextual theology, and so must be recognised here. After teaching theology and church history in Chiengmai (from 1960), he was director and dean of the Southeast Asia Graduate School of Theology and a teacher of religious studies in Dunedin, New Zealand, before teaching ecumenics and world Christianity in New York. His fundamental move in theological focus occurred while still in Chiengmai, when he turned from studies of Aquinas, Luther (subject of his dissertation in 1959) and Barth (subject of his first book in 1966), to begin theologising from the life of northern Thai farmers. From this came the collection of papers first published in a mimeographed volume, *Waterbuffalo Theology - A Thai Theological Notebook* (Singapore, 1970), written to "the theological students of South East Asia".

Koyama sums up the challenges which *Waterbuffalo Theology* addresses in three points: to articulate Jesus Christ in words that are culturally appropriate, yet also criticising and reforming culture where necessary, in the formation of 'theology in loco'; to be inter-personal, and not inter-doctrinal, in the processes of dialogue and "mutual enrichment'; and to pursue ecumenical theology which is committed to ecological health and justice. In his Epilogue to the 25th anniversary edition of *Waterbuffalo Theology* - "My Pilgrimage in Mission" (reprinted from IBMR), Koyama outlines a pilgrim's progress from early theological study, to its Thai reshaping, followed by a decolonialisation of theology in the work of ATESEA/ SEAGST and later teaching appointments. It concludes with reflection on the enormity of violence everywhere in world, which though struggled against within each living religious tradition, remains a mystery only to be exposed through the mystery of the Eucharist.

In his other writings of biblical and "secular" meditations, in his works on missiology and contextual theology, and in his theology of the Cross, Koyama has been deeply concerned to "demonstrate concretely" and through poetic intuition, God's presence and grace with human suffering and violence, human justice and compassion. Writing of the Christian history of Asia, he early identified the paradox of "gun and ointment" there, and returns later again and again to affirm that theology must always involve an "ethical walking" with the marginalised, the homeless and the stranger. Throughout Asia, Africa and in western countries, he has been theological companion and catalyst in all attempts to do theology with the actual circumstances of suffering and with aspiring men and women. This he terms "hot" theology, for it is historical, committed and public in its action, and constantly accompanied by God who experiences the same history and is wholly committed to God's people.

Selected References
Works by Koyama Kosuke
> *Pilgrim or Tourist.* Singapore: CCA, 1974.
> *Waterbuffalo Theology.* London: SCM Press; Maryknoll, NY: Orbis Books, 1974. (25th anniversary revised and expanded edition, Orbis Books, 1999).
> *No Handle on the Cross.* London: SCM Press; Maryknoll, NY: Orbis Books, 1976.
> *50 Meditations.* Belfast: Christian Journals, 1975. Maryknoll, NY: Orbis Books, 1979.
> *Three Mile an Hour God.* Maryknoll, NY: Orbis Books, 1980.
> *Biblical Meditations on Contemporary Issues.* 3 vols. (In Japanese). Tokyo: Doshin Publishing House, 1984-85.
> *Mt Fuji and Mt Sinai: A Critique of Idols.* London: SCM Press; Maryknoll NY; Orbis Books, 1985.
> "We Had Rice With Jesus." In *Theology and Action*, edited by Oh Jae-shik and John C. England. Tokyo and Perth: EACC, 1972.

"Gospel and Japanese Spirituality." (In Japanese). *Fukuin to Sekai* (1986).
"Participation of Culture in the Transfiguration of Humanity: Forms of Ecumenical Theology in Asia." *Asia Journal of Theology* 7.4 (1993).

2.5.18. Arai Sasagu (1930-)

After studies with Goro Mayeda at Todai (with Yagi, Tagawa, Satake) and at Erlangen, Arai taught primitive Christianity at Aoyama Gakuin, and then was professor at Tokyo University (1969-1991). Studies and writing on Gnostic writings and problems of formation of the canon were followed by articles on the distinctions between orthodoxy and heresy and on the recognition of women, in the context of both early Gnostic and Christian movements. His major contributions to contemporary theology and social concern have been in studies of the life of Jesus and his companions within the particular socio-political context of Palestine. They include sociological studies of biblical religion similar to those of Sekine Masao; on christology, creatively interpreting Nag Hamadi writings (in *The Gospel of Truth*, 1966); and on Gnosticism (in *Primitive Christianity and Gnosticism*, 1971).

One of Arai's key works was *Jesus and His Time*, in which he summed up many of his christological concerns, presenting a more fully human and contextualised portrayal of Jesus within the concrete situation of his people. Contrasting Mark's "simple" narrative with Matthew's and Luke's more 'theological' treatments, he sees here the importance of social strata in New Testament writers who, on the evidence of their language, often belonged to the petite bourgeoisie. Jesus' sayings and actions are, however, a threat to authority in giving priority to love and questioning the reasons for their suffering. He obviously disturbed the existing social order by responding directly to people's needs, identifying with those discriminated-against and freeing them for a fuller life, while also urging both oppressed and oppressors to reform themselves in order to restore relationships. Jesus, therefore, is to be understood not just "Christologically" but also humanly and politically.

In later writings Arai returned also to treatment of the New Testament canon and its interpretation, and also of women's role in the New Testament and early church in dialogue with feminist theologians. Although the New Testament writings, apart from Mark, Luke and John, are largely ambiguous or chauvinist regarding the role and status of women, Arai finds the Gospel of Thomas - which also evinces patterns of thought similar to those of India - gives, as do Gnostic movements in west Asia, a high evaluation of women, in contrast to developing discrimination in the churches. Affirming that the Gospels themselves were born within the culture and society of their times, Arai finds in the historical and mental background of Jesus' stories new resources to live together without present class consciousness and discrimination. In a recent book on discrimination (1999), Arai analyses those elements, found in the Bible as well, which legitimate discrimination today, but declares we must affirm the "affirmative heritage" also there, which leads us to "co-living" as humans. Arai here applies the theological methodology of Kuribayashi (2.5.28.) to "restructure and reorganize over again from the perspective of the victim" in our approach to the Bible.

Selected References
Works by Arai Sasagu

> Die Christologie des Evangelium Veritatis. Eine religionsgeschichtliche Untersuchung. Leiden: Brill, 1964.
>
> Die Christologie des Evangelium Veritatis (The Christology of the Gospel of truth). Leiden, Brill, 1964.
>
> Genshikirisutokyo to Gunoshisushugi (Primitive Christianity and Gnosticism). Tokyo: Iwanami Shoten, 1984 (1971).
>
> Shokikirisutokyoshi no shomondai (Problems of early Christian history - A viewpoint in the present day). Tokyo: Shinkyo Shuppansha, 1979 (1973).
>
> Iesu to sono jidai (Jesus and His time). Tokyo: Iwanami Shoten, 1988 (1974).
>
> Iesu Kirisuto. Tokyo: Kodansha, 1984 (1979).
>
> Kakasaretu Iesu - Tomasu ni yoru fukuinsho (The hidden Jesus - the Gospel according to Thomas). Tokyo: Kodansha, 1984.
>
> 'Dodansha' Iesu (Jesus the companion). Tokyo: Shinchi Shobo, 1985.

Shin-yakuseisho no joseikan (Views on women in the New Testament). Tokyo: Iwanami Shoten, 1988.
Discrimination and Living-Together in the Bible. Tokyo: Iwanami Shoten, 1999.
"Jesus and Women around Him." *Bulletin of Research in Christian Culture* 10 (1988).

2.5.19. Takayanagi Shunichi sj (1932-)

The early work of Takayanagi Shunichi is found in a series of collected addresses and monographs on 20th century doctrinal theology, as well as on cultural history, sociology, urban history, the history of utopias, and in comparative studies of Japanese and European civilisation. By the late 1970s he was publishing a series of studies in the life, death and resurrection of Jesus as these are presented in the writings of Japanese theologians and writers. They include Arai Sasagu - an exegesis of Jesus' death; Yagi Seiichi - in dialogue with Buddhism; Takizawa Katsumi - in a theology of religions; Endo Shusaku's portrait of Jesus; and Inoue Yoji's writing on the 'face of Jesus'.

A later series of writings followed on central theological emphases of European theologians and writers (including Christology, Messianism and Creation, the Holy Spirit, the Trinity, Promise and Hope, Aesthetics, and God's Mystery). Hermeneutic issues and critique of neo-Chalcedonianism have also featured in his writings. Takayanagi has also published three volumes of christology, is presently the editor of *The New Catholic Encyclopedia of Japan*, and in a recent major study reflects upon the post-modern role of the Church and of theology.

Selected References

Works by Takayanagi Shunichi

Kindai bungaku no naka no Kirisutokyo (Christianity in modern literature). Tokyo: Nansosha, 1981.
Seisho no kami to hito (Christian anthropology). Tokyo: Nansosha, 1983.
Yutopia-gaku kotohajime (History of utopias). Tokyo: Fukutake Shoten, 1983.
"Christology and Post-war Theologians in Japan." In *Postwar trends in Japan: studies in commemoration of Rev. Aloysius Miller,*

S. J., edited by Shunichi Takayanagi and Kimitada Miwa. Tokyo: University of Tokyo Press, c1975.
"Towards a Japanese Christian Theology." *Japan Missionary Bulletin* 10 (1976).
"Jesus - His Non-political and Political death on the Cross." *Japan Missionary Bulletin* 9 (1979).
"Between Fact and Truth - Endo Shusaku's Powerless Jesus." *Japan Missionary Bulletin* 11 (1979).
"Hermeneutics, Anamnesis and Experience." *Catholic Studies* 18.35 (1979).
"Kirisutoron no Dento" (Christological tradition). *Katorikku Kenkyu* 41.1 (1982).
"Neo-Chalcedonianism: its Significance in the History of Christology." *Katorikku Kenkyu* 47 (1986).
"Modernity and After. The Church, Theology and the World on the Threshold of the Third Millennium." *Katorikku Kenkyu* 68 (1999).

2.5.20. Yagi Seiichi (1932-)

Yagi's studies of Uchimura and Kierkegaard, and in New Testament under Mayeda Goro, were followed by work in Gottingen with Ernst Kasemann and studies of Bultmann. He also encountered Zen Buddhism at that time in what he regarded as a religious experience which added to the phase of I-Thou in Christian conversion, the phase of subject-object integration in Buddhist enlightenment. Both brought experience of transcendental reality, beyond subject-object distinctions, as the ground of religious existence, which he termed "topos". In Zen he found "a parallel existential self-understanding" with Christianity, and found the basis of Christianity to be not atonement and resurrection, but "the Logos, which works everywhere to actualize religious experience". Results of these experiences would be seen in Yagi's continuing efforts to move beyond any "German activity" in theology and also to form bridges between both New Testament and systematic theologies and between Buddhist and Christian thought.

In his work on hermeneutics (*The Formation of New Testament Thought*, 1963), Yagi understands the Christ-kerugma of early Christianity as an interpretation - through "pure intuition" - of enlightenment. What Jesus called "the reign of God", was in fact what the primitive church called "Christ", in its continuing experience of the resurrection. Thus he terms this the "order for integration", similar to Buddhist "mutual interaction" (*engi*) of the ego and knowledge. New Testament thought, therefore, does not proceed by subject-object distinctions, but in a union of these. Yagi also finds parallels to the trends in christological development in the early church towards a "humanistic theology of love", in the history of Buddhist movements culminating in Zen.

A series of six books then traced his movement to studies in the philosophy of religion in dialogue with Buddhism, and in continuing debate with Takizawa and others on the relationship of Buddhist and Christian thought (from *Christ and Jesus*, 1969 to *The Point of Contact of Buddhism and Christianity*, 1975). Agreeing with Takizawa's distinction between the primary and secondary contacts of God with human beings, he maintained against Takizawa, that "pure intuition", or "immediate experience" is in fact a satisfactory basis for religious cognition. He believed that Takizawa discussed more on the basis of Nishida's "ambiguous" approach to experience than on the reality of the experience itself. In this reality, Yagi believes, there is both a "field of integration" between absolute and relative, recognised by both Buddhist and Christian, but also the experience of transcendence, not normally present in Buddhism. Yet in dialogue, both ourselves and the traditions to which we belong can change constructively, as we affirm authentic understanding in the other. In both Mahayana "inter-relatedness" and Christian "love as the source of all", there is movement away from ego, and life in mutual interdependence. Such thought had its impact upon social developments in the 1970s in Japan, but has also opened new paths for theological reflection and dialogue in Japan and in the West.

Selected References
Works by Yagi Seiichi
> *Shinyaku Shiso no Sei-ritsu* (The formation of New Testament thought). Tokyo: Shinkyo Press, 1962.
> *Biblical Jesus and Modern Thinking* (Seisho no Iesu to Gendai no Shii). Tokyo: 1965

Seisho no Kiristo to Yesu (The biblical Christ and existence). Tokyo: Shinkyo Shuppansha Press, 1967.
Kirisutokyo wa Sinji-uruka? (Can we believe in Chrisianity?) Tokyo: Kodansha, 1970.
Bukkyo to Kirisutokyo no Setten. (Buddhism and Christianity). Tokyo: Hozokan Press, 1975.
Die Front-Struktur als Brucke vom buddistischen zum christlichen Denken. Munich: Chr, Kaiser Verlag, 1987.
Shukyo to gengo shukyo no gengo (Religion and language, religious language). Tokyo: Nihon Kirisutokyodan Shuppankyoku, 1995.
"The Dependence of Japanese Theology upon the Occident." *Japan Christian Quarterly* 30 (1964).
"Buddhist Atheism and Christian God." In *Gott in Japan*, edited by Yagi Seiichi and Ulrich Luz. Munich: Chr. Kaiser Verlag, 1973.
"Buddhism and Christianity." *NEAJOT* 20/21 (1978).
"Japanese Christian Theology in Encounter with Buddhism." *Buddhist Christian Studies* 2 (1982).
"Buddhist Philosophy and New Testament Theology." *Buddhist-Christian Studies* 19 (1999).
—, and Leonard Swidler. *A Bridge to Buddhist-Christian Dialogue.* Tokyo: Paulist Press, 1990.
Barksdale, J. "Seiichi's Typology of New Testament Thought." *NEAJOT* 17 (1976).

2.5.21. Aiko Carter (fl. 1970-1990)

After taking up staff responsibilities with the Japan National Christian Council, Aiko Carter became (from 1978) a central figure in the development of programmes for women's study, action and theological reflection in Japan. "I had been fascinated", she recounts, "by women of past times who stood up in the midst of a patriarchal society and never, ever gave up their dreams [and] resisted being locked in the traditional ready-made status of women ... Although many Christian publications were available for men, women's voices were not recognized. In order for women to express their experience, wisdom, and reflections, we needed space where we could freely search the personal puzzle, and accept the uniqueness of the individual ... a newsletter was initiated so that each was able to express themselves through prayers, and poems from the deep places of human hearts. This was a process not of judging others but of creating a shining hope in our hearts."

Carter's work through the Women's Committee of the NCCJ, was also linked to programmes of the CCA, Korean Church Women United, the Women's Commission of the Ecumenical Association of Third World Theologians, and the Asian Women's Resource Centre for Culture and Theology. Activities included surveys of the work and participation of women in the church, a regular *Newsletter*, seminars for women theologians of Japan, Korea, and minority groups, a multi- religious Women's Study Group to study sexuality in different religious orientations, and Buddhist-Christian "ecumenical" prayer action for peace.

Carter's articles in NCC Newsletters and in Japanese magazines, regularly reported her work for political prisoners in Korea and the Philippines; victims of Japan's imperialist, commercial and tourism practices in many countries; for stateless Okinawan children; for the victims of nuclear and environmental destruction in Pacific Islands; and participation in the Asian Women's Solidarity Forum. The conferences, forums and encounters always included other dimensions and studies, and liturgies were shared which reinterpreted biblical teachings of compassion and justice for the experiences of suffering and struggling women at the bottom of society. And for Aiko Carter, "'Doing God-talk' was one of the ways of being with and making solidarity with women who sought help with day-to-day existence as they faced acutely difficult problems ... a suffering God was with those who struggled in pain" and who prayed to "She Who Is".

Selected References
Works by Aiko Carter

> Articles in *In God's Image* (Journal of Asian Women's Resource Centre for Culture and Theology) Nov. (1983), Dec.-Feb. (1985/6), 14.3 (1995), 18.4 (1999).
> Christian Women's Conference - Japan. *Japan Society and Women: Its Problems and Women's Involvement.* Morioka: Hokushu Printing, 1979.

NCCJ Women's Committee. *Josei to Shingaku no Kai kiroku* (Women doing theology report). Tokyo: NCCJ, 1984. (et seq. in succeeding years).
Women, Religion, and Sexuality: Studies on the Impact of Religious Teachings on Women, edited by Jeanne Becher. Geneva: WCC Publications, 1990.
"Shuchi Kato on Meiji Literature - A Review Article." *Japan Christian Quarterly* 46.4 (1980).
Watanabe Mine. "Women's Issues." In *Christianity in Japan 1971-1990,* edited by Kumuzawa Yoshinobu and David Swain. Tokyo: Kyo Bun Kwan; Cincinnati: Friendship Press, 1991.

2.5.22. Tagawa Kenzo (1935-)

Following studies in Tokyo and Strassbourg, Tagawa wrote a number of volumes which developed the theses of Etienne Trocmé regarding the early church. He was also strongly influenced by Simone Weil's turn from institutions to a more radical following of Jesus, and by the Marxist poet Yoshimoto Ryumo. In a study of Mark's gospel as an entry to the history of primitive Christianity (1968), he presents Mark as a Galilean writing in opposition to the kerugmatic Christ as the eschatological Son of God in the Jerusalem community. Mark is thus presenting a more human Jesus who is yet beyond all our attempts to label him, even with christological titles. This was followed by *Formation of Critical Subjects* (1971) in which he considers Simone Weil, Endo Shusaku and Hirata Atsutane; and then by a fuller commentary on Mark (1972). In a later book on Jesus (1980), Tagawa describes him as one who was identified with people suffering both from Roman and Jewish oppressions, and who himself subverted these authorities in quite paradoxical ways. There was, therefore, a strongly critical and societal thrust to these New Testament studies, which found in Christian history and theology a process of "transcendentalizing" for both Jesus and the church, whereby the realities of human life are glossed over and the victimised and exploited are ignored. For Tagawa the life and teaching of Jesus means supremely that to be "in Christ" means to be in the world, in solidarity with workers and victims.

From this analysis, Tagawa came to see in the actions of contemporary church leaders - regarding for example, the Christian

Pavilion at Expo '70 - some of the same kerugmatising intentions discernible in Paul's writings and opposed by the writer of Mark's gospel. Becoming spokespersons in the movements which were campaigning against perceived injustices in church and society, and against the institutionalising of the Christian community, Tagawa and his colleagues raised, and also suffered, severe tensions within the church which would divide churches and districts, and fragment theological faculties throughout the country for almost 15 years. Tagawa and others, including Hori Mitsuo, Takao Toshikazu and other staff members of theological colleges in Tokyo in particular, would be forced to leave their faculties. This series of events was itself part of a much wider societal turbulence in Japan over issues of international relations, war responsibility, industrial development and discrimination against minorities. Tagawa and his colleagues had found, especially in the radical Zenkyoto movement, a clear demonstration of love, self-negation and justice which was in marked contrast to the "Alliance of Egoists" which confronted them in political and religious institutions. The significance of Tagawa's work - along with similar responses by such theologians as Takizawa (2.5.3.) and Arai (2.5.18) - lies at least partly in the hermeneutic process by which detailed New Testament study, along with exposure to social movements, provides insight for contemporary social and political struggle. Others in the next two decades would assume this as the basis for their socio-theological reflection and action. (See eq. 2.5.26, 2.5.27, 2.6.3.1, 2.6.5).

Selected References
Works by Tagawa Kenzo

Miracles et Evangile: la pensée personnelle de l'évangéliste Marc. E´tudes d'histoire et de philosophie religieuses. no. 62. Paris: PUF Universitaire de France, 1967.

A Phase of the History of Primitive Christianity (Genshi Kirisutokyoshi no ichidanmen). Tokyo: Keisho Shobo, 1968.

Maruko Fukuinsho Chukaisho (Commentary on Mark). Tokyo: 1972.

Tachitsukusu Shiso (Thoughts that keep standing). Tokyo: Keisho Shobo, 1972.

Iesu to iu Otoko. (A Man called Jesus). Tokyo: Sanitsu Shobo, 1980.
Shukyo Towa Nanika (What is religion). Tokyo: Daiwa Shobo, 1984.
Shiso no kiken ni tsuite: yoshimoto takaki no tadotta kiseki (A Study of Yoshimoto Takaki, 1924-). Tokyo: Inpakuto Shuppankai, 1987.
Shomotsu to shite no shin'yaku seisho. (The New Testament as a book). Tokyo: Keisoshobo, 1997.
"People and Community in the Gospel of Matthew." *Christianity and Culture* (1967).
"The Yagi-Takizawa Debate." *NEAJOT* 2 (1969).
Takao Toshikazu. *Death and Rebirth of the Christian University.* Tokyo: Shinkyo Shuppansha, 1969.
—. "Can a Christian be a Marxist?" *Japan Christian Quarterly* (1975).

2.5.23. Yamada Keizo sj (1936-)

Yamada Keizo was a professor in Sophia University in Tokyo and now works in East Timor. He is committed to ecumenism and liberation theology, and he believes that Christ has to be communicated to the common man in Japan in a simple and understandable manner, in a way that the ordinary non-Christian Japanese would be able to accept. This communication has to be carried out not as a dogma, but as a road to happiness, based on the record of the Gospels. The Christian apostolate, he believes, should therefore be basically action-oriented.

Commitment to ecumenism has meant 30 years' active cooperation with Protestant groups such as the NCCJ and along with Cardinal Shirayanagi in leadership of the World Conference on Religion and Peace. He believes that we need to actively struggle for the sake of peace and social justice by co-operating with Buddhist and Shinto groups, not just within Japan but within the region of Asia as a whole. This is to be in solidarity with nations such as Korea and the Philippines, and in widening efforts to include the whole of Asia. Commitment to liberation theology has meant long involvement in the formation of Basic Christian Communities, for he believes the minority status of Christians in Japan requires stress upon these: namely groups in which there is no distinction of nationality, caste, creed, or race. In articles and books he writes fully of the need for social analysis, for peacemaking, for a preferential option for the poor and for recognition of the attitudes to Japan held by Asian sisters and brothers, along with Asian views of human rights.

Selected References
Works by Yamada Keizo

Liberation Theology. Tokyo: Iwanami Shoten, 1985.
The Challenges facing the Japanese Church in the 21st century. Tokyo: Shinseisha, 1998.
Business Ethics and Organization Leadership. Tokyo: Asahi Shoten 1989.
The Japanese Church within an Asian Neighborhood. Tokyo: Shinseisha 1999.
"The Challenge from Asian Neighbors and the Response from the Japanese Church. Human Rights and their Relation to Japan." *Japan Missionary Bulletin* 34.11 (1980).
"Witness to the Social Dimension of the Gospel." *Japan Missionary Bulletin* 37.4 (1983).
"Pastoral Action and Social Analysis." Article series in *Japan Missionary Bulletin,* from 38.6 (1984).

2.5.24. Momose Fumiaki sj (1940-)

Momose Fumiaki has been for several years professor of dogmatic theology at Sophia University in Tokyo. Christology has always been a major concern for Momose in a series of writings over the last 25 years which have included presentations of the life, ministry and resurrection of Jesus in relation to the Christian church, to evangelisation and to Japanese culture. He has, however, come to locate these enquiries as a study and pattern of belief that emerges from below; from the historical Jesus and His meaning for people today in their life of faith and witness, in the actual situation of Japanese society and culture. Such an approach to our understanding of and trust in Jesus, he believes, is also the best means of evangelisation where people are.

Momose is also committed to ecumenical exchanges and collaboration and has written fully on these. He believes that the central issue facing the Christians of Japan is the question of ecumenism, namely unity and cooperation between the various denominations of Christianity. Before we proceed with inter-religious unity, which is likely to become one of the major topics of theological reflection in the 21st century, he believes, it is important that Christians be united among themselves. Unity with other religions presupposes unity among ourselves, he would affirm. And this is all the more important when we consider the fact that Christians in Japan constitute a very small minority. This unity is, in his writing, also necessary in the task of creating a theology specific to Japan. Only when Christians are well grounded in the basics of Christian faith, doing their theological research and rediscovering their unity, can we speak of Japanese theology and carry out effectively the necessary task of inculturation.

Selected References
Works by Momose Fumiaki
> *The Study of Jesus Christ. Christology from Below.* Tokyo: Saint Paul's Press, 1976.
> *To Know Christ.* Tokyo: St Paulin's Press, 1976.
> *Christ and His Church.* Tokyo: St Paulin's Press, 1988.
> "Validity and Problems of a 'Christology from Below'." *Katorikku Kenkyu* 27.2 (1988).
> "'Christology from Below' considered as a Method of Evangelisation." Article series. *Japan Mission Journal*, from 48.1 (1994).
> "Karuto to Shukyo no Shikibetsu" (Discernment of cult and religion). *Yori Kyoiku no Tomo* 93/94 (1996).
> "Kirisuto no Fukkatsu wo Konnichi Donoyoni Tsutaeruka" (How to explain the resurrection of Christ today). In *Fukkatsu Shinko no Rikai wo Motomete,* edited by H. Inoue. Tokyo: St Paulin's 1997.
> "Katorikku to Purotesutanto no Kyokai Rikai" (Understanding of the Church by Catholic and Protestant). *Katorikku Kenkyu* 66 (1997).
> "Jesus Christus in der Begegnung mit der japanischen Kultur." In *Reflektierter Glaube,* edited by H.L. Ollig and O.J. Wiertz. Egelsbach; Frankfurt a.M.; Muenchen: 1999.
> (In Collaboration) *Kirisutokyo no Shingaku to Reisei* (Theology and spirituality of Christianity). Tokyo: St Paulin's 1999.

2.5.25. Nobuhara Tokiyuki (1937-)

Nobuhara Tokiyuki studied at the School of Theology, Doshisha University and the Claremont Graduate School of Theology. Currently professor at Keiwa University, he is also project director of the Japan Society for Process Studies. His earliest writings arose out of close association with, and concern for, individuals suffering severe discrimination in Japan, especially Koreans and Burakumin. More recently he has concentrated on articulating a Buddhist-Christian theology which blends the thought of the 'Kyoto School' of philosophers with process theology. He has also made particular study of the theological dimensions of loyalty, in both Christianity and Buddhism.

A main focus of these and other writings, however, is to portray the role of compassion and just actions within national and global society, with a particular concern for the poor and dispossessed. Nobuhara's writings also include studies of Whitehead, Hartshorne, Nishitani and Takizawa, and appraisals of the philosophy of Nishida Kitaro in the light of process theology.

Selected References
Works by Nobuhara Tokiyuki

Now Exposing Our Wounds - Letters Exchanged with Kim Kiro in Prison. Tokyo: Kyo Bun Kwan, 1971.

Bukyoteki Kirisutokyo (The truth of Buddhistic Christianity). Tokyo: Korosha, 1987.

Musha no Tame Fukuin (The Gospel for the have-nots). Fukuoka City: Sogensha, 1990.

Shiseishin no Shangaku (Theology of loyalty). Tokyo: Korosha, 1997.

"Sunyata, Kenosis, and Jihi or Friendly Compassionate Love: Toward a Buddhist-Christian Theology of Loyalty." *Japanese Religions* 4 (1989).

"Toward a Global Hermeneutic of Justification in Process." *Buddhist-Christian Studies* 12 (1992).

2.5.26. Kinukawa Hisako (1938-)

Kinukawa Hisako received her doctoral degree from San Francisco Theological Seminary and returned to teach at Tokyo Women's

Christian University, International Christian University, and Lutheran Theological Seminary. She has been deeply concerned to establish a Japanese feminist perspective in biblical study and in theological construction, placing both exegesis and critical reflection firmly within the Japanese context. She has also been closely involved in the development of programmes and networks in Japan for feminist theology and biblical interpretation from a feminist perspective (see 2.2). "I have kept one dream swelling in my heart for the last ten years", she wrote in 2000. "That was to found an institute of feminist theology where women and men who are interested in advocating such a perspective can get together, further our study academically, and integrate it with the work of ministry." This was begun with Chung Sook-ja through the Doctor of Ministry programme in 1993 and following years. The dream was further fulfilled when, with Satoko Yamaguchi, the Center for Feminist Theology and Ministry in Japan was formed after ten years of preparation and shared dreams (see above p.374).

In her writing Kinukawa utilises historical-critical tools and those of cultural anthropology, along with the particular theological insights of Japanese women. She has placed in question both the androcentric bias of much biblical interpretation, and the patriarchy and ethnic exclusivism of Japanese society, and applies careful study of Jesus' relationships with women as portrayed in the gospels directly to the life situation of Japanese women, that of ethnic minorities in Japan, and particular struggles for justice such as that by the "comfort women" of the Second World War. In her full study of Mark's Gospel, Kinukawa affirms that the Jesus movement was "inconceivable without women disciples ... [for] women's commitment and Jesus' radicalism dismantled the barriers and made them void". Her own commitment continues in working for the restoration of human dignity for exploited women throughout Asia, through, for example, the Violence against Women in War Network (2.2.). She now teaches biblical studies, feminist theology and gender issues at several colleges in Japan. Kinukawa is also active in commissions of the NCCJ and is co-director of the Center for Feminist Theology and Ministry in Japan

Selected References
Works by Kinukawa Hisako

Seisho no Feminizumi (Women in the Bible - to become subjects of history). Tokyo: Yorudan Publishing, 1987.

Women and Jesus in Mark. A Japanese Feminist Perspective. Maryknoll, NY: Orbis Books, 1994.

Reading the Bible in the Eyes of Women. Tokyo: UCCJ Board of Publications, 1995.

"Women Disciples of Jesus." In *God's Image* 11.4 (1992).

"Doing Theology in Asia: A Japanese Feminist Perspective." Proceedings of the Congress of Asian Theologians (CATS). Hong Kong: CCA, 1998.

"Toward a Household of Unity in Christian Faith from a Feminist Perspective." In *CTC Bulletin: Ecumenical Formation as Churches of Asia Move Towards the New Millennium.* Hong Kong: CCA, December 1998.

"My Story." In *Women Moving Mountains: Feminist Theology in Japan,* edited by Margaret Warren. Kuala Lumpur: AWRC, 2000.

"The Miracle Story of the Bent-over Woman in Luke 13:10-17: An Interaction-centered Interpretation." In *Transformative Encounters: Jesus and Women Re-viewed,* edited by Ingrid Rosa Kitzberger. Leiden: Brill, 2000.

—, ed. *Quilting Voices of Diverse Lives in Japan.* Special Issue of *In God's Image* 18.4 (1999).

—, and Arai Sasagu. "Ima Seisho wo Yomu towa." Contemporary Reading of Biblical Texts. *Kyodan Times* 4244 and 4246, 1991.

2.5.27. Honda Testuro (1942-)

Honda Testuro, a Francisan, studied at the Vatican Biblical Institute in Rome and later became rector of St Antonio's Seminary, Tokyo, and Franciscan superior in Japan (1983-1989). On a visit to the Kamagasaki area, Osaka, where many without homes or work live, he "found Jesus Christ in the poorest, the homeless, and the jobless". Putting aside his Franciscan habit and his position as superior, he then took up ministry in Kamagasaki, working at the *Furusata no Ie* (the people's home), which is the Catholic shelter in this area for the poorest, homeless and jobless. There he has identified himself with their struggles for basic human rights, and in establishing the *Shitugyosha Renraku Kyougikai* (the jobless liaison office) in order to establish basic rights to employment.

Re-reading the New Testament from within the situation of the poorest and their agony, he has produced original translations of the Greek text into Japanese. These are designed to correct the misunderstandings of traditional interpretations which, he maintains, have substituted a false charity for the loving justice of God in oppressive societies. In two other books he presents the experience of those standing alongside, and living with, the homeless and jobless in Kamagasaki. Honda affirms that he has found Jesus Christ among these, that many live "in Christ's way", and that in their struggles for justice, shelter and employment he is only a follower, struggling beside them.

Selected References
Works by Honda Testuro

New Testament Translations thus far published (Sinseisha Publishing, Nagoya) are those of the Gospels *Matthew, Mark, Luke and John, the Acts of the Apostles, and the Letters to the Corinthians*.

Chiisakusareta Monono Gawani Tatsu Kami (God stands with the smallest). Tokyo: Shinseisha, 1990.

Zoku Chiisakusareta Monono Gawani Tatsu Kami (A sequel to God stands with the smallest). Tokyo: Shinseisha, 1992.

"Evangelism - Is Sowing or Reaping Sufficient?" *Japan Missionary Bulletin* 45.4 (1991).

2.5.28. Kuribayashi Teruo (fl. 1980 -)

Kuribayashi Teruo has, in his fieldwork, doctoral studies and writings, provided a thorough exploration of new directions for theology in Japan, on the basis of Buraku experience. In his major work *Theology of the Crown of Thorns*, he points out that the "declaration of liberation" of the National Levelers' Association founded on March 3, 1922, witnesses to the cross-suffering of Jesus Christ and to the biblical Exodus experience. In vivid terms he admonishes us to adopt the "crown of thorns", which the Association put in their flag, as the symbol of Japanese Christian churches instead of the cross-symbol. And this is because it was chosen by the discriminated-against people themselves and because we must fully accept their suffering-and-hope experience.

The book presents a comprehensive development of christology, the doctrine of God and of ecclesiology in the light of the struggles of discriminated-against Buraku people. Kuribayashi critically examines the history, faith-content and doctrine of established Japanese Christianity and works in close dialogue with liberation theology, Black theology and Minjung theology. It is a unique theological attempt to thoughtfully re-read the Bible from the viewpoint of the common people, finding souls responding to God in the depths of their folk-stories and experience. In his ethical writings Kuribayashi responds to ethical tasks in the contemporary world, by addressing many problems of a global scale which are now becoming evident in the world: the frequent inter-racial and inter-religious conflicts, the exhaustion of natural resources, inequality of distribution and environmental deterioration which accompany the processes of economic globalization.

Selected References
Works by Kuribayashi Teruo
> *Theology of the Crown of Thorns: Liberation of Discriminated-against-Buraku and Christianity.* Tokyo: Shinkyo-Shuppansha, 1991.
> *Theology of Japanese Folktales.* Tokyo: UCCJ Board of Publications, 1997.
> "Recovering Jesus for Outcasts in Japan - From a Theology of the Crown of Thorns." *Japan Christian Review* 58 (1992).
> "Theology of Crowned with Thorns: Buraku People and the Church in Japan." In *Christ and God's People in Asia*, edited by Dhyanchand Carr. Hong Kong: CCA, 1995.
> —, ed. *Lecture Course "Contemporary Christian Ethics." Volume 4: Living in the World.* Tokyo: UCCJ Board of Publications, 1999.

2.5.29. Iwashima Tadahiko sj (1943-)

Iwashima Tadahiko obtained his doctorate in theology at Munster and is currently professor of dogmatic theology in the Faculty of Theology of Sophia University. He has studied and written on the theology of religions, and the thought of Bernard Lonergan, and was a member of the (Roman Catholic) International Theological Commission.

For Iwashima, principal issues facing Christianity in Japan today include inculturation and ecumenism. The deep roots which Japanese people have in Buddhist and Shinto cultural traditions, he believes, require the communication of the Gospel in ways that do not alienate them from these roots, yet which offers them fuller purpose of life. And in the Asian region, although recognising great cultural diversities, Iwashima considers that collaborative courses of action on the basis of shared understandings and traditions are possible with colleagues in northeast Asian countries. Because the average Japanese Christian tends to choose his particular denomination of Christianity more by chance encounter than by serious reflection, and because denominational divisions have been imported from Europe or America, these should not be important in Japan, but be left to the countries of their origin. And because all religions are based on "experience", they have in this sense a common foundation and common elements which should be enhanced, even while we ourselves recognise the uniqueness of Jesus Christ and undertake dialogue on the basis of genuine faith in Jesus Christ.

Selected References
Works by Iwashima Tadahiko
>   *Menschheitsgeschichte und Heilserfahrung. Die Theologie von Edward Schillebeeckx als methodisch reflektierte Soteriologie.* Düsseldorf: 1982.
>   "Concerning the Theology of Religions - Reflections Based on a Study of P. Knitter." *Katorikku Kenkyu* 25 (1986). In Japanese with English summary.
>   Salvation in Jesus - Considerations about the Logic of the Kingdom of God." *Katorikku Kenkyu* 25.50 (1986).

2.5.30. Watanabe Hidetoshi

Watanabe Hidetoshi has been minister at Naka Church, Nippon Kirisutokyodan (UCCJ) in the Kotobuki area of Yokohama since 1987. Many jobless and homeless live in this area, along with many legal and illegal migrant workers from the Philippines, Korea, China and elsewhere. Some of these meet regularly at the Naka Church and church members there are involved in social service with the local community. Watanabe provides leadership in these programmes and from reflection upon such struggles has come to use "the methods of theology of revolution" in his reflection and writings. His theological writings, as for example, *Mission and Biblical Interpretation in the Modern World* (1986), arise directly from pastoral experience in this context. They include not only critical reflection upon the life-situation of people in such districts as Kotobuki, but also pursue a re-interpretation of biblical texts. Focussing upon particular social issues, he utilises insights from revolutionary Christian theologies and explores contemporary theologies of mission and of liberation as these are related to concrete Japanese communities. Most of Watanabe's works are yet to be translated from the Japanese, but a selection is given below with titles in English.

Selected References
Works by Watanabe Hidetoshi
> *Personalities in the Bible.* Tokyo: Publication Board of the Kyodan, 1976.
> *Liberation to Love, Expository Sermons on Galatians.* Tokyo: Shinkyo Shuppansha, 1980.
> *Mission and Biblical Interpretation in the Modern World.* Tokyo: Shinkyo Shuppansha, 1986.
> *Visiting the Liberation Theology - People and Churcnes in the Philippines.* Tokyo: Shinkyo Shuppansha, 1988.
> *A Marginalized Corner is Heaven.* Tokyo: Shinkyo Shuppansha, 1995.
> *Towards the Age of Migrants - Mission and Theology in 21st Century.* Tokyo: Shinkyo Shuppansha, Forthcoming.

2.5.31. Yamano Shigeko

Yamano Shigeko was early concerned for industrial mission and has been active for almost 20 years in ecumenical and international education and advocacy. She wrote her M.Phil. thesis on industrial mission in England, and upon return to Japan in 1983, started to work with the Center for Asian Women Workers' Fellowship, which was related to the URM network of CCA. She worked with the CCA-URM Committee between 1985 and 1990, and on the staff of the NCCJ she was executive director of the Center for Christian Response to Asian Issues between 1987 and 1992. Building on the work of Kurata Masahiko, Yamano developed the activities of the Center, which has the chief purpose of raising consciousness among Japanese Christians about major human issues in the region through seminars, research and publications. Publications include the monthly *Asia Tsushin* (Asia Correspondence) with its bi-monthly English edition, the *Asian Issues Series*, and occasional publications in Japanese, including translations of important documentation.

Yamano has been long concerned for theological education - especially for women - in both formal and informal settings, and has also collaborated in a number of studies of Christian social ethics and the social ministries of churches in Japan. Since 1992 Yamano has taught courses on missiology (Mission in Japan's Context) and on the history of Asian Christianity at the Central Theological College, Tokyo, and also acts as director for fieldwork programmes there. Since 1998 she has been an ordained priest of the *Nippon Seikokai* (Japan Anglican Church). Her main theological concerns remain the doing of theology in its Asian context, particularly from women's experiences and perspectives.

Selected References
Works by Yamano Shigeko
"A Critique of British Industrial Mission as a Response to Industrial Society in Britain." M.Phil. Thesis, University of Leeds, 1982.
"Restoring Right Relationship between Nature and People." *Tugon* 12.2 (1992).
"North and South Relations and the Church." In *Jissen Shingaku Sosetsu* (Practical theology. A general survey), edited by K. Kanda, Sekita Hiroo and Z. Moreno. Tokyo: Kyodan Shuppansha, 1993.
"Urban Rural Mission and the Asian Women." In *Perspectives and Issues of Theology in Japan—What can Theology do? Proposals from 25 Persons*. Tokyo: Shinkyo Shuppansha, 1993.

—, with Alan Suggate. *Japanese Christians and Society*. Berne: Peter Lang, 1996.
See also *Asian Issues Series,* and *Asia Tsushin* (CCRAI).

2.5.32. Oda Takehiko (1953-)

Following studies at Sophia University (M.Th. 1981), Pontifical Gregorian University (Lic.Miss. 1987, and Ph.D.1988 - on new movements for Japanese parochial communities), Oda became co-pastor of the Osaka Cathedral, and later secretary of the Archdiocese of Osaka. He has also been researcher, Japan Catholic Research Institute for Evangelization (1990 -1999), and one of the experts of the Special Assembly for Asia of the Synod of Bishops (1998). From April 1999 he has been a member of team ministries in Osaka and associate professor of theology at Sapientia University in Osaka.

Oda's theological concerns, apart from the established content of systematic theology, include the mission and role of the church in the pluralistic society of Japan, the role of lay Christian movements, collaborative ministries and various aspects of inculturation. Regarding inculturation he has made particular studies of the post-synodal Apostolic Exhortation "Ecclesia in Asia" and has also recently explored the basis and possibilities for the study of missiology in Japan

Selected References
Works by Oda Takehiko

"Inculturating the Church in Japan." *The Japan Missionary Bulletin* (Spring 1992); *Catholic International* 3.15 (1992) and as "Japon: l'inculturation de l'Eglise." *La Documentation Catholique* 2055 (1992).

"Response to the Holy Spirit: Lay Christian Movements Today." *The Japan Missionary Bulletin (*Autumn 1992).

"The Society We Live in." *Japan Missionary Bulletin* (Spring 1994).

"Fukuin wo akashi suru kyoudou senkyou shiboku." (The collaborative ministry as witness of the Gospel). In *Iyashi no Fukuin,* edited by Sakuma Tsutomu. Tokyo: San Paulo, 2000.

2.5.33. Yamashita Akiko

Yamashita Akiko has been a staff member of the NCC Study Center, Kyoto, for many years and a researcher in religious studies in Japan and the Asian region. She is also active in Japanese women's theology and through PTCA, with Asia-wide programmes for the development of creative Asian theologies. In her theological research and writing she has particularly focused upon such subjects as shamanism in Korea and new religious movements in Japan, along with theological interpretations of changes in popular religion in Japan.

Yamashita has a particular concern for the role and status of women in religion, and also for women's theology throughout the Asian region, and has both researched and published on these issues. Yamashita defines "Asian women's theology" as "a theology being done by Asian women who want to change both the traditional church and its traditional theology", both of which are oppressive to women. Breaking through the barriers within women, both church and society require, she believes, "fresh encounters with neighbors from other faith communities." At the same time, study must be given to the particular socio-historical contexts of women, to core symbolisms in Christianity and in Asian religio-cultural resources, and to the concrete experience of women within those traditions. The "challenge to do a radically new theology" can be furthered best by such a "life dialogue" through which "women can revive their full humanity in body and soul".

Selected References
Works by Yamashita Akiko

> *Senson to onna no jinken* (War and women's rights: The present-ness of "comfort women"). Tokyo: Akashi Shoten, 1997.
> *Azia no onnatachi to shukyo* (Women and religions in Asia). Osaka: Kaiho Shuppansha, 1997.
> "Tenrin-O and Henjo-Nanshi: Two Woman Founders of New Religions." *Japanese Religions* 2 (1990).
> "Feminizumu to okaruto bhumu" (Feminism and occultic boom). Co-authored. In *Bunka no nakana onnato otoko* (Women and men within culture). Kyoto: Sagano Shoin, 1992.
> "Kindai Nihon no Kirisutokyo to Minshu Shukyo" (Christianity and popular religion in modern Japan). In *Kindai Nihon no Kirisutokyo to Joseitachi* (Christianity and women in modern Japan). Tokyo: Shinkyo Shuppansha, 1995.

"Korean Shamanism and Christianity: A Shaman's Story." *Japanese Religions* 21.2 (1996).
"The 'Eschatology' of Japanese New, and New New Religions." *Japanese Religions* 1 & 2 (1998).
"A Review of Asian Women's Theology: From the Perspective of Women's Life Dialogue in Asia." *In God's Image* 18.1 (1999).

2.5.34. Kawamura Shinzo sj (1958-)

Kawamura Shinzo received his Ph.D. from Georgetown University in Washington D.C., and is currently a lecturer in church history in the Faculty of Theology of Sophia University, Tokyo. His primary focus of research is upon Christianity in 16th century Japan, but he places this and the experience of Japanese during the Pacific war, within the settings and issues of lay women and men and their movements in Japan today.

A firm believer in ecumenical dialogue, Kawamura is also interested in working towards the "Japanization of Christianity", believing that the central message of Christianity is universal, and is not confined to a particular culture, community or race. Christianity has therefore to be inculturated within the nation of Japan. During the 16th century, Christianity in Japan was community-based, and the people organised all religious activities by themselves without the dominance of the clerics, he recounts. Christianity at that time was a movement of the lay people, and not of the clergy. Kawamura believes that even today in Japan, the Church of the laity has yet to be formed: the Church should become a people's Church, not clergy-dominated, as present theologies of mission and church in Japan require. Despite the activities of lay movements such as Young Christian Workers, the many articles written by, and the many statements from, the hierarchy show that the full role of lay people in leadership and theological reflection is yet to be accepted.

Selected References
Works by Shinzo Kawamura

"Making Christian Lay Communities During the 'Christian Century' in Japan. A Case Study of Takata District in Bungo." Ph.D. Diss., Georgetown University, 1999.

Senkoku Shakai ni okeru kirishitan no aikoku to keiken (The piety and devotion of the Christians of war-time Japan). K*irishitan bunka kenkyukai kaihou* 115 (2000).

"Juroku seiki Nihon ni okeru Yoroppa Kirisutokyo soshiki (confuraternitas) no doonyuu, nihon senkyo saishoki no Hougou kyoudoutai no rootsu wo megutte" (The introduction of the organisation of European Christian believers (confraternitas) in 16th century Japan, revolving around the roots of the Bungo Christian community of the earliest period of the Japanese mission). *Katorikku Kenkyu* 67 (1988): 1-57.

2.5.35. Kohara Katsuhiro (1965 -)

Kohara Katsuhiro gained his Th.D. at Doshisha University, Kyoto and is an associate professor of theology there. He is also a pastor of the United Church of Christ in Japan and secretary-general of the Japan Association of Religion and Ethics. In teaching and writing he specialises in Christian thought (systematic theology) and comparative religious ethics. Amongst his chief theological concerns are contemporary ethical problems, feminist theology, ecology, eschatology, just-war theory, and inter-religious dialogue. While the traditional eschatology tends to be male-oriented, and presupposes a catastrophic end of the world, Kohara is interested in reforming eschatology through a feminist and ecological perspective. This would be an "ecological eschatology" he writes, which could draw also on recent theologies of creation such as that of Moltman. The relationship of ecological concern to eschatology through ecofeminism is necessary, he believes, in order to present the possibility and necessity of societies which are sustainable. Kohara has also written on religious pluralism in modern theology, justice and peace in multi-religious society, the future of bioethics and Christianity, the dramaturgy of God in which nature, religion, history and body form the stage, and has also co-authored works on the historical development of eschatology and on the European Union.

Selected References (In Japanese)

with K. Kanda et al. *Life and Death*. Tokyo: United Church of Christ in Japan Publication, 1999.

with N. Miyatani et al. *The Meaning of Sex: From the Christian Perspective.* Tokyo: Shinkyo-Shuppan-sha, 1999.

"The Gender of God: A Dialogue with Feminist Theology." *Religion and Society* 4, 1998 .

"A Theological Study on Understandings of the Body." *Studies in Christianity* 59/2, 1998.

"On the 'Imago Dei': A Response to Feminism and Ecology." *Theological Studies in Japan* 37, 1998.

"A Foundation of Ecological Eschatology. *Studies in Christianity* 60/2, 1999.

"A Hermeneutical Study of Eschatology: Apocalypticism and Thought of Wisdom." *Studies in Christianity* 61/2, 1999.

"Christianity and Life Science: Focusing on Responsibility." *Studies in Christianity* 62/1, 2000.

"The Past, Present, and Future of Korean and Japanese Societies from the Perspective of Eschatological Thought." *Studies in Christianity* 63/1. Forthcoming, in Japanese and Korean.

2.6. Other Sources for Contextual Theology
2.6.1. In Selected Catholic Periodicals

Of the two principal Catholic theological journals in Japan, *Katorikku Kenkyu* (Catholic Studies) was established during the war years, and Oriens Institute (2.4.1.) has published the *Japan Mission Journal* (formerly *Japan Missionary Bulletin*) since 1961. *Katorikku Kenkyu* publishes articles and study reports, largely in Japanese, giving much attention to studies in historical theology of the West. *Japan Mission Journal* is bilingual and carries reports on Christian education, liturgy, catechetics, ecumenical, literary and inter-religious topics. It has pioneered cross-cultural discussion on such crucial subjects as ancestor veneration, Zen meditation, the meaning and role of Shinto customs, traditional Japanese dance and festivities, the writings of Endo Shusaku and others. It also features and reports on official Church documents.

From the late 1970s on, Sasaki J. Hiroshi produced a series of studies on contextual theology in Japan, dealing with religiosity of the Japanese, the processes of inculturation, God's word in Japanese tradition and the pastoral implications of a localised church. Throughout the 1980s various series of articles were published in the journal on inculturation within Japanese history, culture and religion. Series authors included: Kaneko Kennosuke, Okada Takeo, Honda Masaaki, Jan van Bragt (2.5.14), Ernest Piryns and Obata Yoshinobu. Writers in the *Bulletin* and *Journal* on these subjects and the doing of theology in Japan during the 1980s and 1990s included Kishi Hideshi, Sakamoto Takashi, Fujiwara Takanori, Mushakoji Kinhide, Onodera Isao, Oda Takehiko, Patrick O'Donoghue, Terao Toshiyoshi, Robert Kisala and Echizen Kiroku. Women writers on related topics included Takeda Misako Maria, Mori Setsuko, Yuguchi Yuriko, Grace Mary Kuji, Arai Sayoko and Iyori Naoko. Along with the writings by Yamada Keizo on social concerns, peace and human rights, Yuasa Makoto wrote on Sanya and the homeless, and Kasuya Koichi on theology and the Buraku Liberation movement.

Regular articles also appeared from Jan Swyngedouw - on "a Church with a Japanese Face", and on Japanese rituals and festivals; from Edmund Piryns - on inter-faith dialogue, Taoism, Buddhism, content of the faith in Japanese context, and on underprivileged minority groups; from Thomas Imoos - on Folk Religion, Shintoism and the Japanese sense of the Sacred; and from Jan van Bragt - on a wide range of inter-faith theological issues (see 2.5.14 above). Nishio Masaji's series of articles, "Before the Century Closes - The Catholic Church in Japan", began in 1996.

In *Katorikku Kenkyu* Obata Yoshinobu's articles surveyed theological discussion of inculturation, and related this to contemporary society, to ecology, liturgy and house churches, while Tsuchiya Yoshimasa and Nakagawa Akira wrote on language and culture, the church in Japan as "overlooked", and the role of migrants to Japan in inculturation.

Significant articles in other journals of the period include: Inagaki Ryosuke, "Scholastic Studies in Japan: A Survey." *NEAJT* (March 1970); and Edmund Piryns, "Encounter of the Christian Message with Japanese Culture - a contribution to a Japanese Contextual Theology." *Japan Christian Quarterly* 50.1 (1984); and Nemeshegyi Peter, "Theology of the Way: An Attempt of Inculturated Theology in Japan." *Studia Missionalia* 45 (1996).

Selected References

Kaneko Kennosuke. "The Mentality and the Spirit of the Japanese in their Culture." *Japan Missionary Bulletin*, from 37.1&2 (1983).

Okada Takeo. "Searching for the Point of Contact between Everyday Life and the Gospel." *Japan Missionary Bulletin*, from 36.8 (1984).

Swyngedouw, Jan. "In Search of a Church with a Japanese Face." *Japan Missionary Bulletin*, from 37.1&2 (1983).

Honda Masaaki. "Towards Rediscovering the Mother Principle. A Contribution to the Japanese Understanding of God." *Japan Missionary Bulletin,* from 37.3 (1983).

Kasuya Koichi. "A Catholic Commentary on 'A Theology of the Crown of Thorns'." *Japan Mission Journal* 47 (1993).

Obata Yoshinobu. "Inculturation in Quest of Theological Understanding." *Katorikku Kenkyu* 23.45 (1984).

Piryns, Edmund. *Japan and Christianity: Towards the Overcoming of a Dilemma.* Utrecht, Lannoo: P Tielt, 1971. Also published as Oriens Studies 3. Tokyo: Oriens Institute for Religious Research, 1974.

—. "Contextual Theology: the Japanese Case." *Philippiniana Sacra* 14.40 (1979).

—. "The Message of Jesus Christ and Japanese Culture, Evangelization and Inculturation in the Japanese Context." *Philippiniana Sacra* 20.59 (1985).

Terao Kazuyoshi, comp. *Annotated bibliography of Christianity in Japan.* Nagoya: Nanzan Shukyo Bunka Kenkyujo, 2000.

Sasaki J. Hiroshi. "Some Pastoral Considerations Regarding Contextual Theology in Japan." *Philippiniana Sacra* 14.40 (1979).

Shimamoto, Sr. M. "Japanese Spirituality and the Religious Life." *Japan Missionary Bulletin* 38.11 (1984).

Takagi Takako, Francis. "Inculturation and Adaptation in Japan Before and After Vatican Council II." *Catholic Historical Review* 79 (1993).

2.6.2. Other Socio-Theologians Working Since the 1960s

Amongst the many who have taught and worked in lay and study-centers, universities, protest movements, and social action centres since the early part of this period, Iisaka Yoshiaki and Shiozuki Kentaro must be mentioned as scholars in political science and international relations as well as in theology; Nakajima Masaaki and Shoji Tsutomu as leaders in NCCJ networks and ecumenical reflection; Robert Fukada, Hirata Satoshi, Arai Toshitsugu and Koyanagi Nobuaki as providing resource and direction for laity formation and urban mission; Lee In Ha, John H. McIntosh, and Lee Chong-il as pastors and leaders in Korean centres and churches; Yamano Shigeko (Ms), and Matsui Yayori (Ms) as researchers and animateurs on social issues and women's theology; Tsukada Osamu, Nambara Shigeru, Nagatoshi Sanpei, Kurata Masahisa, Ooshima Koichi, Inoue Yoshio and Miyata Mitsuo as writers on the church and political religion in Japan and on Tenno issues; Watanabe Minoru, Robert Witmer, Shiraishi Nabe, Kaneko Keiichi and John H.McIntosh as advocates for the rights of minorities.

Of these, Shiozuki Kentaro has also been particularly concerned for the Asian context of Japanese Christianity, and Shoji Tsutomu has in many articles related social issues to "Jesus the Companion". Robert Fukada has also written extensively on Kagawa Toyohiko and on urban pastoral issues, and Hirata Satoshi has written on action-oriented inter-faith dialogue and also on education for liberation and development. Arai Toshitsugu has also published volumes on Christian and laity education and spirituality (with the CCA, the WCC and with Japan Christian Academies). Kurata Masahisa (d.1997) wrote especially on the experience of Koreans under Japanese rule - using both Japanese police authorities and Korean archives as sources, and on the experience of minority groups suffering discrimination in Asia. Kim Sungjae (1952-) succeeded Lee In Ha as general secretary of the Korean Christian Church in Japan and has written much on the missiology for that community from the perspective of post-colonial theories and the social context of an ethnic minority. His writings also include studies of *ger* (sojourner), diasporas, and also of the concepts for "constructing co-habitant society."

Selected References
> Fukada, Robert M. "New Frontiers of Encounter and Witness." *International Review of Mission* 54.214 (1965).

—. "A Theology in Search of Human Community." *NEAJOT* 1 (1980).

—, ed. *God's people in Asian Industrial Society*. Kyoto: Committee on the Witness of the Laity, EACC, 1967.

Hirata Satoshi. "The Modern Significance of Christian Social Education - A Challenge to the Church." *Breakthrough* 27 (1970).

—, ed. *On The Scene: Reality Ministry in Japan*. Kyoto: Kansai UIM, 1975.

Iisaka Yoshiaki. "Reformation of Society and Service." In *Toward the New Form of Service in Japan*. Tokyo: Christian World Service, 1961.

—, et al. *Heiwa no kadai to shukyo* (Religious aspects of peace and peace movements). Tokyo: Kosei Shuppansha, 1992.

Kim Sungjae. "Sabetu Shakai no Shuen Kara Kyosei Shakai no Furontia." Parts 1-3. (From margin of discriminatory society to frontier of co-habitant society 1). *Hukuin to Sekai* 57.7; 57.8; 57.9 (1998).

—. "Sinso to Siteno Uchinaru Geru" (Inner *Ger* as the depth of mind). *Hukuinsenkyo* 52.7 (1998).

—. "Minzoku Zaini Chikankoku chosenjin" (Ethnicity of Koreans in Japan). *Current Christian Ethics* 3 (1999).

Koyanagi Nobuaki. "Give us Back our Humanity." *Japan Christian Quarterly* 37.4 (1971).

—. "Christian Work in the Yoseba: Kamagasaki, Sanya, Kotobuki, Sasajima." In *Christianity in Japan 1971-1990*, edited by Kumuzawa Yoshinobu & David Swain. Tokyo: Kyo Bun Kwan; Cincinnati: Friendship Press, 1991.

Kurata Masahisa. *Tennosei to Kankoku Kirisutokyo* (The emperor system and Christianity in Korea). Tokyo: Shinkyo Shuppansha, 1991.

—. *Rinjintoshitino Ajia* (Asia as a neighbour). Tokyo: Nihkirisuto Kyodamn Shuppan, 1993.

—. *Mainoriii o Tabisuru* (Visiting minority groups). Tokyo: Sofukan, 1998.

Lee In Ha. "Jinken to shosusha mondai" (Human rights and the problem of minorities). In *Minshu no shingaku o mezashite* (Toward a theology of the people), edited by CCA. Tokyo: Shinkyo Shuppansha. 1983.

—. *Myonichi ni ikiru kiryu no tami* (Living as pilgrim people tomorrow). Tokyo: Shinkyo Shuppansha, 1987.

McIntosh, John H. *Closing Statement and Appeal as Minister and Missionary, 1993.* Both in Japanese and in English, and available from KCC in Osaka.

Shiozuki Kentaro. "Rapid Urbanization and Christian Responsibility." *Japan Christian Yearbook* (1968).

Shoji Tsutomu. "Sin and Suffering: Japan and the Peoples of Asia." *Japan Christian Quarterly* 47.1 (1981).

—. "The United Church of Christ in Japan: Its Sin and Rebirth." *Mid-stream* 27 (1988).

Watanabe Minoru. *Studies on the History of Unliberated Buraku* (Mikaiketsu Burakushi no Kenkyu). Tokyo: Yoshikawa Kobunkan 1965, 1969.

Witmer, Robert. *Land of Elms: The History, Culture, and Present Day Situation of the Ainu People.* Toronto: United Church Publishing House, 1998.

2.6.3. Other Protestant Theologians Contributing to Contextual theology

A selection of these would have to include the following:

2.6.3.1. Biblical Studies

Sekine Masao (1912-) was a colleague of Mayeda Goro (1904-1980) who taught many of the influential New Testament scholars of the 1960s-1970s, and was an influential teacher of Old Testament Studies, not using theological categories but aiming to find the "essence of a culture" through history of thought and sociology. Sekine also reflected theologically on the paradoxes of faith within "faithlessness", and of love within "lovelessness". His writings include the sociological setting of Old Testament religion, and also commentaries on, for example, Jeremiah, Job, Psalms.

Satake Akira was also a student of Mayeda with Arai Sasagu and similarly attained a high level of New Testament scholarship in Japan with commentaries on Philippians, Revelation and Galatians. He also contributed to programmes of ecumenical theology and action.

2.6.3.2. Theologies of Church Life

Ishida Yoshiro of Tokyo Lutheran Seminary principally studied aspects of church life in Japan - its self-understanding, and ministry, with writings also on the Uemura-Ebina debate, the Mukyokai, and changing concepts of mission.

Shimizu Keizo has explored frontier situations for faith, evangelism and the life of new churches, portraying challenges and dilemmas faced by those in frontier ministries in Japanese society.

Kanda Kanji has written, and edited or co-authored works in pastoral theology, including ecumenical perspectives on the Eucharist, resources for practical theology and issues of life and death .

2.6.3.3. Bi-Cultural Theologians

Matsuoka Fumitaka worked in ministry in Indonesia and later as ICU Chaplain. His particular interest is in the processes of indigenisation which he studied both in Indonesia and Japan, later writing on issues for Asia-American churches.

Mochizuki Kenihiro taught at McGillivary Faculty of Theology at Chiang Mai in Thailand, and has written on Jesus Christ and the church in the world, on inter-faith dialogue and theological education, and on the SCM, and the role of intellectuals in society.

Sawa Masahiko had a ministry in Korea, later working with Tomisaka Christian Center and Seisho Seminary in Tokyo before an early death (ca. 1991). His major interests were in the history of Korean Christianity, and the mutual relations between Japanese and Korean Christians. A posthumous manuscript on these was later published as *The History of Korean Christianity* (1995).

Selected References

Matsuoka Fumitaka. "An Asian Church: on the Indigenising process of Christianity." *SEAJOT* 13.2 (1972).
—. "Theologia in loco et tempore - A Methodological Reflection." *Humanities* 12 (1977).
— . "The Christology of Shusaku Endo." *Theology Today* (1982)
Mochizuki Kenihiro. God, Man and Society. Chiang Mai: Church of Christ in Thailand, ?1983.
Sawa Masahiko. "Christian Identity in Japan: Self-Discovery through Encounter." *The Japan Christian Quarterly* 44:2 (1978).

—. "To Learn From The Korean Church." *Kirisuto Shinbun* (Christ newspaper) (February 18, 1984).

2.6.3.4. SEMINEX

In a special role are the SEMINEX group of former faculty members of Aoyama Gakuin who in the wake of controversies and divisions in universities and colleges, from 1968 on, continued teaching and writing as an "underground" centre for theological education and publication. Key members of the group included Makoto Mizuno, Kida Kenichi and Sekita Hiroo. Despite restricted conditions they also continued publishing the journal *Kirisutokyo Ronshu* (Essays on Christianity) and also occasional collections of articles such as *Jissen Shingaku Sosetsu* (Practical theology: a general survey, 1993).

Selected References

Kanda Kanji. *A Modern Eucharist: From the Perspective of the Ecumenical Movement*. Tokyo: United Church of Christ in Japan Publication, 1997 (In Japanese).

—, Sekita Hiroo and Morino Zenemono, eds. *Jissen Shingaku Sosetsu* (Practical theology: a general survey). 2 vols. Tokyo: Kyodan Shuppansha, 1993.

Mizuno Makoto. "*Field Education Groping for a Living Theology.*" *NEAJOT* 9 (1972).

—. *Christian Education as Promise for the Future in Japan*. Tokyo, Kyodan Shuppansha, 1991.

Satake Akira. *The Apostle Paul* (Shito Pauro). Tokyo: Nihon Hoso Shuppan Kyokai, 1981.

—. "Symbol of Hope and Signal of Action" and "Grace that enables us to share in Christ's works of Grace." In *To Set at Liberty Those Who are Oppressed*. CCA Eighth Assembly. Singapore: CCA, 1985.

Sekita Hiroo. *Our Faith*. Tokyo: UCCJ Board of Publications, 1983.

2.6.3.5. Protestant Journals

Amongst these *Fukuin to Sekai* (Gospel and World) has played an important role in the publishing of a wide range of Christian comment and theological reflection since 1952, with particular concern to relate Christian faith to the realities of life in Japan. Read by pastors, ministers, congregations, theologians and theological students, the journal holds radical and wide theological perspectives in its editorial stance, providing evangelical messages with a sharply critical eye to approach social and mission realities in Japan. Asian, American, Latin American, and European theologians have also been introduced through this journal. Amongst the many subjects included have been articles on Problems of Mission in Japan (1954, 1972 ...); Church responsibility for Asian countries (1963, 1973, 1980 ...);The Japanese Church and the World Church (1958, 1968, 1982, ...); Christian arts and literature (1957, 1976, 1987...);Church responsibility for the World War II (1960, 1967, 1987...); Problems of the Yasukuni Shrine and the Tenno System (1968, 1978, 1989...); the imagery and language of Japanese theology, and new understandings of Christology (passim); problems of minorities and human rights (1955, 1974, 1984...); along with many other pastoral and missional concerns, and major social and ethical issues faced by Japanese Christians. A wide range of Japan's theologians and educators have written for the journal.

The Japan Society for Christian Studies, which is a large Christian academic society in Japan, holds annual and district conferences as well as publishing *Nihon no Shingaku* (*The Japanese Journal of Theology*). This publishes a wide range of scholarly papers and book reviews, from theologies of peace and development, of ethnic and minority issues, or of the Christian university, to studies of western theologians and philosophers both ancient and modern. Not all the articles, therefore, deal with the issues of contextual theology in Japan, but this society encourages all areas of research related to Christianity and provides a forum for scholarly cooperation.

A significant number of expatriate scholars and writers have also contributed extensively in journal articles (and often monographs) on contextual Japanese theology. Included amongst these, to give only a small selection, are Louis N. Grier (d.1982) and Robert G. Steiber, in work with Japanese Buraku; David Swain - formerly of the WSCF, *Japan Christian Quarterly* and *Japan Christian Review*; Norbert Klein - formerly of the Japan Christian Academies; Charles Iglehart (b.1882), Richard Drummond and

James Phillips (1929-) in historical and ecumenical studies; Raymond Hammer (1920-), David Reid (1927-) and Michael Pye (1939-) in cultural and religious studies; Mark R. Mullins, Wilfred Dehn and Richard Fox Young in studies of Christianity and society.

Selected References

Aug Nishizaka. "Eizo to gengo" (Image and language). *Fukuin to Sekai* 42.13 (1987).

Caldarola, Carlo . "Pacifism among Japanese Non-church Christians," *Journal of The American Academy of Religion.* 41 (1973).

Ichida Yoshiro. "Towards a Self-understanding of the Church in the Context of Contemporary East Asia." *NEAJOT* 15 (1975).

—. "The Church is Emerging: The Ministry of the People of God." *Japan Christian Quarterly* 45.1 (1979).

Iwai, F. "Suffering and Hope in Rural Mission." *Fukuin to Sekai* Sept. 1954

Mullins, Mark R. *Christianity Made in Japan: A Study of Indigenous Movements.* Honolulu: University of Hawaii Press, 1998.

—. "The Situation of Christianity in Contemporary Japanese Society." *The Japan Christian Quarterly* 55.2 (1989).

—. "The Transplantation of Religion in Comparative Sociological Perspective." *Japanese Religions* 16.2 (1990)

Reid, David. *New Wine: The Cultural Shaping of Japanese Christianity.* Berkeley: Asian Humanities Press, 1991.

Shimizu Keizo. *Kenkyo no Kyokai* (Frontier churches). Tokyo: Kyodan Shuppankyoku, 1978.

Suzuki, Masahisa. "Independence in Japanese mission." *Fukuin to Sekai* , Sept. 1954

Swain, David and Masayoshi Sugimoto. *Science and Culture in Traditional Japan.* Rutland, VT: Tuttle, 1989 (1978).

Symposium. "Looking for the True Peace in Vietnam." *Fukuin to Sekai*, Sept.1973.

Theme articles. "Who is Jesus". *Fukuin to Sekai* December 1973.

— "Women and Theology."*Fukuin to Sekai* , May 1988.

— . "Dialogue with Minjung Theology."*Fukuin to Sekai* April 1985.

Yoshida Megumi. "Visiting contemporary Chinese Christian artists." *Fukuin to Sekai* March 1999.

2.6.4. Other Catholic Scholars and Writers

The writings of the Catholic physician Nagai Takashi (1908-1951), who wrote while suffering from terminal radiation disease following the Nagasaki Atomic holocaust, have had exceptional influence both within and outside Japan. People of all classes, conditions and beliefs have read them, and until his death visited Nagai as one who found hope in the ashes, saw that "everything within and without is God's gift" and who condemned no one. For him, even such suffering as was known at Nagasaki and Hiroshima held intense value when transformed in the human spirit as offering for the atonement and peace of others. His teachings hold added significance and poignancy arising as they did from a Christian community that had suffered centuries of the most intense persecution. He has been internationally acknowledged to be an outstanding patriot, humanist, mystic and saint, teaching and living that not suffering, but selfless and transformative response to suffering is the deepest human and religious reality. His key work, *The Bells of Nagasaki*, has gone through many editions, but his theological insights and life have yet to receive full study.

The novelist Endo Shusaku (1923-1996) has played a unique role in stimulating theological reflection both in his fiction and drama, and in his life of Jesus. Influenced by Bernanos, Mauriac and Claudel, he was even more influenced both by encounters with the history of Christianity in Japan, which he felt had haunting parallels to his own life in his century, and with the life of Jesus in Palestine and Jesus' identification with the poor, the rejected and the criminal. Literary studies in Lyon were soon followed by his first novel *Yellow Man* (1955). *Sea and the Poison* (1957) deals with responsibility for evil and sin; *Silence* (1966) presents the experience of martyrdom and betrayal for Japanese Christians of the 17th century; and *Samurai* (1980) is a study of faith and sacrifice. Impressed by the differences between eastern and western views of the world, Endo pictured Japan as the engulfing "swamp" which has absorbed and neutralised Christianity, yet in both *Wonderful Fool* (1959) and *A Life of Jesus* (1973) he presents vivid portrayals of the one who suffers with us, powerless, leaving with us the mystery of a continuing presence despite all. *The River Crowned* (1994) reveals his continuing religious search during travels in India.

Other writers in this period who were sympathetic to or adherents of Catholicism, have both taught and written on aspects of Catholic philosophy, history and belief. Anzai Shin (1923-1998) was professor of sociology at Sophia University, with special concerns for the sociology and philosophy of religion, for religious education, and in the social analysis of Christian missionary work. Hori Ichiro (1910-1974) taught the history of Japanese religions at Todai University and advocated a more open approach by the Church to Japanese culture. For him, Christianity possesses a vision of the future which provides strong incentive for progressive social forces. Toda Yoshio (b.1917), who specialised in the history of religious thought at Kokugakuin-daigaku, recognises the inspiration of the historical Jesus - along with that of Buddha and Shinran - and "discovers religious realities not through the agency of the Church, but directly in contact with Christ found in the words of the Bible." He acknowledges the large contribution of former Christian leaders in theology and social action, but also argues for openness to Japanese forms of thought and feeling, such as those found in documents of the *Kakure Kirishitan*. Kamishima Jiro (b.1917), professor in Japanese political history and folklore at St Paul's University, also recognises the contribution of Meiji and Taisho Christians, but is concerned at the break between some traditional Christian approaches in Japan, and deep-seated emotions of Japanese people. Understanding of urban Japanese culture and the achievement of Church unity are also important for him. Other writers included Tanaka Kotaro (1890-1974) on natural law and Matsumoto Masao (1910-1998) in neo-Thomistic studies.

Other Catholic writers of biography or fiction include Tanaka Chikao (1905-), Ohara Tomie (1912-), Shimao Toshio (1917-1986), Yasuoka Shoutarou (1920-), Miura Shumon (1926-), Kaga Otohiko (1929), Sono Ayako (1931-), Ariyoshi Sawako (1931-1984), Takahashi Takako (1932-), Inoue Hisashi (1934-), Kisaki Satoko (1939-) and Moriuchi Toshio (1936-).

Selected References

Brannen, Noah S. "Three Japanese Authors Look at Jesus: A Review." *The Japan Christian Quarterly* 54:3 (1988).

Endo Shusaku. *Silence*. Tokyo: Kodansha International, 1982. (Sophia University and Tuttle, 1969.)

—. *Wonderful Fool*. Tokyo: Tuttle, 1974.

—. *A Life of Jesus*. Tokyo: Tuttle, 1979.

Matsuoka Fumitaka. "The Christology of Shusaku Endo." *Theology Today* (1982)

Nagai Takashi, Paul. *The Bells of Nagasaki*. Tokyo: Kodansha International 1984. (1949).

—. *Rosario no Kusari* (The Rosary chain). Tokyo: Chuo Publishing Co., 1959. Partly translated in *Japanese Religions* 12.1 (1981).

Japan Missionary Bulletin 21.1-6 (1967).

Japanese Christian Identity: Personal Portraits of Faith. Hong Kong: Federation of Asian Bishops' Conferences, 1999.

Hall, Douglas J. "Rethinking Christ. Theological Reflections on Shusaku Endo's Silence." *Interpretation* 33.3 (1979).

Sato Yazumasa. *Endo Shusaku to Shiina Rinzo*. Tokyo: Kanrin Shobo, 1994.

Spae, Joseph J. *Christian Corridors to Japan*. Tokyo: Oriens Institute, 1965.

—. *Christianity Encounters Japan*. Tokyo: Oriens Institute, 1968.

Suzuki Norihisa, and Joseph J. Spae. *Nihonjin no Mita Kirisutokyo*. Tokyo: Oriens Institute, 1968.

2.6.5. Other Texts in Prophetic Theology - 1980-2000

The selection below includes further books that have been written as a Christian contribution to Japanese society and Asian society at large. They provide examples of contextual Japanese theology, often problem-posing in thrust, written by Japanese writers and mostly in Japanese. They focus on the issues for Christians and the churches, concerning workers, the disabled, minorities and discrimination, social concern, war responsibility and the Tenno system.

2.6.5.1. The Period 1980 - 1990

i) Tsukada, Osamu. *Symbolic Emperor System and Christianity*. Tokyo, Shinkyo Shuppansha, 1981. This is a collection of treatises by the author, who argues that the symbolic emperor system, now making an appearance in a new form, is a basic attack upon the Japanese Christian Church and its theology. He insists that our urgent missionary task requires a liberation from the ideology of the Tenno System.

ii) Nakadaira, Kenkichi. *Commissioned to the World: On The Social Participation of Christians.* Tokyo: Shinkyo Shuppansha, 1982. The author engaged himself as a Christian lawyer, to struggle for the cause of basic human rights, beginning with a lawsuit on the constitutional issue of religion and state. Although focussed upon the controversial issues regarding religious freedom, the book is filled with the author's selfless commitment and generous devotion.

iii) NCCJ Committee of the Differently Abled and Social Concern, ed. *That the Works of God might be Manifest.* Tokyo: Shinkyo Shuppansha, 1984. In this book Christians with different disabilities bear witness to the ways in which they believe God is still able to use their lives and bodily experience. They are able to witness clearly to this in their struggle against the discrimination and injustice which attack the weak and vulnerable.

iv) *A River without Bridges. An Encounter with the Japanese Buraku. The Writings of Louis N. Grier.* Tokyo: Nihon Kirisuto Kyodan Buraku Liberation Center, 1986. Louis Grier's sermons and Bible studies from the thirty-three years of his pioneering ministry are here collected. All these writings wrestle - as Grier did throughout his life - with the problems of discrimination and violence experienced by the Buraku.

v) Committee Searching for Peace and Extinction of Nuclear Weapons, ed. *Peace of Christ.* Tokyo: Shinkyo Shuppansha, 1987. This book explores the church's mission of justice, peace and reconciliation in the present circumstances of mass production and stockpiling of nuclear weapons. The standpoint taken is that of careful biblical study and the papers are a collection of the main lectures presented at the Hiroshima Peace Seminar which began in 1983.

2.6.5.2. The Period 1990 - 2000

i) Fukase Chuichi. *The Japan Constitution of Peace and the Gospel*. Tokyo: Shinkyo Shuppansha, 1990. The author, who has committed his life to deepening the meaning of the Constitution and its practice, explores here the "right of peaceful existence". He confronts the "structure of Emperor System" as a scholar of the Constitution and on the path of searching for the gospel of peace.

ii) Yamazaki Washio. *The Passion of theHoliness Church During the War*. Tokyo: Shinkyo Shuppansha, 1990. The sufferings and 'passion' of Holiness church groups, which began in June 1942, was the most serious experience of oppression in the modern history of Japanese Christianity. This book documents the testimony and researches of 70 kinds of witness by over 60 pastors, their families and lay believers.

iii) Japan Society of Systematic Theology, eds. *Theology of Bodiliness*. Tokyo: Shinkyo Shuppansha, 1990. A pioneering enterprise to take ecological problems as a theological task. Ecological issues which have reached crisis point at the end of the 20th century are explored from the perspective of "bodiliness" and life in the natural world.

iv) Linuma Jiro. *The Emperor System and Christians*. Tokyo: UCCJ Board of Publications, 1991. The author here searches for a way of true Christian living in Japan in relation to the Tenno system. Reflection is based in the agony and thought of both Japanese and Korean Christians who have been confronted with the emperor system as a symbol of Japanese people's integration since the Meiji Era.

> See also NCC Daijosai Mondai Shomei Undou Center (Signiture campaign anti-Daijosai). 1990 booklet series *Kirisuto-kyo to Tennousei* (Christianity and emperor system) booklets 1-6.

v) Lee In Ha. *As You Love Yourself*. Tokyo: UCCJ Board of Publications, 1991. The author, who came to Japan to study from the still-colonised Korea, was challenged by the Bible to become a Korean resident minister in Japan. He searches for a relationship with Japanese neighbours of equal and mutual co-partnership and out of deep pains develops biblical interpretations which challenge Japanese society.

vi) NCCJ Committee of the Differently Abled and Social Concern. *Toward Theology of the Differently Abled*. Tokyo: Shinkyo Shuppansha, 1993. Provides the lectures and speeches conducted in the interchange seminars of the National Organisation of Christian Differently Abled Groups. Theological reflection upon being differently abled is included, along with appeals for the Church to take up the problems of the differently abled persons in a positive stance of cooperative living.

> See also: Tokyo Group to Think About the Problem of the Differently Abled. *Against the Wall of "Common Sense": Witnesses of 21 Differently Abled Persons*. Tokyo: Shinkyo Shuppansha, 1994; National Association of the Differently Abled Groups, ed., *Joyful Life: On the Birth Diagnosis*. Tokyo: Shinkyo Shuppansha, 2000.

vii) Shiraishi Nabe. *Having Lived As An Ainu*. Tokyo: UCCJ Committee of Education, 1993. A record of the oral history of an old Ainu woman: her childhood experience, experience of Ainu culture, the relation of the Ainu with nature, and the events of their history. She eloquently reveals both her strong personality and the realities of struggling against discrimination.

viii) National Federation of Kyodan (UCCJ) Women's Societies. *Thinking of a Human Being in Relation to Discrimination*. Tokyo: Shinkyo Shuppansha, 1994. Examines the histories of discrimination in Japan, and the present situations of those groups still discriminated against: Buraku, women, the handicapped, Ainu, Korean residents in Japan, and poor workers. It also presents records of those people who by their actions have investigated the roots of prejudice and discrimination, and in the Bible have searched for its solution. See also: Kaneko Keiichi (xiii below).

ix) Christian Liaison Group for the Abolition of Capital Punishment. *The Abolition of Capital Punishment and Christianity*. Tokyo: Shinkyo Shuppansha, 1994. This is the first project that wrestles with the institution of capital punishment, in which the state deprives its citizens of their human right to life. Along with

38 statements of Christians of diverse experience and situation - many based in theological reflection - basic sources on the issues involved are provided.

x) Inoue Yoshio. *With the Post-War History of Christianity.* Tokyo: Shinkyo Shuppansha, 1995. A collection of 41 statements and testimonies, wrestling with the problems of church and society. The Church's responsibility for politics and for the welfare of the state is presented from a theological perspective and in the context of post-war Christian history in Japan.

xi) Bucho Takeda. *The Church for the World: From War-Responsibility to Environmental Responsibility.* Tokyo: Shinkyo Shuppansha, 1995. The author sees the problem of confession for war-guilt as an essential condition for the church's present life in the histories of both Japanese and German churches. His studies sharply analyse the historical war responsibility of the Kyodan (UCCJ) and outline the contents of a new faith-confession that centres on environmental responsibility.

See also: Tomisaka Christian Center, ed., *Ecology and Christianity.* Tokyo: Shinkyo Shuppansha, 3rd Printing, 1996.

xii) Kaneko Keiichi, ed. *Lecture Course "Contemporary Christian Ethics," Volume 3: Living in Japan.* Tokyo: UCCJ Board of Publications, 1999. On the basis of accepting war-responsibility, this course questions what it means to "live" together with those who are discriminated against now: minority people, such as Burakumin, Korean residents in Japan, the Ainu, the foreign migrant workers, the homeless labourers, the "handicapped," and the people of Okinawa.

xiii) Institute of Research, UCCJ. *The Historical Records of the United Church of Christ in Japan.* 5 vols. Tokyo: UCCJ Board of Publications, 1997-1998. These historical records cover comprehensively all data of the history of the Kyodan (UCCJ), including those materials discovered in the process of editorial work. "Readers may be shocked", writes the Rev'd. Kaino Nobuo, of the Research Institute, "by the volume of material recording the naked truth about negative aspects of the Kyodan's history, namely, its actions during World War II, which the compilers have made no attempt to hide. It is this honest facing of its history as fact, however, that will enable the church to move on and to develop its future vision."

2.6.6. Institutes, Movements, Associations
2.6.6.1. Catholic Bishops' Conference

The Conference of Catholic Bishops in Japan was first established in 1941 as "Nippon Tenshu Kokyo Kyodan" (The Japanese Catholic Religious Body) including churches and religious orders, becoming in 1945 "Tenshu Kokyo Kyoku Remmei" (The Catholic Inter-diocesan Federation). Since then its activities, carried out through 23 committees, include Inter-Religious Matters, Ecumenical Matters, Scriptural and Doctrinal Matters, the Buraku Problem, and the Registration of Foreigners Problem, matters Concerning the Catholic Church in China, and matters Concerning Combined Korean-Japanese History. The Conference early adopted as its own FABC statements on the local church as a "church incarnate in a people, a church indigenous and inculturated", understood as a church "in continuous, humble and loving dialogue with the living traditions, the cultures, the religions in brief, with all life-realities of the people in whose midst it has sunk its roots deeply and whose history and life it gladly makes its own." In 1967, approval was given for the new catechism based on the spirit of Vatican II and a revised lectionary for Mass. The localising of the church also meant study and action upon many major social and political issues. Following the earlier establishment of the Commission for Social Activities, and later the Japan Catholic Council for Justice and Peace (1970) and the Committee on Human Rights and Welfare (1983), the Bishops' Conference has made regular proposals to government, and also issued Pastoral Letters, Petitions to Government, protest letters and statements of people of the discriminated-against: Buraku, Korean minority, Asian women in Japan, separation of Church and State on peace concerns, the Alien Registration Law, the Yasukuni Shrine, and other issues of social justice. These campaigns have often been in joint action with the National Christian Council.

Contextual Theology in Japan

Significant actions and affirmations that reveal the theological bases of the Bishops' Conference include the following: "Basic Policies and Priorities of the Catholic Church in Japan" were adopted and announced at the ordinary assembly of the bishops in June 1984, including statements that the good news of salvation is to be brought to each and every person, and that salvation is not an individual affair but is to penetrate the whole of society, with a special concern for the marginalised. In September 1986, at the fourth plenary session of the Asia-wide FABC held in Tokyo, Archbishop S. Shirayanagi, president of the Bishops' Conference of Japan, made a formal apology for the wartime responsibility that he said must be borne by Japan and the Catholic Church of Japan for the tragedies and atrocities of the Second World War. In 1987 in Kyoto, the First National Incentive Convention for Evangelization was held on "Building an Open Church", a theme involving the reconsideration of how Japanese Catholics were to live the faith based on the realities of daily life and to evangelise starting from the social conditions in Japan. Then in 1993 in Nagasaki, the Second National Convention was held on "Finding the Ideal of Evangelization from the Realities of Family Life". The Conference understands that the great longing for true human living of the family at present is a cry for salvation, a longing for Christ the Savior, even among those who have no awareness of it. In 1997 the Conference issued "A Plea for Better Treatment of Foreigners Held as Prisoners in Japan" and a Petition for the Ratification of the "international Convention for the protection of the rights of migrant workers".

Perhaps their most important steps theologically have been taken in response to the preparatory document (*Lineamenta*) issued by the Vatican in Preparation for the 1997 Asian Synod of Bishops. The Conference declared: "Since the questions of the *Lineamenta* were composed in the context of Western Christianity, they are not suitable ... From the way the questions are proposed, one feels that the holding of the Synod is like an occasion for the central office to evaluate the performance of the branch offices ... The judgement should not be made from a European framework, but must be seen on the spiritual level of the people who live in Asia." They then presented their proposals for the Synod regarding method, process, aims, leadership and doctrinal content. In their view the central concerns were to be: Asian theology which speaks to us through Christ's living presence, nourishing the faith, liturgy, social issues, Asian spirituality and inculturation of the Gospel, inter-faith dialogue, with in addition "a new look at the connection between the Churches in Asia and the Holy See to consider a system of establishing relationships not based on 'centralization' but on 'collegiality'. We ask the Holy See", they concluded, "to give more recognition to the rightful autonomy of the Local Churches".

Selected References

See *Japan Mission Journal* (formerly *Japan Missionary Bulletin*) for official Statements.

Catholic Bishops' Conference of Japan. *Katorikku Nyumon* (New introductory catechism for adults). Special editorial Board of the Catechetical Committee, 1971.

—. "Preaching the Gospel in Society." Bishops' Pastoral Letter, 1972.

—. "Evangelization in Japan." Episcopal Commission for Evangelical and Pastoral Activities, 1976.

"The Desire for Peace - the Evangelical Mission of the Church in Japan." Bishops' Conference Pastoral Letter, 1983.

"Life a Gift of God." Bishops' Conference Pastoral Letter, 1984.

"Veneration of the Blessed Mother on the occasion of the Marian Year." Bishops' Conference Pastoral Letter, 1987.

"Towards Overcoming Buraku Discrimination." Episcopal Commission for Social Activities, 1992.

"Seeking the Kingdom of God Which Transcends Differences in Nationality." Episcopal Commission for Social Activities, 1993.

"No One Can be Excluded from the Kingdom of God." *Catholic International* 4 (1993).

"A Plea for Better Treatment of Foreigners Held as Prisoners in Japan." Plea of the Bishops' Conference, 1997.

The General Secretariat, Catholic Bishops' Conference of Japan. *The Catholic Church in Japan: an Historical Overview*. Tokyo: Japan Catholic Center, 1995.

—. *The Catholic Church in Japan: Present Structure and Activities*. Tokyo: Japan Catholic Center, 1996.

Contextual Theology in Japan

Catholic Bishops' Conference of Japan, 1984-1997. *Documents in English*. Tokyo: The General Secretariat Catholic Bishops' Conference of Japan, 1998.

Official Response of the Japanese Church to the Lineamenta. Catholic Bishops' Conference of Japan, 1996. See also *Adoremus Bulletin* 5.10 (2000).

2.6.6.2. Ecumenical and Scholarly Institutes

Many such institutes have been established by Christian universities and colleges but only a few important examples can be mentioned here to indicate the extent of activity undertaken.

Sophia University, Tokyo, has a full range of research institutes including the following: the Institute of Christian Culture / Oriental Religions (1969) researches many aspects of Christianity including its cultural heritage and development, along with specialised research into a variety of eastern religions; the Institute for the Study of Social Justice (1981) conducts interdisciplinary studies of diverse problems related to justice both in Japan and elsewhere, in relation to practical outcomes; the Institute of Comparative Culture (1981) promotes research and learning, lectures and seminars in comparative culture; the Institute of Asian Cultures (1982) is devoted to the study of various aspects of traditional cultures throughout Asia, with a special focus on Southeast Asia, South Asia and the Middle East.

Institutes at the International Christian University, Tokyo, include: The Institute for the Study of Christianity and Culture (1963) which focuses on research on Christianity's impact on eastern and western cultures; The Institute of Asian Cultural Studies (1971) focuses on the study of the cultural characteristics of Asian societies, including Japan, and their historical development from a global perspective; The Peace Research Institute (1991), an outgrowth of the course on "Peace Studies", which has been offered since 1984, was established for the purpose of strengthening and promoting peace research at ICU, based upon the ideals of the foundation of the University.

Amongst many other universities and colleges possessing relevant institutes, library resources or research programmes are

Aoyama Gakuin University (Tokyo), Tokyo Union Theological Seminary, Japan Lutheran Theological College (Tokyo); Central Theological College (Tokyo); Tokyo Catholic Seminary, Rural Evangelical Seminary (Tsurukawa Institute), St Paul's Rikkyo University, Doshisha University (Kyoto), Kwansei Gakuin University (Nishinomiya), Sapientia University (Eichi Daigaku, Osaka), Seinan Gakuin University (Fukuoka), Meiji University (Tokyo), Waseda University (Tokyo), and Kyoto University.

Ecumenical social concern centers are also contributing to contextual theology and include the Nippon Christian Academies at Hakone, Oiso, Kyoto and Sapporo; the Korean Christian Center, Osaka; the Student Christian Centers at Kobe and Waseda, Tokyo; the Mt Rokko YMCA Center, and Tomisaka Christian Center (2.6.6.4.). See also the commissions and institutes of the Catholic Bishops' Conference (2.6.6.1.) and the National Christian Council (2.6.6.3). In some cases, local churches have developed significant programs of theological reflection (2.6.6.5.).

See also above for student movements (2.1.1, 2.1.3); inter-faith centres (2.4)); womens' associations (2.2.); social concern centers (2.3); CCRAI (2.5.31, 2.6.6.3); SEMINEX (2.6.3.); and the section Other Protestant Theologians (2.6.3.).

Selected References

Asian Cultural Studies. The Institute of Asian Cultural Studies, International Christian University.

Bulletin of the Nanzan Institute for Religion and Culture. (Since 1976).

Fujimori Hajime. *Ajia no naka no Nihon to Kirisutokyo undo nashonaru na mono to sekaiteki na mono no aida.* Japanese and Christian movements in Asian Context - 5. Articles in English. Tokyo: Nihon YMCA Domei, 1983.

Fukuin Senkyo. Oriens Institute for Religious Research.

Hirata Satoshi, ed. *On The Scene: Reality Ministry in Japan.* Kyoto: Kansai UIM, 1975.

Institute of Asian Cultures Discussion Papers. Various series. Sophia University.

Kattorikku Kenkyu. Theological Society of Sophia University.

Humanities (Christianity and Culture) The Institute for the Study of Christianity and Culture, International Christian University.

Japan Mission Journal (formerly *Japan Missionary Bulletin*) Oriens Institute, Tokyo.

Japanese Religions - NCC Study Center, Kyoto. Bi-annual. Also publishes *Deai - Kirisutokyo to Shoshukyo*, in Japanese.

Japanese Journal of Religious Studies - Nanzan Institute, Nagoya. Quarterly.

Koyanagi Nobuaki. "Christian Work in the Yoseba: Kamagasaki, Sanya, Kotobuki, Sasajima." In *Christianity in Japan 1971-1990*, edited by Kumuzawa Yoshinobu and David Swain. Tokyo: Kyo Bun Kwan; Cincinnati: Friendship Press, 1991.

Monograph Series *Christianity in Japan, Protestantism in Asia*, et seq. 1960- . The Institute of Asian Cultural Studies, International Christian University.

Shoji Tsutomu. "Sin and Suffering: Japan and the Peoples of Asia." *Japan Christian Quarterly* 47.1 (1981).

Suggate, Alan M. with the assistance of Yamano Shigeko. *Japanese Christians and Society*. Studies in the intercultural history of Christianity 98. Bern and New York: Peter Lang, c1996.

2.6.6.3. National Christian Council in Japan (NCCJ)

The Japan Federation of Christian Churches (1911) had become the National Christian Council of Japan (1922) which was re-formed in 1947 (NCC in Japan from 1985). Membership currently includes seven national churches, eight ecumenical associations - including the YWCA and the YMCA - and 19 affiliated churches and organisations. The NCCJ seeks to express the unity of the member churches and organisations in Jesus Christ, promote their collaborative works in the fields of mission, education and service, and contribute to the ecumenical movement throughout the world. This has meant the nurturing of relationships between the churches of Japan, and with churches and projects outside Japan, in their common mission. For these purposes the Council has developed many divisions and committees for particular tasks, including those for Christian literature, Urban-Rural Mission, Women's concerns, Buraku People, Disabled Persons, Shinto and the State, Migrant Workers, International Affairs and Peace and Nuclear Issues. The Council has also initiated or collaborated in the study of Japanese Religions (see 2.4.2.) and in many social and political campaigns for justice and peace, including those on the issues of labor, discrimination against minorities, nuclear development and the Yasukuni Shrine, as well as those concerning China, North and South Korea, Taiwan and the Philippines. In 1981 the Center for Christian response to Asian Issues was established by the Council (See above 2.5.31). Letters and statements have also been regularly sent on behalf of the NCCJ members and affiliates, to sister churches - to establish solidarity, and to Japanese and world governments - to advocate specific causes of peace and justice.

Increasing co-operation with the Roman Catholic Church has developed in the last 20 years, in such activities as justice and peace activities, preparation of the Common Bible, service to day-labourers, advocacy for the rights of Korean citizens, opposition to the role of the Yasukuni Shrine and solidarity with Korean and Philippine churches in similar concerns.

Theological reflection has been integral to almost all of these activities, and often has been focussed in programmes of seminars, workshops and publication. Leading figures in the NCCJ who have contributed further to contextualising theology in Japan include Nakajima John Masaaki, Shoji Tsutomu (2.6.2.), Lee In Ha, Aiko Carter (2.5.21.), Yamano Shigeko (2.5.31.), Kurata Masahiko, Maejima Munetoshi and Otsu Kenichi. Much of the theological reflection emanating from or stimulated by the Council has been published by the nine publishers associated with its work through the *Nikkikan* (Japan Christian Publications Distribution Company); in particular by the *Kyo Bun Kwan* (Christian Literature Society), *Shinkyo Shuppansha* (Protestant Publishing Co.), *Yorudansha* (Jordan Press), the United Church of Christ Board of Publications, Seibunsha (formerly Lutheran Literature Society), and the YMCA Press.

Selected References
    See also references under Theology, Culture and Society (2.3.) and Inter-faith Encounter and Reflection (2.4.).
    Articles, reports and statements have appeared in the *Japan Christian Yearbook* (1932-1942, 1950-1970; formerly the *Japan Mission Yearbook* 1903-1910 and the *Christian Mission in Japan,*

Formosa and Korea,1911-1932); as well as in such periodicals as *Japan Christian Activity News*; *Fukuin to Sekai*, *Asian Issues Series,* and *Asia Tsushin* (CCRAI) and the *Japan Christian Quarterly*. The *Yearbook* was succeeded by the omnibus volume *Christianity in Japan, 1970-1990* (Kumuzawa and Swain,1991), and, for the *Japan Christian Quarterly* also, by *The Japan Christian Review* (1992-1998).

Kumuzawa Yoshinobu and David Swain, eds. *Christianity in Japan 1971-1990.* Tokyo: Kyo Bun Kwan; Cincinnati: Friendship Press, 1991.

Kurata Masahisa. *Taikenteki Ajia Handbook* (Asian handbook through experience). Tokyo: YMCA Shuppan, 1985.

Lee In Ha. *As You Love Yourself.* Tokyo: UCCJ Board of Publications, 1991.

Linuma Jiro. *The Emperor System and Christians.* Tokyo: UCCJ Board of Publications, 1991.

Moriyama Shigeko. "The Anti-emperor and Anti-Yasukuni movements." In *Peace Consultation on Japan/U.S. Military Cooperation in Asia and the Pacific.* Tokyo: Christian Center for Response to Asian Issues, 1989.

NCCJ Social Department. *The System of Licensed Prostitution in Japan: Report of an Investigation by the Social Department, National Christian Council of Japan, July 16, 1925.* Tokyo: Japan Advertiser Press, 1925.

NCCJ Committee of the Differently Abled and Social Concern. *Toward Theology of the Differently Abled.* Tokyo: Shinkyo Shuppansha, 1993.

NCC Daijosai Mondai Shomei Undou Center (Signiture campaign anti-Daijosai). *Kirisuto-kyo to Tennousei* (Christianity and emperor system) booklets 1-6, 1990.

NCCJ Women's Committee. *Josei to Shingaku no Kai kiroku* (Women doing theology report). Tokyo: NCCJ, 1984. (et seq. in succeeding years).

Nihon Kirisutokyo Kyodikai. *The Work of the National Christian Council; a Liaison Organ of Christianity in Japan.* Tokyo: National Christian Council [n.d.]

Phillips, James M. *From the Rising of the Sun, Christians and Society in Contemporary Japan.* Maryknoll, NY: Orbis Books,1981.

Suggate, Alan with Yamano Shigeko. *Japanese Christians and Society.* Studies in the intercultural history of Christianity 98. Bern and New York: Peter Lang, c1996.

2.6.6.4. The Tomisaka Christian Centre

The Tomisaka Christian Centre, of the Christian East Asia Mission Foundation in Tokyo, has maintained its research and publishing activities since 1983, with the policy of carrying out interdisciplinary research into issues of Christian social ethics. Each study group consists of around 10 members and continues its collaborative research over several years. The long-term director has been Dr. Suzuki Shozo. From this work have come the following books:

Tomisaka Christian Centre, eds. *People Open a New Age: A Dialogue between Japan and Korea on Minjun (People's) Theology.* Tokyo: Shinkyo Shuppansha, 1990. Japanese and Korean theologians, write here on the theological movement has had a radical impact upon theologies throughout the world since the 1970s and that it offers essential resources for theology in both Japan and Korea.

Tomisaka Christian Centre, eds. *Theological Criticism of the Emperor System.* Tokyo: Shinkyo Shuppansha, 1991. This book considers the emperor system viewed from the perspective of the Bible, theological criticism, and wider problems concerning the emperor system. Ten writers address the emperor system as a theological task and criticise its religious aspect, especially that of the deification of the human being.

> See also: Iwate Support Association of Unconstitutionality. *The Document of the Struggle of Iwate Unconstitutionality-Law-Suit of Yasukuni Shrine: Like an Ishiwari-Zakura (Rock-breaking Cherry Tree).* Tokyo: Shinkyo Shuppansha, 1992:
> - an epoch-making verdict after more than 10 years' struggle.

Tomisaka Christian Centre, eds. *Theology of "Genba" Utterances from the Living Spot.* Shinkyo Koinonia 13. Tokyo: Shinkyo Shuppansha, 1993. The product of interdisciplinary and co-operative work over four years from the 'living spots' of Japanese mission. Theological reflection here arises from 'hot' discussion of the human stories arising within the participants' involvements in the sharp experiences of frontier mission in Japanese society. These included resistance to Narita airport construction, solidarity with Filipino people in Japan, resistance to nuclear development projects, and revelation of God through marriage. Theologies of story, journalism and of the 'living spot' were explored.

Selected References
>Amongst the 16 books now published by Tomisaka Christian Centre are: *Christianity and the Formation of the Modern Emperor System* (1996); *Ecology and Christianity* (1996); *Psychological Suffering and its Relief* (1997); *Historical Resource Materials on Japanese-Korean Christian Relations II, Scientific Technology and Christianity* (1999); and *Courage for Farming Life* (2000).
>
>The forthcoming volume *Mission and Theology in East Asia* (In Japanese. Tokyo: Shinkyo Shuppansha), is also to be published in English. This has been prepared by the Research Group on East Asian Mission and Theology and provides a new paradigm for doing - and living - theology in East Asian contexts. It draws on new elements of Minjung theology, feminist theology, theology of revolution, biblical theology, social ethics, and psychology.

2.6.6.5. The Hyakunincho Church, Nippon Kiristo Kyodan (UCCJ)

As example of many local churches which have published reflections from innovative ministries.

Founded in November 1970, the Hyakunincho Church has initiated ministries in which socio-political issues are addressed, authoritarian and oppressive structures are challenged, and relationships of trust have been established - on the basis of the Kyodan's confession of responsibility in the Second World War - with Christians in, for example, Korea and the Philippines. Particular relationship has developed over 20 years with the Jam Sil Central Church of the Korean Presbyterian Church in Seoul. This has led to joint studies and action concerning Korean re-unification, communications between Korean and Japanese, and the role of their churches together in contemporary Asia. Ministers of the church have collaborated with others in a history of these relationships (see below).

Roman Catholics, Buddhists and Muslims, also share in the activities of Hyakunincho Church, and with other members accept responsibility to speak "Shoushi" in place of a sermon or preaching, during the Service. This is held in a dining room which is rented from Nippon Christian Kyofukai, where they then have lunch together as Communion, followed by responses to the shared "Shoushi", all sitting in a circle. This is for them "theology in the midst of daily life". Worship is also held at the church cemetery on anniversaries to commemorate the dead.

In all these activities the minister (the Rev'd Ka Jung-soon - the first pastor to be invited to Japan from Korea) here shares as a member, and stresses in his ministry that Asian Christian belief requires coexistence with the poor in working for their liberation. The church has a missionary in the Philippines and supports women and men missionaries from the Philippines ministering to Filipinos in Tokyo.

Selected References

"*ROBA* (Ass)." Newsletter of Hyakunincho Church. (The title is taken from the sculpture of the Japanese Christian artist, Goro Kakei, "Ass and a disciple").

Aso Toshifumi, Kida Kenichi, Dohi Akio, Yoshimatsu Shigeru and Shoji Tsutomu. *Higashi Ajiano Heiwato Kirisutokyo (East Asian peace and Christianity: the last Twenty Years of Church Solidarity between Japan and Korea)*. Tokyo: Shinkyo Shuppansha, 1999.

2.7 Philosophical Theologians

A number of Japanese theologians have concentrated on philosophical or theological questions raised by western theology, often with only passing reference to either Japanese Christian thought or life. A selcection of these follows:

Nakagawa Hideyasu (1908-) taught at Hokaido University in Sapporo and at International Christian University, Tokyo, and combined a deep knowledge of the New Testament with the penetrating understanding of modern existentialism. His writings on these subjects, as well as on prayer, the Bible, the Christian university, and on Christian faith in art and within history, span more than half a century and have had wide influence.

Odagiri Nobuo (1909-) was a physician proposing a more biblical christology in which he affirmed that though there were no biblical texts declaring Jesus was God true belief sees him as purely the Son of God, else the soteriological significance of the cross is nullified. He debated this with Kitamori and others and organised series of lectures later published as *Christological Studies* (1968).

Noro Yoshio (1925-) was partly influenced by Odagiri, and by Kitamori, but more by existential philosophers, western theologians and by Nishida Kitaro. Using these sources, along with his own existential experience of Buddhism and Christianity, his theology presents history as a dialogue between God and the life of human beings, which is however too brief for achieving unity with God which will come only after innumerable rebirths (*samsara*) at the consummation of history. Noro also studied John Wesley's life and work and called for theology to address Japanese tradition and also social concerns.

Miyata Mitsuo (1928-) studied theology from his conviction that western political thought cannot be understood without an understanding of theology. He specialised in modern German political thought, believing its spiritual dimensions to be highly important also in Japan's history. He has also written on Christian ethics, faith and the Bible, the meaning of humour in the light of Christian faith and sought to relate political thought to cultural and artistic creativity in Japan.

Odagakai Masaya's primary influences in his philosophical theology were Hiedigger, Ebeling and Fuchs, along with Nishida Kitaro. With comparatively brief references to "oriental thought", and to the relationship between Buddhism and Christianity, he focusses upon the issues of duality in faith and reason, belief and unbelief. Consideration of the absolute and the relative in God and humanity lead him to picture the Trinity as being comprised of God, human being, and the duality of divine and human (i.e. Holy Spirit).

Sato Toshio (1923-) has studied 19th century (western) theology and, although critical of Barth, draws both on him for his dogmatics, and on Troeltsch for cultural ethics. He has also produced historical surveys of theology in the West, and of Japanese Christianity.

Ariga Tetsutaro (b.1889), Miyamoto Takenosuke (b.1905) and Muto Kazuo (b.1913) dealt in their writing with theological themes, but in the framework of philosophical questions: symbolical theology and ontology, primarily in the church 'fathers' (Ariga); philosophy as symbol, drawing on dialectical theology (Miyamoto); and the philosophy of religion, drawing upon such diverse sources as Kirkegaard, Nishida and Kant (Muto). All three, however, did consider some of the questions regarding indigenisation in occasional articles: Ariga also writing on the history of Christianity in Japan; Miyamoto also on Christian Education; and Muto on Kierkegaard, Tanabe and, with others, on Communism and Christianity.

Ohki Hideo (1928-) has published two books on Puritan ethics, volumes on Barth and Brunner and also articles on ethical questions involved when Christians seek to act in the modern world. In the book co-authored with Furuya Yasuo (see 2.5.11 above) he also questions whether there can be a Japanese theology. In his thought, Japanese theology is one which totally questions Japan from a theological - that is "God's" - point of view. It is therefore more concerned with a theological critique of Japanese subjectivity, with Japan as a theme of theology, than with the faith insights and experience of Japanese within particular contexts.

Selected References

 Odagiri Nobuo, ed. *Kirisuto ron no kenkyu* (Study of christology). Tokyo: Shinkyo Shuppansha, 1968.

 —. *Shingaku to irȳo to no aida* (Christianity and medicine). Tokyo: Sobunsha, 1983.

 Noro Yoshio. "Christ and History." *NEAJOT* 2 (1969).

 —. *Existential Theology and Ethics* (Jitsuzonronteki Shingaku to Rinri). Tokyo: Sobunsha, 1970.

 —. *Kami to Kibo* (God and hope). Tokyo: Kyodan Shuppan Kyoku, 1980.

 —. *Kirisutokyo to Minshu Bukkyo, Yujika to Renge* (Christianity and popular Buddhism - cross and lotus flower). Tokyo: Nihon Kirisutokyodan Shuppan Kyoku, 1991.

Odagaki Masaya. *God in Contemporary Thought* (Gendai Shiso no nakano kami). Tokyo: Shinchi Shobo, 1988.
—. *Hermeneutical Theology* (Kaishakugakuteki Shingaku). Tokyo: Sobunsha, 1975.
—. *To an Unknown God* (Shirarezaru Kami ni). Tokyo: Sobunsha, 1980.
Sato Toshio. *The Loss and Restoration of Religion* (Shukyo no soshitsu to kaifuku). Tokyo: Nihon Kirisutokyodan Shuppankyoku, 1978, 1988.
—. *Nihon no Kirisutokyo to Shingaku* (Japanese Christianity and theology). Tokyo: Kyodan Shuppankyoku, 1968.
Ariga Tetsutaro. "Christian Mission in Japan as a Theological Problem." *Religion in Life* 27.3 (1958).
—. "Some Further Thoughts on Indigenization." *Japanese Religions* 3.4 (1963).
—, and Uoki Tadaichi. *History of Christian Thought* (Kirisutokyo shisoshi). Tokyo: Kyobunkan, 1951, 1955, 1959.
Miyamoto Takenosuke. *The Basic Problems of Christian Ethics* (Kirisutokyo rinrigaku no konponmondai). Tokyo: Tokyodo Shuppan, 1968.
—. The Collected Writings of Miyamoto Takenosuke (*Miyamoto Takenosuku chosakushu*). 2 vols. Tokyo: Shinkyo Suppansha, 1991-92.
Miyata Mitsuo. *Miyata chosakushu* (Selected works of Miyata Mitsuo - on the theme of Bible and faith). 7 vols. Tokyo: Iwanami Shoten, 1996.
—. *Jyujika to Haakenkuroiz* (Cross and swastika - social thought of the anti-Nazi struggle). Tokyo. Shinkyo Shuppansha, 2000.
Muto Kazuo. *A New Possibility of the Philosophy of Religion* (Shukyotetsugaku no atarashii kanosei). Nishinomiya: Kokusai Nihon Kenkyusho, 1974.
—. *Theological and Philosophical Essays* (Shingakuteki, shukyotetsu - gakuteki ronshu). 3 vols. Tokyo: Sobunsha, 1980, 1986, 1993.
Nakagawa Hideyasu. *Kindai teki Ningen to Kirisutokyo* (Modern man and Christianity). Tokyo: YMCA Shuppan, 1957.
—. *Inori to Chinmoku*. (Prayer and silence). Tokyo: Sobunsha, 1988.
—. *Tokino Hazamani Tatsu* (Standing between the times). Tokyo: Kobundo, 1999.

Ohki Hideo. *The Ethical Thought of Puritanism* (Pyuritanizumu no rinrishiso). Tokyo: Shinkyo Shuppansha, 1966.

—, and Furuya Yasuo. *Nihon no shingaku* (Theology of Japan). Tokyo: Yorudansha, 1989.

2.8 Supplementary Bibliography II

2.8.1. Journals and Periodicals - a selection

Bulletin of the Nanzan Institute for Religion and Culture. Since 1976.

Bulletin - United Church of Christ in Japan. Research Institute on the Mission of the Church. Since 1963.

Christ and Society. Frontier Union Newsletter. ca. 1951-1955.

Fukuin Senkyo. Oriens Institute for Religious Research, Tokyo.

Fukuin to Sekai (Gospel and world - monthly since 1952). Tokyo: Shuppansha. Superseded *Kirisutokyo Bunka* (Christian culture) and *Fukuin to Jidai* (Gospel and the times), both 1946-1956.

Japan Christian Activity News - NCCJ, Tokyo. Quarterly.

Japan Christian Quarterly. Quarterly 1926-1991. Tokyo: Kyo Bun Kwan. Superseded *Japan Evangelist*, continued by *Japan Christian Review* - annual to 1998.

Japan Mission Journal (formerly *Japan Missionary Bulletin*) Oriens Institute, Tokyo.

Japanese Religions - NCC Study Center, Kyoto. Bi-annual. Also publishes *Deai - Kirisutokyo to Shoshukyo*, in Japanese.

Japanese Journal of Religious Studies - Nanzan Institute, Nagoya. Quarterly.

Josei to Jinken (Women and human rights). Kyodan Women Clergy Caucus, from 1888.

Kattorikku Kenkyu (Catholic studies). Theological Society of Sophia University.

Kirisutokyo Kenkyu (Studies in the Christian religion). Doshisha University. Semi-annual since 1923.

Kirisutokyo shakai mondai kenky (Study of Christianity and social problems) Doshisha Daigaku Jinbun Kagaku Kenkyujo. Annual since 1958.

Kirisutokyo Ronshu (Essays on Christianity - since 1953). Tokyo: Aoyama Gakuin Daigaku.

Kirisutokyo nenkan (Christian Yearbook). Kirisuto Shimbunsha.

Koe (Voice - since 1891). Catholic Osaka Diocese.

Kyodan Newsletter. United Church of Christ in Japan.

Nihon no Shingaku (Japanese theology - 1945-1961 in one volume, thereafter annually from 1962). Tokyo: Japan Society of Christian Studies.

Nippon Sei Ko Kai Newsletter. (Anglican Church of Japan, since 1988).

Research Institute of Christian Culture of Sapientia University. (Catholic).

Shingaku (Journal of Theology). Tokyo Shingaku Daigaku, Kyo Bun Kwan.

The Catholic News (Catholic English news organ, formerly *Tosei News*). Since 1981.

The Tokyo Mission Reserch Institute News Letter. (Catholic).

See also: *Tezukuri no Kyokai* (The Church of our own making), *Inochi no Kotoba* (The Living Word), *Shinto no Tomo* (Friend of the laity), *Seisho no Kyokai* (The Bible and the Church), *Voices from Japan, Monumenta Nipponica, In God's Image*.

2.8.2. Monographs, Collections, Articles

Amakawa Junjiro. *An Aspect of the Adaptation of "Protestant ethics" to Meiji Japan*. Nishinomiya: Kwansei Gakuin University, 1975.

Anzai Shin. *Nanto ni okeru Kirisutokyo no juyo* (Christianity and society, Ryukyu Islands). Tokyo: Daiichi Shobo, 1984.

Breen, John and Mark Williams, eds. *Japan and Christianity: Impacts and Responses*. Basingstoke, Hampshire: Macmillan Press; New York: St. Martin's Press, 1996.

Bunnosuke Sekine. *Nihon Seishin Sho to Kirisutokyo* (The Spiritual history of Japan and Christianity). Osaka: Sobinsha, 1962.

Caldarola, Carlo. *Uchimura Kanzo to mukyokai: shukyo shakaigakuteki kenkyu* (Uchimura Kanzo and Mukyokai: A sociology of religion approach). Tokyo: Shinkyo Shuppansha. 1978.

—. *Christianity: The Japanese Way.* Leiden: Brill, 1979.

Catholic Committee for Buraku Issues. *Education Materials for Human Rights. Tokyo: 1994.*

Chi Myon-kwan et al., eds. *Historical Resource Material on Japanese-Korean Relations: Records of Christians in Agony*. Tokyo: Shinkyo Shuppansha, 2000.

Copeland, Rebecca. *Lost Leaves: Women Writers of Meiji Japan*. Honolulu: University of Hawaii Press, 2000.

Davis, Winston. *Japanese Religion and Society: Paradigms of Structure and Change*. Albany: State University of New York Press, 1992.

Eiichi Amemiya, and Gen Morioka, eds. *Nihon kirisuto kyodan gojunenshi no shomondai* (Problems in the fifty year history of the United Church of Christ in Japan). Tokyo: Shinkyo Shuppansha, c.1998.

Finkbeiner, Siegfried. "Christian-Buddhist Encounters." *Japanese Religions* 16.2 (1990).

Hammer, Raymond. *Japan's Religious Ferment*. London: SCM Press, 1961.

The Church's Role in Urbanized Japan. Christian Witness in a Transitional Society, 12th Hayama Missionary Seminar, Amagi Sanso, edited by Carl C. Beck. Tokyo: [s.n.], 1971.

Equipping the Laity for Service: M*ajor Papers at the Nineteenth Hayama Missionary Seminar, Amagi Sanso, 5-7 January 1978*, edited by Carl C. Beck. Tokyo: [s.n.] 1978.

The Christian Gospel and its Ethical Implications for Japanese Society: Major Papers at the Twenty First Hayama Missionary Seminar, Amagi Sanso, January 7-9, 1980, edited by Marin F. Moorhead. Tokyo: [s.n.], 1980.

Hitt, Russell T. *Sensei. The Life Story of Irene Webster-Smith.*New York: Harper,1965.

Honda Masaaki. *Choetsusha to Jiko* (The transcendant and the self). Fukuoka: Sogensha, 1990.

Ikuo Natsunaga. "A New Quest for Japanese Christology? A Current Issue for Theology in Japan." *The Japan Christian Quarterly* 52:3 (1986).

Ishida Yoshiro. *An Investigation into the Controversy between Uemura and Ebina from 1901 to 1902 and its Implications for the Development of Christian Theology in Japan*. Microform. 1971.

Iwamura Shinji. *Sandaime no Kirisutokyo: dento bunkato no taiketsu kara shinkae*. Tokyo: Shinkyo Shuppansha, 1990.

Kazusa Hideo. *Endo Shusaku ron*. Tokyo: Shunjusha, 1987.

Kida Kenichi. *Isuraeru Yogensha no Shokumu to Bungaku* (Service and writings of the Israelite prophets). Tokyo: Nihon Kirisutokyodan Shuppankyoku, 1976.

Kirishitan no shima Amakusa (Amakusa, the Kirishitan island). Kumamoto: Kumamoto Catholic Church, 1981. Text in Japanese with some English sections.

Kodera, T. James. "A Vortex of East and West: Watsuji Tetsuro's Phenomenology and the Problem of Contextualization." *The Ecumenical Review* 35:3 (1983).

Kasuya Koichi. "A Catholic Commentary on A Theology of the Crown of Thorns: The Buraku Liberation Movement and Christianity." *Japan Mission Journal* 47.1 (1993).

Kuribayashi Teruo. *Nihon minwa no shingaku*. Tokyo: Nihon Kirisuto Kyodan Shuppankyoku, 1997 (1998).

Lee, Robert. *Stranger in the Land: A Study of the Church in Japan*. London: Lutterworth Press, 1967.

McAlpine, Pauline Smith. *Japanese Hymns in English*. Tokyo: Tsunobue Sha, 1975.

Maruyama Masao. *Nihon no Shiso* (Thought of Japan). Tokyo: Iwanami Shoten, 1961.

Masao Abe. "Man and Nature in Christianity and Buddhism." *Japanese Religions* 7.1 (1971).

Mataix A., Soma Nobuo and Sakae Shinji, eds. *A Liberation Theology for Japanese Society - Suggestions for the Future*. Tokyo: Chuo Shuppansha, 1986.

Minoru Kiyota, assisted by Byron Earhart, Paul Griffiths and James Heisig. *Japanese Buddhism: its Tradition, New Religions, and Interaction with Christianity*. Tokyo and Los Angeles: Buddhist Books International, c1987.

Mitsuo Fukuda. *Developing a Contextualized Church as a Bridge to Christianity in Japan*. Microform, 1956. Includes bibliography (leaves 238-261) and index. Ann Arbor, MI: UMI, 1993.

Morita Yuzaburo. *Modernity of Christianity* (Kirisutokyo no kindaisei). Tokyo: Sobunsha, 1972.

Mullins, Mark R. and Richard Fox Young, eds. *Perspectives on Christianity in Korea and Japan: The Gospel and Culture in East Asia*. Lewiston, NY: Edwin Mellen Press, 1995.

Muto Kazuo. "Christianity and the Notion of Nothingness." *Japanese Religions* 21.2 (1996).

Nakaji Shimao. *Like the Wind*. Kyoto: Hieishobo, 1963.

Naohiro Kiyoshige. "Jesus in Japanese Christian Thought: Uchimura and Kagawa." *The Japan Christian Quarterly* 49:1 (1983).

Nihon Kirisuto Kyodan. *Fukuin no dochaku Nihon Kirisuto*. Christian ministry series 6. Tokyo Nihon Kirisuto Kyodan Shuppanbu 1962.

Nishiyama Shigeru. "Indigenization and Transformation of Christianity in a Japanese Community." *Japanese Journal of Religious Studies* 12.1 (1985).

Ogawa Keiji. *Die Aufgabe der neueren evangelischen Theologie in Japan*. Basel, F. Reinhardt, 1965.

—, and Ji Myeong-Goan, eds. *Nikkan Kirisutokyo kankei shishiryo* (Historical materials on Christianity in Japan and Korea). Tokyo: Shinkyo Shuppansha, 1984.

Oguri Hitoshi. "The Japanese Industrial Society and Christianity." In *1999 Graduate Students' Conference on North East Asia Church History: Korea*, ed., 76-80. The Korea Academy of Church History, Seoul: 1999.

Park Heon-Wook. "The Problem of Secularization in Asian Countries - Toward Cultural Identity and Modernization in Asian Countries." *Transactions of the Institute for Japanese Culture and Classics* 51 (1983).

—. "Miehajimeta kirisuto no kunan" (Beginning to see the suffering of Christ). *Fukuin Shinbun* 461 (1989).

Reid, David. "Secularization Theory and Japanese Christianity: The case of the Nihon Kirisuto Kyôdan." *Japanese Journal of Religious Studies* 6.1-2 (1979).

—, et al. *Kiku to Katana to Jujika to* (Chrysanthemum, sword and cross). Tokyo: Nihon Kirisuto Kyodan Shuppankyoku, 1976.

Sato Yazumasa. *Nihon kindaishi to Kirisutokyo* (Japan and Christianity) Tokyo: Kanrin Shobo, 1997 (1868).

Shimizu Mazumi. *Das "Selbst" im Mahayana-Buddhismus in japanischer Sicht und die "Person" im Christentum im Licht des Neuen Testaments.* Leiden: Brill, 1981.

Shishido Yutaka. "Christian Peace Activities in Postwar Japan." In *Called to Be Peacemakers,* edited by Suguru Matsuki and David L. Swain. Tokyo: Japan Ecumenical Books, 1989.

Swyngedouw, Jan. *Wa to Bun no Kozo* (The structure of apportioned harmony). Tokyo: Nihon Kirisuto Kyodan Shuppan Kyoku, 1981.

Takeda Torao, et al. *Nihon gendai bungaku to Kirisutoky* (Christianity and literature). Tokyo: Ofusha, 1974.

Terazono Yoshiki, ed. *Brennpunkte in Kirche und Theologie Japans* (Focuses in church and theology of Japan). Neukirchen Vluyn: Neukirchener Verl., 1988.

Thelle, Netto R. "A Barthian Thinker between Buddhism and Christianity: Takizawa Katsumi." *Japanese Religions* 8.4 (1976).

Tokichi Ishii. *A Gentleman in Prison. With Confessions of Tokichi Ishii Written in Tokyo Prison,* translated by Caroline Macdonald. London: SCM Press, 1923.

Tokunaga Michio. "A Japanese Transformation of Christianity." *Japanese Religions.* 15.3 (1989).

Tomura Masahiro. *Japanese Fascism and the Problem of the Yasukuni Shrine* (Nihon no Fashizumu to Yasukuni Mondai). Tokyo: Shinkyo Shuppansha, 1974.

Uda Susumu. *Kami no keiji to Nihonjin no shukyo ishiki: gendai ni okeru senkyojo no "sesshokuten" o saguru* (God's revelation and Japanese religiosity). Tokyo: Hatsubai Inochi no Kotobasha, 1989.

Unuma Hiroko. *Kindai Nihon no Kirisutoky oshiso katachi.* Tokyo: Nihon Kirisuto Kyodan Shuppankyoku, 1988 (1989).

Waldenfels, H. "A Japanese Theology for Japan." *Japan Missionary Bulletin* 28.8 (1974).

Yamamoto Shichihei. *The Spirit of Japanese Capitalism and Selected Essays*. (A Protestant ethic in a non-Christian context). Lanham, Md.: Madison Books, 1992.

Yoshimoto Takaaki. *Zen Kirisutokyo ron shusei*. Tokyo: Shunjusha, 1988.

Yoshimoto, Tadasu. *A Peasant Sage of Japan. The Life and Work of Sontoku Ninomiya.* London: Longmans, 1912.

— JCE with AC, CV, KH, KHs, YM

7 Contextual Theology in Korea

1 **Introduction**
  1.1 Bibliographies and Guides
2 **The Christian Movement in Korea to 1919**
  2.1 Politics of Chosun Korea and the Christian Movement
    2.1.1. Catholic Beginnings; **2.1.2.** Confrontation between Korean Catholic Scholars and the Chosun Government; **2.1.3.** Early Catholic Writings; **2.1.4.** Roman Catholic Presence and Thought 19th-early 20th centuries; **2.1.5.** Forerunners in Catholic Contextual Theology
      2.1.5.1. Kim Dae Kun, Andrea (1821-1846); **2.1.5.2.** Choi Yang Up, Thomas (1821-1861); **2.1.5.3.** Suh Sang Don, Augustine (1850-1913); **2.1.5.4.** Ahn Chung Geun, Thomas (Ahn Joong Keun, 1879-1910)
    2.1.6. Protestant Mission in Modern Chosun (1876-1919)
      2.1.6.1. Education, Publishing and Missiology
    2.1.7. Writing and Reflection by Women
      2.1.7.1. Women Doing Theology - Catholic 1; **2.1.7.2.** Women Doing Theology - Protestant 1
3 **Korean Christian Movements to 1945**
  3.1 Transitions for Korea and Korean Christians
  3.2 Korean Christian Movements under Japanese Colonial Occupation: 1910-1945
    3.2.1. Colonial Rule, Independence and Socialism; **3.2.2.** Development of Indigenous Theological Movements under Japanese Colonialism: Contextual Protestant Theology 1
      3.2.2.1. Choi Byung Hyun (1858-1927); **3.2.2.2.** Byron Yun Chi Ho (1864-1894); **3.2.2.3.** Song Chang Keun (1898-1951); **3.2.2.4.** Chung Kyung Ok (1903-1945); **3.2.2.5.** Kim Kyo Shin (fl. 1930-1940.); **32.2.6.** Others

4 **Supplementary Bibliography 1**
   4.1 Catholic Resources
   4.2 Protestant Resources

5 **Korean Theological Movements in the Divided Nation from mid-20th Century 1**
   5.1 Historical Setting
   5.2 Roman Catholic Presence and Thought
      5.2.1. The Pastoral Congress of the Korean Roman Catholic Church; **5.2.2.** Contextual Catholic Theology 1
         5.2.2.1. Chou Jai Yong, Paul (1894-1975); **5.2.2.2.** Bang Yu Ryong Leo, Andrea (1900-1986); **5.2.2.3.** Yun Hyung Joong, Matthew (1903-1979); **5.2.2.4.** Youn, Eulsou (1907-1971); **5.2.2.5.** Choi Min Soon, John (1912-1975); **5.2.2.6.** Sun Jong Wan, Laurence (1915-1976); **5.2.2.7.** Lee Moon Geun, John (1917-1980)
      5.2.3. Contextual Catholic Theology 2
         5.2.3.1. Chi Hak Soon, Daniel (1921-1993); **5.2.3.2.** Choi SukWoo, Andrea (Ch'oe Sok U, 1922-); **5.2.3.3.** Kim Su Hwan, Stephen (1925-); **5.2.3.4.** Lee Won Sun Eusebius (1926-); **5.2.3.5.** Shim Sang Tae (1940-); **5.2.3.6.** Chong Ho Kyong (1940-); **5.2.3.7.** Ri Je Min; **5.2.3.8.** Min Kyong Suk, Anselm (1940-); **5.2.3.9.** Kim Jin So Daegun, Andrea (1940-); **5.2.3.10.** Kim Chi Ha (Kim Hyung, 1941-); **5.2.3.11.** Kim Sung Tae, Joseph (1942-); **5.2.3.12.** Ham Se Ung, Augustine (1942-); **5.2.3.13.** Cho Kwang, Ignatius (1945-); **5.2.3.14.** Pastoral Congress 1984.
   5.3 Contextual Protestant Theology 2
      5.3.1. Inter-faith, Political and Ecumenical Theology; **5.3.2.** Particular Theologians
         5.3.2.1. Kim Jae Joon (1901-1987); **5.3.2.2.** Ham Sok Hon (1901-1989); **5.3.2.3.** Yun Sung Bum (1916-1980); **5.3.2.4.** Kim Chung Choon (d.ca.1987); **5.3.2.5.** Yu Dong Shik (1922-); **5.3.2.6.** Byun Sun Hwan (1927-1996); **5.3.2.7.** Mun Dong Whan, Stephen (c.1930 -)
      5.3.3. Minjung Theology and Minjung Theologians. Contextual Protestant Theology 3

Contextual Theology in Korea

      5.3.3.1. Key First Generation Minjung Theologians
          5.3.3.1.1. Suh Nam Dong (1918-1984); **5.3.3.1.2.** Ahn Byung Mu (1921-1997); **5.3.3.1.3.** Hyun Young Hak (1921-);**5.3.3.1.4.** Suh David Kwang Sun (1931-); **5.3.3.1.5.** Kim Yong-Bock (1938-)
      5.3.3.2. Second Generation Minjung Theologians
          5.3.3.2.1. Kang Won Don; **5.3.3.2.2.** Lee Jung Hee; **5.3.3.2.3.** Park Jae Soon; **5.3.3.2.4.** Park Sung Joon
      5.3.3.3. Third Generation of Minjung Theology - Protestant
          5.3.3.3.1. Choi Hyeong Mook (1961-); **5.3.3.3.2.** Kim Jin Ho (1962-)

6 **Women Doing Theology - Theological Movements from mid-20th Century 2**
  6.1 Women Doing Theology - Protestant 2
      6.1.1. Park Soon Kyung (1923-); **6.1.2.** Lee Oo Chung (1923-); **6.1.3.** Lee Park Sun Ai (d. 1999); **6.1.4.** Choi Man Ja (1943-); **6.1.5.** Chung Hyun Kyung (1956-); **6.1.6.** Park Kyung Mi (1959-); **6.1.7.** Kang Nam Soon; **6.1.8.** Choi Young Sil; **6.1.9.** Other Contextual Women Theologians - Protestant; **6.1.10.** Women's Theological Institutes/Associations - Protestant
          6.1.10.1. Korean Church Women United (KCWU - 1967); **6.1.10.2.** Korean Association of Women Theologians (KAWT - 1980); **6.1.10.3.** Korean Association of Feminist Theology (KAFT - 1985); **6.1.10.4.** Korea Association of Christian Women For Women Minjung (KACWWM - 1986); **6.1.10.5.** Korea Women Church (KWC - 1989); **6.1.10.6.** Ewha Institute for Women's Theological Studies
  6.2 Women Doing Theology - Catholic 2
      6.2.1. Han Soon Hee, rscj (1939-); **6.2.2.** Kim Ok Hee, Anna (ca. 1940-); **6.2.3.** Lee Hae In, Claudia (1945-); **6.2.4.** Kim Sung Hae, sc (ca.1945); **6.2.5.** Choi Hae Young ssc (Choi Hye Yeong, 1955-); **6.2.6.** Kang Young Ok, Lucia; **6.2.7.** Catholic Women's Institutes
          6.2.7.1. *Cham Saram Doe-eo*; **6.2.7.2.** Korean Catholic Women's Community for a New World (KCWC)

7 Other Contextual Theologies of the Late 20th Century

7.1 Contextual Protestant Theology 3

7.1.1. Cheung Ha Eun; **7.1.2.** Chang Chun Ha; **7.1.3.** Han Wan Sang; **7.1.4.** Kang Won Yong; **7.1.5.** Park Pong Bae; **7.1.6.** Mun Ik Kwan; **7.1.7.** Kim Kwan Suk; **7.1.8.** Min Kyung Bae; **7.1.9.** Lee Chang Shik; **7.1.10.** Among many others; **7.1.11.** Keel Hee Seong; **7.1.12.** Noh Jong Sun; **7.1.13.** Oh Jae Shik; **7.1.14.** Expatriate Koreans; **7.1.15.** Other Contributions

7.2 Catholic Contextual Theology 3

7.2.1. Rhee Soun Seong, Peter (1950-); **7.2.2.** Kim Jung Shin (1952-); **7.2.3.** Park Il Young, John (1952-); **7.2.4.** Kim Ung Tai, Joseph (1954-); **7.2.5.** Byun Hee Sun, Anselm (1954-); **7.2.6.** Sim Jong Hyeok (1955-); **7.2.7.** Kim Hyoung Tae, John (1956-); **7.2.8.** Bae Kyung Min, Peter(1957-); **7.2.9.** Hwang Jongryul Leo (1957-); **7.2.10.** Kwak Seung Ryong, Pius (1958-); **7.2.11.** Kim Nyung (1958-); **7.2.12.** Cha Dong Yup Norbert (1958-); **7.2.13.** Kim Min Soo Ignatius (1956-); **7.2.14.** Other Contemporary Catholic theologians

7.2.14.1. Other Priest Theologians; **7.2.14.2.** Other Lay Catholic Theologians

7.3 Selection of Other Contextual Sources

7.3.1. Christian Poets - a Selection; **7.3.2.** Theological Journals - Protestant; **7.3.3.** Theological Journals - Catholic

7.4 Thematic Selections

7.4.1. Theology and Hermeneutic; **7.4.2.** Inter-faith Encounter and Studies; **7.4.3.** Religion and Society

7.5 Institutes, Movements and Associations - Protestant

7.5.1. National Council of Churches in Korea (NCCK); **7.5.2.** Christian Literature Society of Korea (1890); **7.5.3.** Other Institutes and Movements

7.6 Institutes, Movements and Associations - Catholic

7.6.1. Catholic Bishops' Conference of Korea (Hanguk Chinjugyo Chugyodan); **7.6.2.** Woori Theology Institute; **7.6.3.** Korean Christian Thought Institute (1992); **7.6.4.**

Seton Research Center; **7.6.5.** Shinangin Academy (Academy for the Faithful, 1998); **7.6.6.** Catholic Publishing House ("Kyung Hyang Japji Sa", "Catholic Cheong Nyun Sa", 1886-); **7.6.7.** Benedict Press (1909-); **7.6.8.** The Korean Catholic Farmers' Movement (KCFM, 1964); **7.6.9.** Other Catholic Institutes

8 Supplementary Bibliography 2
8.1 Catholic Resources; **8.2** Protestant Resources

1 Introduction (For pre-1800, see chap. 2 above)
Although Roman Catholic Christianity remained proscribed until late in the 19th century, and Protestant Christianity effectively arrived only in the 1880s, a very large and rapidly growing body of writing in Korean theology and church history is available for study. The large proportion of this is yet to be translated from Korean (mostly in *hangul* script) but much has also appeared in western languages. Among the chief guides to this extensive literature are volumes listed below.

1.1 Bibliographies and Guides

Courant, Maurice. *Bibliographie Coréene*. 3 vols. Paris: Libraire de la Société Asiatique de l'Ecole des Langues Orientales Vivantes, 1894-96.

Han Yong Je. *Han'guk Kidokkyo munso undong 100-yon* (100 years of literary movement of Korean Christianity). Seoul: Kidokkyo Munsa, 1987.

—. *Han'guk chonggi kanhaengmul 100-yon* (100 years of Korean Christian periodicals). Seoul: Kidokkyo Munsa, 1987.

Hwang Yang-su. *Han'guk Kidokkyo munhaksajok koch'al. Sangdae* (A study on the formation of Korean Christian literature). Seoul: Kiye Mun'gwan, 1991.

Kim Bong Hee. *Han'guk Kidokkyo munso kanhaengsa yon'gu, 1882-1945*. (Publication and distribution - Christian literature 1882-1945). Seoul T'ukpyolsi: Ihwa Yoja Taehakkyo Ch'ulp'anbu, 1987.

Kim Yong-Bock. *A History of Theological Development in Korea*. Seoul: Mimeo'd, 1981.

—. *Bibliography on the Korean Church* (1985) and *Annotated Bibliography on Minjung Theology* (1989). Mimeo'd.

Lee Chang-Sik. "A Historical Review of Theological Thought for the Last One Century in Korea." *East Asia Journal of Theology* 3.2 (1985).

Min Kyong-bae. *Han'guk Kidokkyo sahoe undongsa: 1885-1945* (A history of social movements in Korean churches). Seoul: Taehan Kidokkyo, 1987.

No Ko-su. *Han'guk Kidokkyo soji yon'gu* (Study of Christian bibliography of Korea). Pusan-si: Yesul Munhwasa, 1981.

Ryu Dong Shik, ed. *Hankuk Eni Kitokkyo Sasang* (Christian thought of Korea. Memorial 200th vol. of "Christian Thought" Magazine). Seoul: Christian Literature Society, 1975.

—. *A History of Korean Theological Thought* (in Korean). Seoul: Jun Mang Sa, 1982.

Sim Sang-t'ae. *Han'guk Kyohoe wa sinhak: chonhwan'gi ui sinang ihae*. (Korean church and theology). Seoul: Song Paoro Chulpansa, 1988.

Song Gil-Seob (Song Kil Sop). *Kankoku Shingaku Shisoshi* (A history of Korean theological thought). Seoul: Korean Christian Publishing, 1987.

Yi Man-yol. *Han'guk Kidokkyo munhwa undongsa* (Cultural history of Christian movement in Korea). Seoul: Taehan Kidokkyo Ch'ulp'ansa, 1987.

2 The Christian Movement in Korea to 1919
2.1 Politics of Chosun Korea and the Christian Movement

See Northeast Asia: 16th to 18th centuries - Korea, vol. 3, chap. 2 above.

2.1.1. Catholic Beginnings

(1784 to 1801 - The Embryo period; 1801-1876 - The Ordeal of the Church)

Informal contacts of Japanese Catholic believers with Koreans and conversions of Koreans in Japan are now known to have begun in the late 16th century, although any connection with later Christian communities is yet to be traced (see de Medina, 1991). In the following period numbers of Korean scholars of the Silhak (*seohak*: "western learning," also 'Catholic faith') movement undertook continuing studies of European sources, including those mediated through Ricci and his colleagues in China. The Catholic movement in Korea is, however, usually said to begin in 1784 when Yi Sung Hun, who with his colleagues was visiting Beijing, was baptised. After Seung Hoon's return from Beijing, he baptised the members of the "western learning" community represented by Pyuk Lee, to form the first Korean Catholic faith community in the spring of 1784. This spread out quickly from its center, Seoul, to other areas, in lay-led churches which, despite persecution, fully maintained Catholic beliefs and rituals, including the Mass.

At first the alienated literati of the Chosun Dynasty in the late 18th century had studied Catholic philosophy as part of their effort to reconstruct Neo-Confucian metaphysics. But as Catholic practices became widespread among both the learned and unlearned, it developed into a strong religious faith clearly countering the Neo-Confucian belief system and social practices. Earlier moderate responses by "Right Teaching" leaders were now replaced with severe repression. When Rome prohibited ancestor worship among Korean Catholics, the Korean Catholics had to face the most violent persecutions of the Confucian government of Chosun Korea, especially in 1801, 1839 and 1866-1871. The first 100 years of Korean Catholic history is a history of bloody persecution and a large body of Catholic writing from this period therefore consists of confessions of faith and the lives of martyrs. However, a number of exceptional scholars, learned in secular disciplines as well as in Catholic teaching, were able to produce works important for both Korean theology and for social and political reconstruction (see 2.1.3.).

Selected References

Choi Suk Woo, Andreas. *A History of Korean Catholic Church* (in Korean). Seoul: Institute of Korean Church History, 1982.

—. *L'Erection du premier Vicariat Apostolique et les Origines de Catholicisme du Coree*. Suisse: n.p., 1961.

Cho Kwang. *A Study in the Catholic Movement in the Later Chosun Period*. Research Seoul: Institute for Korean Church History, 1983.

Dallet, Ch. *Histoire de l'eglise en Corée*. 2 vols. Paris: Victor Palme, 1874. Translated into Korean by Ahn Eung Lyul and Choi Suk Woo. 3 vols. Seoul: Bundo Press, 1979-1980. In English - *A History of Korean Catholic Church*. Hong Kong: M.E.P., 1924.

de Medina, Juan G. Ruiz. *Origenes de la Iglesia Catolica Coreana desde 1566 hasta 1784*. Rome: Institute of History, Society of Jesus, 1986. English translation, Seoul: Royal Asiatic Society, 1991.

Kim Chang Mun and John Jae-sun Chung, eds. *Catholic Korea, Yesterday and Today*. Seoul: Korea Catholic Pub. Co., c1964.

Latourette, K.S. *A History of the Expansion of Christianity*. Vol. 3. London: Eyre and Spottiswood 1945- .

Lee Neung Wha. *History of Korean Christianity and Diplomacy* (in Korean). Vol. I. Seoul: Chosun Kidokkyo Jangmoon Sa, 1928.

Ryu Hong Lyul. *The History of Korean Catholic Church* (in Korean.). 2 vols. Seoul; Catholic Press, 1975.

The Institute of Korean Church History, ed. *A History of Korean Church* (in Korean). Vol. I. Seoul: The Christian Literature Press, 1989.

Yu Chai-shin, ed. *The Founding of Catholic Tradition in Korea*. Studies in Korean Religion and Culture 7. Mississsauga, Ontario: Korean and Related Studies Press, 1996.

2.1.2. Confrontation between Korean Catholic Scholars and the Chosun Government

Among the issues of ideological and cultural conflict between the Catholics and the neo-Confucian scholars, the concept of a personal and creator God was the basic issue. The Christian God is termed in Korean *Chun Ju*, or the Lord of Heaven, who is above human kings and emperors. Failing to recognize the absolute power of the king was condemned as political treason and ideological heresy. Nevertheless, Christian apologetic writings came from many Catholic authors, including Yi Pyok, Kwon Chul Shin, Kwon Il Shin, Chong Yak Jong, Chong Yak Jun, Chong Yak Yong (3 Jung brothers), Yi Ka Hwan and others. (See vol. 3, chap. 2 - Northeast

Asia: 16th to 18th centuries - Korea). The first Korean Catholic apologetics for Christianity was authored by Jung Ha Sang, who wrote on the issue of ancestor worship which the Catholics refused to perform - *Sang Jae Sang Suh* (A letter to the prime minister, 1801). Government critics included Yi Ik, Ahn Jung Bock, Sin Hu Dam and Park Jung Hong. Although Yi Ik recognized *Chun Ju* (the *tianzhu* of Ricci) as *shangdi*, he rejected the doctrines of incarnation, revelation and miracles as absurd, illogical and irrational (see Yi Ik, 1988). Ahn Jung Bock argued that it was blasphemy to say that *Chun Ju* or the Lord of Heaven became incarnate as a human being and died on the cross. Sin Hu Dam is another scholar critical of Catholic teachings, but who affirmed *tianzhu* and *shangdi* as the Lord and creator of heaven and earth. Park Jung Hong also criticizes the Catholic faith in "On Foreign Religion."

The Chosun Government issued its Edict Against the Catholic Movement, *Toh Sa Kyo Moon* (Message from the throne on extermination of the subversive learning), on December 22, 1801, leading to the Shin Yu Persecution. The incident of the *Letter on Silk*, written by Hwang Sah Yung to the Bishop in Beijing, requesting intervention by the Chinese Emperor and western powers on behalf of religious freedom in Korea, only served to intensify the persecution. The *Chuk Sa Yun Eum* (Message of the throne against the evil teaching) was later issued (1839) by King Hun Jong's Queen mother and condemns the Catholic religion as a heterodoxy that rejects Confucian ethics, loyalty to the king and the state, and the virtue of filial piety. Although the persecution of Kee Hae (1839) followed, Catholic faith was preserved in scattered and fugitive communities, subject to constant harassment but maintained by itinerant leaders (see e.g. Sayers, 1987).

Selected References

Choo Myung Joon. "The Catholic Faith Activities of the Jung Yak Yong Brothers." In *Jun Ju Sa Hak* (Historical studies of Jun Ju) (in Korean). Vol I. Seoul: Institute of History of Jun Ju University, 1984.

Choi Suk Woo, Andreas. "The Western Thoughts of Da San" (in Korean). In *Jung Da San and His Time*. Seoul: Min Eum Sa, 1986.

Chong Yak-jong, Augustine. *Chu-Gyo Yo-Ji* (Essence of the Lord's teaching). 2 vols., c.1795. Reprinted in *A Korean Theology. Chu-Gyo Yo-Ji: Essentials of the Lord's Teaching by Chóng Chong Yak-jong Augustine (1760-1801)*, by Hector M.G. Diaz. Immensee: Neue Zeitschrift fur Missionswissenschaft, 1986.

Dallet, Ch. *Histoire de l'eglise en Corée*.

Grayson, James Huntly. *Early Buddhism and Christianity in Korea: A Study of the Implantation of Religion*. Leiden: Brill, 1985.

Hahn Moo-sook. *Encounter: A Novel of Nineteenth-Century Korea*. Berkeley: University of California Press, 1992. (Closely based on historical sources.)

Ki Hae Il Ki (The Journal of 1839). Seoul: MinWa Soo Dang, 1905.

Kum Chang T'ae. "The Doctrinal Disputes between Confucianism and Western Thought in the late Chosun Period." In *The Founding of the Catholic Tradition in Korea*, edited by Yu Chai-shin. Mississauga, Ont.: Korean and Related Studies Press, 1996.

Lee Won Soon. *A Study on the History of Western Learning* (in Korean). Seoul: Il Jee Sa, 1986.

Sayers, Robert, with Ralph Rinzler. *The Korean Onggi Potter*. Washington: Smithsonian Institution, 1987.

Yi Py-ok. *Song Gyo Yo Ji* (Essentials of the holy teaching). Seoul, n.p., c.1784.

Yi Ik. *Songho Sonsaeng Munjip* (Complete works of Sungho Yi Ik). Seoul: Munjip Pyonchan Wiwonhoe, 1988.

2.1.3. Early Catholic Writings

Major Christian writings from the period were shaped both by extensive knowledge of western and Chinese philosophy, religion and science and by Korean theological insights and social concerns which were formed independently of missionary teaching. Christianity is most frequently presented as their own religion for Koreans, and as a faith which would solve this world's suffering and bring national reconstruction.

The writings also include hymn sequences and extensive catechisms or outlines of the faith. See vol. 3, chap. 2, Korea section, for the thought of early scholars: Yi Pyok (1753-1786) who sought to harmonize the ethical ideas of traditional Confucianism with the moral theology of Roman Catholicism (*Essentials of the Holy Teaching*, 1784); Jung Yak Jong Augustine (1760-1801) who produced a systematic presentation of Christian doctrine in Confucian and Korean context (*Essence of the Lord's Teaching*, c.1795); Yi Sung Hun (1756-1801), who in his poetry pictures the quest for true friendship and includes songs of praise to *Tianzhu*.

Those working in the first decades of the 19th century include the following: Chong Yak Yong ("Tasan", 1762-1836) was an expert on Confucianism, and regarded Yi Pyok as his mentor. He was a prolific writer on all aspects of Korean society, an encyclopaedist and advocate of systematic reform in all areas of government, economy, and law. His principal writings were originally printed in 48 volumes (1818) and were later issued in the four volumes of *Mongmin Simso* (A book for the mind of the shepherds of people) (Seoul: Hwangsong, 1902). His 40 volumes of *Kyonse, Yap'yo* (Proposals for government reform) were left unfinished in 1817.

Other Catholics who advocated religious freedom, social equality, improvements in rural and urban life and socio-economic reform include Pak Che Ga (1750-1815), Jung Ha Sang (fl.1820, son of Chong Yak Jong), Kang Wan Suk (d.1801) and Sin Tae Bo (d.1827). (See vol. 3, chap. 2 - Korea). Jung Ha Sang in particular is known for his *Sang chaesang so* (To the heavenly lord, a letter to the prime minister), written in prison. In this he draws similarities between Confucian and Catholic teachings, but also affirms the universal characteristics of truth and the universal appeal of Christianity.

Volumes of letters are extant from a number of those imprisoned, including Kim Chong Han (d.ca.1815), and (Lugarta) Lee Soon Yi (*Okchung Sogan* - Letters from prison. See 2.1.7.1.below). Catholic hymns in *hangul* (Korean characters) date from the time of persecution in early decades of the 19th century, with a large number appearing in the mid-century. These were written both to confess Christian faith and also to defend its place within Korean society. In this they show different emphases from the earlier songs to *Tianzhu*.

Letters, poems and other writings are extant from this period for Kim Dae Kun, Choi Yang Up, Suh Sang Don and Ahn Chung Geun - for these see entries below (2.1.5.).

It should also be noted that the Korean Catholic Church began the translation of the Bible in the late 19th century and although still in process, this is an important influence on the contextualizing of all theology.

Selected References

Cho Kwang. *A Historical Study of Catholicism in the Late Chosun Dynasty* (in Korean). Seoul: Korea University, 1988.

Diaz, Hector M.G. *A Korean Theology. Chu-Gyo Yo-Ji: Essentials of the Lord's Teaching by Chóng Chong Yak-jong Augustine (1760-1801).*

Joe, Wanne J. *Traditional Korea: A Cultural History*. Seoul: Chung'ang University Press, 1972.

Kang Wi-jo. "Early Korean Contact with Christianity and Korean Response: an Historical Introduction." In *Korea's Response to the West*, edited by Jo Yung-hwan. Kalamazoo, MI: Korea Research and Publications, 1971.

Kim, Andreas Jeong-soo. *Katechese und Inkulturation: Dargestellt am Beispiel der Geschichte der Katholischen Kirche im Korea 1603-1983*. Frankfurt: Peter Lang, 1987.

The Letter on Silk (Hwang Sah Yung Baik Suh). In *Study Resources for the Korean Church History*. Seoul: Institute for Korean Church History of the Catholic University of Korea, 1966.

Setton, Mark. *Chong Yagyong: Korea's Challenge to Orthodox Neo-Confucianism*. Albany, NY: State University of New York, 1997.

Takashi Konoi. "The History of the Relationship between Japanese and Korean Christianity in the 16th/17th Centuries". *Samok* 252 (1999).

Yi Won-sun. "The Consciousness of Western Learning Among Scholars of the Practical Learning in the Latter Part of the Chosun Period." *Yoksa kyoyuk* 17 and 18 (1973).

Yu Chai-shin, ed. *The Founding of the Catholic Tradition in Korea*. Mississauga, Ont.: Korean and Related Studies Press, 1996.

2.1.4. Roman Catholic Presence and Thought 19th-early 20th centuries

Between the persecutions of 1815 and 1839, the first Korean bishopric was established in 1831, making the Korean church independent of Beijing. Bishops in the following decades included B. Bruguire, Laurent Imbert, Jean Ferreol, Simeon Berneux and Marie-Nicholas Daveluy. Their Korean assistants in translation and writing included Hyon Sok Mun, Hwang Sok Tu and Choe Chi Hyok. But these and their bishops along with many priests, both Korean and French, catechists, both women and men, and others (to more than 16,000), were martyred in the severe persecutions of 1839, 1846 and 1866. The first Korean priests, Kim Tae Kun and Choi Yang Up (for these see 2.1.5.1 and 2.1.5.2.), and others were also killed at this time. Until 1886, Catholic communities were proscribed, harried and subject to random attack, imprisonment and killing on a major scale. Extensive records and testimonies are extant (see e.g. *Fathers of the London Oratory*, 1859, and Ryu, 1962). The experience of such suffering inevitably brought changes in Catholic understanding of the faith, which became now "more emotional and increasingly eschatological in content" (Min, 1985). This was to weaken the earlier intentions for social reform, seen in the life and theology of the Chong brothers and their colleagues (see 2.1.3). Writings from this period are largely apologetic and for these, for Catholic hymns and other manuals, a wood-block printing house had been set up in 1859. Gospel anthologies like *Songgyong Chikhae* would later follow.

The granting of religious freedom in 1886 ended the protracted ordeal of Korean Catholics and allowed the establishment of churches in main cities along with orphanages and homes for those needing special care. (An early orphanage, *L'oevre de la Sainte-Enfance*, had been formed in 1864). Under bishops such as J. Blanc and G. Mutel churches grew rapidly and from the 1890s on, Catholics became widely accepted for their participation in the "national enlightenment movement" and for their opposition to Japanese colonization. The *hangul* weekly *Kyonghyang Sinmun* was inaugurated by Catholics in 1906 to call for internal national reforms and self-reliance. Catholic laymen such as Suh Sang Don,

Ahn Chung Geun, (for these see 2.1.5.3. and 2.1.5.4.), An Myong Gun and Yi Ki Dang were among the leaders of anti-Japanese and pro-independence movements and following 1919 (the *Samil* movement - see 3.2.1.), some were members of the Korean government in exile.

Throughout this period, and despite the turbulence and distress suffered by Catholic communities, contextual theological understanding was nonetheless growing and its interpretation in life and in fragmentary documents clearly contributed to the formation of a more humane Korean society. The historian Cho Kwong outlines such contributions to include the propagation and practice of social equality, respect for rights of women and care for children, the accelerated formation of *hangul* culture and the offering of alternative models for political systems, civil law and individual conscience. Since the work of Yi To Gi, there had also been the understanding by some leading Catholics that as Christianity was a "universal truth" Korea's "closed culture" could not permanently refuse to welcome it. For Buddhism, Taoism and Confucianism were also "foreign" they declared, but still part of Korea's cultural and religious life, which, after all, was not equivalent to Chinese culture. The "foreign" could both contribute richly and still grow in indigenous forms (Cho, 1996).

Selected References

A Collection of Dissertations on the History of the Korean Churches in Commemoration of the Sixtieth birthday of Father Ch'oe Sok-u. Seoul: Research Institute for Korean Church History, 1982.

Cho Kwang. *Choson hugi Ch'onjugyosa yon'gu.* (Etude sur histoire du catholicisme a la periode posterieure de Chosun). Minjok munhwa yon'gu ch'ongso 21. Seoul: Koryo Taehakkyo Minjok Munhwa Yon'guso, 1988. (Reprint, Seoul: Korea University 1990).

——. "The Meaning of Catholicism in Korean History." In *The Founding of the Catholic Tradition in Korea*, edited by Yu Chai-shin (1996).

Choi Suk Woo. *A Quest for Korean Catholic History.* Seoul: Research Institute for Korean Church History, 1982.

Fathers of the London Oratory. *The New Glories of the Catholic Church*. London: Richardson & Son, 1859.
Kim Chin So. "A Study of the Texts of Catholic Hymns." *Studies of the History of Churches* 3 (1981).
Launay, Adrien. *Les Missionaires Francais en Corée*. Paris: 1895.
Min Kyung Bae. *A History of the Korean Churches*. Seoul: Christian Literature Society, 1974.
——. "A History of Christianity in Korea." In *Asia and Christianity*, edited by M.D. David. Bombay: Himalaya Publishing, 1985.
Ryu Hong Yul. *Hankuk Chunjo Kyo Hoi Sa*. (History of Roman Catholic Churches in Korea). Seoul: Catholic Press, 1962.
Yi Man Yol. "The Birth of the National Spirit of Christians in the Late Chosun Period." In *Korea and Christianity*, edited by Yu Chai Shin.
Yi Sung Nyong. "On Studies of the Korean Language by Catholic Fathers." *Asian Studies* 8.2 (1965).
Yu Chai-shin, ed. *The Founding of the Catholic Tradition in Korea*. 1996.

2.1.5. Forerunners in Catholic Contextual Theology

2.1.5.1. Kim Dae Kun, Andrea (1821-1846) was sent to Macao in 1836 as one of the first four seminarians. Following ordination as deacon in 1844, and a period of ministry in Korea, Kim was ordained in Shanghai by Bishop Jean Ferreol (1845) as the first Korean Catholic priest. While ministering in Korea, he also searched for a safe route by which foreign missioners could enter and leave the country and this led to his arrest in 1846, along with several believers. Though he was tortured severely many times, he kept his faith and died for it, being later canonized in Seoul by Pope John Paul II (1984).

Kim Dae Kun left 21 letters and one report on the young Korean Catholic Church written in Seoul (1845). He also made a map of Korea (1845) and a map of the world (1846). His deep desire was that freedom of religion be accepted for the health of the nation's life, but death was the price of his new vision of the world.

2.1.5.2. Choi Yang Up, Thomas (1821-1861) was also sent to Macao in 1836 with three others as the first Korean seminarians. He was ordained in Shanghai (1849) by Bishop Maresca and entered Chosun at the end of the same year. He ministered throughout Korea, as the second Korean priest, for 12 years during severe persecutions. Weakened by overwork Choi suddenly died of typhoid fever in 1861.

Choi's writings included letters, poems and translations. His Latin translations of the works of martyrs of 1839 and 1846 (1847) were utilised as the basic material for Pius IX's declaration of *82 Korean Venerables* (1857). He wrote 19 letters and many songs of Cheon-ju (God) in a Korean literary form, *Gasa*, composed of rhythmical words (*Cheon-ju Gasa*). He also translated into Korean and revised several Chinese-written catechetical works such as "Prayers of the Holy Church" and "Essential Teachings of the Holy Church."

2.1.5.3. Suh Sang Don, Augustine (1850-1913) was born in Seoul 1850, a descendant of one of Korea's first Catholic martyr families. He suggested a movement for redemption of the national debt borrowed from abroad, especially from Japan (1907) and it was eagerly responded to by many groups throughout the nation. This protest movement against Japan's politico-economic domination, however, was suppressed by the Japanese imperial forces in 1910. Although it failed, the movement inspired nationalist concern in many Koreans and the collected money was spent for universities established by civilians. Suh has been remembered for his "Prospectus of the Movement for Redemption of the National Debt" and as a pioneer of the resistance movement against Japanese imperial domination.

2.1.5.4. Ahn Chung Geun, Thomas (Ahn Joong Keun, 1879-1910) entered the Roman Catholic Church in 1897 and was a General of the Korean Righteous Army in conflict against the Japanese armies (1908). After three defeats he worked for other effective means to obtain independence for Korea. In that process, on October 26th, 1909, Ahn shot Hirobumi Ito, who was one of the most influential contemporary politicians of Japan, at Harbin, Manchuria. Ahn was executed by the Japanese on March 26, 1910.

Having been remembered since as the 'sun of Korea', however, Ahn has enabled many to participate in showing the justice of God for his beloved Korean and Eastern Asian minjung. He wrote his biography in the Port Arthur prison (December 1909 to March 1910) and "A Vision of Asian Peace" (uncompleted, March 1910).

Selected References

> *A Collection of the Letters of Fr. Kim Dae Kun Andrea.* Translated by Cheong Jin Suk and Choi Seok Woo. Seoul: Research Institute for Korean Church History, 1996.
> *A Collection of the Letters of Fr. Choi Yang Up.* Translated by Cheong Jin Suk. Seoul: Pauline Press, 1995.

Ahn Joong Keun. *Autobiography of Ahn Joong Keun* (in Korean). Seoul: Friends of Ahn Joong Keun, 1979.
Cho Kyu-Sik. "The Spirituality of Yang Eob Chio (Choi Yang Up, 1821-1861)." *Samok* 164 (1992).
Choi Suk Woo. *A History of Korean Catholic Church* (in Korean). Seoul: Institute for Korean Church History, 1982.
—. *A Quest for Korean Catholic History.* Seoul: IKCH, 1982.
Institute for Korean Church History, ed. *A History of the Korean Church* (in Korean). Vol. I. Seoul: IKCH, 1989.
Posthumous Works of Ahn Chung-geun, edited by Y.H. Shin. Seoul: Yokminsa, 1995.
Ryu Hong Yul. *Hankuk Chunjo Kyo Hoi Sa* (History of Roman Catholic Churches in Korea). 1962.
Suh Sang Don. "Prospectus of the Movement for Redemption of the National Debt." *Daehan Maeil Sinbo* (Daehan Daily Mail). (Feb. 22, 1907).

2.1.6. Protestant Mission in Modern Chosun (1876-1919)

Although Protestant presence in Chosun Korea is usually dated from 1884, when American missionaries entered Seoul through Inchon Harbor, there is evidence for earlier missionary activity in the period 1876 to 1884 (from the Korea-Japan Amity Treaty of 1876 to the Korea-US Amity Treaty of 1882). This roughly corresponds to the period of Chosun opening to the western world. Some initial contacts were made by the Protestant Karl Friedrich Gutzlaff from China in 1832 and are recorded in his journal. Alexander Williamson was based in China but arranged for other missionaries to travel to Korea. Attempts were made by Robert

Jermain Thomas to enter Korea (1866); Arthur W. Douthwaite worked there as a medical missionary for a period; and John Ross and John MacIntyre went to Manchuria to begin translating the Bible into Korean *hangul*.

With the help of Korean translators such as Paik Hong Joon and Lee Eung Chan, Ross published a Korean language text-book for the missionaries, *Corean Primer* (1877), and in the next 10 years completed the first Korean New Testament. In order to disseminate the Korean version of the Bible to the Korean people in Manchuria and also in Korea, colporteurs were trained. Their contribution in the early 1880s and later years should be noted and commended.

Meanwhile Lee Soo Jung, who was a consular envoy to Japan in 1882, became Christian while there and began translating the Bible into Korean. While he was enlisting new believers to study Christian doctrine he urged American missionaries to come to Korea. A year after the Presbyterian medical doctor Horace N. Allen was appointed physician to the foreign legation (1884), Methodist and Presbyterian missionaries arrived in Inchon Harbor. From the USA were William B. Scranton, Mary F. Scranton (his mother) and Henry G. Appenzeller, along with John W. Heron and Horace G. Underwood from Japan. Missionaries of other denominations soon followed: J.S. Gale from the YMCA of Toronto University (1888); the Australians J.H. Davies and his sister May Davies (1889); C.J. Corfe (later bishop) and E.B. Landis of the Church of England (1890); L.B. Tate, his sister M. Tate and others from the southern Presbyterian Church in the US (1892); C.F. Reid of the Methodist Episcopal Church (1896); R. Grierson, D.M. McRae and W.R. Foote of the Presbyterian Church in Canada (1898); and M.C. Fenwick, R.A. Hardie, W.J. McKenzie and O.R. Avison, also from Canada. The Salvation Army began its mission in 1908, and the Oriental Missionary Society from Japan in 1901 for which two Korean graduates later began mission work in 1907. Seventh Day Adventist work was begun by W.S. Smith (1905); and brief missions were begun by the Russian Orthodox Church (1898) and American Baptists.

Selected References
First Contacts:

> Knox, G.W. "A Macedonian from Corea." *FM* (June 1883).
> —. "Japan and Korea." *FM* (September 1884).
> Loomis, H. "The First Korean Protestant in Japan." *KMF* (July, 1883).
> Orr, J. "The Gospel in Corea." *UPMR* (June 2, 1890).
> Paik, George. *The History of Protestant Mission in Korea, 1832-1910.* Seoul: Yonsei University Press, 1971 (1927).
> Rhodes, H.A. "The First Protestant Missionary to Korea." *KMF* 27.11 (1931).
> Ross, J. "The Christian Dawn in Corea." *MRW* (April, 1890).
> —. "The Gospel for Corea." *Quarterly Record of the National Bible Society of Scotland, (NBSS).* (October, 1882).
> —. "A Bright Light in Northern Korea." *FM* (September, 1886).

American Missions:

> The American Bible Society (ABS) *Report for 1886*: 144.
> *The Annual Report of the Missionary Society of the Methodist Episcopal Church* (ARMS), 1884.
> Hunt, Everett. N. *Protestant Pioneers in Korea.* Maryknoll, NY: Orbis Books, 1980.
> Maclay, Robert S. "Korea's Permit to Christianity." *MRW* 9 (1896).
> Rhodes, Harry A. *History of the Korean Missions, Presbyterian Church USA: 1884-1934.* Vol. I. Seoul: Chosun Presbyterian Church USA, 1934.
> Underwood, Horace G. *Call of Korea: Political - Social - Religious.* New York: Fleming H. Revell, 1908.
> Underwood, Lilias Horton. *Fifteen Years among the Topknots, or Life in Korea.* New York: The American Tract Society, 1904.

Other Protestant Missions:

> Brown, G.T. *Mission to Korea.* (Richmond?): Board of World Missions, Presbyterian Church USA, 1962.
> Fenwick, M.C. *The Church of Christ in Corea.* New York: George H. Doran, 1911.
> "General Work of the Salvation Army in Chosun." *KMF* 35.2 (1939).
> Kerr, E. and G. Anderson. *The Australian Presbyterian Mission in Korea 1889-1941.* Australian Presbyterian Board of Missions, 1970.

Minutes of the Annual Meetings of the Korean Mission of the Methodist Episcopal Church, South, 1897: 3-6.

Rutt, R. *A Biography of James Scarth Gale and a New Edition of his History of the Korean People.* Seoul: Royal Asiatic Society Korea Branch, 1983.

Trollope, M.N. *The Church of Corea.* London: Mowbray, 1915.

2.1.6.1. Education, Publishing and Missiology

Protestant missionary activities from the beginning included medical care, for women as well as men, along with education, media and communication. The new mission schools such as *Bae Jae Hak Dang* (1886), the Underwood Orphanage and *Ewha Hak Dang* (1886) would later develop into Bae Jae University, Yonsei University and Ewha Womans University respectively. In the field of media and communication, the translation of the New Testament was completed in 1900 and the Old Testament in 1910. Hymn books in the Korean language were published by the denominations with a common hymnal published for the use of both Methodists and Presbyterians in 1908.

In Christian literature, the Korean Tract Society was formed in 1888 and published periodicals and tracts in *hangul*. In 1897 Appenzeller began publishing *The Christian Advocate* and Underwood began printing *The Christian News,* two newsletters which were merged in *The Church Herald*, 1907-1910. In 1892 H. Holbert published *The Korean Repository,* and in 1905 *The Korea Review.* In 1900, *The Transaction of the Korea Branch of the Royal Asiatic Society* was published and in 1905 *The Korean Mission Field.* A printing press was imported for Bae Jae School in 1889 and as the "Trilingual Press" printed materials in English, Chinese and Korean. The new printing house was therefore named "Trilingual Press," later becoming the Korea Methodist Publishing House (1899). In 1890 the Korean Religious Tract society was established, later to become the Korea Christian Literature Society (KCLS).

The theology informing much of this publishing reflected more narrowly conservative understandings of belief, mission and church. But some missionaries and their Korean colleagues were committed to broader views of education and social responsibility and were sensitive to people's traditions and aspirations (see 3.1). At the same time strong motivation for Christian mission led many to seek new missiological insights for ministry within Korea's social and religious context. In 1890, John L. Nevius had presented his "three-self" principles for the development of Korean Christian mission, advocating self-propagation, self-government and self-support in order to make the Korean churches independent, self-reliant and aggressive native churches. Adopted as official mission policy by the United Council of Presbyterian Missions (1893), these provisions declared that preference in evangelism was to be given to the laboring class rather than the upper class, and that therefore "All Christian literature should be published in Korean and not in Chinese." This policy was implemented and made a significant impact on the future development of the indigenous Korean churches and their theologies.

Selected References

Annual Reports of the Board of Foreign Mission of the Presbyterian Church in the USA (ARPC); and of the *Missionary Society of the Methodist Episcopal Church.*

The Christian Advocate of the Methodist Episcopal Church and *The Gospel in All Lands* of its mission board. See also *The Korean Mission Field.*

Clark, Allen D. *History of the Korean Church.* Seoul: Korean Christian Literature Society, 1961 (1930).

Clark, Charles Allen. *The Korean Church and the Nevius Methods.* New York: Fleming H. Revell, 1930: 118-119.

Paik, George. *The History of Protestant Mission in Korea, 1832-1910.* Seoul: Yonsei University Press, 1971. Originally published Pyong Yang: Union Christian College, 1927.

Reynolds, W.D. "Fifty Years of Bible Translation and Revision." *KMF* 31.6 (1935).

Scranton, W.B. "Historical Sketch of Korea Mission of the Methodist Episcopal Church." *(KRP)* (July 1898).

Underwood, Horace G. *Call of Korea: Political - Social - Religious.*

Vinton, C.C. "Presbyterian Mission Work in Korea." *MRW* 9.6 (1893).

Williams, F.E.C. and Bonwick, G., eds. *The Korea Missions Year Book.* Seoul: The Christian Literature Society of Korea, 1928.

2.1.7. Writing and Reflection by Women

There is increasing research and writing being devoted to both the traditional situation and roles of Korean women and to the movements by which these have been, and are being, changed. It is in the context of these studies that our present knowledge of writing by Christian women must be placed (see 2.1.7.1, 2.1.7.2.).

Selected References

Cho Hae-joang. "Korean Women and Their Experiences in the Traditional World." In *Korean Women and Culture,* edited by The Research Institute of Asian Women. Seoul: The Research Institute of Asian Women, 1998.

Choi Hyae-weol. "Women's Literacy and New Womanhood in Late Choson Korea." *Asian Journal of Women's Studies* 6.1 (2000).

Choi Sook-kyung. "Formation of Women's Movement in Korea: From the Enlightenment Period to 1910." In *Challenges for Women: Women's Studies in Korea,* edited by Sei-Wha Chung. Seoul: Ewha Womans University Press, 1986.

Kim Yung-Chung. "Women's Movement in Modern Korea." In *Challenges for Women: Women's Studies in Korea*, edited by Sei-Wha Chung. Seoul: Ewha Womans University Press, 1986.

Koh Hesung Chun. "Women's Contributions to Korean Culture." *Korean Culture* 8.3 (Fall 1987).

Lee In-ho. "Women's Liberation in Korea." *Korea Journal* 17.7 (July 1977).

Lee Kyu Hwan. "Early Status of Women's Education in Korea." *Koreana Quarterly* 5.3 (Autumn 1963).

Nahm, Andrew Changwoo. "Korean Women's Modernization Movement, 1896-1945." In *Proceedings of the Tenth International Symposium on Asian Studies, volume 2.* Hong Kong: Asian Research Service, 1989.

Oh, Bonnie B. "From Three Obediences to Patriotism and Nationalism: Women's Status in Korea to 1945." *Korea Journal* 22.7 (1982).

"The New Cultural Movement for Korean Women: Women's Studies in the Early 1920s." In *Korean Women and Culture,* edited by The Research Institute of Asian Women. Seoul: The Research Institute of Asian Women, 1998.

2.1.7.1. Women Doing Theology - Catholic 1

From the early 1800s, we have records and writings from Catholic women in various roles despite the pervasive conditions of severe persecution and hardship. Some like Kang Wan Suk, Kim Yon I and Chong Pok Hye were vigorously active in relief and social work and catechetics. Others like Mme Kwon, Mme Yu (Cecilia), Theresa Kwon and Chong Chong Hye (Elizabeth) were noted for their courageous care of families under persecution and final martyrdom, as well as for their work in literacy, circulating letters and distributing materials. Some such as Kang Wan Suk (a charismatic leader), Kim Hui In, Han Shin Ae and Kang Kyong Bok established communities of women who were unmarried or widows. These included all social classes from nobility to serfs and undertook routines of prayer, study and service. From interrogation records it is clear that many of these women possessed and studied Catholic literature: Han Shin Ae, for example, possessed 38 titles and Kim Hui In, 18. Missionary and evangelistic work by Catholic women, even when in exile or in prison, is also well recorded in the first half of the century. Those such as Kang Wan Suk (Columba) worked within a Confucian society alongside men in organized missionary activity, upheld the persecuted, refused to take part in patriarchal family life, and rejected the ideology regarding male heir succession.

Most notable are the writing activities of women such as Yuhandong Kwon, Yi Lugarta and their associates. From the first came *Onhaeng Shillok* (Written records of words and acts) written as an educational manual for women and including both Silhak material (see 2.1.1.) and also sections of Matteo Ricci's *Tianzhu shiyi* (The true meaning of the Lord of Heaven). Such writings as these, along with the many translations by Catholic women, were part of the basis for Ching Yak Chong's *Chugyo Yoji* (Summary of Catholic Teachings) (see vol. 2, chap. 2 above - Korea). Lee Soon Yi (Lugarta)'s most important writing is her *Okchung Sogan* (Letters from prison) which shows, in her reflections, her dedication to traditions of Catholic asceticism and filial piety and her consolation for the persecuted in the Korean context of Confucian morality. Many other prison diaries and letters are extant for Catholic women in this period. It is to be noted that the practice of virtuous acts by such women as these was both their response to hardship and intense suffering and also a way to realize the teachings of Catholic faith.

Due to the changed socio-political circumstances of mid-century, including episcopal encouragement for widows to remarry, the activities of women's communities changed, but many like Hyon Kyong Nyon continued their ministries as teachers, catechists, pastors and nurses. Although finally martyred, the sisters St. Hyeo Im (Columba) Kim and St. Hyeo Joo (Agnes) Kim, courageously protested at police practices so that from that time women prisoners were no longer normally subject to sexual violence. Later in the century many would be noted for their leadership in patriotic and pro-independence movements. Notable here was the Catholic patriot Cho Maria, the mother of Ahn Joong Keun (see 2.1.5.4.; 3.1.).

Selected References

Cho Hae-joang. "Korean Women and Their Experiences in the Traditional World." In *Korean Women and Culture,* edited by The Research Institute of Asian Women. Seoul: The Research Institute of Asian Women, 1998.

Cho Kwang. "The Meaning of Catholicism in Korean History." In *The Founding of the Catholic Tradition in Korea,* edited by Yu Chai-shin.

Choi Hyaeweol. "Women's Literacy and New Womanhood in Late Choson Korea." *Asian Journal of Women's Studies* 6.1 (2000).

Choi Sook-kyung. "Formation of Women's Movement in Korea: From the Enlightenment Period to 1910." In *Challenges for Women: Women's Studies in Korea,* edited by Sei-Wha Chung.

Chong Sok-ki. *Han'guk Kidokkyo yosong inmulsa* (Introduction to a history of Korean women). Seoul: K'umnan Ch'ulp'ansa, 1995.

Kang Young Ok. "Women's Movement in Korean Catholic Church." *Review of Catholic Church History in Korea* (Institute of Korean Church History) 4 (2000).

Kim Ok Hy. *Hanguk Ch'onju-gyo Yosong-sa* (Women in the Korean Catholic Church). Seoul: n.p. 1991.

—. "Study on *'Onhaeng Shillok'* of Mme Yuhandong Kwon." *Hanguk Hakpo* 27 (1982).

—. "Women in the History of Catholicism in Korea." *Korea Journal* 24.8 (1984).

Kim Sung Hae. *A Religious-Theological Interpretation of Women in East-Asian Tradition.* Mimeo'd. for *Amor VII* (Asian Meeting of Religious, October 12, 1985).

Li Wan Yung. "The Role of Religious Women in Korea." *Samok* 95 (1984).

O Kyong Hwan. "Status of Women in the Korean Church." *Kyonghyang Japji* 12 (1985).

Oh, Bonnie B. "From Three Obediences to Patriotism and Nationalism: Women's Status in Korea to 1945."

Samok Special Issue "Identity and Role of Women in the Catholic Church." 217 (1997).

2.1.7.2. Women Doing Theology - Protestant 1

Later in the century, Protestant women also played a crucial role in the life and mission of the Korean churches, but have seldom had access to publication for their writings and theological reflections. Expatriate women had been in the forefront of mission work since the 1880s, especially as qualified teachers and physicians. Educators such as Alice Rebecca Appenzeller (1885-1950, president of Ewha University) were also noted for their liberal theologies, which were devoted to local church development, and which were followed by such eminent nationals as Helen Kim (1899-1970, also president of Ewha University). (For letters by Appenzeller see Fisher, 1977, and papers by Kim are cited by Weber, 1966.) From groups of patriotic women, including students, protesting against Japanese oppression, we have stories and confessions such as those for Kim Maria (1894-1944) and Yoo Kwansoon (1904-1920), along with others like Cho Maria.

By the 1890s groups of women were being trained at colleges such as Ewha and the Neel and Clark Bible Institutes and were exercising many ministries as Bible Women, although writing very little themselves and never being accorded full recognition by most male church leaders. During the period of Japanese occupation the use of *hangul*, in which such women were educated, was proscribed so that few writings of any sort by women appeared. However as male leaders were largely imprisoned in those years, the leadership of women was all-important. Women such as Mrs Yi, the close associate of Mattie Tate, came to exercise effective ministries as evangelists, educators, preachers and pastors. These roles were maintained and continued to develop throughout the turmoil of the early 20th century, although the less formal training women often received, and sometimes their affinities with traditional ("shamanist") culture, still distinguished their teaching from that of many male colleagues who are influenced by more neo-Confucian roles in learning and vocation (see Chou, 1995).

Although initially only a section of the Japan YWCA, the YWCA in Korea "was a natural part of the independence movement" and was founded as an independent movement by Helen Kiteuk Kim and Mrs Pilley Kim Choi in 1922. Associated with them were others such as Yu Kak Kyung, and Lee Hyo Duck. Two years later 15 branches were active. Among other women who were prominent in YWCA leadership, ecumenical animation and education in these decades, a key figure was Esther Park, YWCA national general secretary 1947-1968 (see Kim Oh, n.d.). The return of men to leadership roles, especially after 1945, meant that women were again marginalized. The ongoing struggles for survival and education placed most heavy demands on women during years of civil war and intense industrialization. From such movements as the YWCA, however, along with those from colleges and universities like Ewha and Hanil, came a number of educated Christian women contributing faith and life to Korea's church and society despite colonial oppression, economic struggle and civil war. Their lives and reflections are yet to be fully studied, although some volumes are now appearing. Among these is the study of Lee Tai Young of Pyongyang and Ewha University (Strawn, 1988) who is recognized internationally for her work in legal aid, women's rights and family law.

Selected References

Chou Fang-lan. "Bible Women and the Development of Education in the Korean Church." In *Perspectives in Christianity in Korea and Japan*, edited by Mark R.

Mullins and Richard Fox Young. Lewiston, NY: Edwin Mellen Press, 1995.

Chun Chae-ok. "Korean Protestant Women in Mission." In *Korean Church Growth Explosion*, edited by Bong Rin Ro and Marlin L. Nelson. Seoul: Word of Life Press; Taichung: Asia Theological Association, 1983.

Fisher, J. Earnest. *Pioneers of Modern Korea*. Seoul: Christian Literature Society of Korea, 1977.

Harvey, Youngsook Kim. *Six Korean Women: the Socialization of Shamans*. St Paul, MN: West Publishing, 1979. (Includes a Christian convert, Deaconess Chang).

Kim, Helen (Kiteuk). *Rural Education for the Regeneration of Korea*. Thesis, New York, 1931.

—. *Grace Sufficient: The Story of Helen Kim by Herself*, edited by J. Manning Potts. Nashville, Tenn.: Upper Room, 1964.

—. "The Asian Churches and their Mission." In *Christ Seeks Asia*, edited by Ro Bong Rin. Hong Kong: Asia Theological Association, 1969.

Kim Oh Hyun-ja. *Life Abundant: Life of Miss Esther Park*. Seoul: Korea YWCA, n.d.

Kim Yong-Bock. "Women's Movement in Modern Korea." In *Challenges for Women: Women's Studies in Korea*, edited by Chung Sei Wha.

Lee Hyo-Chae. "Protestant Missionary Work and Enlightenment of Korean Women." *Korea Journal* 17.11 (1977).

Lee Kwang-Soon. "Korean Women's Understanding of Mission: The Role of Women in the Korean Presbyterian Church." PhD dissertation, School of World Mission, Fuller Theological Seminary, 1985.

Lee Kyu Hwan. "Early Status of Women's Education in Korea." *Koreana Quarterly* 5:3 (1963).

Strawn, Sonia Reid. *Where There is No Path: Lee Tai-Young; Her Story*. Seoul: Korean Legal Aid Center for Family Relations, 1988.

Weber, Hans-Ruedi. *Asia and The Ecumenical Movement 1895-1961*. London: SCM Press, 1966.

Yi Tok-chu. *Han'guk kyohoe ch'oum yosongdul: ch'ogi Han'guk kidokkyo yosong 28-in ui iyagi* (First women of the Korean Church: stories of 28 women in the early Korean church). Seoul: Kidok Kyomunsa, 1990.

3 Korean Christian Movements to 1945
3.1 Transitions for Korea and Korean Christians

In the late 19th century Chosun Korea was in a time of critical transition. Following Japan in 1876, the western powers also forced Korean doors to open to trade and exchange: the USA and Germany arrived in 1882; Great Britain, Russia and Italy in 1884; and France in 1886. The ruling élites were divided into the conservatives who wished to maintain the "closed door" policies of the "hermit nation," and the liberals who advocated open door policies. These led in the Kapshin coup d'état (1884), and in 1892 restless farmers in the southwestern provinces rose up against the corrupt and oppressive Chosun court. The conflict which followed between Chinese and Japanese armies on the Korean peninsula (the Sino-Japanese War) ended with the devastating defeat of China (1894). At the same time the independence movement was growing steadily, with the establishment of the Independence Club and the publication of a Korean daily newspaper, *The Independence (Dok Lip Shin Moon)*. However the Chosun Government acted to disband these (1898), arresting and imprisoning leading members on charges of treason. Among them were many Christian leaders who would later become nationally prominent following their prison years from 1898 to 1904.

In 1903, the Seoul YMCA (see Kang, 1990; David, 1998) was established and its leaders would play a significant role in both independence and socialist movements. In April 1907, *Shin Min Hoe* (The New People's Party) was organized as an independence movement to oppose Japanese aggression in Korea. Although this was a secular political party, Christian leaders were actively involved. Japanese response to the formation of the new Christian youth organization and of the independent political party was to arrest the leaders on charges of conspiracy for the assassination of Governor General Terauchi in 1910. This incident was called "the 105 men Incident," because of the number of Christian leaders who were imprisoned as a result. Korean Christian independence movement leaders, including both Protestants and Catholics, maintained their nationalist solidarity despite the opposition of some western missionaries. There were also a number of Catholic laymen's resistance movements which opposed Japanese colonization in Korea and sought to protect suffering Korean people from their depredations. Some Catholics like Ahn Joong Keun Thomas were directly involved in the assassination of the first Japanese Governor General Ito Hirobumi. While in prison in China awaiting his execution, Ahn recorded his life in an autobiography (see Ahn, 1979).

Selected References

Ahn Joong Keun. *Autobiography of Ahn Joong Keun* (in Korean). (1979).

Brockman, F. "Mr. Yi Sang Chai." *KMF* 7.8 (1911).

Brown, A.J., ed. *Conspiracy Case, Japanese Colonial Government: Selected Correspondence, Reports and Miscellaneous Papers.* PCUSA Board of Foreign Missions, Korea, 1912.

Choi Myung-Keun. *Changes in Korean Society between 1884-1910 as a Result of the Introduction of Christianity.* New York: Peter Lang, 1997.

Clark, Donald N. *Christianity in Modern Korea.* Lanham, MD: University Press of America, 1986.

David, M.D. *A Symbol of Asian Solidarity: A History of the Asia Alliance of YMCAs.* Hong Kong: Asia Alliance of YMCAs, 1998.

Gale, J.S. *Korea in Transition.* New York: Young People's Mission Movement, 1909.

Han Woo-keun. *The History of Korea,* translated by Kyungshik Lee, edited by Grafton K. Mintz. Seoul: Eulyu Publishing, 1970.

Harrington, Fred Harvey. *God, Mammon, and the Japanese: Dr. Horace N. Allen and Korean-American Relations, 1884-1905.* Madison, WI: University of Wisconsin Press, 1966.

History of Independence Movement. Resource Material 6. Seoul: Committee for National History Publication, 1983.

Kang Moon Kyu. *The Korean YMCA Movement.* Seoul: National Council of Korea YMCAs, 1990.

Kang Wi Jo. *Christ and Caesar in Modern Korea: A History of Christianity and Politics.* Albany, NY: State University of New York Press, 1997.

Kim In Soo. *Protestants and the Formation of Modern Korean Nationalism, 1885-1920: A Study of the Contributions of*

Horace G. Underwood and Sun Chu Kil. Asian Thought and Culture 16. New York: Peter Lang, 1996.

Kim Young-chung, ed. and trans. *Women of Korea: A History from Ancient Times to 1945.* Seoul: Ewha Womans University Press, 1976.

Korean Information Papers, Foreign Mission Board of Presbyterian Church. New York.

Lee Ki-baik. *A New History of Korea.* Cambridge, MA: Harvard University Press, 1984: chaps. 13 and 14.

Lee Kwang Lin. "Christian Faith in Prison of the Old Chosun." In *Issues in the Korean Enlightenment History*, 218-222. (In Korean). Seoul: Il Jo Kak, 1986.

Lee (Yi), Man Yul. *Lectures on Korean Church History* (in Korean). Seoul: Taehan Kidokkyo Ch'ulp'ansa, 1987.

Lee Neung Wha. *History of Korean Christianity and Diplomacy* (in Korean). Vol. I. Seoul: Chosun Kidokkyo Jangmoon Sa, 1928.

Palmer, Spencer J. *Korea and Christianity: The Problem of Identification with Tradition.* Seoul: Hollym Corp. Publications, 1967.

Wells, Kenneth M. *New God, New Nation: Protestants and Self-Reconstruction Nationalism in Korea 1896-1937.* Honolulu: University of Hawaii Press, 1991.

3.2 Korean Christian Movements under Japanese Colonial Occupation: 1910-1945

3.2.1. Colonial Rule, Independence and Socialism

An historical overview of Korea under Japanese colonial rule would have to include the following events and movements which shaped the dominant conditions for Christian witness, struggle and reflection:

1910 - Final annexation of Korea by the Japanese Empire;

1911 - The "105 Men Incident" or "The Christian Conspiracy Case" (see 3.1);

1919 - The March First (*Samil*) Independence Movement (see below);

1931- Japanese invasion of China and establishment of the puppet Manchu Kuo;

1937 - Official Japanese declaration of war against China;

1938 - Japanese assimilation policy for Korean people enforced: change of all family names to Japanese form; use of Japanese language in all public schools and churches; Shinto shrine worship forced on all Korean Christians.

1943 - Conscription of Koreans in the Japanese Imperial Army (approximately 200,000 until the end of the War); drafting of laborers to work in Japan's war industry - mostly in hard manual labor (approx.130,000 drafted 1939-45);

1944 - Drafting of young Korean women as "comfort women" for sexual slavery in the Japanese front-line camps throughout Asia (estimated at 200,000);

1945 - Defeat of Japan; liberation and division of Korea.

On March 1, 1919, the leaders of resistance movements against Japanese colonial rule, had issued their declaration of independence which was read in a public park in Seoul, triggering nationwide demonstrations demanding national independence. Among the 33 signatories of the declaration, 17 were Christian leaders. The Japanese police fiercely suppressed the uprising by shooting the demonstrators, burning churches and imprisoning the leaders of the movement. The nationwide demonstration lasted for a year and incurred further persecution. The movement (March First Independence Movement - termed *Samil* in Korean) has, however, come to be the outstanding example and symbol for nationalist aspiration and one of the sources for indigenous and *minjung* theology.

The Japanese colonial government later initiated the so-called "politics of cultural rule," which guaranteed partial freedom of speech and press and some other reforms in colonial rule. In 1920 a new socialist party was organized in Seoul, under the name "Chosun Laborers Welfare Association," although this led to conflict with the Christian churches and the assassination of some Christian ministers. Other Christian leaders attempted to open dialogue with socialism in order to bring about reform of the

Christian churches regarding participation in social concerns. In February 1927, two associations for the independence movement were born, the *Shin Kan Hoe* for men and the *Keun Woo Hoe* for women, as vehicles for the collaboration of socialists and Christians in the name of nationalism. Leaders of *Shin Kan Hoe* included Lee Sang Jae, Jo Byung Ok, Lee Kap Sung and Jo Man Shik, all of whom had participated in the March First Independence Movement. Feminist leaders in the *Keun Woo Hoe* included Kim Helen, Yu Kak Kyung and Lee Hyo Duck, among others.

From 1935 the Japanese colonial government in Korea forced Korean schools and church leaders to pay respect to Shinto Shrines as symbols of Japanese Imperial rule. This was strongly opposed by Korean church leaders and missionaries as interference with religious belief. Christian resistance against the Shinto shrine worship was led by Choo Ki Chul, senior pastor of the San Jung Hyun Presbyterian Church in Pyongyang. He was martyred in prison on April 21, 1944, after seven years of imprisonment. Some 2000 Christians were arrested at this time and among them 50 were martyred in prison. Two hundred churches were also shut down by the Japanese authorities due to refusal of homage to Shinto shrines. The question as to whether such recognition was a religious or purely cultural practice had become a major theological issue for Christians, although the larger theological question was of course raised by Japanese colonial domination itself, along with its methods of enforcement. It was not surprising that during the last two decades of Japanese colonial rule major steps would be taken for the articulation of Korean contextual theologies (see 3.2.2.).

Selected References

Japanese Colonial Rule and Response:
Hankuk Minjung Sa Yonku Hoe (Study group of Korean *minjung* history), eds. *A History of Korean Minjung II* (in Korean). Seoul: Pul bit, 1986.
Kang Man Kil. *A History of Modern Korea* (in Korean). Seoul: Chang Jak Kwa Bi Pyung Sa, 1984.
Kang Tong Jin. *A History of Japanese Invasion Policy* (in Korean). Seoul: Hankil Sa, 1980.

Kang Wi Jo. *Religion and Politics in Korea under the Japanese Rule*. Studies in Asian Thought and Religion 5. Lewiston, NY: Edwin Mellen Press, 1987.

Kim, C.I. Eugene and Dorethea E. Mortimore, eds., *Korea's Response to Japan: The Colonial Period 1910-1945*. Kalamazoo: Western Michigan University, 1977.

Jun Taek Bu. *A History of the Korean YMCA Movement* (in Korean). Jung Eum Sa, 1978.

Lee Ki-baik. *A New History of Korea*. Cambridge, MA: Harvard University Press, 1984.

Song Kun Ho. "Korea under Japanese Imperialism and Christianity." In *Nationalism and Christianity* (in Korean). Seoul: Minjung Sa, 1981.

Suh Kwang-sun David. *The Korean Minjung in Christ*. Hong Kong: The Christian Conference of Asia, 1991: 31-35.

March 1st Movement:

Armstrong, Robert C., ed. *The Christian Movement in Japan, Korea and Formosa: A Year Book of Christian Work*. Tokyo: Christian Federation in Japan, 1921.

Board of Foreign Missions, Presbyterian Church in USA. *The Eighty-Third Annual Report*, 1920.

Kim Yong-Bock. "Samil Undong Gwa Hangug Krisdo ui Kobaeksinang." (Independence movement and Korean Christianity's Confession of Faith.). *Sinhak Sasang* 24 (1979).

Lee Man Yul. "The March First Independence Movement and Christianity." In *Korean Christianity and Historical Consciousness* (in Korean). Seoul: Jishik San Up Sa, 1981.

Lee Tae Yong. "Women's Movement after the March First Independence Movement." In *Collection of Papers Celebrating the 50th Anniversary of the March First Independence Movement* (in Korean). Seoul: Dong A Daily, 1969.

Smith, Frank Herron. *The Other Side of the Korean Question*. Seoul: Seoul Press, 1920.

Song Kun Ho. "The March First Independence Movement and Christianity." In *Korean Christianity and the Third World* (in Korean). Seoul: Pul Bit, 1981.

Socialism and Korean Christianity:

Choi Eun Hee. *Until We Recovered the Motherland*. Vol. II (in Korean). Seoul: Tam Koo Dang, 1973.

Fisher, J.E. *Democracy and Mission Education in Korea.* New York: Columbia University Press, 1928. Reprinted Seoul, Yonsei University Press, 1970.

Kang In Koo. "Anti-Christian Movement in the 1920's and Korean Christianity." In *Studies in the History of Korean Christianity* (in Korean). Vol. 9, 1986.

Kim, Helen. *Grace Sufficient.*

Kim Jun Yup and Kim Chang Soon. *The History of Korean Communist Movement.* Vols. I and II (in Korean). Seoul: Korea University Institute of Asian Studies, 1969.

Lee Dae Wi. "Socialism and Christian Thought" (in Korean). *Chung Nyun* 3.5 (1923).

Lee Moon Won. "Shin Kan Hoe and Lee Sang Jae." In *A Study in Wolnam Lee Sang Jae* (in Korean). Seoul: Jong Ro Publishing Co., 1986.

No Chi Soon. "A Study of Christian Socialism in the Korean YMCA under the Japanese Rule." In *Korean Christianity and Socialism under the Japanese Rule* (in Korean), edited by Kim Heung Soo. Seoul: The Institute of History of Korean Christianity, 1992.

Song Kun Ho. "Shin Kan Hoe Movement." *A History of Modern Korea.* Vol. II (in Korean).

Shinto Shrine Issue:

Kang Wi Jo. *Christ and Caesar in Modern Korea: A History of Christianity and Politics.* Albany, NY: State University of New York Press, 1997.

Kim Yang Sun. *Ten Years of Korean Christianity after the Liberation [1945]* (in Korean). Seoul: Presbyterian Church of Korea, 1956.

Kim Song-gon. *Korean Christianity and the Shinto Shrine Issue in the War Period, 1931-1945: a Sociological Study of Religion and Politics.* Hull: The University of Hull, 1989.

Kim Sung-t'ae. *Han'guk Kidokkyo wa sinsa ch'ambae munje* (Korean church and the Shinto shrine issue). Seoul: Han'guk Kidokkyo Yoksa Yon'guso, 1991.

Kin Nam-sik. *Sinsa ch'ambae wa Han'guk Kyohoe* (Shinto nationalism and Korean Church). Soul: Saesun Ch'ulp'ansa, 1990.

Lee Kun-Sam. *The Christian Confrontation with Shinto Nationalism.* Philadelphia: Presbyterian and Reformed Publishing Company, 1966.

Min Kyung Bae. *The Martyr, Choo Ki Chul*. Seoul: 1985.
Rhodes, Harry A. and Archbald Campbell. *History of the Korean Mission, Presbyterian Church in the USA, Vol. II (1935-1959)*. New York: Commission on Ecumenical Mission and Relations, UPCUSA, 1964.

3.2.2. Development of Indigenous Theological Movements under Japanese Colonialism: Contextual Protestant Theology 1

Little theological activity was undertaken in the first decades of Protestant presence (1885-1915), when faith understanding was largely that of the conservative missionaries, most of whom had no positive appreciation for Korean culture or religion. However, the concentration upon a mission to working classes and women which was included in "three-self" principles, and the sensitivity of some expatriates to nationalist aspirations, already laid some of the grounds for contextual reflection. This was also true of the political commitment of Korean Christian leaders like So Jai Pil, Yun Chi Ho and Lee Sang Jae (see 3.2.1), of the Independence Club (1890s), the YMCA (from 1903) and of the progressive New People's Party (1907).

A germinal stage of Korean theology began in 1916 with the publication of the quarterly *World of Theology* by the Methodist Theological Seminary, edited by Yang Ju Sam. This was followed by the Presbyterian quarterly *Theological Instruction* (1918), the monthly *New Life* (1923) and the *Sungso Chosun* (Bible and Korea, 1927-1942). By 1928 all these journals regularly included the writings of Korean scholars, of whom many of the Methodists in particular were open to biblical criticism, to nationalist concerns and to study of Korean culture. They were joined in the 1930s by Presbyterians such as Kim Yong Ju, Kim Ch'un Bae (see 3.2.2.6.) and Kim Jae Joon (see 5.3.2.1.), who would later lead in the formation of the Presbyterian Church of the Republic of Korea (PROK) and its seminary Hankuk. The most authoritative account of indigenous theological development during this period is found in Yu Dong shik (1982), who presents a number of indigenous Korean theologians and theological "schools" in the period of

Japanese colonialism. See also Yu (1976), Kim (1981), and Keel (1987).

3.2.2.1. Choi Byung Hyun (1858-1927) was a classical Confucian scholar and was active in the movement for national independence. He was ordained in 1902 as one of the first ministers in the Methodist Church in Korea and was a long associate of H.G. Appenzeller with whom he participated in the translation of the Korean Bible. He taught world religions at the Union Methodist Theological Seminary (1923-1927), publishing more than 60 volumes in Chinese and Korean along with articles in the theological periodicals *Shin Hak Wol Bo* (The Theology Monthly*)* and *Shin Hak Se Kye* (The Theological World) on the issues of indigenization of Christianity in the cultural-religious context of Confucianism, Buddhism and Shamanism. He distinguished the Gospel from Christianity as a religion and saw affinities between Confucianism and Christianity. Yu Dong Shik (Yu, 1982) claims that Choi was the first original Korean theologian and that he was a "religious liberal thinker" at the time.

Among other theologians who showed theological interest in Korean religions at this time were Ch'ae P'il Gun (1885-1973) and Chung Kyong Ok (1903-1945 - see 3.2.2.4.). Ch'ae taught courses on world religions and later wrote *A Treatise on Comparative Religion*.

3.2.2.2. Byron Yun Chi Ho (1864-1894) was baptized in 1887 in China, studied theology at Vanderbilt and Emory in the 1890s and returned home in 1895 to serve the government as acting minister of education. After a brief stay in France, he became president of the Independence Club and the *Independence Daily Newspaper*. After five years of exile in the countryside, he was appointed foreign minister in 1904 until the Japanese took over foreign affairs from Chosun in 1905. He was imprisoned on charges of involvement in the Conspiracy Case of 1911-1913. He served as general secretary of the YMCA and president of Yun Hee College of Korea during the trying years of Pacific War.

3.2.2.3. Song Chang Keun (1898-1951), one of the leading liberal theologians, was raised in the Canadian missionary territory of northeast Korea. He studied theology in Japan (Aoyama Gakuin), at San Francisco and Princeton, and later earned his Th.D. from Iliff School of Theology and the University of Denver in 1930. His major publication was on Christian ethics, a lengthy article on ethical problems of Christians in Korea. He contributed to *Shinhak Jee Nam* (Theological Instruction), a publication of the Presbyterian Theological Seminary, such articles as "Problems in Christian Ethics" (15.1); "The Mission of Korean Church Today" (15.6); "Theologians and Preachers" (15.4); and "The Crisis of Korean Christianity" (16.3). Yu Dong Shik (Yu, 1982) categorizes him as the first Korean social ethicist who took seriously the particular situation of Korean Christians.

3.2.2.4. Chung Kyung Ok (1903-1945), a Methodist preacher and theological educator, studied in Doshisha University, Kyoto and Garett School of Theology at Northwestern University in Chicago. He was a liberal theologian who introduced Karl Barth to Koreans and authored an early systematic theology book in Korean, *The Principles of Christianity* (1934), along with *An Introduction to Christian Theology* (1939). Regarding other religions, Chung believed that God speaks not only through the biblical witness, but also through culture and history. For him, other religions also contained revelation. His *Introduction to Christian Theology* is still in use today.

3.2.2.5. Kim Kyo Shin (fl. 1930-1940) was a student of Uchimura Kanzo of the *Mukyokai* (non-church) movement in Japan and was the publisher of *Songso Chosun*. Like Uchimura for Japan, Kim also wrestled with the question of a genuinely Korean Christianity. Recognizing that western Christianity, and western "Christian" culture's institutions and politics could not be the true gospel for Korea, he first advocated a return to the biblical Gospel which alone could save his beloved Korean people. But this Gospel must be understood fully within the situation of Korean people and therefore is to be liberated from western ecclesiastical traditions and control.

3.2.2.6. Others mentioned by Yu include Kim Yong Ju, Kim Ch'un Bae, Lee Yong Doh and Kil Sun Joo. Both Kims were censured by the Presbyterian General Assembly (1924) for criticizing scripture: Kim Yong Ju for rejecting the Mosaic authorship of Genesis, and Kim Ch'un Bae for declaring that Paul's injunction to stop women speaking was merely a localized custom of one particular church two thousand years ago. Lee (1901-1933) was a Methodist revivalist who claimed to have mystical experience of Christ, but was condemned by church authorities as a "heretical mystic." His letters were edited by Pyun Chong Ho in 1934. Yu also names him as a great revivalist who established the Pentecostal revival tradition of the Korean churches. Kil (1869-1935) was a pioneer preacher in the Presbyterian Church of Korea with a strongly conservative yet nationalist faith. He was one who signed the 1919 Independence declaration and he authored a book on apocalyptic theology (1930). Others for whom we have documents or poetry of confession and resistance in this period include Chu Ki Chol, Kim Se Young, Kim Kyu Sik, Ahn Chang Ho, Yun Ding Ju, Suk Jin Young, Ban Byub Sub and Park Du Chin (See 3.2.1.).

Selected References

See the journals *World of Theology*; *Theological Instruction*; *New Life*; *Sungso Chosun* (Bible and Korea); *Hak Wol Bo* (The Theology Monthly*)* and *Shin Hak Se Kye* (The Theological World).

Choo Chai Yong. "The Theology of Yang Ju Sam." *Theological Studies* 29 (1988).

Chung Kyung Ok. *The Principles of Christianity.* Seoul: the Korea Methodist Theological Seminary, 1934.

—. *An Introduction to Christian Theology.* Seoul: the Korea Methodist Theological Seminary, 1939.

Han Sung-hong. *Han'guk sinhak sasang ui hurum* (Trends of Korean theological thought). 2 vols. Seoul: Changnohoe Sinhak Taehakkyo Ch'ulp'anbu, 1996.

Hong, Harold S., Ji Won Yong and Kim Chung Choon, eds. *Korea Struggles for Christ; Memorial Symposium for the Eightieth Anniversary of Protestantism in Korea.* Seoul: Christian Literature Society of Korea, 1966.

Kang Wi Jo. *Christ and Caesar in Modern Korea.* Albany, NY: State University of New York, 1997.

Keel Hee Sung. "Korean Theology: Past and Present." *Inter-Religio* 12 (1987).
Kim Jae Joon. *A Historical Sketch of the Development of the Hankuk Theological Seminary ... and the Formation of the Presbyterian Church in the Republic of Korea.* Seoul; Mimeo'd, 1958.
Kim Yong-Bock. "Korean Christianity as a Messianic Movement of the People." In *Minjung Theology: People as the Subjects of History,* edited by Kim Yong-Bock, with Intro. by D. Preman Niles. Singapore: Christian Conference of Asia, 1981; Maryknoll, NY: Orbis Books, 1983.
—. *A History of Theological Development in Korea.* Seoul: Asian Institute for Christian Studies, Mimeo'd, 1981.
Sunoo, Harold Hakwon. *Repressive State and Resisting Church: the Politics of CIA in South Korea.* Fayette: Korean American Cultural Assoc. CMC, 1976.
Testimonies of Faith in Korea. Geneva: World Alliance of Reformed Churches, 1989.
Yu Dong Shik. "Rough Road to Theological Maturity." In *Asian Voices in Christian Theology,* edited by Gerald H. Anderson. Maryknoll, NY: Orbis Books, 1976.
—. *A History of Indigenous Korean Christian Thinking* (in Korean). Seoul: Jun Mang Sa, 1982.

4 Supplementary Bibliography 1
4.1 Catholic Resources

Byun Ki-yung Peter, ed. *The Founding Fathers of the Catholic Church in Korea: 1779-1831.* Seoul: Committee for Bicentennial Commemorative Projects of the Catholic Church in Korea, 1984.
Choi Suk Woo (Seogu). "The Founding of the Catholic Church in Korea." *Samok* 91 (1984).
—. "The Introduction of Catholicism and the Change of Political Culture in the Late Choson Dynasty." (in Korean). In *State Power and Christianity*, edited by Hanguk Kiddokyo Sahoe Munje Yonguwon. Seoul: Minjungsa, 1982.
Collected Articles on Korean Church History. (Series of vols.) Seoul: Institute for the Studies of Church History in Korea, 1982-.

Han'guk Kat'ollik Taesajon P'yonch'an Wiwonhoe. *Han'guk Kat'ollik taesajon* (Korean Catholic encyclopedia). Seoul: Han'guk Kyohoesa Yon'guso, 1997 (1985).

Institute of Korean Church History, ed. *Martyrs and Witnesses*. Seoul: IKCH, 1982.

Kim Chang-Seok and Lee Choong-Woo. *Holy Places of the Korean Martyrs*. Seoul: Lay Apostolate Council of Korea, 1986.

Kim Se-yun and Donald Baker. *Choson hugi yugyo wa Ch'onjugyo ui taeri* (Confucianism confronts Catholicism in the late Choson dynasty). Series: Pusan Kyohoesa Yon'guso yon'gu charyo ch'ongso. Seoul, T'ukpyolsi: Ilchogak, 1997.

Kusuda, Onosaburo. *Chosen Tenshukyo shoshi* (A concise history of Chosun Catholic church) (in Japanese). Tokyo: Ozorasha, 1996.

Lee Jai-Hyung. *Das traditionelle Verhaltnis von Politik und Religion in Korea und die christlichen Missionen*. Thesis, University of Hamburg, 1979.

Mun Kyu-hyon. *Minjok kwa hamkke ssunun Han'guk Ch'onju kyohoesa* (History of Catholic church in Korea). Seoul: Pit Ture, 1994.

No Kil-myong. *Katollik kwa Choson hugi sahoe pyondong* (Catholics and social change in the late Choson). Minjok munhwa yon'gu ch'ongso 18. Seoul: Institute for the Cultural Studies of Korea, Korea University, 1988.

Pak An-sik. *Han'guk sun'gyoja yolchon: yonggi wa kwanyong ui yoksa*. Seoul: T'ukpyol-si: Songumsa, 1974. (Collective biographies of Christian martyrs - Korea).

4.2 Protestant Resources

Blair, William Newton and Bruce F. Hunt. *The Korean Pentecost and the Sufferings which Followed*. Edinburgh, Carlisle, Pennsylvania: Banner of Truth Trust, 1977.

Chung Chai Sik. "Protestantism and the Formation of Modern Korea, 1884-1894." Ph.D. dissertation, Boston University, 1964.

—. "Christianity as a Heterodoxy: an Aspect of General Cultural Orientation in Traditional Korea." In *Korea's Response to the West*, by Jo Hung-hwan. Kalamazoo, MI: Korea Research and Publications, 1971.

Chung, David and Oh Kang-nam, ed. *Syncretism : The Religious Context of Christian Beginnings in Korea.* Suny Series, Korean Studies. Albany, NY: State University of New York Press, Forthcoming.

Chung Tae Ui. "A Narrative of Christianity in Social Change in Korea since the 17th Century." *Journal of Sciences and Humanities* 14 (1961).

Federal Council of the Churches of Christ in America. *The Korean Situation: Authentic Accounts of Recent Events by Eye Witnesses.* New York: The Commission on Relations with the Orient of the FCCC, 1919.

Han'guk Kidokkyo Yoksa Yon'guso. *Han'guk Kidokkyo wa yoksa* (Korean church and history). Seoul: Kidok Kyomunsa, 1991.

Huntley, Martha. *To Start a Work: The Foundations of Protestant Mission in Korea (1884-1919).* Seoul: Presbyterian Church of Korea, 1987.

Jo Byung Ok. *A Memoire.* (in Korean). Seoul: Minkyo Sa, 1959.

Kim Hung-su. *Ilcheha Han'guk Kidokkyo wa sahoejuui* (Korean Christianity and socialism under Japanese colonial rule). Seoul: Han'guk Kidokkyo Yoksa Yon'guso, 1992.

Kim Kwang-su. *Han'guk minjok Kidokkyo paengnyonsa* (Korean Christianity history for one century). Seoul: Han'guk Kyohoesa Yon'guwon: ch'ongp'an Kyomunsa, 1978.

Kim In-su. *Han'guk Kidok kyohoe ui yoksa* (History of Korean Christian church). Changnohoe sinhak taehakkyo 100-chunyon kinyom ch'ongso IV. Seoul: Changnohoe Sinhak Taehakkyo Ch'ulp'anbu, 1997.

Kum Chang-t'ae. *Han'guk chonggyo sasangsa, Yu Tong-sik kongjo* (History of Korean religious thought). Seoul: Yonse Taehakkyo Ch'ulp'anbu, 1986.

Lee Yeong-Heon. *Kankoku kirisutokyo shi* (A history of Korean Christianity). 2nd ed. Seoul: Concordia, 1980.

McKenzie, F.A. *Korea's Fight for Freedom.* New York: Fleming H. Revell, 1920.

Noble, Mattie Wilcox, ed. *Victorious Lives of Early Christians in Korea.* Seoul: Christian Literature Society, 1933.

Park Jihang. "Trailblazers in a Traditional World: Korea's First Women College Graduates, 1910-1945." *Social Science History* 14:4 (1990).

Ryang, J.S. "The Aims of Methodist Union in Korea." *The Korea Mission Field* 7 (1927).

Sim Il-sop. *Han'guk minjok undong kwa Kidokkyo suyongsa ko: minjok, kyohoe, t'och'akhwa* (A study on national movements and the historical situation of the acceptance of Christianity in Korea). Seoul: Asea Munhwasa, 1982.

Yi Nung-hwa. *Choson Kidokkyo kup oegyosa* (Choson Christianity and diplomatic history). Seoul: Minjok Munhwasa, 1980.

Yi Tok-chu. *Ch'ogi Han'guk Kidokkyosa yon'gu* (Study in early Christianity in Korea). Seoul: Han'guk Kidokkyo Yoksa Yon'guso, 1995.

5 Korean Theological Movements in the Divided Nation from mid-20th Century 1

5.1 Historical Setting

The first years of this period began with the division of Korea, immediately following the liberation from Japanese colonial rule at the end of World War II in 1945, and ended with the April 1960 student revolution and the downfall of the Syngman Rhee regime. This was followed by the military coup of Park Chung Hee in May, 1961. In this period also devastating civil war (1950-1953) was fought between communist North Korea (Democratic Peoples' Republic of Korea-DPRK) supported by Soviet Russia, and capitalist South Korea (The Republic of Korea) supported by the USA. The tightly patrolled Demilitarized Zone (DMZ) has continued to divide the Korean people until the present.

Christian churches in the North were well established even under the severe persecution of Japanese authorities, but they now had to face the oppression of the North Korean communist regime. (For North Korea see chapter 8.) During the Korean War some three million people, the majority of whom were committed Christians, fled to take refuge in the South. There the US military authority befriended Christian leaders and churches grew rapidly as the former missionaries returned from exile and internment overseas during the Pacific War. Syngman Rhee had sought to undergird his government's anti-communist ideology by enlisting Christian support, but this and other theological differences would now divide the churches. The Presbyterian Church of Korea (PCK), easily the largest of all Protestant churches, lost a more liberal wing which formed the ecumenical Presbyterian Church of the Republic of Korea (PROK, 1951), and a politically anti-communist and theologically anti-ecumenical wing, which formed the National Assembly of Evangelicals (NAE, 1959).

Following the downfall of Syngman Rhee, progressive and ecumenical church leaders responded to criticism from outside and inside Christian communities and called for the repentance and reform of both church and state. The 1960s, in particular, was also the decade of Korean Christians' political awakening under the military dictatorship of President Park Chung Hee. Cautious but strong voices were published against the military takeover in a monthly theological journal, *Kidokkyo Sasang* (The Christian Thought), the only Protestant theological journal at the time. When the Park government pushed for diplomatic normalization with Japan in 1964, Protestant leaders such as Kim Jae Joon, Ham Sok Hon, Kang Won Yong (for these see 5.3.2.1.; 5.3.2.2.; 7.1.4.), Hahn Kyung Jik and Kang Shin Myung, along with writers and university professors, protested against the unfair negotiation of war reparations and against the Japanese invasion of the Korean economy. When President Park moved to revise the constitution to allow him a third term as president, progressive Protestant leaders organized a national coalition, led by Kim Jae Joon, to resist this. They were soon joined by Catholic colleagues who deeply shared the same concerns for human rights and social justice. The Park regime was nevertheless extended in 1970, and in 1972 Park declared martial law and promulgated the so-called *Yushin* Constitution to allow him to stay in office for life.

Under this harsh and pervasive military rule, and amid often brutal processes of rapid economic development, numerous sagas of suffering, struggle and resistance were played out in prisons, factories, classrooms and churches. A flood of writing and reflection emerged as the vigorous witness and theology of faith was lived out.

Selected References

Ahn Byung-Mu. "The Korean Church's Understanding of Jesus: An Historical Review." *International Review of Mission* 74.293 (1985).

Editors' Committee on North Korean Church History of the Institute of Korean Christian History. *The History of the North Korean Churches.* Seoul: Institute of Korean Christian History, 1996.

Emergency Christian Conference on Korean Problems, ed. *Documents on the Struggle for Democracy in Korea.* Tokyo: Shinkyo Shuppansha, 1975.

Han Young Je. *Chosen Kirisutokyo Shi* (A history of Christianity in Korea). Tokyo: Nihon Kirisutokyodan Shuppan Kyoku, 1991.

Hong Yon Ho. *Study of the Christian Youth Movement at the End of the Chosun Dynasty.* Seoul: PCK Religious Education Department, 1976.

Kang Wi Jo. *Christ and Caesar in Modern Korea: A History of Christianity and Politics*, especially Chaps. 9, 10 and 11. Albany, NY: State University of New York Press, 1997.

Kim Yang Son. *Ten Years of Liberation of the Korean Church.* Seoul: PCK Education Department, 1956.

Sawa Masahiko, Kim Sook Ja and Kang Moon Kyu. *A Study of Christianity in North and South Korea* (in Korean). Seoul: Min Jung Sa, 1997.

Sohn Hak-Kyu. *Authoritarianism and Opposition in Korea.* London and New York: Routledge, 1989.

Suh Kwang-sun David. *The Korean Minjung in Christ*, especially chap. 2. Hong Kong: CCA, 1991.

—, ed. *Korea 100 Years.* Special Issue of *International Review of Mission* 74.293 (1985).

T.K. *Letters from South Korea.* Tokyo: Iwanami Shoten, 1976.

Yu Chai-Shin, ed. *Korea and Christianity.* Studies in Korean Religions and Culture 8. Seoul, Berkeley, Toronto: Korean Scholars Press, 1996.

5.2 Roman Catholic Presence and Thought

In the period following the events of *Samil* (see 3.2.1.), and despite continuing sporadic persecution, Catholic life and mission was further strengthened by the coming of other congregations, among them Maryknollers, Columbans and additional numbers of Benedictines. Confrontation with Japanese authorities was reduced by papal permission for Catholics to pray at Shinto shrines from 1936 and the first Korean bishop, No Ki Nam, was consecrated in 1942. Final years of the Pacific War, and the ensuing events of national division, large-scale displacement of people and civil conflict (1951-1953), greatly restricted all Christian activities. But rapid growth followed in the 1950s and 1960s, not least from the large numbers of Catholic refugees fleeing from North Korea. The Bible had been translated by Catholics, and a hierarchy was established for South Korea in 1962 - both moves laying foundations for contextual Catholic theology. By this time also many Catholics were sharing in the movements for democracy and human rights which would continue until 1989. There was now a greater sense of social concern, a readiness for critical speech and action among members of worker, student and clergy movements, and a growing concern for national unification.

Catholic periodicals such as *Kyongghyang Sinmun*, *Kyongghyang Chapchi* and *Catholic Youth* had been recommenced after 1953, and now became vehicles for social criticism and resistance to military dictatorship. This was encouraged by the outcomes of the 2nd. Vatican Council recently concluded. The College of Bishops strongly advocated measures to restore human dignity and the spiritual values of love and justice from the mid-1960s, through Pastoral Letters and in joint declarations on issues of social equality and political corruption, and Cardinal Kim Su Hwan (Stephen, see 5.2.3.3.) spoke publicly concerning issues of human rights and North-South relationships (from 1969). There had been increased ecumenical cooperation between Catholics and Protestants since 1963, although there was as yet no wide recognition of social and humanitarian concerns, nor of the issues for indigenous Korean theology. Im Jin Chang et al. (1975) concludes from extensive surveys that there is "little perception of the need to indigenise" even though for some the largely western character of church was "the greatest problem." The same surveys showed some concern for the social role of religion, with 70% citing injustice and corruption and 40% the rich-poor gap. Few clergy and lay people, however, valued social works as a part of corporal mercy if this did not serve evangelism. Biernatski concludes that until the conscientizing events of 1974-5, the theology of many Catholics remained individualistic and pietistic.

But oppressive political and economic measures were to change this for many. The collaboration of priests throughout the country, which was already begun with Catholic student and young worker movements, along with Protestant colleagues in the struggle for human rights and democratization, was now strengthened through such associations as the National Catholic Priests' Corps for the Realization of Justice (NCPCRJ). There followed in the 1970s and 1980s a stream of prayer movements, protest fasts and declarations, demonstrations and arrests, in which cathedrals such as Myong Dong in Seoul came to be centers for resistance, teach-ins and contextual articulation. Large industrial conflicts, as well as the arrest of such figures as Bishop Chi Hak Soon (Daniel - see 5.2.3.1.) served to mobilize further Catholic action which also received added impetus in the wake of bi-centenary celebrations in 1984. In that year the "Pastoral Congress of the Korean Roman Catholic Church" was held and this would have wide impact on Catholic theology in Korea (see below). By now another major concern was peaceful national reunification, and in 1985 the bishops established a committee for North Korean Mission, and in 1988, the Catholic Institute for Reunification.

At the same time, movements for indigenous leadership, liturgy and theology were also gaining in strength. However there were yet no specific attempts to formulate a political or *minjung* theology, although the large body of writings from the democratic and mission struggles of the 1960s and 1970s provided rich groundwork for this. A number of Catholic journals (see 7.3.3. and 7.4) began publishing studies of South American and Asian theologies from the late 1970s and further sources came from those like Ham Sye Ung and Chong Ho Kyong (see 5.2.3.6.) of the Catholic Farmers' Movement in the late 1980s. From the mid-1980s much wider discussion of indigenization and many more writings on contextual theology came from Catholic scholars, clergy and lay people. By 1988 a series of symposia and seminars had been held on such topics as the "Prospect for Indigenization of the Catholic Church in Korea," with long series of articles being published. Issues that were initially considered included inculturation of the liturgy, Korean historical sources, Korean religious traditions, church pastoral councils and lay participation, ecumenical relations, the role of women, and shared ministries. A wide range of other subjects soon appeared, in missiological, pastoral, socio-ethical, hermeneutic, feminist, inter-faith, political and ecological studies (see e.g. 5.3.1.).

Selected References

Choi Suk Woo. *A Quest for Korean Catholic History.* 1982.
—. *History of Korean Catholicism.* 1982.
—. "Korean Catholicism Yesterday and Today." *Korea Journal* 24.8 (1984).
Ham Se Ung. "Activities of the Catholic Church for Social Justice in the 1970s." *Catholic Journal for Social Science* 3 (1983).
Han Yong Hui. *A History of the Catholic Human Rights Movement in Korea.* Waegwan: Benedict Press, 1984.
Im Luke Jin-chang, Min Anselm Kyongsuk and William E. Biernatzki. *Korean Catholicism in the 1970s: A Christian Community comes of Age.* Maryknoll, NY: Orbis Books, 1975.
Kang Wi Jo. *Religion and Politics in Korea under the Japanese Rule,* Vol. 5, Studies in Asian Thought and Religion, chap. 12. Lewiston: Edwin Mellen Press, 1987.
—. *Christ and Caesar in Modern Korea.*
O Kying Hwan. "Justice, Peace, Unification and Church." *Catholic Journal for Social Science* 5 (1984).
Shim Sang Tae. "Issues on Theological Inculturation." In *Christ and Salvation: A Supplementary Volume,* 326-386. Seoul: St Paul Press, 1984.
Young Soon Song and Japanese Catholic Council for Justice and Peace, eds. *"A Declaration of Conscience." The Korean Catholic Church and Human Rights.* 3 vols. Probe Third World studies. Maryknoll, NY: Orbis Books, 1983.
Yu Hang Yol. *A Revised History of the Korean Catholic Church.* Vol. 2. Seoul: Catholic Publishing House, 1975 (1962).
Yun Min Gu. "Inculturation of Liturgy." *Journal of Ministry* 114 (1987).

Yu Chai Shin, ed. *Korea and Christianity*. Studies in Korean Religion and Culture 7. Seoul, Berkeley, Toronto: Korean Scholar Press, 1996.

5.2.2. Contextual Catholic Theology 1

5.2.2.1. Chou Jai Yong, Paul (1894-1975) was ordained 1918 and worked as the chief director of two Dioceses: of Chunju in 1942-1946 and of Taegu in 1946-1948. After he resigned from the office of Taegu Diocese 1948, Chou began a concentrated study of Catholic Church history in Korea. He wrote several books in Korean, including *The Idea of the Lord of Heaven in Ancient Confucianism* (1958) and *Defending Korean Catholic Church History* (1970).

5.2.2.2. Bang Yu Ryong Leo Andrea (1900-1986)
Bang Yu Ryong was ordained in 1930 and while ministering in Gaesung Parish, he established a women's religious community, Sisters of the Korean Martyrs (1946). He also established for men the Clerical Congregation of the Blessed Korean Martyrs in Seoul (1953). He himself entered this religious community in 1957 and taught the members of the two Congregations. Until he died in 1986, he worked to systematically develop the spirituality of men and women using fully Korean sources rooted in the lived faith and spiritual dedication of Korean martyrs. In works such as *Light of the Soul* (1980) this was based on his understanding of "No-Self in Christ."

5.2.2.3. Yun Hyung Joong, Matthew (1903-1979) was ordained in 1930 and served as the editorial chief of the *Catholic Cheong Nyun* in 1933-1936 and of *Kyung Hyang Japji* in 1937-1945. He also worked as the president of Kyung Hyang Shinmun in 1945-1949 and as the publisher of the *Catholic Cheong Nyun* in 1947-1960. He worked as a representative member of the Korea National Association for Democracy Recovery, in opposition to Park Chung Hee's military regime in the 1970s. Yun wrote several books in Korean including *Foundational Issues of Religion* (1952) and *Introduction to the Essential Teachings of the Catholic Church* (1957).

5.2.2.4. Youn, Eulsou (1907-1971) was the first Korean Catholic Priest to receive the Ph.D. from the Sorbonne University in 1939 with his thesis, "History of the Theory of Korean Confucianism." In the thesis, he argued that Confucianism had become the core of Korean thought and the motivating force of its culture and it was thus the starting point of the fields of politics, economics, society, culture, administration, history and literature. In working to illuminate the meaning which Confucianism gives to the life of Koreans, he was an inculturated theologian, well ahead of his time. Under Japanese colonization, he was well known as a patriot, social worker, and the founder of the "Blessed Sacrament Sisters of Charity" in Korea (1956). His teachings on what is true happiness, charity, equality in human beings, human dignity in God, and on mission based on true happiness forms a unique body of thought.

5.2.2.5. Choi Min Soon, John (1912-1975) was a Catholic priest who served as the president of the *Catholic Times* and *Taegu Daily Mail* in the 1950s. He studied spirituality at Madrid University in the early 1960s and taught at Seoul Seminary from 1965. Before he died in 1975, he left many widely-used translations including *The Psalms* (1968) - used as the text of the liturgy in the Korean Catholic Church; *The Divine Comedy* (1957-60); and *Confession* (1965) among others. He also published several poetry collections such as *Nim* (1955) and *Bam* (1977) in which his theological thought can be discerned.

5.2.2.6. Sun Jong Wan, Laurence (1915-1976) was ordained 1942 and studied economics and law in Japan. With the liberation of Korea from Japan (1945) he taught at Seoul Seminary for three years. Following theological study in Rome (1948-1952) he served as professor again at Seoul Seminary and started to translate the texts of the Hebrew Bible into Korean. In 1960, he established a women's religious community, Sisters of the Annunciation, committed to care for the most alienated people in Korea. Sun worked as a member of the Committee for the Common Translation of the Bible, translating many Old Testament books. This Bible was published in 1977 as the first significant result of ecumenical cooperation between Korean Catholic and Protestant Churches.

His writings in *Following Christ* (1977) and *A Priest Who Lived in the Bible* (1984) were published posthumously.

5.2.2.7. Lee Moon Geun, John (1917-1980) was ordained 1944 and studied Catholic Church Music at the Pontifical Institute of Sacred Music in Rome (Doctorate in Sacred Music 1955). He then taught at the Seoul Seminary and Seoul National University. Working for the inculturation of Catholic music in Korea, he published many articles and composed several examples of sacred music including: "Hymn for the Korean Beatified Martyrs"; "Hymn for the Beatified Martyrs in 1866"; "Hymn for Father Kim DaeKun Andrea" and "Korean Sacred Music for Mass." His collected works have been published (1977) in a volume for his 60th birthday.

Selected References

Bang Yu Ryong. *Light of the Soul,* edited by Kim Ok Hee, Seoul: Soon Kyoeui Maek, 1980.

Choi Min Soon. *Nim* (The Lord). Seoul: KyungHyang Japji Sa, 1955.

—. *Bam* (the Night). Seoul: Paulist Press, 1977.

Chou Jai Yong. *The Idea of the Lord of Heaven of Ancient Confucianism and the Issue of Ancestral Worship* (Seoul: KyungHyang Japji Sa, 1958. Rev.ed. Catholic Publishing House, 1988.

—. *Defending Korean Catholic Church History* . Seoul: CBCK, 1970.

Lee MoonGeun. "History of Sacred Music." (25 articles) *Catholic Cheong Nyun* (April1956 to April 1958).

—. *The Collected Works in Honor of the Sixtieth Birthday of Father Lee Moon Geun John.* Seoul: Han Gang Parish Publishing Committee, 1977.

—. *Korean Catholic Hymnbook.* Seoul: Kyung Hyang Japji Sa, 1948.

—. *Selected Catholic Sacred Songs.* Seoul: Kyung Hyang Japji Sa, 1957.

Sun JongWan. *Following Christ.* Seoul: Catholic Publishing House, 1977.

—. *A Priest Who Lived in the Bible.* Seoul: Paulist Press, 1984.

Youn Eul-sou. "History of the Theory of Korean Confucianism." Ph.D. Thesis. Paris: Sorbonne University, 1939.

Yun Hyung Joong .*Foundational Issues of Religion.* Seoul: Kyung Hyang Japji Sa, 1952.
—. *Introduction to the Essential Teachings of the Catholic Church.* Seoul: Kyung Hyang Japji Sa, 1957. Rev. ed. Catholic Publishing House, 1989.
—. *Witness to the Truth.* Seoul: Kapjin Press, 1959.

5.2.3. Contextual Catholic Theology 2

Contextual Catholic theology would develop much further in the period following 1945, with extensive reconstructions being undertaken in Korean church history, in liberalizing and social theologies, and in pastoral, *minjung* and feminist theologies. Prominent in these concerns have been Choi SukWoo, Kim Sou Whan, Lee Won Sun, Chi Hak Soon, Min Kyong Suk, Kim Jin So, Kim Chi Ha, Kim Sung Tae, Ham Se Ung, and Cho Kwang. (For sections on women doing theology see 6.2; and for further names see 7.2 below).

5.2.3.1. Chi Hak Soon, Daniel (1921-1993)

Chi Hak Soon was bishop in Wonju Diocese and bishop-moderator of the Korean JOC (Young Christian Workers) in the 1970s. He was also a sponsor of the Catholic Farmers' Movement and a close associate of Kim Chi Ha (see below 5.2.3.10. and 7.6.8.). He took an active part in movements for democracy, clean government and human rights at the time of the Yushin constitution (1971-), including protest masses, petitions and demonstrations. For this he was imprisoned (1974) but continued to write protest letters, and a public Declaration of Conscience, along with statements to defend Protestant ministers and activists against government harassment and arrest.

In letters from prison he declared that Christian love is "neither a warm reception for the temptor nor ... blind obedience to those who threaten," but is rather a refusal to "forget those who are naked and forsaken ... groaning in pain [and] imprisoned for speaking out of their conscience honestly and fearlessly." He wrote also of reconciliation which "is neither yielding to the powerful nor standing silent in the face of falsehood and injustice [but rather] must be sought by the powerful from the powerless who have been arbitrarily oppressed." In response to the arrest of priests like Choi Ki Shik (1982) he portrays the social meaning of priesthood in modern society through a full study of Jesus' life and ministry with the poor, the weak and the alienated. The model for mission and ministry even under military dictatorship is this identification with poor people in all our actions.

Selected References
Works by Chi Hak Soon
> *My Story during the Communist Regime.* Seoul: Catholic Publishing, 1958.
> "Report to the Vatican Secretariat of State." *IDOC Document* 157/ 003 (1974).
> "Confessing Christ in Korea. Letters from Prison." *International Review of Mission* 64.253 (1975).
> "The Crisis in the Korean Church and its Solution." Seoul: Mimeo'd, Aug. 1976.
> "Korea: Making Martyrs." *Newsweek* (Aug.5, 1974).
> "The True Image of a Priest." In *A Declaration of Conscience. The Korean Catholic Church and Human Rights.* Vol. 3, edited by Young Soon Song et al. Probe Third World Studies. Maryknoll, NY: Orbis Books, 1983.
> *Interview with Mark Raper.* Asia Bureau Australia News 25 (1975).

5.2.3.2. Choi Suk Woo, Andrea (Ch'oe Sok U, 1922-)

Choi Suk Woo was ordained in 1950 and received his doctoral degree in theology from the University of Bonn (STD, 1961) with the dissertation on the origins of Catholicism in Korea which was also then published. He established the Research Institute for Korean Church History in 1964. His research covers the whole history of the Korean Catholic Church in order to integrate church history into Korean national history and to popularize Catholic Church history.

With Ahn Eung Ryul, Choi Suk Woo translated into Korean, and annotated the *Histoire de L'Eglise de Corée* (vols. 1-3) of Charles Dallet (1874) at the Benedict Press 1980. (This is one of the most comprehensive studies on Korean Catholic Church history). While serving as the Director of the Committee of Korean Catholic Church History, he is also working for a project to write the whole history of the Korean Catholic Church. In addition to many historical writings, Choi has written much on the process of inculturation in Korea and on the issues for Catholic presence and mission in today's Korea.

Selected References
Works by Choi Suk Woo (In Korean)
> *A Study on the History of Korean Roman Catholic Church* I-III. Seoul: Institute for the Studies of Church History in Korea, 1982, 1991, 2000.
> *A Quest for Korean Catholic History.* 1982.
> The Korean Mission Field. Vol. 1-36. Seoul: The Institute for Korean Church History, 1986.
> *Church History in North Korea.* Seoul: The Institute for Korean Church History, 1996.
> "L'Érection du premier Vicariat apostoloque et les origines du catholicisme en Corée." *Nouvelle Revue de Science Missionnaire* (1961).
> "Korean Catholicism Yesterday and Today." *Korea Journal* 24.8 (1984).
> "Inculturation in East Asia: Focusing on the Korean Church." *Kyohoesa yongu* 7 (1990).
> "Korean Catholicism Yesterday and Today" (in English). In *The Founding of Catholic Tradition in Korea,* edited by Chai-Shin Yu. Mississauga: Korean and Related Studies Press, 1996.
> Institute for Korean Church History. *Korean Church History, I & II* (in Korean). Seoul: Kidok Kyomunsa, 1993.

5.2.3.3. Kim Su Hwan, Stephen (1925-)

Cardinal Kim was born in Taegu, studied philosophy at Sophia University in Tokyo, theology at the major seminary of Seoul and later, sociology at the University of Munster (Germany). He was then editor of the Korean national Catholic weekly (1964), first bishop of Masan (1966), Archbishop of Seoul (1968) and Cardinal in 1969. He was one of the "founding fathers" of the Federation of Asian Bishops' Conferences (FABC) and became a widely influential leader throughout all of Korean society, advocating people's participation, democratic reforms, human rights and the defence of working people. He has spoken out - sometimes rebuking

Korea's presidents - on the growing disparity between rich and poor sectors, the primacy of justice-and-peace endeavors for people of religious belief and the necessity today of inter-religious dialogue for human solidarity and lasting peace among nations. Such stands have also led him to publicly defend not only Catholics but also Protestants wrongly accused of subversive activities.

For Kim, the Church is to turn outwards; the Church is mission: its *raison d'être* is the redeeming presence and action of the crucified and risen Christ operative in history and in the world. A key model for this is the basic ecclesial communities which he sees as a sign of creative vitality within the Church, an instrument of formation and evangelization, and a solid starting point for a new society based on a 'civilization of love'. On mission practice he believes the goal to be "pre-evangelization which is expressed simply by our very presence among people as believers in Christ ... within the community, in which we can directly and indirectly share the mystery of God and the love of Jesus." On inculturation he has declared that "the Christian message will remain an idiom foreign to our cultural soil" unless the "valid spiritual values" of Korea's and Asia's traditions are integrated. In many other articles he has presented the demands of holistic mission within Korean (and Asian) contexts, the present-day profile of Jesus for this and the centrality of people's solidarity in such mission.

Selected References
Works by Kim Su Hwan

"The Church in Asia: An Examination of Conscience." *Omnis Terra* 35.3 (1971).

"Discovering the True Face of God." *Teaching All Nations* 11.4 (1974).

"Evangelization in the Asian Context." In *Mission Trends 2*, edited by Gerald H. Anderson and Thomas F. Stransky. New York: Paulist Press; Grand Rapids: Eerdmans, 1975.

"Costly Discipleship." *CCA News* (May 1976).

"A Call for Human Rights and Democracy." *IMCS Document Service* 10 (1979).

"Jesus' Evangelization." *Philippiniana Sacra* 15.43 (1980).

"The Church and People of Asia." *IMCS Document Service* 3 (1980).

"The Missionary Vocation of the Korean Church." *Japan Missionary Bulletin* 37 (1983).
"Reflections on Being a Bishop." *FABC Paper* 35 (1983).
"The Korean Church - A Success Story." *Japan Missionary Bulletin* 42.4 (1988).
"A Place to Live: Asian People's Dialogue," and "For a Culture of Life and Peace in Solidarity with the People." *Weltkirche* (1989).
"Mission to Asia." In *In Honour of Stephen Cardinal Kim Sou Hwan on his 75th Birthday. EAPR* 34 (1997).
"Mission to Asia Special Address at the East Asian Pastoral Institute, July 31, 1997." *EAPR* 34 (1997).
Cosmao, V. "Kim: un Cardinal sur la Breche." *Foi et Developpement* 73 (1980).

5.2.3.4. Lee Won Sun, Eusebius (1926-)

Lee Won Sun worked as Chairman of the National Institute of Korean History in 1994-1999. He has contributed to widening the horizon for the study of the histories of the Catholic Churches of Japan, China and Korea by using a comparative historical approach. He has also become known as an expert on the history of the Japanese Catholic Church and his work, *A Study of the History of "Western Learning" in Korea*, is now translated into Chinese. He published many articles especially on the acceptance by Korean intellectuals of Catholicism as an academic subject. He has also written on the related issues of the origin of the Korean Catholic Church. As a founding member of the Research Institute for Korean Church History (see 5.2.3.2.) he has collected and studied the Chinese materials written by several Chinese missionaries and Chinese and Korean scholars.

Selected References
Works by Lee Won Sun

History of the Korean Roman Catholic Church. (in Korean)Seoul: Tamkudang, 1970.

A Study of the History of "Western Learning" in Korea (in Korean). Seoul: Iljisa, 1986. (Also translated and published by the Chinese Institute for Social Sciences, Beijing).

Essays on the Korean Catholic Church (in Korean). Seoul: The Research Institute for Korean Church History, 1988.

5.2.3.5. Shim Sang Tae (1940-)

Shim Sang Tae is professor at Suwon Catholic Seminary and director of the Korean Christian Thought Institute (1992, see 7.6.3.). He studied at the Archdiocesan Catholic Seminary, Seoul, and at the Universities of Innsbruck and Munster, receiving his doctorate at the University of Tubingen. He is a priest-theologian prominent in systematic theology, developing in particular a theology of inculturation through dialogue between Christian truths and Korean thought.

Shim believes that Catholic truths have to be studied more deeply, and at the same time, we must search for the meaning of the Gospel in Korean culture and thought. Regarding fundamental problems in contextualizing theology, he considers the character of Latin American and western theologies, of African and Asian theologies and then focuses upon Korean theology within the context of Korean realities. He has also written, for example, on Christology, Christian anthropology, the responsibility of the church for the sanctification of society, the attitude of the church towards other religions, the resurrection faith of the church, national unification, human freedom, the church and Jubilee, and the ecological crisis. In addition, Shim has taken the initiative to introduce western theology to the field of Korean Catholic theology in order to search for Christian universal truths more deeply.

Selected References
Works by Shim Sang Tae

- *Han'guk kyohoe wa sinhak: chonhwan'gi ui sinang ihae* (Korean church and theology: understanding faith in transition ages). Sinhak sonso 14. Seoul: Song Paoro/St Paul, 1988.
- *Anonymous Christians: Critical Study on the Theory of Karl Rahner* (in Korean). 2nd ed. Seoul: St. Paul Publications, 1989.
- *Human Being: Introduction to Theological Anthropology* (in Korean). Seoul: Seokwang, 1989.
- *Korean Church in the Period of the 2000s*. Seoul: St. Paul Publications, 1993.
- *Introduction to Christology*. Puchon: University of SongSim, 1994.
- *The Third Millenium and New Evangelization of Korean Church*. Hwasung: Korean Christian Thought Institute, 1998.

Korean Church and Theology in the 3rd Millenium. Seoul: Pauline Press, 2000.
"Fundamental Problems in Contextualizing Theology." *Samok* 87, 88, 89, 90 (1983).
"Study of the Concept of God in the writings of B. Welte" (In dialogue with Eastern philosophy). *Collectanea Catholica* 9 (1983).
"The Significance of an Inculturation of Christian Theology." *Samok* 186, 187 (1984).
"The Church as the Kingdom of God" (In its call for freedom). *Samok* 96 et seq. (1984-1986).
"Liberative Elements in Christian Salvation." *Inter-Religio* 17 (1990).
"Inculturation of the Concept of Person." *Samok* 202, 203 (1995).
"The trend of modern theology?" *Pastoral Review* 195.4 (1995).
—, et al. *Introduction to Christianity* (in Korean). Puchon: University of SongSim, 1991.

5.2.3.6. Chong Ho Kyong (1940-)

Chong Ho Kyong is a priest who has written theological works from grassroots perspectives, particularly from the standpoint of farmers during the dictatorship of the 1970s and 1980s. He has been director of the Catholic Farmers' Movement since 1966 (see 7.6.8.) and has developed a pastoral theology of farmer's ministry. In the 1980s he wrote out of the experience of the farmers' struggles for livelihood and recognition, presenting his theological reflections in the form of essays and stories. He declares that "the basis for indigenous farmers' theology will be found along with the beginning of farmers' mission."

Chong thus believes that present work to restore human dignity is more important than scholarly research into Korean culture, although he has also recently interpreted eastern thought in Christian terms. Here he takes the festival mood and conviviality of shamanism, where healing and liberation occurs (*kut*) as the image for Jesus' acts of healing and liberation. He draws on imagery of "the power of God within us," or "little God" which is similar to "Heaven-in-man" (sic) of the *Donghak* movement. He also draws on Buddhist stories and *yin-yang* thought to portray a theology which arises from the realities of people's aspirations and struggles rather than from any intellectual construction.

Selected References
Works by Chong Ho Kyung
> *Community of Sharing and Serving: Pastoral Theology for Farmers* (in Korean). Waegwan: Benedict Press, 1984.
> *Reading the Zangja*. Seoul: Hatvit Pub., 2000.
> "Movement for Life Community." *Community Culture* 3 (1986).
> "The Catholic Farmer's Movement." *Sinhak Jonmang* 67 (1984).
> Korean Catholic Farmers' Assoc. *Hebang Hashinun Hananim* (Liberating God - A Creed for the Farming Community). Seoul, Bundo Publications, 1987.

5.2.3.7. Ri Je Min

The main area of Fr. Ri Je Min's theological work is that of ministry, which he believes to be the whole reason for being Church, that is to serve the world. For him, ministry is a fundamental obligation that Jesus gave to Christians. Theology is therefore a reflective action for pastoral practice and a dialogue between pastoral environments, the Christian Gospel and pastoral practices. His theological works are thus a reflection on Korean pastoral ministry, and his theological method and attitude are based on an understanding and concept of ministry and church in the light of the Second Vatican Council. In his view, the Council was an attempt to view Christian tradition through present perspectives and was an event to define the reason, as in all ministry, for being Church in the modern world. He has developed his works based on an understanding and concept of ministry and church in the light of the Second Vatican Council.

Selected References
Works by Ri Je Min
> *Church, A Chaste Prostitute: the 2nd Vatican Council and the Korean Catholic Church* (in Korean). Waegwan: Benedict Press, 1995.
> *The Face of God* (in Korean). Seoul: Bible Life, 1998.
> *We are the Church* (in Korean). Waegwan: Benedict Press. Forthcoming.

5.2.3.8. Min Kyong Suk, Anselm (1940-)

Educated at Fordham University (Ph.D. 1974) and Vanderbilt University (Ph.D. 1989), Min's main concern has been to reconstruct Christian theology in a way that is both faithful to the best of the Christian tradition and responsive to the needs of liberation and pluralism in a globalizing world. His interest in liberation came to expression in his *Dialectic of Salvation: Issues in Theology of Liberation* (1989). His interest in the problem of living together with diverse peoples comes to fruition in a forthcoming collection of essays, *Solidarity of Others in a Divided World: A Postmodern Theology after Postmodernism* (Trinity Press International). As a theologian, however, always sensitive to his Korean roots, he has also contributed works on Asian theology, Korean Catholicism, and Korean American Christianity.

Selected References
Works by Min Kyong Suk

> *The Spiritual Ethos of Korean Catholicism: Catholic Socio-religious Survey of Korea, Part 1 - Findings of Content Analysis.* Seoul: Sogang University Research Institute, 1971.
> *Dialectic of Salvation: Issues in Theology of Liberation.* Albany: SUNY Press, 1989.
> "Asian Theologians." In *A New Handbook of Christian Theologians,* edited by Donald W. Musser and Joseph L. Price. Nashville: Abingdon, 1996.
> "The Political Economy of Marginality: Reflections on Jung Young Lee's Theology of Marginality." *The Journal of Asian and Asian American Theology* 1 (1996).
> "From Tribal Identity to Solidarity of Others: Reflections on a Divided Korea." *Missiology* (July 1999).
> "From Autobiography to Fellowship of Others: Reflections on Doing Ethnic Theology Today." In *The Journeys at the Margin*, edited by Peter C. Phan and Jung Young Lee. Collegeville, MN: Liturgical Press, c1999.
> *Hangook Kyohoe 2000* (Korean Christianity 2000: Beyond Ecclesiocentrism and Authoritarianism). Seoul: Benedict Press, 2000.
> "From the Theology of Minjoong to the Theology of the Citizen: Reflections on Minjoong Theology in 21st Century Korea." *The Journal of Asian and Asian American Theology* 5. Forthcoming.
> Co-author. *Korean Catholicism in the 1970's.* Maryknoll NY: Orbis Books, 1975.

5.2.3.9. Kim Jin So Daegun, Andrea (1940-)

Kim Jin So was ordained 1972 and is now president of the Research Institute for Honam (southwest Korea) Church History. His studies have focused on Korean Catholic Church history in terms of the life of *minjung*. Through his theological studies, in particular on *Gasa Cheon Ju* (see his *Songs of Faith Living of the Children of God*), he contributed to the recovery of a community-consciousness for Catholics. This was especially based upon the life and witness of those who lived during the first 100 years of the Korean Church. He published *A History of the Diocese of Chonju* from his twenty-year long study in this field. As one of the most ardent advocates for the popularization of Korean Catholic Church history, he regularly lectures for the Catholic faithful throughout Korea.

Selected References

Works by Kim Jin So Daegun

> *Sinbaram Sa-neun Boram* (The land cherishing the faith) (in Korean). Seoul: The Research Institute for Korean Church History, 1987.
>
> *A History of the Diocese of Chonju* (in Korean). Seoul: Big Bell Press, 1998.
>
> "An Essay on the Thought of Cheon-ju Gasa" (in Korean). In *Monographic Collection of the Korean Church History in Commemoration of Sixty Years of Age of Father Choi Suk Woo*. Seoul: The Research Institute for Korean Church History, 1982: 279-310.

5.2.3.10. Kim Chi Ha (Kim Hyung, 1941-)

Kim Chi Ha was born in Cholla Do province, studied at Seoul National University and participated both in the 1960 student revolution which removed Syngman Rhee from power, and in the protests against the security treaty with Japan in 1965. After periods in prison and sanatoria, he wandered the countryside, living with poor farmers and writing. Through association with the Catholic Farmers' movement, and Bishop Chi Hak Soon, he became a Christian. Despite repeated illness and imprisonment in the years that followed, Kim continued writing and became known nationally and internationally as a foremost critic of social injustice, political corruption and violence. In his poetry he conveys directly the bitter experience of poor farmers, workers and prisoners which he has shared, and which is the sustaining motivation for his own intellectual pilgrimage.

But there are deeper levels of his thought which draw not only on long Korean traditions of dissent, such as the *Donghak*, but also upon shamanist insights and imagery along with Catholic social teaching. In poems and dramas, declarations of conscience and longer studies he has presented a comprehensive picture of the "kingdom of God in the Eastern Sea" and of the coming of personal and social salvation - which for him are wholly integral - for all Koreans. His deep concern for suffering and downtrodden outcasts in Korean society leads him both to give vivid images of genuine justice and mutual fellowship in a renewed social collective, and also to advocate and work for concrete means to these: the formation of actual collectives and cooperatives, along with profit-sharing and land redistribution. For the *minjung*, God will be rice, he affirms. In all his work, the model and source is the outcast Jesus who in his continuing passion brings salvation both as food and as forgiveness. Not surprisingly these and other aspects of his thought contributed much to the formulation of *minjung* theologies.

Selected References
Works by Kim Chi Ha
> *Kim Chi Ha Jenshyu* (An anthology of Kim Chi Ha). Tokyo: Hanyangsa, 1977.
> *The Gold Crowned Jesus and Other Writings*. Maryknoll, NY: Orbis Books, 1978.
> *The Middle Hour: Selected Poems of Kim Chi Ha*. New York: Human Rights Publishing Group, 1980.
> *Bab* (Rice). Seoul: 1984.
> *Southern Land Boat Songs*. Seoul: Dooreh, 1985.
> *Nam* (South). 3 vols. Seoul: ?1987.
> *Katsujin* (The man who lives vividly). Tokyo: Ochanomiza-shobo, 1989.
> *Tonghak Iyagi* (The story of Tonghak). Seoul: Sol Publishing, 1994.
> "Declaration of Conscience" (1975). In *Letters from South Korea*, by T.K., 389-408. Tokyo: Iwanami Shoten, 1976.

—, and Tomiyama Taeko. *At Midnight* (in Japanese). Tokyo: Doyo Bijutsu Sha, ?1974.

Kim Heup Young. "A Tao of Asian Theology in the 21st Century: from the Perspective of the Ugmch'i Phenomenon." *Asian Journal of Theology* 13.2 (1999).

Nicholas, Adolph. "A Theological Appraisal of Kim Chi Ha's Thought." In *A Declaration of Conscience. The Korean Catholic Church and Human Rights.* Vol. 1, edited by Young Soon Song et al. Probe Third World Sudies. Maryknoll, NY: Orbis Books, 1983.

Suh Nam Dong. "Toward a Theology of Han." In *Minjung Theology: People as the Subjects of History*, edited by Kim Yong-Bock, with Introd. by D. Preman Niles. Singapore: CCA, 1981; Maryknoll, NY: Orbis Books, 1983.

5.2.3.11. Kim Sung Tae, Joseph (1942-)

Kim Sung Tae was ordained in 1966 and served as Executive Secretary of the Committee for Promoting Christian Unity and Interreligious Dialogue for twenty years from 1981. His work has concentrated on Korean church history as both the roots for present mission and a contribution to the world church. He is also an expert on the history of the Oxford Movement in the 19th century. He contributed his studies of "Korean Catholic Church History" in 42 articles to *Kyung Hyang Japji* (issued by CBCK) in the mid 1980s. As the president of the Research Institute for Korean Church History, he aims to integrate the historical heritage of the Korean Catholic Church not only into the world Christian movement, but also into the long tradition of Catholic Christian theology.

Selected References

Works by Kim Sung Tae

Church in History - A Selection of Essays on the Church History (in Korean). Waegwan: Benedict Press, 1985.

A History of the Catholic Church I (in Korean). Seoul: St. Paul Publishing Company, 1986.

5.2.3.12. Ham Se Ung, Augustine (1942-)

Ham Se Ung was ordained in 1968 and was one of the founding members of the Association of Priests of Korea for the Realization of Justice (1974). He introduced the study of liberation theology in the mid-1970s and later wrote on feminist theology (from 1990). He has opened a way for Korean Christians and for many Korean people to rediscover the spiritual and social value of solidarity with the poor and oppressed. These were especially people who were suffering under the military dictatorships of the former three presidents, Park Chung Hee, Chun Do Hwan and Roh Tae Woo. He is now focusing his theological efforts to renew the relationships between lay people, clergy and religious and between Koreans in South and North Korea for the future of the nation. He now serves as the president of the Pastoral Institute of Joys and Hopes (Gaudium et Spes). His writings have in particular related biblical teaching and theology to major political and social issues in Korea.

Selected References
Works by Ham Se Ung
> *The Suffering Land and the Holy Land*. Seoul: Durhe, 1984.
> *Jesus Who Came to Give Sword*. Seoul: Bit Du Rhe, 1993.
> *The Yoke and the Cross: Church's Social Critical Function*. Seoul: Bit Du Rhe, 1993.

5.2.3.13. Cho Kwang, Ignatius (1945-)
Cho Kwang has contributed to constructing the historical foundations for research in Korean thought including that of Korean Catholicism. As a specialist in the late history of Chosun, he has worked to integrate Korean Catholic Church history into the Korean *minjung*'s historical realities. In particular he has translated and annotated several documents of Korean Catholic Church history as a member of the publishing committee of the "Study of Korean Martyrs." He is now working on the second volume of the fifth Study in this series: "Condemning the Wicked Learning and Recommending the Righteous Teaching" (important material for the first Korean Catholic faith movement of the early 19th century, issued by the officials of the Chosun government). He has also written studies of Korean Catholic writers of that time who are significant in the development of contextual theology, including Chong Yak Yong and Ahn Chung Geun.

Selected References
Works by Cho Kwang
- *A Study of the History of Korean Catholicism in the Late Chosun.* Seoul: Institute of National Culture of Korea University Press, 1988.
- *Two Hundred Years of the Korean Catholic Church.* Seoul: Hait Bit Press, 1989.
- *Condemning the Wicked Learning and Encouraging the Right Teaching I.* Seoul: Korean Martyrs Exaltation Committee (Forthcoming).
- "A Study on Yak Yong Jeong's Consciousness of Civil Rights." In *Essays on Minjung,* edited by The Korea Theological Study Institute. Seoul: Korea Theological Study Institute 1984: 289-340.
- "Patriotic Enlightenment Movement and Independence Fight of Chung-geun Ahn." *Research Journal of Korean Church History* 9 (1994).

5.2.3.14. The Pastoral Congress of the Korean Roman Catholic Church

This was held in 1984 to commemorate the bicentennial of Catholic Christianity in Korea and was one of the most important attempts of the Korean Catholic Church to inculturate its Christian faith. Inculturation was there declared to be "based on the incarnation of Jesus that constitutes the essence of Christian faith ... the Church as the body of Christ concretizes the Gospel in its own time and culture and historical context in the same way that ... Jesus embodied the gospel in his time and culture and historical context" (*Proposal for the Laity*, 122).

To adapt the salvific message to a concrete culture and history is not a relativistic activity, the Congress declared, but a universal sign of the true Catholic Church and this is the way of inculturation. Regarding evangelization the Congress stated: "Therefore the Church should continuously attempt to talk with its own national culture, its society, its scholarship, its other religions and non-Catholic Christians in order to prepare the incarnation of the Word of God today and here" (*Proposal for Mission* 3). When we see the core of inculturation to be God himself, this model can give rise to new and radical meaning because of the universal character of

God, the origin of all our being. All people therefore, including other religious believers, are the agents who nurture the life-bearing energy of God and enjoy and share in incarnating the reign of God in the local community within Korean religious traditions.

The twelve documents issued by the Congress take the form of *Proposals: for Clerics; for the Religious; for Laity; for Liturgy; for Piety Movements; for the Local Church; for Catechism; for Family Ministry; for Special Ministries; for Mission; for Social Ministry; and for Church Management.* Seoul: Catholic Publishing House, 1984.

See also Pastoral Congress Committee for the bicentennial of the Catholic Church of Korea. *An Introduction to the "schemata" of the Pastoral Congress of Korea.* Seoul: Pastoral Congress Committee, n.d.

5.3 Contextual Protestant Theology 2
5.3.1. Inter-faith, Political and Ecumenical Theology

During this period, major theological concerns came to include theologies of mission, biblical hermeneutic, contextualization, human rights and church and society concerns, study of Korean culture, sources for *minjung* theology and movements for reconciliation and reunification. Along with the work of pre-war theologians, calls from Asian colleagues for "contextualization" of the Christian Gospel stimulated many Korean theologians. A number of theologians began studying traditional religions of Korea, such as Confucianism, Shamanism and Buddhism in order to explore indigenous ways of doing theology in their own religious and cultural world. Prominent among these scholars were Yun Sung Bum, Yu Dong Shik, Byun Sun Hwan and Kim Chung Choon (see 5.3.2.3.; 5.3.2.5.; 5.3.2.6.; 5.3.2.4.). These and others would also forge new paths in biblical scholarship and interpreting the gospels within the Korean context: see for example Kim Jae Joon, Kim Chung Choon, Lee Oo Chung and Ahn Byung Mu (see 5.3.2.1.; 5.3.2.4.; 6.1.2.; 5.3.3.1.2.). For others, such as Mun Dong Whan, Kang Won Yong and Lee Chang Shik (see 5.3.2.7.; 7.1.4.; 7.1.9.), theologies of mission were intimately related to tasks of theological education and lay formation, while for these and others such as

Mun Ik Kwan, Kim Kwan Suk and Han Wan Sang (see 7.1.6.; 7.1.7.; 7.1.3.), a central focus for education, writing and action was a necessity in the struggles for democracy and civil liberties.

In the 1960s, and with the rise of state organized economic development plans, labor issues and industrial and urban missions concerns emerged as a context for Korean theology. Ecumenical urban industrial mission organization (UIM) was created in the industrial areas of Seoul and Inchon Harbor and student movements became involved in the struggles of workers, farmers and urban poor in work for community organization. These groups and others also became active in the 1970s in struggles for democracy and human rights under the repressive military Yushin government of Park Chung Hee. Such theological ferment would also contribute much to the movements in *minjung* theology (see also 5.2.3.9.; 5.2.3.10.; 5.2.3.13.; 6.1.5.; 6.1.10.4.).

Chief among ecumenical agencies working on such issues was the National Council of Churches in Korea (NCCK), with special concerns for prisoners and their families, for poor workers and dissident teachers and writers. Through its many commissions and in association with many other networks, the NCCK regularly organized many different activities, from prayer meetings to demonstrations, from petitions to prison visiting, from legal aid to seminars, conferences and workshops. As the democracy movement developed, the NCCK also organized a commission on national reunification and reconciliation to study and promote the mission of the Korean churches to reach out to both governments of the North and the South for reconciliation and peaceful reunification. Following a number of consultations over five years, commission members drafted the "Declaration of the Churches of Korea on National Reunification and Peace," which was adopted unanimously by the General Assembly of NCCK in February, 1988. Most of the commission members were *minjung* theologians such as Suh Kwang-sun, Kim Yong-Bock and others. (The theological agenda of *minjung* theologians from the 1980s onward has focused around the reunification issue.)

Contextual Theology in Korea 541

A large number of scholars and writers, teachers and activists contributed to contextual Korean theologies in this period and only a selection of these can be introduced here (see also 6 - Women Doing theology). Many of these were either staff members or students of Christian seminaries and universities, pastors and lay leaders in frontier mission projects or staff and members of the many ecumenical, theological and democratic associations. Among these last key groupings were the Student Development Service Corps (SDSC) of the YMCA and the Korean Student Christian Federation (KSCF), commissions of the National Council of Churches, the Mission to Labor and Industry (later UIM), Korean Christian Academy, Hankuk Seminary and two faculties of Yonsei University, the National Protestant Clergy's Corps for the Realization of Justice (NPCCRJ), the Korea Christian Institute for Social Justice and Peace and other Christian movements and centers such as Seoul Metropolitan Community Organization (SMCO), the Korea Theological Institute, the Christian Institute for Justice and Development, and many associations and institutes initiated by women theologians (see 6.1., 6.2.). Many Catholic movements such as Young Catholic Workers, the Catholic Farmers' Movement, and the National Catholic Priests' Corps for the Realization of Justice (NCPCRJ) were often also closely involved (see 7.6.).

From all these came communiqués and petitions, trial accounts, statements, poetry, articles and letters which include extensive theological reflection and construction (see also 2.1.7.1.).

Selected References

    Adams, Daniel J. "The Roots of Korean Theology." *Taiwan Journal of Theology* 7 (1985).

    Cho Seung Hyuk. *Realization of Urban Industrial Mission* (in Korean). Seoul: Minjung Sa, 1981.

    Chon Taek Bu. *The History of the Korean Ecumenical Movement.* Seoul: NCCK, 1979.

    Clark, Donald N. *Christianity in Modern Korea.* Lanham, MD: University Press of America; New York: The Asia Society, 1986.

    Emergency Christian Conference on Korean Problems, ed. *Documents on the Struggle for Democracy in Korea.* Tokyo: Shinkyo Shuppansha, 1975.

Kang Wi Jo. *Religion and Politics in Korea under the Japanese Rule*. Vol. 5, chap. 12. Studies in Asian Thought and Religion. Lewiston, NY: Edwin Mellen Press, 1987.

—. *Christ and Caesar in Modern Korea*. Albany, NY: State University of New York, 1997. See especially Chap. 15, "Christianity and the Politics of Reunification," and Appendix C for a full text of "Declaration of the Churches of Korea on National Reunification and Peace."

Kim Yang Sun. *Ten Years of Korean Christianity after the Liberation [1945]* (in Korean). Seoul: Presbyterian Church of Korea, 1956.

Kim Yong-Bock. *A History of Theological Development in Korea* (English and Korean versions). Seoul: Asian Institute for Christian Studies, Mimeo'd, 1981.

Min Kyung-Bae. "The Resistance History of Korean Protestantism." In *Hankuk Eni Kitokkyo Sasang* (Christian thought of Korea. Memorial 200th volume of "Christian Thought" magazine), edited by Ryu Dong Shik. Seoul: Christian Literature Society, 1975.

National Council of Churches in Korea, ed. *History of Christian Movement for Democracy in Korea*. 7 vols. Seoul: NCCK, ?1985.

—. *The Church in Korea*. Seoul: NCCK, 1961.

—. "The KNCC Declaration on the Occasion of the 10th Anniversary of the 1988 Declaration" (in Korean). *The Church and the World* (Dec. 1998).

Yu Dong Shik. *A History of Korean Theological Thought* (in Korean). Seoul: Jun Mang Sa, 1982.

Sohn Hak-Kyu. *Authoritarianism and Opposition in Korea*. London and New York: Routledge, 1989.

Suh Kwang-sun, David. *The Korean Minjung in Christ*, especially chapters 2:3 and 7. Hong Kong: CCA, 1991.

Young Soon Song and Japanese Catholic Council for Justice and Peace, eds. "*A Declaration of Conscience*." The Korean Catholic Church and Human Rights. 3 vols. Probe Third World studies. Maryknoll, NY: Orbis Books, 1983.

5.3.2. Particular Theologians

For Protestant indigenous theological movements in this period - in addition to Kim Jae Joon and Ham Sok Hon (see 5.3.2.1.; 5.3.2.2.) - three outstanding theologians were one-time faculty members of

Contextual Theology in Korea

Korea Methodist Theological Seminary in Seoul: Yun Sung Bum, Byun Sun Hwan and Yu Dong Sik. Others with entries below include, Kim Chung Choon and Mun Dong Whan. Others to be mentioned later include Cheung Ha Eun, Han Wan Sang, Chang Chun Ha, Kang Won Yong, Lee Chang Shik, Min Kyung Bae, Mun Ik Kwan, Kim Kwan Suk and Park Pong Bae (see 7.1.5.). For Catholic theologians see 5.2.3.

5.3.2.1. Kim Jae Joon (1901-1987)

Kim Jae Joon was perhaps the most eminent, and controversial, of Protestant theologians during the period between the 1940s to the 1980s. He graduated from Aoyama Gakuin (Japan), and studied Old Testament theology at Princeton and Western Theological Seminaries (USA). From 1933, he taught theology at Pyongyang and was the first Old Testament theologian to introduce the historical critical method of interpretation of the Scriptures. Due to his method of theological education and theology, he was tried for "heresy" in 1951, but led in the establishment of the Presbyterian Church in the Republic of Korea (PCROK). He taught at Chosun Theological Seminary (of the PCROK) in Seoul, continued editing theological journals he had founded (*Crusader* and *Third Day*) until 1975, and was a leading ecumenical theologian and social critic until his death.

With colleagues, he pioneered in the development of a Korean theology which arose from the historical, cultural and political context of Korea. "We are called," he wrote in a *Crusader* article in 1956, "to erect the liberating history of Christ within the history of this nation, so that Korean history itself may be transformed" (Kim, 1976). For him, the sovereign grace of God in Jesus Christ is found in the concrete world of human struggle, creativity and suffering. The image of Christ's life, death and resurrection are central throughout his teaching and writing, and by the early 1970s when military dictatorship had intensified in Korea, Kim's theology came to center more on Christ's suffering servanthood. More than a doctrine, the cross had become "nails in my hands and feet," in suffering for justice and human rights shared with many compatriots. Nor was it only a death "died for me ... the cross is heavier than that," he wrote in 1974. It is both the sign and power of resistance to entrenched evil; it is obedience to God rather than to human beings; it is the means whereby both body and spirit are transformed (*Third Day* 1976). But the suffering of the cross - from doing and declaring the truth of justice and peace - is inseparable from the "third day" of resurrection - restoration of human life in both persons and society.

The many volumes of his collected writings, all in incisive and exemplary Korean style, cover a very wide range of contemporary Korean issues. They include papers on major theological themes, on nationalism, Korean culture and Christian social concerns, on "faith's adventure with Christ," and "man and woman - so loved," along with biblical studies and commentaries, sermons and lectures, "light" essays and letters. For an account of the rise of PCROK and Kim's theological education, see Kim Yang Sun (1956); for outlines of his thought, Kim Chung Choon (1972) and Yu Dong Shik (1976).

Selected References
Works by Kim Jae Joon (in Korean)

>*Introduction to the Bible.* Seoul: n.p., 1960.
>
>*Jeo Jak Jeon Jib.* (Collected writings of Kim Jae Joon), edited by Chung Woong Sup. 5 vols. Seoul: Committee of Changgong Works Publication, 1971.
>
>*Beom Gang Ki* (The way I see things). In *Collected Essays.* 6 vols. Toronto: Independent Newspapers, 1981-1984.
>
>"The Matter of Participation in History and Our Existence." *Christian Thought* (March 1958).
>
>"Christ, Church and Society in Korea." *Church and Society* (EACC) 5 (1962).
>
>"Signing of the Korea-Japan Agreement and the Attitude of the Christians." *The Presbyter Circular* (August 1965).
>
>"The Present Situation and Future Prospect of the Korean Church" (in English). In *Korea Struggles for Christ,* edited by Kim Chung-chi, Harold Hong and Ji Won-yong. Seoul: Christian Literature Society, 1966.
>
>"Struggle against Injustice Is Also a Religion." *Sasanggye.* (July 1967).

"The Theology of Historical Participation." *The Third Day* (July 1971).

"Theology of the First (Jael) Day." *The Third Day* (April 1973).

"The Logic of the Third Day and the Tomorrow of History." *The Third Day* (Oct. 1974).

"Theology of Resistance." *The Third Day* (April 1976).

Chon Kyong Yon. "On Kim Chae-jun." *Sasanggye* (April 1966).

Kim Chung Choon. "On Dr. Kim Chae-jun." *Theological Studies* 13 (1972).

Kim Yang Sun. *Ten Years of Korean Christianity after the Liberation [1945]* (in Korean). Seoul: Presbyterian Church of Korea, 1956.

Yu Tong Shik. "The Flow of Korean Theology No. 7: Kim Chae-jun." *Christian Thought* (July 1968). See also Ryu Tong-shik. "Rough Road to Theological Maturity." In *Asian Voices in Christian Theology*, edited by Gerald H. Anderson.

5.3.2.2. Ham Sok Hon (1901-1989)

Ham Sok Hon - sometimes called the Korean Gandhi - was born in northern Korea, studied in Japan and participated in the *Mukyokai* (Non-Church Movement) there. A teacher and farmer, he was associated with Lee Sang Hun in the Osan School and was imprisoned many times in Korea by Japanese, Communists and later military dictators. With colleagues he founded the magazine *Bible Korea* and was later provincial director of education. Moving from earlier more exclusive understandings of Christian truth, he came to recognize the insights of other Korean faiths and wrote of the "Eternal Christ" who was present not only in Jesus of Nazareth but also in each person and in Korea's history of suffering. He later became a Quaker, actively dedicated to democracy, reconciliation and peace, and is internationally revered for this as 'Teacher Ham.'

Along with biblical meditations and poetry, Ham has written extensively on the history of the Korean people, seeking a "coherent thread of meaning running through human affairs." For this he weaves together history, philosophy, religion and aspiration in which morality, suffering and acknowledgement of responsibility contribute to a new human evolution. Although geography, national character, colonialism and neo-colonialism have all brought great suffering to Korea, there is yet also a divine intent. Within the suffering there lies great promise; awaiting Koreans is a global mission for peace and benevolence, for fully developed community and personality. This can come, Ham believes, through a harvesting of experience, a critical return to eastern wisdoms and a questing meditation which responds to God's over-arching and all-embracing purpose.

In his writings on Minjung Theology Ham deepened the understanding of *minjung* by using the metaphor of *ssi-al* (seed grain) to picture the inner life of the *minjung* as grass seed; the Spirit sleeping within everyone. "Ssial is me, the real me" he wrote. "It is a person without any clothes; true and real. The only thing existing is 'al' or one grain. The one 'al' is known as 'I' on this side and God, heaven, or Braman on the other side." The *minjung* must therefore be able to approach God who exists deep inside themselves and has a creative, mighty power of life. The *minjung*, or *ssi-al*, must directly encounter God within them. "Let us wake up and call for me-God sleeping and waiting inside me," Ham declares. "... each 'Ssial' together with other 'Ssials' must open a new era and nation with the beginning of a new millenium."

His works in Korean on many related subjects total more than 30 volumes.

Selected References
Works by Ham Sok Hon
> *Kicked by God*. Philadelphia: Quaker Fellowship of Friends World Committee, 1969.
> *Ssi-al: Song of the People. Poetry Anthology* 2. Seoul: n.p., 1971.
> *Meditations at Pendle Hill* (largely on John's Gospel). Seoul: Monthly Meeting, n.d.
> *Albatross* (Collected essays). Seoul: P'yongbom Sodang, 1982.
> *The Queen of Suffering. A Spiritual History of Korea*. London: Friends' World Committee for Consultation, 1985.
> *Collected Works*. 5 vols (in Korean). Seoul: P'yongbom Sodang, ?1992.
> Han Young Sang. "Interview with Ham Sok Hon." *Mahndohng* (1986).

Kim Kyoung Jae. "A Study of Ham Sok Hon's Thought of the People." *Theological Studies* 30 (1989).

Lee Yoon Gu. "Sok Hon Ham: A Wandering Albatross." Seoul: Mimeo'd, 1985.

Kim Sung Soo. *Ham Sok Hon: Voice of the People and Pioneer of Religious Pluralism in Twentieth Century Korea: Biography of a Korean Quaker.* Seoul: Samin. Forthcoming.

5.3.2.3. Yun Sung Bum (1916-1980)

Yun Sung Bum graduated from Doshisha University in Japan, studied under Karl Barth and received a doctorate at Basel University in Switzerland (1960). After brief pastoral work, he was appointed to the faculty of Korea Methodist Theological Seminary (1946) and served until his death in 1980 as seminary president. He was a forerunner in developing a Korean indigenous theology, interpreting the concept of Trinity by the ancient Korean national mythologies of divine figures. In his main volume on Korean theology (1972) he constructed a theology based on *sung* (sincerity) as interpreted by the 16th century Neo-Confucian Yi Yul Guk. Although urging Koreans to take seriously the "cultural a priori" in their theology, his approach was rather to seek a Christian understanding of Confucian thought. He published numerous articles on indigenization of Christian theology in Korean, along with a number of books outlining his Korean theology.

Selected References

Works by Yun Sung Bum

Kidokkyo wa Han'guk sasang (Christianity and Korean thought). Seoul: Taehan Kidokkyo Sohoe, 1965.

Hankuk Kok Shinhak: Sung Ei Hai-suk-hak (A Korean-style theology: hermeneutics of Sung). Seoul: Sun Myoung Moon Wha Sha, 1972.

"A Theological Approach to the Indigenization of the Gospel. *NEAJOT* 3 (1969).

"Theology of Sincerity." *NEAJOT* 5&6 (1970/1971).

"Korean Christianity and Ancestor Worship." *Korea Journal* 13.2 (1973).

"Christian Confucianism and an Attempt at a Korean Indigenous Theology." *NEAJOT* 24.25 (1980).

Yu Dong Shik. *A History of Korean Theological Thought* (in Korean). Seoul: Jun Mang Sa, 1982.

5.3.2.4. Kim Chung Choon (d.ca.1987)

Kim Chung Choon a highly qualified scholar in the Hebrew scriptures, was professor of Old Testament at Hankuk Seminary and was its president (1961-1962; 1969-1976). Full studies of Hebrew writings led to the publication of two widely-used textbooks, and his long-term interest in the indigenization of theological education led to a series of writings on such issues (1962-1974) and to the development of parallel courses in Old Testament theology and Korean history.

From such work Kim Chung Choon consistently drew conclusions for the method and content of theological education, for study of ecology and for the practice of ministry in Korea. He was closely associated with Kim Jae Joon (see 5.3.2.1.) of whose theology he wrote studies, and also with the *Third Day* group. The present experience of the cross by Korea's suffering people under dictatorship recurs again and again in his writings and this is perhaps most sharply addressed in a study of Psalm 22 where the agony of apparent desertion by God remains central. Writing of crucifixion and resurrection, Kim is most critical of those who peddle false hopes and false peace and affirms that true hope can only come through the acceptance of suffering. There can be no "3rd day" without the "1st day" where Jesus died because of corrupt politicians supported by the authority of the church, as happens today, Kim declared.

Selected References
Works by Kim Chung Choon

Sickness unto Life. Seoul: Christian Literature Society, ?1949.

Understanding the Old Testament. Seoul: Hankuk Seminary 1976 (1971).

"The Church and the Problem of Indigenization." In *Korea Struggles for Christ*, edited by Harold S. Hong, Ji Won Yong and Kim Chung Choon.

"Indigenization of the Church." *Church and Society* (EACC) 2.7 (1968).

"Living Theology and Indigenization." *NEAJOT* 8 (1972).

"Contextualization of Theological Education." *NEAJOT* 12 (1974).
A Pastoral (Indigenous) Study of 2nd Isaiah" *Activity Report* 1 (1975).
"Theology of the Afflicted in the Motive of the Exodus Event." *Theological Studies* 19 (1977).
"Suffering and Hope in the Asian Context." *Theological Studies* 18/19 (1977).
"A Theological Understanding of Korean History." *Theological Thought* 17 (1977).
"Toward a Christian Theology of Man in Nature." In *The Human and the Holy*, edited by Emerito Nacpil and D.J. Elwood.
"A Study of Psalm 22." *Theological Studies* 20 (1979).
"The Hope: God's Suffering in Man's Struggle." *Reformed World* 36.1 (1980).

5.3.2.5. Yu Dong Shik (1922-)

Yu Dong Shik graduated from Korea Methodist Theological Seminary, studied at the Boston School of Theology (USA), the Ecumenical Institute in Bossey, Switzerland, and received his doctoral degree from Kokgaku Daigaku in Japan. He taught theology at Korea Methodist Theological Seminary and Yonsei University School of Theology until his retirement in 1987.

One of Yu's major works was the study of Korean indigenous religion, especially Shamanism, for which he held positive appreciation. With a strong missiological concern, he sought to understand traditional Korean religion from the perspective of the Gospel in order to further the indigenization of Christianity. He wrote extensively on Shamanism and Korean folk religions and on their relationship to Christianity, on Korean culture and church history, and on feminist theology and the Korean church. Some of his most valuable writing in books and articles has also been on the history of Korean theology, and for this he has also edited collections of survey articles from, for example, the journal *Sasang* (Christian Thought Magazine).

Selected References
Works by Yu Dong Shik

Korean Religions and Christianity (in Korean). Seoul: Korea Christian Literature Society, 1965.

Han'guk chonggyo wa Kidokkyo (The Christian faith encounters the religions of Korea). Seoul T'ukpyolsi: Taehan Kidokkyo Sohoe, 1965 (1990 printing).
History and Structure of Korean Shamanism (in Korean). Seoul: Yonsei University Press, 1975.
Folk Religion and Korean Culture (in Korean). Seoul: Hyundae Sasang Sa, 1977.
Tao and Logos. Seoul: Christian Literature Society, 1978.
A History of Korean Theological Thought (in Korean). Seoul: Jun Mang Sa, 1982.
Kankoku no Kirisutokyo (Korea's Christianity). Tokyo, University of Tokyo Press, 1987.
Poong Ryu Do and Korean Theology (in Korean). Seoul: Jun Mang Sa, 1992.
Korean Religions and Korean Theology. Seoul: The Korean Theological Studies Institute, 1993.
"The Religions in Korea and the Personality of Koreans." In *Korea Struggles for Christ,* edited by Harold S. Hong, Ji Won Yong and Kim Chung Choon. Seoul: Christian Literature Society of Korea, 1966.
"Chondo-Kyo: Korea's only Indigenous Religion." *Japanese Religion* 5.1 (1967).
"Religion and Changing Society of Korea." *East Asian Cultural Studies* 11.1-4 (1972).
"The World of Kut and Korean Optimism." *Korea Journal* 13.8 (1973).
"Rough Road to Theological Maturity." In *Asian Voices in Christian Theology,* edited by G.H. Anderson.
"Christ in Korea: Suffering and Hope." *NEAJOT* 16 (1976).
"Man in Nature: An Organic View." In *The Human and the Holy: Asian Perspectives in Christian Theology,* edited by E.P. Nacpil and D.J. Elwood. Manila: New Day Publishers, 1978.
"Shamanism: A Dominant Folk Religion of Korea." *Inter-Religio* 5 (1984).
"Culture and Theology in Korea: The Pung-Ryu Theology." *East Asia Journal of Theology* 3.2 (1985).

5.3.2.6. Byun Sun Hwan (1927-1996)

Byun graduated from Korea Methodist Theological Seminary, studied systematic theology at Drew University Theological School (USA), and earned his doctorate from Basel University in

Switzerland. His doctoral dissertation was on the theology of indigenization of a Japanese theologian, Yagi Seiichi. He was an advocate of Christian-Buddhist dialogue throughout his entire life. Because of this, he was tried by his Methodist church and "excommunicated" and dismissed from presidency of Korea Methodist Theological Seminary a year before his death. An authoritative book on his life and theology was published in 1992 in honor of his retirement, with a complete bibliography and a collection of his papers published in 1996.

Selected References
Works by Byun Sun Hwan
> *Inter-faith Dialogue and Asian Theology.* Collection of papers of Byun Sun Hwan (in Korean). Seoul: The Korea Theological Study Institute, 1996.
> *Religious Pluralism and Korean Theology* (in Korean). Seoul: The Korea Theological Study Institute, 1992.
> Yu Dong Sik. *A History of Korean Theological Thought* (in Korean). Seoul: Jun Mang Sa, 1982.

5.3.2.7. Mun Dong Whan, Stephen (c.1930-)

Mun Dong Whan taught Christian Education at Hankuk Theological Seminary and was a key theologian of mission and education for the PROK and the Korean Council of Christian Education in the 1970s. Closely associated with movements for democracy and human rights, he led in the establishment of the House of Daybreak collective in Seoul and, along with fellow evicted teachers, the Mission Education Institute. He sought to orient all theological and lay education towards social and community goals and suffered eviction from his faculty, imprisonment and exile from Korea for his commitments.

Mun was convinced that in order to do theology Koreans must fully know their own situation and people, critically study the Bible and the precise liberation which Jesus brings, and then develop their own 'theology of liberation.' He therefore wrestled in his writing with the teachings that come from suffering, and also those from human joy, with accessible resources for faith and education, and with the theology which arises from awareness and struggle. These concerns he would continue upon return to Korea.

Selected References
Works by Mun Dong Whan
> *So that We may Become Human Again.* Seoul: Christian Literature Society, 1971.
> *Ningen Kaiho toKirisutokyo Kyoiku* (Human liberation and Christian education). Tokyo: Shinkyo Shuppansha, 1975.
> *Korean Minjung Theology.* New York: Union Theological Seminary, 1981.
> *Arirang Gogae Guoyak* (Education of Arirang Hill). Seoul: Korea Theological Research Institute, 1985.
> "First Century Christ for 20th Century Korean Youth." DRE thesis, Hartford Theological Seminary, 1961.
> "Towards a Project-centered Theological training." *NEAJOT* 1 (1968).
> "Mission Education and the Search for Community." *NEAJOT* 11 (1973).
> "Doing Theology in Korea with Reference to Theological Education from a *Minjung* Theological Perspective." *East Asia Journal of Theology* 4.2 (1986).

5.3.3. Minjung Theology and Minjung Theologians - Contextual Protestant Theology 3

Minjung theology, which developed more fully in the 1970s, has become known as a Korean theology of 'liberation.' Its roots lie in the history of Korean people's movements for livelihood and justice, especially those arising in the 19th and early 20th centuries, and in the critical theologies which radical and nationalist Christians evolved under successive colonial (Japanese) and military (Park Chung Hee and successors) regimes. Most important of these movements were the *Donghak* (eastern learning), along with the anti-Japanese movements of 1895-1945; the movements for indigenous leadership and theology in Protestant churches (see 3.2; 5.3); and the democratic, urban-industrial mission and student movements which developed from the late 1950s on. *Donghak* drew upon indigenous and popular religious traditions to oppose feudal and colonial oppression, notably in widespread uprisings in 1864 and 1894, and its blend of Buddhist, Confucian, Shamanist and Christian elements with a strong egalitarianism remains a strong influence in Korean social and religious thought. Under successive military dictatorships in the 1960s and 1970s, the struggle for basic human rights and democratization, and against the oppressive process of rapid economic development and militarization, were opposed by student, worker and clergy groups who also expressed their emerging theologies in letters, poetry, prayers and manifestos (see also 7.3.1.).

By the early 1970s also, groups of theologians and lay people in seminaries, social concern centers and universities were studying and articulating people-oriented theologies within Korean situations. In doing this they used renewed studies in Korean mission and church history; reoriented biblical study, especially of the synoptic gospels; the resources of Korean popular culture and contemporary literature; and critical socio-political analysis and reflection. For many such theologians the crucial element was their direct experience of surveillance and eviction, demonstrations, arrest and imprisonment, which for some brought major redirections in their theology. A stream of letters from prison, prayer vigil meditations, confessions, poems, statements and declarations all made significant contributions. Statements presented by prisoners at the many summary trials form a large class of theology-in-process and among the authors here are Lee Mun Young, Park Hyung Kyu, Mun Dong Whan, Suh Nam Dong, Kim Kwan Suk, Ahn Byung Mu, (Mrs) Lee Tae Young, Lee Hae Dong, (Ms) Lee Oo Chung and Ham Sok Hon, along with Catholics such as Kim Chi Ha, Mun Jung Hyun, Shin Hyun Bong and Tji Hak Soon. See especially the poetry of Kim Chi Ha (5.2.3.10.) and issues of such bulletins as *Korea Communiqué*, *Christian Activity News*, *Korea Theological Study Institute Activity Report* and *Korea Scope*.

Major proponents of *minjung* theology in the 1970s were Ahn Byung Mu, Hyun Young Hak, Kim Yong Bock, Suh Kwang Sun (David) and Suh Nam Dong (for these see 5.3.3.1.2.; 5.3.3.1.3.; 5.3.3.1.5.; 5.3.3.1.4.; 5.3.3.1.1.), who actively participated in the people's movement and reflected on their experience of acting in solidarity with the struggling *minjung* of South Korea. Other theologian activists who contributed to these movements include Kim Jae Joon (see 5.3.2.1.), Stephen Cardinal Kim, Kim Chung Choon, Mun Dong Whan, Han Wan Sang, Moon Cyris Hee Suk, Park Sang Jung and Oh Jae Shik (for these see 5.2.3.3.; 5.3.2.4.; 5.3.2.7.; 7.1.3.; 7.1.14.; 7.1; 7.1.13.). Along with these were theological teachers and leaders of student, worker, women's and clergy movements who have also written and worked for such concerns. Among other leaders in these movements who should be mentioned and whose writings are available are Ro Chung Hyun, Cho Seung Hyuk, George Ogle, Lee Chang Shik, Kim Yong Koo, Min Kyung Bae, Mun Ik Kwan and In Myung Jin.

The 1980s saw the emergence of two significant groupings. The first was the *minjung* church movement and the development of theology by the *minjung* themselves, initiated by 'second-generation' *minjung* theologians such as Kang Won Don, Lee Jung Hee, Park Jae Soon and Park Sung Joon (see 5.3.3.2.1.; 5.3.3.2.2.; 5.3.3.2.3.; 5.3.3.2.4.) who were active in urban and industrial contexts. The second was that of feminist *minjung* theologians, who made use of their indigenous Korean heritage, especially from shamanist traditions. For both there was also the challenge to more openly address Marxist and 'Ju Che' ideologies, the issues of unification and inter-faith coexistence. Feminist *minjung* theologians included Choi Man Ja, Lee-Park Sun Ai, Lee Oo Chung, along with Cho Wha Soon and others (see 6.1.4.; 6.1.3.; 6.1.2.).

In the 1990s, the (largely Protestant) Association of Minjung Theologians was formed, and later a group of 'third-generation' *minjung* theologians (see 5.3.3.3.) furthered the movement. Parallel movements among Catholics have also long been active in the development of people-oriented and socially transformative theologies. (See e.g. 5.2.3). *Minjung* theologians have found radical contextual insights in the Bible, in Korean Christian history and in Korean society and culture, along with solidarity with similar movements across the 'third world.' They have also worked for the renewal of church and society and taken up the issues of peace, justice and the reconciliation of a divided Korea. As Korea faces a financial crisis at the close of the century, *minjung* theology has been challenged anew by the plight of the *minjung*, who are faced with sudden unemployment, deprivation and a new economic exploitation as a result of globalization policies.

Selected References

Ahn Byung Mu. "Jesus and People (Minjung)." *CTC Bulletin* 7.3 (1987).

Christian Institute for the Study of Justice and Development. *Democritization Movement and the Christian Church in Korea during the 1970s.* Seoul: CISJD, 1985.

—. *People's Power, People's Church. A Short History of Urban Poor Mission in South Korea.* Hong Kong: CCA-URM & ACPO, 1987.

Cho Seung Hyuk. *Presence of Christ Among Minjung.* Introduction to Urban-Industrial Mission in Korea. Seoul: CISJD, 1981.

Emergency Christian Conference on Korean Problems, ed. *Documents on the Struggle for Democracy in Korea.* Tokyo: Shinkyo Shuppansha, 1975.

IDOC. *Mission through People's Organization: South Korea.* The Future of the Missionary Enterprise 7. Rome: IDOC, 1974.

Kim Chang Nak. "Minjung's Movement in the 1970s and Minjung Theology." *Theological Studies* 28 (1987).

Kim Kyung-Jae et al. *Chun Whan Kieu Minjung Shinhak* (Minjung theology in the transition period). Seoul, Hankuk Shinhak Yeon Ku Seo, 1992.

Kim Yong-Bock and Kyung Jae Kim. "80 Nyundae ui Hanguk Sinhak ui Jonmang" (An overview of Korean theology in the 1980s). *Sinhak Sasang* 24 (1979).

Korean Theological Study Institute. *1980 Nyon Dae Hankok Minjung Shinhak Chonkye* (The development of *minjung* theology in the 1980s). Seoul: KTSI, 1990.

Lee Jung Young, ed. *An Emerging Theology in World Perspective: Commentary on Korean Minjung Theology.* Mystic, CT: Twenty-Third Publications, 1988.

Ogle, George E. *Liberty to the Captives. The Struggle against Oppression in South Korea.* Atlanta: John Knox, 1977.

Min Young Jin et al. *Minjung Theology Debate in Korea.* Seoul: Korea Christian Academy, 1983.

Park Ik Soo. "A Biblical Understanding of the Development of the Minjung Church." *CTC Bulletin* 1&2 (1989).

Park Jae-Soon. *Minjung Theology and 'Sial' (Seed) Thought*. Seoul: Hanwool, 1990.
Suh Nam Dong. "Moonwha Sinhak, Jungchi Sinhak, Minjung Sinhak" (Cultural theology, political theology, and *minjung* theology). *Sinhak Sasang* 42 (Autumn 1983).
Weems, Benjamin B. *Reform, Rebellion and the Heavenly Way*. Tucson: University of Arizona Press, 1964.
Wells, Kenneth M., ed. *South Korea's Minjung Movement: The Culture and Politics of Dissidence*. Honolulu, University of Hawaii Press, 1995.
Young Soon Song and Japanese Catholic Council for Justice and Peace, eds. *A Declaration of Conscience. The Korean Catholic Church and Human Rights*. 3 vols. Probe Third World Studies. Maryknoll, NY: Orbis Books, 1983.

5.3.3.1. Key First Generation Minjung Theologians
5.3.3.1.1. Suh Nam Dong (1918-1984)

Suh Nam Dong was first widely known as a skilled interpreter of western theology, but turned from this following the period of his imprisonment, to concentrate upon the experience of oppressed Korean people and the sources for indigenous theology in Korea. Making particular studies of the *Donghak* movement and the work of Kim Chi Ha, he came, in major articles, to relate the experience of exodus and cross as known in today's life and witness in Korea, to the revolutionary *minjung* within Korea's history. At the center is the Korean Christ who is at the same time the suffering Korean people (*minjung*) and also the means of their salvation. Suh introduced the concept of *han*, a unique Korean word for the feelings of injustice imposed on the poor and oppressed, as central to theological understanding in Korea. The *minjung* movement thus seeks to overcome and liberate the deep-seated *han* of the people. Suh also illuminates the Jesus event as an archetype of liberation being experienced within Korea's history, and proposes a "pneumatological synchronic interpretation" in order to re-actualize the Jesus event here and now.

Selected References
Works by Suh Nam Dong

Jonwhansidae ui Sinhak (Theology in the changing society). Seoul: The Korea Theological Study Institute, 1976.

Minjung Sinhak ui Tamgu (Development of *minjung* theology in Korea), Seoul: Han'gilsa, 1983; Seoul: The Korea Theological Study Institute, 1990.

"Chongmalon gwa Hyukmyung" (Eschatology and revolution). *Sinhak Sasang* 7 (Winter 1974).

"Yesu, Kyohoesa, Hanguk Kyohoe" (Jesus, church history, Korean church). *Kidokkyo Sasang* 201 (1975).

"Minjung ui Sinhak" (Theology of *Minjung*). *Kidokkyo Sasang* 203 (1975).

"Han ui Saje" (The priest of *Han*). *Hyunjon* (June, 1979).

"Minjung iran Nuguinga?" (Who are the *minjung*?). *Hyunjon* (May, 1980).

"Jesamsekye ui Sinhak" (The Third World theology). *Sinhak Sasang* 34 (1981).

"Minjung Sinhak Soko" (A manuscript about *minjung* theology). *Hyunjon* (Sept./Oct., 1981).

"Han gwa Minjung Sinhak" (*Han* and *minjung* theology). *Kyohoe Yonhap Sinbo* (United Church Newspaper) 27 (June, 1982).

"Moonwha Sinhak, Jungchi Sinhak, Minjung Sinhak" (Cultural theology, political theology, and *minjung* theology). *Sinhak Sasang* 42 (1983).

"Ilryurul Wihyuphaneun Jukeum ui Seryukdul" (The Power of death threatening the human race). *Kidokkyo Sasang* 300 (1983).

"Suh Nam-Dong ui Sinhak Sasang" (Theological thought of Suh Nam Dong). *Sinhak Sasang* 46 (Autumn, 1984).

"Theology as Story-telling: A Counter Theology," and "Cultural Theology, Political Theology, and *Minjung* Theology." *CTC Bulletin* 5.3-6.1 (1984/85).

"Du Iyagi ui Habryu" (Confluence of two stories). In *Minjung gwa Hanguk Sinhak* (*Minjung* and Korean theology). Seoul: The Korean Theological Study Institute, 1985: 237-276.

5.3.3.1.2. Ahn Byung Mu (1921-1997)

Ahn Byung Mu, in his early days, was fascinated with existentialism, which led him to study Bultmannian New Testament theology in Germany. Ahn is widely regarded as laying the foundation for the biblical interpretation of *minjung* theology, in particular through his thorough terminological studies of the synoptic gospels. Ahn's concern with the present context of *minjung* reality helps to identify a "stream of volcanic lava" which penetrated throughout the Bible. His interpretation represents an attempt to synchronize the *minjung* tradition in the Bible with present Korean experience, without ignoring the historical distance. He therefore interprets the *ochlos* (downtrodden) as portrayed in the gospel of Mark as being the *minjung* of the time of Jesus. Furthermore, Ahn claims that the Jesus event of the cross and resurrection was a collective event of *minjung* in their struggles for liberation, and one into which Korean people are entering now.

Ahn was the founding editor of *Sinhak Sasang* (Theological Thought) and is a prolific author of many books and scores of articles, not only on the major concerns of *minjung* theology which he relates to both national tasks and to church reform, but especially on the role of Jesus with *minjung*, *ochlos* and church, and in liberation and hope. He has written also on issues of peace and justice in Korean society, the Jesus image of Korean churches, the Jesus movement, and the church of *minjung*.

Selected References

Works by Ahn Byung Mu

> *Yuksawa Jeungon* (History and witness). Seoul: The Christian Literature Society of Korea, 1972.
> *Haebangja Yesu* (Jesus, the liberator). Seoul: Hyundae Sasangsa, 1979.
> *Yoksa Ape Minjung gwa Doburo* (Facing history with the *minjung*). Seoul: The Korea Theological Study Institute, 1986.
> *Minjung Sinhak Iyagi* (Story of *minjung* theology). Seoul: The Korea Theological Study Institute, 1987.
> *Minjung Sagon sok ui Krisdo* (Christ in *minjung* event). Seoul: The Korea Theological Study Institute, 1989.
> *Galilaea ui Yesu* (Jesus of Galilee). Seoul: The Korea Theological Study Institute, 1990.
> *An Pyong-mu chonjip* (Complete collection of writings of Ahn Byung-mu). 6 vols. Seoul: Han'gilsa, 1993- .
> *Kraedo Dasi nakwonero Whanwonsikigi Anatda - Minjung Sagon ui Maeg* (The vein of *minjung* event). Seoul: The Korea Theological Study Institute, 1995.
> *Kuwone Iruneun Kil* (The way to salvation). Seoul: The Korea Theological Study Institute, 1997.
> *Uriwa Hamke Haneun Yesu* (Jesus with us). Seoul: The Korea Theological Study Institute, 1997.

Saengmyungeul Salineun Sinang (Faith to be lived). Seoul: The Korea Theological Study Institute, 1997.

"Sunansa esu Bon Maga ui Sinhak" (Mark's theology and suffering history). *Sinhak Sasang* 1 (Winter 1973).

"Yesu ui Heemang" (Jesus' hope). *Kidokkyo Sasang* 188 (1974).

"Krisdokyo wa Minjung Ono" (Christianity and *minjung* language). *Hyunjon* 108 (May 1980).

"Minjung Sinhak ui Songsojok Keungo" (Biblical foundation of *minjung* theology). *Kyohoe wa Sekye* (Sept., 1981).

"Yesu wa Minjung" (Jesus and *Minjung*). *Sinhak Sasang* 50 (Autumn, 1985).

"The Transmitter of the Jesus Event." *CTC Bulletin* 5.3 - 6.1 (1984/1985).

"Jesus and People (Minjung)." *CTC Bulletin* 7.3 (1987).

"Yerusalem Songjon Chejae wa Yesu ui Daegyol" (Jesus' confrontation with the social system of the Jerusalem temple). *Sinhak Sasang* 58 (Autumn 1987).

"Mateo ui Minjung jok Minjokjui" (*Minjung* nationalism in the Gospel of Matthew). *Sinhak Sasang* 78 (1992).

5.3.3.1.3. Hyun Young Hak (1921-)

Hyun Young Hak was formerly professor of Religion and Culture at Ewha Womans University and active in the movement for *minjung* theology from the 1970s. His particular contribution was in the study and interpretation of traditional folk culture in Korea from the *minjung* perspective. From a detailed analysis of such scenes in the masked dances as those of the Old Buddhist Monk, The Three Yangban (Aristocrats), Old Woman Miyal and the Cripple, Hyun identifies a stance of "critical transcendence" taken by the *minjung*, which performs a social role in making survival, criticism and struggle possible. His major contribution is the discovery that the Korean *minjung*'s mask dances imply a process for the resolution of the *minjung*'s *han*. Also implied in his interpretation are issues in the theologies of secularization, politics, liberation and the missio dei, as well as of laughter, play and festivity. In writing also on the 'religion of *han*,' Hyun distinguishes the three faces of *han* which are expressed by the *minjung*, as 'priestly' (for resignation and adjustment), 'prophetic' (for struggle and justice) and the 'servant-king' (holding the first two together with satire and laughter).

Selected References
Works by Hyun Young Hak

> *Yesu ui Talchum: Hanguk Krisdokyo ui Sahoeyunri* (Mask dance of Jesus: social ethics of Korean Christianity). Seoul: The Korea Theological Study Institute, 1998.
>
> "Hanguk Talchum ui Sinhakjok Ihae" (Toward a theological understanding of the mask dance in Korea). *Sinhak Sasang* (Sept., 1980).
>
> "Jesamsekye ui Sinhak" (The Third World theology). *Sinhak Sasang* 34 (1981).
>
> "A Theological Look at the Mask Dance in Korea." In *Minjung Theology: People as the Subjects of History,* edited by Kim Yong-Bock.
>
> "Theology with Sweat, Tears, and Laughter." *CTC Bulletin* 4.1 (1983).
>
> "Theology as Rumourmongering." *CTC Bulletin* 5.3-6.1 (1984/1985).
>
> "Minjung Theology and the Religion of Han." *East Asia Journal of Theology* 3.2 (1985).
>
> "Cripple's Dance." *East Asia Journal of Theology* 3.2 (1985).
>
> "Minjung, Konan ui Jong, Heemang" (*Minjung*, suffering servants, hope). *Sinhak Sasang* 51 (Winter 1985).
>
> "Minjungsoge Sungyuksin Haeya" (Incarnation into *minjung*), 15-8. In *Minjung gwa Hanguk Sinhak* (*Minjung* and Korean theology). Seoul: The Korea Theological Study Institute, 1985.

5.3.3.1.4. Suh Kwang Sun, David (1931-)

Suh Kwang Sun holds a Ph.D. in religion from Vanderbilt University and taught theology and philosophy in Ewha Womans University in Seoul. A founding member of the Korean Minjung Theology Movement, he has written numerous articles for national and international ecumenical theological journals along with books in Korean and English. He is currently director of the Asian Christian Higher Education Institute of the United Board for Christian Higher Education in Asia. From delving into Korean religious phenomena in the light of *minjung* tradition, Suh has been able to demonstrate that *minjung* theology is directly rooted in the religious tradition of the *minjung*. He has explored the *minjung* tradition in Korean Buddhist history and also discovered that shamanist traditions are a repository of cultural essence of the *minjung*. He names this "a religion of *han*."

Selected References
Works by Suh Kwang Sun

Hanguk Kidokkyo wa Jesamsekye (Korean Christianity and the Third World). Seoul: Pulbit Publication, 1981.

Theology, Ideology and Culture. Hong Kong: WSCF, Asian/Pacific Region, 1983.

Hanguk Kidokkyo ui Sae Insik (The new understanding of Korean Christianity). Seoul: The Christian Literature Society of Korea, 1985.

Bungori ui Norae (A song of the dumb: A collection of Suh Kwang-sun's sermons). Seoul: Chongusa, 1985.

Han ui Iyagi (The story of *han*). Seoul: Chungnoru, 1986.

The Korean Minjung in Christ. Hong Kong: CCA, 1991.

Kidokkyo Sinang gwa Sinhak ui Bansong (Christian faith and theological self-criticism). Seoul: Ewha Womans University Press, 1995.

Hanguk Kidokkyo Chongchi Sinhak ui Jongae (Development of Korean political theology). Seoul: Ewha Womans University Press, 1996.

—, ed. *Korea 100 Years.* Special Issue of *International Review of Mission* 74.293 (1985).

"Kyheo Pakedo Kuwon i Inna?" (Is there salvation outside the Church?). *Sinhak Sasang* 39 (Winter 1982).

"Diakonia ui Hyundaejok Uimi" (Contemporary meaning of diakonia). *Kidokkyo Sasang* 300 (June 1983).

"Han ui Saje" (The priest of *han*). *Kidokkyo Sasang* 300 (June 1983).

"Called to Witness to the Gospel Today: The Priesthood of 'Han'." *CTC Bulletin* 5.3-6.1 (1984/1985).

"Minjung gwa Sungryong (*Minjung* and the Holy Spirit), 302-318. In *Minjung gwa Hanguk Sinhak* (*Minjung* and Korean theology). Seoul: The Korea Theological Study Institute, 1985.

"Hanguk ui Minjung Sinhak" (*Minjung* theology of Korea). In *Minjung Sinhak ui Tamgu* (The search for *minjung* theology), by Suh Nam Dong. Seoul: Hankilsa, 1983.

"Shamanism and Minjung Liberation." In *Asian Christian Spirituality: Reclaiming Traditions,* edited by Virginia Fabella, Peter K. H. Lee and David Kwang-sun Suh. Maryknoll, NY: Orbis Books, 1992.

5.3.3.1.5. Kim Yong Bock (1938-)

Following doctoral studies at Princeton University, Kim Yong Bock worked with CCA URM in Tokyo, was co-director of the Christian Institute for Justice and Development, Seoul, taught theology and missiology at the Presbyterian Theological Seminary, Seoul, and was president of Hanil University, Wonju. He has been active in many national and regional ecumenical programs in urban-rural mission, conscientization and theological reorientation.

From studies of Christian mission in Korea, and of people's movements such as the *Donghak,* Kim Yong Bock became one of the early articulators of the theological and historical bases for *minjung* theology. He has particularly emphasized that the *minjung* movement is a messianic political movement and that the Christian koinonia has been the paradigmatic community, which under successive oppressions, has striven for the transformation of Korean society. It is also central to his theology that "the people are the subjects of their own historical destiny" and that their social biography is to be interpreted in the light of Jesus' own biography. In many writings in *minjung* theology and related areas, Kim has also focused on linguistic dynamics, political participation, confessions of faith, and on the role of the *minjung* in relation to Third World movements and religions.

Selected References

Works by Kim Yong Bock

> *Minjung gwa Kidokkyo* (*Minjung* and Christianity). Seoul: Hyungsongsa, 1988.
>
> *Messiah and Minjung: Christ's Solidarity with the People for New Life.* Hong Kong: CCA URM, 1992.
>
> —, ed. *Minjung Theology: People as the Subjects of History,* with Introd. by D. Preman Niles. Singapore: Christian Conference of Asia, 1981; Maryknoll, NY: Orbis Books, 1983.

Contextual Theology in Korea

"Sanup Sunkyo ui Sinhakjok Baekyung gwa Keungo" (The theological background of Urban Industrial Mission and its source). *Kidokkyo Sasang* 23.11 (1979).

"Korean Christianity as a Messianic Movement of the People." In *Minjung Theology: People as the Subjects of History,* edited by Kim Yong-Bock.

"Hanguk Minjung gwa Kidokkyo" (Korean *minjung* and Christianity). In *Hanguk Yoksa wa Kidokkyo* (Korean history and Christianity). Seoul: Hyungsong Publication, 1981; Taehan Kidokkyo Sohoe, 1983.

"Hanguk Yoksa wa Mesia Chongchi" (Korean history and Messianic politics); and "Hanguk Kyohoe ui Yoksa Chamyo Jontong" (The tradition of historical participation in the Korean church), 159-172. In *Hanguk Yoksa wa Kidokkyo* (Korean history and Christianity). Seoul: Christian Literature Society, 1983.

"Theology and the Social Biography of the Minjung." *CTC Bulletin* 5.3-6.1 (1984/85).

"Minjung Sinhak gwa Asia Sinhak" (*Minjung* theology and Asian theology). *Sinhak Sasang* 56 (Spring 1987).

"Minjung Kyohoeron Siron" (A *minjung* ecclesiology). *Sinhak Sasang* 63 (Winter 1988).

"Minjung Sinhak gwa Tochakwha Sinhak" (*Minjung* theology and indigenous theology). *Kidokkyo Sasang* 390 (June 1991).

"Minjung gwa Kwonryok" (*Minjung* and power). In *Sinhak hamyo Sarang hamyo.* Seoul: Moonhak gwa Jisongsa, 1996.

5.3.3.2. Second Generation Minjung Theologians

In the 1980s a new generation of *minjung* theologians emerged, drawing on such further resources as cultural dimensions of the *minjung* movement, Marxist thought and the democratization movement. They have both furthered the concerns of earlier *minjung* theologians and critically reflected upon their work. Significant figures have been Kang Won Don, Lee Jung Hee, Park Sung Joon and Park Jae Soon.

5.3.3.2.1. Kang Won Don

Kang Won Don has studied both theology and sociology, and has developed his theological approach through a dialogue with Marxism. This led him to study ideological issues, hermeneutics and methodology. He has also written on the *minjung* and democratic movements, on reunification and on Suh Nam Dong's theology. All articles are in Korean.

Selected References
Works by Kang Won Don
> *Mul ui Sinhak* (Theology and materialism). Seoul: The Korea Theological Study Institute, 1989.
> "New Horizon of the Theological Hermeneutics - Accommodation of Minjung Culture Movement in Minjung Theology." *Sinhak Sasang* 53 (Summer 1986).
> "On the Praxis of Christians for Overcoming the Division and Reunification of Korea." In *Logics of Transformation and Reunification.* Seoul: Sagechul, 1987.
> "Some Strategies of Korean Christians for Democratization in Korea." *Sinhak Sasang* 58 (Autumn 1987).
> "The Characters of Korean Christianity in the Perspective of the National-Democratic Movement in Korea: From the End of 3.1 Movement through the Mid 1930s." *Sinhak Sasang* (Spring 1988).
> "The Subject and Methodology of Suh Nam Dong's Theology." *Sinhak Sasang* 70 (Autumn 1990).

5.3.3.2.2. Lee Jung Hee

Lee Jung Hee was deeply involved with the *minjung* culture movement and his theological imagination is rooted in the encounter of the Jesus movement and the Korean *minjung* movement for cultural liberation. His writings have included studies of the liberative elements of biblical, cultural and religious sources, along with papers on spirituality, eschatology and political imagery. All writings but the 1992a article are in Korean.

Selected References
Works by Lee Jung Hee
> *Salim ui Sangsangryuk* (Imagination of living). Seoul: Dasankeulbang, 1992.
> "The Book of Revelation and Minjung." *Sinhak Sasang* 58 (Autumn 1987).
> "Confluence of the Liberating Culture in the Bible and Minjung Culture." *Sinhak Sasang* 60 (Spring 1988).

"Cultural Strategy of Minjung Theology for the Establishment of Liberating Culture." *Sinhak Sasang* 79 (Autumn 1992).

"Political Imagination of Shamanism." In *Hanguk Jongkyo wa Hanguk Sinhak* (Korean religions and Korean theology). Seoul: The Korea Theological Study Institute, 1992.

"Liberation Spirituality in Dae-dong Gut." In *Asian Christian Spirituality: Reclaiming Tradition,* edited by Virginia Fabella, Peter K. H. Lee, and David Kwang-sun Suh. Maryknoll, NY: Orbis Books, 1992a.

"There is No Minjung Language, There is No Minjung Era." *Sinhak Sasang* 81 (Summer 1993).

"Let's Play for a Happy Event of This House: A Shamanistic Worldview." In *Song Kee Deuk Hoegap Kinyum Nonmunjip* (Essays in celebration of Song Kee Deuk's sixtieth birthday). Seoul: The Korea Theological Study Institute, 1993.

"The Eclipse of God." *Sidae wa Minjung Sinhak* 4 (1997).

"Eschatology and Violence." *Jinbo Pyungron* 5 (Autumn 2000).

5.3.3.2.3. Park Jae Soon

Park Jae Soon was initially influenced by an indigenized Christian movement which inherited traditional *minjung* thought. His strong involvement in the democratization movement led to his frequent imprisonment which caused him severe physical harm. Nevertheless Park has been articulating major theological themes in a series of books as well as in articles which arise from the *minjung* context, and are written in *minjung* language. He has been concerned to relate *minjung* theological tasks and method to national and cultural movements, the Jesus movement and the church, and to Christian doctrines of the Messiah, the Cross and redemption. A major study presents the communal, "life-restoration" and table-fellowship dimensions of the Jesus movement in the context of both Israel and of contemporary Korea. Most of his writings are in Korean.

Selected References

Works by Park Jae Soon

Yesu Undong gwa Babsang Kondongche (Jesus Movement and dining table community). Seoul: Chunji Publication, 1988.

Juche Sasang gwa Minjung Sinhak (Juche thought and *minjung* theology). Seoul: Pulbit, 1989.

Minjung Sinhak gwa Ssial Sasang (*Minjung* theology and traditional *minjung* thought). Seoul: Chonji Publication, 1990.

Yollin Sahoerul wihan Minjung Sinhak (*Minjung* theology for the open society). Seoul: Hanul, 1995.

"Minjung Culture Movement and Korean Church." *Sinhak Sasang* 53 (Summer 1986).

"Ssial Thought and Minjung Theology." *Sinhak Sasang* 66 (Autumn 1989).

"Minjung Theology and the National Theology." *Sinhak Sasang* 81 (Summer 1993).

"The Basic Concepts and Methodology of Minjung National Theology." *Sinhak Sasang* 84 (Spring 1994).

"A Dogmatic Retrospect and Prospect of Minjung Theology: In terms of Minjung's Suffering and Resurrection." In *Minjung Sinhak Ibmoon* (Introduction of *minjung* theology). Seoul: Hanul, 1995.

"A Theological Study on Minjung Messiah." In *Minjung eun Mesia inga* (Is *Minjung* the Messiah?). Seoul: Hanul, 1995.

"The Cross - From Death to Living Together." *Kidokkyo Sasang* (March 1996).

"Minjung Redemption and Justification by Faith." *Kidokkyo Sasang* (December 1997).

"Jesus Movement and Korean Theology." In *Jiguwha Sidae ui Hanguk Sinhak* (Korean theology in globalization). Seoul: Hanbit, 1997.

"Minjung Theological Understanding on the Seeds." In *Minjung ui Sahoejonkiwa Kidokkyo ui Mirae* (Socio-biography of *minjung* and the future of Christianity). Seoul: The Korea Theological Study Institute, 1998.

5.3.3.2.4. Park Sung Joon

Park Sung Joon earned his doctorate in theology from Rikkyo University in Tokyo, studied at Union Theological Seminary and later joined the Pendle Hill Quaker community in Pennsylvania. He had previously lost parents and siblings during the Korean War, survived by working as an errand boy and, by self-study, qualified for university. While studying economics in Seoul National University he organized "The Economic Welfare Society" (EWS), a Christian student organization, from which many social activists and civil movement leaders later emerged in the 70s and 80s. The curriculum of the organization extended to history, theology and social sciences, including Marxist theories. During a long imprisonment (1968-1982) he studied theology. He then worked as research staff of KTSI (Korea Theological Study Institute) and later continued his theological study in Japan while working as assistant director for Tomisaka Christian Center.

Park Sung Joon has led *minjung* theology study groups for theologians in Korea and Japan, written a number of key documents on *minjung* theology and now teaches *Minjung* Theology and Peace Studies at Sung-Kong-Hoe University. He expounds his *minjung* theology drawing on his prison experiences as well as his life experience as a member of the *minjung*. "I am trying to contribute to the development of Minjung theology in 21st Century," he writes, "by searching for and adding a spiritual dimension to it." He also chairs the movements "A School On the Move" and "Nonviolent Peacewave." His series of twelve articles on *minjung* theology appeared in *Fukuin-to-Sekai* (The Gospel and The World): from June 1996, to September1997.

Selected References:
Works by Park Sung Joon
> *Review of Minjung Theology on the Threshold of the 21st Century - Seeking a new horizon for the understanding of 'Minjung'* (in English). Mimeo'd. Tolyo: 1999.
> *The Formation and Development of Minjung Theology in 1970s and 1980s* (in Japanese). Tokyo: Shinkyo Shuppansha, 1997.
> *Vitality of East Asian Christianity: Challenges To Mission and Theology in Japan* (in Japanese). Tokyo: Japan: Shinkyo Shuppansha, 1997.
> "Re-examining A Theology of Minjung - In pursuit of a new horizon in the understanding of 'minjung'." In *Mission and Theology in East Asia* (Japanese and English versions). Edited by Park Sung Joon and Yoshida Megumi (Tokyo: Shinkyo Shuppansha). Forthcoming.

5.3.3.3. Third Generation of Minjung Theology - Protestant
In the 1990s a new generation of *minjung* theologians has emerged within the rapidly changing social conditions of Korea. They are now grouped with the Christian Institute for the 3rd Era. Despite

differences in social, theological or inter-faith commitment, this generation pays special attention to the processes of resistance and obedience as these are manipulated in Korean society. They believe that the necessary theological steps now involve deeper sociopolitical criticism which includes critical analysis of the key historical *minjung* events of the previous century, as well as of the distortions of popular resistance movements for the maintenance of conservative centers of power. This leads to an analysis of power processes in every dimension of daily life and especially in all mass media, and also to a 'deconstruction' of the confining powers of government, commercial and church institutions in daily microexperience. The *minjung* are now, therefore, to be understood as those who maintain a "resistance consciousness" to continuing abuse of authority and wealth. These theologians also recognize that on the macro level the socio-political processes by which obedience or resistance are maintained require both analysis and reconstruction in an era when former concepts of "God's omnipresent power" no longer function. The third generation *minjung* theologian defines such a theoretical reconstruction as the development of 'Cultural-Politics' shaped by the *minjung*'s lived theology.

5.3.3.3.1. Choi Hyeong Mook (1961-)

Choi Hyeong Mook had first contributed to the development of the second generation of *minjung* theology in the 1980s as a student, writing on important problems, especially concerning Marxism and Christianity. In addition to these his attention later moved to include not only the tasks and future of *minjung* theology, but also biblical studies, biblical hermeneutics, the character of liberating communities and theological reflection upon political and economic problems - including political ethics, foreign labor, the homeless, economic justice in the time of globalization, jubilee and the rights of women. All writings below are in Korean.

Selected References
Works by Choi Hyeong Mook
> *Sahoe Byonhyok Undong gwa Kidokkyo Sinhak* (Social revolution and Christian theology). Seoul: Nathan Chulpansa, 1992.

Minjung Sinhak gwa Jongchi Kyongje (*Minjung* theology and political economy). Seoul: Dasankeulbang, 1999.

"The Developing Succession and Prospect of Minjung Theology." *Hanguk Kidok Chongnyun Hyubuihoe Hoebo* 86.1 (1986).

"Korean Christian Theology in Revolutionary Times." In *Sinhak gwa Silchon II* (Theology and Praxis II), edited by KSCF. Seoul: Minjungsa, 1988.

"Methods of Biblical Interpretation in Korean Minjung Communities." *Sinhak Sasang* 63 (Winter 1988).

"Ideological Questions of Minjung Theology - Social Alternative of Minjung Theology." In *Yesu, Minjok, Minjung* (Jesus, national people, and *minjung*). Seoul: The Korea Theological Study Institute, 1992.

"Toward a Political-Economical Ethics in Minjung Theology I." *Sinhak Sasang* 83 (Winter 1993).

"Times of Minjung - Reality of Transformation and Theological Tasks." *Sidae wa Minjung Sinhak* 2 (1995).

"Minjung Theology." In *Kidokkyo Baekkwa Sajon* (The Christian encylopaedia). Seoul: Kidok Kyomunsa, 1996. (A new edition revised and enlarged).

"Tradition and Minjung Theology." *Sidae wa Minjung Sinhak* 4 (1997).

"Some Issues of 1990's Minjung Theology." In *Minjung ui Sahoe Jonki wa Kidokkyo ui Mirae* (Social biography of *minjung* and future of Christianity). Seoul: The Korea Theological Study Institute, 1998.

"Minjung Theology and God's Kingdom - Human Life against Efficiency of Capital." In *Hananim Nara, geu Haesok gwa Silchon* (God's Kingdom, its interpretation and praxis). Seoul: The Korea Theological Study Institute, 2000.

— (co-author). *Hamke irknun Kuyak Songso* (Reading the Old Testament together). Seoul: The Korea Theological Study Institute, 1991.

5.3.3.3.2. Kim Jin Ho (1962-)

Kim Jin Ho graduated from Sogang (1985) and Hanshin (1990) universities and has combined the pastorate of a *minjung* congregation with continued theological study, writing and animation. He is a central figure in the Christian Institute for the 3rd Era and has concentrated on the reinterpretation of *minjung* theology in the setting of cultural-politics since the early 1990s.

He has also initiated studies of "the historical Jesus in Korea," and promoted 'the Christianity of no-Church' in this study. He has also dialogued with critical humanists and social scientists in Korea, and is insisting on the recovery of theology within a daily praxis. Among scores of writings are included those on Ahn Byung Mu's theory of *ochlos*; on the biblical foundations, genealogy and Messiahology of *minjung* theology; on 'post-scriptural' and deconstructed biblical approaches; on the social history of the Jesus movements and alternative Christian movements; and on ideology, justice and politico-economic praxis in the time of globalization, neo-liberalism and hoped-for reunification. All writings below are in Korean.

Selected References
Works by Kim Jin Ho

Silchun jok Kristo rul Yuhayo (Christianity toward praxis). Seoul: Nathan Chulpansa, 1992.

"The Eschatology in the Old Testament Apocalyptics. An Essay from the Perspective of the Class Theory." *Sinhak Sasang* 74 (Fall 1991).

"Minjung as the Subject of History - A Reappraisal on 'Minjung' of Minjung Theology." *Sinhak Sasang* 80 (Spring 1993).

"The 'Crisisology' of Minjung theology reflects the Poverty of the Theory of Praxis!" *Iron* (The Theory) 8 (Spring 1994).

"For the Horizontal Extension of Minjung Theology toward Cultural-Politics." *Sidae wa Minjung Sinhak* 3 (1996).

"Beyond Triumphalism, Toward Restoration of Jesus." *Dangdae Bipyong* (Contemporary Criticism) 8 (Fall 1999).

"The Bible, Reading again - In Search of the Post-Scriptural Reading." *Jinbo Pyungron* 3 (Spring 2000).

"Reading Bible as Understanding Our Contemporary Minjung-Event - A Critique of Chung Yon-bok's Book 'Beautiful Human, Beautiful God'." *Sidae wa Minjung Sinhak* 6 (2000).

"Jesus Movement and the Other Minjung Movements of Palestine in the First Century A.D. - From the Viewpoint of the Theory of Social Movement." In *Hananim Nara - geu Haesok gwa Silchon* (The Kingdom of God - the hermeneutics and praxis). Seoul: The Korea Theological Study Institute, 2000.

—, ed. *Yesu Rnessans - Yoksa ui Yesu Yonku ui Saeroun Jipyung* (Jesus Renaissance - the new horizon of the historical study on Jesus). Chunahn: The Korea Theological Study Institute, 1996.

— (co-author). *Hamke irknun Kuyak Songso* (Reading the Old Testament together). Seoul: The Korea Theological Study Institute, 1991.

— (co-author). *Hamke irknun Sinyak Songso* (Reading the New Testament together). Seoul: The Korea Theological Study Institute, 1991.

6 Women Doing Theology - Theological Movements from mid-20th Century 2

6.1 Women Doing Theology - Protestant 2

In the late 1970s feminist consciousness increased, and the ecumenical movement began to include the leadership of women. In Ewha Womans University in 1975 an elective course on "Feminist Study" was introduced to present feminist issues as academic issues, and this led to the establishment of the Institute of Feminist Studies, the first of such institutes in Korea. In the early 1980s the Korean Association of Women Theologians (KAWT, see 6.1.10.2.) was formed. Church Women United and the Institute for Korean Feminist Theology followed; Korea Women Church began its activities in 1989, and in the 1990s the Association of Feminist Theology (see 6.1.10.3.) developed within the Korean Association of Christian Studies. Along with associations of women ministers and many other groups and associations, these networks have been concerned to support and enhance the role of women theologians in Korea, and also to promote indigenous Korean women's theology. An important methodology for Korean women in such work is that of *hyun jang*, which commences with the concrete issues of everyday life and includes social analysis and Bible study, leading to critical theological reflection.

Important women writers in these movements include Choi Man Ja, Choi Young Sil, Chung Hyun Kyung, Kang Nam Soon, Kim Ae Young, Kim Yoon Ok, Lee Kyung Sook, Lee Oo Chung, Lee Un Sun, Lee Park Sun Ai, Park Kyung Mi, Park Soon Kyung and Sohn Seung Hee (for these see below). Among many others who have published theological reflection (selected below) should be noted Ahn Sang Nim, Kim Myoung Chin, Kim Young Hee, Sook Ja Chung, Young Sook Park, Yong Ja Kim, Kim Young (Sawa), Han Kuk Yeum, Kim Jeong Soo, Yoo Cheun Ja, Kim Myong Hi, Sun Soon Hwa, Cho Wha Soon, Han Mi Ra and Pak Song Ja. Most of their writings have of course appeared in Korean-language journals, of which there is a very large number, along with a smaller number of English-language journals (see 7.3.2.; 7.4). Most accessible is the international journal *In God's Image*, founded by Sun Ai Lee Park and colleagues (See 6.1.3. and also vol. 1, chap. 3), which issues special Korean volumes (see for example 11.2, 1992; 15.2, 1996; 18.3, 1999) and also regularly publishes the articles and poetry of Korean women.

For the particular writings of selected theologians see entries below.

Selected References

Ahn Sang-nim. "Feminist Theology in the Korean Church." *In God's Image* (June, 1988).

—. "Doing Theology with God's Purpose in Korea." In *Doing Theology with God's Purpose in Asia*, edited by Yeow Choo Lak and John C. England. Singapore: *ATESEA Occasional Papers* 10 (1990).

—. *Sung Shinhak Yiyaki* (The story of feminist theology). Seoul: Kidokkyo Seo Hoe (CLSIC), 1992.

Chang Sang. "Mission and Competence of Church Women in Korea." *In God's Image* (Dec.1985/Feb. 1986).

Cho Wha Soon. *Let the Weak be Strong. A Woman's Struggle for Justice*. Bloomington: Meyer Stone Books, 1988.

Chung Hyun Kyung. *Struggle to be the Sun Again: Introducing Asian Women's Theology*. Maryknoll, NY: Orbis Books, c1990.

Dong Joo-lee. "A Study of Hinduism for Indigenisation of the Gospel." *Korea Journal of Theology* 1 (1995).

'Han' Theology in a Divided World - Struggle for Food, Justice and Freedom. A Collection of Papers and Discussions of the Northeast Asia Subregional Women's Consultation (Kwangju-Korea, 1989). Hong Kong: CCA Women's Concerns, 1991.

Han'guk Kidokkyo Hakhoe (Korean Association of Christian Studies). *Yosong sinhak kwa han'guk kyohoe* (Feminist theology and Korean church) (in Korean and English). Ch'onan-si: Han'guk Sinhak Yon'guso, 1997.

Han'guk Yosinhakja Hyopuihoe. *Hamkke ch'amyohanun yosong sinhak* (Doing feminist theology together). Seoul: Taehan Kidokkyo Sohoe, 1991.

Han Kuk-yeum. "Jubilee and Ecofeminist Theology." *In God's Image* 14.3 (1995).

Han Yuk-yom. "Mariology as a Base for Feminist Liberation Theology." In *Asian Women Doing Theology,* edited by Dulcie Abraham et al. Hong Kong: AWRCCT, 1989.

Kim, Marion Kennedy, ed. *Once I had a Dream: Stories told by Korean Women Minjung.* Hong Kong: DAGA, 1992.

Kim Myoung Chin (Mrs). "A Mother's Prayer." In *Testimonies of Faith in Korea.* Geneva: WARC, 1989.

Kim Young (Sawa). "My Journey in Mission: a Korean-Japanese Woman Pastor's Story." *Missiology* 15 (1987).

—. "Searching for the Lost Coin." *In God's Image* 11.2 (1992).

Kim Young-hee. "Theological Reflection on the Situation of the Urban Poor." *In God's Image* (April, 1985).

Lee Oo Jung. *In Search for Our Foremothers' Spirituality.* Seoul: AWRCCT, 1994.

Lee, Maria In-bok. *Joy Where there is Sadness.* Seoul: Woo Jin Publishing, 1994.

Lim Hee Sook. "Two Bible Studies; Eve as Mother of Life; Magnificat." *CTC Bulletin* 9.2&3 (1990).

Sun Soon Hwa. "Women Ministers and the Oppressed in Korea: the Meaning of their Ministry for Theology and Social Change." *In God's Image* 11.2 (1992).

6.1.1. Park Soon Kyung (1923-)

Park Soon Kyung studied at Seoul University (B.A.), Emory University (B.D.), and Systemic Theology at Drew University (Ph.D.). She was professor of Christian studies at Ewha Womans University (1966-88) and has been vice-president of the Union of National and Democratic Unification Committee, the first president of the Korean Association of Feminist Theology, and is the present dean of the Meetings for Peaceful Reunification. While drawing on neo-orthodox theologies she also articulates new meanings of Christ, church, humanity and creation. She also presents a "new theological methodology from Korean women's perspective" (Chung, c1990). Her writings address issues from all her major involvements, as well as the relationship between Korean women's struggle and that of other 'third' world peoples.

Selected References
Works by Park Soon Kyung
> *The Korean Nation and the Task of Women's Theology*. Seoul: Daihan Keedokyo Suhwhe, 1983.
> *The Kingdom of God and the Future of the Nation* (in Korean). Seoul: Korean Christian Books Press, 1983.
> *National Reunification and Christianity* (in Korean). Seoul: Han Kil Press, 1986.
> *The Suffering and Triumph of Unification Theology* (in Korean). Seoul: Han-Ul, 1992.
> *The Future of Theology for Unification* (in Korean). Seoul: Sa-Gue Press, 1997.
> *Feminist Theology, Church Reform, Social Transformation, Korean Feminist Theology* (in Korean). Seoul: KAWT, 2000.
> "Position Paper of the Korean Women's Theological Consultation." *In God's Image* (April 1985).
> "Reunification of Korea and the Task of Korean Feminist Theology." *In God's Image* (June 1988).
> "National Reunification and Minjung Theology - Toward a New Development of Minjung Theology." *Theological Thought* (Spring 1993).
> "Discourse on Minjok-Minjung Theology" (in Korean). *Theological Thought* 83 (1993).
> "Suffering and Jubilee of the Nation." *Theological Thought* 89 (1995).
> Chung Hyun Kyung. *Struggle to be the Sun Again: Introducing Asian Women's Theology*. Maryknoll, NY: Orbis Books, c1990.

6.1.2. Lee Oo Chung (1923-)

Following studies at Hanshin University, Seoul, and Emmanuel College, University of Toronto, Lee Oo Chung taught at Hanshin University and Seoul Women's University. She has been president of Korean Church Women United and also of the Korean Association of Women Theologians and vice-president of the WCC

Contextual Theology in Korea 575

World Mission Committee. In the AWRCCT she has coordinated and edited writing projects and written on women's history, spirituality and theology within the context of Korea's traditional and modern cultures. Here her major concerns include the development of women's aware action in politics and as leaders of social change, for reform, peace and social justice. Her biblical studies have appeared in a number of journals.

Selected References
Works by Lee Oo Chung

> *Traces of Korean Christian Women's Centenary* (in Korean). Seoul: Minjung Press, 1985.
> *In Search for our Foremothers' Spirituality.* Seoul. AWRCCT, 1994.
> "Our Context and Feminist Theology" (in Korean). In *Women's Theology and Humanization*, edited by KAWT. Seoul: KAWT, 1987
> "The Concept of Shalom in Old Testament." In *Women of Courage: Asian Women Reading the Bible,* edited by Lee Oo-chung et al. Seoul: AWRC, 1988.
> "Bible Study on Peace and Unification." *In God's Image* (June 1988).
> "Feminist Theological Hermeneutic of Peace and Unification" (in Korean). Korean Feminist Theology and National Unification. Seoul: KAWT, 1989.
> "Korean Traditional Culture and Feminist Theology" (in Korean). In *The Task of Korean Women's Theology.* Seoul: KAWT, 1985.

6.1.3. Lee Park Sun Ai (d. 1999)

Lee Park graduated from Yonsei University, completed postgraduate study at Emory University (USA), and was ordained minister by the Disciples of Christ. Already known as a poet and theologian, she undertook women's studies and human rights projects while living in Singapore and there founded, with colleagues, the journal *In God's Image* and later the Asian Women's Resource Centre for Culture and Theology. These have played a seminal role in women's theology both in Korea and in the region as a whole.

In her writings Lee Park presents the struggles of Asian women and the resources in both theology and culture which are available to them, moving freely from biblical study to events of national history and the concrete details of women's life. In theological method she insists first on seeing these details; then on analysis of the structures which oppress women; full study of the transformed roles which Jesus brought, and brings, to women; and then social and theological reflection on the eschatological marks of Jesus' life that are already promised in women's lived experiences.

Selected References
Works by Park Sun Ai Lee

"Asian Women's Theological Reflection." *East Asia Journal of Theology* 3.2 (1985).

"Understanding the Bible from Women's Perspective." *In God's Image* (Dec.1986).

"Envisioning a Future Church as an Asian Woman." Osaka: mimeo'd, 1990.

"The Forbidden Tree and the Year of the Lord." *In God's Image* 11.3 (1992).

—, and Virginia Fabella, eds. *We Dare to Dream: Doing Theology as Asian Women*. Hong Kong: AWRCCT; Manila: EATWOT, 1989.

Choi Man Ja. "The Herstory of the Rev. Sun Ai Lee-Park." *In God's Image* - Special Issue Celebrating the Life and Ministry of Sun Ai - 18.3 (1999).

Chung Hyun Kyung. *Struggle to be the Sun Again: Introducing Asian Women's Theology*. Maryknoll, NY: Orbis Books, c1990.

6.1.4. Choi Man Ja (1943-)

Following study at the United Theological School of Yonsei (M.A.) and at San Francisco Theological Seminary (D.Min.), Choi Man Ja taught at Ewha Womans University, the Episcopal University and the Korean Association of Women Theologians. She has also been first president of the Institution of Asian Feminist Theological Education, president of Korean Feminist Academy, coordinating team member for the Asian Women's Resource Centre for Culture and Theology and vice-president of the Theological Academy of

Korean NCC. From early concern for biblical and feminist theology, Choi has come to teach, write and mobilize in a wide area of women's theological concerns, including Christology, methodology and spirituality. She has also recently written on the relation between the Bible and other religious traditions, on tools to interpret the Bible and on post-colonial hermeneutics.

Selected References
Works by Choi Man Ja
   New Heaven New Earth New Women (in Korean). Seoul: Biblical Life Press, 1992.
   "Feminist Christology." In *Asian Women Doing Theology, Asian Women's Resource Centre for Culture and Theology*, edited by Dulcie Abraham et al. Singapore: AWRCCT, 1987.
   "Feminine Images of God in Korean Traditional Religion." *In God's Image* (June 1989).
   "Asian Feminist Theology and Its Method." In *Journey for Life and Liberation* (in Korean). Asian Christian Women and Cultural Studies. Seoul: Korean Christian Books Press, 1999.
   "For the Culture of the Subjective Church Women in 21st Century" (in Korean). *Christian Thought* (1999).
   "Korean Christian Tradition and Spirituality of Women" (in Korean). *Spirituality and Feminist Theology* (1999).
   "Understanding of Sexuality in a Feminist Theology" (in Korean). *Christian Thought* (1996).
   "Journey for Survival and Liberation. Attributes and Methodology of Asian Feminist Theology." *In God's Image* 18.3 (1999).

6.1.5. Chung Hyun Kyung (1956-)

Chung Hyun Kyung studied at Ewha Womans University, at Claremont Theological Seminary, and undertook her Ph.D. work in feminist theology at Union Theological Seminary, New York. She has been professor of Christian studies in Ewha Womans University and is currently professor at Union Theological Seminary. Apart from addressing particular issues for Korean women's and men's theology such as pluralism, *minjung* theology, koinonia and pneumatology, Chung has surveyed types of women's theology and the history and concerns of Asian women's theology. Here she presents fully the effective methodology that combines storytelling, critical awareness, biblical and theological reflection. And in these she calls for openness to the compassionate Holy Spirit so that through metanoia we may change to "Life centrism, the habit of interconnection and the culture of life."

Selected References
Works by Chung Hyun Kyung
> *Struggle to be the Sun Again: Introducing Asian Women's Theology.* Maryknoll, NY: Orbis Books, c1990.
> "Your Comfort vs. My Death: A Korean Women's Reflection on Military Sexual Slavery by Japan." In *Min Jung Theology*, Chunan: Institute of Korean Theology Press, 1995.
> "Woman, Mission, and Pluralism: What is the Problem?" *Christian Thought 425* (1994).
> "Minjung Theology and Koinonia in Life" (in Korean). *Theological Thought* 83 (1993).
> "Come Holy Spirit, Renew the Whole Creation." *In God's Image* 11.3 (1992).
> "Welcome the Spirit; Hear Her Cries: The Holy Spirit, Creation, and the Culture of Life." *Christianity and Crisis* 51.10-11 (1991).
> "Korean Feminist Theology and Minjung Theology." *International Symposium Materials of Korean Minjung Theology*, 1992.
> "Types of Women's Theology & Some Critical Reflection to the Reception in Korean Content). *Christian Thought* 11 (1989); 1 (1990).
> "Han-pu-ri: Doing theology from Korean Women's Perspective." In *We Dare to Dream: Doing Theology as Asian Women*, edited by Virginia Fabella and Sun Ai Lee Park.
> Thomson, Heather. "In the Basement of a Broken Building. Chung Hyun Kyung and Asian Feminist Theology." *Eremos Supplement* 16 (1994).

6.1.6. Park Kyung Mi (1959-)

Park Kyung Mi has specialized in New Testament studies, gained her Ph.D. from Ewha Womans University and is now New Testament professor of Christian studies at Ewha University. Along with particular biblical studies she has written on feminist interpretation of the Bible, the social setting of New Testament writings and on the coming challenges for Asian feminist theology.

This she believes must develop as a "theology of life," cultivate communal views of human life and render inviolable dignity to the human person. Drawing on the thought of Choe Che U (founder of the *Donghak*), on Ham Sok Hon (see 5.3.2.2.), Kim Chi Ha (see 5.2.3.10.) and on interdisciplinary studies, Park calls for a return to self-emptying, solitude and service. This will involve, she believes, a new feminine asceticism in both social and religious contexts by which women reshape society through new levels of social cooperation, justice and creativity.

Selected References
Works by Park Kyung Mi
> *New Heaven, New Earth, New Woman* (in Korean). Seoul: Biblical Life Press, 1992.
> "Women under the Cross" (in Korean). *Biblical Life* (March 1990).
> "Genealogy and Women." In *Women of Courage: Asian Women Reading the Bible*. Seoul: AWRC, 1992.
> "Rachel Wailing." *In God's Image* 12.4 (1993).
> "The Meaning of Paul's use of 'Soma' for Human and Nature's Common Things" (in Korean). *Korean Feminist Theology* 14 (1993).
> "Come, Spirit of Creator! Korean Church and Feministic Interpretation of Bible" (in Korean). *Christian Thought* (Feb.1998).
> "Process of Patriarchy of the Early Church and Household Codes in the Pastoral Epistles" (in Korean). *Theological Thought* 102 (1998).
> "The Korean Church and Feminist Biblical Interpretation" (in Korean). *Journey for Life and Liberation* (1999).
> "A Preview of Challenges for Asian Feminist Theology in the 21st Century." In *PTCA Convocation 2000 Handbook*, edited by Salvador Martinez. Chiangmai: PTCA, 2000.

6.1.7. Kang Nam Soon

Kang Nam Soon studied theology at Methodist Theological Seminary, Seoul, Bonn University and Drew University (Ph.D.). She is adjunct professor of Methodist Theological Seminary in Seoul and San Francisco Theological Seminary, USA, dean of the Program for Theology and Cultures in Asia (PTCA) and has been visiting professor at Cambridge University, England. Along with concerns for feminist theology and ministries, Kang has also written on inclusive theologies, post-colonial discourse and the contradictions within Asian feminist theology. Here she is concerned to analyze the structures which support patriarchal ideology, even within the advocacy for Asian identity and post-colonial endeavors. Kang then describes the goal for Asian feminist theology as "humanism-feminism" which is directed towards the realization of the common humanization of women and men. A final outcome of such endeavors would then be the dismantling of feminist theology.

Selected References
Works by Kang Nam Soon

> *Contemporary Feminist Theology* (in Korean). Seoul: Christian Literature Society, 1994.
>
> *Feminism and Christianity* (in Korean). Seoul: Christian Literature Society, 1998.
>
> "Ecumenical Feminist Theology" (in Korean). *Theology and Korean Church* (1997).
>
> "A Bridge of Inclusiveness of Gender, Race, and Culture: Constructing a Theology of Inclusiveness." *Quarterly Review* (Summer 2000).
>
> "Terrorism of Truth?: The Challenge of Postmodernism and Its Implication for Religion in the New Millennium." *Journal of Korean Christianity* 17 (2000).
>
> "Journey Without Map: Multiple Paradigms of Feminist Ministry Moving Beyond Feminine Ministry" (in Korean). *Women and Ministry* (Summer 2000).

6.1.8. Choi Young Sil

Choi Young Sil, has specialized in New Testament/feminist theology, graduating from Ewha Womans University (Ph.D.). She is also pastor of the Episcopal University, president of the Institute for Korean Theology and president of the Korean Feminist Academy. Along with feminist and hermeneutic studies of New Testament women and theology, Choi has written on women in church history, on aspects of Korean women's experience, and also on the potential within *han* and within Jubilee.

Selected References
Works by Choi Young Sil

Women of the New Testament (in Korean). Seoul: Korean Christian Books Press, 1997.

"Jubilee in Realization from a Perspective of the New Testament - Centered around the Accounts of Luke. *Christian Thought* 72 (1991).

"Korean Feminist Theology from the Biblical Perspective (I and II)" (in Korean). *Christian Thought* (1992).

"The Early Christian Women's Ministry as a Cornerstone" (in Korean). In *Feminist Theology and Korean Church*. Korean Christian Theological Discourse 14. Seoul: Institute of Korean Theological Studies Press, 1997.

"Korean Feminist Theology Blossoming out of the Abyss of 'Han'" (in Korean). *Theological Thought* 100 (1998).

"Peace of Jesus in the Gospel of John" (in Korean). *Theological Thought* 107 (1999).

"Hermeneutic Model of the New Testament - From the Perspective of Korean Women's Experience" (in Korean). *Journey for Life and Liberation* (1999).

6.1.9. Other Contextual Women Theologians - Protestant

A further selection of women doing theology would include Sohn Seung Hee, Lee Kyung Sook, Kim Yoon Ok, Lee Un Sunn and Kim Ae Young.

Sohn Seung Hee has studied Christian education and feminist theology at Ewha Womans University (Ph.D.) and is now professor there, dean of the Feminist Theological Academy and president of the Korean Association of Feminist Theologians. Her writings include studies of feminist theology, philosophy and spirituality.

Lee Kyung Sook studied at Ewha Womans University and pursued studies in Old Testament at Göttingen University (D.Theol.). She is now a professor at Mok-Won University, and concurrently also professor of Ewha Womans University. There she is also dean of the College of Humanities and dean of Ewha Institute for Women's Theological Studies. Her writings include biblical, hermeneutic and liberation studies.

Kim Yoon Ok studied at Suk-Myung University, at Han-Shil Theological Seminary and also at Goethe University, Germany. She is coordinator of the Committee of Christian Presbyterians, co-representative of the Committee of Korean Feminist Theologians and of the Committee of Peaceful Women. She has written on feminist theology in relation to experience and history.

Lee Un Sun's studies in theology and in education were at Ewha, at Methodist Theological Seminary, at Sung Kyun Kwan University and at Basel University (D.Theol.). She has been visiting professor at Northwestern University (USA), and at present is professor of the philosophy of education at Sejong University, Korea. Her writings relate feminist theology to Confucian, post-modern and ecological issues.

Kim Ae Young studied at Hanshin Theological Seminary and Ewha Womans University (Ph.D.). She is now professor of feminist theology at Hanshin University, associate pastor of An-Yang Sae-Bit Church and co-representative of the Committee of Korean Feminist Theologians. Her writings consider life-community, globalization and national unification.

Selected References

Sohn Seung-Hee. *Korean Religion and Women's Studies* (in Korean). Seoul: Ewha Institute of Korean Culture Studies Press, 1984.

—. *Understanding of Feminist Theology* (in Korean). Seoul: Institute of Korean Theological Studies Press, 1989.

—. "Korean Church and Women's Spirituality." *Korean Church and Spirituality* (1988).

—. "Church Women and Healing" (in Korean). *Christian Thought* (Oct. 1996).

—. "Feminist Theology and Korean Church" (in Korean). In *Feminist Theology and Korean Church*. Korean Christian Theological Discourse 14. Seoul: Institute of Korean Theological Studies Press, 1997.

—. "Woman and Moral Subjectivity: Woman and Philosophy" (in Korean). *Philosophy and Reality* (March 1997).

Lee Kyung Sook. *Women in the Old Testament* (in Korean). Seoul: Korean Christian Press, 1994.

—. *Christianity and the World* (in Korean). Seoul: Ewha Womans Univ. Press, 1996.
—. *God, History and Women in the Old Testament* (in Korean). Seoul: Korean Christian Books Press, 2000.
—. "Liberation of Women and Biblical Interpretation" (in Korean). *Doing Theology with Love: In Honor of Dr. David Kwang-Sun Suh*. Seoul: Moonhak-kwa Jisung Press, 1996.
—. "Hermeneutic Task of a Feminist Theology in Asia" (in Korean). *Christian Thought* 453 (1996).
—. "The Concept of Church as the Community of YWHW" (in Korean). *Church and Feminist Theology* (1997).
—. "The Resurrection of New Millennium Conquers the Culture of Death" (in Korean). *Christian Thought* 496 (2000).
Kim Yoon Ok. "Church and Church Women" (in Korean). *Peacemaking Women* (1992).
—. "Feminist Theological Reflection on Korean Christian Women's Experience." *Experience of Korean Women* (1994).
—. "Criticism of Korean Preaching from the Feminist Perspective" (in Korean). *The Church and Feminist Theology* (1997).
—. "Ecological Feminist Theology" (in Korean). *Woman, Peace, and Life* (1993).
—. "Korean Church Women's Movement since 1970s" (in Korean). *Journey for Life and Liberation* (1999).
Lee Un Sun. *Korean Feminist Theology in Postmodern Era* (in Korean). Wae-Kwan: Bun Do Press, 1997.
—. "Postmodernism, Asian Thoughts and Feminism" (in Korean). *Thought of Christianity* (May 1991).
—. "What to say a Korean Ecofeminist Theologian" (in Korean). *Thought of Christianity* (Jan. 1996).
—. "Confucianism and Feminism in Korea." *In God's Image* 18.3 (1999).
—. "Korean Feminist Theologians' God-Talk - Its Diversity and Perspectives" (in Korean). *Journey for Life and Liberation* (1999).
—. "On Religion in the New Millennium World" (in Korean). *Theological Thought* (Spring 2000).
Kim Ae Young. *The Horizon of Korean Feminist Theology* (in Korean). Seoul: Han-Ul Press, 1995.
—. "National Unification and Women." *Christian Thought* 376 (1990).
—. "Feminist Theological Approach of Family in Globalization" (in Korean). *Christian Thought* (July, 1997).

———. "Regeneration toward Life Community and the Mother Holy Spirit" (in Korean). *Christian Thought* (May 1999).
———. "Cultural Transition and Discourse of Nation, Family, and Woman" (in Korean). *Korean Feminist Theology* (Summer 1999).

6.1.10. Women's Theological Institutes/Associations - Protestant

A selection of the more important of these would include - along with such others as the Korean Feminist Theology Academy, the Institute of Asian Christian Women's Culture and the AWRCCT - Korean Church Women United, the Korean Association of Women Theologians, the Korean Association of Feminist Theology, Korean Association of Christian Women For Women Minjung, Korea Women Church and the Ewha Institute for Women's Theological Studies.

6.1.10.1. Korean Church Women United (KCWU - 1967)

KCWU's aims include the building of unity and reconciliation among church women from different denominations, cooperation in social mission and church reformation within Korea and globally. KCWU is also committed to participation in the anti-war, anti-nuclear and peace movements, efforts to assist A-bomb victims and to a program for reducing the defense budget. KCWU works to help those who are forgotten reclaim their human rights and is committed to working to reverse destruction to the environment.

6.1.10.2. Korean Association of Women Theologians (KAWT - 1980)

KAWT has as its purposes the continuing humanization for women, the democratization of the Korean church, and the furthering of justice, peace and the integrity of creation in this world. These were to be fostered and developed through the establishment and spreading of feminist theology. The association has been active in advocacy, publication and theological training, along with a range of seminars, conferences and workshops. They also support projects for women in all situations of oppression and discrimination. Since 1988 KAWT has published a quarterly journal, from 1990 called

Korean Feminist Theology. Also from KAWT and related movements have come a series of significant documents, including "Theology and Women" (a series of seven seminar lectures); "The Task of Korean Feminist Theology" (Report of the first consultation on Asia Feminist Theology); along with "The Social Reality and Korean Feminism in Asia Feminist Theology"; "Research of the Actual Condition of Women in Ministry" and "Korea Woman's Theology and Reunification of Korea" (KAWT Papers).

6.1.10.3. Korean Association of Feminist Theology (KAFT - 1985)

KAFT has participated in women's liberation movements in the Korean context and has endeavored to develop genuinely "Korean" theology. Its aims include the reformation, reflection, and criticism of patriarchal rules and consciousness, both in Korean society and church. The purpose of KAFT is to decolonize both western language and the culture embedded in Korean religion and society, and thus to discover the authentic message of Christianity within the context of Korean language, culture, religion and society.

6.1.10.4. Korea Association of Christian Women For Women Minjung (KACWWM - 1986)

KACWWM is an ecumenical organization of progressive Christian women and has actively participated in social movements to transform Korean society. This organization affirms that every person is created to enjoy freedom and equality and shares the longings of women to establish an equal society between men and women. It is active in advocacy and campaigns concerning legislation, industry and media policies affecting women. KACWWM also published the monthly magazine *Christian Women* (1988), later changed into *Good News for Women Workers,* and the book *Women and the Bible-Exodus*.

6.1.10.5. Korea Women Church (KWC - 1989)

KWC is a faith community initiated by ecumenical church women with non-church women. Women Church stands on Christian truth which is rooted in the liberation of human beings. It is firstly a worship community without a hierarchical structure but in full partnership. "We share the life of Jesus Christ with Korean and foreign suffering people, especially oppressed women, for their liberation and healing." KWC is active in reshaping liturgy, hymns and theological studies to show fully mutual and equal liberation. It also publishes materials for the expansion of Women Church, mostly in Korean.

6.1.10.6. Ewha Institute for Women's Theological Studies

The Ewha Institute for Women's Theological Studies was founded in 1993 at Ewha Womans University to conduct and promote research in women's theological issues and to foster a range of educational activities. This it has done by holding open forums for feminist theological issues and conducting week-long seminars for church women in Korea and Asia. The Institute has also published the journal *Ewha Journal of Feminist Theology*, since 1996.

Selected References

Korean Association of Feminist Theology. *Experience of Korean Women* (in Korean). Seoul: Korean Christian Literature Society, 1994.
—. *Bible and Feminist Theology* (in Korean). Seoul: Korean Christian Literature Society, 1995.
—. *Church and Feminist Theology* (in Korean). Seoul: Korean Christian Literature Society, 1997.
—. *Spirituality and Feminist Theology* (in Korean). Seoul: Korean Christian Books Press, 1999.
Korean Association of Women Theologians. *The Context of Korean Women's Theology.* Seoul: KAWT, 1985.
—. *The Task of Korean Women's Theology.* Seoul: KAWT, 1985.
—. *Women's Theology and Humanization.* Seoul: KAWT, 1987.
—. *Jubilee, Reunification and Feminist Theology* (in Korean). Seoul: KAWT Press, 1992.
—. *The United Participation of Feminist Theology.* Seoul: Korean Christian Literature Society, 1992.
—. *Korean Women Minjung Ministries: Their Lives and Works* (in Korean). Seoul: KAWT, 1994.
—. *Sexual Violence and Christianity* (in Korean). Seoul: Feminist Theology Press, 1995.

—. *Sex Education Book for Christian Young Generation* (in Korean). Seoul: KAWT Press, 1999.

—. *Women Psalm from the Women's Perspective in the Korean Peninsula* (in Korean). Seoul: KAWT Press, 2000.

Korea Women Church, eds. *Collections of Sermons* 1,2,3,4; *Collections of Worship Orders* 1,2,3; *Collections of Drama Manuscripts*.

—. Volume Series: *Korean Woman Jesus*; *Our Hymn Book*; *Worship for Creating Community*; *Worship for Story-telling of Women*.

6.2 Women Doing Theology - Catholic 2

In the period following the Pacific and Korean wars, women would continue to struggle within the patriarchal Korean Catholic Church, for recognition both for the diversity of ministries they performed and fostered, and for their work in teaching, animating and writing. Although forming the majority, women have still been marginalized, and often victimized, and leadership in diocese, parish and even in women's associations is male-dominated. The writings of only comparatively few have gained publication, and the contribution of many women to statements, reports and declarations remains largely hidden. Catholic women are, however, fully conscious of the history of life, faith and commitment of many women martyrs in Korean Church history and on that basis are "moving from being a silent majority to being a speaking church of women ..." A growing number of historical studies such as those of Anna Kim Ok Hy (Hee) also provide resources for this.

Women have also shared in the movements for democracy and human rights and their writing appears in documents from the 1970s and 1980s of women's congregations and such groupings as the United Conference of Superiors for Catholic Women's Religious Orders. Later they would be joined in this by certain of the Diocesan Women's Councils, a Catholic Women's Theological Group and (forthcoming) the Women's Committee of the Catholic Bishops' Conference. For many it has become important to study the actual situation of Catholic women in Korea (see KCWC 6.2.7.2.); to foster alternative and community forms of church (see 6.2.7.1.); or to become "a praying women's church ... calling upon God as both Father and Mother," and "a speaking Sophia-God Church."

Among known authors (see 6.2.7.1.), Han Soon Hee has written and co-authored articles and books on doctrinal, ecological and feminist concerns; Kim Sung Hae has published comparative studies in Christian, Chinese and Korean religious traditions and spirituality; Choi Hae Young has written on a wide range of biblical, sacramental, christological and feminist concerns; Kang Young Ok has concentrated in writings upon the Catholic women's movement and women's culture in Korea. Kim Jeong Ja has written on the basic community of women's ecclesia: "A Church from Below." Other theologians include Cho Tae Yon and Lee Jae Sook (in biblical studies), along with Song Ho Seok, Jeong Soon Ja, Lee In Bok, Pak Choon Cha, Hwon Bong Cheol, Pak Hye Ran, You Heung Sik, Shin Gyo Seon and Anna Kim. Other women religious writing on spiritual theology, ecofeminism, theological method, gender issues, people's solidarity and participatory democracy, and silenced voices of the Korean church, include Leo Kim, Silvia Chung, Cecelia Han, Yang Hee Ok, Miriam Kim Hyun Ok and Cheon Se Hyung.

Selected References

Choi Hae Young. "Theological Reflection on Korean Catholic Women's Faith Experiences: Focusing on 35-60s Middle-aged Women." *Junmang* (Theological Perspective) 129 (2000).

—, et al. *Research on Aspects of Professed Religious and Candidates in Korean Women's Congregations* (4). Korean Association of Major Superiors of Women's Religious, 1999.

Han Soon Hee. "The Open Existence of Women and the Open Churches." *Journal of Junmang* (Theological Perspective) 109 (1995).

—. "Alternative Christian Life Styles for the Third Millennium: In Perspective of Ecofeminism." *Journal of Anthropological Studies* 1 (2000).

Kang Young Ok. "Women's Movement in Korean Catholic Church." *Review of Catholic Church History in Korea* 4 (2000).

—. "Women's Culture in the Context of Christianity in Korea." *Women's Culture in East Asia* (2000).

Kim Jeong Ja. " The Korean Voices of the Silent Church." Seoul: Mimeo'd, 2000.

Kim Sung Hae. *A Religio-Theological Interpretation of Women in East Asian Tradition.* AMOR (Asian Meeting of Religious) 7. Seoul: Mimeo'd (1985).

Li Wan Yung. "The Role of Religious Women in Korea." *Samok* 95 (1984).

O Kyong Hwan. "Status of Women in the Korean Church." *Kyonghyang Japji* 12 (1985).

Samok Special Issue "Identity and Role of Women in the Catholic Church." 217 (1997).

United Conference of Superiors for Catholic Women's Religious Orders. "Forgiveness, Reconciliation, Love - A Prayer on Behalf of our Country, Feb.9th 1980." In *A Declaration of Conscience. The Korean Catholic Church and Human Rights.* Vol. 1, edited by Young Soon Song. Maryknoll, NY: Orbis Books, 1983.

6.2.1. Han Soon Hee, rscj (1939-)

Han Soon Hee has studied education at Yonsei University, Seoul (M.A.), and pastoral studies and spirituality at Notre Dame (M.SA) and Loyola Universities (M.PS), USA. She is Sylvia visiting professor, department of religious studies of the Catholic University, Puchon City, Kyonggi-do, teaching in spirituality and prayer, pastoral theology and theological reflection. She has also been district superior of the Society of the Sacred Heart in Korea and directress of the novices, and is participating member of EATWOT, the FABC Ecumenical Committee, the Christian Unity and Inter-religious Dialogue Committee of Catholic Bishops' Conference of Korea, and the Catholic Feminist Theologians' Association. She has written much on pastoral theology, spirituality (including Julian of Norwich), alternative lifestyles and open churches, inter-religious and ecumenical dialogue, and ecotheology.

Selected References
Works by Han Soon Hee

Introduction to Christology. Puchon: University of SongSim, Publishing Department, 1994.

Human Person and Natural Environment. Chang Dong Wha Center of Anthropological Studies in the Catholic University of Korea. Forthcoming.

"The Open Existence of Women and the Open Churches." *Junmang* (Theological Perspective) 109 (1995).

"A new Relationship between the Human Person and Natural Environment." *Journal of the Science of Humanity* (1996).

"Alternative Christian Life Styles for the Third Millennium: In Perspective of Ecofeminism." *Journal of Anthropological Studies* 1 (2000).

"A New Perspective of Obedience: Commitment to live religious life by its fullness." *Junmang* (Theological Perspective) 131 (2000).

—, et al. *Introduction to Christianity*. Puchon: University of SongSim, Publishing Department, 1991.

6.2.2. Kim Ok Hee, Anna (ca. 1940-)

Kim Ok Hee is a religious from Changyong, who studied Korean history at Seoul National University (M.A.) and history at Universitie de Paris-Sorbonne (Ph.D.) Her doctoral thesis was "Le Role de Yi Pyok dans l'introduction et Diffusion du Catholicisme en Coree" (1977). She is curator of Oryundae Martyrs' Memorial Museum, director of the Research Institute of Korean Catholic Culture and professor of Suwon University (department of history). Her writings are particularly concerned with the history of Korean Catholics, especially early Catholic thought in Korea, along with the lives of martyrs. Along with a number of monographs she has also written articles on "The Acceptance of Western Studies and Their Ways of Thinking"; on "The Symbolic System of Sungkyoyogie"; on "Practical Science and Early Korean Catholicism"; and on "The History of Korean Catholic Religious."

Selected References

Works by Kim Ok Hee

Kwangahm Yi Pyok's Western Studies. Seoul: Catholic Publishing, 1979.

The History of the Religious Riot of Chejudo in the year of Shinchuk. Diocese of Cheju, 1980.

The Light of Soul. Sisters of the Korean Martyrs, 1980.

The Life of Martyrs. Seoul: Hakmoonsa, 1983.

The Biographies of the Martyrs. Seoul: Hakmoonsa, 1983.

Rev. Choi Yangup and the Christians' Village. Seoul: Hakmoonsa, 1983.

"Women in the History of Catholicism in Korea." *Korea Journal* 24.8 (1984).

6.2.3. Lee Hae In, Claudia (1945-)

Lee Hae In entered the convent of the Olivetan Benedictine Sisters in Pusan in 1964 and made her perpetual vows in 1976. She studied English literature at St. Louis University in the Philippines (1975) and comparative religion at Sogang University in Seoul (1985). She had her debut as a poet 1970 and, though a Catholic nun, she has been named one of the most beloved poets in Korea: even students in elementary, middle, and high schools are reading with pleasure some of her poems and essays which are put in their Korean Language texts. She also teaches a course: "Poem and Spirituality in Everyday Life" at the Catholic University of Pusan. Based on her religious spirituality and poetic reflections which relate trivial and ever-changing things to the infinite, she is communicating the compassionate love of God to many, from her religious house "the Land of Dandelion."

Selected References

Works by Lee Hae In

My Land of Dandelion (in Korean). Seoul: Catholic Publishing House, 1976.

Setting My Soul in Fire (in Korean). Waegwan: Benedict Press, 1979.

Though I Am a Half Moon Rising Tonight (in Korean). Waegwan: Benedict Press, 1983.

The Face of Time (in Korean). Waegwan: Benedict Press, 1989.

Prayers of Four Seasons (in Korean). Waegwan: Benedict Press, 1993.

At the Sea Again (Korean-English) Seoul: Parkwoosa, 1998.

The Sea of Dandelions (in English). Peperkorn, 2000.

On a Journey (Korean-English) Seoul: Parkwoosa. Forthcoming.

6.2.4. Kim Sung Hae, sc (ca.1945)

Kim Sung Hae teaches in the department of religious studies at Sogang University, and is director of the Seton Inter-religious Research and Spirituality Center, Seoul. Her major studies and writings are on Chinese religious tradition and on Confucianism, Buddhism and Shamanism in relation to Christian faith. They include comparative studies of biblical and Confucian traditions of "the sage," of harmony between God and all creation, and also of meditation traditions, which offer resources for contemporary spirituality and life.

In writing of contextual theology, she identifies two main streams in the doing of theology using Asian resources: that of "liberation" theology and that of inculturation theology. In the Korean context, Kim sees the first arising from the experience of struggles for livelihood and human rights, while the second arises firstly from study of the Korean cultural tradition. She calls for an inculturation which starts from below and also includes the insights and wisdom of eastern spirituality. Kim finds occasional examples where these two streams converge, as in the work of Chong Ho Kyong (see 5.2.3.6.), and the Catholic Farmers' Movement (7.6.8.), which shows how concerns for liberation and inculturation "may meet at a deeper level."

Selected References

Works by Kim Sung Hae

> *The Righteous and the Sage. Comparative Study of the Ideal Images of Man* (sic) *in Biblical Israel and Classical China.* Seoul: Sogang University Press, 1985.
>
> *Kurisudogyo wa mugyo* (Christianism and shamanism). Seoul: Paoro Ttal, 1998.
>
> "Partners for Dialogue: the Search for Discriminating Norms." *EAPR* 4 (1985).
>
> *A Religio-Theological Interpretation of Women in East Asian Tradition.* AMOR 7 (1985).
>
> "A Reflection on 200 years of Catholicism and 100 years of Protestantism in Korea." *Zeitschrift fur Missionskunde und Religionswissenshcaft* 69.2 (1985).
>
> "Liberation and Inculturation: Two Streams of Doing Theology with Asian Resources: A Report on the Catholic Church in South Korea." *Inter-Religio* 12 (1987).
>
> "Silent Heaven giving Birth to a Multitude of People." *Ching Feng* 31.4 (1988).
>
> "The Concept of Religion from the Perspective of the Basic Structure of Chinese Religious Tradition." *Tripod* 68 (1992).
>
> "The Confucian Sage." *Inter-Religio* 22 (1992).

"Active Contemplation: A Confucian Contribution to Contemporary Spirituality - A Study on Quiet Sitting in Korean Confucianism." *Ching Feng* 38.1 (1995).
"The Kingdom of God as the Christian Image of Harmony." *Inter-Religio* 29 (1996).
"The Korean Liberation Theology from a Confucian Perspective." *Theological Thought* 92 (1996).

6.2.5. Choi Hae Young, ssc (Choi Hye Yeong, 1955-)

Choi Hye Yeong studied arts at Ewha Womans University, Seoul, (M.A. 1987) and gained her doctorate in New Testament theology from Sogang University, Seoul (1996). She is now associate professor and dean, department of religious studies at the Catholic University of Korea. She has also been director of the Catholic Women's Research Institute of Korea and executive member of the Catholic Association of Feminist Theologians, as well as participating in programs of inter-faith dialogue, religion and peace, and in the United Religions Initiative, Korea.

Along with broader religious studies she has studied and written on the New Testament from a feminist perspective. She has also written studies of prayer in the Bible, prayers of Jesus, prayer in Paul; other biblical studies of Jesus' cry on the cross, the glory of God and Jesus Christ and a new interpretation of God the Father. Her articles include papers on the church and sacraments, and on early Christian house churches. A main focus here is upon women's role and leadership. Studies on a new paradigm of theology and feminism are forthcoming.

Selected References

Works by Choi Hye Yeong

The Lord's Prayer. Seoul: Bible Life Press, 1988.
God, Open My Mouth: Prayers in the New Testament. Seoul: Woori Theology Institute, 1999.
Salvation in Different Religions. Seoul: Chang Press, 1993.
The Way with Jesus Christ: Introduction to Christology. Songsim University Press, 1994.
Anthropology. Seoul: The Catholic University Press, 1977.
Report: 11 Ways of Theological Methodology (11). Seoul: Bible Life Press, 2000.

Open Religion and Peace Community. DaEwha Press, 2000.

"Sexuality of Jesus in Christology of the Third Millennium." *Junmang* (Theological Perspective) 116 (1997/1).

"Body and Spirit." *Journal of Anthropological Studies* 1 (2000).

"Theological Reflection on Korean Catholic Women's Faith Experiences: Focusing on 35-60s Middle Aged Women." *Junmang* (Theological Perspective) 129 (2000).

"The Task of Evangelization from Women's Perspective." *Korean Christian Thought* 9. Forthcoming.

"Introducing Western Feminist Theologies." In *Believing for Understanding, Understanding for Believing: The Commemorative Publication for Prof. Yang Mo Chung's Retirement.* Waegwan: Benedict Press. Forthcoming.

—, et al. *The Truth of Christian Faith: Introduction to Christianity.* Songsim University, 1991.

6.2.6. Kang Young Ok, Lucia

Kang Young Ok studied literature and systematic theology at Ewha Womans University, Seoul (M.A. 1983), dogmatic theology at the University of Fribourg, Switzerland (Lizentiat 1988) and at Sogang University, Seoul (Ph.D. 1997). She has been lecturer in theology at Sogang University and Daegu Catholic University, a committee member of the Association of Korean Catholic Women's Theology and of the Office of Evangelization, Archdiocese of Seoul. She is now Research Fellow at the Catholic University, Seoul, and one of a team of scholars researching "The Catholic Church in the 100 years of Korean history."

In *Suffering, the Standpoint of Belief* (1999), which is the published version of her doctoral thesis, Kang answers the question, "What is the Christian soteriological answer to the suffering of the people in the Korean socio-political context?" She writes that Christian truth should be embodied in the Korean cultural-religious context and socio-political background, because it must be reinterpreted in each time and in each place. She therefore discusses "the unique Christian truth" in relation to the problem of suffering, and in comparison with the interpretations of other religions (Buddhism, Confucianism, Taoism). Kang is particularly studying the women's movement and the impact of Christianity, which was initially an egalitarian influence for "the equality of man and woman who are created as Image of God," on Korean society. Such a Christian identity for women, she believes, declined as Christianity became more institutionalized, and this must now be rebuilt.

Selected References
Works by Kang Young Ok
> *Suffering, the Standpoint of Belief* (in Korean). Seoul: Woori Theological Institute, 1999.
> "The Christian Understanding of Suffering." Ph.D. diss., Sogang University, Seoul, 1997.
> "Women's Movement in Korean Catholic Church." *Review of Catholic Church History in Korea* (2000).
> "Women's Culture in the Context of Christianity in Korea." *People and Culture* 9.13 (2000).

6.2.7. Catholic Women's Institutes

6.2.7.1. *Cham Saram Doe-eo* (To be a Real Human Being - since 1987).

Cham Saram Doe-eo is a monthly journal directed by a laywoman, Agnes Han Hyeon, and has greatly contributed to introducing and spreading a progressive perspective of Christian identity within the Catholic Church in South Korea. Since the late 1980s it has published in English and Korean writings by Korean Catholics which are not readily accepted by more official publications. Now appearing as a most influential periodical book, *Cham Saram Doe-eo* has disseminated the idea of non-institutional 'community' (or *Gong-dong-che*) in Catholic church life and this has been welcomed by Catholic grassroots workers and later by members of the hierarchy. The concept had been influenced by Basic Christian Communities and the theology of liberation, but without this magazine's influence, the term would have been used only by a few church academics and activists. The magazine has no recognized office or editorial committee, is financed non-commercially by optional donation only, and publicized and distributed only by word of mouth. Yet it has helped the present Korean church to rediscover its mission and nature as community.

Originally, in 1987, *Cham Saram Doe-eo* started as the newsletter of a small Catholic group who desired a simple Christian life. It was supported by the office of Caritas Coreana, a social arm of the Korean Bishops' Conference, of which at that time Agnes Han was one of the three staff members. Soon its name was changed into *Hana Doe-eo* (To be One) and it became an independent magazine, later to be named *Cham Saram Doe-eo* (To Be a Real Human Being). Under the same publishing name, more than a hundred leaflets and books on church renewal and contextual theology have been published and distributed to make known thought and experience - mainly in Asia and in the USA - that is focused on the poor of God, Christian poverty, inter-religious dialogue and concerns of women.

6.2.7.2. Korean Catholic Women's Community for a New World (KCWC)

KCWC is a voluntary lay women's group set up in April 1993 to improve the situation of women both in the Church and in society. The goals of KCWC are to create solidarity among Catholic women, to address women's issues both within and outside of the Church, to promote the personal growth of women, to contribute towards reform in the Church, and to build a just and peaceful society. It has greatly contributed to raising feminist perspectives and to disseminating women's issues in the Korean Catholic Church: for example, the comfort women's issue (women forced into sexual slavery by the Japanese military during World War II), and the movement to abolish unequal family laws. It has also made proposals for a women's apostolate to the Korean Bishops' Conference and the FABC. Among its publications, *Why Do You Speak With Her?* was produced for use in workshops studying the Bible from a feminist perspective and has been reprinted twice. In conjunction with Woori Theology Institute, KCWC undertook a pioneering survey of the situation and self-understanding of Catholic women in Korea.

7 Other Contextual Theologies of the Late 20th Century
7.1 Contextual Protestant Theology 3

Very many teachers, ministers, writers and activists have also contributed through their ministries, writings, and community

Contextual Theology in Korea

leadership to Korean contextual theologies in this period. A selection of earlier theologians, along with some of their key writings is given first below, along with a brief reference to many others. These are then followed by a selection of later scholars. Among those to be noted are teachers and researchers in Korea such as Keel Hee Seong and Noh Jong Sun, ecumenical theologians working both in Korea and the region such as Oh Jae Shik, and theologians based firstly in North America such as Lee Jung Young, Cyris Moon Hee Suk and Park Andrew Sung. To represent many others, the following should be noted: Park Sang Jung (of the WCC and CCA), Ahn Jae Woong (of WSCF and CCA), Kang Moon Kyu (of the WSCF and YMCA), Kim Heup Young (of Kangnam University), Kim Chang Nak (of Hanshin University), Yang Kwon Sok, Sohn Kyoo Tae and Lee Jeong Ku (of Sungkonghoe Anglican University), Park Kyung Seo (of the KCA and WCC), Lee Moon Jang (of the Center for the Study of Christianity in Asia) and Daniel Adams (of Hanil University). See, however, the bibliographies and guides in 1.1 above, and in 8.2.; 11 below, for further references.

7.1.1. Cheung Ha Eun, who gained his Th.D. from Pittsburgh University, was professor of social ethics at Hankuk Theological Seminary and the United Graduate School of Theology, Yonsei University. He was an early supporter of efforts towards indigenous Korean theology. See for example his:

> "The 80-year History of Korean Christian Social Ethics - A Look at Nationalism and Socialism." In *Korea Struggles for Christ,* edited by Harold S. Hong, Ji Won Yong and Kim Chung Choon. Seoul: Christian Literature Society of Korea, 1966.
> "Image of the Minister in Social Change." *NEAJOT* 1 (1968).
> "The Silence of God: A Theological View." *Japan Christian Quarterly* 54.3 (1988).

7.1.2. Chang Chun Ha graduated from Korea Theological Seminary (1947) and devoted his life's work to reflective and critical journalism. Despite extreme hardship and harassment, during the next 20 years he founded and edited a series of dissident magazines which were dedicated to building national unity, independence and human community. Following *Tungpul* (Lamp, 1944), *Chaedan*

(Altar, 1946) and *Sasang* (Thought, 1951) came the internationally-known *Sasangge* (World of Thought), a wide-ranging intellectual and opposition-orientated journal with wide influence in Korea. He was imprisoned in 1967 and murdered in 1975. See his:

> "My Life with Magazines." In *Listening to Korea*, edited by Marshall R. Pihl. New York: Praeger, 1973.

7.1.3. Han Wan Sang, a theologically-informed sociologist, taught at Seoul National University. He was dismissed from his teaching post twice, in 1975 and in 1989, following which he was imprisoned for political reasons. He served the government, first as minister of reunification and later as minister of education, under the democratized government, 1990- . He is the author of many books and was also active in the struggle of Korean people for human rights and democracy. In his studies of Korean society, church and mission he urges the Christian Church to share struggle and suffering on "the road to Jericho" if it is to recover a clear sense of identity through open and inclusive response to the lives of their people in the midst of social change. See for example his:

> *Han'guk kyohoe, idaero chohun'ga?: Han'guk kyohoe munje palgul chongdam* (Are Korean churches on the right direction?: Conversations on the problems of Korean churches). Seoul: Taehan Kidokkyo Ch'ulp'ansa, 1982.
>
> "The Unification of the Nation and the Response of the Church." *Christian Thought* (December 1971).
>
> "The Christian Church and Problems of Mission." In *Christian Thought of Korea,* edited by Ryu Dong Shik. Seoul: Christian Literature Society, 1975.
>
> "Meditations." In *Varieties of Witness*, edited by D. Preman Niles and T.K. Thomas. Singapore: CCA, 1979.

7.1.4. Kang Won Yong was the founder of the Korean Christian Academy and a prominent ecumenical leader both in Korea and the Asian region. He has been deeply concerned for the role of the church in nation-building, and for the formation of lay people for this, both in rural and urban contexts. Outspoken in criticism of political corruption and Christian timidity from the 1960s on, Kang sought, through fostering the role and insight of "intermediate social groupings," to break through the feudalistic "house of thinking" of

Koreans, and to oppose the rigidities of materialism and dogma. See for example his:

> *Zwischen Tiger und Schlange* (Between tiger and snake). Beiträge aus Korea zu Christentum, Entwicklung und Politik. Erlangen: Ev.-Luth. Mission, c1975.
> "Korean Church in the World Community." *Koreana* 3.7 (1961).
> "The Church and Nation Building." *SEAJOT* 6.2 (1964).
> "A Critical Review of Lay Training in Asia." *Asia Focus* (EACC) 4.3 (1969).
> Kim Nam-jo, Yun Hu-jong and Yi Kye-gyong oe. *Kang Won-yong kwa ui mannam kurigo yosong undong* (Meeting of Kang Won Yong and the feminist movement). Seoul: Yosong Sinmunsa, 1998.

7.1.5. Park Pong Bae taught Christian ethics at the Methodist Theological Seminary, Seoul, with particular concerns for indigenization in the context of both traditional Korean culture and religion, and of contemporary socio-political change. Of three approaches to such indigenization he proposed the 'middle way' between exclusivism and relativism: that of 'transformationism,' whereby theology provides resources for the reshaping of both inherited tradition and social structures. See for example his:

> *The Encounter of Christianity with Traditional Culture and Ethics in Korea: an essay in Christian self-understanding.* [microform, Yale Univ.] 1970.
> "Christianity in the Land of Shamanism, Buddhism and Confucianism." *NEAJOT* 14.1 (1972).
> "Indigenization of Korean Christianity." In *Christian Thought in Korea*, edited by Ryu Dong Shik. Seoul: Christian Literature Society, 1975.
> "Liberation and Community." *Theological Thought* 19 (1977).

7.1.6. Mun Ik Kwan was professor of Old Testament at Hankuk Seminary, and later general secretary of the Korean Bible Society. Since the 1970s, he has provided prophetic leadership, both regarding issues of democracy and human rights, and in movements for reunification. He has been frequently imprisoned as a result. He is also a poet with three published volumes of verse. His writings have appeared in *Korea Communiqué, Third Day, Theological Thought* and elsewhere. See for example his:

There is No Place to Stand Behind Me. Seoul: Practice and Literature Publishing, 1984.
"Desolate Korean Religion: New Propositions to Make Christianity an Aboriginal Faith." *Sasanggye* 7 (1964).
"Painful Melody." *Third Day* 4 (1973).
"The Purpose of the Fast." *Korea Communiqué* 41 (1981).
"Bread and Freedom." In *Tarakwon '83*, edited and published by CCA, Singapore, 1983.
Paekpom Thought Research Institute. *Late Spring: The Soul Pleading for a Dream. Mun Ik Kwan Anthology.* Seoul: Hwada Publishing, 1987.

7.1.7. Kim Kwan Suk specialized in Christian ethics, and directed Korean Christian Broadcasting before serving as general secretary of the NCCK through the turbulent years of the 1970s and 1980s. He was a central figure in campaigns to achieve Christian freedom under military dictatorship, as these were maintained through, for example, the "Thursday Prayer Meetings" and expressed through such documents as the *Declaration for National Democratic Salvation*. See his regular editorials in *Christian Activity News* and also NCCK Statements in, for example, the IDOC FME Dossier 7 (1974). See also:

"The Church and National Unification" (In Korean). *Christian Thought* (December 1970).
"Christmas Message." *NCCK Activity News* 12 (1974).
"A Korean Experience." *International Review of Mission* (July 1980).
Emergency Christian Conference on Korean Problems, ed. *Documents on the Struggle for Democracy in Korea.* Tokyo: Shinkyo Shuppansha, 1975.

7.1.8. Min Kyung Bae studied in Seoul and at Aberdeen, and was long-time professor of church history at Yonsei University School of Theology. He became very widely recognized as Korea's pre-eminent Protestant church historian and was also closely associated with movements for social reform and contextual theology. He sought both to correct misinterpretations of Korea's Christian history and to recover neglected aspects of that which offered creative resource for present tasks in mission and theology. See his titles below (all in Korean):

A History of the Korean Churches. Seoul: Christian Literature Society, 1974.

A History of the National Church Movements in Korea. Seoul: Yonsei University Press, 1974.

A Centennial History of the Presbyterian Church in Korea. Seoul: General Assembly of the Presbyterian Church in Korea, 1984.

A History of the Social Movements of the Churches in Korea. Seoul: Christian Literature Society, 1985.

"National Identity in the History of the Korean Church." In *Korea and Christianity,* edited by Yu Chai Shin. Mississauga, Ont.: Korean and Related Studies Press, 1996.

"Christian Missions and the Modernization of Korea," 22-33. In *1999 Graduate Students' Conference on North East Asia Church History: Korea,* edited by The Korea Academy of Church History, Seoul: 1999.

7.1.9. Lee Chang Shik studied at Queen's Theological College, Canada, and Union Theological Seminary, New York, and was professor of historical theology and church history at Hanshin University, Seoul. He was active in moves for Korean indigenous theology, and wrote on this as well as on the changes needed to shape both devotional life and theological education for historical and life issues, and for community transformation. See his:

A History of Christian Thought. Seoul : Christian Literature Society of Korea, 1963.

Modern Ecclesiology. Seoul: CLSK, 1969.

"The Way to Form Korean Christian Theology." *Christian Thought* (1973).

"A Study of a Chinese Nestorian Sutra, 'Jesus Messiah'." *NEAJOT* 13 (1974).

"Theological Education in Korea, Past, Present and Future." *NEAJOT* 28/29 (1982).

7.1.10. Among many others to be mentioned for related writings at this time are Park Pong Nang, Park San Kyong and Chi Dong Shik in systematic theology; Han Tae Dong and Choo Chai Yong in church history; Kim Yong Ok, Mun Sang Hi and Park Tae Son in biblical studies, along with Kim Chan Kuk, Kim Kwang Shik, Park Hyung Kyu, Lee Mun Young, Chang Il Cho, Maeng Yong Gil, Chi Myong Kwan, Kim Young Koo and Edward W. Poitras.

Selected References

Chang Il Cho. "The Philosophy of Social Enlightenment." *Theological Studies* 19 (1977).

Choo Chai Yong. "A Brief Sketch of Korean Christian History from the Minjung Perspective." In *Minjung Theology: People as the Subjects of History,* edited by Kim Yong-Bock.

Kim Chan Kuk. "The Biblical Basis of Human Rights." *Christian Thought* (Feb. 1974).

Kim Kwang Shik. "The Indigenisation of the Korean church." *Christian Thought* (Feb. 1973).

Kim Yong Ok. "Korean Theology within Asian Theology." *Christian Thought* (Sept. 1971).

Lee Mun Young. "The Vision of the Church - Religion and Politics." *Third Day* (Feb. 1975).

Maeng Yong Gil. "Towards a Theology of Togetherness for Academic Formation in Northeast Asia." *NEAJOT* 26/27 (1981).

Min Kyung Bae. *The History of Korean Protestantism* (in Korean and Japanese). Tokyo: Kyodan, 1974.

—. "History of Resistance of Korean Protestantism." In *Christian Thought in Korea*, edited by Ryu Dong Shik.

—. "Christianity in Korea." In *Christianity in Asia,* edited by T.K. Thomas. Singapore: CCA, 1979.

—. "On the Question of Understanding Korean Churches." *NEAJOT* 24/25 (1980).

Park Hyung Kyu. *Haebonge Kilmocke Suh* (Road to liberation: collection of sermons). Seoul: Sasang-sa, 1974.

Park Pong Nang. "A Theological Understanding of the Indigenization of Christianity." *NEAJOT* 3 (1969).

Poitras, Edward W. "Christian Identity in Korea Today." *Japan Christian Quarterly* 44.2 (1978).

7.1.11. Keel Hee Seong has been staff member of the Institute for Religion and Theology and professor in the department of religion, Sogang University, Seoul, and is a student of both Christianity in Korea and of Buddhism across the Asian region. His writings include studies of Christian theology within Korean culture and of the liberative elements in Mahayana Buddhism, including those of Zen and Pure Land traditions. He has written a full study of Shinran and outlined a Buddhist perspective for Christology, for which he employs the image and role of the Bodhisattva. Here he finds convergences - and differences - in the roles of Jesus and the Bodhisattva, in respect to freedom and detachment, the distinctions between good and evil which "create love and compassion," and the similar generative roles of "emptiness," for the Bodhisattva, and of divine love, for Jesus.

7.1.12. Noh Jong Sun. Following studies in Seoul and Princeton, Noh has taught at the School of Theology, Yonsei University, and written critically of First World theologies, along with studies of liberation, just revolution, story theology and revolutionary theology. He calls for a new unitive, ecological and humanitarian theology which challenges dependencies on destructive industry, on "division psychosis" and on non-liberative theologies. In a vivid parable for social and theological action, he pictures the ashes of the victims of authoritarian violence once thrown into the Imjeen River as the "silver fish" which will flow as the river does through all man-made barriers. A "theology of silver fish" finds paths to liberation through suffering and self-determination by drawing on hidden natural forces and rejecting all divisive dualisms.

7.1.13. Oh Jae Shik studied at Seoul National and Yale Universities, was staff member of the YMCA and the KSCF during the 1960s, and from 1971, was secretary for Urban Rural Mission for the CCA, based in Tokyo. The move from "student activism to organizing workers, farmers, and minorities, fighting against the Asian militarized development ideology," was the major redirection for both his activism and theology. He played a seminal role in the development of people's theology in context throughout the Asian region. After a term with the WCC, he returned to Korea and in the 1990s became president of World Vision Korea. Oh's later writings reflect his commitments to reconciliation and reunification, and to a new international order to be based on understanding and compassion for human beings. Such an order, he declares, stresses cooperative people-oriented structures and allows private ownership only for the survival and integrity of human beings. (See also vol. 1: chap. 3.)

7.1.14. Expatriate Koreans. To represent the many Korean theologians who are based for their teaching largely outside Korea,

Lee Jung Young, Cyris Moon Hee Suk and **Andrew Sung Park** can be mentioned here, for they provide examples of those who have provided major resources for both Korean and Asian Christian theology. Lee (d.1996) in particular, has provided full-scale studies both of Trinitarian belief in the Asian context and of major classics of Asian religion within the global context. Among his later writings, he declares that "all traditions must return to their margins" and roots, which always define the center and provide the source for transformation. Marginality is the place for movement, servanthood and resurrection. Moon is an Old Testament scholar who has often written on *minjung* theology in the perspective of the Old Testament and on biblical and *minjung* cultures. Park's main work has been to draw on both eastern and western religious traditions to build a contemporary theodicy based on *han* in Korean experience.

7.1.15. Among **other contributions** in teaching and writing to contextual theology in recent years are those made by **Kim Kyong Jae, Lee Jong Bae** and **Park Jong Chon.** Kim Kyong-jae teaches systematic theology at Hanshin University and has made contributions to the theology of *minjung* - in particular in *Donghak* studies - to hermeneutic studies and also to the theology of culture and religions. Lee Jong-bae has written on the indigenization of theology and the theology of culture and religions. He has recently worked at developing a theology of life utilizing teachings and wisdom of Korean and eastern religions and Christianity. Park Jong Chon has worked on the indigenization of Korean theology, theology of culture, and more recently on the "Search for Yellow Jesus from the Perspective of *Donghak*."

Selected References

Ahn Jae Woong. *The Image of God in Minorities.* WSCF Book 10. Hong Kong: WSCF Asia-Pacific, 1984.
—. *God in Our Midst.* WSCF Book 19. Hong Kong: WSCF Asia-Pacific, 1995.
Keel Hee Seong. *Understanding Shinran: A Dialogical Approach.* Nanzan Studies in Asian Religion 6. Fremont: Asian Humanities Press, 1995.

—. "Korean Theology: Past and Present." *Inter-Religio* 12 (1987).
—. "Zen and Minjung Liberation." *Inter-Religio* 17 (1990).
—. "Jesus, Bodhisattva, God of Mercy" (in Korean). *Samok* 168 (1993).
—. "Can Korean Protestantism be Reconciled with Culture? Rethinking Theology and Evangelism in Korea." *Inter-Religio* 24 (1993).
—. "Jesus the Bodhisattva: Christology from a Buddhist Perspective." *Buddhist Christian Studies* 16 (1996).
Kim Heup Young. *Toward a Theo-Tao (Toeui Sinhak)* (in Korean). Seoul: Dasan Geulbang, 2000.
—. "The Study of Confucianism as a Theological Task." *Korea Journal of Theology* 1 (1995).
Kim Kyong Jae. *Hermeneutics and Theology of Religions* (in Korean). Chonan: Korea Institute of Theology, 1994.
—. *Christianity and the Encounter of Asian Religions.* Leiden: Boekencentrum, 1994.
—. "Soowoon's Experience of Shichonju and The View of God in Donghak" (in Korean). *Sunghok Journalism Review* 8 (1998).
Lee Jong-bae. *Korean Theology of Life.* Seoul: Gamshin, 1996.
—. *Reliving of Theology and Spiritualization of Theology.* Seoul: CLS, 1999.
—. "Korean Reflection in the Christian Anthropology and Soteriology." *Korea Journal of Theology* (1995).
Lee Jung Young. *The Theology of Change. A Christian Concept of God in an Eastern Perspective.* Maryknoll, NY: Orbis Books, 1979.
—. *Marginality: the Key to Multicultural Theology.* Minneapolis MN: Fortress Press, 1995.
—. *The Trinity in Asian Perspective.* Nashville; Abingdon Press, 1996.
—, ed. *Ancestor Worship and Christianity in Korea.* Lewiston, NY: Edwin Mellen Press, 1988.
—. "Christian Indigenization in Korea." *Asian Pacific Quarterly of Cultural and Social Affairs* 18 (1986).
Moon, Cyris Hee Suk. "An Old Testament Understanding of Minjung." In *Minjung Theology: People as the Subjects of History,* edited by Commission on Theological Concerns of the CCA, 123-137. Maryknoll: Orbis Books, 1983.
—. *A Korean Minjung Theology - An Old Testament Perspective.* Hong Kong: Plough Publications; Maryknoll, NY: Orbis Books, 1985.

—. "Culture in the Bible and the Culture of the Minjung." *Ecumenical Review* 39.2 (1987).
Noh Jong Sun. *First World Theology and Third World Critique.* Hambden Conn.: Center for Asian Theology, 1983.
—. *Religion and Just Revolution: the Third World Perspective.* Hambden Conn.: Center for Asian Theology, 1984.
—. *Liberation of First World Theology. A Critique of Reinhold Niebuhr.* Seoul: NCCK; Quezon City: NCCP, 1987.
—. *Yitaki Shinhak* (Story theology). Seoul: Hanwul Academy, 1993.
—. *Liberating God for Minjung.* Seoul: Hanwul Academy, 1994.
Oh Jae-Shik. "Towards a New Pilgrimage." In *Towards a Theology of People,* edited by Oh Jae Shik. Tokyo: CCA URM, 1977.
—. "Human Rights in Asia and the Japanese Church." *Fukuin to Sekai* 3 (1980).
—. "Mission and Development." *International Review of Mission* 73.290 (1984).
Park, Andrew Sung. *The Wounded Heart of God: The Asian Concept of Han and the Christian Doctrine of Sin.* Nashville, Abingdon Press, 1993.
—. "Minjung and Púngryu Theologies in Contemporary Korea: a Critical and Comparative Examination." Ph.D. diss., Graduate Theological Union, 1985.
Park Jong Chun. *Crawl With God, Dance in the Spirit: A Creative Formulation of Korean Theology of the Spirit* (in English and Korean). Nashville: Abingdon Press; Seoul: CLS, 1998.
Park Kyung Seo. *Reconciliation Reunification. The Ecumenical Approach to the Korean Peninsula.* Hong Kong: CCA, 1998.
Park Sang-jung. *Han'guk kyohoe wa ek'yumenik'al undong* (Korean churches and the ecumenical movement). Seoul: Taehan Kidokkyo Sohoe, 1992.
—. *Ecumenical Praxis and Democracy in Asia. Biblical and Critical Reflections.* Hong Kong: WSCF Book 17. Hong Kong: WSCF Asia-Pacific, 1993.

7.2 Catholic Contextual Theology 3

Theological writing by Catholic scholars and activists has in recent decades taken up many issues for the inculturation of theology, including religious pluralism, sacramental theology, *minjung* and third-world theologies, spirituality, sociology and church-state concerns, evangelization and pastoral ministries.

7.2.1. Rhee Soun Seong, Peter (1950-)

Rhee Soun Seong has shown his deep concern for inculturation of Catholic Sacraments in a series of writings since 1980s. His main ideas for this have been presented in articles appearing in Korean periodicals, mainly in *Shinhak Junmang* (quarterly, Kwangju Catholic University, see 7.3.3.). Many of his writings there are comparative studies which relate Korean cultural traditions to aspects of Catholic faith. He entered the congregation of Claretian Missionaries in 1999 and since then his thought has develped further. Based on a theological respect for the cultural and religious heritage of diverse nations and regions, he is now deeply interested in forming a new solidarity especially with people living in the "third world," including China. This he sees as a sharing of "the consoling presence of the Lord."

Selected References
Works by Rhee Soun Seong

"An Aspect of the Inculturation of Early Christian Community." *Shinhak Junmang* 58 (1982).

"The Comparative Study of Catholic Ritual and the Traditional One of Korean Mouism I-II." *Shinhak Junmang* 112-113 (1996).

"The Comparative Understanding of Symbolic Actions of Korean Mouism and the Catholic Mass for the People." *Shinhak Junmang* 115 (1996).

"The Comparative Understanding of the Experience of God in Korean Mouism and the Christian Church." *Shinhak Junmang* 121 (1998).

7.2.2. Kim Jung Shin (1952-)

Kim Jung Shin is a church architect as well as a professor of architectural history. He has contributed to the systematization of Catholic architectural history in Korea in a series of surveys and also through an inductive method of typological analysis. He has consistently tried to see the developing process of Korean Catholic Church architecture from the receiver's standpoint, thus breaking from a stylistic view of history which centers around western architecture. In addition to this research, he has also designed twenty churches during the 1990s. His church architecture starts from an investigation of intrinsic value and local tradition and his architectural language consistently relates to human life, practical theology, Korean tradition and Korean context.

Selected References:
Works by Kim Jung Shin
> *History of Catholic Church Architecture.* Seoul: The Research of Foundation of Korean Church History, 1994.
> *Gosan Catholic Church.* Gosan, Taegu: 1994
> *Suckchondong Catholic Church.* Seoul: 1995
> *Young-Aham Mansoori Secondary Station.* Young-Aham: 1998
> "A Theological Study on the Tabernacle of Modern Catholic Church." *Journal of Architectural History* (Seoul) 1 (1992).

7.2.3. Park Il Young, John (1952-)

Park Il Young has tried to provide better foundations for understanding religion in Korean society from the point of view of the common people, the *minjung*. He sees in the religiosity of *minjung* the driving force of Korean culture. For the inculturation and practice of Christian belief which is faithful to the concrete multi-religious context, he refers especially to shamanism. This he sees to be the basic religious phenomenon of Korean people and the core of Korean culture itself. On this basis he has attempted to articulate the central dynamics of religious life and action in which common people have been deeply rooted and which they have lived out. His writings deal extensively with Korean Shamanism and its relation to Christian practice and belief.

Selected References
Works by Park Il Young
> "Minjung, Schamanismus und Inkulturation. Schamanistische Religiositaet und Christliche Orthopraxis in Korea." Diss., Universitaet Freiburg, 1988.
> *Understanding Korean Shamanism* (in Korean). Waegwan: Benedict Press, 1999.
> *Korean Shamanism and Christianity* (Korean). Waegwan: Benedict Press. Forthcoming.

"Communion Feast in Korean Shamanism." *Korea Journal* 31.1 (1991).
"Dynamic Religiosity. Insight from Korean Folk-Religion." *Journal of Dharma* (Sep. 2000).

7.2.4. Kim Ung Tai, Joseph (1954-)

Kim Ung Tai has contributed to developing the inculturation of Christian theology of Korea since the 1990s. His attention has now moved to the ways in which Christianity can be open to the religious pluralities of Korea, in searching for the relations between Christian identity and the missionary task. To fulfil this concern he is searching not only for fuller participation in the ecumenical movement but for ways of establishing greater harmony with those of other faiths through meeting and dialogue. His writings therefore include books and articles on missiology, catechesis, the ecumenical movement and religious dialogue. All writings are in Korean.

Selected References
Works by Kim Ung Tai

Seongyo-eui Yeoksa-wa Gaenyeom (History and concept of mission). Seoul: The Catholic University of Korea Press, 1992.

Obun Myeongsang Kyori (Five minutes meditative catechesis: catechesis for men of today). Seoul: Catholic Publishing House, 1995.

Saesul-eun Sae Budae-e (The new wine into fresh wineskins: the reality of the life of faith and the task of religious education). Seoul: Paulist Press, 1995.

Jonggyo-eui Hyeondaejeok Jeokeung (The contemporary adaptation of religion: centering around the inculturation of Korean Christianity). Seoul: The Catholic University of Korea Press. Forthcoming. (Includes in English "The Reality and Prospect of Inculturation of the Korean Christianity," read at the International Symposium on "Process and Perspective of the Asian Church's Inculturation" held by the Pastoral Institute of Korea on the 17-18th, Nov. 2000).

7.2.5. Byun Hee Sun, Anselm (1954-)

Byun Hee Sun sj received his Ph.D. in theology from Boston College (1995) and has taught theological methodology as the first

Lonergan specialist in Korea. In order to develop an authentic Korean theology, he has searched for a common ground for theology in Korea and for Korean Catholic theological groups. He has therefore endeavored to establish inculturation as the basic task. For this he is also trying to provide a common method for doing theology, focused on an authentic process of the theologians' own religious experience and upon the social and cultural levels of conversion in the Korean context. Here the doing of theology is related directly to the theologian's personal experience within Korean society.

Selected References
Works by Byun Hee Sun

"The Reality of God is the Subject-matter of Theology: A Study of Bernard Lonergan's Position." Ph.D diss., Boston College, 1995.

Economy of God: Economy of the Human Heart. Koreawon, 1998.

Theological Anthropology. Korean Studies Information Press. Forthcoming.

"A Study for Lonergan's Notion of Conversion: Conversion and Doing the Theology of a Theologian." *Theological Perspective* (Summer 1999).

"Bernard Lonergan's Notion of Economic Value of Morality." *Theological Perspective.* Forthcoming.

7.2.6. Sim Jong Hyeok (1955-)

Sim Jong Hyeok focuses his research as a Jesuit priest on the Spiritual Exercises of St. Ignatius of Loyola in relation to Confucian cultural tradition. His doctoral study was a hermeneutical study on the idea of *cheng* (sincerity); a key Confucian concept, to be applicable for further developing an inculturated Christology in the Korean cultural context. Other recent writings (in Korean) touch on broad spiritual issues, such as the "discernment of spirits," spiritual direction and ecological and environmental issues. These are considered from the perspective of the Ignatian tradition, located in the social, cultural, and religious context of Korea.

Selected References:
Works by Sim Jong Hyeok

"The Christological Vision of the Spiritual Exercises of St. Ignatius of Loyola and the Hermeneutical Principles of Sincerity (Ch'eng) in the Confucian Tradition." STD Thesis, Pontifical Gregorian University, Rome, 1991.

"A Theological Evaluation of Minjung Theology from the Perspective of Inculturation in Christology." *East Asian Pastoral Review* 29:4 (1992).

"The Notion of Sincerity (Ch'eng) in the Confucian Classics." *Journal of Chinese Philosophy* 21 (1994).

"The Notion of Sincerity (Song/Ch'eng) From a Neo-Confucian Metaphysical Perspective." *Acta Koreana* 4. Forthcoming.

7.2.7. Kim Hyoung Tae, John (1956-)

As a lawyer, Kim Hyoung Tae is serving as the president of the Korean Catholic Human-Rights Commission. In this capacity he pleaded before the court for Lim Su Kyung and Fr Mun Kyuhyun who visited North Korea for the Korea unification movement in 1989. (Mun had returned to South Korea by crossing the Demilitarized Zone, the first South Korean to do so). Kim has also undertaken a project to communicate the relationship of law to the living of the faith. Here he presents faith as a joyful partnership with a "just living of the laws." This is in order to attain a society in which the marginalized people whose rights were violated can receive the peace and justice of the reign of God. His writings in these areas are found in a long series of 55 essays in the journal *Kyung Hyang Japji*.

Selected References

Kim Hyoung Tae. "The Ladder of Jacob." (Article series.) *Kyung Hyang Japji* (Jan. 1997 to Dec. 2000).

7.2.8. Bae Kyung Min, Peter (1957-)

Fr Bae Kyung Min, gained the master's degree in systematic theology at the Seoul Catholic University in 1988 and his doctorate at the missiology graduate school, Urban Pontifical University (1988). He was nominated to be the executive secretary of the Evangelization Committee of the Catholic Bishops Conference of

Korea in 1999. He now lectures in missiology at the Suwon Catholic Seminary. He also carries out research into inculturation theology with the Korean Christian Thought Institute, works as the secretary of the National Pastoral Conference and in a small Catholic community. His writings have dealt with the hermeneutics and praxis of missiology in Korea.

Selected References:
Works by Bae Kyung Min
> "The Hermeneutic Approach to the World Mission of Modern Church through the Principal Concepts of the Gospel." Diss. (in Italian), Urban Pontifical University, Rome, 1998.
> *World Evangelisation, Missiology of Modern Church* (in Korean). Waeguan: Benedict Press. Forthcoming.

7.2.9. Hwang Jong Ryul, Leo (1957-)

Hwang Jong Ryul is a lay theologian holding the M.A. (Seoul Catholic University, 1993), and the A.BD. (Duquesne University, 2000). He has undertaken the construction of methods for doing theology in ways compatible with formative Korean historical and cultural traditions and true to the reign of God proclaimed by Jesus. His theological concern lies also in integrating faith, reason and practice with creative and genuine faithfulness to experiential realities of the *minjung*. The issues of subjectivity in doing and living theology, and in spirituality, are here central. His theology has also a socio-historical character as revealed especially in his work: *When Faith and National Consciousness Meet* (2000). Hwang has written for *Bitdure* (the weekly of the Association of Korean Catholic Priests for the Realization of Justice), and has lectured for the Korean Christian Thought Institute's "Inculturational Theology Program."

Selected References
Works by Hwang Jong Ryul
> *The Structure of Korean Theology.* Seoul: Kooktaewon, 1996.
> *Reading the Bible-History in the Perspective of God's Reign.* Seoul: Kooktaewon, 1997.

> *When the Faith and National Consciousness Meet - A Theological Response to a Korean Roman Catholic Chung-geun Thomas Ahn's Shooting of Hirobumi Ito.* Waegwan: Benedict Press, 2000.
> "Spirituality of Korean Christians of the Twenty-first Century." 1 & 2. *Common Good* 17-18 (Seoul: 1996).
> "If Korean Theology Re-reads the Gospel according to Matthew." 1-12. *Christian Thought* (Forthcoming).
> "Methodology and Practice of Korean Theology: A Korean Roman Catholic Approach to Doing Theology with Minjung." Ph.D. diss., Duquesne University, USA. Korean translation forthcoming from Benedict Press.

7.2.10. Kwak Seung Ryong, Pius (1958-)

Kwak Seung Ryong is currently working as a member of the Pastoral Institute for Inculturation Research of CBCK and a member of Korean Christian Thought Institute. In his theological work and writing he has contributed in particular to developing the theology of inculturation and pastoral research for the parish communities of Korea. For an inculturated Korean theology he has drawn especially on Eastern and Russian Orthodox theology and he has published writings on aspects of these in the *Philokalia* and in Dostoevsky. His interest is now moving towards an interdisciplinary harmony of biblical-systematic-spiritual-pastoral concerns in theology, as the basis for the inculturation of Korean theology.

Selected References

Works by Kwak Seung Ryong

> *Christ, Kenosis-Fullness according to the Later Dostoevsky.* Rome: Gregorian University Pub., 1995.
> *A Reum Da Um eui Sa Rang* (Philokalia: Christian spirituality of the East). Seoul: Mannam, 1997.
> *Sungbu wa Sungja wa Sungryung kwa hamche* (With the Father and the Son and the Holy Spirit). Seoul: Catholic Publishing House, 1999.

7.2.11. Kim Nyung (1958-)

Kim Nyung has contributed to the study of Church-state and Church-society relations, an important research field in Catholic church history and in the political history of Korea. His major work dealt with the Catholic Church's socio-political involvement opposing the authoritarian Korean state in the 1970s and 1980s. In addition to this, his attention has now moved to more recent periods and issues, such as the role and prospects of the Catholic citizens' movement as a part of civil movements in contemporary Korea. He pursues social science researches drawing on Catholic social teachings and focusing on issues of human rights, social justice, democracy, and education.

His writings include several articles on the influences of, and restraints in, the Catholic Church's socio-political involvement, on human rights and democracy in Korea and on the emphasis of Catholic universities on humanity education as a response to the rapidly changing society.

Selected References
Works by Kim Nyung
> "Politics of Religion in South Korea, 1974-1989: The Catholic Church's Political Opposition to the Authoritarian State." Ph.D. diss., The University of Washington, 1993.
> *Hanguk Chungchi wa Kyohwae-Kukga Galdung* (Korean politics and church-state conflicts). Seoul: Sonamu, 1996.
> *Kyohwae wa Kukka* (The church and state). Inchon: The Catholic University of Inchon, 1997. (co-author).

7.2.12. Cha Dong Yup, Norbert (1958-)

Cha Dong Yup was ordained as a priest of the Inchon Diocese in 1991. He earned his doctorate in pastoral theology with the dissertation: "Study on Methods of Evangelization through Small Christian communities" (1996). A central concern has been for him the nurture and support of diverse pastoral ministries and through his work he has contributed to building a healthy consciousness of ministry in the Korean Catholic Church. Two books on these subjects are forthcoming from Korean publishers. His theological interest is now moving towards forming an appropriate pastoral model which is responsive to paradigm shifts in the religious environment of Korea in the 21st century. His most recent writings are therefore focussed on "What Catholics believe in the Korean Context" and are planned to appear shortly.

Selected References
Works by Cha Dong Yup

> *Foundation of Community Ministry.* Seoul: Catholic Publishing House. Forthcoming.
> *The Network of the Word.* Seoul: Pulpit Media. Forthcoming.
> "Study on Methods of Evangelization through Small Christian communities." Ph.D. diss., University of Vienna, 1996.
> "The Desirable Authority of the Church." *Spiritual Life* 15 (1998).
> "Virtues of Pastors in the New Age." *Samok* 154 (2000).

7.2.13. Kim Min Soo, Ignatius (1956-)

Kim Min Soo was ordained in 1985 and earned his doctorate in mass communication from Pennsylvania State University (1997) with a dissertation entitled: "Historical and Comparative Analysis of Globalization through Communications Technology in the West and Asia." Upon returning to Korea he worked for the Pyonghwa Broadcasting Cable Television (PBC-Cable TV) for four years and he is now secretary for Social Communication of the Korean Bishops' Conference. His special interest in study and communication is that of ministry within Korean culture. Convinced that an evangelization of culture is called for at this time, he is continuing research on the nature and tasks of theology on the basis of Korean cultural experience. This can be termed a cultural theology set within a unique Korean situation in which new media such as the internet are flooding contemporary Korean society. He is currently writing a twelve article series on "New Culture Pastoral" which is scheduled to appear in the journal *Pastoral*.

Selected References (In Korean)
Works by Kim MinSoo

> "Inisian Theory: Its Application to South Korea." *Sungkok Journalism Review* 6 (1996).
> "Evangelization of Culture." Article series 1-7. *Pyonghwa Shinmun.* Forthcoming.
> "The Public Interest in Religious Broadcasting: A Case Study of Korean Religious Cable TV." *Journal of the Asian Research Center for Religion and Social Communication* 1.1. Forthcoming.

7.2.14. Other Contemporary Catholic theologians
7.2.14.1. Other Priest Theologians

Among other priests who have written on biblical interpretation, church history, social teaching, hermeneutics, liberation theology, unification and church reform are the following:

Chung Yangmo has studied the New Testament using historical criticism and hermeneutical methodology. He has taken initiatives in Bible annotation and the theology of religion and has written much about church reform. He has also produced a new interpretation of early apostolic teachings.

Mun Kyuhyun is committed to a faith-based praxis for political democratization and unification. He insists upon the importance of the role of Christians for unification in particular, and was arrested because of an illegal visit to North Korea. He has written extensively on Korean Catholic history which he studies from the perspective of unification.

Kim Chunho has mainly studied Catholic social teaching, liberation theology and Marxism and has interpreted these from a dialectical perspective. He is deeply concerned for reform of the Catholic Church.

Suh Kongsuk was a professor of religion at Sogang University. He has criticized the authoritarian Korean Church and is very interested in the hermeneutic reinterpretation of Christian dogma, advocating far-reaching renewal.

Selected References

Chung Yangmo. *The Gospel of Luke; A Bicentennial Anniversary Bible*. Waegwan: Benedict Press, 1990.

—. *The Teachings of Twelve Apostles*. Waegwan: Benedict Press, 1992.

Kim Chunho. *Catholic Church and Social Reform*. Waegwan: Benedict Press, 1999.

Kim Seung Hea. "Minjung Theology observed on the basis of Confucian tradition." *The Theological Thought* 92 (Spring 1996).

Moon Kyuhyun. *The History of the Korean Catholic Church* (I & II). Seoul: Vitture Publishers, 1994.
—. *Socialism and Catholic Social Teaching.* Waegwan: Benedict Press, 1991.
Park Jun Young. "The New Foundation of Theology for Catholic Action in the 1990s." In *The Church in the Age of Revolution.* Seoul: Society of Catholic Youth Theologians, 1991.
Suh In Suk, Paul. *The Poor in the Bible* (in Korean). Seoul: Sogang University, n.d.
Suh Kongsuk. *It has to be Renewed.* Waegwan: Benedict Press, 1998.

7.2.14.2. Other Lay Catholic Theologians

A number of Catholic writers are creative theologians who have published both monographs and articles, sometimes in association with Woori Theological Institute (see 7.6.2.; For Hwang Jongryul, Kim Hyoung Tae, Kim Jung Shin, Kim Nyung and John Park Il Young, see 7.2.9.; 7.2.7.; 7.2.2.; 7.2.11.; 7.2.3.). Their works cover such subjects as spirituality, ecclesiology and church history, biblical study, bio-ethics, Christian community, civil society and socio-economics.

Sung Yeum is a lay professor at Sogang University who studied medieval Latin literature and philosophy. He introduced Latin American liberation theology to Korea in the 1970s and has more recently written essays on church reform.

Kim Subok has also introduced the approaches and concerns of liberation theology to Korea. He operates a publishing company, 'Work and Play,' and has written about political democratization and church reform.

Kim Hangsup is a professor of religion at Hanshin University who studied economic theology in Brazil as a member of Woori Theology Institute. He has introduced economic theology to Korea and developed theological criticism concerning the Asian economic crisis.

Park Hyunjoon is director of the Woori Theology Institute and has studied liberation theology and church reform since the 1980s.

Recently he has written and worked for church reform through the perspective of a theology of community.

Park Moonsu is a lay person interested in pastoral theology. He has studied church reform and women's religious congregations, and has tried to analyze religious life scientifically. His major subject is Christian ethics in the age of information.

Kang Inchul is a professor of religion at Hanshin University. He has studied religious social work in Korean Protestant and Catholic churches, and the dynamic relationship of the Korean Church to civil society.

Selected References (In Korean)

> Hwang Jongryul. *The Structure of Korean Theology*. Seoul: Guktaewon, 1996.
> —. "History and Structures of Korean Inculturated Theology." (12 articles) *Samok* (1995).
> Kang Inchul. *The History of Korean Social Change and Society in the Period of U.S. Military Administration*. Daejun: Hanlim University, 1999.
> Kim Hangsup. *The Challenge of Life Sciences and Christianity*. Kwangju: Work and Play, 2000.
> Kim Subok. *Good News from the Scripture*. Seoul: Woori Theology Institute, 2000.
> Park Hyunjoon. *The Hierarchy of the Christian Church and Lay People*. Seoul: Jangsin University. Forthcoming.
> —. "The Understanding and Evaluation of Korean Catholic Church on *Minjung* Theology." Mimeo'd, 2000.
> —. "The Christian Spirituality and Community." Woori Theology 1. Seoul: Woori Theology Institute. Forthcoming.
> Park Moonsu. *Korean Religious Culture and the New Age Movement*. Seoul: St. Paul Publications, 1998.
> —. "Korea Catholic Church and *Minjung* Theology." *The Times and Minjung Theology* 1 (1994).
> Sung Yeum. *Religious Tolerance and Christianity in the Age of Religious Pluralism*. Seoul: Minji Pub. Forthcoming.

7.3 Selection of Other Contextual Sources
7.3.1. Christian Poets - a Selection

There is a long and rich tradition of writings by Catholic poets such as Kim Chi Ha (see 5.2.3.10.) and Lee Hae In, Claudia (6.2.3.)

Contextual Theology in Korea

as well as of Protestant poets, which along with the work of other nationalist or dissident writers, have proved valuable contributions to Korean theological endeavors. Some examples are extant from earlier periods of persecution in the 19th century and others emerged during the time of Japanese or subsequent military regimes. Many such poets, Christians and others, suffered severely for their beliefs and writings in those times. An early example would be the "Poem of God" by Choe Yong Eob (Yang Eob Chio, d.1861), one of the first two priests ordained. A small selection from different groups of poets in the 20th century would include the following:

In the time of Japanese colonial rule **Chong Chi Yong** (1903-?) studied at Doshisha University, Kyoto, published poetry in the journal *Simunhak* (1930-31) and edited *Munjang* (1939-41). His *Collected Poems* (1935) appeared in a revised edition in 1946. *White Deer Cascade* appeared in 1941 (see Ko won 1970, Lee 1990).

Ku Sang (b.1919) studied in Japan and published his poetry first in North Korea (1946). Many volumes followed, including *Wastelands of Fire* (1956), *Diary of the Fields* (1967), *The True Appearance of the Word* (1980) and *St Christopher's River* (1986). Selections have been published in English in 1990 and 1991.

The woman poet **Kim Namjo** first published her writing in 1953 and most recently in 1993. She is known for the strong feeling and clear diction of such poems as "Candle Light," "Love," "The Winter Christ," "Morning Prayer," and "For you My Beloved." A selection of her work was also published in English in 1993.

Mun Ik Kwan (see 7.1.6.) was professor of Old Testament at Hankuk Seminary, and since the 1970s has been a leader in movements for democracy and reunification, resulting in frequent imprisonment. His poetry has appeared in many periodicals and in three volumes of verse. Two anthologies of his writing have also been published.

One example from many other poets, not necessarily Christian, but who have had wide influence in the movements for democracy and human rights, is **Yang Song U** (fl. 1970). Poems such as "The Winter Republic" (1975) and "The Notes of a Slave" (1977) were first published in Japan (*Fukuin to Sekai*), but led to his imprisonment. He has pictured the poet's role as that of an honest prophet for the future of Korean people.

Others from whom similar poetry has come include Koh Un, Sr. Lee Hae In (see 6.2.3.), Kim Chunt'ae, Park Hyung Kyu, Cho Nam Ki, Kim Myoung Shik and Kim Min Gi. Other poets' work appeared along with that of Kim Chi Ha in such volumes as *Cry of the People and Other Poems* (1974), in anthologies such as *Testimonies of Faith in Korea* (1989), and in journals such as *Samok, Sinhak Sasang* and *In God's Image*. (See 6.1; 7.3.2.; 7.3.3.) Expatriates such as Richard Rutt and Kevin O'Rourke have written poems in the Korean Sijo tradition.

Selected References

Cho Kyu Sik. "The Spirituality of Yang Eob Chio (1821-1861)." *Samok* 164. (1992).

Cho Nam Ki. *Resurrection. Anthology of Rev'd Cho Nam Ki* (in Korean). Seoul: Poet Publishing, 1978.

Kim Chi Ha et al. *Cry of the People and Other Poems*. Hayama: Autumn Press, 1974.

Kim Nam Jo. *Selected Poems of Kim Namjo*. Cornell East Asia Series. Ithaca: Cornell University, 1993.

Ko Won. *Contemporary Korean Poetry*. Iowa City: University of Iowa Press, 1970.

Ku Sang. *Wastelands of Fire. Selected Poems of Ku Sang*. London and Boston: Forest Books, 1990.

—. *A Korean Century: River and Fields*. London and Boston: Forest Books, 1991.

Lee, Peter H. *Modern Korean Literature*. An Anthology. Honolulu: University of Hawaii Press, 1990.

Mun Ik Kwan. *There is No Place to Stand Behind Me* (in Korean). Seoul: Practice and Literature Publishing, 1984.

Paekpom Thought Research Institute. *Late Spring: The Soul Pleading for a Dream. Mun Ik Kwan Anthology*. Seoul: Hwada Publishing, 1987.

Sin Kyu Hho. *Han'guk Kidokkyo siga yon'gu* (Christian poetry, literature, and criticism). Seoul: Ihoe Munhwasa, 1999.

Yang Song-u. *The Notes of a Slave*. Special Issue of *Korea Communiqué* 23 (Aug. 1978).

7.3.2. Theological Journals - Protestant

See also Institutes, Movements and Associations (7.5) and Thematic Selections (7.4).

Apart from those Protestant theological journals mentioned in 3.2.2., others are important for including theological writings. Amongst many others, these include *Chung Nyun* - (The Youth), *Yoksa kyoyuk* (Historical Education), *Hyunjon* (Presence), *Sidae wa Minjung Sinhak* (Minjung Theology and the Times), *Jinbo Pyungron* (The Radical Review) and *Hanguk Kidok Chongnyun Hyubuihoe Hoebo* - Bulletin of EYCK (Ecumenical Youth Council of Korea).

Of particular importance for contextual writings are *Sinhak Sasang* (Theological Thought) and *Kidokkyo Sasang* (Christian Thought). These journals have in recent decades published articles on almost every aspect of Korean theologies, including: studies in biblical interpretation; Christology; theology of the Spirit; spirituality and theology of religions; *minjung* community; Bible interpretation and messianism; feminist theology and theology of life; mission in pluralist society; ecclesiology and the 21st century; ecology; sacramental theology; Christianity and humanism; national unity and reconciliation; Shamanism / *Donghak* and Christianity; and Buddhist and Confucian perspectives on *minjung* and liberation theology; globalization; social ethics; science and theology; national and international economics; the 'Liberal' - 'conservative' encounter; ecumenical theologies; civil society and Korean community.

Notable earlier journals which included significant materials by both Catholics and Protestants were *Korea Communiqué* (writings and poetry on human rights and social justice, published by the Emergency Christian Conference on Korean Problems (Japan - 1975-?1982); and *Inculturation* (published by the Columban Fathers, Korea - 1988-1995). Both of these were published in English.

Sinhak Sasang has in recent years also published collections of articles on important themes, including "The Role of the Asian Church for Peace in Asia" (94, 1996); "A Paradigm of Post-Colonial

Theology" (95, 1996); "Ahn Byung Mu's Theology and Thought" (96, 1997); "The New Dimensions of Pastoral Ministry in the Korean Church" (97, 1997); "Visions of Christian Mission in the 21st century" (98, 1997); and "Korean Theology and its Context" (105, 1999).

Recent article series in *Kidokkyo Sasang* have included: "Feminist Movements and Interpretation of the Bible" (470, 1998); "Reunification and Reconciliation" (488, 1999); "Western Theology and Korean Theology" (502, 2000); and "Sources of Spirituality" (504, 2000).

A selection of other Protestant journals which are significant for Korean contextual theology would include the following:

i) English Language: *Ewha Journal of Feminist Theology; Korean Journal of Theology; Yonsei Journal of Theology; Theology and Society* (Hanil); the *Journal of Korean Christianity;* and *In God's Image.*

ii) Korean Language: *Biblical Life; Church and Feminist Theology* (KAFT), *Experience of Korean Women* (Christian Books Press); *Hanguk Kidok Chongnyun Hanshin Bulletin* (Hanshin University); *Hyubuihoe Hoebo* (EYCK); *Journey for Life and Liberation* (IACWC); *Korean Church and Spirituality; Korean Feminist Theology; Min Jung Theology; New Heaven, New Earth, New Woman* (Biblical Life Press); *Peace-making Women; Sidae wa Minjung Sinhak* (Contemporary and *Minjung* Theology); *Sallim* (Ch'onan-si); *Saembawi* (Seoul); *Sinhak gwa Silchon II* (Theology and Praxis II - KSCF*); Spirituality and Feminist Theology* (Christian Books Press); *Thought of Christianity* (CLS); *Women and Ministry, Woman, Peace, and Life; Yonhap Sinhak Taehagwon* (Yonsei Journal of Theology).

Selected References

A selection of contextual articles (in Korean) from two principal journals mentioned above would include, for *Sinhak Sasang* (in chronological order):

    Kim Chang Lark. "Minjung Theology as Narrative Theology." 64 (1989).

Kim Kyung Jae. "Recent Currents of Systematic Theology in Korea." 64 (1989).
Lee Jong Bae. "Critical Comment on Korean Theology of Inculturation." 66 (1989).
Kim Jin. "Shamanism and the Theology of 'Han'." 67 (1989).
Shu Chang Won. "Minjung Theology and Feminist Theology." 69 (1990).
Kim Sung Jae. "The Methodology of Minjung Theology." 95 (1996).
Jeong Chong Hun. "The Theological Foundation of Social Mission." 98 (1997).
Kim Kyoung Jae. "The Christology of Suh Nam Dong." 99 (1997).
Sohn Kyoo Tae. "Study of the Social Mission of the Korean Church." 100 (1998).
Choi Young Sil. "Korean Feminist Theology beyond the Scope of 'Han'." 100 (1998).
Han Kee Chae. "The Confluence of Two Narratives for Minjung Ethics." 105 (1999).

Recent contextual articles from *Kidokkyo Sasang* would include:
Lee Kyung Sook. "The Hermeneutic Tasks of a Feminist Theology in Asia." 453 (1996).
Chung Jin Hong. "Christianity and Shamanism." 456 (1996).
Song Sung Jin. "Love and Truth, Beauty and Goodness and our Sacramental Life: A Christian Neo-Confucian Dialogue." 462 (1997).
Kim Eun Soo. "A Critical Study of Polarization in the Understanding of Mission." 457 (1997).
Park Kyung Mi. "The Korean Church and Feminist Biblical Interpretation." 470 (1998).
Lee Hyun Mo. "The Democratisation of the Church and her Mission." 472 (1998).
Chai Soo Il. "Theological Criticism of the International Monetary Fund." 473 (1998).
Kim Sang Il . "The Encounter of Gnosticism and Feminist Theology." 475 (1998).
Yoon Won Keun. "The 'Third Way' and the Kingdom of God." 483 (1999).
Lee Chun Jin. "Mission and Culture in Korea." 496 (2000).

7.3.3. Theological Journals - Catholic

See also Institutes, Movements and Associations (7.6) and Thematic Selections (7.4).

Catholic journals of theological importance include *Samok*, *Cham Saram Doe-eo*, *Catholic Theology and Thought* (for these see below), *Catholic Thought Today* (Catholic Bishops' Conference of Korea, Seoul), *Collectanea Catholica* (Catholic College, Seoul), *Shinhak Junmang* (Daegun College, Kwangju), *Genuine People* (formerly *Let's Be One* - Catholic Human Development Committee) and *Reason and Faith* (Kwangju Catholic College). Contents of these journals have been indexed in the bi-annual *Theology in Context* (Aachen) since 1983.

Of particular importance for writings in contextual theology is the Pastoral Review *Samok*, published (in Korean) by the Pastoral Institute of Korea, Seoul. In addition to significant individual articles (see below), special issues of *Samok* have included the following: "Social Justice and the Church" (22, July 1972); "Social Participation by the Church" (37, Jan. 1975); "Christianity and Culture" (45, March 1977); "Shamanism and Christianity" (55, Jan. 1978); "Catholicism and Korean Culture" (64, July 1979); "Church and State" (83, Sept 1982); "Inculturation of the Gospel" (90, 91, Dec. 1983, Jan 1984); article series on "Pastoral Directives for Inculturation" and "Perspectives for Inculturation"(1985); Confucian, Taoist, I-Ching Understandings of Women (105, 109, 112, 1986); "Reunification of Korea" (136, 1990); "Spirituality in the Korean Catholic Church" (211, 1996); "The Jubilee Year" (216, 1997); "Identity and Role of Women in the Catholic Church" (217, 1997). Article series include: "Jesus and Church" (*minjung* facing structural evil) (85, 86, 1983); "Project Commission Reports: Inculturation in Korea" (16 reports in vols.114-150); "Catholic Church in Korean State and Society" (130, 1989; 143, 1990); "Role of Women on the Church" (151, 1991; 186, 1994; 199, 1995); Ecology and Development (171, 1993); Theology of Religions (1994/1995); a series on "The Inculturated Concept of Person" (1995-1996); "Jubilee and the Korean Catholic Church" (240, 1999); "Ecotheology" (12 articles by Moon Yeong Seok, 1999).

The journal *Catholic Theology and Thought* (Catholic University, Seoul), is also a significant source for contextual theology and among article series published by this are those on the themes of Christian Anthropology (7, 1992); Basic Christian Communities (9, 1993); Industrialization, Mammonism, Social Ethics (10, 1993); Christian Humanism in the Bible (17, 1996); Views of Life in Faith Traditions (20, 1997); Christianity and Other Faiths (21, 22, 1997); Ecotheology, Bible and Church (25, 1998); Authority and Power in Korean Society (23, 1998); Capitalism, Social Welfare and the Poor (29, 1999).

For major areas of contextual theology writers in these journals include the following:

On aspects of **Inculturation**: Jeong Hogyeong, Min Yongjin, Ham Seung, Kim Song Te, Choi Sogu, Na Wongyun, Kim Yong Sik, Choi Byonguk, Jeong Yangmo, Lee Soon Seong, Kim Ung Tae, Cho Kwang. Park Il Yeong, Zung Ha Young, Sean Dwan, Hugh McMahon and Robert Brennan. On **Interfaith** concerns: Kim Nak Phil, Choi Ki Bok, Park Il Yeung, Hong Yoon Shik, Lee Soon Seong, Yoon Ho Jin, Jung Gak, Cho Heung Youn, Kim Seong Nye, Yoon Toung Hae and Lee Chan Soo. On issues of **Faith and Society, Social and Political Theology:** Yang Song-u, Kim Shun Ho, Kim Dae Jung, Han Hong Soon, Kim Jeong Hee, Koo Ja Ryong, Ku Beong Jin, Ri Yong Hoon, Lee Ho, Lee Chang Yeon, Lee Hyeon Sook, Lee Seong Bae, Shin Young Bok, Haw Hyen, Ham Sei Ung, Park Moon Su.

A diverse stream of writings has come from many others. Examples of those writing on **Korean Spirituality** are Kim Chang Yeol, Chun Dal Soo, Park Jae Man and Kim Bo Rok; on **Ecotheology**, Chun Hun Ho, Chung Hong Kyu, Moon Yeong Seok and Lee Jae Don; on **Reunification**, Shim Sang Tae, O Kyong Hwan, Yang Han Mo, Baik Nam Ik, Kim Jun Ho, Kim Nam Sik and Kim Choon Ho; on **Catholic Art/Dance in Korea**: You Keun Choon, Pahk Han Jin, Jeong Jae Man and Jin Kyo Hoon; on **Christology**: Zung Tae Hyoun, Seo kong Seok, Kim Kwang Sik, Choi Hye Yeong, Lee Hong Yeon, Lee Sun Seong and Kim Kyoung Jae; on **Biblical Hermeneutic**: Lim Sook Hee, Lee Yeong Heon, Shin Kyo Seon, Shin Sung Hwan, Park Rae Sik and Bang Sang Man; on **Missiology**: Kim Moon Hwan, Kim You Chul, Kim Hak Lyeol, Kim Joon Chul and Jeong Chong Hun.

Notable earlier journals which included significant materials by both Catholics and Protestants were *Korea Communiqué* (writings and poetry on human rights and social justice, published by the Emergency Christian Conference on Korean Problems (Japan - 1975-?1982); and *Inculturation* (published by the Columban Fathers, Korea - 1988-1995). Both of these were published in English.

Selected References

Brennan, Robert. "Inculturation of the Common Tabernacle." *Inculturation* 5.1 (1990).

Cho Hung Youn. "The Influence of Shamanism on Korean Christianity." *Korean Christian Thought* 5 (1997).

Commission for Inter-Religious Dialogue: "Dossier on Jesus Christ." *Samok* 225 (1997).

Dwan, Sean. "Theological Notes on Inculturation." *Inculturation* 3.1 (1988).

Ham See Hung. "Fundamental Reflections on the Renewal of the Church in Democratization." *Samok* 132 (1990).

Han Sang Jin. "The Meaning of Socio-Political Responsibility." *Samok* 145 (1991).

Jeong Da Sik. "Christian Community and Evangelism." *Samok* 87 (1983).

Ku Sang et al. "Inculturation of the Gospel" (Restoring, evaluating traditional culture). *Samok* 90 (1983); 91 (1984).

Kang Byoung Kwon. "Theology of Inculturation in Korea." *Korean Christian Thought* 5 (1997).

Kim Chun Ho. "The Development of Korean Society and Social Ethics." *Sinhak Jonmang* 128 (1989).

Kim Dae Jung. *Prison Writings*. Berkeley: University of California, 1987.

Kim Jeong Soo. "Korean History of the Catholic Faith." *Sinhak Jonmang* 81 (1988).

Kim Seong Te. "The Historical Meaning of the Catholic Church: its Subjectivity." *Samok* 91 (1984).

Kim Shin Ho. "The Meaning and Significance of Liberation and Freedom." *Samok* 192 (1995).

Ku Byeong Jin. "Politics and Ethics." *Samok* 159 (1992).

Lee Soon Seong. "The Korea Shamanistic Gut and Christian Eucharist." *Sinhak Jonmang* 115 (1996).

Lim Chae Chung. "The Teaching of Minjung Theology." *Samok* 174 (1993).

McMahon, Hugh. "Reflections on an Inculturation Experience." *Inculturation* 6.2 (1991).

Moon Yeong-seok. "Introduction to Eco-theology" (Series of 12 articles). *Samok* 240-252 (1999).

Oh Kyeung Whan. "Marxism and Theology of Liberation." *Samok* 116 (1988).

—. "Theological Foundation of the Justice Movement of the Church." *Samok* 136 (1990).

—. "Social Teaching of the Church, Social Welfare and Common Goods." *Samok* 213 (1996).

Park Sang Bae. "Political Involvement of the Church and Pluralistic Society." *Samok* 30 (1973).

Yang Han Mo. "The Unification of Korea and a Perspective of the Catholic Church." *Catholic Journal for Social Science* 5 (1984).

7.4 Thematic Selections

To provide further examples to those already mentioned, writings in the areas of theology and hermeneutic, inter-faith encounter and studies in religion and society, are listed below.

7.4.1. Theology and Hermeneutic

Han Kee Chae. "Narrative Ethics in a Minjung Context." *Asian Journal of Theology* 11.2 (1997).

Kim Chang Nak. "Peace Movement in the New Testament." *Theological Studies* 31 (1990).

Kim Heup Young. "A Tao of Asian Theology in the 21st Century: from the Perspective of the Ugmch'i Phenomenon." *Asian Journal of Theology* 13.2 (1999).

Koh Jae Sik. "Minjung Theology and Liberation Theology." *Theological Studies* 28 (1987).

Lee Jung Bae. "Korean Reflection on Christian Anthropology and Soteriology." *Korea Journal of Theology* 1 (1995).

Lee Moon Jang. "Identifying an Asian Theology: A Methodological Quest." *Asian Journal of Theology* 13.2 (1999).

Park Ik Soo. "A Biblical and Historical Understanding of the Development of the Minjung Church." *CTC Bulletin* 8.1&2 (1989).

Park Tong-whan. "The Relation of Theory and Praxis in Korean Thought." *Theological Thought* 21 (1978).

Pyun Sun Hwan. "Dewesternization and Third World Theology." *Theological Thought* 46.3 (1984).

Yang Guen Seok. "A Pre-colonial Reading of the Bible in Korea: its Hermeneutical and Missiological Implications." *CTC Bulletin* 16.1 (1999).

Yim Tae Soo. "Interpretation of the Old Testament from the Perspective of Minjung Theology." *Asian Journal of Theology* 14.1 (2000).

Yong Nak Heong. *Reformed Social Ethics and the Korean Church.* New York, Peter Lang, 1997.

7.4.2. Inter-faith Encounter and Studies

Adams, Daniel J. "Ancestors, Folk Religion and Korean Christianity." In *Perspectives in Christianity in Korea and Japan*, edited by Mark R, Mullins and Richard Fox Young. Lewiston, NY: Edwin Mellen Press, 1995.

Cheon Jun Ku. *Liberating Shamanism: a Spiritual Resource for Korean Christians.* Grand Rapids, MI: UMI Dissertation Services, c1996.

Chong Chae-sik. "Confucian Tradition and Nationalist Ideology in Korea." In *South Korea's Minjung Movement: the Culture and Politics of Dissidence,* by Kenneth M. Wells. Honolulu: University of Hawaii Press, c1995.

—. *Korea: the Encounter Between the Gospel and Neo-Confucian Culture.* Gospel and Cultures Pamphlet 6. Geneva: WCC Publications, 1997.

Han Tai Dong. "Meditation Process in Cultural Interaction: A Search for a Dialogue Between Christianity and Buddhism." *NEAJOT* 3 (1969).

Kim Heup Young. *Wang Yang Ming and Karl Barth: a Confucian-Christian Dialogue.* Lanham, MD: University Press of America, 1996.

Na Chae Woon. "Filial Piety in Confucian Thought." *NEAJOT* 28/29 (1982).

Kim Kyoung-Jae. *Christianity and the Encounter of Asian Religions: Method of Correlation, Fusion of Horizons, and Paradigm Shifts* in the Korean Grafting Process. Zoetermeer: Uitgeveriji Boekencentrum, 1995.

Park Pong Bae. "The Confucian Moral Philosophy of Harmony." *NEAJOT* 9 (1972).

Pyun Sun Hwan. "Other Religions and Theology." *East Asia Journal of Theology* 3.2 (1985).

7.4.3. Religion and Society

Abelmann, Nancy. *Echoes of the Past, Epics of Dissent: A South Korean Social Movement.* Berkeley: University of California Press, 1996.

CCA and International Christian Network for Democracy in Korea. *Reunification, Peace and Justice in Korea: Christian Response in the 1980s.* Hong Kong: CCA, 1988.

Kim Yong-han. *Pyonghwa tongil kwa Hanguk Kidokkyo: pogumjuuijok tongil sinhak ul hyanghayo* (The peaceful unification and Korean Christianity). Seoul: Pungman, 1990.

Kim, Nyong. *Han'guk chongch'i wa kyohoe-kukka kaltung* (Korean politics and church-state conflicts). Seoul: Sonamu, 1996.

Choi Myung-keun. *Changes in Korean Society between 1884-1910 as a Result of the Introduction of Christianity.* Asian Thought and Culture 20. New York: Peter Lang, 1997.

Choi Sung and others. *Korean Situation in 1992.* Seoul: CISJD, 1993. (Annual).

Christian Institute for the Study of Justice and Development. *Lost Victory. An Overview of the Korean People's Struggle for Democracy 1987.* Seoul: Minjungsa, 1988.

Lancaster, Lewis R. and Richard Payne, eds. *Religion and Society in Contemporary Korea.* Berkeley: Institute of East Asian Studies, 1996.

Ogle, George E. *South Korea: Dissent within the Economic Miracle.* London and New Jersey: Zed Books, 1990.

Sohn Hak-Kyu. *Authoritarianism and Opposition in Korea.* London and New York: Routledge, 1989.

7.5 Institutes, Movements and Associations - Protestant

7.5.1. National Council of Churches in Korea (NCCK)

The NCCK is a key association for many Protestant churches in all aspects of mission, education and theology. It has developed from the General Council of Evangelical Mission in Korea (1905) and the Korean National Council of Protestant Churches (1924). With national independence in 1945, the NCCK worked to share the Gospel with all Korean people, to build unity and cooperation among all churches in Korea, and with churches around the world. From the 1960s the NCCK has, through many agencies, focused on mission with the marginalized poor, farmers and laborers, on issues of human rights and democracy, on peace and reunification of the Korean peninsula, and on responding to voices of Korean-origin in China, Japan and Russia. Theological reflection and prayer, ministries of women and men and social action have been integral to all its activities.

The NCCK publishes *Activity News* (English) and *The Church and the World* (Korean) which feature papers on Korean ecumenical theological developments along with theological statements of the NCCK. The council now plans to issue a series of documents on issues of peace and reconciliation, the Korean crisis, participation of women, establishment of an ecumenical community in Northeast Asia, an alternative global community, and the creation of wider networks for communication and co-operation in mission and human solidarity. In regard to these issues, a recent statement declares that "we seek an alternative global economic structure and life on the basis of economic theology, economic ethics and life theology. We warn against the devastation of humanity and nature by capitalistic power, and seek the practice of economic justice based on our faith."

7.5.2. Christian Literature Society of Korea (1890)

The CLSK was founded as The Korean Religious Tract Society at the Rev'd. Underwood's house and in 1919 was renamed The Christian Literature Society of Korea. Throughout the 20th century, and despite the destruction of material during times of war, the inter-denominational CLSK has published a very wide variety of books and Christian materials. These have included the ecumenical hymn-books *Hapdong Chansongga* (1949), *Kaepyon Changsongga* (1968), and *Hankook Chansongga* (1983); *The Christian Encyclopedia* (1972), a series of Bible translations and New Testament Commentaries (50 volumes by 1998), and continuing series of works in Korean theology, church history and biography.

With its associated agencies the Hyondae Sasangsa (1972) and Korea Christian (1976) publishing houses the CLSK had by 1990 published a total of 2,887,907 copies of 420 different kinds of books. More recent volumes have included not only professional theological books but books for lay people, along with works on contextual theologies, feminist theologies, church and society issues, theology of Korean culture and *minjung* theology.

7.5.3. Other Institutes and Movements

The number of other theological institutes and networks, centers and journals in Korea is very extensive and a complete listing is not possible here. A selection of representative institutes which also publish journals would include those already mentioned under 5.3.1. above, along with study institutes at such universities and colleges, as Hanshin, Yonsei, Ewha, Sunshil, Keimyung, Kang Nam, Han Nam and Korea universities. A small selection follows of other institutes which provide important resources for the development of Korean theologies, including women's theology and *minjung* theology. Many of these are associated with the NCCK.

Christian Institute for the Study of Justice and Development has published regular bulletins and books, including the annual *Korean Situation*. It has been concerned not only to analyse church and society issues and political and economic developments but also to stimulate the development of "the new indigenous Korean theology."

The Korea Theological Study Institute has long published the quarterly journal *Sinhak Sasang* (Theological Thought) along with series of monographs and documents dealing with issues of contextual, minjung and feminist theologies. See e.g. Kim Ee Kon

(1985), and Sohn Seung Hee (1990). (See also 5.3.3.1.2. and 5.3.3.2.4. above).

Korean Association of Accredited Theological Schools publishes the *Korean Journal of Theology* and also papers and reports from conferences and seminars. It also co-operates in Asia-wide ecumenical programs and in the publishing of the *Asia Journal of Thelogy*, with SATHRI (see vol. 1) and ATESEA (see vol. 2)

Korean Association of Christian Studies (Han'guk Kidokkyo Hakhoe) arranges regular conferences and symposia and publishes occasional collections of papers. Since 1990 see e.g. *Korean theology and integrity of creation* (1992), *The Task of Korean Theology in 21st century* (1994), *National Reunification and the Christian Church of Korea* (1994) and *Feminist Theology and the Korean Church* (1997).

The Research Institute of Minjung Theology since 1995 has been publishing the *Minjung Theology series* 1 and 2, including such titles as *An Introduction to Minjung Theology*, and *Are the Minjung Messiah?* (see 5.3.3.2.3. above).

Christian Institute for the 3rd Era, the grouping of '3rd Generation' Minjung Theologians (see 5.3.3.3.).

Institute for Cross-Cultural Studies, Taegu, issues *Taegu Tongso munhwa* (Journal of the Kyemyong Taehak Tongso Munhwa Yon'guso).

The Korea Institute for Social Justice and Peace has published a number of "Mooks," and other materials on Korean indigenous theological movements.

Systematic Theology Society in Korea, Seoul, publishes the *Korea Journal of Systematic Theology,* from 1997- .

Selected References

Chon Taek Bu. *The History of the Korean Ecumenical Movement* (in Korean). 1979.
Christian Institute for the Study of Justice and Development. *Korean Situation*. Seoul: CISJD (Annual).
—. *Democatization Movement and the Christian Church in Korea During the 1970s*. Seoul: CISJD, 1985.

Han'guk Kidokkyo Hakhoe (Korean Association of Christian Studies). *Ch'angjo ui pojon kwa Han'guk sinhak* (Korean theology and integrity of creation). Seoul: Taehan Kidokkyo Sohoe, 1992.

Han Yong Je. *Han'guk Kidokkyo munso undong 100-yon* (100 years of literary movement of Korean Christianity). Seoul: Kidokkyo Munsa, 1987.

—. *Han'guk chonggi kanhaengmul 100-yon* (100 years of Korean Christian periodicals). Seoul: KidokKyo Munsa, 1987.

Hwang, Yang-su. *Han'guk Kidokkyo munhaksajok koch'al. Sangdae* (A study on the formation of Korean Christian literature). Seoul: Kiye Mun'gwan, 1991.

Kim Ee Kon. *The Rapid Change of Mood in the Lament Psalms.* Seoul: Korea Theological Study Institute, 1985.

Korean Association of Feminist Theology, ed. *Feminist Theological Thought.* 3 vols. Seoul: Christian Literature Society of Korea, 1993, 1995,1997.

Lee Kyung Sook. *Women in Old Testament.* Seoul: CLSK, 1994.

National Council of Churches. *The Church in Korea.* Seoul: NCCK, 1961.

—. *The National Council of Churches in Korea.* Seoul: NCCK, c.1990.

Sin, Kyu-ho. *Han'guk Kidokkyo siga yon'gu* (Christian poetry, literature and criticism). Seoul: Ihoe Munhwasa, 1999.

Sohn Seung Hee. *Understanding Feminist Theology.* Seoul: Korea Theological Study Institute, 1990.

Yonse Taehakkyo. *Kidokkyo komunhon chonsi mongnok* (Catalogue of Christian books and periodicals exhibited). Seoul: Yonse Taehakkyo Chungang Tosogwan, 1968.

Yun, Ch'un-byong. *Han'guk Kidokkyo sinmun, chapchi paengnyonsa, 1885-1945* (100 years of Christian newspapers and periodicals). Seoul: Taehan Kidokkyo Ch'ulp'ansa, 1984.

7.6 Institutes, Movements and Associations - Catholic

7.6.1. Catholic Bishops' Conference of Korea (Hanguk Chinjugyo Chugyodan)

Following the establishment of the Korean hierarchy in 1962, a College of Bishops was formed, later to become the Catholic Bishops' Conference of Korea (CBCK). The Conference formed four Episcopal Commissions in 1981: for Clergy and Religious, for Doctrine, for Mission and Pastoral Affairs, for Social Affairs;

and later added two special commissions for the Great Jubilee of the Year 2000, and for the Reconciliation of Korean People.

In the last three decades the CBCK, or groups of its bishops, have made a number of declarations and statements both on pastoral concerns of the church and on major social and political issues. These have been published in the CBCK's media and also in the main Catholic journals (see references below). Among major issues which the bishops have addressed have been the wrongful arrest and imprisonment of priests and lay people (both Catholic and Protestant), the imposition of martial law and the Yushin constitution (early 1970s), the forced closure of the 'Laborers Classroom' (1977) and harassment of social and community workers, the suppression of Unions and industrial workers (1978), the conditions for foreign workers (a recurrent concern), responsibility for failing to oppose the Japanese occupation during World War II, opposition to the cloning of human embryos and the present-day tendency of some priests to embrace 'rampant materialism.'

Many of these statements affirm important theological positions in response to contemporary situations. The Statement on Foreign Workers, for example, declares that "the riches of creation are to be considered as a common good of the whole of humanity. ... The jubilee year was meant to restore this social justice." The bishops have apologized for failures under Japanese rule and ask all churches throughout the country to repent past and present sins committed by the Korean Church, and for the "self-serving" attitude of the Church. It also mentions the Church's "insufficient" modern-day role as a guardian of social morals, human rights and dignity as well as economic justice in times of social conflicts, corruption, political upheavals and economic opportunism.

Bishops of Japan and Korea now meet regularly to seek "a common view of the history their countries share" and to broaden their dialogue to include pastoral practices, youth exchanges, vocations and the formation of seminarians in both countries. The Pastoral Institute of the Conference conducts research and study, as well as seminars and conferences on a wide range of pastoral and inculturation questions. It also publishes the Pastoral Review *Samok* (see 7.3.3.).

Selected References

The publishing department of the Catholic Conference of Korea produces the periodicals *Kyonghyang Magazine* (Korean / monthly), *Catholic Thought Today - CBCK Bulletin* (Korean / bi-monthly), *CBCK Newsletter* (English / quarterly), and *Documenta Catholica* (Korean / quarterly). CBCK also publishes *Daily Mass* (Korean / monthly), along with liturgical books, catechisms, ecclesiastical documents and other books.

The Catholic Church in Korea. Seoul: Bicentennial Episcopal Commission, 1984.

"Declaration by the Korean Bishops' Conference on the Problem of Unification of South and North Korea." *Samok* 128 (1989).

"How to Meet the Requirements of the Korean Faithful. Discussion on the Mission and Responsibilities of the CBCK." *Samok* 181 (1994).

"Statement by the Korean Bishops' Conference on Foreign Workers 25 June 1997." *CBCK Newsletter* Document File V3.00.

"Reform and Reconciliation" Seoul: CBCK n.d.

Research on Korean Society. Seoul: Catholic Commission for its Bicentennial Celebration, 1985.

7.6.2. Woori Theology Institute

Woori Theology Institute was established in 1994 for the purpose of church reform and the evangelization of society. It was begun by young scholars committed to the struggle against the dictatorship of the 1980s and is the only theological institute run by laity in the Korean Catholic Church. The ultimate purpose is to do 'Woori theology,' which means for the Institute and its partners, seeking for Korean experiences of God through Korean historical life, to be described in Korean language. Woori Theological Institute has focused its studies and reflection, symposia and publications on church reform and on proposals for pastoral policy through a scientific analysis of pastoral reality.

Selected References (in Korean)

Park Taesik. *Church and History.* Seoul: Woori Theology Institute, 1999.

Lee Chunghee. *The Last Supper of Jesus and the Holy Supper of the Early Church*. Seoul: Woori Theology Institute, 1999.

Woori Insitute. *The Asian Economic Crisis and the Role of the Church: IMF, Human Rights, and the Church*. Seoul: Woori Theology Institute, 1998.

—. *Study on the Faith and Situation of Korean Catholic Christians*. Seoul: Catholic News Paper, 2000.

—. *Study on the Activities of the Korean Catholic Church related to the IMF Economic Crisis*. Seoul: Woori Theology Institute. Forthcoming.

"Symposium on the Task and Vision of Catholic Ministry for Unification at the Present." Seoul: Woori Theology Institute, 1995.

"Symposium on the Korean Catholic Church-The Present State of the Church." Academic Paper. Seoul: Woori Theology Institute, n.d.

Weekly Magazine: 'Good News in the Period of Separation' (weekly, 1991-) Seoul: Woori Theological Institute.

7.6.3. Korean Christian Thought Institute (1992)

Korean Christian Thought Institute (KCTI) aims to promote the inculturation of Christianity and to enrich the universal Church through in-depth research on questions related to Christianity in Korea. It brings together clerics, religious, and laity who are interested in inculturation with discussion papers presented at regular study meetings, lectures and seminars.

Seminars held have included, in 1992, "The Present State Faith in Korea"; and "Pioneers of Inculturation in Korea" [on the thought of the Catholic lay leader, St. Chong Ha Sang (1795-1839) and the Protestant pastor, Choi Pyong Hon (1858-1927)]: in 1993, "The Historical Process of Inculturation" [the Early Church's Inculturation]. Since 1994, seminars have included a series on "The Gospel's encounter with the truth of the other religions"; Buddhism (1994-95), Shamanism (1996), Confucianism(1997-98), Taoism (1999). Papers from the seminars appear in the Annual Report of KCTI, *Korean Christian Thought*.

Selected References

Why Do You Speak With Her? Seoul: Living with Scripture, 1995.
Survey on the Situation and the Consciousness of Korean Catholic Women. Seoul: Woori Theology Institute & KCWC, 2000.
Shim Sang Tae. *The Third Millennium and New Evangelization of Korean Church.* Hwasung: Korean Christian Thought Institute, 1998.
—. *Faith in New Millennium: the 60th Anniversary Memorial Book.* Hwasung: Korean Christian Thought Institute, 2000.

7.6.4. Seton Research Center

Seton Research Center of the Sisters of Charity of Seton Hill was founded for the Inculturation of Korean Spirituality and Interreligious Dialogue. It publishes *The Spirituality Journal* (1990) and books concerning spirituality. Since 1994 it also conducts Interreligious Dialogue programs to foster undersatnding of traditional cultural thought in the pluralistic religious situation of Korean society.

The monthly Interreligious Dialogue Lecture Series has included:

"Zen Buddhism and Christianity" (1994), "Religious Life in Buddhism and Christianity" (1995), "Confucianism and Christianity"(1996), "Korean Shamanism and Christianity" (1997), "Daoism and Christianity"(1998), "Korean New Religions and Christianity"(1999), and "Pilgrimage in Christianity and Buddhism"(2000).

Future programs are planned on the inculturation of Christian spirituality in Korea, including studies and lectures concerning religious practices and ecological, issues in various Korean faiths.

7.6.5. Shinangin Academy (Academy for the Faithful, 1998)

"Shinangin Academy" was established by Catholic lay people involved in the social justice movement and now has a wholly lay steering committee that includes Catholics and Protestants. Its purpose is to study and share modern understandings of Christian tradition and scriptures along with the Asian cultural and religious heritage, in association with those of other denominations and of other faiths. The focus is on inter-religious dialogue and the renewal of Korean Christianity, leading to a Korean way of spirituality and of doing theology in the context of Korea. Subjects under the theme "various echoes of the Good News" have included Eastern Spirituality, Jesus and Buddha, the *Tao te ching* of Lao-Tzu, *Analects* of Confucius, *Bhagavadgita*, Mahayana Buddhistic Reading of John's Gospel, Yoga for Beginners, Zen Buddhist Exercise, Christology, Historical Jesus and Korean Christians, and Korean Theology for Koreans.

7.6.6. Catholic Publishing House ("Kyung Hyang Japji Sa", "Catholic Cheong Nyun Sa", 1886-)

Catholic Publishing House was established by E.J.G. Coste mep. Early publications included G. Mutel's *The Stories of the Martyrs in 1866* (1895), along with *A Short Introduction to the Gospels* (1897), and *Prayers of the Holy Church* (1907). Its publications did much for the development of the modern Korean language. CPH commenced the weekly *Kyung Hyang Shinmun* (1906), although under Japanese rule only its supplement *Bogam* continued. It became a monthly magazine entitled *Kyung Hyang Japji* (1911-1945, 1946-1950, 1953-). CPH also issued the *Catholic Cheong Nyun* (later *Chang Jo* - Creation, 1971-1972) for contemporary intellectuals during 1933-1936, 1947-1950 and 1955-1971, and also the widely influential *SoNyun* (The Youth, from 1961). CPH now publishes the series "Korean Catholic Culture Library," in order to root the long Christian faith tradition in Korean society.

7.6.7. Benedict Press (1909-)

The Benedict Press was founded by the Benedictines on their arrival (1909) to further cultural mission through publishing and printing. From the early 1930s, Benedictine missionaries translated and published the Latin Mass, and also sacred songs, into Korean. In the early 1940s, sections of the New Testament were translated into contemporary Korean and published. Following dissolution in North Korea (1946, 1949), the press reopened in Waegwan (1962), South Korea. Benedict Press began in the 1970s to publish Third World theologies, including liberation theologies and Asian theological voices. It also introduces the works of contemporary Korean theologians to foster authentic Korean spirituality and theology. Since1981, the Press has translated and published annotated books of the Greek New Testament by Korean Catholic scholars along with the annotated Korean edition of the New Testament and the annotated translations of early Christian Fathers and now aims to publish many more authentic Korean spiritual and theological works to be shared among Koreans.

7.6.8. The Korean Catholic Farmers' Movement (KCFM, 1964)

The Movement was first formed under the J.O.C. of Korea, becoming independent in 1971. It has fostered laity formation, reflection and action on politico-economic problems and farmers' rights, regardless of their faith, and also for democracy, for livelihood, human rights and social justice in agricultural areas. From the early 1980s KCFM began a new movement for "Life and Community" on the basis of the subjective identity of farmers. It includes such projects as the "direct trade of agricultural products between consumers and farmers," "Korean Traditional Wheat (Woorimil) Revival Movement," and the "Revival Movement for Agricultural Communities."

Through these activities KCFM offers models and practical alternatives for saving the earth, "the table," and also rural societies themselves, in solidarity also with city-dwellers. As a Catholic NGO based on several renewed agricultural communities, KCFM provides new ministry models for the Catholic Church in rural districts. It also provides practical guidelines for Korean farmers in achieving an independent agricultural economy for the nation's survival, a healthy environment, reduction of armaments and rejection of the politico-economic domination by the so-called "First World." It is now associated in these tasks with the ecumenical Korea Christian Farmers Federation (See also Chong Ho Kyong 5.2.3.6.).

Selected References

Chong Ho Kyung. *Community of Sharing and Serving: Pastoral Theology for Farmers* (in Korean). Waegwan: Benedict Press, 1984.

—. "The Catholic Farmers' Movement." *Sinhak Jonmang* 67 (1984).

Hebang Hashinun Hananim (Liberating God) - A Creed for the Farming Community. Seoul, Bundo Publications, 1987.

Korea Christian Farmers Federation. Seoul: KCFF, 1984.

"Manifesto by the Korean Catholic Farmers' Organization; Liberation of Farmers and the Uniting of the Korean People." *Kyong-Hyang* 78.12 (1986).

7.6.9. Other Catholic Institutes include:

The Catholic University of Korea College of Theology (Seoul) has a large theological library, museum and three research institutes and publishes *Catholic Theology and Thought* (See 7.3.3.) and *Collectanea Theologica*.

Institute for the Study of Religion and Theology, Sogang University. Occasional publications are issued.

Korean Institute for the Study of Catholicism has issued a number of historical and theological studies.

8 Supplementary Bibliography 2
8.1 Catholic Resources

Buchmeier, Francis X. *The Catholic Church in South Korea: Social Involvement and Church Growth. Pro Mundi Vita Dossiers* 1 (1986).

Catholic Institute for International Relations, in association with the Korean Ecumenical Education Programme. *Disposable People: Forced Evictions In South Korea* 1988); *South Korea Profile* (1989) and *The Reunification of Korea* (1989).

Cho Kyu Man. "A Study of the Theological Interests in 1974-1995: Graduation Theses of Catholic University Theologies." *Catholic Theology and Thought* 20 (1997).

Ch'oe Ki-Pok. "Ancestor Worship: From the Perspective of Confucianism and Catholicism." In *Ancestor Worship and Christianity in Korea,* edited by Jung Young Lee. Lewiston, NY: Edwin Mellen Press, 1988.

The Commitment of the Laity in Church's Mission with Special Reference to Implementing Social Teaching: the First Asian Laity Meeting, 4-9 September 1994, Korea [Atti di congresso]. Seoul: Catholic Lay Apostolate Council of Korea, 1995.

The Constitutions of the Catholic Committee of Korea. Text in Latin, Korean and English. Seoul?: Catholic Committee of Korea, 1961.

Daniels, M.J. *Through a Rain Spattered Window. Essays on Korea*. Seoul: Taewon Publishing Co., 1973.

——. *The Pine Tree*. Seoul: Samsung Moonwha Pub. Co., 1975.

Digan, Parig. *Churches in Contestation. Asian Christian Social Protest*. Maryknoll, NY: Orbis Books, 1984.

England, John C. "Kim Chi Ha and the Poetry of Christian Dissent." *Ching Feng* 21.3 (1978).

Han'guk Kat'ollik Munhwa Yonguwon. *Han'guk chont'ong sasang kwa Ch'onjugyo* (Korean traditional thought and Catholic teaching). Seoul T'ukpyolsi: T'amgudang, 1995.

Huang, Joseph. "Korean Catholic and Korean Church." *Collectanea Theologica Universitatis, Fujen* 64, 1985.

Im Jinchang, Luke. *Social Development of Korea and the Role of the Catholic Church*. Seoul: Social Research Institute, Sogang University, 1976.

Kim Jang Tae. "Traditional Korean Culture and Catholic Thought." In *"A Declaration of Conscience." The Korean Catholic Church and Human Rights*. Vol. 2, edited by Young Soon Song. Maryknoll, NY: Orbis Books, 1983.

Kim Jin-Hong. *I Will Awake the Dawn*. Lima, Ohio: Fairway Press, 1991.

Kim Kwang-Won. "Zur Theologie der Negation: Versuch Einer Koreanischen Kontextellen Theologie im Gesprach mit dem 'Hwaom' Buddhismus Uisangs." Thesis. Bonn, Catholic Faculty, 1990.

Kim Mong Woon. "Catholicism and Social Change in Korea." In *"A Declaration of Conscience." The Korean Catholic Church and Human Rights*. Vol. 2, edited by Young Soon Song. Maryknoll, NY: Orbis Books, 1983.

Ryu, Hae-Wuk. "Love in the 'Contemplatio' of the Spiritual Exercises of St. Ignatius and 'Han' in the Korean culture." STL Thesis, Weston School of Theology, 1992.

Thalman, Eugene. *Let Your Heart be Bold. A Study on Church and National Security in Korea, Philippines and Taiwan. Part 1 - Korea*. Hong Kong: Center for the Progress of Peoples, 1985.

Yi Man Yol, et al. *The Korean Christian Church and the National Movement.* (in Korean). Seoul: Posong, 1986.

8.2 Protestant Resources

Chang Soo Young. "Two Intellectuals Voice Different Views on Cultural Direction of Korea." *Korea Times* (October 7, 1992).

Chi Myong Kwan. *Modern History and the Church of Korea.* Tokyo: Shinkyo Shuppansha, 1975.

Chi Pyong-gu. *Syamanijum kwa Han'guk kyohoe* (Shamanism and Korean church). Seoul: Saehan Kihoek Ch'ulp'anbu, 1996.

Chung Sei-wha, ed. *Challenges for Women: Women's Studies in Korea.* Seoul: Ewha Womans University Press, c1986.

CISJD, eds. *Nationalism and the Christian Church* (in Korean). Seoul: Minjungsa, 1981.

From the Womb of Han: Stories of Korean Women Workers. Hong Kong: CCA-URM, 1982.

Goh Jung-hi and Lee Geonyong. *Songs For Jubilee* (words and music). Manila: AILM, 1991.

Han Yong-Un. *Han Yong-un Chonjip* (Complete collection of Han Yong-un). Seoul: Singu Munhwasa, 1973.

Han'guk Kidokkyo hakhoe yokum. *Isipilsegi Han'guk sinhakui kwaje* (Task of Korean theology in the 21st century). Seoul: DaehanKidokkyo sohoe, 1994.

Han'guk Kyohoe Sahak Yon'guwon. *Han'guk Kidokkyo sasang* (Korean Christian theological thoughts). Seoul: Yonse Taehakkyo Ch'ulp'anbu, 1998.

Han'guk Sahoesa Yon'guhoe. *Hyondae Han'guk ui chonggyo wa sahoe* (Religion and society in modern Korea). Seoul: Munhak kwa Chisongsa, 1992.

Hansin Taehakkyo Sinhakpu. *Kurisudokyo wa munhwa* (Christianity and culture). Osansi, Kyongkido: Hansin Daehakkyo Chulpanbu, 1996.

Harvey, Youngsook Kim. "The Korean Shaman and the Deaconess: Sisters in Different Guises." In *Religion and Ritual in Korean Society,* edited by Laurel Kendall and Griffin Dix. Berkeley: Institute of East Asian Studies, University of California, 1987.

Hong Yi-Sup. *Korea's Self-Identity.* Seoul: Yonsei University Press, 1973.
Hong Chong-gil. *Han'guk kyohoe nun i minjok ul ch'aegim chilsu innun'ga* (Christian responsibility and the fate of the nation). Seoul: Turanno, 1995.
Kang Won-Oon. *Mul eu Shinhak* (A theology of matters). Seoul: Ran UI, 1992.
Kang In-ch'ol. *Han'guk Kidok Kyohoe wa kukka, simin sahoe, 1945-1960* (Korean Christianity, the state and civil society). Seoul: Han'guk Kidokkyo Yoksa Yon'guso, 1996.
Kim Ch'an-guk. *Songso wa hyonsil* (The Bible and contemporary society). Seoul: Taehan Kidokkyo Sohoe, 1992.
Kim Chang-nack. "Justification by Faith - A Minjung Perspective." *Chicago Theological Seminary Register* 85 (1995).
Kim Dong Soo and Byong Suh Kim, eds. *Human Rights in Minority Perspectives.* Montclair NJ: Association of Korean Christian Scholars, 1979.
Kim Kwang-sik. *Sinang e ui ch'odae* (Invitation to the Christian faith). Seoul: Taehan Kidokkyo Ch'ulp'ansa, 1984.
Koh Hesung Chun. "Women's Contributions to Korean Culture." *Korean Culture* 8.3 (1987).
Korean National Commission for UNESCO, ed. *Main Currents of Korean Thought.* Seoul: Si-sa-yong-o-sa Publishers; Arch Cape: Oregon, 1983.
Kuster, Volker. *Theologie im Kontext. Zugleich ein Versuch uber die Minjung-Theologie.* Nettetal: Steyler Verlag, 1995.
Lee In-ho. "Women's Liberation in Korea." *Korea Journal* 17:7 (1977).
Lee Kwang-Rin. "Progressive Views on Protestantism (II)." *Korea Journal* 16 (1976).
Lee Sang-Bok. *A Comparative Study between Minjung Theology and Reformed Theology from a Missiological Perspective.* New York: Peter Lang, 1996.
Lee Sang Hyun, ed. *Essays on Korean Heritage and Christianity.* Princeton: Association of Korean Christian Scholars, 1984.
No Ch'i-jun. *Han'guk Kaesin'gyo sahoehak: Han'guk kyohoe ui wigi wa chonmang* (Sociology of Korean Protestant churches: Crisis and future outlook). Seoul: Hanul, 1998.

Pak Sun-gyong. *Minjok t'ongil kwa Kidokkyo* (National unification and Christianity). Seoul: Han'gilsa, 1986.

—. *T'ongil sinhak ui kot'ong kwa sungni* (Theology of reunification: The suffering and victory). Seoul: Hanul, 1992.

Park Jong-chun. "A Paradigm Change in Korean Indigenization Theology: from a Theology of 'Sincerity' to 'Interliving' Theology". *Korean Journal of Systematic Theology* 1 (1997).

Rhee Jong Sung. "Writings on Christology in Korea." *NEAJOT* 2 (1969).

Rhim Soon-Man. *Women of Asia: Yesterday and Today (India, China, Korea, Japan)*. New York: Friendship Press, c1983.

Shu Chang Won. "Minjung Theology and Feminist Theology." *Sinhak Sasang* 69 (1990).

Son Seung Hee. "Minjung Theology from the Perspective of a Feminist Theology." *Sinhak Sasang* 66 (1989).

Song Kil-sop. *Han'guk sinhak sasangsa* (History of Korean theological thought). Seoul: Taehan Kidokkyo Chulpansa, 1987.

Songs of the Minjung. Jesus Sets Free to Serve. Seoul: Ecumenical Youth Council in Korea, 1985.

Suh Chang-won. *Che 3-segye sinhak* (Theology of the Third World). Seoul: Taehan Kiddokkyo Sohoe, 1993.

Sung Kap-sik. *Hyondae sahoe wa Kidokkyo* (Modern society and Christianity). Seoul: Taehan Kidokkyo Ch'ulp'ansa, 1987.

Sunoo, Harold Hakwon and Kim Dong Soo, eds. *Korean Women in a Struggle for Humanization*. Memphis: Association of Korean Christian Scholars in North America, 1978.

Yi Tong-ch'ol. *Turora mongmuldul a* (Listen, you eggheads!). Seoul: Tonggwang Ch'ulp'ansa, 1985.

Yu Chai-Shin, ed. *Korea and Christianity*. Studies in Korean Religion and Culture 7. Seoul, Berkeley, Toronto: Korean Scholar Press, 1996.

Yun Kyong-no. *Han'guk kundaesa ui Kidokkyosajok ihae* (Understanding the history of modern Korea from the perspective of church history). Seoul: Yongminsa, 1992.

— DSKS, JCE and HJR with KJK, LKJJ, PHJ

8 A Note on Contextual Theology in North Korea

1 Church and Historical Context

Following the Pacific and Korean wars, the large Christian communities in North Korea were drastically reduced through migration to the South and periodically severe persecution, with numbers of clergy and lay people being imprisoned and killed in the early 1950s. Many churches and temples were taken over by the state and converted to secular use although the 1948 constitution permitted "freedom of religious belief and of conducting religious services." Article 54 of the 1972 constitution, however, stated that "citizens have religious liberty and the freedom to oppose religion." In the 1992 constitution, Article 68 grants freedom of religious belief and guarantees the right to construct buildings for religious use and religious ceremonies. The article also states, however, that "No one may use religion as a means by which to drag in foreign powers or to destroy the state or social order." Although there have been annual meetings (outside Korea) with North Korean Christians since 1966, the first full reports of Christian activity in North Korea came from Pastor Ki Joon Koh in 1981, one of the representatives of the Federation of Korean Christians (FKC) attending an international meeting in Vienna. His reports of approximately 5,000 practising Christians and about 500 house churches meeting regularly, were largely confirmed by ecumenical visits to North Korea in 1982. Two full-time ministers were then working in Pyongyang, and it was reported that the FKC had a three-year theological education program there for training pastors through the Pyongyang Divinity School (established in 1972). The FKC was then described as a semi-official organization, similar to the TSPM in China. Following visits by WCC staff in 1985, North Koreans were allowed to attend another International Seminar of

Christians of the North and South for the Peace and Reunification of Korea in Switzerland, 1986, as part of the Tosanzo process for reconciliation and unification. In 1988 two new churches, the Protestant Pongsu Church and the Catholic Changchung Cathedral, were opened in Pyongyang, and international representatives attended. In the same year a building for the FKC was also erected in Pyongyang and a new Roman Catholic association was established.

By the early 1990s there were three official churches in Pyongyang and the total number of Christians was reported to be over 10,000 Protestants (*Kiddokkyo*), with about 5,000 Catholics (*Chonjugyo*), ranging in age from 30 to 60 years (Total population is approximately 24,500,000). Increasing humanitarian needs since 1995 have led to many Christian (and other) relief organizations receiving fuller welcome and these have included Church World Service, delegates from the Vatican, WCC ACT, and other agencies such as Christian Friends of Korea and Cornerstone Ministries International. These have carried out a variety of programs including food aid, medical work, and educational and agricultural assistance. Some staff members have had opportunity to make contact with the house churches. Catholic visitors in 1997-2000 have included Joseph Jung Kwang Ung, head of Seoul archdiocesan Committee for National Reconciliation, and two lay persons, a team to monitor the distribution of 2,000 tons of corn donated by Seoul archdiocese and four priests and two sisters of the Catholic Priests' Association for Justice (CPAJ) who celebrated a Mass with 250 Catholics at Changchung Catholic Church in Pyongyang.

Protestant visitors have included Manchurian Christians and those from South Korea such as Mun Ik Kwan (see p.599 above), Kim Dong Wan and NCCK delegates, and staff members of the WCC and the CCA.

Despite greatly increased contacts and exchanges, the degree of religious liberty permitted is the subject of differing reports. Christian leaders in the North, such as Pastor Chang Sung Bok at Pongsu Church in Pyongyang, insist there are no controls or religious persecution, that there are almost 20 active Christian pastors and that most church activities are very similar to those of the South. Samuel Chang Jae On, president of the (North) Korean Roman Catholics' Association (KRCA), also affirms that there is full freedom to meet either in churches or in homes. Others say that the church activity they have seen appears to be staged, and some also allege that persecution still occurs. The Reverend Kim Dong Wan of the (South) NCCK reported that despite his visits to churches in the North, it was "impossible to tell how much they represent genuine opportunities for worship, or are simply showcase churches for visitors." Yet many house churches are meeting, although widely scattered, small numbers of North Korean evangelists are moving across the country, more than 50,000 copies of the Bible have been printed by the FKC, and many informal contacts continue between groups and individual Christians in North and South Korea. There are also reports of activities by the (North Korea) Missionary Association of Korean Women. Recent visits (1999-2000) by WCC, CCA and WARC personnel have built further ecumenical relationships.

Selected References

Chang Sang Loi. "The North Korean Catholic Church." *Inculturation* 6.1 (1991).

Chong-Sik Lee and Se-Hee Yoo. *North Korea in Transition* (Korean Research Monographs, No 16). Berkeley: Institute of East Asian Studies, 1991.

Chung Chong Shik and Kim Gahb Chol. *North Korean Communism: A Comparative Analysis.* Seoul: Research Center for Peace and Unification, 1980.

Cuny, Jean-Michel. "Une Eglise Particulièrement Silencieuse: Corée du Nord." *Spiritus* 29 (1988).

Editors' Committee on North Korean Church History of the Institute of Korean Christian History. *The History of the North Korean Churches.* Seoul: Institute of Korean Christian History, 1996.

Han Young-Je. *Church History in North Korea* (in Korean). 2 vols. Seoul: The Institute for Korean Church History, 1996.

Kim Hung-su. *Haebang hu Pukhan kyohoesa: yon'gu, chungon, charyo* (History of the North Korean church since 1945). Seoul: Tasan Kulpang, 1992.

Kim Kwang-su. *Pukhan kidokkyo t'amgusa* (A history for Christianity in Northern Korea). Seoul: Han'guk Kyohoesa Yon'guwon, 1994.

Kim Son Hwi. "Christianity in the DPRK." *The Peoples' Korea* (1997).

Kim Yong-han. *Pyonghwa tongil kwa Hanguk Kidokkyo: pogumjuuijok tongil sinhak ul hyanghayo* (The peaceful unification and Korean Christianity). Seoul: Pungman, 1990.

Kong Dan Oh and Ralph C. Hassig. *North Korea through the Looking Glass*. Washington: The Brookings Institution, 2000.

Lee Man Yul. *History of North Korean Christianity* (In Korean). Seoul: Institute of Korean Church History, 1996.

Park, Kyung Ae. "Women and Revolution in North Korea." *Pacific Affairs* 65:4 (Winter 1992-93): 527-545.

Pukhan kyohoesa. *Han'guk Kidokkyo Yoksa Yon'guso Pukhan Kyohoesa Chipp'il Wiwonhoe chium* (History of Christianity in North Korea). Seoul: Han'guk Kidokkyo Yoksa Yon'guso, 1996.

Rhim Soon Man. "Women of North Korea: Yesterday and Today." *Asian Studies* 13:1 (April 1975): 55-76.

Sawa Masahiko. "Human Rights of the Christian Minority in North Korea." NEAJT 28/29 (1982).

—, Kim Sook Ja and Kang Moon Kyu. *A Study of Christianity in North and South Korea* (in Korean). Seoul: Min Jung Sa, 1997.

Wells, K.M. "Protestantism in North Korea: An Explanation." *Religion in Communist Lands* 11.2 (1983).

Yang Han Mo. "The Unification of Korea and a Perspective of the Catholic Church." *Catholic Journal for Social Science* 5 (1984).

2 Theology in Context

Courses for theological education are slowly increasing, from largely interim programs to a curriculum at the Pyongyang Divinity School that is reported to include Old Testament and New Testament studies, pastoral theology, historical theology, a history of Christianity in Korea and other theological studies. Reports also talk of 35 graduates of the school taking holy orders by 1999, and of novice Roman Catholic priests being sent to study in Rome. There are very few writings available from North Korean Christians since 1953, apart from a small number of biographical accounts. Articles such as that of Kim Chang Joon on Marxism and Christianity earlier, and the many articles in South Korean journals since 1980 on reunification and reconciliation (see e.g. 5.3.1., 6.1.1., 7.3.2., 7.3.3. above), do provide sympathetic insight and reflection. Documents have also come from the series of Dialogue Conferences between North Korean and overseas Korean Christians (almost 20 conferences since 1981 - see Cho Eunsik). Amongst the few statements that are available from Christians in the North, that of Hwang Shi Chon and Kim Nam Hyok, director of the international department and deputy director of the organizational department, respectively, of the Central Committee of the FKC, provide some indication of theological response in this context. Missionary activities by churches they feel, have to be "in keeping with the actual situation of our country." It is therefore "mainly focused on individuals such as by house-to-house visits," although some missionary associations, such as the Missionary Association of Korean Women, are active in this. However, they declare the most important task of the FKC to be that of leading Korean Christians to "work for the construction and reunification of our country...As the solidarity of the whole nation is the only way to realize a lasting peace in our country, Christians in north and south Korea and overseas should be united first," they declare.

The setting for this understanding of Christian mission, and for any theological study, as for any theological expression in North Korea, is partly shaped by the *juche* philosophy of Kim Il Sung. Some Christians there have affirmed similarities between this "guiding idea" and Christian faith, in a shared emphasis on human value, service and love for neighbor. Young Chil Kim, a senior researcher of the Committee for Peaceful Unification declares that the *juche* 'idea' also supports human dignity and deliverance for the poor, and recognizes that liberation theology and its social reforms are close to this. The *juche* philosophy differs from other Marxisms in stressing subjectivity and creativity, and proponents such as Young Chil Kim, Jang Yup Hwang and Seung Duk Park accept a role for religion, viewing primitive Christianity as a genuine religion for the *minjung*, meeting the desperate needs of the poor.

There is, however, no place here for a theocentric or christocentric world view, for "man (sic) is the master of everything...of the world and his own destiny" and this applies to all aspects of life, personal and political. In this anthropocentric political philosophy, identity is to be found only in the collective and man has power to decide every part of his destiny. Most theological discussion emerging from North Korea has, however, centered on the *juche* philosophy, and it has stimulated a considerable body of writing, through its interpretation of humanism and "human remodelling," of the *minjung* and their situation and of the character of primitive Christianity (For an accessible outline and bibliography see Cho below).

Selected References

An Pu-sop. *T'ongil kwa Pukhan son'gyo chollyak* (Religion and state North Korea, Christianity and politics). Seoul: Peduro Sowon, 1991.

Belke, Thomas J. *Juche: A Christian Study of North Korea's State Religion*. New York: Living Sacrifice Book Company, 1999.

Cho Eunsik. "Dialogue between North and South Korean Christians." *Dialogue* (Colombo) 28. Forthcoming.

Choi Suk Woo. *Church History in North Korea*. Seoul: The Institute for Korean Church History, 1996.

"Declaration of the Churches of Korea on National Reunification and Peace." KNCC, Feb. 1988. In *Christ and Caesar in Modern Korea*, by Wi Jo Kang. Albany, NY: State University of New York, 1997.

Hong Dong Keun. *Juche and Minjung Theology* (in Korean). Pyongyang, 1987.

—, and Hakwon Sunoo. *The Juche Idea and Christianity*. Los Angeles: Bookmi Juche Sasang Yeonkoohwe, 1990.

Hong Sung Hyun. "The *Juche* Idea and Christian Thought" (in Korean) In *Reunification and Theology of National Church*, edited by Tongil Shinhak Dong Jee Hwe. Seoul: Hanool, 1990.

Institute of Korea Church History Studies. *Bookhan Kyohwesa* (A history of North Korean Church) (in Korean). Seoul: Institute of Korea Church History Studies, 1996.

Kang In Chul. "The Logic of Mutual Understanding between the *Juche* Idea and Christianity of North Korea (in Korean). *Minjokkwa Shinhak* (Nation and Theology) 2 (1994).

Kang Wi Jo. *Christ and Caesar in Modern Korea*. Albany, NY: State University of New York, 1997. Chap. 15, "Christianity and the Politics of Reunification."

Kang Young Ahn."Christianity and Juche Philosophy" In *National Reunification and Christian Church of Korea* edited by Korea Association for Christian Studies.Seoul: Korean Inter-Varsity Press,1994.

Koberlin, Gerhard. "Okumenischer Dialog mit Nordkorea." *Junge Kirche* 49 (1988).

Lee, David. "Re-examining North Korea Missions. Background Study for a Church-Planting Movement." Thesis, Korea Baptist Theological Seminary, 1999.

Park Joon Young. "Dialogue between the *Juche* Idea and Christianity" (in Korean). *Sahwewa Shinhak* 2 (1992).

Park Seung Duk. "*Juche's* New Perspective on Christianity" (in Korean). In *Kidokkyowa Juche Sasang* (Faith and *Juche* Philosophy). Seoul: Shinangkwa Jisung Sa, 1993.

Park Soon Kyung. *The Suffering and Triumph of Unification Theology* (in Korean). Seoul: Han-Ul, 1992.

Park Kyung Ae. "Women and Revolution in North Korea." *Pacific Affairs* 65:4 (Winter 1992-93): 527-545.

Rhim Soon Man. "Women of North Korea: Yesterday and Today." *Asian Studies* 13:1 (April 1975): 55-76.

"The Spiritual Struggle for Korea." Mimeo'd, Cornerstone Ministries International, (1997).

Samok. Special issue "Reunification of Korea" (in Korean). *Samok* 136 (1990).

9 A Note on Contextual Theology in Macau

1   Historical Setting
2   Christian Mission and Publication
3   Theological Reflection and Education
    3.1 Manuel Teixeira (1912-)
4 Supplementary Bibliography

1 Historical Setting

Following Portuguese arrival in the mid 16th century, the peninsula rapidly became an intermediary post in the profitable trade between China and Japan, and between these and Europe, a position it retained until the early 19th century. The port was both a gateway to China and also for some centuries the only meeting point between western and East Asian cultures. It was also, therefore, an obvious base for early Roman Catholic, and later Protestant, mission work, study and exchange. Since the 17th century it has possessed many features of a tolerant and "cosmopolitan centre [and] a meeting point for cultures, ethnic groups, beliefs, and languages ... a nerve centre for the diffusion of knowledge" (Ricci Institute, Macau). The major cultural influences which have made Macau a unique society in the region have remained those of China and of Portugal, along with the pervasive roles of religious belief and mercantile activity. Macau merchants and Jesuit missionaries have long been the key actors in shaping Macanese culture and, over almost three centuries, in the exchanges between European and Chinese civilizations.

After more than four centuries of ambiguous relationships with China, Macau reverted to China in 1999, becoming a Special Administrative Region (SAR) with a degree of autonomy. The Basic Law and the1998 Religious Freedom Ordinance require religious organisations to be registered, but provides for freedom of religion

A Note on Contextual Theology in Macau 653

and prohibits discrimination on the basis of religious practice. Religious bodies have access to electronic media, they may maintain relations with religious groups abroad and missionaries are also free to carry out mission work. According to recent census figures, of the population of 450,000, 16.8 % are Buddhist, 8.4% are Christian, 60.9% have no religious affiliation and 13.9 % are "other" (a combination of Buddhist, Taoist and Confucian).

Selected References

Barry, Peter. "Macau: Center for Cultural Exchange." *Tripod* 114 (1999).

Cheng, Christina Miu Bing. *Macau: a Cultural Janus*. Hong Kong: Hong Kong University Press, 1999.

Fei Cheng Kang. *Macao 400 years*. Shanghai: Shanghai Academy of Social Sciences, 1996.

Gomes, Luiz Gonzaga. *Bibliografia Macaense*. (Macao): Instituto Cultural de Macau, 1987 (1973).

Hoe, Susanna. *Chinese Footprints: Exploring Women's History in China, Hong Kong and Macau*. Hong Kong: Roundhouse Publications, 1996.

Longsitai Zhu et al. *Historical Sketch of the Portuguese Settlements in China and of the Roman Catholic Church and Mission in China*. Beijing: Dongfang chubanshe, 1997.

Montalto de Jesus, C.A. *Historic Macao*. 2nd ed. Hong Kong; Oxford: Oxford University Press, 1984 (1922).

Porter, Jonathan. *Macau, the Imaginary City: Culture and Society, 1557 to the Present*. New Perspectives on Asian Studies. Boulder, CO.; Oxford: Westview Press, 1996.

Roberts, Elfed Vaughan, Ling Sum Ngai and Peter Bradshaw. *Historical Dictionary of Hong Kong & Macau*. Asian historical dictionaries 10. Metuchen, NJ; London: Scarecrow Press, 1992.

Yee, Herbert. "Macau's Mass Political Culture: Continuity and Change." *Tripod* 114 (1999).

2 Christian Mission and Publication

The first Roman Catholic priest arrived in Macau in 1521, in 1569 the Santa Casa da Misericordia (Holy House of Mercy) was founded, and Macau became a diocese for all of the "Far East", in 1576. St. Paul's College was founded as a university in 1594, but

St Joseph's Seminary not until 1728, under Jesuit, and later Lazarist, direction. The early period of Christian history is chiefly notable however for Macau's role as a base for wide-ranging ventures and exchanges in Catholic mission - to Japan, Indo-China, the East Indies, the Philippines and to China itself. Amongst the leaders in such ventures were Alessandro Valignano, Matteo Ricci, Francis Xavier and Michele Ruggieri. Their writings would have wide influence on mission theology both in China and beyond (See chap. 2 above). A rich tradition of Christian art and architecture also was developed by religious orders in Macau, including Mannerist, Rococo and Romantic styles, and this added to the resources of regional Christian mission.

In the 19th century, Macau would play a similar role in Protestant mission, to China in particular, as the base for missionaries such as Robert Morrison, Liang Fa (Leung Faat / Leong Kung-fa - see chap. 3 above), S. Wells Williams and Lewis and Henrietta Shuck. Protestant mission work was then geographically confined to Macau and Guangzhou, where it depended largely on the goodwill of merchants, and there was initially minimal contact between the missionaries and the Chinese. Missionary activity was therefore mostly literary in nature, with much work on translation of the Bible and compilation of Christian tracts and dictionaries; those of Robert Morrison, Elijah Bridgman and S. Wells Williams being published in Macau. *The Memorial of Protestant Missionaries* (1867) lists missionary publications, many of which were published at the Macau presses of the East India Company and the Albion Press. (This was Morrison's own press, later managed by S. Wells Williams.) The Morrison Education Society was founded in 1834, and in 1835 Karl and Mrs Gutzlaff founded a school, at which Rong Hong (Yung Wing, 1828-1912) studied. Rong Hong would later investigate Chinese coolie traffic, graduate from Yale University and, until 1881, direct the Chinese Educational Mission to the USA.

In this period (the 19th century) all Catholic religious orders were banned (1834), Hong Kong became a separate prefecture but the missions in Singapore and Malacca came under Macau jurisdiction (1866-1981). Catholic churches, charitable and relief organisations faced heavy demands in the following years, from catastrophic storms and from the repercussions of conflicts and revolutions in China (1901, 1925-1945, 1949 on, and 1967). A small number of publications came in the late 19th and early 20th centuries from such presses as the Imprimerie de l'Orphelinat de l'Immaculée-conception, the Impresso na Typographia do Seminario and the Typographia Mercantil. In the post-war period, however, energies could be put to new initiatives in education, publication and communication. Schools and colleges were founded or restored by Anglican, Baptist, Methodist, Lutheran, and Assemblies of God churches, and the activities of ecumenical associations developed. These included the YMCA, YWCA, the Macau Christian Literature Association, and the Macau Christian Music Association.

In 1956 the Catholic diocese in Macau founded a weekly newspaper, *O Clarim* (edited since 1985 by Albino Pais), expanded the *Boletim Eclesial* (formerly the *Boletim eclesiastico da diocese de Macau*, since 1903) and founded the Dom Policarpo Library and São Paulo bookshop. Beginnings were also made towards setting up a recording studio for radio and television. In 1977 all these activities were organised under the Centro Diocesano dos Meios de Comunicação Social (CDMCS), led by Fr Américo Casado and Sr Maria Pia Cantieri. In the last 20 years publication of Christian materials, including theological reflection, has steadily increased.

Selected References

Carmo, António. *A Igreja católica na China e em Macau no con* ... (1997).

Gu Changsheng. *Rong Hong: xiang xifang xuexi di xian qu.* Shanghai: Shanghai renmin chubanshe: Xinhua shudian, 1984.

Harrison, Brian. *Waiting for China*. Hong Kong: Hong Kong University Press, 1979.

Meco, J. *The Art of the Azulejo in Portugal*. Lisboa: Bertrand Editora, 1988.

Memoria sobre a Diocese de Macau: pelos missionarios da mesma diocese. Macau: Impresso na Typographia do Seminario, 1896.

Neves, Artur Augusto. *Macau, mae das missoes no Extremo Oriente*. Macau: Tip. Salesiana, 1957.
Pereira, F.A. Baptista, ed. *Os Fundamentos da Amizade, Cinco Séculos de Relacões Culturais e Arísticas Luso-Chinesas*. Lisbon: Centro Científico e Cultural de Macau, Lisbon, 1999.
Paton, David MacDonald. *R.O.: the Life and Times of Bishop Ronald Hall of Hong Kong*. Hong Kong; Gloucester: Diocese of Hong Kong and Macao, 1985.
Teixeira, Manuel. *Macau e a sua diocese*. 16 vols. Lisboa: Agência Geral do Ultramar, 1940-1977.
—. *A Imprensa Periódica Portuguesa no Extremo-O*. (The Portuguese periodic press in the Far East). Macau: Noticias,1965.
—. *Exposição bibliográfica* (Bibliographical exposition). Macau: Direcçao dos Servicios de Educaçao de Macau, 1986.
(For other works by Manuel Teixeira see 3.1.)
The Jesuits 1594-1994: Macao and China, East meets West. Special Issue *Review of Culture*; no. 21 (2nd series) Macau: Instituto Cultural de Macau, 1994.
Wylie, Alexander. *The Memorial of Protestant Missionaries to the Chinese: Giving a List of their Publications, and Obituary Notices of the Deceased; with Copious Indexes*. Taipei: Ch'eng-Wen Publishing, 1967.

3 Theological Reflection and Education

Theologically the role of early missionaries based in Macau continues to have wide influence in many parts of the Asian region. (See especially Matteo Ricci, Alessandro Valignano and successors, vol. 3, chap. 2 , 2.1.2., 2.1.14.) This has come, for example, from the principles for "sinicised" mission, which Valignano in particular enunciated, and which have provided important sources for contemporary missiology. However, any study of contextual theology from Macau since 1800 has to consider many different levels of theology in reflection, action and writing. Amongst others, these would include the theology which guided Macau's long Catholic tradition of humanitarian service through such agencies as the Santa Casa da Misericordia; the life-stories of civic and church leaders; the pastoral letters, commentaries and other publications from Catholic orders and ecumenical agencies; along with the writings of particular authors and institutes. Amongst the latter are the following.

The extensive historical works of Manuel Teixeira over more than 70 years include strong humanist concerns and place all narratives of the history of church and faith in Macau firmly within the context of Macau's intellectual life and of its civil and political context (see 3.1 below). By the late 20th century there came other initiatives in theological writing, education and publication. Pastoral Centres were established in 1976, to be followed by Catechetical centres and lay associations founded by Bishop Lam Ka-tseung. Publications have issued from these programmes and from the Pontifical Council for Justice and Peace which initiated a series of Regional Seminars, in which, for example, Peter Chung of Macau has spoken on "Post-colonial Autonomy and the Nation-State: The Future of Macau." The Diocese of Macau commenced a two-year "Theology Open Programme for Laity" (1997), and lay-initiated seminars on the theme "Knowing Christ" have been organised. Bible commentaries and biblical-pastoral books have also been published. The Macau Ricci Institute was established (1998) to promote, in co-operation with other scholars, academic research on the intercultural history of Macau; to assess the individual and social impact of the economic development on the cultural traditions of the country, especially in developing a new Chinese economic ethics; to foster mutual understanding among the different spiritual traditions of the Chinese people, and to contribute to the integral human and communitarian up-building of the society. Publications are forthcoming. The Instituto Cultural of Macau also includes historical and theological papers in its quarterly *Review of Culture*, of which volume 21 (2nd series) contains four series of articles on "Christ and Confucius", "The Accommodation", "The Meeting of Cultures" and "Jesuits in China".

Bishop Domingos Lam Ka-tseung, first Chinese bishop of Macau, was a member of the Macau Basic Law Drafting Committee in 1988, and has included political advocacy in his pastoral activity and writing. He has also stressed the need to consider Asian pluralism and Confucian values in all discussions of mission in Asia. Writing in 1999, Lam stresses that "social communications" in the context of inculturation and inter-religious dialogue, are necessary for any "incisive evangelization". Pastoral coordination and fuller mutual understanding must also be built, he declares, between the church and the poor in Macau, and between those of Chinese culture and language and those of Portuguese culture.

Glimpses of people's theology can be seen emerging in a number of recent documents and activities. Fr Joao Evangelista Lau Him-sang, parish priest of St. Lazarus' Church and Catholic cleric on the committee to prepare for the return of Macau to China, raised the "issues concerning ethics and people's rights", and insisted that full dialogue on such issues is necessary. Responding to the preparatory outline ("lineamenta") for the Synod for Asia (1998), groups of religious and lay persons emphasized the need for clergy and laity formation, increased communion between the Church in Macau and the universal Church, and Church participation in social issues. The Rev'd Lam Yam-min, pastor of the Evangelical Church in Macau, who specialises in working among students and youth, is a member of the government people's council, which he believes demonstrates China's respect for religion. "The Church should take the opportunity to contribute to society," he has said, on the basis of full consultation with local people and churches. Legislator Anthony Ng Kuok-cheong, leader of the Union for Democracy Development, has also led in social protests and activism on such issues as the recent incompetence of the government, public order and triad gang crime. Other writers on Macau identity and future include Gary M.C. Ngai, Joao Lourenco, Angela Paulette Yeung, Victoria Lau, Thomas Luk Man Hoi, Peter Chung and expatriates G. Wilczek, Peter Barry, Betty Ann Maheu and Roman Malek.

Selected References

Barry, Peter. "Macau: Center for Cultural Exchange." *Tripod* 114 (1999).

Carmo, António Duarte de Almeida. *A Igreja católica na China e em Macau no contexto do sudeste asiático: que futuro?* Macau: Fundação Macau: Instituto cultural de Macau, 1997.

Lam Ka-tseung, Domingos. "Macao: The New Situation Demands Greater Missionary Impulse." *International Fides* (May, 1999).

Lau, Victoria, Thomas Luk Man Hoi and Peter Chung. "Macau Roman Catholic Church and 1999." *Tripod* 50 (1999).

Medeiros, Antonio Joaquim de. *Lettere pastorali - Cina.* Macau: s.n., 1885?.

Nas pegadas de Xavier (Pursuing the dream: Jesuits in Macau). Macau: Jesuítas em Macau, 1990.

Ng Kuok Cheong, Antonio. "The Relationship between State and Church in Macau in the Perspective of the Civil Community" (in German). In *Origin is Future,* edited by China Center and Institut Monumenta Serica. Sank Augustin: Steyler Publishing House, 1999.

Paton, David MacDonald. *R.O.: the Life and Times of Bishop Ronald Hall of Hong Kong.* Hong Kong; Gloucester: Diocese of Hong Kong and Macao, 1985.

Religião e cultura: simpósio internacional comemorativo (Religion and culture: an international symposium commemorating the IVth centenary of the University College of St. Paul: Macau, 28 de Novembro a 1 de Dezembro de 1994). Macau: Instituto Cultural de Macau, 1994.

Teixeira, Manuel. *Os ouvidores em Macau* (The listeners in Macau). Macau: Impr. Nacional, 1976.

—. "A Igreja em Macau: Historia e actualidade." *Boletim Eclesial* 85 (1990).

Yeung, Angela Paulette. "The Church of Macau in Transition. An Overview of Church Mission in Macau." *East Asian Pastoral Review* 22.1 (1985).

Zheng Weiming, Peter. "Popular faith conceptions in Macau" (in German). In *Origin is Future*, edited by China Center and Institut Monumenta Serica. Sank Augustin: Steyler Publishing House, 1999.

3.1 Manuel Teixeira (1912-)

Manuel Teixeira came to Macau in 1924 as a young seminarian at the S. José Seminary. Under the influence of Fr Régis Gervaix, author of *Histoire Abregée de Macau* (A Concise history of Macau), he committed himself to historical research and since the 1920s has produced a steady flow of histories of Catholic orders, congregations and churches; biographies of bishops and clergy;

studies of the Portuguese presence in countries throughout Asia; and century-by-century works on the history, topography and historical figures of Macau. When directing the *Boletim Eclesiástico da Diocese de Macau,* he gained the collaboration of well-known intellectuals such as Charles Boxer and Jack Braga. He also became a collector of documentation and information on both "the history of the church in Macau [and] the civil history of the territory", which he believes inseparable. He is now an eminent scholar not only on the history, both civic and church, of Macau but also on the wider Portuguese and Christian presence in the Asian region. Along with his numerous articles and books, he continues to write daily columns for the morning paper *Macau Hoje*, thus continuing long activity as columnist, formerly in the *Gazeta Macaense*, with the famous "Little Seeds of Good Sense".

Teixeira is a broadly sympathetic historian who takes seriously the widest range of social, personal and ecclesial history, including the diverse fortunes and failures of the church and its leaders. In a deeply humanist historiography he marries faith to history by blending meticulous archival research with the recognition of transcendent elements present in all the vicissitudes of human striving and suffering. His perspective is both tolerant and philosophical, for he says, "we 'learn' that all great men (sic) have their moments of weakness. And the history of Macau and the Portuguese in the Far East abounds in these men." In his many studies of Macau, China, Japan, Burma, Cambodia, Malaya, Vietnam, Borneo and Singapore, his theology of history presents the "divine" mission being worked out within the (often clearly fallible) "human".

Selected References
Works by Manuel Teixeira

Macau e a Sua Diocese. 16 vols. Macau: Tip. do Orfanato Salesiano, 1940-1979.

Portuguese Mission in Malacca and Singapore 1511-1958. Lisboa: Agencia Geral do Altramar, 1961-1963.

The Fourth Centenary of the Jesuits at Macao. Macau: n.p., 1964.

A Note on Contextual Theology in Macau 661

Macau através dos séculos. (Macau through the centuries). Macau: Imprensa Nacional, 1977.
The Protestant Cemetries of Macau. Macau: Direcçao dos Servicios de Turismo de Macau, 1982?
Os ouvidores em Macau (The listeners in Macau). Macau: Impr. Nacional,1976.
The Japanese in Macau. Macau: Instituto Cultural de Macau, 1990.
"O Futuro de Macau." *Boletim Eclesial* 83 (1985).
"A Situacao de Macau em face da China." *Boletim Eclesial* 83 (1985).
"Praeludio de Macau." *Boletim Eclesial* 84 (1986).
" A Igreja em Macau: Historia e actualidade." *Boletim Eclesial* 85 (1990).
Instituto Cultural. *Mons. Manuel Teixeira "O homem e a obra"* (Wen Dequan shenfu "Zuozhe ji zuopin - Father Teixeira, the man and his work). Macao: Instituto Cultural de Macau: Wenhua sishu zhongyang tushuguan, 1992.

4 Supplementary Bibliography

Agencia Geral do Ultramar. *Instrucao para o bispo de Pequim e outros documentos para a historia de Macau.* Lisboa: Agencia Geral das Colonias, 1943.

Boxer, Charles. *Estudos para a História de Macau.* Lisboa: Fundacao Oriente, 1991.

Bray, Mark and Ramsey Koo, eds. *Education and Society in Hong Kong and Macau: Comparative Perspectives on Continuity and Change.* Hong Kong: Comparative Education Research Centre, 1999.

Catálogo dos manuscritos de Macau. Filmoteca Ultramarina Portuguesa. Lisboa: Centro de Estudos Históricos Ultramarinos, 1963.

Guerra, Joaquim A. de Jesus. *Quadrivolume de Confúcio.* Revised ed. Macau: Instituto Cultural de Macau, 1990.

Gunn, Geoffrey C. *Encountering Macau: a Portuguese City-state on the Periphery of China, 1557-1999.* Transitions - Asia and Asian America. Boulder, CO; Oxford: Westview, 1996.

Leao, Francisco G. Cunha, ed. *Jesuitas na Asia: catalogo e guia.* Macao: Instituto Cultural de Macau; Lisboa: Instituto

Portugues do Patrimonio Arquitectonico: Biblioteca da Ajuda, 1998.

Ljungstedt, Andrew. *Contribution to an historical sketch of the Roman Catholic Church at Macao; and the domestic and foreign relations of Macao.* Canton: s.n., 1834.

Macau: Cidade no Nome de Deus na China, nao ha outra mais leal. Lisboa: Agencia Geral do Ultramar, Divisao de Publicacoes e Biblioteca, 1957.

Malek, Roman, ed. *Macau. Herkunft ist Zukunft.* Nettetal: Steyler Verlag, 2000.

Marques, António Henrique R. de Oliveira. *História dos portugueses no Extremo Oriente.* Lisbon: Fundacao Oriente, 1998.

"New Historical Atmosphere: Macau Catholic Church Ten-day Visit to China." *Yi* (Message) 60 (Dec 1985).

Ramalho, João de Deus. "Macau, padrão espiritual lusíada." *Boletim Eclesiástico de Macau*, 1952.

Revés, Sigismundo and Alberto Cotta Guerra. *O centro de recuperação social da ilha da Taipa, Macau* (The center of social recovery of the island of Taipa, Macau). Lisboa: Agência-Geral do Ultramar, 1962.

Roberts, Elfed Vaughan, Ling Sum Ngai and Peter Bradshaw. *Historical Dictionary of Hong Kong & Macau.* Asian historical dictionaries 10. Metuchen, N.J.; London: Scarecrow Press, 1992.

Santos Domingos, Maurício Gomes dos. *Macau, primeira universidade ocidental do Extremo-Oriente* (Macau, the first western university in the Far East). Macau: Fundacao Macau, Universidade de Macau, 1994 (1968).

Valdez, Henrique. *Por Macau! Artigos e discursos.* Macau: n.p., 1922.

Vasconcellos, Antonio Maria Augusto de. *Sermao pregado na se Cathedral de Macau na primeira dominga de quaresma, 6 de marco de 1881, no qual sam refutados alguns pontos do systema darwiniano, com referencia ao homem e a religiao catholica.* Macau: Typographia Mercantil, 1881.

Yung Wing (Rong Hong). *My Life in China.* New York: Henry Holt, 1909.

10 Contextual Theology in Taiwan

1 **Introduction**
  1.1 People and History
  1.2 Religions
  1.3 Christianity in Taiwan from 17th to 20th Centuries
2 **The Development of Contextual Theology in Taiwan - Protestant Tradition**
  2.1 The Early Context
  2.2 The Emergence of Contextual Theology
    2.2.1. Theological Movements and Praxis
      2.2.1.1. Contextualizing Theology; **2.2.1.2.** The Theology of the Incarnation; **2.2.1.3.** Identifying with the Sufferings and the Hopes of the Taiwanese people; **2.2.1.4.** Aboriginal Theology; **2.2.1.5.** Women Doing Theology; **2.2.1.6** Identifying with the History and Cultures of the Taiwanese people
    2.2.2. Key Theological Writers
      2.2.2.1. Shoki Coe (Ng Chiong Hui / C.H. Hwang, 1914-1988); **2.2.2.2.** Tin Jyigiokk, John (1922-); **2.2.2.3.** Song Choan-seng (C.S. Song, b. 1929); **2.2.2.4.** Kao Chun-ming (C.M. Kao, 1929-); **2.2.2.5.** Wang Hsien-chih (Ong Hian-Ti, 1941-1996); **2.2.2.6.** Lucy T.H. Kao-Loh; **2.2.2.7.** Chen Nan-jou (1944-) and Theology of Identification; **2.2.2.8.** Huang Po-ho (1951-); **2.2.2.9.** Cheng Yang-en; **2.2.2.10.** Tong Fung-wan; **2.2.2.11.** Loh I-To and Contextual Music and Worship in Taiwan
3 **The Development of Contextual Theology in Taiwan - Catholic Theology**
  3.1 Context, Concept and Experience
    3.1.1. Theologizing in Chinese; **3.1.2.** Theologizing in Context; **3.1.3.** Theologizing with Chinese Concepts

3.1.3.1. "Heaven," as it is understood by Chinese people; **3.1.3.2.** In Confucianism
3.1.4. Chinese Spiritual Experiences and Theological Discourses
3.2 Writers and Writings
  3.2.1. The Period from 1950 to 1976
    3.2.1.1. Tien Liang (fl.1960); **3.2.1.2.** Ch'eng Shih-kuang (fl. 1970) and colleagues
  3.2.2. The Period from 1976-2000
    3.2.2.1. Theology by Women Writers; **3.2.2.2.** Lo Kuang, Stanislaus (fl.1985); **3.2.2.3.** Chang Ch'un-shen Aloysius B. (b.1929); **3.2.2.4.** Fang Chih-jung, Mark sj. (b.1926); **3.2.2.5.** Yves Raguin (1912-1998); **3.2.2.6.** Luis Gutheinz sj. (b.1933); **3.2.2.7** Benoit Vermander sj; **3.2.2.8.** Other Writers on Spirituality, Worship and Indigenization

4 Supplementary Bibliography

1 Introduction
1.1 People and History
The population of Taiwan is over 22 million, of whom a little under 2% are aborigines, approximately 85% are ethnically Han people, descendants of migrants from southeast China, and about 13% are descendants of those who arrived after 1949 with the Chinese Nationalists. There are in addition over 300,000 migrant workers. Much of the populace cannot now claim pure ethnic roots: the Taiwanese people are the people who live in Taiwan and identify Taiwan as their homeland. Over the last three centuries, Formosa suffered oppressive colonial rule by the Spanish (1624-1642) in the northern part of Taiwan, by the Dutch (until 1662), by the Manchurian Chi'ng (Qing) dynasty (nominally from 1683, but as a territorial province only from 1887), and by the Japanese (1895-1945). At the end of World War II (1945), the Chinese Nationalist government undertook the military occupation of the island as a trustee on behalf of the Allied Powers. In 1949, when China fell to Communist forces, the Chinese Nationalist government, along with many soldiers and civilians, fled to Taiwan, there to impose

rule, which was followed by the massacre of more than 20,000 Taiwanese on February 28, 1947 - the unforgettable "2-28 Incident." Taiwan was thereafter ruled by Martial Law until 1987.

Except for the brief interlude from 1945 to 1949, Taiwan has been effectively separated from China since 1895. Because of this historical separation, Taiwan and China have developed along separate lines, resulting in quite different political, economic and cultural conditions and identity. The movement for self-determination has grown over 30 years to include large numbers of Taiwanese, including many Christians, who prefer the option of national independence. A most significant development in the history of Taiwan regarding self-determination was the direct election of the president in 1996. In March 2000, the Kuomintang party (KMT), which had ruled Taiwan for 50 years, was defeated by the Democratic Progressive Party (DPP) which advocates the independent sovereignty of Taiwan and its full membership in the United Nations. The KMT government has been proud of rapid economic growth in recent decades, but a high price has been paid for this. For it has brought, for many, bad working conditions, low wages, the prohibition of demonstrations or strikes, high levels of pollution, and increasing extremes of wealth and poverty. Today, though many aspects have changed, social disintegration and ecological deterioration remain major features of life in Taiwan.

Historically the issue of identity is not strange to the Taiwanese, and has been faced many times - by aborigines who are not Chinese, by Han people who have fled from China to Taiwan in different periods, and by many whose lives have been shaped by Japanese or Chinese military rulers. The issue is one of political and cultural identity, where the people of Taiwan are seeking that form of national life, education and creativity, which recognizes the diverse cultures, languages, and folk-culture of Taiwanese in their one homeland.

Selected References
    Chen Tzu-Sung. *Taiwan Consciousness. An Invisible Hand that Rocks the Democratic Cradle*. Microform. Diss. (Ph.D), University of Notre Dame, 1995.

Davidson, James W. *The Island of Formosa, Past and Present.* London: Macmillan, 1903; Taipei: SMC Publishing, 1988. Reprint.

Hsu, Immanuel C.Y. "The Nationalist Rule on Taiwan." In *The Rise of Modern China.* 5th ed. Hong Kong: Oxford University Press, 1995.

Mendel, D. *The politics of Formosan Nationalism.* Los Angeles: University of California Press, 1970.

Ngou, Nai-tek. "Ethnic consciousness, political support, and national identity." In *Ethnic Relations and National Identity.* Taipei: Lan-kiong, 1993.

Su Bing. *Taiwan's 400 Year History, The Origins and Continuing Development of the Taiwanese Society and People.* (Hanji edition.) San Jose: Paradise Culture Associates, 1980; Washington: Taiwanese Cultural Grassroots Association, 1986.

Su Nan-chou. *Chi-tu chiao yu erh erh pa* (Christianity and the event of Feb.28th 1947). Tai-pei: Ya ko chu pan she, 1991.

The Republic of China Yearbook 2000. (http://www.gio.gro.tw/info/book2000, October17, 2000)

1.2 Religions

Recent demographic figures show that the Taiwanese people consist primarily of four ethno-linguistic groupings: the Hoklo people (73.3%), the Hakka people (12%), the Aborigines, (1.7%) and those called "mainlanders" (13%). The majority (75-80%) of the population, especially the Han people, are affiliated with Buddhism, Taoism, or folk beliefs - a mixture of Buddhism, Taoism, Confucianism, folklore and animistic beliefs. Christians, including Protestants and Catholics, consist of only 2-3% of the entire population.

Polytheistic and syncretic, Taiwanese society is dominated by ancestor worship, Taoism and Buddhism. Age-old religious customs and beliefs permeate all levels of Taiwanese culture. Almost all adults in Taiwan, even those not formally subscribing to religious belief, or worshipping regularly at a particular temple, engage in religious practices stemming from one or more traditional Taiwanese folk religions. Most families perform the filial duties of ancestral veneration; and on important occasions, as when a son or daughter takes the university entrance examination, a visit to the temples is made to present petitions and solicit divine assistance. Yet these people are not necessarily Buddhist, Taoist, officially affiliated with any particular temple, or registered with a religious organization. Currently, there are 13 religions recognized by the government: Buddhism, Taoism, Catholicism, Protestantism, Hsuan-yuan Chiao, Islam, Li-ism, Tenrikyo, Baha'i faith, Tien Dih Chiao, Tien Te Chiao, I-kuan Tao, and Mahikarikyo. Altogether, some 47,400 temples and churches can be seen across the island, serving the spiritual needs of the people on Taiwan.

Selected References

> Bo Institute of Taiwan History. *A Bibliography of Taiwanese Folk Belief*. Taipeh: Academia Sinica, 1991.
> Gates, Alan Frederick. *Christianity and Animism in Taiwan*. San Francisco: Chinese Materials Center, 1979.
> Jones, Charles. *Buddhism in Taiwan Religion and State 1660-1990*. Honolulu: University of Hawaii Press, 1998.
> Kramer, Gerald P. and George Wu. *An Introduction to Chinese Folk Religion*. Taipei: published by the authors, 1979.
> Reichelt, Karl. *The Transformed Abbot*. London: Lutterworth Press, 1954.
> Ro, Bong-rin, ed. *Christian Alternatives to Ancestor Practices*. [Tsu hsien ch'ung pai wen t'i]. Taichung: Asian Theological Association, 1985.
> Vermander, Benoit. "Christianity and The Taiwanese Religious Landscape." *The Way* 39.2 (1999).

1.3 Christianity in Taiwan from 17th to 20th Centuries

The history of Christian mission in Formosa/Taiwan came about in three separate waves. The first wave began with the Dutch and Spanish missions in the 1620s. (See vol. 3, chap. 2 above.) A second wave of mission activity began in the 19th century, with the arrival of Dominicans (1859) and Presbyterians (1865). James L. Maxwell began the publication of *Kau-hoe-po* (Church News) in 1885; William Campbell, the church historian, edited a comprehensive Taiwanese Dictionary and laid the foundation for the study on the Dutch mission in the 17th century; Thomas Barclay founded Tainan Theological College (1876) and Taiwan Church Press (1884) and wrote many pamphlets. George Leslie Mackay established Oxford College, the Women's School, and trained 60 native preachers. By the late 1800s, missionaries were coming to adopt a more comprehensive approach to mission, engaging, in addition to evangelism, in medical, educational, and social services.

The Taiwan Synod, the forerunner of the Presbyterian Church of Taiwan (PCT), was formed in 1912, and this also assisted the churches to endure difficult times under the Japanese regime. Missionaries in these new fields of work who have also left writings, some of whom question some aspects of Christianity out of their encounters with local people, include David Landsborough, Marjorie Learner, Campbell Moody, George Ede, Edward Band and George W. Mackay. Women such as Chang Tsong-ming (Mrs. G. Mackay) and Mrs. D. Ferguson, along with women and men graduates of Mackay's "Oxford College for Christian Workers," were active educators and evangelists also. Formosan colleagues and co-workers in this period included Lo Liong (tutor), Phoa Beng-tsu and Lim Hak-kiong (pastors), Lim Ian-sin (teacher), Ng Se-keng, Lim Ang and Ng Tsok-pang (elders), Ko Thian-su (medico and educator), Toh Lau-seng (preacher) and Lim Kiam-kim (See also 2.2.1.4 below).

From 1915 on, while under the Japanese rule, some local leaders, notably Gou Hi-eng, began to advance the missionary principle of "self-support, self-government, and self-propagation." However, it was not until the 1940s that the process of indigenization in leadership began. Taiwanese churches and pastors emerged from war, and the attempts by Japanese to impose Emperor worship, more strongly "confessing the Lordship of Christ." The rapid growth of the aboriginal churches after 1945 was hailed as "the miracle of the twentieth century." Many hundreds of Catholic priests arrived in Taiwan with refugees from the mainland in 1949, and movements for conversions followed among both refugees and Aborigines. From the late 1950s, experiments in the recognition of "Chinese rites" were begun and in this period also the first (modern) Catholic writings in Taiwanese church history and theology appeared. By now the public activities of the Church were closely linked with government policy and statements of the Bishop's Conference strongly supported KMT tenets. The Conference did, however, submit a mildly reformist list of proposals to the KMT Congress in 1976. In the same year, seminars at the Fujen Theologate which was formed in 1968, addressed the problems of industrial workers and of ethnic languages.

After the defeat of the Nationalist regime in China, many other mainstream and independent churches entered Protestant mission along with the Presbyterian Church in Taiwan. In evangelistic work which followed, some movements were more directly "evangelistic" by nature, while others clearly embraced the ecumenical principle of "*missio Dei*." Regular meetings of an Ecumenical Consultative Committee, involving the Catholic and mainline Protestant churches, had begun in 1964, and in following years there were cooperative programs for the university apostolate, book distribution, medical work and a Common Bible. On this foundation a National Council of Churches in Taiwan (NCCT) was later formed.

From the 1970s on, democratic development, membership in the UN and the political future of Taiwan became paramount, although divisive, concerns for many. The PCT called in a series of public statements for social and political reforms, proclaimed the right of Taiwanese people to self-determination, and expressed hope for a "new and independent country." Persecution by the Nationalist regime followed. But the Church's concern for the future of Taiwan has remained strongly linked with "the renewal of the corporate spirituality of the people, as an integral part of the salvific mission of God." Members of other Christian churches, both mainstream and smaller denominations, seldom shared these same convictions, and this opposition stemmed from diverse ideological and ethnic differences in the Taiwanese context. These are also reflected in denominational and theological differences, as well as in pro-or anti-ecumenical rhetoric and in pro- or anti- independence movements.

In 1981, the Vatican reaffirmed links with Taiwan, and a "Year of Evangelization" was declared by the Bishops' Conference in

1983, with emphasis on Bible-reading and prayer. Responsibility for mission now came to be seen as belonging to women, young people, men and women religious, to the Catholic university and seminaries, and to Catholic professionals in the fields of art, science and social communication. Within the rapidly changing political context, many attitudes of both clergy and faithful to social, cultural and political issues were changing. Catholic action in non-government organizations greatly increased, especially in labour concerns and national and international issues. Since 1995 the Catholic Bishops have advocated stronger emphasis on religion and education for the instilling of freedom, democracy and human rights values, opposed revision of the constitution to increase presidential powers, and with other Catholic leaders have supported aborigines in their quest to regain traditional rights (See 2.2.1.4.).

Pro-democratic movements continued, and in 1987 the Martial Law, which had lasted for 38 years, was finally lifted, with democratic elections following in 1991, 1992 and 1996. A new phase of reconstruction and reconciliation among peoples of different ethnicity, culture, language and faith has begun. Presbyterian churches have continued to provide initiatives in educational and socio-political witness, as well as in contextual theological reflection and writing, and some other Protestant churches have further diversified their mission activities.

Selected References

See also references vol. 3, chap. 2: *Groundwork for Asian Theologies North East Asia - Formosa.*

Chen Tzu-Sung. "Taiwan Consciousness." Microform. Ph.D. diss., University of Notre Dame, 1995.

Chung-kuo chu chiao tuan chuan chiao. *Tien chu chiao tsai Taiwan hsien kuang chih yen chiu* (A Study of the Catholic Church in Taiwan ROC). Taipei: Kuang ch'i, 1987.

Covell, Ralph. *Pentecost of the Hills in Taiwan.* Pasadena: Hope Publishing, 1998: chaps. 5 and 6.

Digan, Parig. *Churches in Contestation. Asian Christian Social Protest.* Maryknoll, NY: Orbis, 1984, 103-106.

Fang, Mark Chih-jung. "Common Christian Witness in Asia: Facts and Perspective." In *Towards a "Dialogue of Life."*

Contextual Theology in Taiwan 671

Ecumenism in the Asian Context, edited by Pedro S. de Achutegui sj. Cardinal Bea Studies. Quezon City: Ateneo de Manila, 1976.

Fernandez, Pablo. *One Hundred Years of Dominican Apostolate in Formosa: Extracts from the Sino-Annamite Letters, Dominican Missions and Ultramar.* Translated by Felix Bautista. Quezon City: 1959.

Lai En-tse. "The Task of a Church Historian in Formosa - Church History as a History of Encounter." *SEAJOT* 3.4 (1962).

Lai, John Yung Hsiang. *Tai-Oan Kao-hoe Su-oe* (Topics on Church history). Series of volumes. Tainan: Jin-kong Press, 1990- .

Lin Chih-ping and Wei Wai-yang. *Chi-tu chiao yu Tai-wan* (Christianity in Taiwan). T'ai-pei: Yu chou kuang chuan po chung hsin, 1996.

MacKay, George L. *From Far Formosa.* New York: Revell, 1895.

Pickering, William A. *Pioneering in Formosa.* London: Hurst and Blackett, 1898.

Rubinstein, Murray A. *The Protestant Community in Modern Taiwan: Mission, Seminary and Church.* Taiwan in the Modern World. Armonk, NY: Sharpe, 1991.

Su Hsin-lu. *Chiang Fu-tsung chu* (On Catholic Church in Taiwan). Taipei: Taiwan shang wu yin shu kuan, 1985 (1958, 1961).

Swanson, Allen J. *Taiwan: Mainline Versus Independent Church Growth.* Pasadena, CA: William Carey, 1970.

—. *The Church in Taiwan - A Profile, 1980.* Pasadena, CA: William Carey, 1981.

Tei Jigyoku. "Christianity in Taiwan." In *The History of Christianity in Asia* [1], by Guo Liming et al (in Japanese). Tokyo: Kyobunkan, 1981.

Tong, Hollington K. *Christianity in Taiwan: a History.* Taipei: Printed by China Post, c1961.

2 The Development of Contextual Theology in Taiwan - Protestant Tradition. For pre-1800 see chap. 2 above.

2.1 The Early Context

Overseas missionaries who came to Taiwan in the middle of the 19th century, dressed as Taiwanese, built chapels in the form or style of the Taiwanese traditional building, adapted Taiwanese tunes in hymns and even married Taiwanese women. However, the theology of the Taiwanese churches then was almost entirely western and the attitude towards local cultures was negative. In fact, it was not until the early 20th century that Taiwanese Christian churches began to talk about "self-government, self-support, self-propagation." For Northern Presbyterians this was in 1906, and for Southern Presbyterians, 1915. With control of ministries and administration of the churches largely in the hands of foreign missionaries, it was almost impossible to do contextual theology.

During the Second World War, foreign missionaries were forced to leave Taiwan by the Japanese colonial government. However, the Taiwanese Church did not then become an autonomous Church. The administration was gradually taken over by native ministers, but their theology remained almost wholly western, influenced in part by the return of foreign missionaries as theological educators in most seminaries after WWII. It was therefore only after the celebration of the centennial of missionary work in Taiwan that contextual Protestant theology began to emerge fully.

Note the influence of such Chinese Christian philosophers and educators as Li Ch'un-sheng (1838-1924), Francis Wei Cho-min (1888-ca.1970) and Paul Sih Kwang-tsien (b.1910) on philosophical and cultural studies in Taiwan. Recent colloquia and publications in Taiwan have dealt with aspects of their work.

Selected References

    Beeby, H.D. *Formosa, the Challenge*. Overseas Committee of the Presbyterian Church of England, 1956.

    Chih, Andrew. *Chinese Humanism: a Religion beyond Religion*. Taipei: Fu Jen Catholic University Press, c1981.

    Freytag, Justus. *The Church in Villages of Taiwan; the Impact of Modern Society and Folk-religion on Rural Churches*. Tainan: Research Center, Tainan Theological College, 1969.

    Li, Minghui, ed. *Li Chunsheng di si xiang yu shi dai*. (The times and thoughts of Li Ch'un-sheng). Series: Taiwan yan jiu xi lie. Papers selected from Li Ch'un-sheng ssu hsiang yen t'ao hui, held in Taipei, Mar. 13, 1993. Taipei Zheng zhong shu ju, 1995. Table of contents also in English.

    Li, Huangbin.: *Taiwan di yi si xiang jia : Li Ch'un-sheng*. (Biography and Selections of Li Ch'un-sheng 1838-1924). Series: Sheng huan wen ku. Taoyuan Xian Zhongli Shi: Sheng huan tu shu gong si, 1997. See also "A Brief Biography of Li Ch'un-

sheng." *Newsletter*, 7.4 (1997). Institute of Chinese Literature and Philosophy, Taipei.
Lin, H.S. *Bibliography of Chinese Theology*. (Revision of Thesis by Harvey Chi, c.1980). Taipei: Taiwan Theological Seminary, 1995.
Richardson, William Jerome. "Christianity in Taiwan under Japanese Rule 1895-1945." Microform. Ph.D. diss., New York, St. John's University, 1972.
Rubinstein, Murray A. *The Protestant Community on Modern Taiwan: Mission, Seminary and Church*. Taiwan in the Modern World. Armonk NY: M.E. Sharpe, 1991: chap. 4.
Robinson, Lewis S. "Christianity through the Eyes of Chinese Writers." In *Double-Edged Sword. Christianity and 20th Century Chinese Fiction,* by Lewis S. Robinson, Part II. Hong Kong: Tao Fong Shan Ecumenical Centre, 1986.
Sih, Paul K.T.(Kwang Tsien), ed. *Taiwan in Modern Times*. New York: St. John's University Press, 1973.
— *Chinese Culture and Christianity; Selected Works of Paul K. T. Sih* (Chung-kuo wen hua yü chi tu chiao i). Taipei: China Culture Publishing Foundation, 1957.
Sik Ming Chong. *Transition from Missionary Leadership to Leadership by a Team of Nationals: a Reflective Study of a Taiwan Experience*. Theological Exchange Network Series. (Microform.) Wheaton, Ill: Wheaton College, 1997.
Wei, Francis C.M. *The Spirit of Chinese Culture*. New York: Charles Scribner's Sons, 1947.(Reprinted 2002).
— *Dr Francis C.M.Wei's Writings on Education, Culture and Religion*.Taipei: Hua Chung University, 1980.

2.2 The Emergence of Contextual Theology
2.2.1. Theological Movements and Praxis
2.2.1.1 Contextualizing Theology

Many streams can be seen contributing to the growth of contextual theology in Taiwan, apart from some elements of adaptation and indigenization recognizable in earlier changing patterns of mission there. In the post-war period, a small number of Protestant scholars and writers continued their studies in Chinese literature and culture, and these would come to influence Taiwanese Christian theology. Among those writing on Christianity and Chinese culture in this period, and relating their study to the context of Christianity in

Taiwan, were Wei Cho-min (1888-ca.1970), Paul Sih Kwang-tsien (b.1910), James T.M. Pong (1911-1987), and N.Z. Zia (1892-1992: see also 3.2.2. in chapter 4, Hong Kong). Wei Cho-min wrote much on the convergence of Christianity and Chinese culture, with the concept of a harmonious world culture (*shijie datong wenhua*), while N.Z. Zia was a Christian philosopher who devoted his later years to the construction of an indigenous Chinese theology. In addition a number of other writers embodied Christian concerns or teaching in novels and drama. Amongst these are Hsu Ti-shan (1892-1941) (Xu Dishan,see also chapter 4, Hong Kong), Chu Hsi-ning (b.1927), Ch'i-teng (b.1939), and Ch'en Ying-chen (b.1936), along with two women writers Ti-jan (Evelyn O. Shih, b.ca.1925), and Chang Hsiao-feng (b.1941).

Indigenous churches such as the True Jesus Church, although maintaining firmly conservative formal theologies, also show both a congruence with local folk (and Chinese) tradition - in piety and biblical interpretation, and a measure of acculturation and accommodation - regarding Eucharist, glossolalia and ancestor practices.

Movements arising in the churches, and developments within the changing society of Taiwan, made Christian communities aware of important issues in the lives of marginalized people such as farmers, fishermen, workers, and aborigines. The Presbyterian Church in particular had long worked with some of these groups and was gradually identifying itself with the land and the people who live on the land. From this came awareness both of the contextual realities in Taiwan, and of the indigenous resources of faith and culture held by Taiwanese people. In 1961, Shoki Coe (Ng Chiong-hui, see 2.2.2.1. below), the principal of the Tainan Theological College and Seminary, questioned whether it was appropriate for Taiwanese churches to promote ministries and theology which had been developed by churches of the West in secularized western society. Theological education, he affirmed, has to be an education in its historical situation, so that if Christian communities want to fulfil the mission they received from God, they must have existential communication with the religions and

Contextual Theology in Taiwan 675

cultures of the society to which they belong: this encounter and dialogue is the way to construct a native theology.

In the same period new patterns of education and social mission emerged in lay-training programs and social concern institutes. Initiatives of the EACC in laity formation, and the models of European Lay Academies led to the establishment of Christian Academies (1967) in Tainan - with leadership by John Jyigiokk Tin (2.2.2.2.) and later Sun Hong-tsurn; and in Taipei, led by Cheng Lien-te, and later by Shang Jeng-tzong. The Taipei Women's Development Center was established in 1984. These institutes engage in a wide range of social, occupational and educational ministries, which provide a bridge between church and society through dialogue, education and cooperation on issues of social tension, legislation, minority concerns and social justice. From them have come conference and course reports, research studies, contextual reflection and liturgies (See *Taiwan Church Weekly*, *ACISCA News*, *EACC/CCA News*). Lay movements like the YMCA, the Ecological Theological Center and student groups have also initiated educational and social action programs, from which theological reflection has arisen (See also 2.2.1.6. below).

Selected References

Coe, Shoki. *Joint Action for Mission in Formosa; a Call for Advance into a New Era*. New York: Commission on World Mission and Evangelism, WCC: Friendship Press, 1968.

Conference of Bishops. *Sinicization - the Church as a Living Community - the Gospel of Christ in Modern China. Proceedings of National Pastoral Workshops of the Catholic Church in the Republic of China*. Tainan, 1969.

Feng Xiang. "People's Theology in Taiwan." *Ching Feng* 25:3 (1982).

Freytag, Justus, ed. *Junge Kirchen auf eigenen Wegen: Analysen u. Dokumente* (Young churches on their own ways: analyses and documents). Perspektiven der Weltmission 2. Frankfurt/Main: Lembeck, 1972.

MacLeod, Alexander N. *A Bibliography of Chinese Theological Books*. Alumni collection prepared for the Taiwan Association of Theological Schools. Taipei: China Sunday School Association, 1973]

Ma Min, ed. *Francis C.M. Wei's Writings on Christianity.* Hong Kong: Institute of Sino-Christian Studies, 2000.

Pong, James T.M. *Dialogue Between Christianity and the Non-Christian Religions.* Taipei: Episcopal Church Press, 1976.

—. *Christian Doctrine and Chinese Religious Thought.* Taipei: Taiwan Diocesan Press, 1979.

Sih, Paul K. T. (Kwang Tsien). *Chinese Culture and Christianity; Selected Works of Paul K. T. Sih* (Chung-kuo wen hua yü chi tu chiao i). 1957.

Wang Hsien Chi (Wang Xianzhi). *Taiwan xiangtu shexue lunwenji* (Essays on Taiwan's indigenous theology). Tainan: Taiwan Church Press, 1988.

Wan Hsien-fa et al., eds. *Dr Francis C.M. Wei's Writings on Education, Culture and Religion.* Taipei: Dr Francis C.M. Wei Memorial Hall, Huachung University, 1980.

Wei, Francis C.M. *The Spirit of Chinese Culture.* 1947 / 2002.

— *Dr Francis C.M.Wei's Writings on Education, Culture and Religion.*1980.

YMCA, ROC. *Records of the Young Men's Christian Association of the Republic of China.* Held in Yale University Divinity School Library, n.d.

Zia, N.Z. *Philosophy of Religion.* Tai-chung, Taiwan: Tung-hai University Press, 1980.

2.2.1.2. The Theology of the Incarnation

Following the centennial celebrations for Protestant mission in Taiwan, the "New Century Mission Movement" emphasized the role of the churches in rapidly changing Taiwanese society. This was therefore, not only a missionary movement, but also a theological renewal movement for the Church. It was a movement challenging the Christian communities to go into the world for the changing of the world. This was a further dimension of contextualization. C.S. Song (see 2.2.2.3.), who had succeeded Shoki Coe at Tainan, then proposed a "theology of the Incarnation" for the churches. This was a theology related to the reality of Taiwanese society; not a theology borrowed from western churches, but one emerging from the context and situation of the people, a theology "renewed in the light of God's Word and the needs of the world." Thinking from the context and situation of the people became the way of doing theology, both for Song and the many he inspired in many countries.

Here, too, is the beginning of a Theology of Identification rooted in the identification of God with Israel, and through Jesus Christ, with all human beings. Contextual theology in Taiwan emerges only from identification with the Taiwanese people, their sufferings and hopes. Through identification, Christian communities are participating in these sufferings and in the hope of liberation: and they are thereby directly involved in the history and cultures of the Taiwanese people. From this arises their contextual theology in Taiwan.

Other theologians and writers - apart from those in individual separate entries below - who have contributed to aspects of such theology include Hsiao Ching-fen, Ingram Hsieh, Kao Chun-ming, Tung Fang-yuen, Chen Chu-hsien and Wu Fu-ya (For the last mentioned see 2.2.1.5).

Selected References

Chen Jiahn-yuen. "Mission of Sacrifice: A Reflection on the Death of Cheng Nan-jung." *ATESEA Occasional Papers* 10 (1990).

Hsiao, Ching-fen. "Asian Theology in Retrospect and Prospect." *NEAJOT* 18/19 (1977); *SEAJOT* 19.1 (1978).

—, and Ingram Samuel Seah. "Creativity, Integrity and Solidarity in Theological Education." *East Asia Journal of Theolog* 2.2 (1984).

Hsueh Po Tsan. " 'The Kingdom of God' in the Context of Taiwanese Folk Religions." *Taiwan Journal of Theology* 18 (1996).

—. "Basic Elements and Interpretation of Ecumenical Missiology." *Taiwan Journal of Theology* 19 (1997).

Song Choan-seng. *Towards A Theology of the Incarnation*. Tainan: n.p.,1965.

—. *The Church in Taiwan on the Move: the New Century Mission Movement*. Tainan: Tainan Theological College, Research Center, 1966-1968.

Sawatzky, Sheldon Victor. "The body of Christ Metaphor: an Interpretation to Stimulate Taiwanese Mennonite Reflection on the Nature and Task of the Church within Chinese Society." Ph.D. diss., Fuller Theological Seminary, School of World Mission, 1980.

2.2.1.3. Identifying with the Sufferings and the Hopes of the Taiwanese People

In the 1970s, as part of movements against the KMT government in Taiwan, the PCT in particular issued three public statements, namely, "Statement on Our National Fate"(1971), "Our Appeal"(1975), and "The Human Rights Declaration"(1977). These public statements could be seen in part as resulting from the renewal of theology of the Taiwanese Presbyterian Church. In this renewal of theology, the Christian communities realized that the Church is deeply concerned with the people's vital concerns. Along with movements in Taiwan society (including "Formosan Christians for Self-Determination"), and the work of courageous writers, editors and intellectuals, the church, through these public statements, was trying to identify the sufferings of the Taiwanese people, and to participate in the struggle for self-determination. These statements and the ministries out of which they arose, therefore comprised part of the praxis for contextual theology in Taiwan.

It was on the basis of the Public Statements of 1971-77, that the new Confession of the Presbyterian Church in Taiwan was accepted in 1985. Speakers declared of this that "[the Church] is both universal and rooted in this land, identifying with all its inhabitants, and through love and suffering becoming the sign of hope." Here too, discussion and the approval of the Confession was part of the praxis in identifying with the sufferings and the hopes of the Taiwanese people, an important step in contextual theology.

Kao Chun-ming (C.M. Kao), general secretary of the Presbyterian Church in this period (see 2.2.2.4.), was notable for his courageous but modest leadership. Despite harassment and imprisonment, he and his colleagues Hsu T'ien-hsien, Lin Hung-hsuan and Liu Fung-sung, continued their writing - in poems, hymns, letters and statements - on themes of harmony, fortitude in suffering, the life of Jesus, peace and justice. Among long-term expatriate workers who were identified closely in such endeavors were Boris Anderson, Elizabeth Brown, Daniel Beeby and James Sutherland.

Selected References

Huang Wudong. *The History and Development of the Presbyterian Church of Taiwan.* Taipei: Vanguard Press, 1988.

Hsueh Po Tsan. "Preparing the People's Hope - Singing an Old Taiwanese Folk Song 'Po Poah Bang' with New Vision." *ATESEA Occasional Papers* 11 (1991).

Ming, Anne. *Taiwanese Voice.* London: Division of International Affairs, British Council of Churches, 1981.

Presbyterian Church in Taiwan Public Statements, 1971-1992. Taipei: The General Assembly of the Presbyterian Church in Taiwan, 1992.

Taiwan - Its International and Ecumenical Status and Role. A Report of the International Forum, February 1994. Taipei: General Assembly of the Presbyterian Church in Taiwan, 1994.

Testimonies of Faith. Letters and Poems from Prison in Taiwan. Selected, edited and translated by Choan-seng Song. Geneva: World Alliance of Reformed Churches, 1984.

The Presbyterian Church in Taiwan Under the Cross. New York: Formosan Christians for Self-Determination, 1978.

The Presbyterian Church in Taiwan (http://www.pct.org.tw/english/introe.htm)

Wong Chong-Gyiau. "The emergence of political statements and political theology in the history of the Taiwanese Presbyterian Church." Ph.D. diss., Boston University, 1992.

2.2.1.4. Aboriginal Theology

The roots of aboriginal theology can be seen in middle decades of the 20th century, in the ministries and reflections of pastors, evangelists and teachers such as Chi Wang (see 2.2.1.5.), Dawai (Liu Fu Ch'ang) and Wiran (Kao T'en-wang) - all of whom suffered severely from Japanese persecution. Wiran preached also in Japan in the 1950s, and was outspoken there on the inhumanities of Japanese soldiers and police in Taiwan - another form of liberation praxis. Contributions from Taiwanese and expatriates to mission among aborigines in this period - in pastoring, teaching, translation - were also significant. Notable among Taiwanese were Lo Hsien ch'un - pastor, linguist and scholar - and Hu Wen-ch'ih, whose writings provide a rare reflection upon Aboriginal life and witness (Hu Wen-ch'ih, 1984).

The quality of aboriginal faith and their tacit theology can be seen in a study made in 1957: "I have never known a people whose conception of God is so entirely one of love as is that of the people ... [the] community of believers is a great and joyful fact in [their] lives" but "the true nature of the Church (in Ami 'the body of God') is expressed by faith and activity ..." It is "the heart of our Lord Jesus Christ on earth," declared an Ilan woman (Vicedom, 1967).

The studies made by such centers as the Institute of Ethnology at Academica Sinica in Taipei have raised the profile of Aboriginal culture, and mother tongues in particular, as does the Formosan Aboriginal Culture Village in Nantou county. A newly-developed sense of identity has led movements for human rights (among Sediq and Ami communities), in protest at government policies on land, natural resources and disposal of nuclear waste. In these, Christians have played leading roles, sometimes leading to their imprisonment and to reflection upon this.

More recently, Kao Wang-chin, a Tayal theological professor in Yu-Shan Theological College and Seminary, and influenced by the theological method of C.S. Song, has written a theological reflection on the history of his own tribe. In this Kao Wang-chin has said that the aborigines had an Exodus-like experience, and the stories of the aborigines have meaning for all people who value human life. Professor Peter Ming-yu Chang was another theologian who tried to reinterpret aboriginal stories and to discern their theological meanings. Kao Wang-chin, now the principal of Yu-shan seminary, should also be noted here. There is also a Research Centre for Urban Aboriginal Theology at Taiwan Theological College and Seminary (Taipei).

Selected References

Ch'en Ch'ien-wu. *Taiwan P'ingputsu Ch'uanshuo* (Oral tradition of Taiwan's Pepohoan). Taipei: Kuoli Chungyang T'ushukuan, 1993.

Covell, Ralph. *Pentecost of the Hills in Taiwan*. Pasadena: Hope Publishing, 1998.

Fey, Virginia and Afo Apak. *Amis Culture* (Ami Tsu Wenhua or O'Orip No 'Amis). Taipei: Bible Society of Taiwan, 1993.

Hu, Wen-ch'ih. *Yiwang Szi K'an Shenlen* (Reflecting on God's power in the past). Taipei: Ta Kuang Publisher, 1984.
Kao Wang-Chin. *The Aboriginal People: Rather Dying than Surrendering* (in Chinese.) Chiayi: Hsin Fu Press, 1995.
Lin, Yvonne Mai-jung, ed. *Community Control, Cultural Dignity and Economic Value. Asian Consultation on Tourism and Aboriginal Rights.* Taidong: Huadong Community Development Center, 1992.
Shephard, John R. "Plains Aborigines and Missionaries in Ch'ing Taiwan, 1859-1895." Unpublished ms., Stanford University, 1988.
Shih Lei. "Social Contact and Religious Change among the Formosan Aborigines." *New Asia Academic Bulletin* 6 (1986).
Stainton, Michael Stuart. "Return our Land. Counterhegemonic Presbyterian Aboriginality in Taiwan." (Microform). Thesis, Toronto: York University, 1995.
Vicedom, George. *Faith That Moves Mountains. A Study of the Tribal Church in Taiwan.* Taipei: China Post, 1967.
Whitehorn, John and Edward Band. *He led Them on: the Story of the Christian Movement among the Paiwan Tribe of Formosa.* London: British and Foreign Bible Society, 1955.

2.2.1.5. Women Doing Theology

Taiwanese women have long played a prominent part in the life and witness of the churches, as Bible Women, pastors' wives and teachers. But their thought and even their lives have seldom been recorded. One for whom we have a full account is Chi-oang (Chi Wang Yiwal, 1872-1946) the committed Christian teacher, evangelist and courageous peacemaker for aboriginal peoples. Along with her teaching of repentance, faith and prayer, Chi-oang declared often that "the God of Creation was the one true God who had created all people." Despite regular surveillance and interrogation by Japanese police she persisted in her ministries from which emerged both aboriginal movements and churches.

More critical feminist theology in Taiwan has been published only in recent decades. The Taiwan Association of Theologically Trained Women was established in October, 1981, and now has almost 200 members. With the aims of mutual support, theological reflection and Christian proclamation, the Association has held retreats and workshops, developed a library, conducted surveys and organized a network for visitation, advocacy and evangelism. A central concern has been the holding of "Seminars on Feminist Theology" and the preparation of related publications. In 1991 the Women's Work Committee of the PCT initiated new training courses and published the book *Educate Women in Mission*.

Among those who have been active in writing, Wu Fu-ya and Su So-jin have written theological and historical surveys on biblical sources, the role of the women in the Taiwanese Church, and the theological reflection of Taiwanese women. Wu Fu-ya has also published poetry (in, for example, *In God's Image*) and collaborated in theological reflections upon sustainable development movements. Chuang Shu-jen has written biblical studies and on Asian mission. Other women writers include Yvonne Lin Mai-jung, Carol Chou-Adams, Nancy Lin, Nancy Tzu-mei Chen and Lucy Kao-Loh (2.2.2.6.). Writings by these and others now appear more frequently in such journals as *Taiwan Church News* and *In God's Image*, a special issue of which (18.2, 1999) featured a number of Taiwanese women writers. In addition, a group of Christian women have now formed the Ecological Theological Centre to promote a new concept of creation, through different forms of education, action and publishing.

Selected References

Chou-Adams, Carol and Copland, Margaret L. *Chi-oang: Mother of the Taiwan Tribes Church*. Taipei: General Assembly of the Presbyterian Church of Formosa, United Publishing Center, 1962.

Chuang Shu-jen. "The New Mission of Asian Christians." *CTC Bulletin* 9.1 (1990).

Feng Xiang (Kao Teng-shiang / Ko, Tian-hiong / Lucy Kao-Loh). "People's Theology in Taiwan." *Ching Feng* 25:3 (1982).)

Good Stewards, an Environmental Handbook. Taipei: Ecological and Theological Study and Action Group, 1992.

Lin, Nancy. "The Never-ending Stories." *In God's Image* 18.2 (1999).

Su So-jin. *Women's Theology in Taiwan Context*. Tainan: Church Press, 1990.

Wu Fu-ya, *The Image of Women in the Bible*. Tainan: Taiwan Church Press, 1990.
—. *Women in the Christian Church: The Taiwanese Case*. Taipei: The Women's Ministry Committee of the General Assembly of the Presbyterian Church in Taiwan, 1996.
—. "Taiwanese Experience: Looking Back and Moving Forward." *In God's Image* 17.4 (1998).
—. "Reclaim the Sustainable Spirituality of Asia." *In God's Image* 18.2 (1999).
Women's Mission Committee. *Women's Educational Handbook, Volumes I and II*. Taipei: PCT Assembly, 1992.
Wu Shu-huey and Linda Petrucelli. "Taiwanese Women in Mission: A Search for New Roles." *In God's Image* 11.4 (1992).

2.2.1.6 Identifying with the History and Cultures of the Taiwanese people

Besides social involvement such as identification with the sufferings and the hopes of the Taiwanese people, the praxis of contextual theology had another dimension. This meant identifying with the history and cultures of the Taiwanese people and reinterpreting Taiwanese history and cultures from within Christian faith. In this way, the theological meaning of Taiwanese history and cultures can be discerned.

In his book entitled *Christian Mission in Reconstruction* (1975), C.S. Song proposed a new theological approach to mission: doing theology from the creation of God. Traditional approaches to mission were from the perspective only of Redemption, centered upon the Cross of Christ, and personal conversion. However, we should understand mission more from the perspective of creation. If we see Christian mission in that perspective, then all histories, cultures, social changes and even politics outside Israel have their own meanings within the salvific purpose of God. Long before western missionaries came, God has from the beginning been in Asia, for example, sustaining, meeting and calling all peoples. Activities of Christian mission should therefore not reject "non-Christian" cultures, but seek to understand them, to identify with them, and to discern their theological meaning.

These new developments in contextual theology in Taiwan were also trying to discern the theological meaning of Taiwanese history and cultures. This was influenced by the theological method developed in the Asia-wide programs of "Doing Theology with Asian Resources" initiated by Song and an international team (The Programme for Theology and Cultures in Asia - PTCA). Here the whole range of a people's history, culture and religious experience - including the life of their Christian communities - was taken as the primary source for theological reflection and teaching. Study of the histories and experience of western peoples therefore takes second place to discerning the presence of God in a people's own life. Taiwanese theological workers, along with many others in the region, are now learning to reinterpret their own history and cultures, and to discern their theological meaning. These concerns have been also central to the work of the Research Center for Contextual Theology, Taiwan Theological College and Seminary (Taipei), and the Christian Institute for Social Transformation and the Chhut-thau-thin Institute, Tainan Theological College and Seminary (Tainan).

Selected References

Song, Choan-seng. *Christian Mission in Reconstruction - An Asian Attempt*. Madras: The Christian Literature Society, 1975.
—, and Chen Nan-Jou. *Constructing Theology in the Context of Taiwan* (in Chinese and English). Tainan, 1994.
England, John C. and Archie C.C. Lee, eds. *Doing Theology with Asian Resources: Ten Years in the Formation of Living Theology in Asia*. Auckland: Pace Publishing for PTCA, 1993.

2.2.2. Key People
2.2.2.1. Shoki Coe (Ng Chiong Hui / Hwang Chang-hue) 1914-1988.

A Taiwanese born in 1914, and named by his parents Ng Chiong Hue, Shoki Coe was always conscious that because of Japanese colonial rule, military rule by the KMT, and exile from Taiwan, he had never been able to use his native name. He saw the experience of displacement he went through as also the experience his

Taiwanese compatriots faced throughout their history. He thus calls his own theology a theology of "M-kam-goan" (theology of comfortlessness). The concept and contents of contextualizing theology therefore has a deep root in his personal experiences as an exiled theologian from Taiwan. Under his leadership, Tainan Seminary, when opened following the defeat of Japan, became a center of innovative and ecumenical developments throughout the region and beyond. In exile, he joined the staff of the Theological Education Fund (TEF), becoming its director, 1970-77. There he provided leadership in the renewal and diversification of theological education throughout the Third World. In 1973 he became one of four founders of the movement "Formosan Christians for Self-determination."

Shoki Coe's most important writings, 1962-1977, present the life of Jesus (with his friends) as the primary "indigenization" text, and picture the Church as a world-directed servant community amid the processes of industrialization, political struggle and cultural resurgence. The "double wrestle" both with such cultural realities and the living text of Christ's continuing presence brings to birth, he declared, a contextualizing theology.

By raising the question of the relation between text and context, Shoki Coe has consciously tried to find relevant loci for Christian theologies. He contends that "authentic theological reflection can only take place as the *thologia in loco,* discerning the contextuality within the concrete context." With his colleagues he was thus proposing the concept of "contextualization" to replace the then fashionable idea of "indigenization" for theological education, and eventually as a method for theology. By proposing this new concept, Shoki Coe has pointed out that the old method of indigenization derives from the idea of "taking root in the soil," which, however, tends to suggest a static response to the Gospel "in terms of traditional culture: an orientation to the past which may weaken the ability of theologies to respond to the living contexts of people." "Contextuality", he also said, "is the critical assessment of what makes the context really significant in the light of the *missio Dei.* It is the missiological discernment of the signs of the times, seeing where God is at work and calling us to participate in it."

For Shoki Coe, "indigenization is a missiological necessity when the Gospel moves from one cultural soil to another and has to be retranslated, reinterpreted, and expressed afresh in the new cultural soil. It is only right that the younger churches, in search of their own identity, should take seriously their own cultural milieu." However, because indigenization is in danger of being past-oriented "the T.E.F. does not speak about 'contextual theology,' nor 'contextualized theology,' but about contextualizing theology." The theological method proposed therefore emphasized the responses of faith in a dynamic context. "The incarnation," declared Shoki Coe, "is the divine form of contextualization [and] authentic contextualization must be open constantly to the painful process of de-contextualization, for the sake of re-contextualization."

These insights would have wide-ranging impact upon the doing of theology not only in Taiwan, but throughout Asia and the wider world.

Selected References
Works by C.H. Hwang (Shoki Coe / Ng Chiong Hui)
"God's People in Asia Today." *SEAJOT* 5.2 (1963).
"The Life and Mission of the Church in the World." *SEAJOT* 6.2 (1964).
"Text and Context in Theological Education." In *Theological Education and Ministry - Reports from the North East Asia Theological Educators' Conference, Seoul, 1966.* Tainan: Presbyterian Bookroom, 1967.
"Across the Frontiers: Text and Context in Mission." In *Christian Action in the Asian Struggle*, edited by U Kyaw Than. Singapore: CCA, 1973.
"Contextualizing Theology." In *Mission Trends No. 3,* edited by Gerald Anderson. New York: Paulist Press, 1976.
"Contextualizing as the Way Towards Reform." In *Asian Christian Theology: Emerging Themes*, edited by D.J. Ellwood. Philadelphia: Westminster Press, 1980.
Recollections and Reflections. Introduced and edited by Boris Anderson. 2nd ed. New York: The Rev. Dr. Shoki Coe's Memorial Fund, for Formosan Christians for Self-Determination, 1993; Tainan: Church Press, 1994.

England, John C. "Watershed Figures in Asian Theologies 6." *PTCA Bulletin* 5.1 (1992).
TEF Staff. *Ministry in Context. The Third Mandate Programme of the Theological Education Fund (1970-77).* Bromley: Theological Education Fund, 1972.
—. *Learning in Context. The Search for Innovative Patterns in Theological Education.* Bromley: Theological Education Fund, 1973.

2.2.2.2. Tin, John Jyigiokk (1922-)

John Jyigiokk Tin (Cheng Erh-yu) was born in Tangkáng, Taiwan, and graduated from Doshisha University in 1946, from McCormick Theological Seminary, Chicago (Th.M. 1958) and the Graduate School of Ecumenical Studies, University of Geneva (1959). He also did graduate studies at the University of Hamburg (1972-75). He has been professor of Christianity and history, church and society at Tainan Theological College and Seminary (1966-1989), and director, Christian Institute for Social Transformation (1979-). He also founded the Taiwan Christian Academy (1968), and was an initiator and drafter of the PCT "Public Statement on Our National Fate" (1971); and of the "Confession of Faith" of the PCT (1985).

Tin's work and writing has focused chiefly upon the issues of church and society, in theological teaching, in laity education and animation, and in church history, missiology and hymnology. He has been especially critical of KMT autocracy, opposed the equation of anti-communism to the Gospel, and has contributed to the formulation of PCT theology in response to major socio-political events and issues in Taiwan. Along with books, articles and sermons on mission, church history and social ethics in Taiwan, he has written on Homeland Theology. His society-oriented and ecumenical hymns have been widely published and have received international awards.

Selected References

Works by John Jyigiokk Tin (Cheng Erh-yu)
The Religious Identity in Taiwan - A Study of Mentality. Madras, CLS Press, 1992.

Taiwan the Green - Christian Commitments and Poems of the Taiwan Democracy Movement, Taipei: Böng-chhun-hong Press. Forthcoming.

The Christian Faith and Resistance under the Autocracies of the Chiangs. Taipei: Böng-chhun-hong Press. Forthcoming.

"Critical Analysis on the Basic Problems of Mission in Taiwan Today" (in Taiwanese). *Theology and the Church* (June 1961).

"Education for Professional and Non-Professional Ministries." *Theology and the Church* (June 1969).

"Light of the World, Salt of the Earth." *New Songs of Asian Cities.* Tainan: CCA-URM Committee, 1972. Also in *Neue Cantate Domino*, Geneva: WCC, 1974, and *Das Wort der Welt* (Jan. 1975).

"Our Homeland" and "Introducing 'Our Homeland'." *CTC Bulletin* (November 1979).

"Concerning the Problems of Identification of the Government with the People and the Homeland." *CTC Bulletin* (Nov. 1979).

"Christianity in Taiwan." In *Christianity in Asia*. Singapore: CCA Asia Focus, 1979. Also Tokyo: Kyobunkwan, 1981.

"Your Kingdom Come." *International Review of Mission* (Oct. 1980).

"Stand Up! Let Us Go Forward from Here ..." *Theology and the Church* 22.2 (1996).

2.2.2.3. Song Choan-seng (C.S. Song, 1929 -)

Song is one of the pioneers of Asian theologies and of the founders of the Programme for Theology and Cultures in Asia (PTCA), as well as being "the guru of Story Theology." He has been President of Tainan Theological Seminary, on the staff of both the WARC and the WCC, regional professor of theology for the South East Asia Graduate School of Theology (1983), and since 1985, professor of theology and Asian cultures at the Pacific School of Religion (GTU; Berkeley, CA). Following the "Statement on Our National Fate," issued by the PCT in 1971, together with Shoki Coe (Hwang Chang-Hue), Hwang Wu-tong, and Lin Tsung-yi, Song initiated the movement *Formosan Christians for Self-Determination* in order to assist Taiwanese people "to assert their human rights of self-determination for the future of Taiwan and to promote the cause of self-determination in the international community of nations." He was the editor of *Chhut-thau-thin* (Raising the head above the sky, meaning liberation), the occasional journal of that movement.

While Song was associate director of the Secretariat of the Faith and Order Commission, WCC (from 1973), worldwide experiences enriched and deepened his critical theological reflection, especially in the field of Gospel and culture. In his writings since 1977 he presents the histories of peoples as a continuation of God's creation, taking culture and history very seriously in his theology. His theology is a "third-eye theology," or a "theology from the womb of Asia." He emphasizes that "the frontiers of our theology must move from the history of Israel and history of Christianity in the West to the history in which we are involved in Asia" making "a leap from Israel to Asia."

From 1983, Song and other Asian theological leaders conducted Theological Seminar-Workshops that developed into PTCA (Programme for Theology and Cultures in Asia) in 1987. More than 600 Asian theologians and church leaders have participated in these courses of doing theology with Asian resources. To him, culture is the matrix or womb of theology, i.e. "the totality of life is the raw material of theology," and cultures are endowed theological significance.

In 1994 Song completed his three-volume work on Jesus, *The Cross in the Lotus World*. This he describes as "a theological effort to understand Christian faith in the part of the world not dominated by Christianity." The five stages towards a theological reconstruction in the multi-cultural world he suggests are as follows: (1) "Asking a fundamental question," such as "the possibility that God may be working also outside the church"; (2) The story of Jesus as the story of suffering people is the key to unlock the mystery surrounding God; (3) The Reign of God provides the link between stories of Jesus and stories of different cultures. Asian Christians have to discern the stories of God's Reign in Asia and to realize how God is speaking to us; (4) Identifying a theological problem. "With the story of Jesus as the story of God's Reign and with the stories of people in Asia that reflect the story of God's Reign, we return to the Christian church, to its faith and theology and look at it with a new eye"; and (5) Jesus and stories of people. "As the story of Jesus and stories from Asia inter-penetrate each other, a theological space is also opened for the stories of Hebrew Scripture, a theological feast of stories: the story of Jesus, stories from Asia, stories in Hebrew Scripture, and stories from the rest of the world, told as stories of God's Reign."

As early as in 1965, Song proposed a "theologia viatorum" to his colleagues at Tainan Theological College. In 1994, he continues to say that theology is always on the way -"theologia viatorum." His theological journey continues.

Selected References
Works by Choan-seng Song
    Christian Mission in Reconstruction - An Asian Attempt. Madras: Christian Literature Society, 1975; New York: 1977.
    Tell Us Our Names - Story Theology from an Asian Perspective. Maryknoll, NY: Orbis Books, 1984.
    The Five Stages Towards Christian Theology in the Multi-cultural World. Tainan: Tainan Theological Seminary, 1994.
    Third-eye Theology: Theology in Formation in Asian Settings. Maryknoll, NY: Orbis Books, 1979.
    The Compassionate God: An Exercise in the Theology of Transposition. London: SCM Press, 1982.
    The Tears of Lady Meng: A Parable of People's Political Theology. Risk Book Series. Geneva: WCC, 1981.
    Theology from the Womb of Asia. Maryknoll, NY: Orbis Books, 1986.
    The Cross in the Lotus World. Vol. 1: *Jesus, the Crucified People.* New York: Crossroad, 1990; Vol. 2: *Jesus and the Reign of God.* Minneapolis, MN: Fortress, 1993: Vol. 3: *Jesus in the Power of the Spirit.* Minneapolis, MN: Fortress, 1994.
    The Believing Heart: an Invitation to Story Theology. Minneapolis, MN: Fortress Press, c1999.
    Chan, Stephen T. "Narrative, Story and Story-telling: A Study of C.S. Song's Theology of Story." *Asia Journal of Theology* 12.1 (1998).
    Federschmidt, Karl H. *Theologie aus asiatischen Quellen: der theologische Weg Choan-Seng Song's vor dem Hintergrund der asiatischen okumenischen Diskussion* ... Münster: Lit, 1994.

Ngun, Richard. *C. S. Song's Theological Method : an Exposition and Evaluation.* Dissertation. Dallas Theological Seminary, 1994. Published Grand Rapids, Mich.: UMI Dissertation Services, 2000

2.2.2.4. Kao Chun-ming (C.M. Kao, 1929-)

Kao was formerly principal of Yu-Shan Theological College and Seminary (1957-1970) and general secretary of the PCT (1970-1989). Part of this period was spent in prison because of his assistance to patriots wanted by the government. He has been one of the most dedicated pastors to the Taiwanese aboriginal Christian ministry. His letters and poems from prison, along with his theological writings on Taiwan's identity and role as a nation, have been internationally recognized. He has also been leader in fostering Christian participation in social concerns, especially those related to the future of Taiwan. His newly published volume *The Road of the Cross* will be one of the most important historical materials for understanding the social involvement of the PCT in recent decades.

Selected References
Works by Kao Chun-ming (C.M. Kao)
The Road of the Cross: The Memories of C. M. Kao. Taipei: Wang-Chung-Fong Press, 2000.
"Statement on Our National Fate: Motivation Based on Faith and Theology." *Taiwan Church News* (Tai-oan Kao-hoe Kong-Po) 1078 (Mar.1972).
"Poems." In *Testamonies of Faith. Letters and Papers from Prison,* edited by C.S. Song. Geneva: World Alliance of Reformed Churches, c.1983.

2.2.2.5. Wang Hsien-chih (Ong Hian-Ti 1941-1996)

Wang Hsien-chih (Ong Hian-Ti) graduated from Tainan Theological College and Seminary (TTCS) summa cum laude, in 1968, was ordained in the Episcopalian Church, and joined the faculty of TTCS (1975). In his doctoral thesis (1978) Wang expounded the law of nature in Lao Tzu's *Dao De Jing* ("Way and its Power" - the scripture of Taoism) as one of the paradigms for contextualizing Christian theology in the Confucius-dominated culture milieu in Taiwan.

A compassionate and gifted teacher, Wang was also a leader in articulating Taiwanese theology, in both open and clandestine venues, nationally and overseas, in relation to aspirations for homeland, issues of human rights, and of justice and sovereignty. As an Episcopalian, he contributed to the PCT "Declaration of Human Rights" issued in 1977 and the "Confession of Faith" in 1986, and also edited *Taiwan Church News*. He chaired the Commission for Theological Concerns of the Christian Conference of Asia, and after leaving TTCS in 1993 established with other colleagues the Taiwan Institute of Theology and Culture.

In the context of Taiwan's particular historical experience, and as part of further theological reflection on social participation and ministries of social concern, Wang developed a theology of Homeland, based on the role of the promised land in Israelite history and on the six major covenants of the First and New Testaments. Taking the Exodus/nation-building/exiles of Israel as a paradigm, homeland theology affirms that the issues of ethnicity (people), land, power and God are the main theological themes for the Israelites, the Israelis, and the Taiwanese as well. To deal with these themes, socio-historical, cultural and ideological elements in the formation of the Scriptures are studied, and the stories of the people on Taiwan are essential resources for theological deliberation. Homeland theology was therefore born in the particular political and theological milieu of nation-building in Taiwan. For Wang "the idea of a homeland in this new experience of God in Jesus Christ may be conceived as a process of concretion of the Kingdom of God in Taiwan ... [It] has its roots in the struggle ... to establish a new identity for the church and people together as the people of God." For this the stories and experience of Taiwanese people are of central concern as they reflect upon identity and homeland.

Selected References
Works by Wang Hsien-chih (Wang, Xianzhi / Ong Hian-Ti)
> *Tai-wan hsiang tu shen hsueh lunwen chi pien chu.* (Homeland theology in the Taiwanese context). Taiwan Homeland Theology Research Papers, vol. 1. Tainan, Tai-nan shen hsueh yuan, 1988.

"Who are the Taiwanese People: A Theological-Socio-Historical Perspective." *Shen shueh yu chiao hui* (Theology and Church) 17.1 (1986).
"Doing Theology in the New Asia." *Taiwan Journal of Theology* 1.1 (1990).
"The Problem of Religious Fundamentalism in Relation to Ethnicity, Power and Ideology: An Asian Perspective." *The Reformed World* 42 (1991).
"Some Perspectives on Homeland Theology in the Taiwanese Context." In *Frontiers in Asian Christian Theology: Emerging Trends*, edited by R.S. Sugirtharajah, 185-195. Maryknoll, NY: Orbis Books, 1994.
"The Portrayal of the Human One (Son of Man) of John: An Asian Perspective." *CTC Bulletin* 13.3-14.1 (1995-1996).

2.2.2.6. Lucy T.H. Kao (Kao Teng-shiang / Ko, Tian-hiong)

Lucy Kao-Loh was associate professor teaching Christian education at Taiwan Theological College, Taipei, and has worked for many years in Taiwanese and women's theology. She is a scholar in Japanese literature, and participates widely in teaching and ecumenical programs, both in the Asian region and beyond. Since a first article on "People's Theology in Taiwan" (see under Feng Xian above p.682), Kao has written extensively on women's theology in Taiwan and in biblical studies related to this in such journals as *Direction*, *In God's Image* and *Insaka*. In these Kao-Loh moves from contextual studies of, for example, women in the Bible, to contemporary questions of oppression. She is concerned to explore the methodology of women's theology in Taiwan and the Asian context, particularly for the present tasks of both mission and theological construction.

Selected References
Works by Lucy Kao-Loh
"The Challenge to the Church of the Feminist Theology." *Direction* 8 (1989).
"The Cry of the Oppressed: The Methodology of the Feminist Theology." *Direction* 9. (1989).
"The Women and the Bible - I-IV." *Direction* 10-13 (1989).
"Her Name was called 'Life'." *Direction* 14 (1990).

"The First Missionary sent by the Resurrected Lord." *Direction* 15 (1990).
"The Role of the Women in the Church." *Direction* 17 (1990).
"Understanding Eve in Context. *In God's Image* 18.1 (1999).

2.2.2.7. Chen Nan-jou (1944-)

Chen Nan-jou has taught at Tainan and Yu-shan Theological Colleges, Taiwan. For him, theology is always directly related to the reality of the people to whom churches and Christians doing theology belong. Therefore, what is happening to the people of Taiwan is the starting point of doing theology in the Taiwanese context. The sufferings and hopes of the Taiwanese are the realities to be analyzed first in Chen's theology, especially in thinking of the social mission of the Church in the Taiwanese context today.

Taiwanese reality is also the reality of the church in Taiwan, Chen believes. When Taiwanese face a crisis of identity, the church in Taiwan also faces an identity crisis. If the Christian would like to respond to the God of the Exodus and to Jesus' incarnation and Cross and participate in the mission of God in Christ's way in the midst of this identity crisis, he/she has no choice, Chen declares, but to identify with the suffering and oppressed Taiwanese, and to engage in the Taiwanese struggle for liberation and new identity. When the church in Taiwan, faces the possibility of being accused of sedition, and speaks out for the people facing an identity crisis in a situation of political uncertainty, she becomes for Chen and his colleagues the voice of the voiceless people, the conscience of the nation, and a sign of hope - as the Church confesses in the Confession of Faith.

There are two important directions in this Theology of Identification. Firstly, in order to identify with the sufferings and the hopes of the Taiwanese people, theology, praxis and proclamation must be shifted from concern only for personal salvation to concern for the life of the whole person, the whole society, and the whole creation. There are at least two theological aspects which have to be considered. Emphasis must be placed not only on "Christian-centered" programs but much more on "people-centered" programs. Secondly, for Christian communities to identify with the history and cultures of the people of Taiwan, their belief that God is the God of creation must include belief that history is a record of God's activities, and that God can be found within history and cultures. Here is the basis, Chen believes, for a Theology of Identification and the challenge for Christian communities, so that Taiwanese may become the subjects of the history of Taiwan. This theology hopes to discern the theological meaning of the cultures of Taiwan so that all cultures and religions may be mutually respected by all Taiwanese people. Prerequisites for this will be, Chen concludes, dialogue and cooperation with other religious communities, and the growth of ecumenical unity in mission.

Selected References
Works by Chen Nan-jou
> *The Socio-Political Ethics of the Presbyterian Church in Taiwan* (in Chinese). Taipei: Yung Wang Press, 1991.
> *Mission and Ethics* (in Chinese). Chiayi: Hsin Fu Press, 1995.
> "An Introduction to the Theology of Identification." *Theology and the Church* 18.1 & 2 (1990).
> "Involvement of the Presbyterian Church in Taiwan on the Issue of the Future of Taiwan - A Theological Reflection." *Asia Journal of Theology* 9 2 (1995).
> "Proclaiming the Word of God with the Taiwanese Story." *Way - Journal of Taiwan Institute of Theology and Cultures* 1.5 (1997).
> "Interpreting the Bible from the Taiwanese Experience." *Chung Fu Bulletin* 11 (1997).
> "Interpreting the Bible from the Perspectives of Theology and Culture - An Attempt at Constructing a Biblical Hermeneutics from the Taiwanese Christian Identity." *Theology and the Church* 23.2 (1998).
> "Theology of Identification - A Theology Reflection in the Taiwanese Context Today." *Taiwan Church News* 2407 (1998).
> "Human Rights, Human Dignity and the Mission of the Churches amidst a Changing Asia." *Taiwan Journal of Theology* 21 (1999).
> "Doing Theology in the Context of Taiwan - An Example from Social Ethics and Theology of Mission." In *Papers of the Theological Symposium '99 and the 11th General Assembly of NEAATS, January 6-8, 1999.*

2.2.2.8. Huang Po-ho (1951-)

Theology of *Chhut-thau-thin* (metaphorically, raise one's head to see the sky; also used to signify theology of self-determination), Huang declares, is similarly to other Third World theologies, primarily concerned with the well-being of the people in a particular place, Taiwan, with particular attention given to the problem of the identity of the people in that place. Here the former professor of theology (now president) of Tainan Theological College and Seminary, and chairperson of PTCA, has developed a theology of *Chhut-thau-thin* (self-determination) upon two main historical fabrics, namely the mission experiences of the church, and the historical and cultural experiences of people.

Although both emphasize the historical experiences of suffering of the people in Taiwan - in colonization, martial law control, and distortion of identity - homeland theology, on the one hand, begins its theological approach mainly in socio-political analysis. While for Huang, "the theology of *Chhut-thau-thin* has concentrated its methodology more on cultural dimensions in order to penetrate the nature of the suffering experiences of the people and their hope." He contends that "methodologies are determined by resources, and resources are determined by identities," so identity - of theologians and of people - must be considered as a starting point for theology. Huang Po-ho argues that the theme of *Chhut-thau-thin* represents not only a deep cultural expression of the historical experiences of struggling for the people in Taiwan; it also contains a promise for the future with a dynamic hope of liberation envisioned by the people of Taiwan through their life of daily struggle.

In Huang's theology, both freedom and identity are elements to constitute a genuine action of self-determination, so that as long as we continue to confess that the Gospel frees people, and cultures shape people's identities, an exploration on the theme of self-determination must involve theological discourse which interprets both Gospel and cultures. Self-determination understood from this perspective of Gospel and cultures should not only be political, but has to be considered as a way of building up a selfhood for people struggling to be human in their *Imago Dei*. It is through this theological exploration of the socio-political, economic struggles of the people in Taiwan confronted with the Christian proclamation of the Gospel, that the hope of *Chhut-thau-thin* offers the promise of the kingdom of God revealed in the story of Jesus Christ.

Selected References.
Works by Huang Po-ho

> *A Theology of Self-determination*. Taipei: Rice Home, 1990; Tainan: Chhut-Thau-Thin Theological Study Center, 1996.
>
> *A Faith That is Rooted in the Land*. (In Taiwanese.) Tainan: Jenkuang press, 1990.
>
> *Not To Be A Stranger, A Hand Book on Contextual Theology in Taiwan*. (In Taiwanese.) Tainan: Jenkuang press, 1995.
>
> *The Shaping of Christian Identity* (in Taiwanese.) Tainan: Kong Pau press, 1997.
>
> *Lectures for Contextual Theology* (in Taiwanese.) Tainan: Kong Pau Press, 1999.
>
> *Ethical Concern of Contextual Theology* (in Taiwanese.) Tainan: Kong Pau Press, 1999.
>
> "Searching for a Compassionate Human Community." *Asia Journal of Theology* 7.1 (1993).
>
> "Social change and theological development in Taiwan: The case of Chhut-thau-thin (self-determination) theology". *Ching Feng* 39.2 (1996).
>
> "Re-confessing Christian Identity through Telling People Stories in Asia: a Methodological Discussion on Hermeneutical Control." *Ching Feng* 41.1 (1998).
>
> "Theology in Taiwan." In *Dictionary of Third-World Theologies*, edited by Virginia Fabella and R.S. Sugirtharajah. Maryknoll, NY: Orbis Books, 2000.

2.2.2.9. Cheng Yang-en

Associate professor of church history at Taiwan Theological Seminary, Taipei, Cheng has been for some years the editor of the *Taiwan Journal of Theology*, and has also edited a number of symposia volumes in Taiwanese theology. With his chief discipline being that of church history, Cheng's main theological study is of the indigenizing and contextualizing experiences of the history of Christianity in Taiwan. Within that history, he places a particular focus on liberative movements among the marginalized, on the socio-political engagement of the Christian faith, and on the dynamic interaction between religion and politics. From his historical studies, Cheng has concluded that key theological issues are still, as a century ago: Gospel and culture, contextualization, the role of ethnicity and ideology, the relationship of faith to history, and mission as co-suffering with the people.

Selected References
Works by Cheng Yang-en
> *History and Faith: A Christian Perspective on Taiwan and the World* (in Chinese.) Tainan: Jen-Kuang, 1999.
> "The Idea of Tien-Ming in the Book of Historical Documents." *ATESEA Occasional Papers* 4 (1987).
> "The Bible and the Critique of Ideology." NCC Review (India) 116 (1996).
> "Building a Harmonious Society in Taiwan. An Analysis from the Ideological Perspective." *Taiwan Journal of Theology* 18 (1996).
> "A Historical Review of Christianity in Taiwan at the Turn of the Century." *Taiwan Journal of Theology* 20 (1998).
> "A Historical Review of Christianity in Taiwan at the Turn of the Century." In *1999 Graduate Students' Conference on North East Asia Church History*, edited by The Korea Academy of Church History, 51-68. Seoul, 1999.
> "What New Song Shall We Sing? A Review of the Theory and Practice of Asian Theologies from a Taiwanese Perspective." *Taiwan Journal of Theology*. Forthcoming.
> —, ed. *God and Theology: Faith Seeking Understanding* (1) (in Chinese.) Tainan: Jen-Kuang, 1997.
> —, ed. *Human Being and Christian Life: Faith Seeking Understanding* (2) (in Chinese.) Tainan: Jen-Kuang, 1998.

2.2.2.10. Tong Fung-wan

Tong's doctorate was granted by the South East Asia Graduate School, after which he taught at Taiwan Theological Seminary, Taipei. His studies, teaching and writing have concentrated upon the folk religions of Taiwan, which he first considered in doctoral research on "Pa-Kua-Pai" beliefs and practices. But his focus has been primarily upon the place of folk religious studies in the modernizing society of Taiwan, in the endeavors of missiology, and in theological contextualization. He has also studied and written on aspects of Taiwanese and folk customs, on biblical hermeneutics, contextualized mission, and the influence of Taiwanese religions upon political choices. For some years Tong edited the *Taiwan Journal of Theology*.

Selected References
Works by Tong Fung-wan
> *Faith and Custom: Missiological Approach to Contextualized Christianity in Taiwan. Histories and Liturgies from Taiwan's Folk Religions.* Tainan: Taiwan Church Press, 1995.
> "The Contextualization of Christian Mission: A View from the Perspective of Taiwan Folk Religion." *Taiwan Journal of Theology* 3 (1981).
> "The Protective Function of 'Pak-Kua-Pai' on the Door Lintel of the Taiwanese House." Th.D. diss., Southeast Asia Graduate School of Theology, 1983.
> "The Influence of Religious Beliefs on Taiwanese Political Attitudes." *Taiwan Journal of Theology* 10 (1988).
> "A Perspective on Taiwanese Folk Beliefs." *Taiwan Journal of Theology* (1994).
> "The Presbyterian Church and Modernization in Taiwan." *Taiwan Journal of Theology* 17 (1995).

2.2.2.11. Loh I-to and Contextual Music and Worship in Taiwan
Loh gained his doctoral degree in musicology and has been professor, composer and collector not only in Taiwan, but throughout the Asian region. For most of this work he has been based at the Asian Institute for Liturgy and Music (Philippines) and since 1995 he has been president of the Tainan Theological College and Seminary. He has played important roles in the initiation of contextual writing and composing of hymns since 1960. He then began composing in native idiom, and his music for the Passion Play exhibited such an intimate relationship between the Gospel and the people that it gave added impetus to begin the long journey of contextualization of music and worship in Taiwan, and eventually in other Asian countries.

In an initial article in 1984 I-to Loh expounded the meaning of contextualization as being 1) not revivalism, but utilizing elements of native culture which are relevant to the time, place and people; 2) not exclusivism, but the widening of views and becoming more objective in appreciating different Christian statements; 3) not self promotion, but the cultivation of self esteem with a searching for truth, goodness and beauty in Christian arts; and 4) the manifestation of the *Imago Dei*, the development of creativity and participation in God's continuing creation (*Asia Journal of Theology* 4.1, 1990). In applying these concepts to liturgy and music in Taiwan and throughout Asia, Loh's aims have included the renewal of worship to enable more active congregational participation, along with education in Asian liturgy and music to graduate level. In addition he has introduced a wide range of native as well as non-western musical instruments from many Asian countries, in worship and music education. He has also fostered the use of characteristic ethnic features of Taiwanese music, including also other Asian styles, to compose and author new hymns, anthems and liturgical responses for new liturgies.

Selected References

Collections of Hymns by Loh I-to include: (* denotes with cassette) *New Songs of Asian Cities*, CCA/URM, 1972*; *Liturgical Music I* (original compositions), Tainan, 1972; *A Festival of Asian Christmas Music*, AILM, 1984*; *Let the Hills Sing, Tribal Hymns of Taiwan*, AILM, 1986*; *Hakka Songs of Praise*, AILM, 1987*; *Kristus Sundaring Bali* (Christ the Light to Bali), *New Balinese Hymns*, AILM, 1988*; *Rak Pra Jao Rao Pen Thai* (The Love of God Sets Us Free), *New Thai Hymns*, AILM. 1989*; and *Sound the Bamboo: CCA Hymnal 2000* - 315 hymns in 45 languages from 20 countries in Asia. CCA: Taiwan Church Press, 2000.

Works by Loh I-to

Teach Us to Praise: In Search of Contextual Church Music, 20 essays (in Chinese). Tainan: Taiwan Church Press, 1991.

"Toward Contextualization of Church Music in Asia." *Asia Journal of Theology* (April 1989), abridged.

"Contemporary Issues in Inculturation, Arts and Liturgy: Music." In *The Hymnology Annual* 3 (1993).

"Transmitting Cultural Traditions in Hymnody." In *Church Music Workshop: Practical Tools for Effective Music Ministry* 4:3 (1994).
"Asian Resources on Music, Worship and the Arts." *Theology and Church* 22:2 (1997).
"Yinyue, libai yu lingming gengxin" (Music, Worship and Spiritual Renewal). *Theology and Church* 24:1 (1998).
Hawn, C. Michael. "Sounds of Bamboo: I-to Loh and the Development of Asian Hymns." *The Hymn* 49.2 (1998).
Pittman, Don. "I-to Loh: Finding Asia's Cultural Voice in the Worship of God." In *And God Gave the Increase*, edited by June Ramage Rogers. Louisville: 1998.

3 The Development of Contextual Theology in Taiwan - Catholic Theology
3.1 Context, Concept and Experience
3.1.1 Theologizing in Chinese

The majority of Catholic theologians writing in Taiwan work primarily within the context of Chinese culture, and use the Chinese language as their mode of expression. Many are conscious of the rich traditions of Christianity in mainland China, and directly draw on these as resources and models for the present doing of theology in Taiwan. Some see their work primarily as a contribution to Chinese theology as a whole in partnership with colleagues in the People's Republic of China, although from the late 1980s on, an increasing number have also focused attention upon the particular history, mission and thought of Taiwanese and aboriginal Catholics.

Chinese as a linguistic tool deeply differs from other languages such as Greek, Latin or Sanskrit, for its morphology does not distinguish between clear-cut grammatical categories. On the other hand, Chinese characters have a concrete flavor and a suggestiveness of their own and, as a whole, constitute a framework for expressing perception and thought that closely associates form and meaning. Consequently, basic western concepts such as soul, substance, modality are often translated in an approximate way, and finding equivalents for some basic Chinese categories is a painstaking endeavor.

Furthermore, Chinese terminology is rooted in the canon of classical writings which constituted the basis for the development of Chinese culture and philosophy throughout the centuries. This canon plays too important a role not to be a constant reference for the Christian theologian. Roughly speaking, one has to distinguish between two canonical strata: the first is composed of the five "Books" (Books of History, of Poems, of Rites, of Mutations, of Documents), to which all schools refer in one way or another. The second stratum is composed of "Confucian" writings in a stricter sense which is often interpreted ... through a principle of "reason" (*li*) which was seen as an immanent principle directing the wondrous working of the cosmos. Here might be the core of this "cultural-linguistic matrix" which theologians have to deal with.

3.1.2 Theologizing in Context

The context in which the enterprise of theological inculturation is pursued in Taiwan, cannot but be deeply influenced by the traumas of the Communist victory of 1949 and the subsequent historical events that this has represented for the Christian community. As a consequence the theological research which we are concerned with here is conducted in Taiwan, even if it takes into account the entirety of the Chinese cultural sphere. For many Chinese intellectuals or "Christians without Church," the Bible appears now to be a relevant reference for cultural and spiritual reflection, a reference that they widely use for developing a new trend of thought. Hence the threat of a growing gap occurs between the mainstream theological discourse and the positions and interpretations developed on the fringes of Christianity. (See also the debate on "culture Christians" in China, chap.3 above). The second tension arises when a theology concerned with traditional Chinese concepts has to come to terms with the realities of contemporary Taiwanese society. First of all, the debate with Confucianism might have little relevance for a society which has been, in many respects, deeply westernized. Secondly, some sectors within the Church which strive to assert their Taiwanese uniqueness are ill at ease with a discourse defining the task of inculturation only within the frame of "Chinese"

Contextual Theology in Taiwan 703

tradition and concepts. "Inculturation" is to be implemented within a pluralist and somehow divided society.

Theologizing in context also means understanding the way a pluralistic, syncretic and all-encompassing cultural-religious system works: Chinese people have a natural tendency to stress the "unity of all religions," first when it comes to their own tradition (thus postulating the identity of the ultimate meaning of Confucianism, Taoism and Buddhism), secondly when trying to integrate the teachings of religions developed in foreign settings. Such a syncretistic outlook goes along with the overall fluidity of religious affiliations: the concept of "diffused religions" is widely used when observers seek to define the unique intertwining of social and religious rites, as well as the intermingling between different religious creeds and practices which has taken place throughout Chinese history. In Taiwan, recent inquiries confirm that nearly half of the people define themselves as Buddhists when they are asked about their religious affiliation. But further questions about observance of Buddhist beliefs and practices lead to a proportion of Buddhist believers between 7 and 15% of the whole sample (the conservative estimate being probably the more accurate). Furthermore, approximately 7% are self-declared Taoists, and 29% consider themselves as belonging to "folk religion." When it comes to distinguishing between affiliations, beliefs and practices, the matter is so intricate that researchers generally conclude that the most urgent task is to determine what the terms "religion" (the word in itself is recent in Chinese), "Buddhism," "Taoism," etc. mean for ordinary people.

3.1.3 Theologizing with Chinese Concepts
With regard to such an inheritance, it is not surprising that theological inculturation has much to do with semantics: how to understand Chinese notions and theological concepts within a unified frame of thought? In this respect, a few terms deserve special attention.

3.1.3.1. "Heaven," (*dao/tao*) as it is understood by Chinese people, is, at the same time, lofty, anonymous, and the source of endless production. The use of the expression "Lord of Heaven" has led Catholic theologians to emphasize the category of "unity" in the concept of God in order to complement that of "personality" which is more easily stressed within the western tradition: going from "the way of man" (*rendao*) to "the way of heaven" (*tiandao*) is what "The Way" (*dao*), Christ, allows us to do. Nowadays, the emphasis put both by Catholics and Protestants on the notion of *dao*, one of the most deeply rooted notions in the Chinese psyche, testifies to the shift from a God-centered to a Christ-centered theology.

3.1.3.2. In Confucianism, there are two values which are considered as central, both from a personal and a social point of view: those of "filial piety" (*xiao/hsiao*) and "humanity" or "benevolence" (*ren/jen*)." "Filial piety" is the way of attaining self-cultivation and, consequently, of being considered worthy to govern a nation and regulate the world. Many Chinese authors have seen in "filial piety" the key for interpreting the New Testament in a Chinese context. Feeling grateful for the gift of life, being part of this process of transmission from generation to generation, such is the Chinese way of understanding filial piety. Moreover, because filial piety is the natural manifestation of love within the inner heart of man, it is also the root of *ren*, the virtue of humanity. Cultivating filial piety is a way of forgetting oneself by relating to one's origin through an appropriation of the whole process of life. Long ago, the Confucian thinker Han Yu (768-824) said that the virtue of humanity was nothing other than the name given to universal love. In other words, love is rooted in filial gratitude.

Another field open for semantic inculturation is that formed by words such as virtue (*diode/taote*), law (*fa*) and rites (*li*). "Virtue" is traditionally seen as an internal principle which governs one's conduct and deeply influences one's surroundings. By the very fact of being virtuous, a man can deeply change this environment. In contrast, "law" is often accused of being an artificial construct which goes against the natural and virtuous flow of life (See under Aloysius Chang 3.2.2.2.3.). In many respects, "rite" is the best Chinese equivalent for "law" in this context (See under Mark Fang

3.2.2.4.). More recently, attention has been focused on another concept - namely, "energy" (*qi/ ch'i*). The *qi* concept is more specifically rooted in the cosmological and Taoist stratum of Chinese consciousness. The *qi* can to some extent be defined as the power which makes everything grow according to its own nature. It is neither a "material" nor a "spiritual" concept, it rather points out the integrating factor behind the various spheres of natural and human development.

3.1.4. Chinese Spiritual Experiences and Theological Discourses

Chinese theologians have been led to situate the Christian experience vis-à-vis the main Chinese cultural and spiritual traditions, namely Confucianism, Taoism and Buddhism. However, until now the dialogue with the first of these three traditions has been overtly privileged.

An expression "quiet sitting" or "sitting in meditation" (*jingzuo/ ching-tso*) is common to all Chinese spiritualities. However, the Neo-Confucian tradition has given it a particular meaning, which has drawn the interest of several theologians, among them Peter Hu and Aloysius Chang. For them, Oriental spirituality's stress on quietness has helped Catholics to grow in their own faith, to discover aspects of prayer not fully developed within the western Church. At the same time, colloquial prayer and attention to the Word have to remain central in any spirituality rooted in the biblical tradition. "Sitting in meditation" is to develop an attitude of contemplation and respect towards the world, is to awake (*jue/chüeh*) to reality and to strengthen (*jian/chien*) one's own faith by fostering a "recollection that penetrates movement and quietude" as the Neo-Confucians say. Restoring human nature is also a collective process, which is tirelessly pointed out by the Chinese classics. This collective dimension is symbolized by the sacraments of the Church, whose goal is always to establish a new harmony among people, between the human person and the world and, finally, between God and human beings.

It is clear enough that this eulogy of the Neo-Confucianist tradition partly derives from a relative distrust towards the Zen (or Chan) school. Zen spirituality is presented in a few articles, and indeed pervades the spiritual life of a great number of Chinese Christians. But, as noted earlier, theologians often point out that Zen does not hold the written word to be of much value. In purely theological terms, the crux of the matter is generally considered to be the opposing conceptions of accomplishment that can be found in Christianity and Buddhism, the former based on the category of "plenitude," the latter on the category of "nothingness." The new interest in Buddhism that can be sensed in the Chinese theological sphere is partly due to the fact that Buddhism itself is growing and changing at a rapid pace. In the future, theological creativity could then be based on "cooperation" rather than on mere "dialogue."

The premises for a dialogue with the Taoist spiritual tradition are not identical. In so far as "Taoism" is identified with folk religion, the challenge is not generally seen as theological, but rather as pastoral or liturgical. How can the popular sensitivity shown by ordinary people before the mystery of life and death be translated into appealing rites and songs? One suspects that, asked solely in these terms, the question is too restricted. What has already been said about the *qi* concept is a rather good example of the way the dialogue with the Taoist tradition is perceived: breathing is seen here as a metaphor for the work that the Spirit pursues in one's life, and the eucharistic liturgy creates the space and the dynamics in which such an experience can be tasted and expressed. The Taoist "passivity" is, at its roots, a way of entering the liberty of the Spirit. Its anthropological wholeness, that makes it integrate spirit and body into one and the same living unity, helps Christians to penetrate more fully the mystery of the Word become flesh.

Selected References

Chan Shu-fang. "Shanhaijing zhong feng yu long de xiangzheng ji qi shenxueyiyi" (The symbols of phoenix and dragon in the Shanhaijing and their theological meaning). *CTUF* 106 (1995).

Chang Ch'un-shen, Aloysius B. "Confucius, Revelation, Chinese History and Christ." *CTUF* 7 (1971).

—. *The Inculturation of Theology in the Chinese Church*. Asian Theological Search 15. Colombo: Centre for Society and Religion, 1984. Also *Gregorianum* 63 (1982).

Chih, Andrew. *Chinese Humanism: a Religion beyond Religion.* Taipei: Fu Jen Catholic University Press, c1981.

Chuang Ching-hsin. "Fuchuan tan tienfu: yu Taiwan zongjiao wenhua zhong tienfu gu'en de duihua" (God the Father in evangelization: A dialogue with Taiwanese culture and religion regarding its view of the Heavenly Father). *CTUF* 122, 123 (1999).

Fang, Mark Chi-jung. "The Image of Christ Reflected by Confucius." *CTUF* 61 (1984).

Gutheinz, Luis sj. "Speculative Theology and the Chinese Way of Thinking." *Vox Clerici* 4.10 & 11 (1966).

Lai Xiao-zhong. "Taiwan minjian zongjiao yu shengshen: Shengshen nian tan miandui minjian xinyang de fuchuan" (Taiwan popular religion and the Holy Spirit: Considerations on evangelization to popular belief). *CTUF* 117 (1998).

Liu Ching-chang. "Inculturation of the Catholic Church in Taiwan." *CTUF* 111 (1997).

Raguin, Yves. "Les Chinois et la Mystique." *Medecine de l'homme. Revue du Centre Catholique des Medecins Francais* (Paris) 229 (1997).

3.2 Writers and Writings
3.2.1. The Period from 1950 to 1976

The main concerns of Catholic theologians at this time were focused on "the common or similar concepts [in] the Bible and traditional Chinese culture", and the interpretation of the life and actions of Jesus Christ "in terms of the moral virtues which are considered important by the Chinese people" (Chang, 1982, p.20). From 1949-1962 members of the New Clergy Group produced many writings on these subjects, which appeared in the journal *New Vox Clerici*. In this endeavor, some were concerned to recognize fully the similarities between classical Chinese concepts and biblical teachings, while others like Ch'eng Shih-kuang and Chang Wei-tu also outlined major differences between the concepts and methods of western theology and that theology which was growing from within Chinese communities and traditions. The Ricci Institute was founded in Taipei for the study of major religious traditions: and (from 1968) the Fujen Catholic Theologate would become a center for much theological study and writing. In part influenced by Vatican II, a few writers, like Aloysius Chang, also reflected on these traditions in relation to "the history of salvation," both in biblical sources and in the history of Taiwan's people. For other scholars such as Maurus Fang Hao (see Contextual Theology in China, vol. 3, chap. 3) the main concern was to collect and reflect on the history and biographies of the Catholic Church in China in recent centuries.

The context for all these theological developments was, however, that of a divided society - described by a Chinese Catholic scholar as comprising Taiwanese, "mainlander" and aboriginal communities - which was subjected to pervasive military rule. For some decades these divisions and this subjection would also be reflected in the Catholic Church in Taiwan. The recent traumatic history of civil and international war and of complex nationalist and communist movements in China, and of nationalist and independence movements in Taiwan, continued to shape - and often distort - Christian reflection. The writings of many, such as Archbishop Yu Bin (See Contextual Theology in China, vol. 3, chap. 3), therefore expressed opposing positions in these conflicts, more than an articulation of Taiwanese theology.

Selected References

    Chang Ch'un-shen. "The Inculturation of Theology in the Chinese Church." *Gregorianum* (Rome) 63 (1982).
    Charbonnier, J. "La théologie du salut en terre chinoise." *Exchange France-Asia* 5 (1975).
    Chen Jialu. *Tianzhujiao lai Tai chuanjiao yibainian jian shi* (History of one hundred years of Catholicism in Taiwan). Gaoxiong: Tianzhujiao daominghui, 1960.
    Fujen Theological Publications Association. *Theological Dictionary: A One-Volume Encyclopedia of Christian-Catholic Theology.* 2nd ed. Taipei: Kuangchi Press, 1998.
    Gutheinz, Luis. "My Humble View on Theology in China." *Vox Clerici* 6.10 & 11 (1968).
    Humphey, D.A., ed. *Sinicization - the Church as a Living Community: the Gospel of Christ in Modern China.* Taipei: Wisdom Press, 1971.
    —. *The Catholic Church in Taiwan.* Taipei: Wisdom Press, 1974.
    Laurentin, Rene. *Chine et christianisme: après les occasions manqués.* Paris: Desclée De Brouwer, 1977.

Lin Rui-qui. *Haixia liang'an shang de jiaohui huodong de shenxue fanxing* (Theological reflections on the activities of the three Churches in the Chinese Straits). *Collectanea Theologica Universitatis Fujen* 113 (1997).

Loeding, W.J. "Centenary of Modern Catholic Mission on Formosa." *Worldmission* (New York) 11 (1960).

Pro Mundi Vita. *Taiwan. Asia-Australia Dossier* 6. Brussels: Pro Mundi Vita, 1978.

3.2.1.1. Tien Liang (fl.1960)

Tien liang was an important figure working for a Chinese theology in the period 1949-1962 with the "New Voice of Clergy Group." He is known particularly for his systematic treatment of filial piety as comprehending all the major features of Christian life and knowledge. For such a (renewed) piety the holy Trinity is the source, and the life of prayer and action, and all that realizes piety in daily life, is the expression. In this the life and piety of Jesus corrects and renews what is inadequate in Chinese traditional filial piety. Tien's writings were extensively commented on, sometimes most critically. They are found chiefly in the articles listed below.

Selected References
Works by Tien Liang

"My Humble View on the Establishment of a Chinese Catholic Culture." *New Vox Clerici* 5.26 (1959).

"The Sayings of the New Testament and their Value: Concerning the Worship of God with the Virtue of Filial Piety." *New Vox Clerici* 5.27, 5.28 & 5.29 (1960).

Chang Tien-tseng. "After My Reading of 'The Laying of the Foundation of a Chinese Catholic Culture'." *New Vox Clerici* 5.28 (1960).

Chang Ch'un-shen. "The Inculturation of Theology in the Chinese Church." *Gregorianum* (Rome) 63 (1982).

3.2.1.2. Ch'eng Shih-kuang (fl. 1970) and colleagues

Ch'eng was prominent in post-Vatican II discussions of the Taiwan Bishops' Conference, and with others convened a number of colloquia on indigenous theology. His journal articles and books

(1974) played a significant role in exploring the nature of theology in Taiwan. For him it was necessary to leave behind models of western theology and literary style, along with the traditional western boundaries of theological disciplines (See Hsiang Twei-chieh 1977). Moral theology would have to adopt the Chinese ethical system, centered on moral virtues which encourage a "total enculturation of the individual" within community, rather than on (the Catholic) moral law. Here he advocates a blending of dogmatic theology and moral theology into a unity, as Confucianists, Taoists or Mohists have always "united the worship of Heaven with living a human life" (See Chang Wei-tu 1973). For this, both "cultivation" of the Way and grace received through Jesus Christ are necessary.

Others contributing to such theological construction, by explaining the Christian faith by means of key concepts of the Chinese classics, or Chinese traditional ethics and metaphysics, included Chao Pin-shih, Hsiang Twei-chieh, Lo Kuang, Kung Shih-rung and Yang Ku-ch'eng.

Selected References
Works by Ch'eng Shih-kuang
> *The Boundary between Heaven and Man*. Tainan: Tao Publishing Co., 1974.
> "A Few Words Concerning Theological Inculturation." *Vox Clerici* 10.7 (1972).
> Chang, Ch'un-shen. "The Inculturation of Theology in the Chinese Church." *Gregorianum* (Rome) 63 (1982).
> Chang Wei-tu. "Now is the Time for Theological Inculturation." *Vox Clerici* 11.4 (1973).
> — "After My Reading of 'A Few Words Concerning Theological Inculturation." *Vox Clerici* 11.10 (1973).
> Chao Pin-shih. "God and Man Belong to One Family." *Heng Yi Monthly Press* (Oct. 1977).
> Hsiang Twei-chieh. "My Humble View on South Asian Theology." *Vox Clerici* 10.8 & 9 (1972).
> Li Shan-hsiou. *A Study of the Inculturation of the Catholic Church in China*. Taipei: Kuang Ch'i Press, n.d.
> Yang Ku-ch'eng. "What is Theological Inculturation?" *Vox Clerici* 12.7 & 8 (1974).

3.2.2. The Period from 1976-2000

In 1976 the Study Secretariat of the Bishops' Conference of Taiwan declared that the Church should now move more fully to achieve theological adaptation - beyond earlier imitations - since the inculturation of the Republic of China Chinese Church had become the most urgent task. The Draft Plan which was issued for this "stressed a theology which would blend the Gospels with the humanistic spirit of Chinese tradition" (See also Wu Ching-hsiung, 1965). This was to be an incarnation of the Catholic Faith "in the culture and life of the native peoples." Divisions within the Church, however, over the issues of national security and human rights, along with the role of government ideology, was to make such an "incarnation" difficult for some years to come. In 1979 the Bishops' Conference with Major Religious Superiors disbanded the Justice and Peace Committee of the Maryknoll Fathers and issued a letter to all priests forbidding any political involvement. In the same period, however, theologians and bishops came in part to recognize the issues of nationhood and identity for the Taiwanese people, and fostered study on these. The Bishops' Conference also took the unusual step in 1979 of publishing an open letter on the future of Taiwan to all Bishops, Christians and those "committed to justice" worldwide.

By the 1990s, theological studies, in the context of radical societal and political changes in Taiwan, along with insights from the social ministries of the Church, fostered new directions in theological reflection and writing. Many writers, who earlier had limited their concerns to the relationship of the Gospel to Chinese cultural tradition and the traits common to Jesus and Chinese sages, came increasingly to advocate application of the faith to the present context of Christians in Taiwan and to the tasks of fostering identity, justice and peace (Chang Ch'un-shen, 1999a). For most, this is centered upon new insights into the life and message of Jesus Christ, as the basis of the community of the Church and as the central model for all transformative social process (See Vermander, 2000).

A notable development in the cooperative and ecumenical doing of theology in Taiwan in recent years has been the series of Joint

Study Days and Catholic-Protestant Dialogues held in Taipei. These have involved, at different times, the Catholic Theologate at Fujen, the Taiwan Theological College, the Ricci Institute and the Tainan Theological College and Seminary. Reports of these have appeared in the *Collectanea Theologica Universitatis FuJen,* and in the *Taiwan Journal of Theology.* Since 1995 there have also been occasional colloquia, on both convergent and divergent understandings, between Catholic scholars and Buddhist masters.

In their response to the "lineamenta" for the 1998 Synod for Asia, the Taiwan bishops affirmed the Church's efforts in religious dialogue and lay concern for migrant workers, aborigines and other marginalized sectors of society. However, they also expressed reservations about the Church's hierarchical structure, too close relationships between Church and state, weak grassroots evangelization and a lack of religious vocations and Church leadership, as well as concern about moral degradation and other social problems. They further suggested that the Church take up a more actively prophetic role, promote increased sharing among Asian Churches, more lay participation and formation, and evangelization through cultural and social services.

Selected References

Catholics Bishops' Conference. *A Draft Plan for Building up the Chinese Local Church*. Taipei: The Association for the Promotion of Catholic Affairs, 1976.

Catholic Bishops of Taiwan. "To the Bishops of the World, to all Christians, to all Men (sic) Committed to Justice." *Teaching All Nations* 16.3 (1979).

Chang Ch'un-shen, Aloysius B. *Yesu zemmeyang yingxiang le renlei* (How did Jesus influence humankind). Taipei: Kuangchi Press, 1999.

—. "An 'Independent, Autonomous and Self-Administered' Church." *Tripod* 112 (1999a).

Cheung Ka-hing. *Let Your Heart be Bold Taiwan*. Hong Kong: Centre for the Progress of Peoples, 1989.

Chow, Joseph. "Indigenous Theology." *CTUF* 76 (1988).

Fischer, Brigitte. *Neue Dienste in der katholischen Kirche Taiwans: die "freiwillingen Laienapostel" auf Taiwan im Rahmen der* gesamtkirchlichen Fragen nach Bedeutung und Aufgaben der Laien im Glaugensvollzug einer Ortskirche. Supplementa 42. Immensee: Neue Zeitschrift fur Missionswissen-schaft, 1994.

Gutheinz, Louis and Wang Hsien-chih. "Christologie aus Taiwan." In *Der Andere Christus, Christologie in Zeugrissen aus aller Welt*, edited by Hermann Dembowsk and Wolfgang Greive. Erlangen: Verlag der Ev. Luth. Mission, 1991.

Lu, Bosco Ta-ch'eng. "Cong cunyouhua jiaodu kan derijin yuzhou guan de jidulun (Reading the doctrine of the cosmic Christ according to Teilhard de Chardin from an existential point of view)." *Shensi* (Spirit) 34 (1997).

Ryden, Edmund. *The Human Person as the Foundation of Human Rights: Proceedings of the East Asian Regional Seminar of the Pontifical Council for Justice and Peace, Fujen Catholic University, 21-23 November 1999*. Taiwan: Fujen Catholic University, c2000.

Vermander, Benoit. "Blessed are the Peacemakers: Towards an Inculturated Chinese Theology of Peace." *Tripod* 20.115 (2000).

Wu Ching-hsiung. *Chinese Humanism and Christian Spirituality: Essays*, edited by Paul K.T. Sih. New York: St. John's University, 1965.

See also bibliographies below.

3.2.2.1. Theology by Women Writers

Catholic women theologians have contributed significantly in this period to studies of the Gospel and of mission and to the concerns of Taiwanese Christians. Their own experience of inculturation has included the establishment of religious life in Taiwan (see Mary Paul, 1967), involvement in a wide range of pastoral and catechetical ministries, and exposure to major social issues, aboriginal concerns and the arts. From these and their theological research have come many biblical pastoral and spirituality studies, for example from Maria Madore, Magdalena Kwong, Gertrude Chen, Anna Chang, Agnes Lim, Cecilienne Lin, Rosa Chen, Agnes Wong, Sofia Chang, Theresa Wong Yai-chow and Sisters of the Carmelite Order. Writers upon lay participation in church ministries include Theresa Huang, Anna Chang, Maria Chao and Teresa Lee.

Women writers have also addressed inter-faith concerns, aboriginal culture, the Eucharist, Marian devotion, liberation theology and aesthetics. Among others who have published on these and related topics are Martha Hsieh, Cecila Chang, Maria Lim, Theresa Huang, Lucia Marie Chen, Johana Shu, Pauline Cheng, Stephana Wei, Grace Hsu and Teresa Hsieh. The Taiwan Catholic Sprout Women-Concerns Association fosters pastoral concern and reflection on issues facing women, on which it conducts surveys and holds seminars. Since 1990 it has been fostering Asian feminist theological reflection. Leaders who have written on the Association's work include Katherine Ho Li-hsia, a lay woman lecturer at Fujen Catholic University who holds degrees in theology and religious studies, and Theresa Tsou Yih-lan sss,a fully qualified physician and psychiatrist.

Among other women theologians writing on contextual theological issues should be noted Madalena Lau and Grace Hsu - on Confucius and Christ; Agnes Lee - on Chinese cultural consciousness; Madeleine Kwong Lai-kuen - on the "breath" of Christ; Lee Chwen Jiuan - on Taoist-Buddhist insights; Katerina Kao - on Ami culture; Katherine Ho - on active non-violence; and Agnes Lim - on aesthetic experience.

Selected References

 Chang Rui-yun. *Dangdai nuxing dushen jiaoyou-shidai yiyi ji shengzhao fenxiang* (Contemporary celibate Catholic women: meaning for our time and its vocational sharing). Fujen Theological Monographs 47. Taipei: Kuangchi Press, 1999.

 Ho, Katherine. "The Spirit of the Beatitudes in Active Non-violence." *CTUF* 93 (1992).

 Hsu, Aloysius. "Central Themes of Feminist Theology and Spirituality." *CTUF* 105 (1995).

 Hsu, Grace. "'Heart' in the Old Testament and in the Analects of Confucius." *CTUF* 108 (1996).

 Kao, Katerina. "The Harvest Sacrifice of the Ami Tribe and the Eucharist." *CTUF* 89 (1991).

 Ko, Maria. "Cong yesu dansheng erqian nian tan ta de wuqing yu renqing" (The affection of Christ for nature and humanity from the perspective of two thousand years after his death). *Shensi* (Spirit) 34 (1997).

Kwong, Madeleine Lai-kuen. "Le souffle du Christ." In *Le Christ chinois* (homage to Fr. Yves Raguin), edited by Benoit Vermander, cf. especially p.167. Paris: Desclee de Brouwer, 1998.

Lau, Madalena. "The Way of Educating People by Confucius and by Jesus Christ." *CTUF* 70 (1986).

Lee, Agnes. "Marian Devotion from the View-point of Chinese Cultural Consciousness." *CTUF* 78 (1988).

Lee Chwen Jiuan A., with Thomas G. Hand. *A Taste of Water. Christianity through Taoist-Buddhist Eyes*. Mahwah, NJ: Paulist Press, 1989.

Lim, Agnes. "From Inspiration in Arts to Scriptural Inspiration." *CTUF* 74 (1987).

Paul, Sr. Mary, with C. Edmund Fisher. *Nun in Taiwan*. London: Hale, 1967.

Reichl, Helene. "Reflections on Christian Formation and Initiation Sacraments in Taiwan." *Collectanea Theologica Universitatis Fujen* 98 (1993).

Yang, Ruth. "Liberation Theology and Mariology." *CTUF* 117, 118 (1998).

3.2.2.2. Lo Kuang, Stanislaus (fl.1985)

Archbishop Lo Kuang has long contributed scholarly studies to theological debate in Taiwan: on Chinese filial piety in contrast to that of Rome; on the specific character of *jen* (*ren*) in Chinese tradition and its relationship to Christian love; on developments within contemporary Confucianism; theological reflections on creation and anthropology; and such models for present ministry in the early 20th century, as Vincent Lebbe. His contribution has often been to examine more closely the nature of Chinese traditions to clarify their particular nature as ingredients for indigenous theology.

Among other writers on the character of indigenous theology, Luke Tsui has written on doing indigenous theology in China and its relationship to social change, and Abraham Leong on the particular situation of Catholics in Taiwan, as well as in Hong and Macau.

Selected References
Works by Stanislaus Lo Kuang
> "Heaven, Earth and the Universe." *CTUF* 82 (1989).
> "Love in the Bible and Jen in Confucianism." *CTUF* 7 (1971).
> "The Principle of Endless Production." *CTUF* 14 (1972).
> "Encounter of Modern Confucianism and Christianity." *CTUF* 76 (1988) & 85 (1990).
> "The Theological Significance of the Sacrament of Priestly Ordination as Realised in the Lives of Cardinal Tien and Father Lebbe." *CTUF* 87 (1991).
> Leung, Abraham. "Church in Taiwan, HK and Macau." *CTUF* 113 & 114 (1997).
> Tsui, Luke. "Inculturation in China." *CTUF* 71 (1987).
> —. "Christianity and Social Change." *CTUF* 89 (1991).
> Zhou, Joseph. "Christian Norms, Traditional Chinese Norms and the Concept of Natural Law." *CTUF* 72 (1987).

3.2.2.3. Chang Ch'un-shen Aloysius B. (b.1929)

Chang Ch'un-shen sj is possibly the most senior and prolific of Catholic theologians in Taiwan. For over thirty years a regular stream of his writings has appeared in many journals, especially *Collectanea Theologica Unversitatis Fujen*. In these he has contributed to most major areas of discussion in that period - among others, on christology, social justice in Asian perspective, pneumatology, theology of mission, the Church in China, Basic Ecclesial Communities, theology of liberation, Chinese and Ignatian Spirituality.

Chang has struggled to displace the debate about Confucianism from the field of morality to that of salvation history. According to him, the covenant that linked God and the people of Israel was the "social method" which God made available to His chosen ones in order to be saved. Similarly, God made a "revelation" to Confucius which was propagated through him to the Chinese people. "Revelation" does not mean here a list of dogmas, but a kind of spirit and practice. An early article interpreted the history of the Chinese people in the light of the salvation history of Israel. Here he portrayed Confucius as "the Moses of the Chinese Catholic Church" and the Chinese classics as the "Old Testament" of the

Chinese (See p.77 above). The divine Word has had earlier "dialogue" with the Chinese people Chang affirmed, and also with the traditional cultures of native peoples. Among the concerns in his numerous other writings, this relationship of two "salvation histories" has been a major one, and within this, the relationship of personality to the category of unity, that of Chinese spirituality to the restoration of human nature, and latterly, the relationship of Christ to the life of humankind and the present tasks of building a civilization of justice and peace. There he has based his christology - a "Christology of Life," on the approach to life's mystery found in the Chinese philosophy of Fang Dongmei.

Selected references
Works by Chang Ch'un-shen Aloysius B.
"Confucius, Revelation, Chinese History and Christ." *Collectanea Theologica* 7 (1971).
The Inculturation of Theology in the Chinese Church. Asian Theological Search 15. Colombo: Centre for Society and Religion, 1984. Also *Gregorianum* 63 (1982).
Dann sind Himmel und Mensch in Einheit: Bausteine chinesischer Theologie. Theologie der Dritten Welt 5. Freiburg: Herder, c1984. Reprint in translation of essays that originally appeared 1977-1982.
Zhonguo dalu tienzhujiao muling yu shenxue fanxing (Pastoral and theological reflections on the Church in mainland China). Fujen Theological Monographs 45. Taipei: Kuangchi Press, 1997.
Yesu zemmeyang yingxiang le renlei (How did Jesus influence humankind). Taipei: Kuangchi Press, 1999.
"A Critical Review of Chinese Catholic Thinking." *Ching Feng* 22.3 (1979).
"The Inculturation of Theology in the Chinese Church." Special Issue of *Gregorianum* (Rome) 63 (1982).
"The Chinese People and the Revelation." *CTUF* 71 (1987).
"Signs of the Time for the Church in China." *CTUF* 88 (1990).
"Yige shengming de jidulun (A christology of life)." *CTUF* 112 (1997). French version in *Le Christ chinois* (homage to Fr. Yves Raguin), edited by Benoit Vermander, 141-149. Paris: Desclee de Brouwer, 1998.

"The Chinese Catholic Church and Christ's Saving Grace." *Tripod* 104 (1998).

"An 'Independent, Autonomous and Self-Administered' Church." *Tripod* 112 (1999).

—, and others. *Jiaohui benweihua zhi tantao* (Studies on the inculturation of the church). Fujen Theological Monographs 14. Taipei: Kuangchi Press, 1981.

3.2.2.4. Mark Chih-jung Fang sj (b.1926)

Fang has for many years been a senior Catholic biblical scholar in Taiwan pursuing biblical hermeneutics in the western tradition, with a particular concern to apply scripture and the Chinese Classics to the spiritual life. He is also much concerned for ecumenism and inter-religious dialogue and has participated fully in ecumenical theological studies in "the quality of life," and on the "option for the poor." In relation to developments in indigenous theology, he has been concerned to apply a critical spirit to the process of inculturation within Confucian tradition, stressing both the diversity of Chinese culture, and the need for dynamic dialogue between this and the biblical sources. Fang has stressed the prophetic dimension of rites that classical writings also contain; where without love and justice there is no true ritual observance. He has also affirmed that properly performing liturgical rites enables the Chinese Catholic community to reappropriate and reinterpret the symbolic richness of its own cultural inheritance and to unite Christian consciousness.

To express such prophetic dimensions, western distinctions between the natural and the supernatural in commenting on biblical material reflect neither the biblical tradition nor that of Chinese commentary on the classics he believes. In addition there will be here not only adaptation, but also contrast and challenge. This is not least because of the close personal relationship with men and women established by the God of the Bible, especially with the weak, the victimized and the poor, but also because "Jesus Christ sealed his teaching of this love by the sacrifice of his life to be the fountain of new life for all." Mark Fang is a member of the FABC Office of Theological Concerns and has played a key role in drafting such papers of the FABC as *The Spirit at Work in Asia Today*, a document of the Office of Theological Concerns of the Federation of Asian Bishops' Conference (FABC Papers 81).

Selected References

Works by Mark Chi-jung Fang

A Study on the Book of Genesis (in Chinese.) Taipei: Kuangchi, 1989. (4th printing).

A Commentary on Biblical-liturgical Readings. Hong Kong: Catholic Truth Society, 1992.

To taste the Gospel at its Source-Locality. Taipei: Wisdom Press, 1993.

"A Tentative Explanation of the Imitation of Heaven in Matthew's Gospel by Means of the Diagram of Heaven in the Book of Changes." *CTUF* 29 (1976).

"Biblical Hermeneutics in Chinese Setting." *CTUF* 40 (1979).

"A Theology of Spiritual Discernment." *CTUF* 45 (1980): 385-412.

"Building up the Chinese Local Church." *CTUF* 50 (1981): 519-537.

"Sensus plenior in Holy Scripture and in the Chinese Classics." *Bible and Inculturation* (Rome) 1983.

"Image of Christ reflected by Confucius." *CTUF* 61 (1984): 367-374.

"Kongzi suo fanying de jidu mianmao (Images of Christ reflected by Confucius)." *CTUF* 61 (1984).

"A Biblical Sociology: The Preferential Option for the Poor." *CTUF* 66 (1985).

"Chinese Symbols and liturgy." *CTUF* 68-69 (1986).

"Theology of Inculturation in Asia and Latin America." *CTUF* 67 (1986).

"Teaching/Learning in Judeo-Christian Faith and the Promotion of Social Justice." *CTUF* 82 (1989).

"Between Tradition and the Future. Reflections for Ministry Today." *Pacific Theological Review* 25 (1992) and 26 (1993).

"Jidutu kan kongzi yu qi mendizi de guanxi (A Christian looks at Confucius' relationships with his disciples)." *Daofeng* (Logos and Pneuma) 8 (1998).

3.2.2.5. Yves Raguin (1912-1998)

Raguin was a leading authority on Chinese religion and on spirituality East and West, writing more than 20 books on these topics which have appeared in French, Chinese, English, and several other languages. Following work in China (1949) and Vietnam, Raguin was for many years Director of the Ricci Institute for Chinese Studies in Taipei. There he concentrated his studies upon Chinese Buddhism, Taoism and Confucianism and for this engaged in regular dialogue with Buddhist monks and Taoist devotees. In these traditions he found, despite differences of terminology, a "three-level" structure of the human being - body, heart and spirit. The distinction between heart (or soul) and spirit he found especially depicted in Zen traditions, but also in Yoga, as well as in the New Testament. Zen meditation became central to his spirituality, along with Taoist traditions of "sitting in forgetting" and the "emptying of the heart" of both Buddhism and Christianity. In his last book (*Ways of Contemplation*) Raguin has mapped out a descriptive East/West geography of the spiritual world encompassing both Taoist, Buddhist and Christian traditions in addition to others.

Selected References
Works by Yves Raguin
> *Contemplation and Sitting in Silence*. Taipei: Taipei Ricci Institute, 1997.
> *Ways of Contemplation East and West. Part I: the Structure of the Spiritual World. Part II: Travel in the Spiritual World*. Taipei: Taipei Ricci Institute, 1997 and 1998.
> "Deepening our Understanding of Spirituality." In *Spirituality in Interfaith Dialogue*, edited by Tosh Arai and Wesley Ariarajah. Geneva: WCC Publications, 1989.
> "Meditation without Object." *Bulletin of Monastic Interreligious Dialogue* 55 (1996).
> "Evangelisation et Dialogue Interreligieux." *Lumière et Vie* (Lyon) 229 (1996).
> "Les Chinois et la Mystique." *Medecine de l'homme. Revue du Centre Catholique des Medecins Francais* (Paris) 229 (1997).
> "Un Message de Salut pour Tous." *Vie Chrétienne* (supplement) 1996.
> "*Ways of Contemplation East and West. IV Chinese Spirituality.*" Taipei: Ricci Institute. Forthcoming.
> Vermander, Benoit, ed. *Le Christ chinois* (homage to Fr. Yves Raguin). Paris: Desclee de Brouwer, 1998.

3.2.2.6. Luis Gutheinz sj. (b.1933)

Teaching in Taiwan since the early 1960s, Luis Gutheinz has written extensively on many issues facing the Taiwanese churches. Among these have been continuing reflections on the mission of the Taiwan local church: its identity, context, liturgy and theological reflection. The nature of Chinese and Asian theology has been a major concern, as has theological reflection in the Basic Ecclesial Communities and liturgy for the churches in Asia and Taiwan as a sign of salvation in today's society.

In his writing on the language and imagery of indigenous theology, he notes the Chinese love of concrete expressions and intuitive understandings which are close to the thought-forms of the Bible. He believes they also underscore the immanence of the Absolute in a way helpful for Christian theology, so that the fundamental truths of Catholicism can in fact be expressed in terms of the "Way". This Chinese humanism can be affirmed by Christians in an anthropology which has Christ as its centre, and an indigenous theology which therefore urges participation in social tasks for all brothers and sisters. The significance of a cosmic christology for ecological theology, and of Trinitarian doctrine for relationships between Hong Kong and Taiwanese churches are also to be stressed here. In collaboration with Fujen colleagues he has written a trilogy inspired by the Chinese fundamental worldview, although centered on humanity, of seeing Heaven, humanity and earth together as one great unity of all reality. His most recent writing, *China im Aufbruch: Chinesische Kultur und Religion und das Christentum, Theologie Interkulturell* (forthcoming), describes further the process of the inculturation of theology for western audiences.

Selected References

Works by Luis Gutheinz sj

"Speculative Theology and the Chinese Way of Thinking." *Vox Clerici* 4.10 & 11 (1966).

"My Humble View on Theology in China." *Vox Clerici* 6.10 & 11 (1968).

"Asian Theology Begins to Raise Questions" (Parts I and II). *Tripod* 14 (1983); 15 (1983).

"Reflections on the Mission of the Taiwan Local Church." *CTUF* (1983).

"Elements of a Theology of Ecology." *CTUF* 104 (1995).

"Hong Kong's Return and Communion across the Straits." *CTUF* 114 (1997).

"God in Pastoral Work: Our Great Father and Mother." *CTUF* 121 (1999).

—, with Wang Hsien-chih. "Christologie aus Taiwan." In *Der Andere Christus, Christologie in Zeugrissen aus aller Welt,* edited by Hermann Dembawski and Wolfgang Greive. Erlangen: Verlag der Ev. Luth. Mission, 1991.

—, (with others). *Shenxue zhongdi renxue-tiendirenheyi:Ren* (Theological anthropology: Heaven-Earth-Humanity). 3 vols. Fujen Theological Monographs 25, *Humanity* (1991); Monograph 28, *God* (with Peter Chao Sung-chiao) (1992); Monograph 37, *Earth* (with Liao Yong-hsiang) (1994). Taipei: Kuangchi Press. Forthcoming.

3.2.2.7. Benoit Vermander sj

Benoit Vermander is the present director of Ricci Institute, Taipei. Besides assisting in many studies, dialogues and colloquia, he has written extensively on the Chinese and Taiwanese religious context, with special focus on Chinese art as spiritual experience and the renewed understanding of the Chinese diversity that anthropological studies on ethnic minorities bring to us. His main concern is to draw from such resources offered by ancient and present Chinese culture for building up an inculturated and contextualized Christian theology relevant to the challenges that are met today. This means forging a culture of peace, finding an equilibrium between the imperatives of "harmony" and "justice," and devising a strategy of human development and environmental protection.

Vermander's recent book on violence offers an original analysis of the roots of violence in today's East Asian societies, for by placing a particular focus on language, special attention has been paid by the author to those people who are culturally marginalized in the use of various communication channels. In writing upon ecological issues he argues that because any overall developmental model must include all the dimensions of human existence, many elements in the Chinese tradition which run counter to a sound developmental model today must be reformulated.

Selected References
Works by Benoit Vermander

Violence and Politics (in Chinese.) Hsinchuang: Fu Jen University Press, 1995.

Le Christ chinois (sous la direction de Benoit Vermander). Paris: Desclee de Brouwer, 1998.

"Théologiens Catholiques en Monde Chinois." *Nouvelle Revue Théologique* 117 (1995).

"Theologizing in the Chinese Context." *Studia Missionalia* 45 (1996): 119-134.

"Religions in Taiwan: Between Mercantilism and Millenarianism." *Inter-Religio* 32 (1997).

"The Flavour of Heart and Heaven." *Tripod* 18.106 (1998).

"The Nosu of Liangshan." *China Perspectives* 21 & 22 (1999). (Translated from the French, cf. *Perspectives chinoises* 50, 51.)

"Christianity and the Taiwanese Religious Landscape." *The Way: Review of Contemporary Christian Spirituality* 39.2 (1999).

"Blessed are the Peacemakers: Towards an Inculturated Chinese Theology of Peace." *Tripod* 20.115 (2000).

—, and Li Jinyuan. *Veilleur de Jour* (Day watcher). Toulouse: C.361 Publishing House, 1996.

3.2.2.8. Other Writers on Spirituality, Worship and Indigenization

Apart from the groups and individuals already mentioned above, many others have worked in these areas. Sung Chih-ching, Fang Chih-rong and Hu Kuo-chen provide sympathetic yet critical studies of the relationship of Zen meditation to Christian prayer; Joseph Chow has also written on the indigenous theology of worship; Peter Hu Kuo-chen has published a number of historical and pneumatological studies of liturgy, with a particular concern for the communitarian dimensions of liturgy and sacrament. He also defines the process of theological inculturation as finding out a Chinese philosophical system that makes use of the concepts of Heaven and man for interpreting the Scriptures and the dogmas and, through such a system, interpreting anew the more important Chinese classics. Louis Gendron writes primarily as a moral theologian, but deals also with a wide range of pastoral issues including experience of conversion, spirituality and the relation of faith to human rights. Paul Pan Pei-chi has written on indigenous church music, and on the inculturation of contemplation.

Others working on the issues of indigenization and contextualization apart from those already mentioned above include Joseph Vu Kim Chinh (liberation theology), Dong Li (Vincent Lebbe), Chuang Ching-hsin (ecology), Andrew Kim (Buddhism), and Yeh Pao-kuei (feminist theology). The majority of their writings have appeared either in the *Collectanea Theologica Universitatis Fujen*, or in the series of *Fujen Theological Monographs*.

Among a large number of other writers who have published volumes on aspects of Taiwanese church history and theology should be included Li Chih-jen, Milton M. Ch'iu, Ching Liu, Yueh Heng, Lin Chih-p'ing, Yeh Jen-ch'ang, Eric Wang Tsung-chung, Lai Yung-hsiang, Pang Tsang, Yu Chi-ping, Hsiao Yüan, Wo Ti-chia, Su Nan-chou, Kuo Wei-hsia, Chao Wei-chu, Chen Chia-lu, Sun Shang-yang, Chang Feng-chen and Chen Sheng-cheng.

Selected References

Chuang Ching-hsin. Zhongguo sixiang zhong de shengtaiguan (The ecological view in Chinese thought). *CTUF* 104 (1995).

Dong Li. Leimingyuan shenfu yu Zhongguo bendihua (Fr. Vincent Lebbe and inculturation in China). *CTUF* 103 (1995).

Gendron, Louis. "Basic Human Rights." CTUF 65 (1985).

—. *Six Conversion Stories: A Look in Depth*. Hsinchuang: Fu Jen University Press, 1997.

Hu Guo-chen. "The 'Sitting in Meditation' of Chinese Christians." *CTUF* 37 (1978).

Hu, Peter. "Christian Discernment of Spirits and Chinese Spiritual self-examination." *CTUF* 55 (1983).

—. "Jesus in the Ordinary Life." *CTUF* 95 (1993).

—. "Towards a Christian Commentary on the Chinese Classics." *CTUF* 60 (1984).

—. "A Reinterpretation of the Sacrament of Reconciliation." *CTUF* 61 (1984).

Hsu Ke-chih. *Zhonghua lingxiu weilai?* (The future of Chinese spirituality?) Fujen Theological Monographs 41. Taipei: Kuangchi Press, 1996.

Kim, Andrew. "Fojiao yu Tienzhujiao de Zhongguo bendihua zhi lu" (The way of inculturation of Buddhism and the Catholic Church in China). *CTUF* 127 (2001).

Lardinois, Olivier. "Christian Participation in Ethnic Reconciliation in Taiwan." *Collectanea Theologica Universitatis F u j e n* 124-125 (2000).

Pan, Pei-chi Paul. "Indigenous Catholic Music." *CTUF* 102 (1994).

—. "Towards an Inculturational Concept of Contemplation." *CTUF* 112 (1997).

Sung Chih-ching. "Prayer and Sitting in Meditation." *Witness Monthly* 8.9 (1978).

Ryden, Edmund. "Sowing the Seed in Contemporary Chinese culture." *Spirit* 47 (2000).

Vu Kim Chinh, Joseph. *Jiefang shenxue:mailuo zhong de quanshi* (Liberation theology: hermeneutical study of its contextualization). Fujen Theological Monographs 31. Taipei: Kuangchi Press, 1991.

Yang Xin-shi. *Daojiao yu jidu zongjiao lingxue* (Daoist and Christian spirituality). Fujen Theological Monographs 43. Taipei: Kuangchi Press, 1997.

Yeh Pao-kuei. "Tienzhu shengsan yu nuxing shenxue bing jianshi qi benweihua xiangzheng" (The Holy Trinity and feminist theology: An examination of its symbolism for inculturation). *CTUF* 127 (2001).

Yu Chi-ping. "Theology of Filial Piety." *Asia Journal of Theology* 3.2 (1989); 4.1(1990).

4 Supplementary Bibliography

"Acts of the Kaohsiung Buddhist-Christian Colloquium 'Buddhism and Christianity - Convergence and Divergence': Kaohsiung, Taiwan 31 July - 4 August 1995."*Pro dialogo* 90 (1995)

Band, Edward. *Formosa*. Part Two of *Working His Purpose Out: The History of the English Presbyterian Mission 1847-1947*. London: Presbyterian Church of England, n.d.

—, ed. *He Brought Them Out: The Christian Movement among the Mountain Tribes of Formosa*. London: BFBS, 1949.

Barclay, Thomas. "The Aboriginal Tribes of Formosa." In *Records of the General Conference of the Protestant Missionaries of China Held at Shanghai, May 7-20, 1890*, 558-575. Shanghai: American Mission Press, 1890.

Blair, E.H. and J.A.R. Robertson, eds, chaps. 24, 26, 32, 35. *The Philippines Islands 1493-1898*. Cleveland: Arthur H.Clark, 1906.

Chang Feng-chen. *Shen hsueh yu che hsueh* (Theology and philosophy). (Chinese Catholic) Tainan: Wen tao ch'u pan she, 1979.

Chen Chia-lu. *Tienchuchiao lai Tai chuan chiao i painien chien shih*. Kao hsiung: Tien chu chiao tao ming hui, 1960. (On 100 years of the Catholic Church in Taiwan).

Chen Chung-min, Chuang Ying-chang and Huang Su-min, eds. *Ethnicity in Taiwan: Social, Historical, and Cultural Perspectives*. Taipei: Institute of Ethnology, Academia Sinica, 1994.

Chow Lien-hua. "Christ the Transformer of the Chinese Tradition." *Church and Society* (EACC) 4 (1962).

Covell, Ralph R. *The Liberating Gospel in China: the Christian Faith among China's Minority Peoples*. Grand Rapids, MI: Baker Books, c1995.

Ede, George. *The Three Character Classic. A Commentary*. London: ca.1885.

Fu jen ta hsueh shen hsueh chu tso pien i hui pien (Chinese vocabulary of dogmatic theology). T'ai-pei: Kuang ch'i, 1986.

Grichting, W.L. *Value System in Taiwan*. Ann Arbor: Inter-university Consortium for Political and Social Research, ?1972.

Hang Tui-jie, Thaddeus. *Liming qian de Zhongguo Tianzhujiao* (The Catholic Church in Chinese dawn). Taipei: 1963.

—. "The Christian Quest for Truth." *Tripod* 65 (1991).

Hsiang, Paul Stanislaus. *The Making of a Catholic priest*. Taipei: Prophet Press, c1973.

Ion, A. Hamish. *The Cross and the Rising Sun: the Canadian Protestant Missionary Movement in the Japanese Empire,*

1872-1931. Waterloo, Ont.: Wilfrid Laurier University Press, c1990.

Johnston, James. *China and Formosa: The Story of the Mission of the Presbyterian Church of England*. London: Hazell, Watson and Viney, 1897.

Kerr, George H. *Formosa, Licensed Revolution and the Home Rule Movement, 1895-1945*. Honolulu: The University Press of Hawaii, 1974.

King, Ambrose Y.C. "A Non-paradigmatic Search for Democracy in a Post-Confucian Culture: The Case of Taiwan R.O.C." In *Political Culture and Democracy in Developing Countries*, edited by L Diamond. Boulder: L. Rienner Publishers, 1993.

Kuo Wei-hsia and Chao Wei-chu. *Tien chu chiao ta chuan yuan hsiao hsueh hsiao chi feng yu huan ching tan wei* (Catholic church education since 1945). Taipei: Fu jen ta hsueh, 1990.

Lai Yung-hsiang. *Chi-tu chiao Tai-wan hsuan chiao shih wen hsien. Tai-wan Chi-tu chang lao chiao hui pai nien shih* (Centennial history of the Presbyterian Church of Formosa: 1865-1965). Tainan: Chi-tu chiao tsai Tai hsuan, 1984 (1965).

Lamley, Harry Jerome. "The Taiwan Literati and Early Japanese Rule 1895-1915." (Microform) Ph.D. diss., University of Washington, 1964.

Lee Teng-hui. *Love and Faith*. Taipei: Kwang Hwa, 1990.

Lee Yu-yuen. *The Society and Culture of Taiwanese Aborigines*. Taipei: United Classical Publishing, 1982.

Li Khin-hoann. "Language policy and Taiwan Independence." In *Linguistic Politics and Policy*, edited by Si Cheng-hong. Taipei: Chian-ui Press.1996.

Matthias, Christian. "Ruhe xiang xiandai zhongguoren quanshi jidu" (How to explain Jesus Christ to modern Chinese people). *CTUF* 113 (1997).

Mitchell, Donald W. and James a Wiseman, eds. *The Gethsemani encounter: a Dialogue on the Spiritual Life by Buddhist and Christian Monastics*. New York: Continuum, 1997.

Moody, Campbell N. *The Saints of Formosa: Life and Worship in a Chinese Church*. London: 1912.

Ngo Tok-liu. *Fig Tree* (in Chinese). Taipei: Frontiers Publication Society, 1989.

Raber, Dorothy A. *Protestantism in Changing Taiwan: a Call to Creative Response.* Pasadena, CA: William Carey Library, 1978.

Richard, Mrs. "Canadian Presbyterian Mission: Formosa." In *The China Mission Hand-book*, 286-288. Shanghai: American Presbyterian Mission Press, 1896.

Ross, Daniel G. *Chinese and Western Religious Symbols as Used in Taiwan.* Taipei: Fujen University, 1980.

Sasaki Yasuko et al. "Appendix: The Taiwan Mission" (in Japanese). In *Give Us More Light, a History of the Women's Auxiliary of the District of Kyoto 1878-1943*, 79-100. Kyoto: The Women's Association of the Diocese of Kyoto, NSKK, 1998.

Sawatzky, Sheldon. "Chinese Ecclesiology in Context." *Taiwan Journal of Theology* 5 (1983).

Schweizerischer Evangelischer Kirchenband. *Christliches Zeugnis auf Taiwan* (Christian witness on Taiwan), edited by Oekumeni Working Group. Bern: [s.n.], 1991.

Shen hsüeh tz'u tien Fu jen shen hsüeh chu tso pien i hui (Theological dictionary, a one volume encyclopedia of Christian-Catholic theology). T'ai-pei: Kuang ch'i, 1996.

Shephard, John R. *Statecraft and Political Economy on the Taiwan Frontier, 1600-1800.* Stanford: Stanford University Press, 1993.

Shen T.H. (with C.S. Shen.). *Autobiography of a Chinese Farmer's Servant*.Taipei: 1981.

Sovik, Ruth, et al. *Mission in Formosa and Hongkong: studies in the beginning and development of the indigenous Lutheran Church in Formosa and Hongkong.* Minneapolis, MN: Augsburg Pub. House, 1957.

Standaert, Nicolas and Adrian Dudink, eds. *Chinese Christian Texts from the Roman Archives of the Society of Jesus.* 12 vols. Taipei: Ricci Institute. Forthcoming.

Tainan Theological College Centennial Celebration. Special issue, edited by Editorial Board, Tainan Theological College. Tainan: C.F. Hsiao, 1977.

Taiwan Journal of Theology (in Chinese and English.) Taiwan Theological College and Seminary. Annual.

Taiwan Missionary Fellowship. *Taiwan Christian Yearbook*. Taipei: Taiwan Missionary Fellowship, 1954- ca.1972

The Holiness Church of Taiwan. *1976 Anniversary Volume*. Taichung: Holiness Church Press, 1976.

The Taiwan Christian Yearbook [begun 1955]: *a Survey of the Christian Movement in Taiwan, during 1959, with Special Attention to the Ten Years, from 1949 to 1959*. Taichung: Taiwan Missionary Fellowship, 1960?

Ti 2 chieh Chung-kuo cheng chiao kuan hsi kuo chi hsueh shu yen t\ao hui lun wen chi: 1990 (The second international symposium on politico-religious relations in China). Tai-pei: Tan-chiang ta hsueh li shih hsueh hsi, 1991.

True Jesus Church. *Fiftieth Anniversary Volume*. Taichung: True Jesus Publishing Centre, 1977.

Xu Zongze. *Ming Qing jian Yesu hui shi yi zhu ti yao* (Bibliography of Chinese Catholic authors). Taipei: Taiwan zhong hua shu ju, 1958.

Yao Yeuhung. "The Spirituality of Ch'i." *CTUF* 94 (1993).

Ye Weimin. "Christian Art in Taiwan." *Tripod* 106 (1998).

Yeo, Peggy Bee-tin. *Christian communications in Asia*. Taipei, Taiwan: Asia Theological Association, 1980.

—BV, CNJ, CYE, JCE, KTK

Key Bibliographical Sources

Asia Journal of Theology
Includes regular section on Asian bibliographical resources.
P.O. Box 4635, 57 Miller's Road, Bangalore 560 046, India.

Bibliographia Missionaria
Annual classified listing of new publications on non-western Christianity, by country worldwide.
Pontifical Missionary Library, Pontifical Urban University, 00120 Vatican City.

Exchange
Journal of Missiological and Ecumenical Research, issued three times a year. Occasional special issues or bibliographical articles on Asian resources.
c/o Exchange IIMO, Interuniversity Institute for Mission and Ecumenical Research, Heidelberglaan 2, 3584 CS Utrecht, The Netherlands.

International Review of Mission
Quarterly. Includes a regular classified bibliography of mission and church studies from a selection of Asian journals and books.
World Council of Churches,150 route de Ferney, 1211 Geneva 2, Switzerland.

PTCA Bulletin - now Journal of Theologies and Cultures in Asia
Bi-annual publication of the Programme for Theology & Cultures in Asia.
c/o Theology Division, Chung Chi College, Chinese University of Hong Kong, Shatin N.T., Hong Kong SAR.

Theological Book Review

Issued three times a year - classified listing of theological publications primarily from Europe and North America.
Feed the Minds, Albany House, Sydenham Road, Guildford, Surrey GU1 3RY, England.

Theology in Context

Published three times a year. Annotated Bibliography, including summaries and surveys of "Third World" periodicals, books, articles. Lists and abstracts from approximately 50 Asian journals, along with selected books. The print version of Theology in Context will be discontinued at the end of 2002, but MWI-Missio's Yearbook is to be expanded and published annually in German and in four other languages (English, Spanish, French and Portuguese). In addition, the MWI data base will be freely available on the Internet. Up-to-date details from: Institute of Missiology (MWI), Missio, P.O. Box 11 10, 52012 Aachen, Germany.

Contributors to Volume 3

BAM - Sr Betty Ann Maheu mm is Editor of the journal *Tripod* (Ding), Hong Kong.

BV - Dr Benoit Vermander sj, is Director of the Taipei Ricci Institute, Taipei, Taiwan.

CMF - Dr Theresa Chu Mei-fen, has been teaching Christology and Spirituality at the National Seminary in Beijing, China

CNJ - Dr Chen Nan-jou is professor of Christian Ethics, Theology of Mission, Theology and Culture at Yushan Theological College and Seminary, Hualien, Taiwan.

CV - Fr Cyril Velliath, is a member of the Society of Jesus, Tokyo, Japan.

CYE - Dr. Cheng Yang-en is Associate Professor of Church History, Taiwan Theological College and Seminary, and Editor of *Taiwan Journal of Theology*

CYT - Rev'd Chen Yongtao is Instructor at NUTS, and assistant editor of Nanjing Theol Review China.

DSKS - Dr David Suh Kwang-sun is Director of the Asian Christian Higher Education Institute of the United Board for Christian Higher Education in Asia, Hong Kong.

GRW - Dr Guan Rui Wen (Kwan Sui-man) is currently assistant professor at the Theology Division, Chung Chi College, Chinese University of Hong Kong.

HJR - Dr Hwang Jong Ryul is a specialist in Catholic Minjung Theology, Seoul, Korea.

Contributors to Volume 3

JCE -	Dr John C. England was formerly Associate Dean, Programme for Theology and Cultures in Asia, Kyoto, Japan.
JW -	Ms Janice Wickeri is Editor of the *Chinese Theological Review*
KH -	Dr Kajiwara Hisashi, is a professor of Nagoya Gakuin University, Japan.
KHs -	Dr Kinukawa Hisako is professor at Tokyo Women's University, Japan.
KJK -	Dr Kwon Jin Kwan is professor at Episcopal Theological Seminary, Seoul, Korea.
LKJJ -	Sr Leo Kim Jeong-ja, of the Little Servants of the Holy Family of Seoul, Korea.
KTK -	Dr. C. George Guo (Koeh Tiong-kiat), is Plant Physiologist and Program Director, Asian Vegetable Research and Development Center, Tainan, Taiwan.
PHJ -	Mr. Park Hyun Joon, is Director of Woori Theological Institute, Seoul, Korea.
TM -	Dr Takenaka Masao was formerly professor of Christian Ethics at Doshisha University, Kyoto, Japan.
YM -	Ms Yoshida Megumi is Consultant to Tomisaka Christian Centre

Editors

Janice Wickeri was a mission co-worker with the PCUSA in Taiwan and Hong Kong, was formerly managing editor of the Research Centre for Translation of the Chinese University of Hong Kong and has been the editor of the *Chinese Theological Review* since 1985. She is the translator of many literary and theological works from Chinese to English. Recent publications include: *Love Never Ends: Papers of K.H. Ting* (ed. & tr., 2000), named one of Fifteen Outstanding Books in Mission Studies 2000–; *Plurality, Power and Mission* (ed., with Philip Wickeri and Damayanthi Niles, 2000); and *The Oxford Guide to Literature in English Translation* (member of Advisory Board and editor of China section, 2000).

David Kwang-sun Suh, holds a PhD in Religion from Vanderbilt University, and taught theology and philosophy in Ewha Womans University in Seoul, Korea. A founding member of the Korean Minjung Theology movement, he has written numerous articles for national and international ecumenical theological journals along with books in Korean and English. His representative work is *Korean Minjung in Christ* (1991). He was recently Henry Luce Visiting Professor of World Christianity at Union Theological Seminary in New York and Visiting Professor of Asian Theology at Drew University. He is currently working for the Asian Christian Higher Education Institute of the United Board for Christian Higher Education in Asia.

Dr Lily A. Quintos rc, is a religious of the Cenacle and is Director of the Cenacle Retreat House and Center of Spirituality, Quezon City, Philippines. She was the first woman to defend her doctoral dissertation at the Faculty of Theology of the Catholic University of Louvain, Belgium magna cum laude, and has served in international programmes for renewal in religious life as well as in theological education. Her writings and teachings in many countries have included also Buddhist and feminist studies. She has served as Academic Dean and Professor of Moral Theology at the Franciscan School of Theology, Graduate Theological Union in Berkeley, California and now also teaches at the Loyola School of Theology, Ateneo de Manila University.

John Mansford Prior svd (PhD, Birmingham) has worked in eastern Indonesia in cross-cultural mission since 1973. He is Executive Secretary of Candraditya Research Centre for the Study of Religion and Culture, Maumere, Flores, and has lectured in Asian theology in many countries. Since 1987 he has published scores of articles in Indonesian and other journals, 16 original book chapters in collections, and edited or co-edited more than 20 books. He has been lecturer at St. Paul's Major Seminary, Maumere, Flores, Executive Secretary of the SVD Asian Pacific Missiological Education and Research Programme(1994-99) and founding member and first Secretary of SVD Asian Pacific Association of Mission Researchers (ASPAMIR). Since 1992 he has also worked closely with the FABC Office for Evangelization.

Jose Kuttianimattathil sdb, has been Professor of Systematic Theology at Kristu Jyoti College, Bangalore, India and holds a Doctorate in Systematic Theology from the Pontifical Gregorian University, Rome. He has taught philosophy at the Salesian College, Yercaud, Tamil Nadu (1978-1981), systematic theology at Kristu Jyoti College, Bangalore (1987-1990, and 1994-), being also Rector for theology students at Kristu Jyoti College. He is the editor of *Kristu Jyoti*, a youth pastoral, theological and catechetical journal. His previous publications include *Jesus Christ: Unique and Universal* (1990), *Practice and Theology of Interreligious Dialogue* (1995) and a number of articles in scholarly journals.

John C. England has degrees in Humanities and in Theology from New Zealand, Silliman University, the Philippines and the SEAGST. He has been a staff member of the EACC/CCA, Programme Co-ordinator for Tao Fong Shan Ecumenical Centre,

Hong Kong, and Associate Dean for the PTCA. Since 1970 he has worked with centres, movements and seminaries throughout the region, co-ordinated programmes of post-graduate theological education for the Asian region and lectured in Asian theologies in many countries. Along with many articles in international journals, he edited the PTCA Bulletin from 1987-1994, and has written or edited five volumes for EACC/CCA, along with *Living Theology in Asia* (1981, 1982) and the annual series of Occasional Papers of *Doing Theology with Asian Resources* (Singapore). He is co-ordinating writer and editor of *Asian Christian Theologies*.

INDEX OF PERSONS

A

Abe Iso 336, 337, 395
Abe Masao 388
Abe Mitsuko 377
Abe Yoshiya 383
Abercrombie, John 297
Adams, Daniel 597
Adams, J.R. 201
Ahn Byung Mu 539, 553, 557ff., 570
Ahn Chang Ho 512
Ahn Chung Geun, Thomas (Ahn Joong Keun) 486, 488, 490f., 498, 503, 537
Ahn Eung Ryul 526
Ahn Jae Woong 597
Ahn Jung Bock 483
Ahn Sang Nim 572
Aiko Carter 370, 373, 418ff., 460
Akaiwa Sakai 369, 376, 377, 386f.
Akizuki Ryomin 388
Akutagawa Ryonosuke 394
Aleni, Giulio 16, 314
Allam, Cheryl 374
Allchin, George 350
Allen, Horace N. 492
Allen, Roland 170f.
Allen, Young J. 93, 99, 100, 104, 110, 114
Alley, Rewi 172
Alopen 2
Amaladoss, Michael 278
An Chong-bok 29
An Myong Gun 488
Andaryas, Hussain 295
Anderson, Boris 678
Anderson, Rufus 177
Andrews, Mary Elizabeth 104
Anzai Shin 448
Aoki Hiroyuki 403
Aoyama Gen 380
Appenzeller, Alice Rebecca 499
Appenzeller, Henry G. 492, 494, 510
Arai Eiko 374
Arai Hakuseki 25
Arai Osui 328f., 332, 340
Arai Sasagu 370, 413ff., 415, 421, 442
Arai Sayoko 374, 438
Arai Toshitsugu 440
Ariga Tetsutaro 407, 466
Ariyoshi Sawako 448
Armstrong, Robert C. 350
Avison, O.R. 492
Axling, William 350

B

Bae Kyung Min, Peter 611f.
Bai Buntei 25
Baker, Gilbert 239
Ban Byub Sub 512
Band, Edward 668
Bang Yu Ryong Leo, Andrea 522
Bao Guanglin 134
Bao Guangxi 100, 104
Barclay, Thomas 667
Barr, John S. 118
Barry, Peter 88, 270, 277, 285, 658
Basho 403, 405
Beeby, Daniel 678
Bernard, Henri 45
Berndt, Manfred 238, 263
Berneux, Simeon 487
Bianchi, Lawrence 267

Bichurin, Nikita Yakovlevich 105
Biernatski, William E. 520
Bing Xin, see Xie Wanying
Birmingham, Alan 82
Blanc, J. 487
Boxer, Charles 660
Braga, Jack 660
Brandauer, Frederick 239
Bridgman, Elijah C. 99, 105f., 654
Brown, Dr. 315
Brown, Elizabeth 678
Brown, Frank L. 350
Brown, Maria 104
Browne, G.A.M.R. 294
Bruguire, B. 487
Bucho Takeda 453
Buell, Constance 350
Butruille, Emille 45
Byun Hee Sun, Anselm 609f.
Byun Sun Hwan 539, 543, 550f.

C

Cable, Mildred 124
Cai Kuei 124
Cai Sujuan (Christiana Tsai) 109, 120
Campbell, William 667
Candeau, Sauveur 334
Candidus, George 19, 20
Cantieri, Maria Pia 655
Cao Fangyun 120
Cao Jingrong (Cao Ziyu) 98, 100, 104
Cao Shengjie 199
Carroll, Ewing 239
Cary, Otis 350
Casado, Américo 655
Casey, John J. 272
Cha Dong Yup, Norbert 614f.
Ch'ae P'il Gun 510
Chan Chor-choi, Alan (Chen Alan Zuocai) 238, 247, 251f.
Chan, Dominic 273
Chan, Joanna 274, 285
Chan Kai-yung, Anna 257
Chan Ka-wai 263

Chan Kim-kwong 76
Chan, Margherita 275
Chan Shun-hing 247
Chan, Stephen 273
Chang, Aloysius 270
Chang, Anna 713
Chang, Cecila 714
Chang Chih-tung (Zhang Zhidong) 100
Chang Chun Ha 543, 597f.
Chang Ch'un-shen, Aloysius B. 77, 704, 705, 707, 716ff.
Chang Feng-chen 724
Chang Fu-liang 118
Chang Hsiao-feng 674
Chang Il Cho 601
Chang Jae On, Samuel 647
Chang, Joyce 274
Chang Ming-yu, Peter 680
Chang, Pastor 98, 108
Chang, Sofia 713
Chang Sung Bok 646
Chang Tsong-ming (Mrs. G. Mackay) 668
Chang Wei-tu 707
Chang Wen-kai (Zhang Wenkai) 227, 230
Chang Yutang 41
Chao, Jonathan 239
Chao Kuan-hai (Zhao Guanhai) 118
Chao, Maria 713
Chao Pin-shih 710
Chao, T.C. (Zhao Zichen; Chao Tze-ch'en) 118, 130f., 133, 134, 138ff., 237
Chao Wei-chu 724
Charbonnier, Jean 270
Chau, Edward 279f.
Ch'en Ying-chen 674
Ch'eng Shih-kuang 707, 709f.
Ch'i-teng 674
Ch'iu, Milton M. 724
Ch'u, Pastor 98, 108
Chen Alan Zuocai, see Chan Chor-choi, Alan
Chen Chia-lu 724
Chen Chu-hsien 677

Index of Persons

Chen Duxiu 131f., 133
Chen, Gertrude 713
Chen Guoliang 134
Chen, L.T. 118
Chen, Lucia Marie 714
Chen Mengnan 98, 153
Chen Nan-jou 694f
Chen, Rosa 713
Chen, Sanford C.C. 118
Chen Sheng-cheng 724
Chen Tzu-mei, Nancy 682
Chen Weitong, Marc 63
Chen Yuling 120
Chen Zemin 183ff.
Cheng Cheng-yi 237
Cheng Cheng-yi (Mrs.) 124
Cheng Chonggui , Marcus 118, 133
Cheng, Cynnec 268, 278
Cheng, Dominica 274
Cheng Erh-yu, see Tin, John Jyigiokk
Cheng Guanyi (Ruth Cheng) 103, 120, 124, 133, 169
Cheng Jingyi (Andrew C.Y. Ch'eng) 118, 133, 150ff., 154, 157f., 159
Cheng Lien-te 675
Cheng Mao 108
Cheng, Pauline 275, 714
Cheng, Ruth, see Cheng Guanyi
Cheng Wanzhen 93, 103, 120, 121, 169
Cheng Yang-en 697f.
Cheon Se Hyung 588
Cheung, Dominic 268
Cheung Ha Eun 543, 597
Cheung Ka-hing 278
Cheung, Vivian 275
Chi Dong Shik 601
Chi Hak Soon, Daniel 520, 525f., 534
Chi Myong Kwan 601
Chi Wang 679
Chiang, Clara 275
Chien Yu-wen (Jian Youwen) 118
Ching Liu 724
Ching Yak Chong 497
Chi-oang (Chi Wang Yiwal) 681
Chiu, Andrew 238

Chiu Teng-kiat 238, 239
Cho Kwang, Ignatius 488, 537f.
Cho Maria 498, 499
Cho Nam Ki 620
Cho Seung Hyuk 554
Cho Tae Yon 588
Cho Wha Soon 554, 572
Choe Che U 579
Choe Chi Hyok 487
Choe Yong Eob (Yang Eob Chio) 619
Choi Byung Hyun 510
Choi, Enoch 263
Choi Hae Young (Choi Hye Yeong) 588, 593f.
Choi Hyeong Mook 568f.
Choi Ki Shik 526
Choi Man Ja 554, 571, 576f.
Choi Min Soon, John 523
Choi Pyong Hon 636
Choi Suk Woo, Andrea (Ch'oe Sok U) 526f.
Choi Yang Up, Thomas 486, 487, 489f.
Choi Young Sil 571, 580f.
Chong Chi Yong 619
Chong Chong Hye (Elizabeth) 497
Chong, Eric 247
Chong Ha Sang 31, 636
Chong Ho Kyong 520, 531f., 592
Chong Pok Hye 497
Chong Yak Jong, Augustine 3, 29, 30, 482, 485
Chong Yak Jun 482
Chong Yak Yong ("Tasan") 31, 482, 485, 537
Choo Chai Yong 601
Choo Ki Chul 506
Chou Chi-shih Joseph 54
Chou Jai Yong, Paul 522
Chou-Adams, Carol 682
Chow, Joseph 723
Choy, Peter 273
Chu Hsi-ning 674
Chu Ki Chol 512
Chu Mei-fen, Theresa 76, 83f., 88
Chu, T.C. (Mrs), see Hu Binxia

Chuang Ching-hsin 724
Chuang Shu-jen 682
Chui, Jane 263
Chui, Paula 239
Chun Kwang-Rye 374
Chung Hyun Kyung 571, 577f.
Chung Kyung Ok 510, 511
Chung, K.T. 154, 157
Chung, Peter 657, 658
Chung, Silvia 588
Chung Sook-ja 373, 374, 426, 572
Chung Yangmo 616
Chung Yuk-sum 238, 247
Ciƀot, Pierre-Martial 17
Cieslik, Hubert 350
Cioppa, John 270
Clancy, Jack 268, 270, 278
Clark, William 315
Clasper, Paul 263
Coe, Shoki (Hwang Chang-hue / Ng Chiong-hui) 674, 676, 684ff., 688
Collins, Edward 273
Collins, John 268
Constantini, Cardinal 41, 51
Corfe, C.J. 492
Coste, E.J.G. 638
Cotta, Anthony 51
Couvreur, Seraphin 45
Criveller, Gianni 270, 285f.

D

Dallet, Charles 526
Daveluy, Marie-Nicholas 487
Davidson, Flora 294
Davies, J.H. 492
Davies, May 492
Davis, J.D. 350
Dawai (Liu Fu Ch'ang) 679
de Belen, Aquino 3
de Cespedes, Gregorio 23
de Chardin, Pierre Teilhard 48f., 237, 281
d'Elia, Pasquale M. 45
de la Servière, Jean 45
de Moidrey, Joseph Tardif 43

de Moyria de Mailla, Joseph-Anna-Marie 21
de Poirot, Louis 39
de Rotz, M.M. 319
DeForest Charlotte 350
DeForest, John Hyde 350
Dehn, Wilfred 446
del Rosario, Jacintho Esquivel 20
Delaney, Joan 268
Deng, Cora, see Deng Yuzhi
Deng Yuzhi (Cora Deng) 124, 169, 172, 177
Deng Zhao-ming 239, 247
Deutsch, Richard 238, 263
Dewey, John 147
Dilawar Khan 294
Ding Lik-kiu 244
Ding Limei 108, 118, 169
Ding Meiyu (Mary Ting) 169
Ding Shujing (Ting Shu-ching) 103, 120, 124f., 169
Ding Si-ngok, (Mrs) 104
Dogen 403
Doi Masatoshi 370, 380, 382, 390f., 407
Dong Guangqing 665
Dong Li 724
Dore, Henri 43
Douthwaite, Arthur W. 592
Doyle, Frank 82
Drummond, Richard 445
Duan Yinming 66
Dugout, H. 43
Dumoulin, Heinrich 378, 379, 380, 385

E

Ebina Danjo 315, 322, 324f., 329, 331, 332, 335, 355, 443
Ebisawa Arimichi 398
Echizen Kiroku 438
Ede, George 668
Eitel, Ernest John 219f.
Elert, Haakon 383
Elsinger, P. 268
Endicott, James G. 172
Endo Shusaku 415, 420, 447f.

Index of Persons

England, John C. 239
England, Rita M. 239
Enomiya-Lassalle, Hugo (Makibi Enomiya) 378, 384ff.
Etienne Lamotte 393
Eto Naozumi 383
Eunja Lee 374

F

Faber, Ernst 114
Fan Xueyan 76
Fan Yurong 120, 124, 169
Fan Zimei (Fan Tzu-mei; T.M. Van) 117
Fang Chih-jung, Mark 704, 718f.
Fang Chih-rong 723
Fang Dongmei 717
Fang Hao, Maurus 67f., 708
Fang, Mark 270
Farley, Margaret 274
Faust, Allen K. 350
Fedrigotti, Lanfranco 272
Feng Shang-li 239
Feng Xian, see Kao, Lucy
Feng Yingqing 11
Fenwick, M.C. 492
Ferguson, Mrs. D. 668
Ferreol, Jean 487, 489
Fisher, Elizabeth M. 103
Foote, W.R. 492
Foucauld, A.G. 45
Foucquet, Jean Francis 17
Francis, Carolyn 374
Franck, Frederick 380
Franklin, Samuel 395
French, Francesca 124
Fu Tieshan 75, 87, 191
Fucan Fabian 23
Fujiwara Takanori 379, 438
Fukada, Robert 440
Fukansai Fabian 3
Fukase Chuichi 451
Fukunaga Takehiko 377
Fung Chi-wood 262
Fung, Raymond 238, 244

Furet, Louis-Théodore 319
Furuya Yasuo 359, 401ff., 466

G

Gabet, Joseph 297
Gaillard, Louis 43
Gale, J.S. 492
Gamo Ujitsato-ki 24f.
Gendron, Louis 724
Gerlach, Talitha 172
Gervais, Régis 659
Gih, Andrew (Ji Zhiwen) 167
Giles, Herbert A. 114
Gilmour, James 297
Gluer, Winfried 239
Goessens, Robert 298
Goh, Lionel 272
Gong Liren, see Kung Lap-yan
Gong Pingmei 65
Goodrich, Sarah 124
Gore, Charles 356
Gou Hi-eng 668
Gourdon, F.M.J. 45
Gravius, Daniel 20
Grier, Louis N. 445, 450
Grierson, R. 492
Gu Baoluo 232
Gu Luodong 45
Guan Ruiwen, see Kwan Sui-man
Guennou, Jean 45
Gullick, O.H. 350
Gunzel, Margaret 298
Gunzel, Stuart 298
Guo Fangyun 124
Guo Moro 133
Gutheinz, Luis 721f., 724
Gutzlaff, Karl Friedrich 105ff., 491, 654

H

Ha, Joseph 273
Haas, Hans 350
Habito, Ruben L. 380, 383
Hahn Kyung Jik 517
Hall, Ronald O. 171, 222f., 237f.

Ham Se Ung, Augustine 536f.
Ham Sok Hon 517, 542, 545ff., 553, 579
Ham Sye Ung 520
Hamark, Lennart 263
Hammer, Raymond 445
Hamre, Axel 222f.
Han Hyeon, Agnes 595f.
Han Kuk Yeum 572
Han Lin 14
Han Mi Ra 572
Han Shin Ae 497
Han Soon Hee 588, 589f.
Han Tae Dong 601
Han Wan Sang 540, 543, 554, 598
Han Wenzao 191
Han Yu 704
Han, Cecelia 588
Hane Mikiso 371
Hang, T. 63
Hansen, Anders 263
Haouissé, Auguste 54
Happert, Gilbert 20
Harada Sogaku, Roshi 385
Hardie, R.A. 492
Hardy, Mark 82
Hartwell, Charles 104, 114
Haslewood, H.L. 229
Hatano Seichi 343f., 356, 407
Hattori Chiyo 337
Havret, Henri 43
Hayashi Utako 346
He Guanghu 203
Heisig, James 380, 383
Heron, John W. 492
Higa Shuncho 332
Highbaugh, Irma 124
Hiraiwa Yoshiyasu 333
Hirata Atsutane 324f.
Hirata Satoshi 440
Hirobumi Ito 490, 503
Hisamatsu Eiji 380
Hisamatsu Shin-ichi 388
Ho, Agatha 275
Ho, Agnes 275
Ho Chuk-ping 273

Ho Fuk Tong, see Ho Tsun Sheen
Ho Hei-wah 245
Ho Hsiao-hsin, Winnie 247
Ho, Jessica 274, 275
Ho Kai 222
Ho, Katherine
Ho Li-hsia, Katherine 714
Ho Sai-ming 240f.
Ho Tsun Sheen (Ho Fuk Tong) 96f., 108
Ho, William 272
Hobbs, Mary Kay 247
Hodgkin, Henry T. 118
Hoffman, Tim 238
Hoin, Vincente 23
Holbert, H. 494
Holcomb, Chester 104
Holth, Sverre 239
Hon Tai-fai, Savio 272, 286
Honda Masaaki 388, 438
Honda Testuro 427f.
Honda Yoichi 315, 329
Honey, P.J. 82
Hong Iou-han 29
Hong Rengan 228
Hong Tui-kit 272
Hong Xiuquan 101f.
Hong Xiuquan 228
Hori Ichiro 448
Hori Mitsuo 421
Horiguchi Ikiko 374
Hoshino Tenchi 333
Hosokawa, Tama Gracia 3, 23 25
Hou Sheng-ch'ing 108
Howard, Therese 275
Hsi, Pastor, see Hsi Sheng-mo
Hsi Sheng-mo (Xi Shengmo) 98, 108
Hsiang Twei-chieh 710
Hsiao Ching-fen 677
Hsiao Yüan 724
Hsieh Hung-lai (Xie Honglai) 118
Hsieh, Ingram 677
Hsieh, Martha 714
Hsieh, Teresa 714
Hsu (Xu), Candida 3
Hsu Chen-ping, Francis 267

Index of Persons

Hsu Ch'ien 118
Hsu, Grace 714
Hsu, Paul 67
Hsu, P.C. (Hsu Pao-ch'ien; Xu Baoqian) 118, 133, 143f.
Hsu T'ien-hsien 678
Hsu Ti-shan (Xu Dishan) 674
Hu Binxia (Mrs. T.C. Chu) 93, 121
Hu Kuo-chen, Peter 705, 723
Hu Shih 118
Hu Wen-ch'ih 679
Hu Xuecheng 134
Hu Yiku (Y.K. Woo) 118
Huang Huizhen, see Wong Wai-ching, Angela
Huang Po-ho 696f.
Huang Po-lu 43, 44
Huang, Theresa 713, 714
Huang Ying 124
Huang Ziyu 75
Huc, Evariste Régis 45, 297
Hui Zhou, Elizabeth 76
Hullen, Antoon 45
Humbertclaude, Pierre 350
Hun Jong, mother of 483
Hurley, James 268, 273, 278
Hutchinson, Paul 118
Hwang Chang-hue, see Coe, Shoki
Hwang Jong Ryul, Leo 612, 617
Hwang Sah Yung 483
Hwang Shi Chon 649
Hwang Sok Tu 487
Hwang Wu-tong 688
Hwon Bong Cheol 588
Hyon Kyong Nyon 498
Hyon Sok Mun 487
Hyun Young Hak 553, 559f.

I

I Py-ok 29, 30, 31
I Su-kwang 29
Ibuka Kajinosuke 333
Iglehart, Charles 445
Iha Fuyu 331f.

Ii Kyoshi 392
Iisaka Yoshiaki 377, 398, 439
Im Jin Chang 519
Imamichi Tomonobu 366
Imanaka Tsugumaru 325, 336
Imbert, Laurent 487
Imoos, Thomas 379, 438
In Myung Jin 554
Inagaki Ryosuke 438
Inoue Hisashi 448
Inoue Yoji 404ff., 425, 407
Inoue Yoshio 391, 453
Ishida Yoshiro 440
Ishihara Ken 351f., 398
Ishihara Yoshiro 377, 442
Ishikawa Sanshiro 336
Ishiwaki Yoshifusa 380
Isshiki Yoshiko 373, 374, 375, 408f.
Itasaka Bokusai 25
Ito Katsutake 315
Iwashima Tadahiko 429f.
Iwashita Soichi 325f., 327
Iyori Naoko 374, 438

J

Jaeske, Heny A. 297
James, William 147
Janes, Leroy Lansing 315, 320, 324
Jang Yup Hwang 649
Jeong Soon Ja 588
Ji Zhiwen see Gih, Andrew
Jia Yuming 118, 144ff., 154
Jiang Dahui, see Kaung Tai-wai, Joseph
Jiang Hezhen (Anna Kong Mei) 124
Jiang Peifen 190, 199
Jiang Wenhan (Kiang Wenhan) 177, 187
Jin Luxian, Aloysius 75, 79, 87
Jin Yican 66
Jing Dianying 160
Jo Byung Ok 506
Jo Man Shik 506
Jodo Shishu 388
Johnston, William 379
Jones, Dorothy 263

Jones, Francis Price 171
Jones, Henry 377
Joset, Theodore 218
Julian of Norwich 589
Jung Ha Sang 483, 485
Jung Kwang Ung, Joseph 646
Junius, Robertus 21

K

Ka Jung-soon 464
Kadowaki Kakichi, Johannes 380, 403f.
Kaga Otohiko 448
Kagawa Toyohiko 337, 338, 353ff., 356, 357f., 376, 395, 440
Kahn, Ida (Kang Cheng) 120, 124, 125
Kaino Nobuo 453
Kajiwara Higashi 376
Kakehi Mitsuaki 338
Kamishima Jiro 448
Kan Enkichi 337, 338, 355, 356f., 359
Kanamori Tsurin 315, 322, 329
Kanda Kanji 335, 443
Kane, Margaret 243
Kaneko Keiichi 440, 452, 453
Kaneko Kennosuke 438
Kang Cheng, see Kahn, Ida
Kang Inchul 618
Kang Kyong Bok 497
Kang Moon Kyu 597
Kang Nam Soon 571, 579f.
Kang Shin Myung 517
Kang Wan Suk 31, 485, 497
Kang Won Don 554, 563f.
Kang Won Yong 517, 539, 543, 598f.
Kang Young Ok, Lucia 588, 594f.
K'ang Yu-wei (Kang Youwei) 104, 110, 225
Kanno Sugako 346
Kao Chun-ming (C.M. Kao) 677, 678
Kao, Katerina 714
Kao, Lucy T.H. (Kao Teng-shiang / Ko, Tian-hiong) 682, 693
Kao Wang-Chin 680
Kasuya Koichi 438

Katayama Sen 336, 337
Kaung Tai-wai, Joseph (Jiang Dahui) 247, 255f.
Kawai Michi 345, 347f., 408
Kawakami Jotaro 395
Kawamura Shinzo 435f.
Kee Hoe 483
Keel Hee Seong 597, 602f.
Kemp, Hugh 298
Kenji Nakahara 338
Ki Joon Koh 645
Kiang Wenhan, see Jiang Wenhan
Kida Kenichi 444
Kil Sun Joo 511f.
Kim Ae Young 571, 582
Kim, Andrew 724
Kim Chan Kuk 601
Kim Chang Joon 649
Kim Chang Nak 597
Kim Chi Ha (Kim Hyung) 525, 534ff., 553, 556, 579, 618, 620
Kim Choi, Mrs Pilley 500
Kim Chong Han 485
Kim Ch'un Bae 509, 511f.
Kim Chung Choon 539, 543, 548f., 554
Kim Chunho 616
Kim Chunt'ae 620
Kim Dae Kun, Andrea 486, 489
Kim Dong Wan 646, 647
Kim Hangsup 617
Kim, Helen Kiteuk 499, 500, 506
Kim Heup Young 597
Kim Hui In 497
Kim Hyeo Im (Columba) 498
Kim Hyeo Joo (Agnes) 498
Kim Hyoung Tae, John 611, 617
Kim Hyun Ok, Miriam 588
Kim Hyung, see Kim Chi Ha
Kim Jae Joon 509, 517, 539, 542, 543ff., 548, 554
Kim Jeong Ja 588
Kim Jeong Soo 572
Kim Jin Ho 569ff.
Kim Jin So Daegun, Andrea 534
Kim Jung Shin 607f., 617

Index of Persons

Kim Kon-sun, Josaphat 30
Kim Kwan Suk 540, 543, 553, 600
Kim Kwang Shik 601
Kim Kyo Shin 511
Kim Kyong Jae 604
Kim Kyu Sik 512
Kim, Leo 588
Kim Maria 499
Kim Min Gi 620
Kim Min Soo, Ignatius 615
Kim Myong Hi 572
Kim Myoung Chin 572
Kim Myoung Shik 620
Kim Nam Hyok 649
Kim Namjo 619
Kim Nyung 613ff., 617
Kim Ok Hy (Hee), Anna 587, 588, 590f.
Kim Se Young 512
Kim Su Hwan, Stephen 519, 527ff., 554
Kim Subok 617
Kim Sung Hae 588, 591f.
Kim Sung Tae, Joseph 536
Kim Sungjae 440
Kim Tae Kun 487
Kim Ung Tai, Joseph 609
Kim Yang Sun 544
Kim Yon I 497
Kim Yong Bock 540, 553, 562f.
Kim Yong Ju 509, 511f.
Kim Yong Koo 554
Kim Yoon Ok 571, 582, 601
Kim Young [Sawa] 370, 375, 572
Kim Young Hee 572
Kim Young Koo 601
Kinoshita Naoe 336, 395
Kinukawa Hisako 370, 373, 374, 425ff.
Kiong, Simon 43, 44
Kisaki Satoko 448
Kisala, Robert 438
Kisei Chishi, see Sadakata Ryosuke
Kishi Chitose 359
Kishi Hideshi 438
Kishimoto Hideo 382
Kishimoto Nobuta 330, 333

Kitamori Kazoh 369, 396f., 465
Kitamura Tokoku 335, 337
Klein, Norbert 445
Ko, Maria 275
Ko Siu-wah 238
Ko Thian-su 668
Koh Un 620
Kohara Katsuhiro 436f.
Kohn, Livia 375, 383
Kojima Junji 314
Kokyo Shoryaku 314
Kolhatkar, Sonali 295
Kong Mei, Anna, see Jiang Hezhen
Koo, T.Z. 118, 134, 154, 171, 237
Kotoku Shusui 336
Kou, Maria 275
Koyama Kosuke 411ff.
Koyanagi Nobuaki 440
Kozaki Hiromichi 315, 316, 320f., 321, 322, 324, 331, 333, 335, 342
Ku Sang 619
Kuantu 222f.
Kubushiro Ochimi 345
Kuji, Grace Mary 374, 438
Kumano Yoshitaka 359
Kumkuzawa Banzan 25
Kumuzawa Yoshinobu 369, 409ff.
Kung Lap-yan (Gong Liren) 262, 263
Kung Shih-rung 710
Kuo Wei-hsia 724
Kurata Masahisa 432, 440, 460
Kuribayashi Teruo 414, 428f.
Kurihara Sadako 375
Kuroda Nobue 374
Kurosaki Kokichi 323
Kuwahara Shinobu 374
Kuwata Hidenobu 359
Kvan, Eric 239
Kwak Seung Ryong 613
Kwan, Anna Maria 275
Kwan, Carlo 273
Kwan Chun-tong, Thomas 273
Kwan Sui-man (Guan Ruiwen) 263
Kwok Nai-wang (Guo Naihong) 238, 252f.

Kwok Pui-lan (Guo Peilan) 169, 247, 259f.
Kwon Chul Shin 482
Kwon Il Shin 482
Kwon, Mme 497
Kwon, Theresa 497
Kwong Lay-kuen, Madeleine (Magdalena) 274, 275, 282f., 713
Kwong, Magdalena 713
Kwong, Maria 275

L

Labayen, Julio 278
Ladanyi, Laszlo 81f.
Lai Yung-hsiang 724
Lai, Cecila 275
Lai, Clare 275
Lam, Anselm 272
Lam, Anthony 88, 270, 277, 286
Lam, Benedict 272
Lam, Grace 239
Lam Hong-ching 273
Lam Ka-tseung, Domingos 657f.
Lam Wing-hung (Lin Ronghong) 247, 262, 264
Lam Yam-min 658
Landis, E.B. 492
Landsborough, David 668
Larsen, Frans 298
Lau Chin-shek 244
Lau Him-sang, Joao Evangelista 658
Lau Lai-kwan, Maria 275
Lau, Madalena 714
Lau, Maria Goretti (Lau Choi-mei) 76, 270, 274, 277, 281f.
Lau, Victoria 658
Laucaigne, Joseph 313
Laures, Johannes 350
Lazerotto, Angelo 270
Le Tobar, Jerome 43
Learner, Marjorie 668
Lebbe, Vincent (Lei Mingyuan) 41, 50f., 53, 56, 68, 715
Lee, Agnes 275, 714
Lee, Andrina 275
Lee Chang Shik 539, 543, 554, 601
Lee Chi-chung, Archie (Li Zhiiang) 247, 256f.
Lee Ching-chee 238, 247
Lee Chong-il 440
Lee Chwen Jiuan 714
Lee De Pei 62
Lee Eung Chan 492
Lee Gong 272
Lee, Grace 274
Lee Hae Dong 553
Lee Hae In, Claudia 591, 618, 620
Lee, Helen 82
Lee Hyo Duck 500, 506
Lee In Bok 588
Lee In Ha 440, 451, 460
Lee Jae Sook 588
Lee Jeong Ku 597
Lee Jong Bae 604
Lee Jung Hee 554, 563, 564f.
Lee Jung Young 597, 604
Lee Kap Sung 506
Lee King-hung, Peter (Li Jingxiong) 239, 242f., 270
Lee Kyung Sook 571, 581
Lee, Leo 67
Lee, Louis 273
Lee, Lucia 274
Lee Moon Geun, John 524
Lee Moon Jang 597
Lee Mun Young 553, 601
Lee Oo Chung 539, 553, 554, 571, 574f.
Lee Park Sun Ai 554, 571, 575f.
Lee, Ralph 238, 262
Lee Sang Hun 545
Lee Sang Jae 506, 509
Lee Soo Jung 492
Lee Soon Yi (Lugarta) 485, 497
Lee, S.K. 231
Lee Tai Young 500, 553
Lee, Teresa 713
Lee Un Sun 571, 582
Lee Won Sun, Eusebius 529
Lee Yong Doh 511f.

Index of Persons

Legge, James 93, 96, 97, 105f. 222, 224f., 228
Lei Mingyuan, see Lebbe, Vincent
Leo Fung-ming, Josephine 275
Leong, Abraham 715
Leong, Benjamin 272
Leroy, Pierre 49
Leung, Beatrice 270, 274, 286
Leung Ka-ling 262
Leung Ka-lun 247
Leung, Thomas 273
Leung Sui-choh 231
Lew, T.T., see Liu Tingfang
Leyssen, J. 298
Li Andang 14
Li Boyu 60, 63, 66
Li Ch'un-sheng 672
Li Changshou 164
Li Chen 273
Li Chih-jen 724
Li Chuwen 134, 177
Li Guanfeng 124
Li Guoliang 87
Li Han 63
Li Jingxiong, Peter, see Lee King-hung, Peter
Li Jiubiao 12
Li Jiugong
Li Kang-chi 44
Li Lezhi 40
Li Madou (Li Ma Tou) (Matteo Ricci) 11, 29, 45, 53, 55, 66, 67, 314, 497, 654, 656
Li Qizhao 11
Li Shen 270
Li Shiyu, Antonius 63
Li Side 66
Li Tim-oi, Florence 171, 237
Li Wenyu, Laurent 44, 46f.
Li Zhaojiang 232
Li Zhizao (Li Chih Tsao) 11
Liang Ch'i-ch'ao (Liang Qichao) 110, 225
Liang Fa (Leung Faat / Leong Kung-fa) 93, 95f., 99, 654

Liang Qichao 104
Licent, Edward 45, 49
Lim, Agnes 713, 714
Lim Ang 668
Lim Hak-kiong 668
Lim Ian-sin 668
Lim Kiam-kim 668
Lim, Maria 714
Lim Su Kyung 611
Lin, Cecilienne 713
Lin Chih-p'ing 724
Lin Han-ta (Lin Handa) 118
Lin Hung-hsuan 678
Lin Mai-jung, Yvonne 682
Lin, Nancy 682
Lin Quan, Joseph 75
Lin Ronghong, see Lam Wing-hung
Lin Tsung-yi 688
Ling, Esther 275
Linuma Jiro 451
Little, Alice 104
Liu, Andrew C.C. 273
Liu Bo-chin, Victor 238
Liu, Catherine 275
Liu Fu Ch'ang, see Dawai
Liu Fung-sung 678
Liu Liangmo 177
Liu Minglian 87
Liu, Monica 274
Liu, Mrs. Herman C.E., see Wang Liming
Liu Ning 15
Liu Tingfang, Timothy (T.T. Lew) 118, 133, 152f., 237
Liu Xiaofeng 88, 203, 258f.
Liu Xutang, Ludovicus 63
Liu Yuanlong 87
Liu Yuanren 87
Liu Yuanren, Joseph 85f., 87
Lloyd, Arthur 350
Lo Hsien-ch'un 679
Lo Kuang, Stanislaus 710, 715f.
Lo Liong 668
Lo Lung-kwong (Lu Longguang) 257f.
Lo Lun-yen (Luo Lunyan) 118
Loewen, Arley 294

Loh I-to 699ff.
Loh, Lucy, see Kao, Lucy
Lonergan, Bernard 430
Lou Mong-in 29
Lou Tseng-tsiang 52f.
Lourenco, Joao 658
Lu Longguang, see Lo Lung-kwong
Lu Xun 131
Lu Y Doan 3
Lu Yunpeng 87
Lue Yuting 87
Lue Yuting 87
Lui, Ophelia 275
Luk Hung-kay, Bernard 270, 272
Luk Man Hoi, Thomas 658
Lung, Tom 263
Luo Guanzong 177
Lutz, Hans 244, 254, 263
Ly (Li), Andrew 16, 39

M

Ma Ji 76
Ma Xiangbo 40, 46, 47f.
Ma Yinglin 87
Ma Yutian 87
MacDonald, Caroline 345, 347, 350
Macgowan, John 104
MacIntyre, John 492
Mackay, George Leslie 668
Mackay, George W. 668
Mackay, Mrs G., see Chang Tsong-ming
Madore, Maria 713
Maejima Munetoshi 460
Maeng Yong Gil 601
Maheu, Betty Ann 270, 274, 277, 286f., 658
Makoto Mizuno 444
Malek, Roman 658
Man Kit-wah, Eva 274
Mao Tsetung (Mao Zedong) 83
Maresca, Bp. 489
Maritain, Jacques 327
Marnas, Francisque 350
Martin, Mary Louise 270

Martin, W.A.P. 93, 100, 110, 114
Martinez, Bartholomew 20
Mateos, Fernando 82
Matsudaira Nobutsuna 25
Matsui Yayori 371, 373, 440
Matsumoto Masao 366, 367, 448
Matsumura Kaiseki 333
Matsuoka Fumitaka 443
Maxwell, James L. 667
May, John 88
Mayeda Goro 413, 416, 442
Mayumi Mori 374
McCarthy, Jerry 82
McIntosh, John H. 440
McKenzie, W.J. 492
McMillan, Mary 350
McNair, Thomas 350
McNeal, M.B. (Miss) 350
McNeur, George Hunter 114
McRae, D.M. 492
McVeigh, Brian 383
Medhurst, W.H. 97, 105f.
Mei Yunying 120
Mella, Franco 268
Mermet-Cachon, Eugène-Immanuel 319
Metraux, Daniel 383
Mi Hu Yong 109
Miao, Chester S. 118
Miller, Roy 398
Miller, William McElwe 294
Milne, William 95, 99, 105f.
Min Kyong Suk, Anselm 532f.
Min Kyung Bae 543, 554, 600
Minato Akiko 374
Miner, Luella 124
Miura Ayako 377
Miura Riu 337
Miura Shumon 448
Miyabe Kinga 315
Miyamoto Takenosuke 394, 466
Miyata Mitsuo 440, 465
Mizuno Kayano 375
Mochizuki Kenihiro 443
Mommaers, Paul 380
Momose Fumiaki 423f.

Index of Persons

Monroe, Paul 118
Moody, Campbell 668
Moon Hee Suk, Cyris 554, 597, 604
Mori Arimasa 377
Mori Reiko 378
Mori Setsuko 374, 438
Morijon, Pedro 28
Moriuchi Toshio 448
Morris, Christopher 239
Morrison, Robert 92f., 95, 96, 99, 105f., 654
Mostaert, Antoine 45, 297
Motoda Sakunoshin 335
Mou Zongsan 231
Moule, Arthur Evans 114
Mounicou, Pierre 319
Mullins, Mark R. 383, 446
Mun Dong Whan, Stephen 539, 543, 551f., 553, 554
Mun Ik Kwan 540, 543, 554, 599f., 619, 646
Mun Jung Hyun 553
Mun Kyuhyun 611, 616
Mun Sang Hi 601
Murao Moses Shoichi 309
Mushakoji Kinhide 438
Mutel, G. 487
Muto Kazuo 383, 407, 466

N

Nagai Takashi 447
Nagakura Hisako 380
Nagasaka Genichiro 380
Nagashima Tadashige 328
Nagatoshi Sanpei 440
Naizen Joao 28
Nakadaira Kenkichi 450
Nakagawa Akira 438
Nakagawa Hideyasu 464
Nakajima John Masaaki 440, 460
Nakajima Shigeru 336, 338, 355f., 356
Nakamura Masanao 335
Nakaya Yasuko 372
Namae Takayuki 358
Nambara Shigeru 440

Naruse Jinzo 318f.
Nee, Watchman (Ni Tuosheng) 118, 160, 164f.
Neesima, Joseph Hardy, see Niijima Jo
Nemeshegyi, Peter 438
Nevius, John 110, 177, 495
Newell, Helen 104
Newman, Paul 238
Newton, Ella J. 124
Ng Chi-fun, Robert 283f.
Ng, Henry 272
Ng Kuok-cheong, Anthony 658
Ng Lee-ming 238, 247
Ng Se-keng 668
Ng Sui-lai 238
Ng Tsok-pang 668
Ngai, Gary M.C. 658
Ni Tuosheng, see Nee, Watchman
Nichiren 403
Nicolai (Ivan Kasatkin) 328, 350
Niijima Jo (Joseph Hardy Neesima) 316, 317f., 341
Nishida Kitaro 343, 359, 379, 388, 425, 465
Nishio Masaji 438
Nishitani Keiji 343, 380, 425
Nitobe Inazo 315, 331, 332, 347, 398
No Ki Nam 519
Nobuhara Tokiyuki 383, 425
Nodrat, Zia 294f.
Noh Jong Sun 597, 603
Noren, Loren 263
Noro Yoshio 465

O

O'Donoghue, Patrick 438
O'Rourke, Kevin 620
Obata Yoshinobu 438
Oda Takehiko 433, 438
Odagakai Masaya 465
Odagiri Nobuo 386, 465
Ogawa Keiji 359
Ogborn, Kate L. 124
Ogle, George 554
Ogoshi Aiko 374

Oh Jae Shik 554, 597, 603
Ohara Tomie 448
Ohki Hideo 402, 466
Okada Takeo 438
Okano Haruko 375
Okumura Ichiro 379
Okuyama Michiaki 380
Omurasan 346
Ong Hian-ti, see Wang Hsien-chih
Onishi Hajime 329
Onodera Isao 379. 438
Onomura Rinzo 309
Ooshima Koichi 440
Oshida Shigeto 379, 380
Osouf, Peter 313
Ota Julia 28
Ota Yuzo 383
Otsu Kenichi 460
Otsuka Hisao 395
Otsuka Setsuji 336, 357f.
Ou Feng-chi 230
Ou Jifu 273

P

Padilla, Wenceslao 298
Pagell, Edward 297
Paik Hong Joon 492
Pais, Albino 655
Pak Che Ga 31, 485
Pak Choon Cha 588
Pak Hye Ran 588
Pak Marina 28
Pak Song Ja 572
Palladius, Archimandrite (Benedict Petr Ivanovich) 105, 107
Pan, James 238
Pan Lok-sam 222f.
Pan Pei-chi, Paul 724
Pan Sheoshan 201
Pang Tsang 724
Pao Kuang-lin (Bao Guanglin) 118
Park, Andrew Sung 597, 604
Park Chung Hee 516f., 522, 537
Park Du Chin 512
Park, Esther 500
Park Hyung Kyu 553, 601, 620
Park Hyunjoon 617f.
Park Il Young, John 608f., 617
Park Jae Soon 554, 563, 565f.
Park Jong Chon 604
Park Jung Hong 483
Park Kyung Mi 571, 578f.
Park Kyung Seo 597
Park Moonsu 618
Park Pong Bae 543, 599
Park Pong Nang 601
Park San Kyong 601
Park Sang Jung 554, 597
Park Soon Kyung 571, 573f.
Park Sung Joon 554, 566f.
Park Tae Son 601
Pasio, Francisco 28
Paton, David M. 171
Pe Mu, Laurence 108
Peet, Azalia Emma 350
Pei, W.C. 49
Peng Jinzhang 122
Pennell, Theodore 294
Petitjean, Bernard-Thadée 313, 314, 319
Pfister, Louis 43
Phillips, James 446
Phoa Beng-tsu 668
Pi Shushih 60, 63, 65
Pierson, L.H. (Mrs) 350
Pilley, Mrs, see Kim Choi
Piryns, Ernest D. 379, 438
Poitras, Edward W. 601
Pollard, Samuel 201
Pong, James T.M. 674
Porter, Lucius 118
Porter, Mary H. 103, 104
Price, Frank W. 118, 165, 171
Pye, Michael 383, 446
Pyuk Lee 481
Pyun Chong Ho 512

R

Raguin, Yves 719f.
Raimondi, Bp. 267
Rakhel (Rachel) 295

Index of Persons

Rawlinson, Frank Joseph 118, 172
Raymaker, John A. 379
Reichelt, Karl Ludwig 114, 222f., 231, 232ff., 237
Reid, C.F. 492
Reid, David 383, 446
Reid, Gilbert 93, 100, 110, 112f.
Reischauer, A.K. 350
Ren Bing 87
Ren Ch'eng-yuan 98, 109
Repp, Martin 380, 383
Rhee Soun Seong, Peter 607
Ri Je Min 532
Ricci, Matteo, see Li Madou
Richard, Mary Martin 104
Richard, Timothy 93, 99, 100, 104, 110f., 112, 114
Ro Chung Hyun 554
Road, A., see Ladanyi, Laszlo
Roberts, I.J. 102
Rogers, Denis 238, 263
Roggendorf, Joseph 368
Rong Hong (Yung Wing) 654
Ross, John 492
Roy, Andrew 238
Ruggieri, Michele 15, 654
Rui Tao'an 232
Russell, Maud Muriel 172
Rutt, Richard 620
Ryokan 405

S

Sadakata Ryosuke 314
Sailer, Randolph C. 172
Saito Soichi 339
Sajo Jitsunen 333
Sakai Toshihiko 336, 395
Sakaibara Gan 394
Sakamoto Takashi 438
Sakata Hiro 378
Sanderson, Abbe 350
Sansom, G.B. 304
Sasaki J. Hiroshi 437
Sasaki Toyoji 345
Satake Akira 413, 442

Sato Shosuke 315
Sato Toshio 465f.
Satoko Yamaguchi 426
Sawa Masahiko 443
Sawabe (assistant to Nicolai) 328
Sawada Kazuo 326
Sawayama, Paul 318f.
Schall, Adam 15
Schereschewsky, Samuel Isaac Joseph 298
Schmidt, Isaak Jakob 297
Schneder, Anna M. 350
Schwartz, Henry B. 332
Scranton, Mary F. 492
Scranton, William B. 492
Sebes, Joseph 82
Sekine Masao 359, 413, 442
Sekita Hiroo 444
Seung Duk Park 649
Shaeq, Nazira 295
Shang Jeng-tzong 675
Shang Weitang (Huquuig) 14
Shaw, Ella C. 124
Sheepshanks, John 298
Shen Derong 177
Shen, Philip 238, 247
Shen Sizhuang 154
Shen Szu-chuang 118
Shen, T.K. 195
Shen Yifan 195f.
Shen Zigao 177
Shen, Vincent 272, 280
Sheng Junyu 47
Shi Junpu 66
Shi Meiyu (Mary Stone) 103, 120, 124, 125, 154, 169
Shi, Phoebe 169
Shields, Bernard 273
Shigekane Yoshiko 378
Shih, Evelyn O., see Ti-jan
Shiina Rinzo 377, 386
Shim Sang Tae 530f.
Shimada Keiichiro 358
Shimamoto, M. 374
Shimao Toshio 448

Shimazaki Toson 341
Shimizu Keizo 443
Shin Gyo Seon 588
Shin Hyun Bong 553
Shiozuki Kentaro 377, 439, 440
Shiraishi Nabe 440, 452
Shirayanagi, S 422, 455
Shoji Tsutomu 440, 460
Shu, Johana 714
Shu King-shen 52
Shuck, Henrietta 654
Shuck, Jehu Lewis 218, 654
Sih Kwang-tsien, Paul 672, 674
Sih Paul Kwang Tsien 70
Sim Jong Hyeok 610f.
Sin Hu Dam 483
Sin Tae Bo 31, 485
Sloboda, Michael 270, 277
Smith, Arthur H. 104
Smith, C. Stanley 118
Smith, Carl T. 220f., 226
Smith, Emma D. 103, 104
Smith, W.S. 492
So Jai Pil 509
Sohn Kyoo Tae 597
Sohn Seung Hee 571, 581
Song Chang Keun 510
Song Choan-seng (C.S. Song) 278, 281, 676f., 680, 688ff.
Song Ho Seok 588
Song Yuru 153
Sono Ayako 448
Soong Chiao-shun 108
Soong, Veronica 275
Soothill, William 93, 100, 103, 114
Spae, Joseph John 378, 393f.
Spencer, Herbert 341
Spier, Fredrik 383
Stallybrass, Edward 297
Steiber, Robert G. 445
Stone, Mary, see Shi Meiyu
Strong, Augustus H. 145
Stuart, John Leighton 118, 152
Stumpf, Kilian 17
Sturt, Reginald 298

Su Nan-chou 724
Su So-jin 682
Suen Tsong-yi 63
Sugiyama Kenji 338
Sugiyama Motojiro 338
Suh Kongsuk 616
Suh Kwang Sun, David 540, 553, 560ff.
Suh Nam Dong 553, 556f., 564
Suh Sang Don, Augustine 486, 487, 490
Suk Jin Young 512
Sultan Mohammad, Paul 294, 295
Sumiya Mikio 337, 371, 376, 377, 394ff.
Sun Hong-tsurn 675
Sun Jong Wan, Laurence 523
Sun Shang-yang 724
Sun Soon Hwa 572
Sun Yat-sen 116f., 222, 226f., 230
Sung Chih-ching 723
Sung Yeum 617
Sung, John (Song Shangjie) 167
Sung, (Mrs.) F.H. 120
Sutherland, James 678
Suzuki Bunji 308, 336
Suzuki Masahisa 369, 370, 376, 391ff.
Suzuki Shozo 462
Swain, David 445
Swan, William 297
Swanson, Paul 380, 383
Swyngedouw, Jan 379, 438
Syngman Rhee 516f., 534
Sze Lai-shan 245

T

Tagawa Kenzo 370, 376, 413, 420ff.
Taitetsu Unno 380
Takahashi Goro 329, 333f.
Takahashi Takako 448
Takahashi Wataru 366
Takakura Tokutaro 359
Takao Toshikazu 421
Takayanagi Shunichi 415f.
Takeda Cho Kiyoko 371, 372, 398ff.
Takeda Misako, Maria 374, 438
Takenaka Katsuo 337
Takenaka Masao 358, 377, 400f.

Index of Persons

Takeo Tadao (Mrs) 345
Takeoshi Yasaburo (Mrs) 345
Takeuchi Yoshinori 380
Takizawa Katsumi 370, 382, 388f., 407, 415, 417, 421, 425
Talmage, J.V.N. 103
Tam, Stephen 268
Tan, John 273
Tanabe Hajime 343, 359, 380, 396
Tanaka Chikao 448
Tanaka Komimasa 378
Tanaka Kotaro 367, 448
Tanaka Shozo 340f.
Tang, Bishop 61
Tang Junyi 231
Tao Xingzhi 165
Tate, L.B. 492
Tate, Mattie 492, 500
Taylor, Hudson 93, 114
Tchang, Mathias 43, 44
Tchou, M. Thomas 118
Teixeira, Manuel 657, 659ff.
Teng Chih-hui 231
Terao Toshiyoshi 438
Thalman, Eugene 278
Thelle, Notto 380, 382
Thevenet, Jacqueline 298
Thomas, Robert Jermain 492
Thomas, Winburn 350
Ticozzi, Sergio 270, 277
Tien Ju-Kang 201
Tien Liang 709
Ti-jan (Evelyn O. Shih) 674
Tin, John Jyigiokk (Cheng Erh-yu) 675, 687f.
Ting, K.H. (Ding Guangxun) xvii, 180ff., 191, 194, 202, 209, 237, 285
Tji Hak Soon 553
To, Edith 278
Toda Yoshio 448
Togawa Yasuie 333
Togawa Zanka 336
Toh Lau-seng 668
Tokutomi Soho 341f., 342
Tong Fung-wan 698f.

Tong, John 270, 277, 284f.
Tong King-shing 222
Torisu Yoshifumi 380
Trocmé, Etienne 420
Troeltsch, Ernst 356
Tsai, Christiana, see Cai Sujuan
Tsai Jung-fang 219f.
Tsai, Peter (Cai Wenhao) 187
Tsang, Iris 274
Tsang Ka-wai, Calina 245
Tsao Kuei, Agnes 108
Tscepe, Albert 43
Tse, Christine 270, 274, 278
Tse Kam Fong, Cecilia 274
Tseng, P.S., see Zeng Baosun
Tsou Yih-lan, Theresa 714
Tsu Yuyue, Andrew 118, 133
Tsuchiya Yoshimasa 438
Tsuda Umiko 346
Tsui, Bartolomeo 268
Tsui, Luke 715
Tsui Shan-shen 275
Tsukada Osamu 440, 449
Tsukamoto Toraji 323
Tu Shihua 87
Tu Shihua xvii, 75, 80f., 87, 191
Tucker, Henry 350
Tung, Barnabas 160
Tung Fang-yuen 677
Tung, William 238

U

Uchimura Kanzo 315, 321, 323f., 329, 336, 359, 416, 511
Uemura Masahisa 315, 320, 321f., 329, 331, 333, 335, 343, 345, 443
Uenura Tamaki 346
Ukita Kazutami 320, 341
Underwood, Horace G. 492, 494
Unsworth, Virginia 278

V

Vagnone, Alfonso 15
Valignano, Alessandro 15, 23, 654, 656

Valtorta, Henry 267
Van Bragt, Jan 379, 380, 383, 406f., 438
Van Hecken, J. 298
Venn, Henry 177
Verbiest, Ferd 16
Verbist, Théophile 297
Vermander, Benoit 722f.
Villion, Aimé 334f., 350
Vu Kim Chinh, Joseph 724

W

Wahid Khan, Khalilullah 295
Wainwright, Samuel 350
Walne, E.L. 350
Wan, Catherine 275
Wan Wai-yiu, Milton (Wen Weiyao) 238, 262, 263, 264
Wang Ai-tang 229
Wang Boren 66
Wang Cheng-tin 93
Wang Chih-hsin (Wang Zhixin) 93
Wang Hsien-chih (Ong Hian-ti) 691ff.
Wang Liming (Mrs. Herman C.E. Liu) 103, 124, 125, 169
Wang Ming-tao (Wang Mingdao) 118, 160, 162f., 167
Wang Tao 93, 97, 222, 224, 225f.
Wang Tch'ang-tche 43, 44
Wang Tsung-chung, Eric 724
Wang Wei 87
Wang Weifan 193ff.
Wang Yangming 43, 74
Wang Ying-ming 108
Wang Yuk-ch'o 97f., 108
Wang Zheng 12f.
Wang Zhengting (C.T. Wang) 117
Wang Zhiming 201f.
Wang Zhixin (Wang Chih-hsin) 116f., 154
Wang Zizheng 87
Ward, Harry 147
Ward, Jane Shaw 124
Watanabe Hidetoshi 430f.
Watanabe Manabu 380, 383
Watanabe Mine 370

Watanabe Minoru 440
Watanabe Zenda 359
Webb, Paul 238, 263
Wei Cho-min, Francis 118, 672, 674
Wei I-chieh (Wei Yijie) 13
Wei, Paul 160
Wei, Stephana 714
Wei Tsing-sing 67
Weil, Simone 420
White, Laura 121
Wiant, Bliss 171
Wickeri, Janice K. 247
Wickeri, Philip L. 247
Wieger, L. 45
Wilczek, G. 658
Williams, S. Wells 654
Williamson, Alexander 99, 114, 491
Wilson, Christy 294
Wiran (Kao T'en-wang) 679
Witmer, Robert 440
Wo Ti-chia 724
Wolff, Joseph 294
Wong, Agnes 713
Wong, Emily 274, 275
Wong Hee-kam, Edith 274
Wong, Heyward 262, 263
Wong, Joseph 272, 273
Wong, Louise 275
Wong, Phyllis 274
Wong Shing 222
Wong, Teresa 275
Wong Wai-ching, Angela (Huang Huizhen) 261f.
Wong Yai-chow, Theresa 713
Woo, Kate 120
Woo, Y.K., see Hu Yiku
Woodard, William 382
Woods, Henry McKee 114
Wu Cheng-chung, John Baptist 267
Wu Fu-ya 677, 682
Wu Hsiang-hsing 15
Wu, John C.H. (Wu Ching-hsiang) 67f.
Wu Leichuan (Wu L.C.) 118, 130, 133, 134, 141ff.
Wu Li 13, 16, 46

Index of Persons

Wu Mingjie 241f.
Wu Muyi 66
Wu, Rose 263, 264
Wu Ting-fang 222
Wu Xianli 232
Wu Yifang 134, 199
Wu, Y.T. (Wu Yaozong) 118, 133, 134, 146ff., 171, 177, 187, 237
Wu Yu-shan, see Wu Li
Wung Wing 222
Wurth, Elmer 270, 277
Wylie, Alexander 114

X

Xavier, Francis 22, 23, 305, 654
Xie Fuya, see Zia, N.Z.
Xie Honglai 153
Xie Meng 87
Xie Wanying (Bing Xin/ Ping Hsin) 103, 124, 134, 169
Xu Baoqian 118, 124
Xu Candida 13
Xu Chan, Judith 274, 287
Xu Dishan 118, 235f.
Xu Fuguan 231
Xu Guangqi (Hsu Kuang-ch'i) 12, 66
Xu, Paul 46
Xu Qian (Hsü Ch'ien) 116
Xu Shikang 165
Xu Xuchen 11
Xu Zonghai 66

Y

Yagi Seiichi 370, 382, 388, 413, 415, 416ff., 551
Yajima Kajiko 337, 345, 346
Yamada Akira 366
Yamada Kakichi 348
Yamada Keizo 422f., 438
Yamada, Roshi 385
Yamada Waka 346, 348f.
Yamaguchi Kosaku 377
Yamaguchi Satoko 374, 375
Yamaguchi Susumu 393
Yamaji Aizan 341, 342f.
Yamamoto Chiyo (Mrs) 394
Yamamoto Kano 359, 394
Yamamoto Sumiko 398
Yamamuro Gumpei 336, 337
Yamano Shigeko 371, 373, 431ff., 440, 460
Yamashita Akiko 375, 383, 433ff.
Yamazaki Washio 451
Yan Mo 15, 16
Yanagawa Keiichi 383
Yanaihara Tadao 309, 336, 337
Yang Eob Chio, see Choe Yong Eob
Yang Hee Ok 588
Yang Ju Sam 509
Yang Ku-ch'eng 710
Yang Kwon Sok 597
Yang Lingde 66
Yang, Michael 67
Yang Mugu, Arnold 263, 264
Yang Ni 88
Yang Song U 619f.
Yang, Thaddeus 44
Yang Ting-yun 3, 11
Yasui Tetso 346
Yasuoka Shoutarou 448
Yasutani, Roshi 385
Yeh Jen-ch'ang 724
Yeh Pao-kuei 724
Yen, James Y.C., see (Yan Yangchu)
Yen Yang-ch'u (James Y.C. Yen) 93, 118, 165
Yen Yung-kiung (Y.K. Yen; Yan Yongjing) 97, 108
Yeo Khiok-khng 247
Yeung, Angela Paulette 658
Yeung, Michael 61
Yeung, Teresa 274
Yi Ik 29, 483
Yi Ka Hwan 30, 482
Yi Ki Dang 488
Yi, Mrs 500
Yi Pyok 482, 485, 590
Yi San Huan Bei Lee, see Chu Mei-fen, Theresa

Yi Sung Hun 30, 481, 485
Yi To Gi 31, 488
Yi Yul Guk 547
Yin Wen-ka 230
Ying Fuk-tsang 247, 262
Ying Lianzhi, Vincent 44, 47
Ying Yuan-tao (Ying Yuandao) 93, 118
Yip, Francis 238
Yip, William 273
Yoho-ken, Paulo 3, 22
Yokoi Tokio 315, 329f., 331, 332, 342
Yong Ja Kim 572
Yong Yuandao 154
Yoo Cheun Ja 572
Yoo Kwansoon 499
Yoshida Megumi 374
Yoshimitsu Yoshihiko 326, 327f.
Yoshimoto Ryumo 420
Yoshino Sakuzo 336
You Heung Sik 588
Youn, Eulsou 523
Young Chil Kim 649
Young, John 270
Young, Richard Fox 383, 446
Young Sook Park 572
Yu (Cecilia), Mme 497
Yu Bin, Paul 54f. 118, 708
Yu, Carver T. 247, 262, 264f.
Yu Chi-ping 724
Yu Cidu (Dora Yu) 120
Yu Dong Shik 509, 510, 511, 539, 543, 549f.
Yu, Dora, see Yu Cidu
Yu Guozhen 153, 154
Yu Kak Kyung 500, 506
Yu Mong-in 29
Yuan Yuying 121f.
Yuasa Hachiro 398
Yuasa Makoto 374, 438
Yuasa Yuko 370, 374
Yueh Heng 724
Yuen, Mary 274

Yuen, Pauline 275
Yuen, Teresa 275, 277
Yuguchi Yuriko 374, 438
Yuhandong Kwon 497
Yui, David Z.T. (Yu Rizhang) 118, 133, 158
Yuki Hideo 380, 382f.
Yun Chi Ho, Byron 509, 510
Yun Ding Ju 512
Yun Hyung Joong, Matthew 522
Yun Sung Bum 539, 543, 547f.
Yung Wing, see Rong Hong

Z

Zanin, Mario 54
Zeng Baosun (Tseng Pao-suen) 93, 103, 108, 120, 122, 169
Zhang Geng 14
Zhang Jiashu 66
Zhang Junmai 231
Zhang, Mr. 64
Zhang Shijiang, John B. 86f.
Zhang Shilang 65, 66
Zhang Wendao 11
Zhang Xingyao 14, 16
Zhang Zhilai 75
Zhang Zhujun 104
Zhang Zimou 122
Zhao Fusan 177, 186f., 191
Zheng Jianye 187
Zheng Xinrong 232
Zheng Yongfu 226
Zhou Yuxi 232
Zhou Zuoren 133
Zhu Baoyuan 118, 153
Zhuo Xinping 203
Zia, H.L. 118
Zia, N.Z. (Xie Fuya) 118, 146, 231, 234f., 674
Zong Huaide 74f. 75, 82f.
Zottoli, Angelo 46
Zuo Taobei 47

INDEX OF SUBJECTS

A

Aboriginal theology, Taiwan 668, 674, 679f., 681f., 701, 714
Afghan Women's Mission 295
Afghanistan Christian agencies 294
Afghanistan welfare and development programmes 295
"A-ha!" theology 401
Ainu, Japan 442, 452
Alien Registration Law, Japan 366, 454
All Japan Socialist Christians' Frontier Union 377
Amity Foundation 191, 200
Anonymity 25f. See also vols.1 and 2.
Anti-Christian Movement, China 135f., 154
Anti-Mui Tsai campaign, Hong Kong 228f.
Aoyama Gakuin (now Aoyama Gakuin University), Tokyo 308, 316, 413, 444, 458
Apologetics 3, 11, 15f., 19, 20f., 23, 29f., 45, 133ff., 143, 227, 240, 264, 314, 350, 482f., 487
Asian Centre for the Progress of Peoples, Hong Kong 263, 268, 276, 278
Asian Christian Art Association 400. See also vol. 1.
Asian Ecumenical Institute 409
Asian Human Rights Association 247
Asian Institute for Liturgy and Music 699. See also vol.1
Asian Synod of Bishops, Rome 433, 455, 712
Asian Women Workers' Fellowship 373
Asian Women's Resource Centre for Culture and Theology 419, 575, 584. See also vols.1 and 2
Asian Women's Solidarity Forum 419
Association of Catholic Intellectuals, Shanghai 76
Association of Catholic Laity, Japan 309
Association of Feminist Theology, Korea 585
Association of Korean Catholic Priests for the Realization of Justice 520, 536
"Atheism" 41, 54, 56f., 61, 63, 65, 333

B

Bible Women 169, 345, 499, 681
Biblical study / Hermeneutics / Bible
  China 54, 63, 76, 86, 95, 121, 139, 145, 162, 167, 179, 184f., 199, 209f.
  Hong Kong 225, 244, 247, 256f., 258f., 261, 265, 275, 283
  Inner Asia 294f., 299
  Japan 315, 320f, 323, 340, 353, 358, 367, 372ff., 387, 396, 400, 404, 408, 412ff., 416, 419f., 426, 428f., 462, 465,
  Korea 511f., 543, 553, 557f., 564, 570, 577f., 581, 604, 621., 624f., 627f.
  Macau 657
  Taiwan 670, 674, 682, 685, 689f, 693, 699, 702, 705, 707f., 713, 718, 721
Biographies 10, 24f., 43, 55, 67, 98, 108f., 199, 259, 274, 333, 343, 347, 377, 400, 404, 448, 481, 491, 500, 562, 590, 631, 659, 708. See also vol. 1

Buddhist-Christian Conference (1896), Japan 330, 333
Buddhism Christian Dialogue - see Interfaith Encounter. See also vol.2
Burakumin ("Village People") 305, 341, 367, 370, 389, 425, 428f., 438, 445, 450, 452ff., 459
Bushido 321, 323, 331

C

Caritas, Hong Kong 267
Catechetics 10, 13, 15f., 18, 19f., 24, 29f., 39, 51, 74, 99, 126, 267, 273, 275, 284, 286, 487, 609, 657, 713.
Catholic Action 41, 366, 520
Catholic Bishops' Conferences / Colleges
    China 41, 50, 54, 60f., 71, 78f., 80, 85, 87
    Japan 366ff., 454ff., 458
    Korea 587, 589, 596, 611, 615, 633ff.
    Taiwan 668f., 709, 711
    See also Federation of Asian Bishops' Conferences
Catholic Council of the Church in China 41
Catholic Farmers' Movement, Korea 520, 531, 534, 541, 592, 639
Catholic Institute for Reunification, Korea 520
Catholic University of Korea College of Theology, Seoul 638, 640
Center for Christian Response for Asian Issues, NCCJ 373, 409, 432, 460
Centre for the Progress of Peoples, Hong Kong - see Asian Centre for the Progress of...
Cham Saram Doe-eo, Korea 595f.
Chhut-thau-thin Institute, Taiwan 684
China Christian Council 177f.
China Continuation Committee (Edinburgh 1910) 120, 157f.
China Graduate School of Theology, Hong Kong 247, 258, 262, 264

Chinese Catholic Patriotic Association - see Patriotic Assoc. of Chinese Catholics
Chinese Christian Literature Council, Hong Kong 240, 262f.
Chinese Home Mission Society 150, 154
Chinese Christian writings pre-1800 2f., 10-19
Christian arts 3, 9f., 26, 199, 390, 401, 608, 625, 654. See also vol. 1
Christian Conference of Asia 6f., 251, 400, 419. See also East Asia Christian Conference and vol. 1
Christian Industrial Committee, Hong Kong 239, 243f., 246, 253
Christian Institute for Social Transformation, Taiwan 684, 687
Christian Institute for the 3rd Era, Korea 567ff., 632
Christian literature societies
    China 99, 126, 134
    Hong Kong 240, 247, 262f.
    Korea 630f.
    Japan 350, 460
    Macau 655
    Taiwan 667
Christian Manifesto 1950, China 148, 174f.
Christian music - see Hymns and Lyrics
Christian Pavilion at Expo '70, Osaka - see Expo Pavilion
Christian Peace Fellowship, Japan 377
Christian Study Centre on Chinese Religion and Culture, Hong Kong 231, 239. See also Tao Fong Shan Ecumenical Centre
Christian Union China (*Jidutu hui*) 153
Christian writings, pre-1500 1-3. See also vol.1
Christian writings, 16-18th cents. 3-33. See also vol.1
Christian Worker Fellowships, Hong Kong 244, 254
Chung Chi College, Hong Kong 231, 247, 255f., 259, 261f., 263ff.

Index of Subjects

Church and Mission - see Mission and Evangelism
Church and Society - see Socially concerned theology
Church of Christ in China 158ff.
CICM (Scheut Fathers), Mongolia 297
Comfort Women, Japan 374
Committee for Promoting Christian Unity and Interreligious Dialogue, Korea 536
Community Christian Church, Kabul 294
Concordia Lutheran Seminary, Hong Kong 263
Confession of the Presbyterian Church in Taiwan 678
Confession of War Guilt, Japan 370, 391f.
Confucianism - see Inter-faith Encounter
Contextual theology, pre 1800 1-3. See also vol.1
Councils of Churches - see National Christian Councils
Creation-centred theology 179, 184ff., 209ff., 256, 320, 415, 436, 573, 584, 592, 603, 632, 681ff., 695, 715
Cultural Revolution era, China 74ff., 188f.
Cultural studies 12, 24f., 17, 20, 23, 31, 44f., 110-114, 121, 139, 142, 194f., 319f., 330f., 332, 364, 393, 398f., 446, 557, 607f., 674, 684, 689, 702, 722
"Culture Christians", China 202f.

D

Declarations or Statements 47, 62f., 70, 74, 231, 248ff.
Deng Xiaoping's open policy (1978) 70
Denunciation Movement, China 176, 201f. See also 163, 171
Donghak 531, 535, 552, 556, 562, 579, 604
Doshisha University, Kyoto 308, 316f.

E

East Asia Christian Conference 6, 244, 400, 675. See also vol.1

Ecclesiology
  China 62f., 72, 74ff., 148, 151, 153f., 157f., 160f., 177ff., 181f., 191
  Hong Kong 268f., 270f., 275
  Japan 358, 410, 420f., 429, 435, 442f., 454., 463f.
  Korea 538, 562, 565, 573, 587f., 595f., 621, 624f.
  Macau 660
  North Korea 647
  Taiwan 711f., 716
Ecological Theological Center, Taiwan 675, 682
Ecotheology 273, 340 382f., 409, 419, 429, 436, 453, 548, 588, 625, 721, 724
Ecumenical Consultative Committee, Taiwan 669
Ecumenical Theologies passim
  China 49f., 84f., 94, 117, 120-125, 150f., 152, 170f.
  Hong Kong 231, 233f., 237, 239, 242, 251f., 255, 261, 277
  Japan 320, 328f., 333, 338f., 347, 352, 366f., 382f., 409f., 418f., 422ff., 430, 457ff.
  Korea 539f., 556ff., 560f., 573ff., 589, 597, 603, 610, 621, 624f., 630ff.
  Taiwan 675, 685f, 689f., 691f., 699f., 711f., 718
Evangelical Lutheran Theological Seminary, Hong Kong 247
Evangelism - see Theology of Mission and Evangelism
Expo Pavilion, Osaka, 1970 370, 410, 421

F

Federation of Asian Bishops' Conferences 6f., 527. See also vol.1
Fellowship of Evangelical Students, Hong Kong 258
Feminist theology - see Women doing theology

Filial piety 53, 88, 114, 324, 437, 497, 666, 709, 715
Formosan Christians for Self-Determination 678, 685, 688
Footbinding, China, response to 98, 100, 104, 121
Fujen Catholic Theologate, Taipei 669, 707, 712
Fujen Catholic University, Taipei 714

G

General Conference of Protestant Missionaries of China 97, 114. See also vol.1
General Council of Evangelical Mission in Korea 630
God as Trinity 281, 324, 415, 465, 547, 709
  as "male/female" 11f., 328ff., 587
  names for 97, 224, 482f.

H

Hankuk Seminary, Seoul 509
Holy Carpenter Church, Hong Kong 238
Holy Spirit, Pneumatology
  China 95, 142, 145, 160, 179, 185
  Hong Kong 233, 261, 271, 277, 281, 283
  Inner Asia 294
  Japan 320, 329, 355f., 358, 415, 465
  Korea 546, 556, 577f., 606, 621
  Taiwan 706, 716, 723
Holy Spirit Seminary and Study Centre, Hong Kong 263, 276ff., 268, 270, 276ff., 279, 281f., 283f., 285f.
Homeland theology, Taiwan 687, 692
Hong Kong Christian Churches Union 222
Hong Kong Baptist University 264
Hong Kong Christian Council - see National Christian councils
Hong Kong Christian Industrial Committee - see Christian Industrial Committee

Hong Kong Christian Institute 247, 252, 264
House of Daybreak, Seoul 551
Humanism, Humanist 47f., 49, 69f., 117, 147, 184f., 279f., 357, 399, 447, 560, 621, 711
Hymns and Lyrics. See also Christian poetry
  China 138, 152, 171, 366
  Inner Asia 295
  Japan 471, 353f.
  Korea 30ff., 484f., 487, 524, 594
  Taiwan 687, 699f., 702ff., 710, 721

I

Independence Club, Korea 509f.
Indigenisation / Inculturation passim
  China 47f., 51, 61, 93, 117, 120ff., 153ff., 178ff., et seq.
  Hong Kong 232, 240, 242, 250ff., et seq.
  Inner Asia 294f.
  Japan 322, 328ff., 340, 353ff., 372ff., 385ff., et seq.
  Korea 506, 509ff., 547ff., 552ff., 571ff., 599ff., et seq.
  Macau 656ff.
  Taiwan 673, 685, 702ff., 707f. 715, 721, 723f.
Industrial Evangelistic Fellowship, Hong Kong 258
Institutes for Research - see Research Institutes
Intellectual movements, China 44, 131f., 202ff.
Inter-faith Encounter / Dialogue passim
  China 53, 70f., 74, 76, 96f., 106, 110f., 112, 114, 116f., 121, 142
  Hong Kong 224, 231ff., 240, 242, 271, 277, 285, 287, 280
  Inner Asia. See vol.1, chap.1
  Japan 304f., 309, 314, 320, 324, 328, 330f., 332ff., 335f., 340, 350, 363, 366, 368, 377ff., 382f., 384ff., 388f., 390, 397,

Index of Subjects

402f., 406f., 416f., 422, 425, 430, 433f., 437, 459, 463f., 485
Korea 510, 523, 531, 536, 539f., 547, 549, 551, 561, 582, 589, 591ff., 602f., 608, 621f., 625, 628f., 636ff.
Macau 657
Mongolia 299
Taiwan 691f., 698f., 703ff., 714f., 718ff., 722
International Christian University 457
International Institute for Study of Religion, Japan 382
International Movement of Catholic Students - see Student Movements

J

Japan Catholic Council for Justice and Peace 366, 454
Japan Christian Academies - see Nippon Christian Academies
Japan Society for Buddhist-Christian Studies 382, 390
Japan Society of Systematic Theology 451
Jerusalem Principle, China 164
Jesus Christ, Christology
    China 83, 86, 116, 118, 122, 124, 138, 148, 182, 190, 194f., 196
    Hong Kong 233, 260, 275, 281, 283, 285f.
    Inner Asia 295
    Japan 322, 325, 329, 340, 347, 353, 355, 364, 368, 386, 389, 391, 405, 410, 413, 415, 417, 420, 465
    Korea 526, 531, 543, 545, 548, 556ff., 565, 573, 576f., 593, 625
    Macau 657
    Taiwan 668, 676f., 680, 683, 685f., 692, 694, 697, 704, 707, 710f., 714, 716f., 718
Jesus Family, China 160f.
Joint Study Days and Catholic-Protestant Dialogues, Taiwan 711f.
'*Ju Che*' ideologies, Nth Korea 554, 649f.
Justice and Peace Committee of the Maryknoll Fathers, Taiwan 711

K

Kakure Kirishitan (Hidden Christians) 5, 22, 25f., 307, 311f., 313. See also vol.1
Kingdom / Reign of God. See also Socially concerned theology
    China 54, 99f., 102, 111, 121, 138, 147, 159
    Hong Kong 233, 254, 263, 271, 275, 281
    Japan 309, 338, 353, 355f., 377
    Korea 535, 559
    Taiwan 689, 697
Korea Christian Institute for Social Justice and Peace 541, 632
Korea Christian Literature Society - see Christian literature societies
Korean Association of Christian Studies 571, 632
Korean Christian Centers, Japan 370
Korean Christian Academy 541, 598
Korean Christian Church in Japan 372
Korean Student Christian Federation - see Student Movements
Korean Women's Institutes - see Women doing theology
Kumamoto Band (Kyushu) 315, 320, 329, 341
Kyo Bun Kwan - see Christian literature societies
Kyodan (United Church of Christ), Japan 310, 352, 369, 371
Kyodan Confession of Faith, Japan 369
Kyoto School of Japanese Philosophy 343

L

"Lay" theology and formation. See also Women doing theology

China 47f., 51, 62-67, 72, 100, 104, 123f., 136, 151, 165f., 168f., 178, 190f., 197f.
Hong Kong 231, 237, 239, 241, 243ff., 247, 252ff., 268, 273ff., 276
Japan 309, 313ff., 327-333, 336, 338-344, 366, 418f., 433, 435, 440
Korea 520f., 533ff., 537, 539, 541, 551, 554, 595, 598f., 612, 617f., 635, 637f.
Macau 657f.
Taiwan 670, 675, 681f., 687f., 699f., 711f., 713, 719f., 724
Letters, pre-1800 10f., 12f., 15, 17, 19ff., 23f., 28, 30. See also vol.1
Liberation theology 363, 373, 391, 422, 429, 431, 533, 551f., 592, 617, 714, 724
Little Flock, China 160f., 164f.
Liturgy, Worship, Prayer
    China 40, 54, 88, 97, 105, 121, 126, 145, 147, 179, 188f.
    Hong Kong 237, 244, 269, 270f., 273, 275, 278, 286
    Japan 307, 317, 326ff., 357, 366, 385, 390, 418, 437, 464
    Korea 497, 520, 523, 540, 586, 589, 600, 621, 630
    Mongolia 298
    Taiwan 670, 675, 681, 699f., 705, 709, 714, 721, 723f.
London Missionary Society 92, 95ff., 98, 150, 159f., 162, 224f.
Lutheran Theological Seminary, Tokyo 426, 442, 458

M

Macau
    Centro Diocesano dos Meios de Comunicação Social 654
    Christian Literature Association 655
    Dom Policarpo Library 655
    Instituto Cultural of Macau 657
    Morrison Education Society (1839)
    Ricci Institute 657
    St Joseph's Seminary 654
    St. Paul's College 653
    Santa Casa da Mirericordia 653, 656
    São Paulo bookshop
Major Catholic Seminary, Tokyo 309
March First Independence Movement (*Samil*) 488, 505f.
Marxism, Marxian 74, 172, 281, 332, 355, 387f., 391, 395, 554, 563, 567f. See also Socialism
Masked dances, Korea 559
Mary, Mother of Jesus 26, 121, 275, 281, 397, 714
May 2nd meeting (1922), China 157
May 30th incident (1925), China 136, 158
May 4th Movement, China 118, 130ff., 168
Minjung theology 429, 462, 505, 520, 525, 534f., 537, 539f., 546, 552-570, 577, 604, 606, 608, 612, 649
Minority Christians 201f., 338, 425, 454f.
Mission and Evangelism - see Theology of Mission and Evangelism
Mission Education Institute, Korea 551
Missions Etrangère de Paris 319
Mukyokai ("Non-Church"), Japan 308, 323, 443, 545

N

Nanjing Synod (1953) 62
Nanzan Institute for Religion and Culture, Nagoya 379
National Alliance of Social Christianity, Japan 355
National Assembly of Evangelicals, Korea 517
National Catholic Priests' Corps for the Realization of Justice, Korea 520, 541
National Christian Conference, China 155, 156ff.

Index of Subjects

National Christian councils
  China 126, 151f., 158f., 170f.
  Hong Kong 231, 238, 243, 246, 252, 258, 263
  Japan 309, 338f., 370, 373, 382, 418f., 422, 426, 440, 459ff.
  Korea 540, 600, 630
  Taiwan 669
National Protestant Clergy's Corps for the Realization of Justice, Korea 541
Nationalist / Patriotic concerns
  China 47, 51, 54f., 60, 62ff., 64ff., 74ff., 83, et seq.
  Japan 318ff., 329ff., 335ff., 353ff., 376ff., et seq.
  Korea 502ff., 509ff., 522, 535, 543ff., 552ff., et seq.
  Taiwan 669, 673f., 678,ff., 683f. et seq.
NCC Center for the Study of Japanese Religions, Japan 380, 382f., 390
NCCJ Commissions and Committees 339, 373
Nestorian theology 43, 111. See also vol. 1
New Clergy Group, Taiwan 707
New Culture Movement, China 93, 143, 154, 157. See also May 4th Movement
New Life Movement, China 154
New Youth Workers' Night School, Hong Kong 268, 276
Nihon Kirisuto Kyodan - see Kyodan
Nihon Kirisuto Kyokai Domei (Japan Federation of Christian Churches) 338, 459
Nippon Christian Academies 370, 377, 400, 458
Nippon Seikokai 432
Nippon Tenshu Kokyo Kyodan - see Conference of Catholic Bishops in Japan
Noh drama 374, 403
Non-Church Movement - see *Mukyokai*
Northeast Asia Association of Theological Schools 409. See also vol.1

North Korea
  Catholic Committee for North Korean Mission 520
  Catholic Priests' Association for Justice 646
  Dialogue Conferences 649
  Federation of Korean Christians 645ff., 649
  Korean Roman Catholics' Association 647
  Missionary Association of Korean Women 647
  Pyongyang Divinity School 645
  Relief Organizations 646f., 649

O

Okinawa, in Theology 331f.
Oriens Institute for Religious Research, Tokyo 367, 379, 393
Orthodox thought and writing 105, 107, 328, 350, 613
Oxford College for Christian Workers, Taiwan 668

P

Pahakpa (Northern Learning) 31
Pastoral theology
  China 41, 54, 74, 78f., 80, 87, 96, 110, 121f., 123f., 138, 145, 169, 199
  Hong Kong 237, 247ff., 251, 254, 269, 271, 275, 284
  Japan 350, 367, 379, 403, 431, 437, 440, 445, 454, 493
  Macau 656f.
  Korea 521, 531f., 525, 589, 623f., 618, 624, 633f.
  Taiwan 711f., 713, 724
Pastoral Congress of the Korean Roman Catholic Church 520, 538f.
Patriotic Association of Chinese Catholics 60, 64f., 71, 78f., 80, 84. See also Nationalist Concerns
Periodicals
  China 41, 46, 48, 54ff., 62f., 69, 71, 81f., 87f., 103, 116f.,

120f., 126f., 133f., 136, 143, 147, 152, 154f., 162, 169, 172, 178, 187f., 190, 196f., 199f., 203f., 209ff.
  Hong Kong 222, 225, 227, 229f., 239, 242, 247, 254, 258, 263, 267ff., 274f., 277ff., 281, 283ff.
  Inner Asia 295
  Japan 307, 309, 320f., 323, 333ff., 336, 338, 341f., 345, 348, 350, 355, 347, 363, 367, 373f.,. 377, 379f., 383, 387, 393, 419, 432, 437ff., 444ff.
  Korea 487, 494, 509f., 517, 519, 522f., 543, 545, 553, 558, 572, 575, 585f., 595ff., 619, 621ff., 623ff., 630ff., 636ff., 640
  Macau 655, 657, 660
  Taiwan 667, 682, 688, 692f., 697, 699, 707, 712, 716, 724
Poetry, Christian 10, 11, 13f., 30, 116, 118, 124, 133f., 138, 169, 234, 318, 327, 335, 353, 485, 490, 512, 523, 534f., 553, 575, 591, 599, 618ff., 682. See also Hymns, Lyrics
Prayer - see Liturgy, Worship, Prayer
Presbyterian Church of Korea 517
Presbyterian Church of the Republic of Korea 509, 517, 543f.
Presbyterian Church in Taiwan 668f., 674, 678, 691
Programme for Theology and Cultures in Asia 256, 263, 400, 579, 684, 688. See also vol.1
Prophetic witness - see Socially concerned theology
Public Statements of .PCT 1971-77 669, 678, 687f., 692
Publishers and Presses, Christian 76, 126, 147, 267, 278, 350f., 367, 460, 487, 494f.,631, 638f.,654f., 667

R

Reform movement - China 93, 100, 110

Religious freedom 40, 54f., 63, 65f., 71, 645ff.
ren or humanheartedness, China 142, 194f.
Research Institutes 24f., 80, 85, 88, 204f., 220, 238f., 258, 263, 276ff., 366, 367, 379, 380, 382f., 390, 393, 406, 433, 453, 454ff., 457, 462, 526, 529f., 536, 541, 562, 567, 613, 631, 636f., 640, 657, 680, 684, 692. See also Christian Study Centres; Christian Institutes
Reunification theology, Korea 520, 537, 540, 554, 564, 573, 598, 599, 611, 630, 646, 649
Revolutionary Association of Women of Afghanistan 295
Ricci Institute for Chinese Studies, Taipei 707, 712, 720, 722
Rome, relationships with 65f., 68, 72, 75f., 80, 84, 86, 286, 712. See also Asian Synod of Bishops
Russian Orthodox communities, Japan 328, 350
Ryukyu - see Okinawa

S

Sapporo Band, Japan 315, 331
Scheut Fathers - see CICM
Seibunsha (formerly Lutheran Literature Society), Japan 460
Seito Society, Japan 345, 348
Self-determination, Taiwan 665, 678, 696
SEMINEX, Tokyo 444
Shamanism - see Inter-faith encounter
Shin Kan Hoe, Keun Woo Hoe, Korea. 506
Shinangin Academy, Korea 637f.
Shinto - see Inter-faith encounter
Silhak (*seo-hak*: "western learning") 29f., 481, 497, 506
Social Christianity Movement, Japan 309, 356f.
Socially concerned theology
  China 47f., 51, 56, 65f., 75, 84, 97, 99f., 103f., 110f., 112, 116,

Index of Subjects

121f., 124f., 144, 165f., 191f., 210
Hong Kong 218f., 223, 225f., 228f., 230, 232, 237, 239, 243ff., 251ff., 258, 263, 268f., 271, 273, 275, 277f.
Japan 320, 322, 335f., 338ff., 345f., 353, 357ff., 366, 369, 376ff., 395, 400f., 427f., 439ff., 449ff., 462f.
Korea 484, 487f., 490f., 502f., 510f., 517, 519f., 525, 527f., 534f., 537, 543f., 571ff., 575, 579, 611, 613f., 617f., 625, 629ff., 633f.
Macau 658
Taiwan 669f., 675, 678, 687, 691f., 694, 697f., 711
Socialism, Socialist 78f.,. 84, 116f., 148, 184, 190f., 209f., 277, 281f., 309, 329, 331f., 336, 343, 353, 355f., 386, 504f., 507
Society for Community Organization, Hong Kong 244f.
Society for the Diffusion of Christian and General Knowledge 99
Sophia University, Tokyo 308, 457
Southeast Asia Graduate School of Theology 411. See also vol.1
Spirituality 23, 49, 83, 88, 242, 252, 260, 268, 273, 275, 279, 327f., 331, 364, 407f., 440, 520, 523, 577, 581, 588f., 612, 625, 705, 716, 723f.
St Paul's School (now Rikkyo University), Tokyo 308, 316
Student Christian Movement - see Student movements; World Student Christian Federation
Student movements
  China 117, 124, 126, 136, 143, 147, 165, 180
  Hong Kong 237ff., 246, 258, 261ff., 268, 276
  Japan 309, 326, 338, 347, 388, 421, 443, 458
  Korea 499, 519, 540f., 552, 566, 603
  Taiwan 675

Systematic Theology Society in Korea 632

T

Tainan Theological College and Seminary, Taiwan 712
Taiping Movement 101f.
Taiwan Christian Academy 687
Taiwan Institute of Theology and Culture 692
Taiwan Theological College and Seminary, Taipei 712
Tao Fong Shan Christian Institute, Hong Kong 233, 237, 239, 258
Tao Fong Shan Ecumenical Centre, Hong Kong 220, 239, 246. See also Christian Study Centre, Hong Kong
Taoism - see Inter-faith encounter
Tenno issues, Japan 320, 322, 370, 445, 462
The Japan Society for Christian Studies 445
Theological Education Fund 685f. See also vol.1
Theological Method / Reconstruction
  China 66f., 74f., 138f., 142, 145, 147f., 178f., 181f., 184, 189ff., 209ff.
  Hong Kong 231, 242, 254, 256, 258, 261, 264, 269, 275, 280, 284
  Japan 328f., 343f., 358, 364, 369, 373, 390, 393, 405, 411ff., 417, 420f., 426, 429, 431, 434, 436
  Korea 543f., 546, 551, 556ff., 563, 568, 571, 574, 576ff., 588, 609f., 612, 617
  Macau 658
  Taiwan 685f., 689f., 694, 696f.
Theology and Society - see Socially concerned theology
Theology of Mission and Evangelism passim
  China 92f., 106, 142, 145, 147, 151, 157, 162f., 167f.

Hong Kong 218, 222, 237, 243ff., 249, 251f., 254, 266f., 270, 273ff., 277
Japan 336, 338, 370, 377, 390, 392, 395, 400, 409, 412, 423, 427f., 431ff., 435, 440, 443, 445, 450, 455, 459, 462
Korea 481, 487f., 494f., 497f., 519ff., 528, 541, 552-570, 598, 600, 609, 614f., 621, 625, 649
Macau 656ff., 660
Taiwan 669, 683ff., 694, 699, 712, 716, 721

Theology in Action 60, 74 See also vol.1
Theology of Identification, Taiwan 677, 694f.
Theology of the Incarnation, Taiwan 674f.
Three-Self / self reliance Movements 61, 148, 177f., 237, 318, 320, 323, 392, 487, 494, 509, 668, 672
"Third Day" Group, Korea 548
"Thursday Prayer Meetings", Korea 600
Tianzhu shiyi (Ricci) 11ff., 16, 29, 483, 485
Tokyo Theological Seminary 258, 321, 409, 458
Tokyo Women's Christian College 331
Tokyo Women's Christian University 425f.
Tomisaka Christian Center 371, 373, 462f., 567
Tonghak - see *Donghak*
Tosanzo Process for Reconciliation and Unification, Korea 645
True Jesus Church, China 160f.

U

Underground writings 60. See also vol. 2
Union for Catholic Action, China 41
Union Version (UV) of the Bible, China 133
University of the Sacred Heart, Tokyo 374
Urban Industrial Mission 370, 377, 459, 540f., 552ff., 603, 687. See also Christian Industrial Committee; Nippon Christian Academies

V

Vatican II 71f., 74, 76, 80, 82, 368, 519, 532, 707

W

Women doing theology
China 66, 76, 78, 83f., 87, 94, 100, 103f., 120-125, 169, 199f.
Hong Kong 247, 274ff., 259f., 261f.., 263f., 281ff., 286f.
Inner Asia 294, 298
Japan 345f., 347ff., 371-375, 408f., 418f., 425f., 431f, 433f, 438
Korea 496ff., 499f., 554, 571-596, 618f.
Taiwan 681f., 693, 713f.
Women doing theology - Institutes, Associations
China
Jinling Women's Seminary, Nanjing 145
Women's Christian Temperance Union, China 103, 120ff., 123f.
Women's Mission societies 103
Yenching Women's College 134
Young Women's Christian Association 103, 120ff., 123f.

Hong Kong
Association of Major Superiors of Religious Women 281
Hong Kong Women Christian Council 247, 264
Precious Blood Wah Fu Community 282
Young Women's Christian Association 238

Japan
Center for Feminist Theology and Ministry 374, 426

Index of Subjects

Church Women's Congress 373
EATWOT Women's Commission, Japan 419
Fujin Kyofukai (WCTU) Japan 309, 337, 339, 345, 370, 372f., 377, 408
Japan-Korean Resident Women's Theologies Forum 373
Japan Women's College 318
Korean Christian Church in Japan Women's Association 372
National Federation of Kyodan Women's Societies 372, 452
NCCJ Women's Desk 373
Violence against Women in War Network 373, 426
Women Doing Theology Group 371
Women Thinking about Church 373
Women's Christian Temperance Union - see *Fujin Kyofukai*
Women's Committee of the NCCJ 418

Korea
Association of Christian Women For Women Minjung 585
Association of Feminist Theology 573, 585ff.
Association of Korean Catholic Women's Theology, Seoul 594
Association of Women Theologians 571, 584f.
Catholic Feminist Theologians' Association 571
Catholic Women's Theological Group 587
Catholic Women's Community for a New World 596
Church Women United 57, 419, 571, 584
Ewha Institute for Women's Theological Studies, Seoul 586
Feminist Theology Academy 576, 584

Institute for Korean Feminist Theology 571
Institute of Asian Christian Women's Culture 584
Institute of Feminist Studies 571
Institution of Asian Feminist Theological Education, Korea 576
United Conference of Superiors for Catholic Women's Religious Orders 587
Women Church 571, 585f.
Women's Committee of the Catholic Bishops' Conference 587

Taiwan
PCT Women's Work Committee 682
Taipei Women's Development Center 675
Taiwan Association of Theologically Trained Women 681f.
Taiwan Catholic Sprout Women-Concerns Association 714
Woori Theology Institute, Seoul 596, 635f.
World Conference on Religion and Peace 422
World Council of Churches 400, 689
World Student Christian Federation 94, 117, 135, 171, 180, 186, 347
Worship - see Liturgy, Worship, Prayer

Y

Yasukuni Shrine, Japan 309, 366, 370, 382, 460
Yokohama Band 315
Yonsei University, Seoul 541
Young Christian Workers (JOC) 366, 435, 541, 639 See also vol.1

Young Men's Christian Association 94, 126, 165, 321, 335, 338f., 347, 370, 377, 459, 502, 509f., 541, 655, 675

Young Women's Christian Association 94, 103, 124ff., 165, 200, 339, 345, 347, 370ff., 377, 418f., 425f., 431ff., 459, 500, 655

Yu-Shan Theological College and Seminary, Taiwan 680

Z

Zhendan daxue (Aurora University), China 460f.

Zhonghua Jidijiao wenshe (National Christian Literature Association of China) 134

Zikawei (Xujiahui), China - Jesuit foundation 43, 52

WITHDRAWN

BT 30 .A8 A774 2002 v.3 c.2

Asian Christian theologies